COMPENSATING THE
CORPORATE EXECUTIVE

VOLUME I. SALARY, PROFIT PARTICIPATION, AND
DEFERRED COMPENSATION PLANS

VOLUME II. STOCK, PENSION, AND INSURANCE PLANS

COMPENSATING THE CORPORATE EXECUTIVE

SALARY, PROFIT PARTICIPATION, AND DEFERRED COMPENSATION PLANS

GEORGE THOMAS WASHINGTON

JUDGE, UNITED STATES COURT OF APPEALS
DISTRICT OF COLUMBIA CIRCUIT

and

V. HENRY ROTHSCHILD, 2ND

MEMBER OF THE NEW YORK AND FEDERAL BARS

With the Assistance of

THEODORE NESS

MEMBER OF THE
NEW YORK BAR

RUDOLF SOBERNHEIM

MEMBER OF THE DISTRICT OF
COLUMBIA AND NEW YORK BARS

THIRD EDITION

VOLUME I

THE RONALD PRESS COMPANY • NEW YORK

PREFACE

Ten years have passed since V. Henry Rothschild and I wrote the last edition of *Compensating the Corporate Executive*. Those years have seen the disappearance of the federal government's salary stabilization program, and the development, expansion, and widespread use of supplemental forms of compensation. Interest in the whole field of executive compensation has greatly increased. A vast array of material—legal, statistical, and economic—has become available. The problems presented have become increasingly complex and difficult. As a result, it was found impossible to contain the discussion in a single volume and the present work appears in two volumes.

Volume I covers the basic materials relative to compensating the individual executive: practical and policy considerations in fixing his compensation, his salary contract, profit participation, deferred compensation, expense accounts and fringe benefits, with a chapter devoted to the corporate approval required or appropriate under statute, common law, or practice. A chapter is also included about the outside director, his functions and compensation.

The volume constitutes a thorough revision and updating of approximately the first half of *Compensating the Corporate Executive*. An effort has been made to cover the legal and practical problems presented in negotiating the executive's contract and operating under it. The corporate as well as the tax aspects of each typical situation have received intensive treatment.

Much new material is included in the present volume. We have in this edition reviewed the important surveys of compensation statistics published in recent years and have analyzed them giving our conclusions. There has been added a discussion of enforceability of salary contracts and the validity of non-competition provisions, which have become so important in connection with deferred compensation arrangements. The discussion of executive participation in profits has been completely reorganized and expanded. A new formula clause for the determination of profits, worked out by Mr. Rothschild over the years and actually incorporated in a number of functioning plans, is presented. The subject of deferred compensation is now covered in two separate chapters, setting forth the many important legal developments that have taken place in the field.

Included for the first time is an entire chapter devoted to the treatment of expense accounts, perquisites, and fringe benefits. New statutory developments dealing with corporate approval of compensation arrangements, including the Model Corporation Code, sponsored by the American Bar Association, are considered at length. Many other changes and additions have been made with an effort to reflect decisions and other authorities to July 1, 1961. A great deal has also been added to the Appendix, one innovation being the inclusion of a complete model plan for a compensation contract which brings together in one place specific clauses and provisions discussed throughout the book. The model plan is cross-referenced to the pertinent textual discussion.

There is no attempt in our work to suggest ready-made plans for compensation: the needs of individual enterprises are too various. It is hoped that the book may serve as a starting point for corporate managers and their legal advisers in considering the needs of a particular company. It may also prove useful to accountants, investors, government officials, and others interested in the problems of modern business.

Pressure of judicial duties has precluded me from making as substantial a contribution to this volume as I would have wished. Mr. Rothschild, working in consultation with me, has had to carry the principal burden. If I may be permitted to say so, I think he has done an excellent job. Invaluable assistance was given by Mr. Rudolf Sobernheim and Mr. Theodore Ness, attorneys long interested in this field. Both made important suggestions for and contributions to the volume as a whole. Mr. Sobernheim collated much of the statistics and data for the first chapter, collaborated in writing the major part of the new expense account chapter and in rewriting the profit participation chapters, and added new cases to bring up to date the corporate approval chapter and other parts of the volume. Mr. Ness prepared the basic text of most of the two deferred compensation chapters, the tax section of the profit participation chapters, the fringe benefit section of the expense account chapter, and the Model Corporation Code section of the corporate approval chapter, and brought up to date the outside director chapter and certain other portions of the volume. Others assisted in a variety of ways, and their help is described and gratefully acknowledged elsewhere.

GEORGE THOMAS WASHINGTON

Washington, D.C.
January, 1962

ACKNOWLEDGMENTS

It is impossible to give due credit for the assistance received in bringing forth this new edition without mentioning again a few of those who were so helpful to the authors in the preparation of prior editions.

Robert S. Stevens, Dean Emeritus of the Cornell Law School and author of a standard text on corporation law, read over a large part of the manuscript for the first edition. His comments and suggestions proved exceedingly useful.

A chapter of the second edition on federal securities legislation was reviewed by Myer Feldman, formerly Associate Solicitor and Special Counsel to the Securities and Exchange Commission. Mr. Feldman later collaborated in rewriting a major part of that chapter. The revision was published in the form of an article by the Michigan Law Review which, as further revised to reflect subsequent developments, will appear in the second volume of this edition.

Sections of the manuscript for this or earlier editions were read by Dean Rosensteel, Director, Executive Compensation Service of the American Management Association, who contributed valuable information concerning AMA surveys; Nicholas L. A. Martucci, former manager, Compensation Research, National Industrial Conference Board; Louis Loss, member of the faculty of the Law School of Harvard University; Peter F. Drucker, economist; Perrin Stryker, editor, Fortune magazine; J. S. Seidman and William W. Werntz, certified public accountants, and Jack B. Salwen, certified public accountant and member of the New York Bar.

Other members of the New York Bar were equally generous. Carlos L. Israels, Charles C. MacLean, Jr., Peter Miller, and Melvin C. Steen each read two or more chapters and passages suggested by them are included in the text. Chapters or sections of the manuscript for this or earlier editions were also read by Ethan D. Alyea, Laurence F. Casey, George E. Cleary, Roswell L. Gilpatric, Ray I. Hardin, Charles S. Lyon, Samuel A. McCain, Karl R. Price, George C. Seward, Henry Cassorte Smith, and Everett I. Willis, New York attorneys; Robert G. Surridge of Detroit, Michigan; Professor Joseph W. Bishop, Jr. of the Yale University Law School; Frank D. Emerson of the University of Cincinnati Law School; Abner C. Brodie, of the Law School of the University of Wisconsin; Luke

K. Cooperrider of the University of Michigan Law School; and Professor Daniel L. Sweeney of the University of Michigan. All made valuable comments and suggestions reflected in this work.

Government officials were exceedingly courteous and helpful. A special debt is acknowledged in connection with earlier editions to John Lord O'Brian, formerly General Counsel of the Office of Production Management; John P. Wenchel, former Chief Counsel of the Bureau of Internal Revenue; Ralph Dwan, former Assistant to the Chief Counsel and John A. Gilmore, former Special Assistant to the Chief Counsel, and numerous former members of the staff of the Securities and Exchange Commission, including Roger S. Foster, former General Counsel; Harry Heller, John F. Davis, George F. Parlin, Milton Freeman, and Parker Bailey. A special debt in connection with the preparation of material for this edition is acknowledged to David A. Lindsay, former Assistant to the Secretary of the Treasury and thereafter General Counsel of the Treasury; to Harold T. Swartz, Assistant Commissioner of Internal Revenue, and Edward C. Rustigan, former Assistant Head of the Legal Advisory Staff of the Treasury Department.

Acknowledgment is also made to Dr. John Calhoun Baker, formerly of the Harvard School of Business Administration; to Sylvester Garrett, former Executive Director and Acting Chief Counsel of the Wage Stabilization Board; to Edward J. Zuhr, Chief Listing Representative of the New York Stock Exchange; to Ruth Gray and her associate editors on the Michigan Law Review; to the editors of the Yale Law Journal; to Peyton Ford of the District of Columbia Bar, Wendell R. Crockett, Joel Field, Harry K. Schwartz, Roger Kuhn, and Sidney Wolinsky. Valuable help on legal questions was also received from Harry Scott, Jr., Rex Rowland, John W. Reed, and Stanley M. Brown. Particularly valuable contributions were made by Helen Washington of the District of Columbia Bar.

Finally, we gratefully acknowledge the help of Beatrice Schmulling McDermott, librarian at the New York law firm of Dewey, Ballantine, Bushby, Palmer and Wood and member of the New York Bar; of Winifred Ing, librarian at the Washington law firm of Alvord and Alvord; of Janet K. Savage and Eleanor Hall, who helped put the manuscript in shape for the printer; and of Charles F. Hollander and Thomas A. Rothschild, who prepared the table of cases.

While expressing our gratitude, we must add that none of the individuals to whom we are indebted is necessarily in agreement with any views expressed in this book and they are not chargeable with any of the statements which we have made or opinions which we have expressed.

GEORGE THOMAS WASHINGTON
V. HENRY ROTHSCHILD, 2ND

Washington, D.C.
January, 1962

CONTENTS

APPENDIX CONTENTS

COMPENSATING THE CORPORATE EXECUTIVE

CHAPTER 1

PROBLEMS OF EXECUTIVE COMPENSATION

The efficient operation of our business enterprises is of paramount importance to the survival of our nation. We depend upon the abilities, initiative, and energy of those charged with their management. Foreign aid, urban redevelopment, and similar programs will not relieve us of this dependence—quite the contrary is to be expected. In times of emergency, government controls over manpower and materials and the channeling of industry into military production may alter the tasks and functions of private management, but they cannot replace or provide a substitute for those tasks and functions as long as American enterprise endures.

The executive group is relatively small in number [1] and comparatively unorganized; each man, generally speaking, is his own bargaining agent. Yet it is a group which possesses real power. Its abilities are high, and its functions essential. The directors and controlling stockholders, faced with the necessity of providing rewards sufficient to attract and retain capable management, must seek plans of compensation which will reconcile the executive's demands with those of the other groups interested in the enterprise. Reconciliation of these competing claims is not easy. Stockholders will oppose burdensome fixed charges, or rewards of such size as to effect an appreciable reduction in dividends. Among the lower-ranking executives and white-collar employees, some will resent rewards far beyond their own; others will view the payment of high salaries to top executives as a positive stimulus to further effort on their own part. Organ-

[1] Of approximately 51,000,000 men and women employed in business in the United States in 1957, perhaps 175,000 could be considered members of top management and 575,000 members of middle management. See U. S. DEP'T OF COMMERCE, BUREAU OF THE CENSUS, STATISTICAL ABSTRACTS OF THE UNITED STATES 1958, Tables 254, 263, at 203, 211 (1958). The management figures result from a percentage estimate for all management of one and one-half per cent of total business employees, with roughly one-fourth of one per cent estimated as top management executives. See HALL, SOME OBSERVATIONS ON EXECUTIVE RETIREMENT 4, n. 1 (1953). Surveys confined to large companies (20,000 or more employees) assume one per cent of all employees in such companies to be executives and one-tenth of one per cent to be top management. See Bursk, *Thinking Ahead*, 30 HARV. BUS. REV. 141 (1952); Patton, *Are Executives Paid Enough?*, FORTUNE, Jan. 1953, pp. 106–07; ROTHSCHILD, COMPENSATION AND INCENTIVES FOR EXECUTIVES, ENCYCLOPEDIA OF TAX PROCEDURES 965, nn. 1 & 2 (rev. ed. 1960). Consult *infra* note 4.

ized labor will point to executive rewards to justify its own demands. The government, for its part, may regard with disfavor plans which lower the tax payments made either by the company or by its managers, or which are inflationary in tendency or effect. And sitting in judgment is the public. Business and financial writers, columnists, the press in general, and ultimately Congress and the courts will view management rewards critically because of their relative size [2] and because they are often, and sometimes of necessity, fixed by management itself rather than as the result of arm's length negotiation.[3]

Today the corporate executive [4] has attained a status of leadership affecting every facet of society. He occupies positions of decisive

[2] "Within the range of their experience, most persons are satisfied to regard income differences as reasonable. . . . The same sense of equity, however, does not extend for most persons to ranges of earned income far beyond their own, because the going rates at higher levels are indefinite and the equivalence of service and compensation unfamiliar. . . . A salary of $300,000 is so remote from the expectation of most persons that an effort is required to reason about it in the same terms as would apply to a salary of $5,000." Blackett, *Management Compensation,* 11 MICH. BUS. STUDIES, No. 2, at 9 (1953) ; see note 47 *infra.* Cf. Rosensteel, *New Study Shows Executive Pay Trends,* NATION'S BUS., June 1956, p. 74 at 76: "As a people we are rather proud of the high salaries paid to prominent movie stars, athletes, and others, but in the business world there are social, economic and political pressures which fail to credit the individual skills and capabilities required of business leaders." Cf. note 83, *infra.*

[3] The point suggested in the text has been graphically illustrated by a cartoon showing nine or ten men sitting around a table, presumably the directors of a corporation, with one saying: "I think we can be congratulated on our foresight in voting ourselves these increases, thus assuring to the corporation our continuing loyal services." THE NEW YORKER, June 20, 1953, p. 21. *Cf. id.* July 11, 1959, p. 23 (cartoon of a similar group with the chairman saying: "Lest we be accused of contributing to inflation later on, let's vote ourselves a good little raise right here and now."). See typical criticism cited in note 35 *infra.*

[4] For definitions of the term "executive," see HALL, EXECUTIVE COMPENSATION AND RETIREMENT PLANS 3-4 (1951) : "As used in this study, an executive is defined as any policy-making employee earning $10,000 or more yearly, and a top executive is defined as any policy-making employee with earnings at least as large as those of officers, excluding assistant officers"; SANDERS, EFFECTS OF TAXATION ON EXECUTIVES 3-4 (1951) (colloquially: "the people responsible for formulating policies and putting them into effect in business organizations") ; HALL, *op. cit. supra* note 1, at 3-4, who, after considering an executive's compensation as typically $10,000 or more annually, states: "A top management executive is a businessman whose duties are exclusively or partly those of policy determination." *Cf.* ABBOTT, FORBES, AND THOMPSON, THE EXECUTIVE FUNCTION AND ITS COMPENSATION 3 (1957) ("In many companies executives are defined pragmatically as a small per cent of all salaried employees, such as: the top one per cent or some smaller fraction thereof, or all employees receiving more than some fixed amount, such as $20,000."). The executive's task has been defined as "the selection, assignment, and organization of individuals for the profitable and successful use of materials, plant and money." DODGE, AN INTRODUCTION TO THE BUSINESS OF MANAGEMENT (1939), as quoted in Blackett, *supra* note 2, at 10.

For brilliant discussion of the image and function of the corporation and the corporation executive in the 1960's, consult the essays collected in MASON, THE CORPORATION IN MODERN SOCIETY (1960).

importance in government, on boards of educational institutions, in the sciences and the arts. He influences distribution of large sources of wealth, both through the capital controlled by the corporation which he serves and through organizations affiliated with or dependent on his corporation. He has been made the subject of countless studies and analyses; numerous publications and periodicals are directed towards him. His problems are given separate consideration in business and tax forums. His position and its significance have been dramatized in novels and on the stage and screen.

The Background. The current status and recognition of the executive are of relatively recent origin. In the early days of the Republic, the most desirable form of wealth was considered to be land, with the great manorholders and Southern planters occupying the most respected place in society. Great business fortunes were rare. Such as they were, they generally had been accumulated by the leading merchants of Boston, Philadelphia, and New York. The nineteenth century brought with it tremendous growth both in commerce and in manufacturing, and after the Civil War the accumulation and concentration of business wealth proceeded apace. It is estimated that in 1860 there were 500 millionaires in the country,[5] and that by 1892 the number had risen to more than 4,000,[6] including some 1,140 manufacturers, 986 merchants, 468 landowners, 410 transportation magnates, and 356 bankers and brokers.[7] It is hardly probable that any of these men of wealth derived any substantial income from salaries. A Gould, a Vanderbilt, a Wanamaker, or a Carnegie made his money in other ways.

The tremendous industrial expansion of the country in the later years of the nineteenth century and the opening years of the twentieth was accompanied, as we all know, by an increasing concentration of control; mergers took place in every branch of industry, and the merged groups in their turn would join with each other to form even greater aggregations. The men who headed these vast enterprises were generally representatives of the old school—Rockefeller, Duke, Hill, and their compeers. Such men and their immediate lieutenants built up their fortunes not through salaries or other direct compensation from their companies, but through stock ownership and the profits of expansion and promotion. The salaried worker, whether or not he was graced with an official title in the corporate

---

[5] Corey, The Decline of American Capitalism 307 (1934).

[6] Corey, *Fortunes: Private,* 6 Encyc. Soc. Sci. 396.

[7] There were also 286 mine and oil field owners; 168 lumber magnates; 47 cattle ranchers; 65 corporation lawyers; 3 patent holders; and a scattered group in other fields. *Ibid.*

hierarchy, seems to have remained at a financial plane and position infinitely below that of the great leaders of industry. Taussig and Barker found that in the decade from 1904 to 1914 the largest manufacturing companies, those having capital over $1,500,000, paid average yearly salaries of $9,958 to their ranking executives.[8] Similarly, it is said that in 1900 the president of one of the elevated railroads in New York City received yearly compensation of $5,000.[9] Information on these subjects is not plentiful, but such as there is all points in the same direction.[10] In general, the corporate executive simply had no place in the upper income levels.

Later, of course, the picture changed. One by one the old titans passed. Not always were their children able to take their places; often they were definitely unwilling to do so. In one after another of our great corporations the professional executive began taking charge. His influence steadily increased, but so also did his responsibilities. Rewards, too, became greater. Exact figures are hard to obtain, since few companies revealed their salary schedules to the public, or even to their own stockholders. Business tradition forbade discussion of such matters. Average executive compensation in large industry appears to have risen steadily,[11] and by 1928 the executives of some of our largest companies were receiving compensation running as high as $1,000,000 or $1,500,000 annually.[12] This development was accompanied by the rise of new forms of compensation; bonus and profit-participation plans came into wide use. Such plans, which were almost unknown in this country prior to 1914,[13] had by 1929 been adopted by many—if not most—of our large corporations.[14]

[8] Taussig and Barker, *American Corporations and Their Executives,* 40 Q. J. Econ. 1, 19 (1925). This study was based on information received from 400 manufacturing companies. One company paid a salary of $100,000.

[9] N. Y. Times, Oct. 29, 1933, § 8, p. 3, col. 6.

[10] The highest salary found prior to 1900 was one of $75,000 paid to the president of a life insurance company in the 1890's. See Beers v. New York Life Ins. Co., 66 Hun 75, 20 N.Y. Supp. 788 (1st Dep't 1892), where the court speaks of such a salary as "enormous." After the foundation of the United States Steel Corporation in 1901, Judge Gary was reputed to be receiving a salary of $100,000 and a bonus of nearly $400,000. 2 EDITORIAL RESEARCH REPORTS, No. 10 (1935) 237.

[11] Government investigations showed that in 1914 four railroads paid their presidents $75,000 annually; in 1917 the top in one road was $87,500, which went to $100,000 in 1921. By 1929 two railroad executives were receiving $150,000; one received $125,000, and eight received $100,000. 2 EDITORIAL RESEARCH REPORTS, No. 10 (1935) 239.

[12] *Cf.* FTC, REPORT ON THE COMPENSATION OF OFFICERS AND DIRECTORS OF CERTAIN CORPORATIONS (1934), mimeographed, Washington, D.C. See note 23 *infra.*

[13] See *infra* Chapter 3, note 1; Taussig and Barker, *supra* note 8, at 29.

[14] BAKER, EXECUTIVE SALARIES AND BONUS PLANS 16 *et seq.* (1938), states that in 1928 some 64% of a group of companies studied had adopted such plans.

Then came October of 1929. The managerial group, as a whole, seems to have been pretty deep in the market. To make matters worse, corporate earnings fell off, and bonuses contingent upon profits either ceased or were sharply reduced.[15] To compensate for their losses, many executives sought and obtained increases in fixed salaries in 1930 and 1931.[16] While some decline took place in the absolute amounts paid to corporate executives,[17] the purchasing power of the amounts paid was still high and during the depression the executive class as a whole probably suffered less than the rest of the population.[18] In the meantime, working men were being discharged in large numbers, wage levels were falling, and dividends were not being paid.

The high rewards of the boom years gradually came to light as the depression took its course. Stockholder litigation played a part.[19] So also did investigations by equity receivers and bankruptcy trustees after the collapse of certain large companies. Government investigations brought many facts to public attention.[20] Congressional interest in the subject took active form with the passage, on May 29, 1933, of a Senate resolution directing the Federal Trade Commission to make a study of the matter.[21] The Commission thereupon requested over 1,000 large corporations to submit information concerning "salaries, and all compensation, direct or indirect, including that from subsidiary and affiliated companies, paid to executive officers and directors for each year 1928–32, inclusive, and also the rate of salary as of September 1, 1933."[22] The report of the Commission was

[15] *Id.* at 16–27.

[16] REIS, FALSE SECURITY 22–23 (1937).

[17] Between 1928 and 1933, the salaries of the officers of 100 large corporations had on the average fallen less than 3 per cent. See Stryker, *How Much is an Executive Worth?*, FORTUNE, Apr. 1955, pp. 108–09 (citing a Baker study).

[18] See BUREAUCRACY AND TRUSTEESHIP IN LARGE CORPORATIONS 110–12 (Temporary National Economic Committee, Monograph 11, 1940) ; BAKER, *op. cit. supra* note 14, at 14, 20, 235. However, the number of functioning bonus plans declined. *Id.,* at 16–17.

[19] See the discussion of the American Tobacco case, Volume II, Chapter 19.

[20] *Hearings before Subcommittee of the Senate Committee on Banking and Currency,* SEN. RES. 84, SEN. RES. 239, PART 6, 72d Cong., 2d Sess. (1933), Peter Norbeck, chairman, Ferdinand Pecora, counsel.

[21] SEN. RES. 75, 73d Cong., 1st Sess. (1933–34), 77 CONG. REC. 4474, 4475 (1933).

[22] The inquiry, in the language of Senate Resolution 75, was directed to corporations "engaged in interstate commerce (other than public-utility corporations) having capital and/or assets of more than a million dollars in value, whose securities are listed on the New York Stock Exchange or the New York Curb Exchange." The FTC sent out 1,050 questionnaires and received 877 replies; certain corporations, including a number of the largest, refused to report. See 78 CONG. REC. 8481 *et seq.*

rendered to Congress on February 26, 1934.[23] Its publication showed the magnitude of the amounts paid in the boom years.[24]

Resentment against corporate managers began to mount. A more critical attitude toward the rewards of management was reflected in the requirements of disclosure imposed by federal securities and tax legislation,[25] and by other governmental policies adopted by the Roosevelt Administration.[26]

The depression years also brought strenuous efforts by stockholders to set aside the compensation policies of some of the great corporations, and to force a refund of sums received by executives in the boom days. This litigation set the pattern for the stockholders' suits which were instituted in volume during the 1930's and early 1940's. The professional minority stockholder's attorney made his appearance, and his activities eventually brought about the enactment in a number of states of legislation which curtailed the derivative stockholder's action.[27] In a number of companies, efforts were made to organize minority stockholders for the purpose of unseating existing management, and in the ensuing proxy fights executive compensation policies were made an important issue.[28]

These developments gradually brought about a marked change in corporate policy toward executive compensation. With the knowledge that such compensation would be given the publicity attendant upon compulsory disclosure, boards of directors adopted a more

[23] See note 12 *supra*. The report is summarized in N. Y. Times, Feb. 27, 1934, p. 10, col. 1; and, in part, in REIS, *op. cit. supra* note 16, at 273–85 (1937); BAKER, *op. cit. supra* note 14, at 10–27. See also 78 CONG. REC. 3172, 3211, 8481 (1934). The questionnaire form used by the Federal Trade Commission is reproduced in BAKER, *op. cit. supra* note 14, at 257. A few days previously, on Feb. 12, 1934, the Federal Power Commission had reported on the salaries paid by public utilities. See N. Y. Times, Feb. 13, 1934, p. 29, col. 2.

[24] For public reaction at the time, see N. Y. Times, Mar. 3, 1934, p. 12, col. 7, and the proposals of Senator Gore referred to in Volume II, Chapter 16.

[25] Discussed in Volume II, Chapters 16 and 17.

[26] *Id.*, Chapter 16.

[27] E.g., N. Y. GEN. CORP. LAW, § 61-b (1944) (requiring stockholders holding less than 5% of the outstanding shares, unless their stock is worth $50,000 or more, to furnish security for the expenses of the litigation). See also CALIF. GEN. CORP. LAW, § 834; N. J. GEN. CORP. LAW, § 14.3; MD. PUB. GEN. LAW, Art. 16, § 195. For analysis and criticism of the California statute in particular, see Ballantine, *Abuses of Shareholders' Derivative Suits*, 37 CALIF. L. REV. 399 (1949).

[28] Thus the deferred compensation contract of J. Carleton Ward, Jr. (App. E) was a ground for the 1949 proxy fight for control of Fairchild Engine and Airplane Corporation. See Volume II, Chapter 19; 60 YALE L.J. 429 (1951).

cautious approach toward salary and bonus payments and began to look for supplemental methods of compensating their corporate executives. This trend was somewhat accelerated by developments incident to World War II.

Our entry into that war led for the first time to direct governmental control over salaries as part of the effort to prevent runaway inflation.[29] Such control, exercised through salary stabilization measures in effect for the period from 1942 to 1945 and again during the Korean crisis, 1951–53,[30] stimulated deferred compensation and pension plans, which were in general excluded from the operation of stabilization policies.

World War II also brought with it federal income tax rates which made the relatively high pre-existing rates seem modest by comparison. Inflation came.

The post-World War II tax reductions that were effected directly through lower rates, and indirectly through the income-splitting permitted since 1948 upon joint returns,[31] did not restore after-tax executive compensation to the level of the 1920's or the 1930's.[32]

[29] 56 Stat. 765 (1942).

[30] 64 Stat. 798 (1950), as amended by 65 Stat. 134 (1951), and 66 Stat. 296 (1952) discussed in Washington and Rothschild, *op. cit. supra* note 19, at 308 ff.

[31] INT. REV. CODE OF 1954, § 2.

[32] Blackett, *Management Compensation,* 16 MICH. BUS. STUDIES, No. 2, at 35, 45; Roberts, *A General Theory of Executive Compensation Based on Statistically Tested Propositions,* 70 Q.J. ECON. 270 (1956), see note 51 *infra.* Consult SANDERS, *op. cit., supra* note 4, at 85 ff.

Tax rates in 1939 and 1949 and their minimum effect on compensation at various levels are shown by the following tables derived from Blackett, *supra,* at 43:

Salary Level	1939 Tax Rate (Per Cent)	1949 Tax Rate (Per Cent)
$ 60,000	18.2	33.8
80,000	23.6	38.6
100,000	29.0	42.6
140,000	37.4	48.3
180,000	42.4	52.6

For other tables showing the effect of taxes, see CASEY, PAY PLANS § 8104 (1960); ROTHSCHILD, *op. cit. supra* note 1, at 968–69.

The impact of taxes on executive compensation was dramatically illustrated in 1947 by the case of Walter S. Carpenter, Jr., chairman and past president of the du Pont Company. In that year, Mr. Carpenter's annual compensation was $175,000 as compared to $78,570 in 1922. But his net income from that source in 1947 after taxes was $48,251, as against $60,843 in 1922. Letter dated Feb. 16, 1953 from R. E. Manning, of the du Pont Company, to one of the authors. Thus, while over a period of years Mr. Carpenter's annual salary had been increased by almost $100,000, he

Moreover, if loss in purchasing power through impaired value of the dollar is taken into consideration, the executive group seems to have suffered more severely than other groups of employees, with few top executives faring as well in terms of real compensation in the 1950's as in the 1930's.[33] So far as real current compensation is concerned, no change for top executives appears to be in prospect.[34]

This is, of course, only one side of the picture. The other side is reflected in the view that in the past, and particularly in the 1920's and 1930's, management compensation was unduly high. It is implicit in this view that tax and inflation factors have simply brought about a proper and needed adjustment and that, in fact, still further readjustment would be in order. It is also suggested that stock options, pensions, deferred compensation, and other supplemental benefits received by management have more than made up for any loss in real salary.[35]

Whatever the merits of this controversy, there is no doubt that high taxes, always important in the negotiation of employment

---

was earning $12,500 less than he had been earning twenty-five years before, without taking into consideration the loss in his dollar's purchasing power.

Roberts, *supra*, in referring to "the substantial decline in executive earnings during the last decade," gave a table to show that before-tax earnings for the presidents of a group of 100 companies increased in 1950 to 141% of their 1929 before-tax earnings but were only 80% of the 1929 level after taxes. *Id.*, at 270, n. 1. However, the table showed an increase of earnings from 54% of 1929 after-tax earnings to 61% and 80% in 1936 and 1950, respectively. *Ibid.* Consult notes 33 and 67, *infra*.

[33] Consult Bursk, *Lag in Executive Compensation,* 30 HARV. BUS. REV. 141 (1952) ; Rothschild, *The "Inflationary" Lag in Executive Compensation,* PERSONNEL, July 1952, p. 25. See note 32 *supra*.

[34] Proposed amendments to the Constitution would limit income taxes to a maximum of 25% of income. *Cf.* NATIONAL ASSOCIATION OF MANUFACTURERS, FACING THE ISSUE OF INCOME TAX DISCRIMINATION (1956) (suggesting a five-year plan for reducing both individual and corporate tax rates to a top rate of 35%). A former Commissioner of Internal Revenue has urged that the income tax be repealed. Andrews, *Let's Get Rid of the Income Tax,* AM. WEEKLY, Apr. 2, 1956, p. 6. A proposed Twenty-third Amendment to the Constitution would repeal the Sixteenth Amendment. See Sokolsky, *Income Tax Next under Fire,* Rockland County Journal News, Apr. 26, 1961, p. 30, col. 2. As part of a tax reform program entailing elimination of special tax provisions, including those from which executives benefit, a lower tax rate has been proposed. See *infra* note 89.

[35] For representative criticism of executive compensation, consult LIVINGSTON, THE AMERICAN STOCKHOLDER 227 *passim* (1958) ; GILBERT, ANNUAL REPORTS OF STOCKHOLDER ACTIVITIES AT CORPORATION MEETINGS ; MILLS, THE POWER ELITE 118 ff. *passim* (1957) ; Girard, *They Escape Income Taxes—But You Can't,* AMERICAN, Dec. 1952, p. 15 ; KAUFMAN, YOUR RIGHTS AS AN INVESTOR 37 ff. (1956). In 1953, Westbrook Pegler wrote a series of columns attacking the "greedy executive pension racket, the stock-option racket and other grabs of money which should belong to the individual holders of corporation stocks." See N. Y. Journal-American, May 12–14, 23, 1953. For a reply to these columns, see ROTHSCHILD, TAX ASPECTS AND TRENDS IN EXECUTIVE COMPENSATION 40 at 48–49 (American Management Association, General Management Series No. 166, 1953).

arrangements—as in other business transactions—have become and remain today the single most important factor in executive compensation.

Management's Share.

THE AMA SURVEYS. From time to time surveys have been made of executive compensation in relation particularly to corporate earnings, sales, and invested capital. By far the most comprehensive of these surveys have been those conducted by the American Management Association.

Commencing in 1951, the American Management Association has been publishing annual surveys of executive compensation currently based on analysis of reports from several thousand companies. According to the first such survey, relating to compensation paid chiefly in 1950, "executive compensation accounted for a steadily declining portion of company net income as profits increased. The bigger the profit, the smaller the proportion that went to top executives." [36] The same conclusion appears from subsequent surveys.

The 1950 Survey gave a table setting forth executive compensation as a percentage of net profits in companies classified by the size of current profits into five groups, from those with net profits under $500,000 to those with net profits over $15,000,000.[37] A comparison

---

[36] AMERICAN MANAGEMENT ASSOCIATION (AMA), EXECUTIVE COMPENSATION SURVEY, 1950–51, p. 14. In the survey, "compensation" was defined to mean salaries, bonuses in cash or stock, and retirement contributions, excluding fringe benefits and other forms of compensation not measurable in cash.

[37] *Id.* pp. 31, 32. The table given, in a form not reproduced in subsequent editions, was as follows:

Percentage of Net Profits

	Under $500,000	$500,001 to $2,000,000	$2,000,001 to $7,000,000	$7,000,001 to $15,000,000	Over $15,000,000
President	38	6.4	1.9	1.0	.4
No. 2 Executive (including board chairman)	29	4.6	1.5	.7	.3
No. 3 Executive .	21	3.6	1.1	.6	.3
"Working" directors (excluding three highest paid and those not full-time employees) ...	24	5.4	2.2	1.0	1.0
Non-director officers	45	6.9	2.9	1.9	.7
Total	157	26.9	9.5	5.2	2.7

with similar data in subsequent surveys (with the 1954 Survey [38] taken for illustrative purposes) shows little variation in the percentage of net profits paid top executives (Table I).[39]

TABLE I

PERCENTAGE OF NET PROFITS

Position	$500,001 to $2,000,000		$2,000,001 to $7,000,000		$7,000,001 to $15,000,000		Over $15,000,000	
	1950	1954	1950	1954	1950	1954	1950	1954
President	6.4	5.8	1.9	2.0	1.0	1.2	0.4	0.3
No. 2 Executive (including Chairman of the Board)	4.6	4.5	1.5	1.9	0.7	0.95	0.3	0.27
No. 3 Executive	3.6	4.1	1.1	1.3	0.6	0.9	0.3	0.2
Total	14.6	14.4	4.5	5.2	2.3	3.05	1.0	0.77
		(−0.2)		(+0.6)		(+0.75)		(−0.23)

Table I shows few significant variations in the size of compensation paid top executives between 1950 and 1954. Slight decreases, not in excess of one-fourth of one per cent of after-tax profits, occur in the highest and lowest brackets, but compensation increases of about six-tenths to three-fourths of one per cent of net profits are

[38] AMA, EXECUTIVE COMPENSATION SERVICE, TOP MANAGEMENT SURVEY 32–43 *passim* (6th ed. 1955). This survey covered 3,057 companies with 25,315 executives. *Id.*, p. 17. It was based on compensation paid for the calendar year 1954 and fiscal years ending prior to July 1, 1955.

[39] For the 1951 table of the AMA SURVEY, see WASHINGTON AND ROTHSCHILD, *op cit. supra* note 19, at 21. The 1955 SURVEY does not contain a similar table. In order to obtain data for comparison, the average after-tax profits for the various corporate units classified by their sales, as shown on p. *32 et seq.* of the SURVEY FOR DURABLE GOODS MANUFACTURING, NON-DURABLE GOODS MANUFACTURING AND WHOLESALE AND RETAIL TRADE, were averaged in accordance with the after-tax profits groups appearing in the 1951 table. Thus, an average net profits figure was obtained for each class; for instance, in the $500,001 to $2,000,000 net profits class, the average profit per company in the three fields mentioned was $1,076,800. It was against this figure that the percentage represented by the executive's salary was computed. The companies in the three classifications used in the table include 2,519 or about 80% of the companies participating in the survey.

In order to obtain comparable data on compensation paid executives in 1954–55, the average paid to each of the three top executives in companies engaged in durable and non-durable goods manufacturing and in wholesale and retail trade, classified according to size of net profits, was computed and figured as a percentage of net profits in each of the four size classes appearing in the table. Comparison of compensation paid "working" directors and non-director officers as a group had to be omitted since executives below the top three were not listed in accordance with these classifications in the 1954–55 SURVEY.

indicated in the middle-bracket companies whose net profits range from $2,000,000 to $15,000,000.

Companies with less than $500,000 in net profits were excluded from this comparison because data for them appeared insufficient.[40] However, a limited comparison among manufacturing companies indicates a sharp reduction in the percentage of after-tax profits represented by the compensation of the three highest paid executives. Where this pay took 38%, 29%, and 21% of profits in 1950, it took only 15%, 12%, and 11% of net profits on the average to compensate the three highest paid executive positions covered by the 1954 Survey. It is not clear whether this drop is due to the incompleteness of current data, increases in after-tax profits of smaller companies unaccompanied by a comparable rise in executive compensation, or a drop in the compensation paid by relatively small companies to their executives. General data showing a continued rise in executive compensation would, however, render the last hypothesis the least likely .

Table I also shows that the compensation of the three top executives of companies engaged in trade or manufacturing [41] with after-tax profits in excess of $500,000 amounted to from less than 1% to 14% of after-tax profits, depending on company size. Only in companies with less than $500,000 in after-tax profits does this compensation exceed one-third of such profits; more complete data may well show it to be as high as the more than 80% figure developed from the 1950 AMA Survey.

While the compensation of the three top executives as a whole, in terms of a share of after-tax profits, seems to have increased little between 1950 and 1954, executive compensation as a whole increased after 1950. The 1954 Survey gave figures which are summarized in Table II.[42]

[40] For example, with respect to companies engaged in wholesale and retail trade in which small companies are significant, no data were furnished for companies with less than $2 million in sales. Later surveys cover companies with sales volumes of from under $1,000,000 to over $1,000,000,000, with special sections for small companies, million-dollar companies, and divisional positions.

[41] The AMA SURVEY data were not as readily collated for financial companies, utilities, and companies engaged in extracting industries. However, the compensation patterns in these industries generally show no deviation from those of the major groups, though lower levels of compensation commonly appear, as shown in more comprehensive coverages in current surveys. *E.g.*, AMA, EXECUTIVE COMPENSATION SERVICE, TOP MANAGEMENT SURVEY (11th ed. 1960) ; see 198 ff. (Coal Mining, Petroleum, and Natural Gas), 218 ff. (Finance and Insurance), 236 ff. (Public Utilities).

[42] AMA 1955 SURVEY, *supra* note 38, p. 18. A study of the ten-year trend from 1949 to 1958 showed that compensation paid all executives in 1958 was 42.2% greater than that paid in 1949, but the compensation of chief executives was only

TABLE II

| | Per Cent Increase Over Previous Year | | | |
	1951	1952	1953	1954
Profits before taxes	12.7	−11.9	6.7	−5.8
Profits after taxes	−6.3	− 2.4	8.3	4.1
Sales	15.5	5.1	9.9	−2.2
Total compensation	5.4	0.6	5.2	1.8

The percentages in Table II raise a question as to the usefulness of comparing executive compensation with company profits, for executive compensation did not decrease with decreases in profits during the four years covered. Nor does Table II show any correlation between the percentage of increase in compensation and the percentage of increase in profits when profits did increase. All that the table appears to indicate is that aggregate compensation of corporate executives for the four-year period increased without regard to increases or decreases in profits, whether before or after taxes. Before-tax profits decreased in 1952 and in 1954 almost to their levels in 1951 and 1953 respectively, but in both 1952 and 1954 executive compensation continued its upward climb, although at a reduced rate. A closer correlation can be observed between increases (or decreases) in profits before taxes on the one hand and bonuses on the other, but increases in other components of compensation—viz., salaries and pension contributions—made up for decreases in bonuses.[43]

The annual increases in executive compensation shown in Table II do not necessarily mean increases in the compensation of specific executives. The figure is an aggregate for all executive compensation and would increase, for example, with addition of officers or other members to the executive staff as the result of expansion, merger, or other factors.

The AMA Surveys also show a lack of correlation between compensation and sales trends. In 1952, for instance, the percentage increase of executive compensation was only one-eighth of the

24.7% above its 1949 level; in terms of 1949 dollars, executives on the average were found to be earning in 1958 about 27% less than in 1949. AMA, EXECUTIVE COMPENSATION SERVICE, TOP MANAGEMENT EDITION 36 (10th ed. 1959). See note 65 infra.

[43] Ibid. Increases or decreases of before-tax profits in companies included in the survey were: 1951: +12.7%; 1952: −11.9%; 1953: +6.7%; 1954: −5.8%. However, the operation of the tax laws brought quite different results for after-tax profits.

increase in sales, while in 1954 executive compensation rose 1.8% but sales fell 2.2% below those of the previous year.

A correlation does appear between the size of the employing corporation and the amount of the executive compensation which it pays, as evidenced from the data condensed in Table III.[44]

TABLE III

Sales in Millions of Dollars	Average Compensation[a] in Thousands of Dollars			Average Compensation as Percentage of Sales[b]		
	Manufacturing[c]		Whole- sale and Retail Trades	Manufacturing		Whole- sale and Retail Trades
	Durable Goods	Non- Durable Goods		Durable Goods	Non- Durable Goods	
Under 2	216.2[d]	199.9[d]	–	14.0	18.0	–
2–5	284.0[e]	280.9[e]	219.7[f]	8.0	8.0	6.0
5–10	344.0	351.8	296.4[g]	4.5	5.0	3.5
10–25	446.7	450.3	381.1[e]	2.6	2.2	2.1
25–50	558.8	591.0	540.3	1.6	1.65	1.5
50–100	643.8	657.4	565.3	1.0	0.9	0.8
100–200	782.9	766.5	716.7	0.6	0.6	0.47
200–500	1,025.6	958.9	968.3	0.3	0.32	0.26
500–1,000	1,225.7	1,321.6	1,091.0	0.17	0.18	0.15
Over 1,000	2,712.8	1,625.3	1,334.0	0.13	0.09	0.08[h]

[a] Actually not average compensation paid by participating companies, but average cash compensation paid to employees in nineteen or fewer top executive positions, depending on how many are found in a particular sales size class or type of company.

[b] I.e., of the average sales of companies in the particular class.

[c] The inclusion of companies in industries other than trade and manufacturing would not significantly affect the table. The compensation paid by the 538 companies falling into such other industries is generally lower than that of the companies engaged in trade and manufacturing generally. The largest oil companies, ranking among the largest industrial concerns, constitute a significant exception. In dollar terms, at least, they rank well ahead of the larger wholesale and retail trade companies as payers of executive compensation. (AMA 1955 Survey, p. 213.) The average dollar figure was $1,372,000 for companies with over $500,000,000 in sales.

[d] Seventeen positions only.

[e] Eighteen positions only.

[f] Fourteen positions only.

[g] Sixteen positions only.

[h] The corresponding figure for the largest oil companies is 0.1%.

The survey reveals that average sales vary little in amount, within each size group, between durable and non-durable goods manufacturing and companies in wholesale or retail trades; variations do not exceed 10%. There was only one real exception: the very largest durable goods manufacturing companies (those with over $1,000,000,-000 of sales) such as the largest manufacturers of steel, automobiles,

[44] AMA 1955 SURVEY, supra note 38.

machinery, or household and electrical appliances, had average sales of from 16% to 22% higher than companies of similar size in other fields. Average executive compensation [45] paid by the largest companies in non-durable goods manufacturing and trade was about six to eight times higher than that paid by the smallest companies. Among durable goods manufacturing companies it was 12½ times higher. In all other size groups, however, except among the largest and the smallest companies, there appears to be little difference if allowance is made for the nature of the data used.[46]

THE BLACKETT STUDY. Other surveys have attempted to throw light on the structure of executive compensation in relation to company size, profits, and other factors. One, a study by O. W. Blackett, examines the statistical relationship of executive compensation to invested capital and earnings based on analysis of 92 large companies during the ten-year period 1929–38 and the five-year period 1945–49.[47] Professor Blackett assumes that the relationship to earnings provides the best measure of executive compensation since it points up the cost of top management from the stockholder's point of view. In addition, he has compared with company earnings the compensation of the president [48] and of the three highest paid executives. Basically, and without probing the validity of his statistical assumptions, his tables confirm that compensation decreases as a percentage of earnings in proportion to increases in invested capital. Smaller companies with an invested capital of about $10,000,000 (or $10,000,-000 to $50,000,000 of sales) [49] pay their three top executives an average of 11.6% of earnings, while companies with a capital of over $1,000,000,000 pay only 0.3% of earnings. Each of over 90 companies used by Professor Blackett for this part of his study [50] paid in 1953 0.0985% of its average invested capital in compensating its three top executives, a percentage strikingly similar to the average

---

[45] For explanation of this term, see *supra* note a to Table III.

[46] AMA 1955 SURVEY, *supra* note 38, pp. 10, 25. The conclusions stated in the text continue to be borne out by subsequent surveys, in the opinion of Dean Rosensteel, director of the surveys. Letter from Mr. Rosensteel, dated July 11, 1961, to one of the authors.

[47] Blackett, *Management Compensation,* 11 MICH. BUS. STUDIES, No. 2 (1953) (the Blackett Study). The study used a sample of 92 listed companies from 14 industries, excluding deficit companies, railroads, and utilities, for the two periods 1929–38 and 1945–49, both inclusive, *id.* 14–17. Certain results of the study were summarized in Blackett, *Changes in Top Management Compensation,* 5 MICH. BUS. REV. 2 (1953).

[48] Usually the highest paid corporate official.

[49] *Cf.* AMA 1955 SURVEY, *supra* note 38, p. 32 *et seq.*

[50] Blackett, *Management Compensation, supra* note 47, at 36–38.

percentage of invested capital paid by the approximately 2,500 companies which participated in the AMA Survey for 1954.

THE ROBERTS STUDIES. A conclusion generally in accord with the AMA surveys and the Blackett study evolves from technical studies made by David R. Roberts of 392 companies in 1945, 1948, and 1949, and of 939 companies in 1950.[51] All the companies selected were publicly held and about 70% of them were engaged in manufacturing. Examining the relationship between compensation and sales, profits, and profit rate, Dean Roberts concluded that the level of executive compensation was not influenced either by the profits of the employing company or by profitability in terms of the sales dollar, but that it was significantly related to the amount of sales, i.e., to corporate size. In addition, he found that differences in compensation by industry generally reflected only differences in corporate size and became statistically insignificant when the effect of such differences in size was removed.[52]

While the rate of progression in the amount of compensation from one size class to the next was not at all uniform, no example was found in which average compensation in a larger size class was lower than for companies in a smaller size class. Dean Roberts concluded that compensation progressed in amount according to size, although he noted occasional irregularities when compensation trends ran counter to both profits and size.

Based upon the same sample, Dean Roberts later elaborated on his studies and published expanded findings in which he concluded that "the absolute dollar level of a firm's compensation and its relationship to the levels of other companies do not affect incentive." He suggested that "it must be the internal relationships and other arrangements which are vital, the absolute level being important chiefly in so far as it may bear upon them." [53]

THE NEWCOMER STUDY. Other studies accord with the Roberts findings and those set forth above based on the AMA Surveys. A

---

[51] Roberts, *A General Theory of Executive Compensation Based on Statistically Tested Propositions,* 70 Q.J. ECON. 270 (1956) (the Roberts Studies). The Roberts Studies are summarized in Roberts, *New Facts about Executive Compensation,* 44 MGMT. REV. 473 (1955).

[52] Roberts, *General Theory, supra* note 51, at 271. An exception is noted for companies engaged in activities subject to public regulation, such as utilities, airlines, and railroads, which pay less than companies of comparative size in other industries. Dean Roberts concluded that profits and sales are so closely interrelated as to form a single package, but that compensation relates to sales rather than profits to the extent that the package is broken. *Id.* at 276.

[53] ROBERTS, EXECUTIVE COMPENSATION 160–61 (1959).

study by Dr. Mabel Newcomer of compensation paid in 1950 to board chairmen and presidents of 428 very large companies (420 with assets of over $75 million) showed a relationship between remuneration and size but "many and erratic . . . deviations." [54]

THE MASSEY-EMERSON STUDY. Substantial deviations are also apparent from a detailed study of corporations organized in California, Florida, Ohio, and Virginia with securities listed on the New York or American Stock Exchanges.[55] The Massey-Emerson survey compares aggregate remuneration paid to officers and directors in 1950 and 1956 to assets and net income of 22 out of 36 listed California companies, 6 out of 8 listed Florida companies, 63 out of 64 listed Ohio companies, and 23 out of 29 listed Virginia companies. The companies surveyed are ranked in each of the four states by aggregate remuneration, total assets, and net income. In the case of each group, the survey failed to show a significant relation between compensation, asset value, and income at any level.

EARLIER SURVEYS. In 1936 the National Association of Manufacturers made a study of payments by 694 companies.[56] It was found that executive rewards amounted to 3% of total payrolls and 10% of total dividends. A subsequent study by Baker [57] covering the years 1929 through 1936 was more detailed: he found that a group of large companies (51 concerns with assets exceeding $100,000,000 in 1929) paid 3% of earnings to their executives in 1929, and an average of 4.9% for the entire period. Comparable figures for a group of smaller companies (53 concerns with assets less than $10,000,000 in 1936) were 11% and 25.5%, respectively. All of these companies (large and small) had shares listed on the New York Stock Exchange, and the study did not include any closely held companies of small size. Dividend distributions in the large companies stayed at about the same proportion to executive payments: 16 times greater in 1929, and 17 times greater in 1936. In the smaller companies, dividends were 4 times greater than executive cost in 1929, 3½ times greater in 1936. Over the entire period from 1929 to 1936, dividends in

---

[54] NEWCOMER, THE BIG BUSINESS EXECUTIVE 123, 130 (1955). Survey of compensation paid (a) in 1900 by 214 companies with assets of over $25 million, (b) in 1925 by companies with assets of over $50 million, and (c) in 1950 by companies with assets of over $75 million (the Newcomer Study).

[55] Massey and Emerson, *Remuneration of Officers and Directors of Listed California, Florida, Ohio and Virginia Corporations*, 12 UNIV. FLA. L. REV. 156 (1959).

[56] The study itself was semiconfidential, for the benefit of members of the association. The figures quoted are from the association's press release of July 5, 1936.

[57] Baker, *Executive Compensation Payments by Large and Small Industrial Companies*, 53 Q.J. ECON. 404 (1939).

large companies were 14 times more than executive payments; in the smaller companies, 2½ times more. Average payments to individual executives varied little: the top man in large companies averaged $101,000 in 1929 and $93,000 in 1936; in smaller companies, $31,000 in 1929 and $25,000 in 1936. The whole executive group (the top three executives in each company) followed a parallel pattern: the average in large companies was $40,000 in 1929 and $35,000 in 1936. In the smaller companies members of this group averaged $18,000 in 1929 and $14,000 in 1936.

Table IV is derived from a compilation issued by the National Industrial Conference Board, covering over 450,000 manufacturing corporations, and comparing the years 1929 and 1937.[58]

TABLE IV

| | Millions of Dollars | |
	1929	1937
Total income (100% of corporations studied)	$72,224	$62,457
Management expense (officers)	1,172 (6.6%)	1,004 (7%)
Cash dividends paid (gross) $3,159	$2,954	
Less: Intra-corporate dividends 583	617	
Net dividends	$ 2,576	$ 2,337

Gross dividends decreased 6.5%, while management cost decreased 14.3%. The undistributed profits tax in effect for 1937 may have forced a large part of these dividend payments, however. It is also noticeable that the officers' share of total income increased slightly, from 6.6% to 7%.

A more detailed table (Table V) showing the relationship between dividends and executive compensation covers all manufacturing industries.[59]

In a study of over 13,000 textile companies, covering the years 1931 through 1937,[60] Mr. Baker concluded that the smaller companies paid a far higher percentage of earnings to executives than did the large companies; and that, in fact, the stockholders in the smallest companies received little or nothing (in their capacity as stock-

[58] Condensed from Table 5, MEASUREMENT OF THE SOCIAL PERFORMANCE OF BUSINESS 96 (TNEC Monograph 7, 1940). The table was compiled by the Conference Board from official data.

[59] Condensed from Table 2, *id.* at 59. The table was compiled by the authors of Monograph 7 from official data.

[60] Baker, *Executive Compensation by Small Textile Companies,* 20 HARV. BUS. REV. 81 (1941).

TABLE V

Year	Dividends (Excluding Intra-corporate Dividends)		Officers' Compensation	
	Millions	Index 1923–25 = 100	Millions	Index 1923–24 = 100
1929	$2,575	145.2	$1,172	121.3
1930	2,613	147.3	1,096	113.4
1931	1,894	106.8	935	96.8
1932	1,116	62.9	734	76.0
1933	1,009	56.9	706	73.1
1934	1,221	68.8	754	78.0
1935	1,580	89.1	812	84.0
1936	2,405	135.6	951	98.4
1937	2,871	161.8	1,076	111.4
1938	1,668	94.0	956	99.0

holders, at least). The percentage paid to executives decreased "regularly and substantially" as the size of the company increased.

Finally, a Conference Board survey of salaries and pensions in 1949, made in terms of sales, for the three highest paid executives of 1275 companies in 120 industries showed that the cost of executive compensation ranged from 0.05% in some large companies to 6% or more in some of the small ones.[61]

Significance of the Figures. What conclusions can be drawn from this array of surveys and statistics? These appear to be indicated:

1. No specific correlation has yet been established between current remuneration on the one hand, and corporate assets, earnings, or sales on the other.[62] A relationship has been found in one study

[61] COMPENSATION AND PENSIONS FOR EXECUTIVES, NICB Studies in Personnel Policy No. 111 (1950). For subsequent Conference Board reports, see TRENDS IN EXECUTIVE COMPENSATION, NICB Studies in Labor Statistics No. 6 (1951); TOP MANAGEMENT COMPENSATION, NICB Studies in Labor Statistics No. 8 (1953); COMPENSATION OF TOP EXECUTIVES, NICB Studies in Labor Statistics No. 17 (1956); COMPENSATION OF TOP EXECUTIVES, NICB Studies in Personnel Policy No. 173 (1959); TOP EXECUTIVE COMPENSATION, NICB Studies in Personnel Policy No. 179 (1960).

Other surveys include studies published by Dartnell Publications, Inc., and annual summaries of the highest pay published by BUSINESS WEEK.

[62] But cf. Rosensteel, *Executive Compensation: Developing a Balanced Program,* 45 MGMT. REV. 388, 390–91 (1956): "By and large, surveys indicate that the salaries paid for comparable management jobs from one company to another show a rather considerable degree of uniformity. AMA surveys of comparable jobs at top- and middle-management levels show that up to 75 per cent of actual salaries paid fall within a range that has a maximum no greater than 50 per cent more than the minimum. . . . the majority of jobs are clustered at a medium range, the top of

where executive compensation was considered in terms of capital and earnings jointly.[63]

2. A general relationship has been found in most of the surveys between executive compensation and size expressed in terms of assets, earnings, sales, or capital, with executive compensation larger in absolute dollar amount but smaller in percentage in the case of the larger companies.[64]

3. Executive compensation has increased each year since 1940,[65] but its rate of increase has been less than the rate of wage increases for hourly workers,[66] and less than the general rate of expansion of the economy.[67]

4. Notwithstanding annual increases in aggregate executive compensation, salary increases for the highest paid executives in at least the largest corporations have been relatively small and few.[68]

---

which is approximately 50 per cent higher than the bottom." It is believed, however, that Dean Rosensteel, who has directed the AMA Surveys, was referring primarily to surveys confined to companies within an industry or related industries. See *infra* note 74.

[63] Blackett, *Management Compensation, supra* note 47, at 23 *passim.*

[64] Although compensation paid by larger companies is greater than that paid by smaller, the differences have been found not so great as might be expected based on differences in size. NEWCOMER, *op. cit. supra* note 54, at 123, 130.

[65] It has been estimated that top-management compensation increased about 75% over the ten-year period beginning about 1940 and 23% over the five-year period beginning about 1950, and in 1956 was increasing at the rate of 5% per year. Rosensteel, *supra* note 2.

[66] During a comparable period from 1939 to 1950, wage rates in selected manufacturing industries increased by about 130%; between 1950 and 1955 they increased further by approximately another 28%. Increases in these hourly rates in 1956, 1957, and 1958 over the prior year averaged about 4% annually. The movement of hourly wage rates between 1939 and 1957 in the building and retail trades was similar, though the percentage increases were somewhat lower than those for hourly wage rates in manufacturing industries. U. S. DEP'T OF COMMERCE, *op. cit. supra* note 1, Table 283, at 227; and, for 1958 wage rate data, 5 U. S. DEP'T OF LABOR, BUREAU OF LABOR STATISTICS, EMPLOYMENT AND EARNINGS 53 (No. 2, Aug. 1958).

[67] Gross national product, as a measure of the expansion of the national economy, rose by about 183% between 1940 and 1950 and by approximately 37% over 1950 in the year 1955. In 1956, the annual growth rate was 8% and in 1957 slightly below 5%, U. S. DEP'T OF COMMERCE, *supra* note 1, Table 382, at 304; for 1958 figures, see U. S. DEP'T OF COMMERCE, OFFICE OF BUSINESS ECONOMICS, SURVEY OF CURRENT BUSINESS, Table 1, at 6 (May 1958).

[68] *Cf.* NEWCOMER, *op. cit. supra* note 54, at 123–24 (finding that newly appointed executives receive almost as much as those with long service). In the Blackett Study, *supra* note 47, none of the companies paying over $200,000 had increased the salary of its highest paid officer. *Id.,* 45–47. For a specific example, consult Referee's Report pursuant to order dated March 13, 1952, Cohn v. Columbia Pictures Corp., unreported, N. Y. County Clerk's Index No. 9038/1950 (salary of president of motion picture company had remained at $3,500 a week from 1932 to 1952). The discussion is confined to salary increases and does not consider the effect of supplemental compensation and incentives which may have taken the place of salary increases.

5. Increases or decreases in corporate earnings, before or after profits, do not appear to have resulted in proportionate increases or decreases in executive compensation. More than half the time, however, executive compensation, sales, and profit have moved together in the same direction.[69]

6. There may be a relationship between increased executive compensation and increased corporate earnings,[70] but the relationship has yet to be satisfactorily demonstrated.[71]

7. A relationship has been found between the compensation of the highest paid executive and executives immediately below him.[72]

8. Relationships of executive compensation patterns have been found within the same or related industries. Such relationships may be based on historical factors [73] or may result from one company's study of the compensation practices of other companies with which it considers itself comparable.[74] Some industries are high-paying,

[69] Cf. Roberts, *General Theory, supra* note 51, at 279 (finding the three variables moving together in 53% of the cases, with compensation moving in one direction and profits and sales together in another in 27%).

[70] Patton, *Current Practices in Executive Compensation,* 29 HARV. BUS. REV. 56 (Jan.–Feb., 1951) (based on AMA Survey, 1950–51) ; *cf.* Patton, *Annual Report on Executive Compensation,* 34 HARV. BUS. REV. 124, 125 (Nov.–Dec., 1956) : "Industries reporting above-average compensation increases to their chief executives were generally among the biggest sales and profit gainers, while the smallest compensation increases tended to go to the top managements of industries with the poorest sales and profits records."

[71] Corporate size (with which executive compensation has been found to increase) being closely related to total corporate profit, "one would expect to find a statistical relationship between compensation and total profit, and a number of lay writers have been so impressed by its discovery that they have asserted a causal connection." Roberts, *General Theory, supra* note 51, at 292.

[72] "Generally speaking, a president will receive in salary about a third more than his No. 2 man, about twice what his No. 3 man gets, and some three times the salaries paid to those on the fourth rung of management." Stryker, *supra* note 17. For the suggestion that the differential between the top man and the No. 2 man has been widening and that between the second and fifth ranks narrowing, see *id.,* 230–31 (quoting Ralph W. Ells, of Allen-Bradley Co.). *Cf.* Patton, *Annual Report, supra* note 70, at 126 (finding the 1955 percentages of top-man compensation to be 72% for the second rank, 59% for the third, and 52% for the fourth).

[73] In the tobacco industry, for example, major companies which were once a part of the American Tobacco Company for many years had a bylaw providing for incentive compensation for officers and others based on the original American Tobacco bylaw. For the present form of the bylaw see AMERICAN TOBACCO, App. U.

[74] It is for purposes of study and comparison within particular industries that the AMA and other surveys have particular value. *Cf.* Rosensteel, *supra* note 2 at 74: ". . . if you select a group of companies within a given industry and of a given size determined by sales and profits, capital invested and number of employees, you can arrive at usable averages." But even in the same industry, companies with approximately the same sales may pay widely disparate salaries and bonuses. Stryker, *supra* note 17, at 111 (comparing the $225,000 salary in 1953 of the president of Fruehauf Trailer with the $105,000 salary of the president of Mack Trucks and the

others are low-paying, a result which may derive, in some part, from the amount of regulation to which the industry is subject and the size of the companies in the industry.

9. Statistics with respect to executive compensation have been and will continue to be handicapped by the inability to value supplemental benefits, such as contingent or deferred compensation and stock option or stock purchase plans, which may often take the place of salary increases that would otherwise have been granted.

"Reasonable" Compensation and the Businessman.

No satisfactory formula for determining the reasonableness of executive compensation has yet been devised.[75] The market forces of supply and demand are relatively weak in this area.[76]

The corporate executive is likely to think of the compensation problem in terms of rivalry, competition, prestige. How much could he earn with another company in the same line of business, or with a company in another line of business? How much would his company have to pay to obtain someone else of equal ability? How much are others in his company making? What are his friends or associates in other companies being paid?

$258,000 salary of the president of U. S. Steel with the $457,000 salary of the president of Bethlehem Steel). At least in the latter case, the difference may be explained in large part by historical considerations and use of a bonus formula.

[75] The Roberts Studies, *supra* note 51, at 290, suggest as a formula to ascertain the upper limit which a company should be willing to pay an executive "the excess of the firm's total profit under his direction over what it would be under the direction of the best alternative executive plus the amount which would have to be paid in order to secure the latter's services." The lower level would be what the executive could command in his next best employment. *Id.,* 290–91. A more generalized approach is the suggestion that executive compensation should not exceed a specific percentage of corporate net income; as an example, a corporation with earnings of $2½ million a year should not pay more than 20% of net earnings to its ten top executives. The Wolfson Plan for Stockholder Security, Address to New York Financial Writers Association by Louis E. Wolfson, Mar. 2, 1954, at 8, 12.

Job evaluations, with salary ranges up to and including the office of president, have been attempted. E.g., The Basic Ability System of Job Evaluation proposed by Ralph W. Ells, described in Stryker, *supra* note 17, at 230 ff. Their practicality and utility for general use have yet to be demonstrated. "Application of the standard of reasonableness has produced no empirical results, no specific standards, only cursory comparisons of industrial levels, and no limitation on compensation." Mautz and Rock, *The Wages of Management,* 11 U. FLA. L. REV. 474, 508 (1958). See also Patton, *What is an Executive Worth?,* 39 HARV. BUS. REV. 65, 72 (1961) (an executive's worth depends on decisions affecting profits and hence evaluating executive positions "is certainly no science").

[76] *Cf.* the Roberts Studies, *supra* note 51, at 283, concluding that as a result of "extreme immobility," hiring at the trainee level, filling of executive vacancies by promotion, and receptivity by executives only to much bigger jobs "there is a serious weakening of the concept of a 'market for executives,' and accordingly market forces can be expected to exert only a loose constraint over the firm's executive compensation. . . ."

These tests obviously need not reach the same result. A motion picture star may have been receiving $300,000 a year from a movie company; this cannot mean that he is worth $300,000 as an office manager to some other company. Similarly, the chief bookkeeper in a corporation may be paid $10,000 a year, but his inefficiency may have rendered the books meaningless to anyone but himself; he has become indispensable in the sense that if he were to leave the company's employ, it would be months before anyone else could adequately perform the same duties. Under such circumstances, it might be worth while for the company to pay him $30,000 or $40,000 a year to avoid losing him. Far-fetched as these illustrations may seem, they represent a line of reasoning not infrequently heard. If an executive receives an offer of a post with another corporation paying $100,000 a year, he feels that he must be worth $100,000 a year to his present employers. Even though he has not received such an offer, he will feel the same way if someone whom he knows in another company, occupying a position which he considers comparable to his own, is receiving $100,000 a year.[77]

Other factors give the executive substantial bargaining power. There is and always has been a shortage of able executives. The present leader, if he has been even moderately successful in getting to know his staff and in winning their loyalty, has a tremendous advantage—all the forces of inertia tend to keep him in his job.[78] A large corporation depends, after all, on human relationships. An or-

---

[77] For the point that social position is governed by gross salaries, see Drucker, *Keep the Carrot Dangling*, FORTUNE, Oct. 1949, p. 81. *Cf.* ROBERTS, *op. cit. supra* note 53, at 161: "Can it be that in the upper brackets money derives its incentive quality more from the fact that it is a symbol of recognition than from the fact that it is purchasing power?"

[78] In the Roberts Studies, *supra* note 51, the employment histories since age 25 of 500 top executives were studied. Thirty-nine per cent had had only one employer, 22% had had two employers, 15% three, and 24%, or less than one-fourth, had had four or more employers. After attaining the rank of a corporate officer, 87% had never changed employment, 8% had made one change, and only 5% three or more changes. *Id.,* 279 ff. From these figures, Dean Roberts concluded: "Very few corporations lose executives and correspondingly few executives change employers." *Id.,* 279–80. For the view that these figures evidence a substantial degree of mobility among executives, see WHYTE, THE ORGANIZATION MAN 62–63 (1956).

For discussion of the effect of taxation on mobility of executives, with suggestions that plans developed as the result of taxes have impaired such mobility, see SANDERS, *op. cit. supra* note 4, at 33 ff.; HALL, *op. cit. supra* note 4, at 261 ("Progressive personal income taxes have reduced the mobility of executives advancing to higher paid positions from one company to another by reducing the new financial differentials between the highly compensated positions and others"). Consult Joint Committee on the Economic Report, *Federal Tax Policy for Economic Growth and Stability,* 84th Cong., 1st Sess. (Nov. 9, 1955), especially Break, *The Effects of Taxation on Work Incentives* 192, 198. See also Chapter 6, note 116.

ganization is more than a mere chart on paper; it is a collection of individuals who must work together harmoniously. It takes time to learn the ramifications of a great business, and the man on the job finds his purely negative value building up every year. The longer he stays, the harder it will be for the corporation to replace him.

It is also argued that lesser executives and the employees as a whole must have a worth-while goal; that if the salaries of the top executives are low, the morale of the whole organization will suffer.[79] Related to this argument is one having an important bearing upon the payment of high salaries: maintenance of the corporate hierarchy. To maintain the hierarchy—from the general foreman to the chief executive—significant salary differentials are essential.[80] Furthermore, the status of the individual in the organization, and in industry as well, is primarily measured by salary. Accordingly, an executive may seek a salary increase even though his salary bracket is so high as to render the amount of the increase relatively insignificant. Moreover, salary usually measures the amount of supplemental benefits to which the executive may be entitled—the pension that he will receive on retirement, the amount of life insurance protection and medical benefits to which he is entitled under his company's group plans, the amount annually credited to his account under an incentive compensation or profit-sharing plan, perhaps the amount of stock to which he can subscribe under a stock option or stock purchase plan.

Again, it is pointed out that there are fields where the accumulation of wealth may be achieved by the development of new enter-

[79] *Cf.* RUML, TOMORROW'S BUSINESS 112 (1945) : "In an industry-wide sense, top compensation for special qualifications is really being paid not only to the particular individual, but to all who aspire to comparable positions."

Consult E. I. du Pont de Nemours & Co., Annual Report 1949, COMPENSATION OF TOP MANAGEMENT 23, 24:

> While comparison of compensations paid individual executives with identical titles in various companies is not always significant—because of widespread variation in the degrees of authority, responsibility and discretion assigned to them—compensation in any particular company must be commensurate with general competitive conditions imposed by other companies. Further, compensation must be kept in balance with responsibility in order to provide the incentive necessary for advancement through the several levels of responsibility up to the top management, where the ultimate accountability to stockholders rests and where compensation is highest.

[80] "The magnitude of the firm's compensation ceiling, i.e., the compensation of its highest paid official, is important largely through its effect on the internal structure. . . ." Roberts Studies, *supra* note 51, at 294. *Cf.* Stryker, *supra* note 17, at 109–10: "The wide salary spreads in the upper ranks accentuate the major weakness in executive pay scales: the top man's salary is usually too low to permit sufficiently wide pay ranges down the line." Consult Fox, *Top Executive Salary Relationships*, 23 NICB MGMT. REC., Feb. 1961, p. 10.

prises.[81] To the extent that the building up of a fortune in such a manner is possible, must not corporations endeavor to offer similar opportunities in order to attract their fair share of the able people in the community? Must not corporations pay enough to permit their most valued employees to accumulate a reasonable amount of capital, as well as to permit them to maintain a high standard of living?

On the other hand, an argument that high salaries are necessary to dissuade a corporate executive from starting his own business is chiefly theoretical in nature, not so much because the opportunities of establishing a new enterprise may be limited as because the talents of the corporate executive are usually different in nature from those of the successful entrepreneur. The corporate executive must work with and through a corporate organization and with and through people; he will usually be at a loss without an organization at his disposal. The corporate executive plans for the future and is far more of a long-range builder than the entrepreneur, who must inevitably be something of an opportunist.[82]

It has also been argued somewhat as follows: (1) no man can be worth $1,000,000 a year (or $500,000, or $100,000); [83] (2) stock-

[81] See Symposium, *Capitalism and Monopolistic Competition*, 40 AMER. ECON. REV. 67 *et seq.* (May 1950). The position was there strongly expressed that our economy is becoming more rather than less competitive, with past data bearing upon the subject criticized. Wilcox, *On the Alleged Ubiquity of Oligopoly, id.* at 72, 100. See also Drucker, *How Big is Too Big?*, HARPER'S, July 1950, p. 23 and Drucker, *The Care and Feeding of Small Business*, HARPER'S, Aug. 1950, p. 74. It has been said that in 1949 there were 3,700,000 businesses in the United States, the highest number in the history of any country in the world. N. W. AYER & SON, INC., IN BEHALF OF MANAGEMENT 41–44 (1949). The economic significance of these figures, however, was not analyzed. According to the Department of Commerce report for 1950, American business firms in that year totaled over 4,000,000 in number. See N. Y. Times, Feb. 19, 1951, p. 30, col. 5.

[82] *Cf.* Address delivered on Oct. 14, 1949, by Eugene Holman, president of the Standard Oil Company of New Jersey:

. . . the sole proprietor has a definite limit on his life, whereas . . . the managers of a corporation expect the company to continue long after they have left the business scene. As a consequence, the objective of continuity and the long-range view generally weigh more heavily in a corporation's conduct than in that of the individual businessman.

[83] Judge Swan's dissenting opinion in Rogers v. Hill, 60 F.2d 109, 113 (2d Cir. 1932) is often cited for the proposition that no man is worth $1,000,000, but it does not say so.

For a number of years Lewis Gilbert has been proposing a ceiling on executive compensation of $200,000 in the aggregate, including bonuses, with a requirement that no bonus shall equal more than 100% of salary. *E.g.*, GILBERT, EIGHTEENTH ANNUAL REPORT OF STOCKHOLDER ACTIVITIES AT CORPORATION MEETINGS DURING 1957 at 115. However, the ceiling is not intended as an arbitrary sum: "The $200,000 ceiling which we suggest . . . is not final, and we will have no objection if

holders have not been receiving the dividends to which they consider themselves entitled and management should therefore reduce its share of corporate income; (3) it is unfair, and provocative of labor problems, for the president of a company to receive, say, $500,000 a year while workers in the same company may average $100 a week or less. As generalizations, these points are open to debate. How much a man is "worth" to a company cannot be determined satisfactorily if we already have fixed in our minds a definite upper limitation beyond which we refuse to admit that anyone can go. Again, one can be in favor of higher wages in industry without being convinced that reducing the president's salary to some nominal sum is an effective way of achieving the desired result. And one can be in favor of higher dividends for stockholders and still not be convinced that the earnings of a given company will be increased if a cheaper group of executives is hired by that company.

It is further argued that management is in control of the company, sits on both sides of the table, and is thus able to fix its own pay without regard for the interests of stockholders. This point lies at the root of increasingly vocal stockholder and public criticism of executive compensation.[84] To be sure, management will, as a matter of good practice today, and even though not required by law or regulation, submit a plan for its own compensation to stockholders for their approval. But as a practical matter, management will often be in a position to control a majority stockholder vote, with institutional investors and others who hold large blocks giving management their proxy. On the other hand, presentation to stockholders cannot be dismissed as meaningless. It exposes management's proposals to public view and criticism and, like other disclosure requirements imposed by federal securities legislation, serves as a restraint. Further, the requirement of disclosure makes possible the building of opposition to existing management and lays the groundwork for the proxy fight which has become increasingly important as a threat, if not a positive restraint. Finally, to the extent that overreaching can be

---

it is increased to $225,000 or $250,000 in certain cases. It is when we see sums like an aggregate of close to $700,000 that we become critical." *Ibid.* See also LIVINGSTON, *op. cit. supra* note 35, at 88–89. *Cf.* The Wolfson Plan for Stockholder Security, *supra* note 75, at 9 (suggesting that officers' salaries be limited to $50,000 when no dividends have been paid for two consecutive years). See note 2, *supra.*

[84] See note 3 *supra* and related text. For representative criticism, see note 35 *supra.* For judicial regulation, see Chapter 8, text to notes 48 ff. Consult Volume II, Chapter 19.

shown, the courts have been lending an increasingly sympathetic ear.[85]

Another important element in this problem must be recognized. As previously noted, the professional manager has gradually taken on a new and different character : once regarded as a mere hired man, he now presents himself as a leader and policymaker. This increase in prestige and authority has brought with it a demand on his part to share in the profits of the enterprise—to receive the rewards of an owner-controller as well as those of a hired expert. Opinion on this question must be largely conditioned by one's views on the issue of excessiveness of compensation. We are touching here upon the heart of the problem of executive compensation and an extremely important problem of economic policy as well, affecting, in fact, the mainsprings of incentive to business activity.

If we regard the executive as an employee, we think of him as a replaceable cog in a machine. On that basis, it is simply foolish to pay him more than what we think an employee should receive. If we think of the executive as a managing partner, there is basically no more reason to impose a limitation upon executive compensation than upon dividends.[86]

On the other hand, the executive will damage his own cause if he insists upon being given the ultimate dollar to which he believes himself entitled. He must remember that corporate enterprise in this country was originally a means of collecting and using private capital on a fairly limited scale. Some of our corporations have since come

[85] "In the final analysis managerial compensation is not controlled by shareholders; it is not controlled by directors; it is not controlled by the courts. Its form may be altered by the tax structure, but taxes are not a limiting control. Compensation may be restrained by all of these elements with an assist from public opinion. Even this latter factor is diluted by the individual American dream of great wealth and the equation of power and wealth. The ultimate present control is the integrity and conscientiousness of management." Mautz and Rock, *supra* note 75.

[86] See ABBOTT, FORBES, AND THOMPSON, *op. cit. supra* note 4, at 24. As early as 1934, Professor Dodd called the idea that the sole function of business organizations is the production of maximum profit for absentee owners one which "no longer appeals strongly to the community as a social policy." Dodd, *Is Effective Enforcement of the Fiduciary Duties of Corporate Managers Practicable?*, 2 U. CHI. L. REV. 194, 205 (1934). Asking, as between management and stockholders, "Who should be regarded as the entrepreneur and who should have the first claim to profits?" the Roberts Studies, *supra* note 51, at 289, suggested that the stockholder had come "to resemble a creditor in many respects, despite the fact that he is the ultimate risk-bearer." *Cf.* MASON, *op. cit. supra* note 4, at 2: "The equity owner is joining the bondholder as a functionless *rentier*." But *cf.* The Wolfson Plan for Stockholder Security, *supra* note 75, at 6 ("Without capital, management will not have anything to manage."). For a middle-of-the-road viewpoint, see Stryker, *supra* note 17, at 110 ("Managers are neither enterprising capitalists with a claim on the profits nor simply high-priced office help sharing labor's take.").

to serve a different function: they operate substantial segments of the nation's wealth. The work done by the managers of these companies is of high public significance, and in a very real sense these men are public servants. The prestige and perquisites that they enjoy are far from negligible.[87] To a greater extent than is generally conceded, they respect their obligations as public servants, but the very fact that the work they do is of public importance means that pressure will increase to bring them and their enterprises under direct governmental control. Thus, activities in violation of anti-trust laws or other statutes have led to demands for non-payment or repayment of compensation, and secret participation in the profits of firms doing business with the corporation has led to severe condemnation. Management must convince the public that it has set for itself standards of self-denial as well as of efficient performance.

Those who do the work—labor and management—are demanding ever larger shares of the rewards of enterprise. The stockholder may well be caught between the increasing pressures of labor, management, and government, but at least in an expanding economy he has increased income and opportunities for capital gain. The stockholder, too, has the security represented by capital, which management and labor find difficult to accumulate today.

The New Types of Compensation. The search for a solution of issues such as those discussed has played an important part in the development of forms of executive compensation and incentive plans supplementing fixed salary. Chief among these forms are the following:

1. Incentive compensation based on company profits, either on an individual basis or through a group plan.
2. Fringe benefits, perquisites, health and welfare benefits.
3. Deferred compensation arrangements, also on an individual or group basis.

[87] "The opportunities for personal power and for creative work are, if not limitless, certainly very great. In this respect, non-financial rewards may provide a more powerful stimulus than monetary compensation to the business executive in the large corporation." GORDON, BUSINESS LEADERSHIP IN THE LARGE CORPORATION 314 (1945). For a discussion of the nature and importance of non-financial incentives, see SANDERS, *op. cit. supra* note 4, at 21 ff.; HALL, *op. cit. supra* note 4, at 256 ff.; FETTER AND JOHNSON, COMPENSATION AND INCENTIVES FOR INDUSTRIAL EXECUTIVES 54 ff. (1952); *cf.* Given, *Compensating Executives, Nonfinancial Incentives,* 13 NICB MGMT. REC., Aug. 1951, p. 274 (acceptance of non-financial incentives "is more emotional among the lower group of executives, and those headed for those places, than among the seniors").

The view that the prestige and perquisites accorded executives should serve in the place of high compensation is implicit in much of the criticism of executive compensation. *Cf.* LIVINGSTON, *op. cit. supra* note 35, at 88, 91.

4. Stock awards.
5. Stock options.
6. Stock purchase plans.
7. Pension, profit-sharing, and other retirement plans.
8. Life insurance and death benefits.

We have already outlined the background against which these forms of compensation developed and the reasons why both the company and its executives have increasingly sought methods of compensation to supplement salaries.

What is the justification for these special forms of compensation? Why not stick to a policy of fixed salaries, sufficiently generous to satisfy management and revised with sufficient frequency to meet changing needs?

From the standpoint of the investor, and perhaps also from the standpoint of business efficiency, there is much to be said for a compensation policy based only on salaries, if it is administered with judgment and fairness by a directorate in close touch with the problems of the enterprise.[88] Yet incentive compensation and stock plans carry with them their own justification to the extent that they make rewards contingent upon success. Pensions and, perhaps to a more limited extent, deferred compensation and death benefits likewise have aspects of incentive compensation in rendering future rewards contingent upon performance, in furnishing security for later years, and in tending to reduce turnover.

The use of supplemental rewards, then, has been due to many factors, of which the following are probably the most significant:

1. The desire of management to have a direct share in the profits of the enterprise.
2. The desire of stockholders to provide an incentive to management, and obtain increased effort and enthusiasm.
3. The desire of management and stockholders to cut down tax payments by management and by the corporation.
4. The desire of both groups to find means of satisfying management without directly burdening the corporation, e.g., by granting stock rights which can be sold to the public by the recipients, at a profit.
5. Especially over the past two decades, the executive's desire to obtain security for himself and his family upon his death, disability, or retirement, a desire which taxes and inflation have made it impossible to satisfy through savings.

[88] Consult Patton, *Old-Fashioned Initiative for Modern Enterprise,* 32 HARV. BUS. REV. 67 (July–Aug., 1954), criticized in Lasser and Rothschild, *Deferred Compensation for Executives,* 33 *id.* 89 (Jan.–Feb., 1955).

The factors just mentioned must be borne in mind as we study particular forms of compensation in the succeeding chapters. Those who guide corporate policies, and who decide how management is to be compensated, must in their own interest—if in no other—consider the effect their decisions will have on the company's public relations. Stockholders are entitled to demand that corporate policies be framed for their benefit, that compensation plans be drafted with clarity and fairness, and that their terms be fully disclosed. The public is entitled to demand not only that stockholders be fairly treated, but also that corporations and their executives pay their fair share of the tax burden.

Government and Managerial Rewards: Taxation and Control. Many of the complicated arrangements we will study had their origin in a desire to minimize taxes. Two fundamental tax questions must be borne in mind.

1. DEDUCTIBILITY OF THE COMPANY'S PAYMENT. To the extent that compensation paid an executive constitutes a proper tax deduction, the government is in effect paying a percentage of such compensation. For example, assuming a corporate income tax of 52% in a normally prosperous company of any size, a legitimate salary of $100,000 a year will cost the employing corporation only $48,000, with the balance of $52,000 representing the amount which the corporation would otherwise have had to pay in federal income taxes. As corporate tax rates increase, compensation paid to corporate employees costs the corporation less, there is less incentive for the corporation to keep compensation at a low level, and in fact it may try to enlarge its business expense deductions. Taxable income will thus be lowered, and the expenditures will presumably benefit the company—though this is a point that may not be as carefully watched as in other circumstances. In the first World War, as well as in the second and the later Korean emergency, efforts to reduce taxes in this manner, though limited to some extent by salary stabilization, were particularly strenuous and, stimulated by manpower shortages at all levels, accounted in some instances for increased payments to executives during these periods.

Pressure for increased executive compensation is particularly strong in closed companies with stockholder-officers. Taking a larger share of the company's profits as compensation, these officers may—at least in some circumstances—succeed in reducing the tax load on the corporate taxpayer without correspondingly burdening themselves as individual taxpayers. Furthermore, by depleting the corporation's assets, estate and inheritance tax problems are diminished. The government struggles to prevent these results.

2. TAXABILITY OF THE EXECUTIVE. The recipient of compensation usually wants: (a) to avoid paying a tax on a merely illusory benefit, e.g., stock which is never delivered, or which turns out to be worthless; (b) to spread his compensation (and hence his tax payments) over the longest period which can conveniently be arranged, thus obtaining continued income and avoiding higher tax brackets; and (c) to avoid paying an unnecessarily high estate tax. A compensation plan may lose much of its value to the executive (and hence, indirectly, to the corporation) if it imposes on him an unnecessarily high tax burden.

From the tax point of view, the ideal plan is one which has the dual objective of eliminating the executive's tax or at least deferring its payment (and possibly rendering his compensation when received subject to tax only at capital gain rates) and at the same time permitting the employing corporation to obtain a tax deduction for payments as and when made under the plan. Statutes, Treasury Regulations, and court decisions have combined to render attainment of this objective more and more difficult.

3. TAX TRENDS. There is observable a significant government policy to seek to deny the employing corporation the right to a deduction for payments under supplemental compensation plans that are attractive to the executive. The result of this policy may be to make some plans expensive to the corporation since it may either obtain no tax deduction and therefore have to bear the entire cost, or must postpone its tax deduction to a period of uncertain profits and unknown tax rates. Even so, in many cases the total cost to the corporation may be less, for, as the result of a plan, the corporation may pay a lower dollar amount than it would otherwise have to pay for the executive's services, and it may, in addition, gain the use in its business of substantial funds which would otherwise have to be paid out currently.

Another recent trend calls for comment. Particularly in the 1940's and 1950's, tax legislation tended to favor supplemental compensation plans for groups of employees, such as pensions and profit-sharing, group insurance, health and welfare plans, under which important benefits could be enjoyed by executives as part of the group. A trend towards limiting the tax benefits available to top executives under such plans—and under certain other special plans such as stock options—is evident. It finds expression in the viewpoint of Treasury officials, members of Congress, and other influential spokesmen that tax-favored benefits of this nature are the product solely of high taxes, represent special provisions of an undesirable nature, and should be curtailed or eliminated, perhaps as part of a program to make possible lower tax rates for everyone.[89]

4. CONTROLS. The regulation of executive compensation by the federal government has assumed a variety of forms. For the protection of the investor, disclosure of compensation plans and of amounts paid is now required from most of the nation's leading enterprises under federal securities legislation. Indirect controls are imposed on public utilities, airlines, and companies under contract with the federal government. Direct limitations upon managerial rewards were imposed during World War II and during the Korean emergency.

Logical and necessary as these controls may have been in a military economy, limitations on executive rewards cannot be defended as a permanent measure. Every age and every economic system must find an effective means of encouraging enterprise and of bringing forward those individuals who are to keep the system functioning. Our own system, in its earlier stages, relied almost entirely upon rewards which might be gained by a small capitalist investing his

---

[89] Thus, the Treasury Department under Secretary Robert B. Anderson proposed the elimination of capital gains treatment of lump-sum payments under qualified retirement plans and re-examination of the estate and gift tax exemptions conferred on benefits under such plans. See *Hearings before the Senate Finance Committee on Pension Plans for Owner-Managers of Corporations,* 86th Cong., 1st Sess., 2, 8 (1960).

For similar views on these matters, on elimination of capital gains treatment accorded stock options, and, in general, the elimination of provisions that result in different after-tax income for individuals with the same amount of before-tax income, see *General Appraisal of the Income Tax* and *The Relative Role of Income Taxes in the Tax System,* in TAX REVISION COMPENDIUM SUBMITTED TO THE COMMITTEE ON WAYS AND MEANS OF THE HOUSE OF REPRESENTATIVES IN CONNECTION WITH PANEL DISCUSSIONS, beginning Nov. 16, 1959. See, in particular, Surrey, *The Federal Income Tax Base for Individuals,* at 1, 7 ("Over the past decade or so the executive class has been steadily occupied in carving out tax shelters to ameliorate the impact of the high-rate scale.") and Griswold, *The Mysterious Stock Option,* at 1527. The Surrey paper had previously been published. See 58 COLUM. L. REV. 815 (1958) and TAX INSTITUTE, INCOME TAX DIFFERENTIALS 34 (1958). See also papers submitted to the Joint Committee on the Economic Report, in FEDERAL TAX POLICY FOR ECONOMIC GROWTH AND STABILITY, 84th Cong., 1st Sess. (1955) and, in particular, Surrey, *Definitional Problems in Capital Gains Treatment,* 404, 417–18. For a criticism of these views, see Steadman, *Capital Gains as Applied to Executive Compensation,* 16 BUS. LAW. 643, 656 ff. (1961). Consult, generally, Mills, *Are You a Pet or a Patsy?,* LIFE, Nov. 23, 1959, p. 51 (comparing the situation of two fictitious neighbors, each with income of $6,000, who were $2,350 apart in actual real earnings as the result of special tax provisions and fringe benefits) ; Seidman, *Let's Get Off the Tax Road to Ruin,* READERS DIGEST, Apr. 1961, p. 45.

own funds and his own ability in an enterprise of limited size. Today, in an age of automation which is also a corporation age, we must provide sufficient rewards and incentives to the men who guide our business enterprises. These men can no longer expect the same type of reward that they might have gained one hundred years ago. They must find new rewards and incentives within the framework of a changing system.

Whatever the future may hold for business in this country, the problem of adequate incentive to the corporate executive will continue to be of vital importance. The task of a democratic government is not satisfied merely by imposing restraints on business; it must see to it that the rewards of management are sufficient to insure efficiency in enterprise and the encouragement of personal ability.

CHAPTER 2

THE EXECUTIVE'S SALARY CONTRACT

In the present chapter, our discussion is limited to the employment contract of the individual executive on a straight salary basis. This discussion will help provide a background for our treatment in later chapters of more complicated provisions for compensation. We cannot take up the entire law of employment, or even of the employment of executives, but we can present a sufficient outline of the executive's contract to cast light on many of the problems.

It is worth noting at this point that even though the negotiations leading up to the final contract may be characterized by considerable firmness on both sides, they are hardly likely to be carried on in a "pound of flesh" atmosphere. The company's representative does not want to take unfair advantage of one of the present or future executives; in fact, he may not be sufficiently hard-boiled in his attitude, particularly where one of the present managers is concerned. Lack of effective bargaining on behalf of the stockholders' interest has sometimes been apparent.[1]

On the other hand, the executive will seldom insist on a provision obviously detrimental to a corporation with which he intends his future to be identified for an indefinite period—though he may have a rather inflated idea of his worth to the company. Both sides recognize, without much being said about it, that the contract will not be quite so hard-and-fast as it looks on paper. Moreover, the difficulty of proving damages or of securing an injunction or other effective relief against the executive may render the employment agreement more in the nature of a letter of intent designed to crystallize a general understanding of terms than a legally enforceable contract under which the executive may be compelled to render service,[2] at least

---

[1] *Cf.* discussion in Chapter 1, text to notes 84 and 85.

[2] When the executive attempts to breach his contract by working for another, the corporation's sole remedy is usually a suit for such damages as it can prove. See Note, 61 A.L.R.2d 1008 (1958). However, if the executive who breaks his contract can be shown to have skills and abilities which are clearly unique, he, like actors, singers, and others with special and unusual skills, can frequently be enjoined from working for others, even in the absence of an express covenant not to compete. 5 WILLISTON, CONTRACTS § 1450 (rev. ed. 1937) ; 5 CORBIN, CONTRACTS § 1209 (1951) ; 6 *id.*§ 1411; Essex Specialty Co. v. Bueschel, 116 N.J. Eq. 337, 173 Atl. 595 (1934) (inventor and designer employed at manufacturing plant enjoined) ; Harry Rogers

when no provision is made for supplemental benefits contingent on the executive's performance of obligations under the agreement.[3]

If conditions change so that the compensation becomes inadequate, the executive will probably be able to persuade the board of directors to amend the contract to provide for a higher rate. An executive who is held to his contract against his will is not likely to be of much value to the business. If, on the other hand, the company falls on hard times, a request by the board that the executive accept less than the contracted amount will very often be honored. The discussion which follows should, therefore, be read with the realization that any hardships resulting from the operation of the agreement will probably be corrected as they arise by amendatory contracts.[4]

A formal employment contract was once the exception rather than the rule for all executives, other than a few at the top.[5] The

---

Theatrical Enterprises v. Comstock, 225 App. Div. 34, 232 N.Y.Supp. 1 (1st Dep't 1928) (actor enjoined) ; Shubert Theatrical Co. v. Rath, 271 Fed. 827, 20 A.L.R. 846 (2d Cir. 1921) (unique acrobatic services) ; Mission Independent School Dist. v. Diserens, 144 Tex. 107, 188 S.W.2d 568, 161 A.L.R. 877 (1945) (music teacher of unique abilities enjoined) ; cf. Wm. Rogers Mfg. Co. v. Rogers, 58 Conn. 356, 20 Atl. 467 (1890) (corporate officer's services not unique) ; Mantell v. Internat'l Plastic Harmonica Corp., 141 N.J. Eq. 379, 55 A.2d 250, 173 A.L.R. 1185 (1947). However, a recital in the contract that the services are unique is not controlling. Frederick Bros. Artists Corp. v. Yates, 271 App. Div. 69, 62 N.Y.S.2d 714 (1st Dep't 1946), aff'd 296 N.Y. 820, 72 N.E.2d 13 (1947) ; Dockstader v. Reed, 121 App. Div. 846, 106 N.Y.Supp. 795 (1st Dep't 1907). For such a recital, see UNIVERSAL, App. O, ¶ 6.

And under some circumstances a third party who has intentionally induced an executive to breach his employment contract can be sued for such damages as can be shown, or, if the executive's services are unique, the third party can be enjoined from employing the executive. S. C. Posner Co. v. Jackson, 223 N.Y. 325, 119 N.E. 573 (1918) ; Lamb v. S. Cheney & Son, 227 N.Y. 418, 125 N.E. 817 (1920) ; Campbell v. Gates, 236 N.Y. 457, 141 N.E. 914 (1923) ; Harry Rogers Theatrical Enterprises v. Comstock, supra; Essex Specialty Co. v. Bueschel, supra; Savoy Record Co. v. Mercury Record Corp., 108 F. Supp. 957 (N.J. 1952).

[3] See infra notes 6 and 7 and accompanying text.

[4] For a discussion of the legal problems involved in amending a contract, see Chapter 8, text to notes 149 ff.

[5] It has been estimated that only about 10% to 20% of the individuals in top management positions obtain contracts when relocating—principally, they do so when "an element of special risk is involved." BUSINESS WEEK, Mar. 29, 1958, p. 121; id. Apr. 26, 1958, p. 165. To ask for a contract with a well-established concern is "almost bound to give the impression that you lack full confidence in the company—or worse yet—in yourself." Id. Apr. 26, 1958, p. 165. Exceptions given include situations in which the company is in a weak position and "trying to bolster a lagging management team," presumably through additional incentives; or in which an experienced executive is giving up job security and pension and other retirement benefits; or in which the job is overseas and entails moving his family. Id. 165–66. A merger may involve risks justifying a request for a contract. Consult Proxy Statement of The Glenn L. Martin Co., infra note 9.

trend towards deferred compensation [6] and the consideration requirements for stock options [7] have brought about more general use of the
employment agreement. Since the right to receive supplemental benefits, such as deferred compensation and the right to purchase stock, is
usually predicated on performance of the terms of the employment
agreement, observance of these terms may become a matter of real
importance to the executive.

In the numbered paragraphs which follow, there are presented the
individual clauses of a typical compensation contract. These clauses
are brought together and reproduced as a model of a complete compensation contract in Appendix RR. For comparison, copies of the
contracts of the principal executives of a number of large corporations
have been obtained from the files of the Securities and Exchange
Commission and from individual companies or their attorneys.
These agreements, which will be frequently referred to, are reproduced elsewhere in the Appendix.

The Hiring Clause.

• 1. The Corporation agrees to and hereby does employ the Executive, and the Executive agrees to and hereby does enter the employ
of the Corporation [8] as General Manager [or "Chief Executive"] of
the Corporation in charge of the operation of its business and affairs,
subject to the supervision and direction of its Board of Directors, for
a period beginning ...., 19.., and ending
.... 19.., unless such period is extended by
written agreement of the parties or is sooner terminated pursuant to
the provisions of paragraph 5 below.

This clause presents primarily questions relating to the duration of the term and the nature of the position to be occupied. With
regard to the *duration* of full-time or active (as distinguished from
advisory or consultative) services, the usual contract will run for one
or two years, possibly with provisions for renewal; five-year contracts

---

Employment contracts with non-disclosure clauses and provisions for patent
assignments are not unusual for engineers, chemists, scientists, and other professional technicians. See *infra* note 54.

[6] See Chapter 5, note 1.

[7] See Chapter 8, note 87.

[8] If the executive is in the corporation's employ at the time of the contract, the
following language may be used in substitution for that in the text: "The Corporation agrees to continue the Executive in its employ, and the Executive agrees to
continue in the employ of the Corporation. . . ."

are not unusual, and ten-year contracts are sometimes made.[9] Unless intention as to the duration of the contract has been definitely and clearly stated, an officer-executive may be unable to recover damages for a discharge without cause, at least when there is a bylaw or statute giving the board power to remove at any time, at will, or at pleasure.[10] The longer-term contracts are usually found in connection with deferred compensation arrangements pursuant to which future compensation is to be paid, usually on a contingent basis, on retirement or other termination of employment.[11] These arrangements necessitate provision for continued employment until the executive becomes entitled to receive deferred compensation on termination of active services.

Such long-term arrangements may be in effect lifetime contracts for the executive, and pose serious questions of policy and legality. Is it wise for a board of directors to commit the management of the company, or a phase of management, to a specific executive for a period of time longer than the term of the board itself? Is it legal for the board to do so, with particular reference to statutes or bylaws requiring the annual election of officers? On the question of legality, the weight of authority, including the more recent cases, upholds (where no statute dictates otherwise) an employment contract extending beyond the term of the board of directors authorizing the

[9] Two-year contracts are often found as consideration for stock options. For prescribed periods in other situations, see Fibreboard Paper Products Corp., Proxy Statement for Annual Meeting on Apr. 12, 1957 (original employment contract contemplated execution of similar annual employment contracts so long as executive was elected chief executive officer); CHRYSLER, App. HH (five years); The Glenn L. Martin Co., Proxy Statement for Annual Meeting on Apr. 23, 1956 (five-year employment contracts for principal executives of Seaboard Container Corporation on acquisition of its business); General American Transportation Corp., Proxy Statement for Annual Meeting on Apr. 22, 1958 (employment contracts for executives over 60 until age 70, with provision for resignation from offices at age 65 and reduced compensation thereafter); Square D Co., Proxy Statement for Annual Meeting on Apr. 24, 1956 (ten-year employment contract for chairman aged 74).

[10] E.g., Walker v. Maas & Waldstein Co., 104 N.J.L. 341, 140 Atl. 286 (1928); Cohen v. Camden Refrigerating & Terminals Co., 129 N.J.L. 519, 30 A.2d 428 (1943); Hansen v. Stirrat & Goetz Inv. Co., 144 Wash. 118, 256 Pac. 1033 (1927), error dismissed 278 U.S. 561 (1928); O'Donnell v. James E. Sipprell Inc., 163 Wash. 369, 1 P.2d 322, 76 A.L.R. 1405 (1931); Darrah v. Wheeling Ice & Storage Co., 50 W.Va. 417, 40 S.E. 373 (1901); and compare United Producers & Consumers Co-op. v. Held, 225 F.2d 615 (9th Cir. 1955); Dennis v. Thermoid Co., 128 N.J.L. 303, 25 A.2d 886 (1942); Hansen v. Columbia Breweries, 12 Wash.2d 554, 122 P.2d 489 (1942); In re Paramount Publix Corp., 90 F.2d 441, 111 A.L.R. 889 (2d Cir. 1937); Realty Acceptance Corp. v. Montgomery, 51 F.2d 636 (3d Cir. 1930); Cuppy v. Stollwerck Bros., 216 N.Y. 591, 111 N.E. 249 (1916); Hicks v. Haight, 171 Misc. 151, 11 N.Y.S.2d 912 (1939).

[11] See Chapter 5, text to notes 31 ff. passim.

contract,[12] subject to the qualification that the contract must be for a "reasonable" period in the light of all the circumstances.[13]

Insofar as company policy is concerned, the governing consideration, as with other provisions bearing on employment arrangements, must be what the company needs to offer in order to secure the executive's services on a basis with which he will be satisfied. It may be also that in some jurisdictions an executive's contract for life or permanent employment, like those of other employees, would be regarded as terminable without liability at the will of either party, unless it is based upon some consideration given by the employee other than the services to be performed.[14] But there is some author-

[12] United Producers & Consumers Co-op. v. Held, *supra* note 10 (three-year employment contract for general manager extending beyond term of board of directors, not prohibited by Arizona statute or case law, was for "reasonable" period) ; *In re* Paramount Publix Corp., *supra* note 10 (employment contract for a fixed term no more "sterilizes" a successor board than does a long-term lease authorized by a predecessor board) ; Realty Acceptance Corp. v. Montgomery, *supra* note 10 (restraint placed on freedom of future board by five-year contract was not in fact or principle injurious to the public interest) ; Hansen v. Columbia Breweries, *supra* note 10 (employment for term of years does not handicap succeeding board any more than does a lease or other contract extending over long period of years) ; Carney v. New York Life Ins. Co., 162 N.Y. 453, 57 N.E. 78 (1900) (term of office of board authorizing lifetime employment contract may be taken into account in deciding whether contract is reasonable) ; *cf.* General Paint Corp. v. Kramer, 57 F.2d 698 (10th Cir. 1932) *cert. denied,* 287 U.S. 605 (1932) ; Clifford v. Firemen's Mut. Benev. Ass'n, 259 N.Y. 547, 182 N.E. 175 (1932), *affirming* 232 App. Div. 260, 249 N.Y.Supp. 713 (2d Dep't 1931) (lifetime contract not enforceable because board could not impose obligation on corporation to continue for long period beyond its term and thus hamper future boards). See also note 36 *infra,* and accompanying text.

[13] United Producers & Consumers Co-op. v. Held, *supra* note 10 (three-year employment contract reasonable considered against background facts) ; Realty Acceptance Corp. v. Montgomery, *supra* note 10 (five-year contract not fraudulent but reasonable in view of executive's relationship to corporation, and familiarity with and grasp of its business) ; Carney v. New York Life Ins. Co., *supra* note 12, (lifetime contract not reasonable in view of four-year term of board) ; Kline v. Thompson, 206 Wis. 464, 240 N.W. 128 (1932) (contract for indefinite time or for life not reasonable and held void as against public policy because president of corporation gained a personal benefit). *Cf.* Lubrecht v. Laurel Stripping Co., 387 Pa. 303, 127 A.2d 687 (1956).

The giving by the executive of some consideration in addition to services would be a strong factor in determining whether a long-term or life contract is reasonable. Consult cases *infra* note 15.

[14] E.g., Fibreboard Products v. Townsend, 202 F.2d 180 (9th Cir. 1953) (pulp mill worker) ; Chesapeake & Potomac Tel. Co. v. Murray, 198 Md. 526, 84 A.2d 870, 28 A.L.R.2d 920 (1951) (sales agent of telephone directories) ; Lynas v. Maxwell Farms, 279 Mich. 684, 273 N.W. 315 (1937) (manager of milk distributing station) ; Heideman v. Tall's Travel Shops, 192 Wash. 513, 73 P.2d 1323 (1937) (mechanic) ; Skagerberg v. Blandin Paper Co., 197 Minn. 291, 266 N.W. 872 (1936) (engineer-superintendent) ; Heaman v. E. N. Rowell Co., 236 App. Div. 34, 258 N.Y.Supp. 138 (4th Dep't 1932), *rev'd on other grounds,* 261 N.Y. 229, 185

ity that the absence of consideration other than services is merely evidence tending to show that the parties did not intend to make a permanent or lifetime contract.[15] If the long-term arrangement includes provision for deferred compensation, the company need not be bound to continue the executive's employment for his working life but can be kept free to terminate the executive's employment if it is provided that upon such termination the deferred compensation provisions will take effect and the deferred compensation payments commence.

Much can be done to obviate questions concerning a long-term contract by submitting the contract for approval of, or ratification by, stockholders and, at least when substantial obligations are involved, the better practice today is to submit such a contract to stockholders, separately or as part of a company policy or plan for a group of executives.

The closely held company presents a different situation. For it, a lifetime contract may be completely unobjectionable, at least if ratified by the holders of all the outstanding stock.[16]

With regard to the *nature of the position,* many attorneys feel that it is undesirable to hire an executive to serve for a fixed number of years as president, or, indeed, to fill any other bylaw office, since as a technical matter the officers must in most jurisdictions be elected yearly by the board of directors, to serve at the pleasure of the board, and the bylaws may often provide that an officer may be removed at any time by the board with or without cause. From the company's point of view, a desirable form of hiring clause is one which simply "employs" the executive without describing his position; from the

N.E. 83 (1933) (auditor and assistant to president); Mt. Pleasant Coal Co. v. Watts, 91 Ind. App. 501, 151 N.E. 7 (1926) (mine superintendent). But such contracts are not enforceable by the employee when a statute prohibits a contract of that duration. Page v. New Orleans Public Service, 184 La. 617, 167 So. 99 (1936); Hill v. Missouri Pac. Ry. Co., 8 F. Supp. 80 (W.D. La. 1933); Foster v. Atlas Life Ins. Co., 154 Okla. 30, 6 P.2d 805 (1931). Consult Rosen v. Guaranteed Sanitation, Inc., N.Y.L.J., Feb. 14, 1961, p. 14, col. 5 (Aurelio, J., Sup. Ct.) (resignation as officer and director at age 67, on sale by founder of his stock, relinquishment of annual salary of $25,000, covenant not to compete, and occasional advice as called on held adequate consideration for lifetime annual payments of $7,500); Koster v. Warren, 176 F.Supp. 459 (N.D. Cal. 1959) (long-term consultation contracts incident to personnel changes upheld). See Chapter 6, text to notes 90 ff.

[15] Littell v. Evening Star Newspaper Co., 73 App.D.C. 409, 120 F.2d 36 (1941) (suggesting as examples making an investment, resigning from government service, giving up one's own business, releasing a claim); Eggers v. Armour & Co. of Delaware, 129 F.2d 729 (8th Cir. 1942); Savarese v. Pyrene Mfg. Co., 9 N.J. 595, 89 A.2d 237 (1952); Arentz v. Morse Dry Dock & Repair Co., 249 N.Y. 439, 164 N.E. 342 (1928).

[16] The leading case is Clark v. Dodge, 269 N.Y. 410, 199 N.E. 641 (1936).

executive's point of view, the clause may, in lieu of referring to a specific position, define his duties in general terms and engage him to "perform such other functions and services of like scope and dignity as he may from time to time be requested to perform by the Board of Directors of the Corporation." [17]

Ordinarily, however, the executive will insist that the dignity of his position be safeguarded as carefully as the circumstances will permit. This is sometimes accomplished by using a general clause of the type just mentioned, accompanied by a statement that the duties initially to be performed by the employee shall be those of "Chief Executive," "General Manager," "Division Manager of the Company's New York Division," or the like, with the further provision that any change in the duties or rank of the executive shall be only to a post of equal or greater dignity and importance. The executive also may wish to have it provided that any such change shall be made only after obtaining his prior consent in writing, or that he shall not, without his consent, be assigned to duties outside a given state or group of states. [18]

The powers of the executive are seldom affirmatively enumerated, though special circumstances may occasionally make this desirable. [19] If the executive is named to a definite post, the title given may indicate his powers and responsibilities. Further, the executive's duties are generally stated in the clause which is about to be discussed, and

[17] In the following contracts the executive is named to a definite post:
FAIRBANKS, App. A: "General Manager."
COLUMBIA, App. C, ¶ 1: "Senior Executive."
Esquire-Coronet, Inc., Contract with D. A. Smart, Apr. 1, 1937, ¶ 3: "President of the Company, and in the event that at any time the Board of Directors of the Company shall fail to elect him as President of the Company, or shall remove him as President, he shall be free, if he so elects, to cancel this Agreement."
See also U. S. RUBBER, App. B, ¶ 1, under which the executive agrees to serve "in an important managerial or executive capacity with such duties as may be assigned to him from time to time by the Board of Directors of the Company . . ." Cf. ALLIED, App. N, ¶ 1: ". . . as President with duties as shall be assigned to him by the Chairman of the Board . . . ," and U. S. RUBBER, App. B, ¶ 2.
Consult Meck, *Employment of Corporate Executives by Majority Stockholders*, 47 YALE L.J. 1079, 1082 (1938).
[18] See *infra* note 51.
[19] *Cf.* BUSINESS WEEK, Apr. 26, 1958, p. 166, suggesting the desirability of a precise definition of the scope and authority of an executive's position when the position is a new one. For a definition in general terms of the powers of a chief executive, see FAIRBANKS, App. A: "[The Company employs the executive as General Manager] with authority to manage and control all of its operations and to hire and discharge and fix the compensation of all of its employees, excepting the officers thereof elected from time to time by its Board of Directors." See also UNIVERSAL, App. O, ¶ 1.

from this statement of duties a grant of power can no doubt be derived.

The Performance Clause.

• 2. The Executive agrees to devote all of his time, attention, skill, and efforts to the performance of his duties as General Manager [or "Chief Executive"] of the Corporation, and to the performance of all of the duties of office of President of the Corporation or of any subsidiary or subsidiaries of the Corporation, if elected, all under the supervision and direction of their respective Boards of Directors.

This clause is generally somewhat broader in scope than the hiring paragraph, since it is a covenant by the executive rather than by the employer. The executive often agrees to perform any tasks demanded by the directors, and sometimes to perform certain specified duties.[20] He almost always states that he will perform "faithfully and to the best of his ability,"[21] and that he will, perhaps subject to reasonable vacations,[22] give "his entire business time" to the position. Full business time may also be required indirectly by provisions of paragraph 4 of our typical contract.[23]

The Compensation Clause.

• 3. For all services to be rendered by him in any capacity hereunder [including services as an officer, director, member of any committee

[20] See clauses quoted or referred to *supra* notes 17 and 19.

[21] FILENE, App. D, ¶ 4: "Faithfully."

FEDERATED, App. NN, ¶ 6 (faithfully and in conformity with the directions of the board of directors).

FAIRBANKS, App. A: "To use his best endeavor, judgment and energy to promote, improve and advance the business and interests of the Company."

[22] LERNER STORES, App. F, § 1 (". . . to devote his knowledge, ability, and his working time and energy, subject to the right to receive reasonable vacations and subject to absences on account of temporary illnesses, to the business . . ."); CASEY AND ROTHSCHILD, PAY CONTRACTS WITH KEY MEN (1953), Ex. 172 (Universal Pictures Co. and Edward Muhl—leave of absence for a consecutive period of four weeks); FORD, App. I, § 3 ("reasonable vacation periods and other reasonable leaves of absence").

ALLIED, App. N, ¶ 1: "Substantially all of his time and attention."

U. S. RUBBER, App. B, ¶ 2: "Shall devote all of his time and services exclusively to the business."

UNIVERSAL, App. O, ¶ 1: "His exclusive business and working time."

If the executive is to be on a part-time basis or if it is contemplated that he may have other interests, the employment agreement may simply provide that he will devote such time as may be necessary to fulfill his duties under the agreement. *Cf.* FEDERATED Contract, *supra* note 21, ¶ 2: "Such time and attention to the business of the Employer as may be fairly and reasonably necessary." Presumably, time spent on community and charitable affairs, and perhaps service on the boards of banks or other non-competing enterprises as well, may be considered good public relations and in the interests of the employing corporation.

[23] See text accompanying note 30 *infra*.

or otherwise],[24] the Corporation agrees to pay the Executive, so long as he shall be employed hereunder, (a) a fixed salary at the rate of \$...... per annum, payable in equal monthly instalments at the end of each month; and

[Here may follow clauses providing for profit participation or deferred compensation.]

These fixed salary provisions require little comment. The executive nearly always desires a fixed salary, even though he may also be obtaining some special form of compensation.[25]

When the employer has subsidiary or affiliated corporations as part of its system, the executive may be obligated by his contract to serve them as officer or director without additional compensation,[26] or the employer may obligate itself to cause additional salaries to be provided by its subsidiaries or affiliates.[27] The Woolworth contracts have been exceptional in not providing for a fixed salary.[28]

With deferred compensation contracts, the long period of time comprehended may make a specific salary clause undesirable from the point of view of both the executive and company. In such circumstances, if an executive is in the company's employ when the contract is made, the contract may simply provide that the executive shall

[24] The bracketed matter, relating to services as an officer, director, or otherwise, may of course be omitted if inappropriate. For the incidence of executives' independent compensation as directors, see Chapter 9, note 1. The question of reasonableness of salary provisions is discussed under appropriate headings throughout the volume; the index should be consulted. For an expanded paragraph 3, including percentage compensation as well as fixed salary, see Chapter 3, text to notes 18 and 19.

[25] The late Charles M. Schwab believed that the fixed salary should provide a minimum for living requirements, with higher rewards left to depend on an incentive plan. See Volume II, Chapter 19.

[26] UNIVERSAL, App. O, ¶ 1; GOODYEAR, App. JJ, ¶ 2.

[27] For a provision for sharing salary as between a parent and its subsidiaries "in a constantly fluctuating amount," consult Continental Aviation & Engineering Corp., Proxy Statement for Annual Meeting on Mar. 14, 1956. See Contract of Allied Stores Corp. with B. E. Puckett, dated Feb. 1, 1940, by which Allied hired Puckett as general manager of its subsidiary Allied Purchasing Corporation, promising to cause its subsidiary to pay Puckett an additional salary. See also Contract of Reuben B. Bolstad with Paramount Pictures, Inc., dated Dec. 31, 1945, SEC Rep. Form 8K, Mar. 1946. The allocation of salary between companies which are not all included in a consolidated tax return may conceivably present tax problems. Cf. Leedy-Glover Realty & Ins. Co. v. Com'r, 184 F.2d 833 (5th Cir. 1950). Further, the desirability of having such companies become parties to the employment agreement should be considered.

[28] See Periodic Reports by F. W. Woolworth Company to the Securities and Exchange Commission on Forms 8K and 10K. See also BAKER, EXECUTIVE SALARIES AND BONUS PLANS 190 (1938); WINKLER, FIVE AND TEN 61, 106, 125–26, 137, 142 (1940).

receive a salary at a rate fixed by the board of directors from time to time, but at a rate in no event less than that currently paid unless and except to the extent that salaries are generally decreased. Such a provision may be accompanied by a provision for an increase in salary commensurate with general increases to officers and other executives, or may in some other way evidence contemplation of periodic salary increases.[29]

The Covenant Against Competition.

• 4. The Executive agrees that during the period of his employment he will not have any other corporate affiliations without the approval of the Board of Directors of the Corporation. The Executive further agrees that during the period of his employment, and during a further period of two years after leaving the employ of the Corporation, whether upon the expiration of this contract or otherwise, he will not directly or indirectly, for his own benefit, or for or with any person, firm or corporation whatsoever other than the Corporation, engage in the production or the manufacture or the distribution of any products similar to those manufactured or sold by the Corporation during such period of employment.

This clause supplements paragraph 2 (the performance clause). The restrictions imposed on the executive, which vary a good deal in strictness,[30] are of course to be considered in the light of the rule of reason. Such covenants for a definite period of time following termination of the contract of employment should be sustained as valid when found reasonable from the standpoint of the corporation, the executive, and the public interest, taking into account all relevant circumstances. In general, the restraint on the executive must be no more than is necessary to protect a legitimate business interest of the corporation and, from the executive's viewpoint, must not be greater in geographical area and time than reasonably necessary to give this protection.[31]

[29] Cf. The Glenn L. Martin Co., Proxy Statement for Annual Meeting on Apr. 23, 1956 (annual salary for chief executive of $120,000, subject to such increases and additional payments as may be determined by the board of directors).

[30] COLUMBIA, App. C, ¶ 3; UNIVERSAL, App. O, ¶ 1; GOODYEAR, App. JJ, ¶ 1(c). However, some contracts allow a certain degree of outside activity, apparently regardless of its competitive character, e.g., measured by that existing at time of contract. See also Chapter 5, text to notes 36 ff. as to covenants against competition after active employment has ceased during the period when consulting services are to be rendered.

[31] See WILLISTON, op. cit. supra note 1, § 1643 and cases cited. See also McCall Co. v. Wright, 198 N.Y. 143, 91 N.E. 516 (1910); Heinz v. Nat'l Bank of Commerce, 237 Fed. 942 (8th Cir. 1916); Eigelbach v. Boone Loan & Inv. Co., 216 Ky. 69, 287 S.W. 225 (1926); Wahlgren v. Bausch & Lomb Optical Co., 68 F.2d 660

The Incapacity and Death Clause.

• 5. Notwithstanding anything herein contained,

    (a) In the event that the Executive shall, during the term of his employment hereunder, fail to perform his duties hereunder owing to illness or other incapacity and such illness or other incapacity shall continue for a period of more than .... months, the Corporation shall have the right, by notice [32] sent by registered mail addressed to him at ...., to terminate the Executive's employment hereunder as of a date (not less than 30 days after the date of the sending of such notice) to be specified in such notice, and the Executive shall be entitled to receive his fixed compensation as provided in paragraph 3 hereof [33] to the last day of the calendar month in which such notice shall be sent; provided, however, that if, prior to the date specified in such notice, the Executive's illness or incapacity shall have terminated and he shall have taken up and performed his duties hereunder, the Executive shall be entitled to resume his employment hereunder as though such notice had not been given.

    (b) In the event of the Executive's death during the term of his employment hereunder, the Executive's legal representatives shall be entitled to receive his fixed compensation as provided in paragraph 3 hereof [34] to the last day of the calendar month in which the Executive's death shall have occurred.

(7th Cir. 1934), *cert. denied,* 292 U.S. 639 (1934), *rehearing denied,* 292 U.S. 615 (1934); Economy Grocery Stores v. McMenamy, 290 Mass. 549, 195 N.E. 747 (1935); A. Hollander & Son v. Imperial Fur Blending Corp., 2 N.J. 235, 66 A.2d 319 (1949); William N. Frye Inc. v. Weber, 342 Ill. App. 303, 96 N.E.2d 579 (1951); Welcome Wagon v. Morris, 224 F.2d 693, 698 (4th Cir. 1955).

A contract may sometimes be enforced as against an executive whose services are unique even in the absence of a contract not to compete. See cases cited, *supra* note 2. But a recital that the services are unique is not controlling. Frederick Bros. Artists Corp. v. Yates, and Dockstader v. Reed, both *supra* note 2. From the company's point of view, the contract should be so drafted as to evidence the irreplaceable nature of the executive's services. A covenant not to compete may be helpful in this regard.

Consult Chapter 5, text to notes 37–38.

[32] A provision as to notice may be inserted in a later clause in the contract.

[33] In a contract providing for incentive compensation, his fixed compensation "and his incentive compensation" as provided in paragraph 3. For an example of an incentive compensation clause, see Chapter 3, text to note 54. No independent reference to unreimbursed expenses would appear to be necessary for, upon submission of bills or vouchers, such expenses would become an account payable to the executive. To the extent that compensation payable on death was not yet earned and hence was not "non-forfeitable" immediately before the executive's death, the first $5,000 thereof will be free of federal income tax. INT. REV. CODE OF 1954, § 101(b).

[34] If appropriate: "his fixed compensation and incentive compensation."

Many employment contracts do not contain provisions for the termination of the contract prior to the expiration of the fixed term or as to steps to be taken in the event of illness or incapacity. Negotiation on these subjects is likely to be difficult, and both sides will often prefer to leave the matter unmentioned in the contract, to be decided in the best way possible when and if difficulty later arises. Doubtless, however, a reasonable effort should be made to reach a prior agreement on the subject; perhaps certain contingencies can be met by insurance coverage. Provisions terminating the contract in the event of the executive's death, resignation, or permanent disability, and giving a pro rata share of the compensation in such event, are fairly frequent.[35] Contracts which provide for deferred compensation conditioned upon services for a specific period of time will usually make some provision for a disability that may render performance of the services impossible.

Again, many contracts contain no provisions relating to the dismissal of the executive by the directors.[36] In this connection, it should be noted that statutory provisions or corporate bylaws to the effect that the directors may remove any "officer, agent or employee . . . at pleasure" preclude the executive from continuing to hold office but do not necessarily mean that the dismissal of an officer prior to the expiration of his contract term will be without risk to the corporation. If the contract is for a fixed term, the dismissed officer may have an action for damages against the company.[37]

The Merger Clause.

• 6. The Corporation will not consolidate or merge into or with another corporation, or transfer all or substantially all of its assets to another corporation, unless such other corporation (hereinafter referred to as the "Successor Corporation") shall assume this agree-

---

[35] See ALLIED, App. N, ¶ 3; FILENE, App. D, ¶ 3B. For a clause dealing with the disposition of bonuses in the event of death, see Chapter 3, note 99. Lengthy clauses for the termination of the contract will be found in WASHINGTON AND ROTHSCHILD, COMPENSATING THE CORPORATE EXECUTIVE (rev. ed. 1951), App. X, ¶¶ 4, 5, and 6.

[36] ALLIED, App. N, ¶ 3, providing for termination if a successor to executive is elected president of the Company. The Woolworth contracts, referred to *supra* note 28, provide for cancellation by either party on 30 days' notice. But generally top executive employment contracts are for a definite term. FAIRBANKS, App. A; COLUMBIA, App. C.

[37] See *In re* Paramount Publix Corp., *supra* note 10 (interpreting N.Y. STOCK CORP. L., § 60), 50 HARV. L. REV. 518 (1937); Realty Acceptance Corp. v. Montgomery, United Producers & Consumers Co-op. v. Held, Dennis v. Thermoid Co., Cuppy v. Stollwerck Bros., Hansen v. Columbia Breweries, all *supra* note 10. Compare Walker v. Maas & Waldstein Co., and other cases cited *supra* note 10, and see text to note 10 *supra*.

ment; and upon such assumption the Executive and the Successor Corporation shall become obligated to perform the terms and conditions hereof; provided, however, that although the Executive shall be an executive of the Successor Corporation, he need not be named as Chief Executive of the Successor Corporation, and his duties shall be such as shall be prescribed by the Board of Directors of the Successor Corporation.

The problem dealt with in this clause is obviously a delicate one. The executive hardly wishes to interfere with his corporation's proper expansion through combination with another enterprise. In fact, if he is to be head of the combined enterprises, he will usually welcome the idea. On the other hand, the use of the merger or consolidation device to demote or displace an unwanted executive is one which might occur to a hostile board of directors—fruitless as the attempt might ultimately prove.[38] Demotion or displacement as the result of a merger or consolidation is a contingency against which the executive may well seek to guard.

While modern statutes and case law generally provide some means for protecting creditors of a merging corporation,[39] the position of a claimant under a contract naming him as "Chief Executive" of the corporation is a particularly difficult one.[40] What is to be done if Corporation A has a contract with B hiring him as "Chief Executive," Corporation X has a similar contract with Y, and then Corporation A merges with Corporation X? If the parties can agree, well and good.[41] If not, trouble will result. Accordingly, if combinations are probable, the executive will usually try to clarify the situation in advance. Frequently, however, the executive does not succeed in getting a clause as favorable to him as the one which is given

[38] Consult Washington and Fulda, *Protective Coloring in Corporation Law*, 26 MINN. L. REV. 824, 831–34 (1942). See Willey v. Diepress Co., 156 Misc. 762, 281 N.Y. Supp. 907 (Sup. Ct. 1935) (new corporation held liable for unpaid salary obligations of merged company); Small v. Sullivan, 245 N.Y. 343, 157 N.E. 261 (1927).

[39] See STEVENS, CORPORATIONS 917–19 (2d ed. 1949); Note, 15 A.L.R. 1112, 1133 (1921); N.Y. STOCK CORP. LAW, §§ 85, 90. Compare N.Y. STOCK CORP. LAW, § 71 for liability of stockholders for unpaid salaries.

[40] See Washington and Fulda, *supra* note 38.

[41] Thus, the Kaiser-Willys merger agreement contained the following provision: Purchaser [Kaiser] agrees to . . . operate [Willys] . . . as a separate division of Purchaser, and in connection therewith not only to maintain in effect the employment contracts made, prior to the date of this proposal, by Willys or its subsidiaries, but also to continue the employment of the principal officers . . . for a minimum period of two years at not less than the respective salaries they are now receiving.

As quoted in Rosensteel and Baer, *Mergers: Their Effect on Executive Compensation*, 44 MGMT. REV. 490–499 (1955).

above. The problem is often handled by a general provision that the employment contract shall be binding upon any successor of the corporation or its business.[42] When the executive has a deferred compensation contract, a possible solution is to give him an election to terminate his employment contract in the event of a merger or consolidation and thereby accelerate his receipt of deferred compensation. When profit participation or a stock option is given, the merger clause presents special problems.[43]

Inflation Clauses. Provisions protecting the executive against the consequences of currency inflation deserve special mention, though they are not in wide use, at least for salary during active employment.[44] Profit participation and stock option and stock purchase plans will sometimes provide a certain amount of such protection, at least in the case of businesses which are benefited by inflation. Occasionally a cautious executive, uncertain as to what the effect of inflation may be upon the particular business employing him, not only wishes to obtain a percentage of the profits but also seeks a legal basis to substantiate a demand for a higher fixed salary in the event of inflation. The old-fashioned gold clause being no longer available, attention has been turned to various means of establishing a measure of inflation and causing the amount of compensation to be varied accordingly. While this is not the place to attempt to discuss the vast problem of efforts to guard by contract against the consequences of inflation, it may, nevertheless, be pointed out that although the provisions of the gold clause resolution [45] prevent any form of application of the gold clause to any type of domestic obligation,[46] some attorneys

[42] COLUMBIA, App. C, ¶ 5; MANUFACTURERS TRUST, App. PP, § 93. UNIVERSAL, App. O, ¶ 9, also providing for right of cancellation by executive in the event of merger. *Cf.* Esquire Contract, *supra* note 17, ¶ 7: "Anything herein to the contrary notwithstanding, in the event it is determined by the Company to effect a merger or consolidation of the Company with any other corporation or business or to dispose of the entire or substantially the entire business of the Company to another corporation or business, and in that connection it becomes advisable in the judgment of the Board of Directors to modify the terms of employment above set forth, it is understood that the Board of Directors may so modify said terms of employment and in the event [the Executive] is not satisfied with such modification, he shall be released from his obligations hereunder."

[43] See *infra* note 47, and Chapter 3, text to note 100.

[44] For a clause seeking to protect deferred compensation against inflation, see DEVOE AND RAYNOLDS, App. L, and see also Chapter 3, text to note 100.

[45] Joint Resolution of June 5, 1933, 48 Stat. 112 (1933).

[46] Holyoke Water Power Co. v. American Writing Paper Co., 300 U.S. 324 (1937) (gold commodity clause); Guaranty Trust Co. v. Henwood, 307 U.S. 247 (1939) (alternative foreign currency clause); 8 GEO. WASH. L. REV. 232 (1939). In the Henwood case, Mr. Justice Black stated (307 U.S. 258):

Congress sought to outlaw all contractual provisions which require debtors who have bound themselves to pay United States dollars to pay a greater number of dollars than promised.

have considered that a measure of protection could be obtained in the form of provisions basing compensation upon the cost-of-living index or similar indices.[47]

One form of inflation clause, based on the theory that wage rates rise with inflation, provides for pro rata increases in salary if, as, and when wage increases take place. A less frequently found clause is one providing for an increase in salary in the event of a substantial increase in federal income tax rates. Protection against this contingency may be obtained either by direct provision or by tax reimbursement provisions.[48]

In the last analysis, an executive will usually rely for protection against inflation, as well as against other material changes in circumstances during the period when he is actively employed, upon his relationship with and value to the corporation and his consequent ability to secure equitable adjustments in his compensation contract. As we have previously pointed out, an executive is usually not in a formal arm's length relationship with the employing corporation, and its board of directors will rarely hold him to a contract which a material change in circumstances has rendered inequitable.

Other Clauses. The contract provisions discussed above—and particularly those contained in paragraphs 1, 2, and 3—state the usual and essential terms of the executive's salary contract. Additional clauses occasionally found include the expense clause discussed in a separate chapter,[49] and the vacation clause.[50] There may also be clauses protecting the status of the executive,[51] providing for arbitration of difficulties,[52] hinting at future rewards,[53] precluding the corporation from requiring the executive to work elsewhere than in a specific locality, providing for ownership by the corporation of inventions and conceptions developed by the executive and of patents and copyrights,[54] making provision for the sending of notices by one

---

[47] See DEVOE AND RAYNOLDS, App. L, for such a clause.

[48] See WASHINGTON AND ROTHSCHILD, *supra* note 35, at 383. Tax reimbursement provisions are rarely used today.

[49] See Chapter 7, text to note 9 *passim*.

[50] See note 22, *supra*.

[51] UNIVERSAL, App. O, ¶ 1, providing that the duties of the executive shall be "of a dignity consistent with [his] standing and experience . . . in the industry." FILENE, App. D, ¶ 5: the executive is to be furnished "office space and accommodations suitable to the character of his position with the Employer and adequate for the performance of his duties hereunder." See also Avco, App. QQ, ¶ 3. *Cf.* text to notes 17 and 18 *supra*.

[52] See U. S. RUBBER, App. B, ¶ 7, for a standard form of arbitration clause.

[53] For clauses, see Chapter 8, note 155.

[54] AMERICAN CYANAMID, App. K.

Such provisions are often required in the case of engineers. In a survey of 800 companies in major industrial activities employing a significant number of engineers, one-half of 206 responding employers stated that they execute some form

party to the other, and cancelling all previous agreements between the parties.[55] Clauses may also be included providing that the rights of the executive shall not be assignable by him,[56] that the agreement shall be submitted to the corporation's stockholders for approval,[57] that the agreement may not be modified or amended orally, that, unless terminated within a specified period of time prior to its expiration, the agreement shall be deemed renewed on a year-to-year basis on the same terms and conditions. When it can appropriately be negotiated, the corporation may seek a provision pursuant to which, perhaps after a period of time (say, a year or two), the corporation may elect, with or without cause, to pay the executive a fixed or determinable sum related to what would have been his compensation had the contract continued to its end and, on making such payment, to terminate the contract without further obligation or claim for damages, with the executive thereupon similarly released from any further obligation such as a covenant not to compete. Finally, many corporations today have adopted bylaws providing for the indemnification of directors and others against litigation and other expense; in the case of such corporations, parallel indemnification provisions may be included in the employment contracts of their executives.[58]

---

of employment agreement covering patent assignments, non-disclosure of proprietary information, or both. ENGINEERS JOINT COUNCIL, *A Survey of Employer Practices Concerning the Safeguarding of Proprietary Rights.*

[55] ALLIED, App. N, ¶ 7; U. S. RUBBER, App. B, ¶ 8; FILENE, App. D, ¶ 6.

[56] COLUMBIA, App. C, ¶ 5; ALLIED, App. N, ¶ 8; TEXAS, App. II, ¶ 8.

[57] UNIVERSAL, App. O, ¶ 12; TEXAS, App. II, ¶ 9. Many companies, while providing for such approval, also deny that it is legally required. See, e.g., Proxy Statement of E. R. Squibb & Sons, Sept. 28, 1950, p. 6. For a discussion of the point, see Chapter 8, text to notes 101 ff.

[58] These indemnity provisions should be carefully drawn. It may be desirable to limit their scope rather strictly. See WASHINGTON, CORPORATE EXECUTIVES' COMPENSATION 390 *et seq.,* 399 *et seq.* (1942). On the other hand, an employee may properly be indemnified for anything done by him in the normal course of his employment and in his employer's interest, at least when the employee did not know, and could not reasonably be expected to have known, that his conduct was illegal or tortious. See Bishop, *Current Status of Corporate Directors' Right to Indemnification,* 69 HARV. L. REV. 1057, 1065–1068 (1956). The current New York statute dealing with indemnification (Article 6-A of the General Corporation Law) has been construed not to apply to the expenses of a director or officer defending himself against criminal charges, apparently regardless of his guilt or innocence. Schwarz v. General Aniline & Film Corp., 305 N.Y. 395, 113 N.E.2d 533 (1953). Sections 723 and 724 of the New York Business Corporation Law, effective April 1, 1963, however, sanction the indemnification of corporate officers and directors against the expenses, including fines, of criminal prosecutions, even those in which they are convicted or plead *nolo contendere,* "if such director or officer acted, in good faith, for a purpose which he reasonably believed to be in the best interests of the corporation and . . . had no reasonable cause to believe that his conduct was unlawful." Courts have upheld the propriety of a corporation's indemnification of an officer who had

Other clauses which may be found appropriate in specific situations will be found in the model form of contract and in other agreements reproduced in the Appendix.

---

pleaded *nolo contendere* in a criminal antitrust proceeding. Koster v. Warren, 176 F. Supp. 459 (N.D. Cal. 1959) ; Simon v. Socony-Vacuum Oil Co., 179 Misc. 202, 38 N.Y.S.2d 270 (Sup. Ct. 1942), *aff'd mem.,* 267 App. Div. 890, 47 N.Y.S.2d 589 (1st Dep't 1944). But in neither of these cases does it appear that the violation was clear and flagrant ; it seems doubtful that any court would permit indemnification of an employee who had deliberately engaged in conduct which he knew or should have known to be criminal, even if the indemnification provision purported to sanction it. It is understood that none of the executives who in 1961 pleaded guilty in antitrust proceedings against General Electric and Westinghouse was indemnified by those corporations.

CHAPTER 3

PROFIT PARTICIPATION:
THE CONTRACT OR PLAN

Although a great many executives in American industry are paid on the basis of a straight salary with no incentive or bonus arrangement, direct participation in profits by management has a firmly established place in the American business scene and is found in a substantial number of companies and industries.[1] While certain

[1] AMERICAN MANAGEMENT ASSOCIATION (AMA), EXECUTIVE COMPENSATION SERVICE, REPORTS ON METHODS OF COMPENSATING EXECUTIVES, Revn. of Bull. Three, pp. 10–11 (June 1954) ("Executive Compensation Surveys, made by this Service over a period now going into five years have shown that about 45 per cent of the commercial and industrial firms in the United States currently use this form of compensation [viz., incentive compensation] and that if financial and utility companies, where bonus plans are rare, were eliminated, the number of companies with these plans would increase to about 67 per cent."). A subsequent report, giving a later analysis of bonus payments by industry, states that the companies in the Top Management Survey of the Service which paid bonuses increased from 42% in 1953 to 49.3% by 1957, percentages presumably based on the inclusion of financial and utility companies in the Survey and hence to be compared with the 45% figure in the 1954 report. AMA, EXECUTIVE COMPENSATION SERVICE, REPORTS ON METHODS OF COMPENSATING EXECUTIVES, INCENTIVE COMPENSATION, pp. 6–7 (1957). *Cf. A Sharper Eye on Bonuses,* BUSINESS WEEK, Aug. 11, 1956, p. 112 (stating that half the companies on the New York Stock Exchange have bonus plans, a number that has doubled over the preceding decade); Smyth, *Bonus Plans for Executives,* 37 HARV. BUS. REV. 66 (July–Aug., 1959) (stating that "today over half of the larger companies in the country have incentive bonus plans, and the trend is toward an increasing use of them"; they are used in 75% of companies in some industries such as rubber, textile, automobile, and household appliances, but seldom in banks and trust companies, insurance companies, and communication, gas, and electric utilities). The 1950's witnessed a trend toward profit sharing among banks. See N. Y. Times, July 9, 1961, sec. 3, p. 1, col. 4.

Consult BROWER, PROFIT SHARING FOR EXECUTIVES, NICB Studies in Personnel Policy No. 90 (1948), who summarizes the results of a study conducted in 1947 of 132 active plans (analyzed in an appendix to the study) adopted by corporations having an aggregate of 1,000,000 employees. Of some 70 plans providing for current distribution of profits, 25% had been in existence over twenty years; of all the plans examined, 56% had been in existence for ten or more years, and 29% had been in existence for five years or less. For a later study conducted by the NICB of 62 incentive bonus plans in use by 59 companies, see Martucci, *Computing the Executive Bonus Fund,* 27 MGMT. REC. 390 (1955) and Martucci, *Incentive Bonuses for Executives,* 28 *id.* 82 (1956).

Profit-sharing and other bonus plans were little used in this country prior to 1914, though they had long been known in Europe. Taussig and Barker, *American Corporations and Their Executives,* 40 Q.J. ECON. 1, at 29, 43 (1925); BAKER, EX-

52

aspects of the bonus system are still open to question,[2] many of the problems it raises may now be dealt with in the light of a considerable body of practical experience.

To connote a bonus arrangement based on profits, we use in this chapter the term "profit participation" or, interchangeably, "incentive compensation" or "contingent compensation," rather than the term "profit sharing," which has come to refer primarily to a plan qualified under Section 401 of the Internal Revenue Code of 1954 and, hence, open to a relatively large group of employees rather than confined to executives.[3]

ECUTIVE SALARIES AND BONUS PLANS 16 *et seq.* (1938) ; Balderston, *Fundamentals of Profit Sharing,* 9 NICB MGMT. REC. 388 (1947) ; Madden, *A Yardstick for Executive Incentive Plans, id.* at 393 ; PERSONNEL ACTIVITIES IN AMERICAN BUSINESS, NICB Studies in Personnel Policy No. 86 (1947). *Cf.* KNOWLTON, PROFIT SHARING PATTERNS 1 (1954) ("In the year 1900, well within the recollection of many business executives of today, any estimate that there were as many as 100 active profit-sharing plans in the United States would have been challenged as a gross exaggeration."). The Madden report, *supra,* based on a study conducted in 1946 of approximately 3,500 American corporations, found profit-sharing plans in existence in 25.1% of 3,039 manufacturing and 459 non-manufacturing concerns. A similar survey of a somewhat smaller group of companies made in 1939 showed an average of 23.1% as having such plans. *Cf.* NICB Studies in Personnel Policy No. 20 (1940). An earlier survey by the American Management Association of 411 companies in 22 major industries filing data with the SEC showed payment of bonuses in 40% of the companies in 1949 as compared to 20% in 1945. AMA, EXECUTIVE COMPENSATION SURVEY 1950–51, p. 22, summarized in Patton, *Current Practices in Executive Compensation,* 29 HARV. BUS. REV. 56, 61 (1951). Consult later AMA reports cited *supra.* But *cf.* Rosensteel, *New Study Shows Executive Pay Trends,* NATION'S BUSINESS, June 1956, pp. 39, 74 ("In the years we [American Management Association] have been making top management surveys, the number of incentive compensation plans has increased only slightly"). Of 60 companies with sales of $1 billion or more reporting to the American Management Association, 31 paid bonuses. AMA EXECUTIVE COMPENSATION SERVICE, TOP MANAGEMENT REPORT, pp. 66–67 (11th ed. 1960). On the other hand, of 615 companies with annual sales volume of under $10 million, only 231 or 37.5% reported bonus payments. *Id.,* 41.

[2] See Chapter 4, text to notes 1 ff., 79 ff.

[3] Consult, for example, publications of the Council of Profit Sharing Industries and of the Profit Sharing Research Foundation. *Cf.* SANDERS, EXECUTIVE COMPENSATION AND RETIREMENT PLANS 15 (1951) : "Many profit-sharing plans include a large number of employees, and most plans include executives, but those which include only top executives are rare." The term "incentive compensation" is usually reserved, with the term "executive bonus," for a plan confined to executives. Consult Martucci, *Computing the Executive Bonus Fund, supra* note 1 ("Participation in such [incentive bonus] plans is limited to top executives, high-level administrators and other key employees. These limitations distinguish executive incentive bonus plans from profit-sharing plans which are open to all employees."). Consult also Stryker, *The Executive Bonus,* FORTUNE, Dec. 1956, pp. 127, 131 : ". . . profit-sharing payments are usually distinguished from bonuses in that profit-sharing schemes normally predetermine the awards in one fixed ratio to all salaries (e.g., 10 per cent of salaries) whereas the ratio of bonus payments to salary often varies widely between lower and higher echelons of management." Consult also Rosensteel, *supra*

Profit-participation plans are usually discussed in terms of "providing an incentive." An executive, according to the proponents of such plans, should receive a fixed salary sufficient to satisfy his normal needs and to provide fair recompense for normal services; in addition, there should be an "incentive" to induce added effort and bring about improved performance.[4] According to this theory, one might expect a profit-participation plan to result in lower fixed salaries for participating executives than might otherwise have been paid. While many plans of this sort may initially have had this result, a survey conducted in 1947 showed that of the 103 corporations with profit-participation plans that were studied, only 5% paid their executives less than prevailing salaries and about 21% actually paid salaries above average.[5] In an earlier survey of similar scope con-

---

note 1, at 74: "Profit-sharing means different things to different people. Many companies call their bonus or incentive plan a profit-sharing plan. However, in strict terms, profit-sharing is a plan by which some portion of the profits are distributed among all employees of an organization or institution. Executives participate in these plans proportionately the same as any employee participates."

[4] While proof is of course difficult, indications have been found that bonus-paying companies achieve the aim of creating extra profits through additional incentive. AMA, EXECUTIVE COMPENSATION SURVEY 1950-51, supra note 1, at 19-20. Major arguments against profit-sharing by executives are the difficult problems presented in attempting to evaluate each executive's responsibility in the success of the enterprise, and the fact that a substantial portion of profits received will be paid out in taxes, thereby lessening the profit-sharing incentive. For a summary of arguments for and criticisms of profit-sharing plans, see BROWER, op. cit. supra note 1, at 3 ff.; Madden, supra note 1, at 394. [Both as to purpose and details, profit-sharing plans for executives must be distinguished from profit-sharing plans for workers. In general, the latter, together with lower-paid executive personnel, prefer a fixed salary structure to the uncertainties of profit-sharing. Cf. BROWER, op. cit. supra note 1, with PROFIT SHARING FOR WORKERS, NICB Studies in Personnel Policy No. 97 (1948).] On the other hand, a study by Dean David Roberts, based on rate of return on sales, concluded that "in general bonus and deferred compensation plans in common use through 1950 are not associated with greater corporate profitability than the alternative devices, whatever they may be, which are used by other companies." ROBERTS, EXECUTIVE COMPENSATION 93 passim (1959). This conclusion is in conflict with the findings of others. EXECUTIVE COMPENSATION SERVICE, TOP MANAGEMENT REPORT, pp. 21-22 (10th ed. 1959) (from ten-year analysis, 1949-58, it appears that "bonus-paying companies grow faster and produce better performance than those without management bonus plans" and produced a larger return on investment than did the non-bonus companies); e.g., PATTON, MEN, MONEY AND MOTIVATION 134 (1961) ("bonus payers tend to have substantially greater profit increases and return on investment than non-bonus payers").

[5] BROWER, op. cit. supra note 1, at 18-19. As a result of the study which he conducted, BAKER, op. cit. supra note 1, concludes (at 236): "There is no evidence that the use of bonus plans lowered the regular cash salaries paid executives. Instead there is definite evidence that companies paying bonuses paid larger total compensation to their officers than did non-bonus-paying companies." But cf. Smyth, supra note 1, at 68 ("particularly in the case of higher management positions, there has been a tendency to pay a lower base salary if a bonus is also paid"); Howe, Price

ducted in 1937, 50% of the corporations studied were paying less than prevailing salaries.[6] These figures may suggest that after a profit-participation plan has been in operation for a period of time, it may no longer keep fixed salaries at a lower level; for example, a business recession substantially reducing compensation received from the plan may result in increases in salaries which are difficult to eliminate after the recession has run its course.[7] Or the figures may simply indicate that a corporation with a business sufficiently profitable to make a profit-participation plan significant is led in addition to pay fixed salaries as high as or higher than average.[8]

Tags for Executives, 34 HARV. BUS. REV. 94, 98 (May–June, 1956) ("In operations of equal size, bonus-earning managers were found to average 19% less in base salary than nonbonus managers; total compensation of the bonus earners, however, was 7% more than for nonbonus earners").

[6] See PROFIT-SHARING PLANS FOR EXECUTIVES, NICB Studies in Personnel Policy No. 6, at 9 (1938); *cf.* BROWER, *op. cit. supra* note 1, at 19. See Com'r v. Surface Combustion Corp., 181 F.2d 444, 445 (6th Cir. 1950).

[7] The use of profit-sharing plans decreases in periods of depression and increases in times of prosperity. *Cf.* BAKER, *op. cit. supra* note 1, at 16–27. The post-1929 depression had a withering effect on such plans, especially for wage-earners. 60% of 161 wage-earner plans and 8.7% of 92 executive plans examined in 1937 had been abandoned during the depression years. See PROFIT-SHARING PLANS FOR EXECUTIVES, *supra* note 6, at 10; STEWART AND COUPER, PROFIT-SHARING AND STOCK OWNERSHIP FOR WAGE-EARNERS AND EXECUTIVES (1945).

[8] The corporations involved in the Brower study, *op. cit. supra* note 1, were a relatively profitable group. A later survey indicates a bonus range from 23% to 37% of salary for executives other than presidents, and a range from 54% to 84% of salary for corporation presidents. COMPENSATION AND PENSIONS FOR EXECUTIVES, NICB Studies in Personnel Policy No. 111 (1950). The median yield for 109 cash plans was found to be 10% in a study published in 1954. KNOWLTON, *op. cit. supra* note 1, at 24. As the result of more comprehensive surveys, bonus payments have been said normally to average 45% of salary, as compared to 36% in the past, ranging in different industries from 10% to more than 100% in exceptional cases. Rosensteel, *Executive Pay Trends,* NATION'S BUSINESS, Dec. 1958, pp. 37, 44. In the 31 companies with sales of $1 billion or over reporting to the American Management Association, bonus payments represented 73.1% of the $21.9 million in salaries paid to the 301 executives who received them. AMA, TOP MANAGEMENT REPORT, *op. cit. supra* note 1, at 67. In the case of small companies, the bonuses ranged from 21.1% of the salary of the chief executive officer (public utilities) to 46% of such salary (durable consumer products). *Id.,* 41. *Cf.* Stryker, *supra* note 3, at 130 (ratio of bonuses to salaries for all executives "probably not much higher than 15%"). Extra rewards amounting to less than 10% of salary are said to be "ineffective as incentives for executives." *Id.,* 60n. See also Smyth, *supra* note 1, at 68. Typical bonuses at the officer level have been found to amount to 40%–50% of salary, as compared to 20%–30% of salary at the middle management levels. *Id.,* at 67. *Cf.* Martucci, *Incentive Bonuses for Executives, supra* note 1, at 103 (plan of heavy equipment manufacturer resulted in bonuses of 100% of salary for top echelon positions and 66.6% for key supervisory positions). See Stryker, *supra* note 3, at 131 (noting that the four top executives at Bethlehem Steel, General Motors, and Ford received 1955 bonuses averaging 416%, 300%, and 216%, respectively, of their salaries).

Profit-participation awards may be payable in cash, in stock, or in units with value based on the value of stock. The measuring rod of the added compensation is usually corporate profits,[9] but may be dividends,[10] sales of the company or of a particular division,[11] or some other significant figure. The compensation may be set at a percentage fixed in advance by bylaw, or by plan or resolution usually approved by the stockholders,[12] or it may be fixed from year to year by the board of directors.[13] The cash bonus based on a percentage of the company's profits and payable at least once a year is one of the more common forms of incentive compensation,[14] and it is that form which is the principal subject of this chapter.

In granting additional compensation of this type the corporation may provide for a fund in which two or more executives or employees

[9] This is the most common form of profit-sharing. See BROWER, op. cit. supra note 1, at 9. In a survey of 300 profit-sharing companies with a total of over 730,000 employees, conducted by the Profit-Sharing Research Foundation, the most frequently occurring straight percentage of employer contribution to cash plans was 25% by plan count when there were no prior reservations in computing the bonus fund; when there were prior reservations, the commonest percentage rose to 50%. KNOWLTON, op. cit. supra note 1, at 17, 29. Cf. AMA, INCENTIVE COMPENSATION, supra note 1, at 18 (finding the percentages of profits ranging from 1% to 50% but with the most common—one out of every four—based on a distribution of 10%). Ten per cent was also found to be the rate most frequently used in a survey of 125 companies published in 1959, with two-thirds of the plans using between 5% and 12½%; though the rates were generally higher when based on after-tax income, they did not vary proportionately with the federal income tax rate. Simons, A Survey of Incentive Compensation Plans, J. ACCOUNTANCY, Oct. 1959, pp. 49, 53.

[10] E.g., Eastman Kodak Company plan referred to in BAKER, op. cit. supra note 1, at 200; revised Bethlehem Steel Corporation Plan (App. FF) discussed id. at 210. See discussion of the relationship of profit participation to dividends, infra text to notes 34 and 37.

[11] Executives of companies engaged in distribution are often granted additional compensation based on increases in volume of sales, either of the entire enterprise or the branch which they serve. See SAFEWAY, App. P. See also Saltz Bros., Inc. v. Saltz, 122 F.2d 79 (App. D.C. 1941).

[12] With regard to the practice of seeking, and the necessity for, stockholder approval of profit-participation contracts, see Chapter 8, text to notes 108 passim.

[13] BROWER, op. cit. supra note 1, at 9. The Brower study found only a small number of the latter plans. An annual plan may be preferred because of the fluctuating nature of the business. See Proxy Statement, Mar. 10, 1950, of Phelps-Dodge Copper Co. Other large companies with bonus plans on a year-to-year basis are E. R. Squibb & Sons (see Proxy Statement, Sept. 28, 1950, pp. 6–7); Van Raalte Co., Inc. (see Proxy Statement, Mar. 29, 1949); Inland Steel Co. (see Proxy Statement, Mar. 31, 1951).

[14] Profit-participation plans for individual executives were in the past usually on a current distribution or short-term instalment basis, whereas plans serving a larger group of personnel were more often on a deferred distribution basis. BROWER, op. cit. supra note 1, at 7 and Table 3. Today, deferment is frequent for highly paid executives. See Chapter 5, note 1. In a study conducted by the Profit-Sharing Foundation, supra note 9, cash plans predominated in small companies, outnumbering deferred plans by two to one, and were relatively three times as frequent as in large companies. KNOWLTON, op. cit. supra note 1, at 12.

will share,[15] or it may enter into a separate contract with each executive who is to receive a percentage of earnings.[16]

There is no "ideal" form of profit participation; the needs of the individual business must control the substance and form of the final arrangement, and the success of a particular plan will depend upon how well it is adapted to the business methods of the corporation.[17] Since a compensation contract which has worked out well in one business may be unsatisfactory in another, it is inadvisable to rely too completely on any form of model contract. With this caveat, there are given below certain clauses designed for insertion in the form of contract presented in the preceding chapter. References to actual contracts, reproduced in the Appendix, are also given.

The Compensation Clause: The Basis for Profit Participation.

• 3. (a) For all services to be rendered by him in any capacity hereunder, the Corporation agrees to pay the Executive, so long as he shall be employed hereunder,

  (i) a fixed salary at the rate of $.... per annum, payable in equal monthly instalments at the end of each month; and

  (ii) an additional sum (hereinafter sometimes referred to as "the Executive's contingent compensation") equal to ..% of the adjusted consolidated net earnings of the Corporation and its subsidiaries for each calendar year [fiscal year of the Corporation], or portion thereof, during his employment hereunder beginning January 1, 19..,[18] such sum to be computed and payable as provided in paragraph 3(b) below.[19]

---

[15] See Chapter 4.

[16] See, e.g., FAIRBANKS, App. M; ALLIED, App. N.

[17] The possibilities of forms of incentive compensation other than those here discussed should not, of course, be overlooked. Cf. BAKER, op. cit. supra note 1, at 245: "Plans doubtless should be adapted to meet company and industrial needs. . . . Satisfactory solutions in any area will not be 'ready made' ones; rather they will be 'made to order.'" For additional considerations see AMA, EXECUTIVE COMPENSATION SURVEY 1950–51, supra note 1, pp. 24–25.

[18] If the executive's employment does not begin at the start of the corporation's accounting period, it will be advisable to add a clause providing for ratable adjustment of the percentage compensation. This might be either a ratable portion of the earnings of the entire calendar or fiscal year, or a percentage of the earnings actually accruing during the months when the executive is on the job. The question assumes particular importance if the executive is not hired until after the most profitable season of the year has passed.

[19] If a ceiling is to be imposed, the clause may conclude: "provided always that the total contingent compensation payable to the Executive under this contract for any calendar [fiscal] year shall not exceed the sum of $ . . . ," e.g., a sum equal to his fixed salary or a stated percentage thereof. See BROWER, op. cit. supra note 1, at 8–9. For examples, see infra note 36.

The fixed salary provision has been discussed in Chapter 2. As to profit participation,[20] we note, first of all, that the basic figure used is "the adjusted consolidated net earnings of the Corporation and its subsidiaries." This is preferable to "the adjusted net earnings of the Corporation" for the reason that the company which pays such incentive compensation may be a parent corporation as well as an operating company, using consolidated financial statements in reporting to its stockholders.[21] At least the top executives of the parent company will usually perform some services for subsidiaries, if only general supervision. At any rate, companies which report to stockholders on a consolidated basis will normally use that basis in computing participations for executives.[22] Such a basis would appear to be unjustified only when the parent company's executives have no connection whatever with subsidiaries, or in the case of the head of a subsidiary or division concerned only with its operations.[23]

Regardless of the position which we may take as to the suitability of consolidated balance sheets and consolidated income statements as a basis for declaring dividends or for other business purposes, there seems to be no insuperable legal objection to the use of consolidated earnings figures as a base for supplemental compensation.[24] We are,

---

[20] The word "bonus" is in disfavor and is not actually fully descriptive of true profit-sharing. The usual expression is "incentive compensation." See note 3, supra; FAIRBANKS, App. M. BLOOMINGDALE, App. R, ¶ 3, speaks of "a sum based on the net earnings of the Employer"; UNIVERSAL, App. O, ¶ 3, speaks of "a percentage of the consolidated net profits . . ."; NEW ENGLAND, App. Q, ¶ 2(a), speaks of "Percentage Compensation." But see SAFEWAY, App. P, granting a "bonus."

FAIRBANKS, App. M, ¶ (e), provides: "Nothing contained in this agreement shall be construed to give the party of the second part any interest in or to the surplus or net profits of the company, it being agreed that the annual profits thereof are being adopted herein as a standard by which to measure the amount of the additional compensation payable under this agreement."

Properly authorized profit participation is a business expense and not a diversion of shareholders' profits. See 1 WILLISTON, CONTRACTS § 130B (rev. ed. 1936) and cases cited. Non-executive employees, such as salesmen, are frequently hired on a profit-sharing basis. See cases collected in GORDON, EMPLOYMENT AND AGENCY AGREEMENTS 153, 154, 157 (1940).

[21] NEW ENGLAND, App. Q, ¶ 2(a), speaks of "consolidated net earnings"; UNIVERSAL, App. O, ¶ 3, of 'consolidated net profits"; BLOOMINGDALE, App. R, ¶ 3D, "net earnings"; JONES, App. S, of "net profits." See also FAIRBANKS, App. M, ¶ (b). If the employing corporation is a parent company, the expressions "net profits" or "net earnings" are ambiguous and are not to be recommended.

[22] Cf. contracts cited supra note 21. Consolidated income is adjusted by exclusion of income from partly owned subsidiaries and of unconsolidated income from affiliates in the Bonus Plan of Monsanto Chemical Company. See its Proxy Statement dated Feb. 28, 1950, p. 9.

[23] See SAFEWAY, App. P.

[24] Meyers v. Cowdin, 47 N.Y.S.2d 471, (Sup. Ct. 1944), aff'd w.o., 270 App. Div. 827, 60 N.Y.S.2d 129 (2d Dep't 1946), aff'd w.o., 296 N.Y. 755, 70 N.E.2d 555 (1946). Actual transmittal of earnings to the parent, prevented by currency restric-

after all, merely seeking a fair measuring rod of the success of the enterprise, and, in the case of a parent company, a consolidated statement prepared in conformity with good accounting practice doubtless provides such a measure.[25]

A further accounting question relates to the period during which the earnings are to be measured. The usual period is, of course, one year—as a rule the corporation's fiscal year (frequently the calendar year); corporations keep their accounts on a yearly basis, and the authors know of no instance in which profit participation has been computed otherwise. However, it must be recognized that for many businesses the year is not a natural cycle; some companies would be justified in keeping their accounts on a two-year, three-year, or even five-year basis. Occasionally, we find wide fluctuations between the earnings of one business year and the next. The executive may receive a large bonus in the first year and none in the second, whereas if the company had been on a two-year accounting basis, he would have received a bonus of perhaps one-fourth of the amount actually paid. Ideally, it may be that corporations should endeavor to determine what accounting system would properly reflect the conditions prevailing in their particular line of business, and then regulate their bonus payments accordingly,[26] but the practicality of such a plan is open to question.

---

tions or otherwise, is not required for the purpose of computation. Meyers v. Cowdin, *supra;* Epstein v. Schenck, 35 N.Y.S.2d 969, 983 (Sup. Ct. 1939). See text to note 88 *infra.*

[25] For a short treatment of the suitability of consolidated statements generally, see Berle and Fisher, *The Law of Business Accounting,* 32 Cal. L. Rev. 573, 597–99 (1932). A question may arise as to whether companies which are less than wholly owned should be included in the consolidation, though accepted accounting practice usually provides an adequate answer. Consult New England, App. Q, ¶ 2(c) (A) (ii) and ¶ 2(d). See also the bonus plan of Loew's, Inc., which included profits of all companies in which Loew's, Inc. had at least a 25% stock interest (Epstein v. Schenck, *supra* note 24, at 983) and the Monsanto plan, *supra* note 22; General Motors, App. V, ¶ 3.

[26] Numerous arguments are from time to time advanced in favor of the averaging of income over a period of years for the purpose of computing incentive compensation and other payments measured by profits, in cases where fluctuation of income from year to year regularly occurs. See, e.g., O'Leary, Corporate Enterprise in Modern Economic Life 38 (1933). The loss carry-over provisions of Section 172 of the Internal Revenue Code of 1954 (26 U.S.C. § 172) are a partial recognition of the problem. On the whole, however, attempts at averaging income often raise as many problems as they solve. For a criticism of the taxing of earned income "by reference to arbitrary twelve-month cubicles," see Silverson, *Earned Income and Ability to Pay,* 3 Tax L. Rev. 299, 300–01 (1948).

Consult, generally, Kragen, *Effect of Taxation on Individuals with Fluctuating Incomes;* Steger, *Averaging Income for Income Tax Purposes,* and other articles in the section on Taxation of Fluctuating Incomes, 1 Tax Revision Compendium, submitted to the Committee on Ways and Means of the House of Representatives

A step in the direction of averaging-out incentive compensation over a period of two or more years can be made through a provision that the amount available for incentive compensation out of earnings of a particular year need not be distributed entirely in awards for that year,[27] thus permitting amounts earned in a good year to be carried forward for awards in a poorer year. However, failure to distribute over an extended period of time large amounts earned in prior years may result in dissatisfaction among executives who produced the amounts and who may consider that they have at least a moral claim to them in preference to those who joined the company at a later date.

Another step in the direction of averaging-out is a provision for payment of larger awards in instalments over a period of two or more years, thus cushioning the shock of reduced bonuses in lean years.[28]

The compensation clause may place a definite limitation on the amount payable.[29] Sometimes, of course, the executive's compensation is based upon a fixed percentage of the company's net profits, regardless of the extent of the company's earnings. In the event of unexpected success, the company may find itself paying the executive a much larger dollar amount than was contemplated at the time the contract was signed. In such a situation the executive may consent to a reduction in the percentage rate. Even if no such reduction is made, many stockholders—perhaps most—would not object too

in connection with Panel Discussions beginning Nov. 16, 1959, 579, 589 ff.; Driscoll, *Income Averaging for Individual Income-Tax Purposes,* Joint Committee on the Economic Report, FEDERAL TAX POLICY FOR ECONOMIC GROWTH AND STABILITY, 175, 84th Cong., 1st Sess. (1955).

[27] E.g., GENERAL ELECTRIC, App. AA, § II(3) (authorizing allotments for any year not to exceed amounts credited to the Incentive Compensation Reserve for such year plus the amount of any balance carried forward from prior years). A provision authorizing the taking of action in a year subsequent to the year in which awards were earned, which may have the effect of reducing the total awards to less than the total authorized by the plan, may jeopardize the company's tax deduction for the year in which the awards were earned, since the liability of the company will not be based upon facts ascertainable at the close of that year. See discussion, Chapter 4, text to notes 46 ff.

[28] E.g., GENERAL MOTORS, App. W, ¶ 6 (five annual instalments); DU PONT. App. Y, ¶ 12(3) (four annual instalments); FORD, App. CC, ¶9b(2) (*semble*). For other examples, see Chapter 6, text to notes 38 ff.

[29] See note 19 *supra.* A bonus limitation of 100% of base pay, with the added stipulation that annual compensation, including bonuses, shall not exceed $200,000 for any executive has been advocated. See GILBERT AND GILBERT, TWENTY-FIRST ANNUAL REPORT OF STOCKHOLDER ACTIVITIES AT CORPORATION MEETINGS DURING 1960, 106–107 (1961). Consult LIVINGSTON, THE AMERICAN STOCKHOLDER 88–89 (1958). Allegedly excessive incentive compensation resulting from unexpectedly large profits was the ground of judicial criticism in the *American Tobacco* case; see text to note 32 *infra.* In more recent times, it was the basis of a suit against Bethlehem Steel Corporation which was settled. See Proxy Statement for special meeting on July 28, 1959.

strenuously to payment at the original rate, inasmuch as their own profits are being similarly increased beyond their expectations. However, there may be stockholders who will raise objections. Whether these objections are held valid—that is, whether it is believed that a ceiling should be placed upon the amount that management should be permitted to earn—depends on the view taken of the function of management, a matter heretofore discussed.[30]

In an extreme case the courts may intervene. Thus, in the *American Tobacco* case,[31] the Court had before it a bylaw passed in 1912, giving the executives a total of 10% of the net profits of the company above $8,222,248.42. In 1921 the arrangement produced a bonus of less than $360,000 for the managing group; in 1929 the operation of the bylaw produced a bonus of $2,670,000 for the group, paid in addition to salaries and other rewards. The Supreme Court of the United States, sustaining a minority stockholder's complaint, held that "the payments under the bylaw have by reason of increase of profits become so large as to warrant investigation in equity in the interest of the company." [32] The Court's decision might possibly have been different had the facts presented a recent plan rather than an ancient bylaw outmoded by economic developments. As a result of this decision, many lawyers recommend that incentive compensation plans be resubmitted to stockholders periodically.[33]

Apart from the attitude of the courts and the view taken of management's functions and right to compensation, the public relations aspect of the matter must be considered. A large part of the public condemnation of bonus contracts, and much of the litigation which they have caused, has been based on the payment of very large

---

[30] See Chapter 1, text to note 86.

[31] Rogers v. Hill, 289 U.S. 582, 53 Sup. Ct. 731 (1933).

[32] *Per* Butler, J., 289 U.S. 582, 591 (1933). The amounts produced by the bylaw in the years prior to 1921 are not revealed in the opinions or the record on appeal, as the plaintiff made no complaint concerning them. For another instance of compensation in excess of amounts originally contemplated, see the *American Woolen* case, discussed in Baker, *op. cit. supra* note 1, at 227, 228, where stockholders' dissatisfaction led to the termination of the plan. *Cf.* Fogelson v. American Woolen Co., 170 F.2d 660 (2d Cir. 1948). Consult, also, the opinion of Dibell, J., in Seitz v. Union Brass & Metal Mfg. Co., 152 Minn. 460, 468–69, 189 N.W. 586, 589 (1922). See Kennedy, Dividends To Pay 117–18 (1939).

[33] The bylaws of General Motors Corporation require that the directors resubmit the Bonus Plan of the corporation to stockholders at least once every five years. See Proxy Statement for Annual Meeting on May 24, 1957, p. 15. The bylaws of the major tobacco companies have contained similar requirements, probably as the result of the American Tobacco cases, *infra* note 66. For similar provisions in plans more recently adopted, see American Sugar Refining, App. Z, § 90, and that of National Biscuit Company cited in Gilbert and Gilbert, Nineteenth Annual Report of Stockholder Activities During 1958, 110–11 (1959).

amounts arising from unforeseen increases in corporate earnings. Simply from the standpoint of keeping on good terms with stockholders and the public, it may be good policy for executives to agree in advance either to some definite limitation upon the total monetary amount payable to them or to the requirement of a basic or initial return to stockholders before incentive compensation can be paid.[34] Over the years, limiting clauses of this general nature have been used with increasing frequency,[35] often taking one of the following forms:

1. A ceiling may be imposed by inserting a proviso with a flat dollar limitation upon the total payable.[36]
2. A ceiling may be imposed by limiting the incentive compensation bonus in terms of dividends, either earned or paid.[37]
3. Incentive compensation in each year may be limited to a percentage of earnings in excess of a stated return upon invested capital or stated minimum earnings [38] or in terms of some other figure.[39]

[34] As a practical matter, bonuses will rarely be paid, at least to top management, when dividends are omitted. On the other hand, at least one company points out that, irrespective of dividends, it may find it necessary or advisable to pay a bonus to employees of subsidiaries operating in foreign countries, and that outstanding performance may in individual cases warrant a bonus irrespective of dividends. See GILBERT AND GILBERT, *op. cit. supra* note 33, at 111–12. See text *infra* to notes 38, 39.

[35] See BAKER, *op. cit. supra* note 1, at 208. A trend has been found towards deducting earnings on capital before applying the bonus formula to determine the bonus fund; only 36% of plans studied in 1947 made such a deduction as compared to 65% of those studied in 1959. Torrence, *Trends in Executive Bonus Plans,* 22 NICB MGMT. REC. 12, 14 (1960). Approximately one-half of fifty representative plans studied by the American Management Association required a return on capital before applying the bonus percentage, the return ranging from 4% to 17%, with two out of three using from 6% to 10% as the basic deduction. AMA, INCENTIVE COMPENSATION, *supra* note 1, at 19. Consult note 8 *supra*.

[36] E.g., ALLIED, App. N, ¶ 2. See also BROWER, *op. cit. supra* note 1, at App. A, Nos. 32 and 49 (maximum limitations of $350,000 and $200,000 imposed). For a contract conversely imposing a floor, see FAIRBANKS, App. M, ¶ (C) (fixing a $15,000 annual minimum for additional compensation). The employment contract of Louis B. Mayer with Loew's, Inc. provided that Mr. Mayer's total compensation, including profit-sharing, shall not exceed $300,000, formerly $500,000. Proxy Statement, Feb. 15, 1950, p. 5. For a ceiling based on percentage of base pay, see *supra* note 29.

[37] *Cf.* JONES, App. S; BROWER, *op. cit. supra* note 1, at 2, 9–10. See also contracts cited *infra* note 45 and compare notes 44 and 46. Consult *infra* note 49. The bylaws of R. J. Reynolds Tobacco Company (Art. XII) formerly provided for the deduction of dividends upon preferred stock before profit-sharing participation in earnings. Proxy Statement, Mar. 24, 1949, Exs. B, C. Such provisions are more usual in group plans than in individual contracts. For an instance of the latter, see BLOOMINGDALE, App. R, ¶ 3D. *Cf.* employment contract of Louis B. Mayer with Loew's, Inc., *supra* note 36, deducting from profits an amount equivalent to $2 per share on common stock.

[38] See GENERAL MOTORS, App. V, and instances cited *infra* note 52.

[39] AMERICAN TOBACCO, App. U (no profit-sharing in earnings below a certain figure); SAFEWAY, App. P; Curtiss-Wright, Proxy Statement, Mar. 10, 1950, p. 6.

4. A decreasing scale of percentages may be fixed in the contract, as
in the following provision of a contract between Columbia Broadcasting System, Inc., and a former president: [40]

• *Additional Compensation.* As additional compensation, Columbia
agrees to pay, and/or cause its subsidiaries to pay, to [the Executive]
five per cent (5%) of the amount of the annual consolidated net
profits of Columbia and its subsidiaries (hereinafter referred to as
"such net profits") up to $1,000,000, plus four per cent (4%) of the
next $1,000,000 of such net profits, plus three per cent (3%) of the
next $1,000,000 of such net profits, plus two per cent (2%) of
the sum by which such net profits shall exceed $3,000,000.[41]

Clauses such as the one just quoted are frequently used.[42] The
draftsmen may work out other means of limiting the amount receivable in an attempt to meet the needs of a particular business.[43]

Another limitation might be 100% (or any other percentage) of the executive's
fixed salary. See Madden, *supra* note 1, at 399. *Cf.* The Borg-Warner Plan, limiting the bonus to 100% of the first $15,000 of salary, 75% of the next $20,000, and
50% of any amount in excess of $35,000. Proxy Statement, Mar. 27, 1950. The
Ekco Products Plan limits the company's contribution to 15% of the participating
payroll. Proxy Statement, Mar. 17, 1950. *Cf.* Park & Tilford, Inc., Form 8K, filed
Apr. 1948 (bonus limited to 15% of fixed salary). For findings as to the percentage relationship between bonus and salary, see *supra* note 8.

The reverse of the foregoing types of limitation, excluding higher levels of earnings from profit-sharing, is of course possible. See *Summary of Profit-Sharing
Plan of Textile Company,* BROWER, *op. cit. supra* note 1, at 32 (no sharing in profits
in excess of $5,000,000) ; *id.,* 35–36 (bonus not to exceed 6% of real income).

[40] Contract with William S. Paley, Nov. 9, 1937, ¶ 3.

[41] This represents an amendment of a prior contract, which provided for a bonus
of 2½% of the consolidated net profits up to $600,000 and 5% of such profits above
$600,000. *Cf.* The Borg-Warner Plan, *supra* note 39.

[42] See, for example, the plan of Corn Products Refining Company as summarized in BAKER, *op. cit. supra* note 1, at 212. The opposite arrangement—an increasing scale—is of course also possible. UNIVERSAL, App. O, ¶ 3A, B. BLOOMING-
DALE (*cf.* App. R) provides in ¶ 3 for a bonus of 1% on net profits (above preferred
dividend requirements), 1½% additional on that part of such profits which is in
excess of $500,000, and 2½% additional on any part in excess of $1,000,000. See also
the plan of the Continental Oil Company summarized in BAKER, *supra,* and BROWER,
op. cit. supra note 1, at 9. *Cf.* former CBS contract, *supra* note 40.

[43] FAIRBANKS, App. M, presents an interesting plan:

(a) From the net profits of the Company for each calendar year there
shall be deducted a sum equalling four per cent (4%) of the sum of its
average outstanding Common Capital Stock during such year and its surplus
and undivided profits at the beginning of such year as shown by its books of
account, which deductions are hereinafter referred to as "Capital Earnings."
The remainder after the deduction of such "Capital Earnings" from the said
net profits is hereinafter referred to as the "Balance of Profits."

* * * *

(c) Such annual additional compensation shall be that proportion of the
annual salary paid to said party of the second part during such year as said

Clauses limiting profit participation in terms of dividends, such as the second clause mentioned above, are intended to meet possible stockholder objections to the company's failure to declare dividends while paying substantial bonus compensation to executives. Some corporations include in their employment contracts clauses to the effect that no incentive compensation shall be payable for any year in which the stockholders have not received a dividend.[44] This is open to some objection. If the directors are unfriendly to the executives, they could simply fail to declare any dividend. If, on the other hand, they are themselves executives or overfriendly to the executives, they could declare dividends in some small amount for the sole purpose of justifying bonus payments. These objections may be met by a provision for payment of incentive compensation if dividends in a stated amount have been earned, even though not declared and paid, for once the dividend has been earned, it may be argued that the executives should not suffer because of failure of the board of directors for extraneous reasons to declare and pay the dividend to stockholders.[45] Such a provision, while exempting initial yearly profits

---

"Balance of Profits" shall bear to said "Capital Earnings" above described, provided, however, that such additional compensation in any year shall not be less than the sum of Fifteen Thousand Dollars ($15,000.00) for each calendar year during the term hereof.

In the preceding 1938 contract, there was a ceiling on additional compensation of 100% of fixed salary rather than the floor fixed in 1946.

Profit-sharing of division managers and other sales executives is commonly restricted to operations under their control, with administrative expenses of the entire organization prorated among the divisions on a basis proportionate to sales. See SAFEWAY, App. P. A variety of formulae in 25% of 132 plans examined is summarized in BROWER, *op. cit. supra* note 1, at 11–12.

[44] *Cf.,* The Container Corporation bonus fund plan, attached to Proxy Statement for stockholders' meeting of Apr. 25, 1940: ". . . no such additional compensation shall be paid and no liability for such additional compensation shall be created or recorded as to any fiscal year in which no dividend has been paid on the capital stock of the Company." See also discussion of the Bethlehem and Westinghouse plans in BAKER, *op. cit. supra* note 1, at 210, 211, 214, and consult *infra* notes 49 and 51. The Profit Incentive Plan of E. R. Squibb & Sons makes the plan effective only if dividends in a specific amount have been earned as well as paid. See Proxy Statement, Sept. 28, 1950, p. 7. Consult contracts cited *infra* note 52. For a discussion of the point, see International Telephone and Telegraph Corp., Proxy Statement for Annual Meeting dated Apr. 17, 1959; GILBERT AND GILBERT, TWENTIETH ANNUAL REPORT OF STOCKHOLDER ACTIVITIES AT CORPORATION MEETINGS DURING 1959, 101 ff. (1960); AMA, INCENTIVE COMPENSATION, *supra* note 1, at 19–20. For specific clauses, see Simons, *supra* note 9, at 52.

[45] See, for example, *Summary of Profit-Sharing Plan of Oil Refinery,* BROWER, *op. cit. supra* note 1, at 37 ($1.50 per share of common stock to be earned, but declaration of dividend not required); Contingent Compensation Plan of Borg-Warner Corporation, providing for payment of incentive compensation only when corporate earnings equal at least $1 per share (Proxy Statement, Mar. 27, 1950, pp. 5–6). Consult *infra* note 49.

for possible distribution as dividends, does not of course operate as a ceiling after such profits have been earned.[46]

As a matter of practice, however, it appears that many corporations which have omitted a dividend in a particular year simply have not paid executives bonuses for that year.[47] In some instances, this may be due to a renunciation on the part of the executive in the interests of the corporation and its public relations; in others, it may be caused by the executive's belief that if he does not voluntarily waive his bonus, his position in the corporation will be in jeopardy.[48] The matter may be removed from controversy by an express clause of limitation in the contract such as that which we have just discussed.[49]

Limitation of incentive compensation in terms of dividends may be accomplished directly by basing additional compensation not on earnings but on the amount disbursed to stockholders in the form of dividends. A plan of this nature was adopted by Bethlehem Steel

[46] See BROWER, op. cit. supra note 1, at 2, 9–10. Examples are: ALLIED, App. N, ¶ 2; Reynolds Tobacco, supra note 37; JONES, App. S. The formula may vary: a fixed figure per share, or a general reference to regular dividends, or a fair return to stockholders. With reference to the last formula, consult Preinrich, infra note 52. The Bethlehem Steel Plan (App. FF) imposed a ceiling by limiting incentive compensation payments to $\frac{1}{15}$ of the aggregate amount of each cash dividend paid on common stock. See discussion of this provision in Proxy Statement, Mar. 1, 1950, pp. 2–4.

[47] See BAKER, op. cit. supra note 1, at 208.

[48] Such a renunciation, if it takes place after the bonus has been earned and is payable, could conceivably result in a tax problem for the executive. See discussion in Chapter 4, text to notes 50 ff.

[49] At a stockholders' meeting of the Curtiss-Wright Corporation, held on July 2, 1940, a resolution was defeated which proposed that no incentive compensation be paid officers and directors in any year in which a dividend of at least 10 cents a share was not declared on common stock. N. Y. Times, July 3, 1940, p. 31, col. 3. That company's plan was suspended from 1942 to 1950 when it was again put into effect. See Proxy Statement, Mar. 10, 1950.

At a stockholders' meeting of Pan American Airways Corporation on May 16, 1940, a resolution was defeated which proposed that no bonus compensation be paid to officers and employees "unless a dividend of at least like amount is distributed pro-rata among the stockholders." The management resisted this proposal as an unwise restriction on the judgment of the directors. See Proxy Statement, Apr. 26, 1940.

A stockholder's proposal which was defeated at a meeting of Loew's, Inc. proposed that when earnings or dividends were reduced, salaries of executives receiving more than $25,000 a year should likewise be reduced. It was opposed by management upon the grounds, among others, that the executives affected might not have been responsible for the decline in earnings or dividends, and that to retain executives which the company might otherwise lose, the board of directors might be compelled to declare dividends when it was unwise to do so. Proxy Statement, Feb. 15, 1950, pp. 7–8. Cf. The American Tobacco Co., Proxy Statement, Mar. 1, 1950, p. 5 ("The establishment of an arbitrary ceiling beyond which there is no such incentive is inconsistent with the principle of incentive compensation.").

Corporation after previous bonus plans had been attacked in the courts.[50]

Plans of the type just mentioned are open to the objection that the directors (who may include among their number executives participating in incentive compensation) may be tempted to declare a higher dividend than warranted. Although opinions may differ as to the seriousness of this risk, very little protection against it can in any event be obtained through contractual provisions. The stockholders must rely for their protection on the good faith and informed judgment of the directors; if the directors are dishonest or negligent, relief will have to come through an action for violation of fiduciary duty or election of a new board.[51]

Still another approach to the same problem is to base incentive compensation on a percentage of net earnings in excess of a stated return on invested capital or in excess of a stated figure, as in the third limitation clause suggested above.[52] Such a plan has much to

[50] For the present plan, see App. FF. For the earlier version, see excerpts from the Bethlehem Steel Plan given in BAKER, *op. cit. supra* note 1, at 210, 211; see also *id.* at 269. For a digest of the Westinghouse bonus plan see *id.* at 214. Consult BROWER, *op. cit. supra* note 1, at 13–14, suggesting a plan for percentage compensation based upon a hypothetical allocation of shares of common stock to profit-sharing executives, each executive receiving as percentage compensation an amount equivalent to dividends which he would have received if the stock had actually been issued. The suggestion foreshadowed the "dividend unit" plan. E.g., DU PONT, App. X; UNION CARBIDE, App. GG; BETHLEHEM STEEL, App. FF. For a plan based in part upon actual stockholdings, see the Reynolds Tobacco Company bylaw, *supra* note 37. As to stockholders' attacks on the operation of the Reynolds bylaw, see Bookman v. Reynolds Tobacco Co., 138 N.J. Eq. 312, 48 A.2d 646 (1946).

[51] An English commentator has urged that all percentage plans contingent upon dividends be forbidden by statute, arguing that in several instances British companies have been brought to financial ruin as a result of such plans. SAMUEL, SHAREHOLDERS' MONEY 164–66 (1933).

[52] For the invested capital limitation see General Motors Bonus Plan (App. V). See also bonus plans of DU PONT, App. X, and Chrysler Corp., Proxy Statement, Mar. 16, 1950. See also FAIRBANKS, App. M, *supra* note 43; Preinrich, *Profit-Sharing Problems and Their Solution,* 48 J. ACCOUNTANCY 341, 350–53 (1929) (discussing basis of fixing fair return on stockholders' investment).

BAKER (*op. cit. supra* note 1, at 200–01) studying the bonus plans of 30 large industrial companies found that 15 made a deduction in favor of stockholders in calculating the bonus fund, 1 made such a deduction for preferred stock only, 13 made no deduction, 1 gave no information. BROWER (*op. cit. supra* note 1, at 11–12) shows such limitations or specific limitations of a similar nature in 45 out of a total of 79 plans.

The plan formerly in use by The National City Bank was thus described by the court in Gallin v. Nat'l City Bank, 152 Misc. 679, 699, 273 N.Y. Supp. 87, 109 (Sup. Ct. 1934): "After eight per cent had been set aside for the stockholders on invested and employed capital, one-fifth of the total remaining net profits in any one year was apportioned by periodical action of the boards among the executives responsible for the management, and the remaining four-fifths distributed to the stockholders."

The Container Corporation plan (*supra* note 44) provides that from net profits there shall be first deducted "an amount equivalent to 6% of the aggregate of the

recommend it, for it avoids many of the difficulties which have just been discussed and is, in effect, a method of setting aside some return to stockholders on their investment before the executive receives a share in the profits. This type of plan is subject to the drawback that it may induce the executives to cause the company to raise funds through borrowing rather than through the sale of stock; but this is not usually a serious objection. A return on borrowed capital may be required and, if not required, interest on the borrowed funds would reduce the base for incentive compensation awards.

A somewhat similar plan is that of limiting incentive compensation by requiring a return on invested capital. This type of provision, too, is open to the objection that it may encourage borrowing rather than equity financing, as well as to the further objection that it may require revision as the result of consolidations, mergers, or other changes in capital structure. Such objections will not in the usual case be too serious and, if desired, can be met by specific clauses tailored to the circumstances.[53]

The Computation Clause.

• 3. (b) The adjusted consolidated net earnings of the Corporation and its subsidiaries, for the purpose of computing the Executive's contingent compensation under the provisions of paragraph 3(a) above, shall be determined in accordance with accepted accounting practice within 90 days after the end of each calendar [fiscal] year by the independent accounting firm employed by the Corporation as its auditors. The computation by such accounting firm of the net earnings and of the Executive's contingent compensation, made in the manner herein provided, shall be in all respects final and binding upon the Corporation and upon the Executive,[54] and the Corporation

---

Capital Stock and Surplus accounts as at the beginning of the year for which the additional compensation is to be calculated"; the bonus fund is to be 15% of the balance remaining after such deduction.

JONES, App. S, ¶ 2, provides for a share in the profits in excess of $4,200,000 "equivalent to the amount of the annual dividend on 600,000 shares of cumulative seven per cent preferred stock of the party of the first part."

See also *supra* note 38; *cf. supra* note 46.

[53] For a valuable discussion of problems involved in determining the meaning of the term "net profits" in profit participation arrangements, see Note, *Computation of Net Profits in Contingent Compensation Agreements*, 51 COLUM. L. REV. 867 (1951), based on the profit participation clause set forth in the first edition of this treatise, WASHINGTON, CORPORATE EXECUTIVES' COMPENSATION 29–30 (1942).

[54] It may be desirable for express provision to be made that the computation of contingent compensation shall not be affected by allowance or disallowance of any item upon any tax return filed by the corporation. Otherwise, the actual amount to which an executive may be entitled might remain open for several years pending final audit.

shall pay such compensation to the Executive within 120 days after the end of the calendar [fiscal] year in question. For the purpose of computing the Executive's contingent compensation, the adjusted consolidated net earnings of the Corporation and its subsidiaries for the above-mentioned period shall be the consolidated net earnings of the Corporation and its subsidiaries for such period, as certified by the Corporation's independent auditors for the purposes of the Corporation's annual report to stockholders for such period, plus all amounts charged against such consolidated net earnings in respect of the following:

(i) Taxes of the United States and foreign governments (including, but without limitation, excess profits taxes) based upon or measured, in whole or in part, by income of the Corporation or its subsidiaries but exclusive of state and territorial taxes and taxes imposed by political subdivisions thereof;

(ii) Profit participations, if any, which may be payable by the Corporation under any plan or agreement, including this agreement, other than a profit-sharing plan qualified under Section 401 of the Internal Revenue Code or any statutory provision that may hereafter be enacted to replace such section;

(iii) All items of non-recurring loss or other extraordinary charge which, by reason of size, character, or other factors did not, in the sole and uncontrolled judgment of the Board of Directors, arise in the ordinary and usual course of the business of the Corporation and its subsidiaries, including expenses properly attributable to such loss or charge;

less, however, all amounts included in such consolidated net earnings in respect of items of capital gain, non-recurring profit, or other extraordinary credit which, by reason of size, character, or other factors did not, in the sole and uncontrolled judgment of the Board of Directors, arise in the ordinary and usual course of business of the Corporation and its subsidiaries, after deducting expenses properly attributable to such gain, profit, or credit, except and to the extent that the Board of Directors, in its sole and uncontrolled judgment, shall find that the Executive was responsible for such gain, profit, or credit and shall direct the inclusion, in whole or in part, of such gain, profit, or credit in the computation of consolidated net earnings.[55]

[55] If the contingent compensation is to be computed after income taxes, clause "(i)" should be omitted. *Cf.* contract between Loew's, Inc. and Louis B. Mayer, *supra* note 36, providing for the deduction of all taxes "except taxes arising from

In the computation clause, the draftsman's effort is to define and limit the amount available for incentive compensation so as to confine it to sources of income which the executive has aided in producing, and at the same time to attain reasonable ease of administration and calculation. He starts, then, with the accountants' determination of "net earnings"—imperfect though that determination may be [56]—and next states expressly various deductions from income.[57] Operating expenses, of course, must be deducted, and it is possible to go into considerable detail in specifying them.[58] Federal and state income taxes may expressly be made deductible, and the executive's compensation based on a percentage of the net earnings remaining after provision for their payment.[59]

---

profits on sale or exchange of property where such profits are not included as income for [Mr. Mayer's] benefit."

If an after-tax formula is adopted, provision should be made that from items added back or subtracted there should be deducted or added, as the case may be, the income tax or deduction attributable to such items.

[56] See Chapter 4, text to notes 2, 3 ff.

[57] See ALLIED, App. N. FAIRBANKS, App. M, does not specify any deductions. For a detailed statement of deductions from gross earnings, see NEW ENGLAND, App. Q, ¶ 2(c)(B).

[58] *Operating Expenses:* These are usually summarized first by a general formula (see contracts referred to *supra* note 57), followed by specification of particular items deemed especially applicable to the company by the draftsman, such as "interest," NEW ENGLAND, App. Q, ¶ 2(c)(B)(i); "current repairs to and minor replacements of and additions to, and maintenance expenditures upon, the properties and equipment," NEW ENGLAND, App. Q, ¶ 2(c)(B)(iii); "depreciation," NEW ENGLAND, App. Q, ¶ 2(c)(B)(iii); "assessments," "insurance," NEW ENGLAND, App. Q, ¶ 2(c)(B)(ii); "provision for depreciation and depletion, interest charges and all taxes," JONES, App. S, ¶ 2; Loew's, Inc., *supra* note 36 ("except on bonds, mortgages and monies borrowed and amortization of bonuses in connection therewith and in connection with issues of Preferred Stock"; also: "cost of Employees Retirement Plan, including expenses of administration").

Depreciation, repairs, loss of finished product, and insurance are all proper deductions under an agreement to share the "net profits of an enterprise." Stone v. Wright Wire Co., 199 Mass. 306, 85 N.E. 471 (1908); see Stein v. Strathmore Worsted Mills, 221 Mass. 86, 89, 108 N.E. 1029, 1030 (1915).

The propriety of a provision excluding "interest on funded indebtedness" from deductions has been upheld. Diamond v. Davis, 62 N.Y.S.2d 181, 192 (Sup. Ct. 1945).

[59] ALLIED, App. N, ¶ 2; JONES, App. S, ¶ 2; NEW ENGLAND, App. Q, ¶ 2(c)(B)(ii); SAFEWAY, App. P. For illustrative computations in the case of typical income tax and accounting problems arising from profit-sharing contracts, see DARTNELL PUBLICATIONS, INC., SALARY ADMINISTRATION PLANS 31 (1945); Preinrich, *supra* note 52, at 346–49, and Tyson, *infra* note 68. For determining the share of company taxes to be borne by a branch, either by applying the entire company's tax ratio to the branch operations or by treating the branch as an independent enterprise for purposes of such compensation, see SAFEWAY, App. P. See *supra* note 55. For provision for a reduction of the bonus itself if the ratio of taxes to income rises, see UNIVERSAL, App. O, ¶ 3, which also sets forth examples of how the principle shall apply.

A majority of current plans base incentive compensation on operating earnings before taxes,[60] on the theory that the executive has performed his function when the corporate profits have been produced and that management should not either be penalized by an increase in taxes or receive a windfall if and when taxes are reduced.[61] Plans that use after-tax earnings as a base may be justified by the fact that many of management's decisions today have tax implications and effects and, generally, the base for management awards should be the same as that for dividends.[62] Consistent with this theory, however, the executive should receive the benefit of capital and other non-recurring gains, a subject discussed below.[63]

In the absence of specific provision, it has been held that income taxes should be deducted in computing the executive's percentage of net earnings.[64] Inasmuch as the federal income tax and similar taxes can be computed only after the executive's total compensation (provided it is reasonable) is deducted as a corporate expense, it is evident that a specific provision for deductibility of such taxes will require the accountants to employ a little algebra.[65]

[60] "In approximately two out of every three plans with fund formulae, the funds are based on profits before taxes." AMA, INCENTIVE COMPENSATION, *supra* note 1, at 14. In the survey conducted by the Profit-Sharing Research Foundation, *supra* note 9, companies sharing profits before taxes outnumbered companies sharing after taxes by 2 to 1 in the case of cash plans, 4½ to 1 in the case of deferred plans, and 3 to 1 in the case of combination plans. KNOWLTON, *op. cit. supra* note 1, at 29; see also *id.* at 15. For criticism of the before-tax formula, see Stryker, *supra* note 3, at 160 (quoting Royal Little: "This type of incentive payment has encouraged executives to go hell bent on expansion and pressured them into using more and more capital regardless of the return on that capital"); for summary of pro and con arguments, see Simons, *supra* note 9, at 53.

[61] While a bonus windfall based on tax reduction may seem to be a remote contingency, reduction or repeal of a tax such as the excess profits tax in 1945 (59 Stat. 568) may bring about a windfall under after-tax plans then in effect.

[62] Many well-established plans provide for use of "net earnings" reported to stockholders. E.g., GENERAL MOTORS, App. W, ¶ 3(a); GENERAL ELECTRIC, App. AA, § I(3). Some modern plans also use an after-tax base. E.g., RCA Incentive Plan set forth in Proxy Statement for Annual Meeting on May 4, 1954, § IV(a), specifically providing for no adjustment for taxes.

[63] See text to note 76 *infra*.

[64] Where a bonus was given under a directors' resolution which spoke of "net earnings . . . after . . . all expenses . . . [and] depreciation," it was held that state and federal taxes must be deducted before computing the employee's contingent compensation. Fleischer v. Pelton Steel Co., 183 Wis. 451, 198 N.W. 444 (1924). *Cf.* Mencher v. Alden, 41 N.Y.S.2d 678 (Sup. Ct. 1943), discussing excess profits taxes; there, however, the contract provided for non-deductibility of taxes. See also Ransome Concrete Mach. Co. v. Moody, 282 Fed. 29, 35, 36 (2d Cir. 1922). The unqualified term "net earnings" usually refers to net earnings after taxes. E.g., GENERAL MOTORS and GENERAL ELECTRIC, both cited *supra* note 62. But *cf.* Maguire v. Osborne, 384 Pa. 430, 121 A.2d 147 (1956).

[65] See Fuller v. Miller, 105 Mass. 103 (1870). For applicable equations, consult P.-H, PENSIONS AND PROFIT SHARING, § 7104 (1961).

A similar problem, but one of greater difficulty, arises when the corporation employs more than one executive on a profit-participation basis. The question here is whether the compensation of any one executive should be based on a percentage of the net earnings remaining after the compensation payable to the other executives has been deducted as an expense. When a number of executives share in the same bonus fund, the entire fund, including the share of each participant, has been held a proper deduction. In *Heller v. Boylan*,[66] the court had to construe the American Tobacco bylaw under which several officers divided a bonus fund consisting of 10% of net earnings. It was held that the amount of the fund itself should be deducted from net earnings available for distribution under the fund.[67] Thus, if the contract with any single executive fails to provide that incentive compensation payable to the other executives shall not be deducted as an expense, it would appear to be necessary, in the absence of an

[66] 29 N.Y.S.2d 653, 704 (Sup. Ct. 1941), discussed in Volume II, Chapter 19.

[67] The court, at p. 693 of 29 N.Y.S.2d, quoted with approval the following passage from the present volume, as it appeared in an article by Judge Washington in 50 YALE L.J. 35, 51 (1940) :

> A similar problem, but one of much more difficulty, arises when the corporation employs more than one executive on a percentage compensation basis. The question here is whether the compensation of any one executive should be computed as a percentage of the net earnings remaining after the compensation payable to the other executives has been deducted as an expense. If the contract with any single executive fails to provide that the percentage compensation payable to the other executives shall not be deducted as an expense, it is doubtless necessary that this deduction be made, despite difficulties in making the computation. Usage varies as to deducting all or any part of the executive's own compensation. It would seem that only his fixed salary should be deducted.

In line with the last sentences quoted, it would appear that where a single fund is involved, the fund itself should not be deducted as an expense in making the computation. Consult cases cited *infra* note 70, and connected text.

Algebraically, the court's decision in Heller v. Boylan would be expressed as follows:

$$\text{Fund} = \tfrac{1}{10} \ (\text{Net earnings—Fund})$$
$$10 \ \text{Fund} = \quad \text{Net earnings—Fund}$$
$$11 \ \text{Fund} = \quad \text{Net earnings}$$
$$\text{Fund} = \tfrac{1}{11} \ \text{Net earnings}$$

The fund, under this reasoning, equals only one-eleventh (9.09%) of earnings. In fact, the amount the stockholders contracted to pay was one-tenth (10% of net earnings).

The plans of some companies specifically provide that profit-sharing payments shall not be deducted from income. E.g., E. R. Squibb & Sons, Proxy Statement, Oct. 26, 1950, p. 7. *Cf.* Harvey v. Missouri Valley Electric Co., 268 S.W.2d 820 (Mo. 1954) (profit-sharing bonus held properly deducted by cash-basis taxpayer in year of payment rather than year in which profits earned) ; Note, 49 A.L.R.2d 1131 (1956).

established practice of the company to the contrary, that this deduction be made, despite difficulties in making the computation.[68] Usage varies as to deducting all or any part of the executive's own compensation.[69] In the absence of express provision to the contrary, it would seem that only his fixed salary, and not the bonus itself, need be deducted.[70]

We have already referred to the question of whether the executive shall be permitted to share in capital and non-recurring gains.[71] It will be noted that the form given in the text contains a clause seeking to prevent him from sharing in such gains. This represents a relatively recent and apparently sound trend. A contract of Burlington Mills Corporation expressed the underlying idea more simply, and probably as effectively, by providing that the executive is to share in income "from ordinary operations (exclusive of capital and nonrecur-

[68] For sample computations, see Tyson, *Bonus Problems Under the Revenue Act of 1938*, 67 J. ACCOUNTANCY 94 (1939) ; Galitzer, *The Graduated Bonus and the Individual Income Tax Ratio*, 22 TAXES 16, 18–19 (1944). The problems presented are somewhat similar to those that arise in computing the marital deduction under federal estate tax law. In Epstein v. Schenck, *supra* note 24, it was held that failure to deduct the bonus of *A* in computing the bonus of *B* was a practice not "inherently unfair" to the employer, and that where the executives and the board of directors fully understood the facts and had followed this practice consistently for many years, it could not be attacked in a stockholders' action.

[69] ALLIED, App. N, ¶ 2, provides that all compensation payable to the executive himself under the contract shall be deducted as an expense.

BLOOMINGDALE, App. R, ¶ 3D, provides : ". . . there shall not be deducted in determining 'net earnings' or 'basic net earnings' for the purpose of this agreement the amount payable under said clause 3B to the employee hereunder or the amount payable to Harry A. Hatry under a similar clause designated as 3B in an agreement of even date between this corporation and said Harry A. Hatry."

Loew's, Inc., with Louis B. Mayer, *supra* note 36, provides for the deduction of all fixed compensation, but no percentage compensation based on net profits paid or payable to any employee or executive.

See cases cited *infra* note 70.

[70] See Selz v. Buel, 105 Ill. 122 (1882) ; Buning v. Kittell, 7 N.Y. Supp. 485 (Gen. Term, 1st Dep't 1889) ; Briggs v. Groves, 9 N.Y. Supp. 765 (Gen. Term, 5th Dep't 1890), *aff'd mem.,* 132 N.Y. 545, 30 N.E. 865; Holmes v. James Buckley & Co., 165 La. 874, 116 So. 218 (1928) ; Rishton v. Grissell, L.R. 5 Eq. 326 (1868) ; Epstein v. Schenck, *supra* note 24; Gottlieb v. Schenck, 82 N.Y.S.2d 917 (Sup. Ct. 1942) ; Winkelman v. General Motors Corp., 44 F. Supp. 960, 1000 *et seq.* (S.D.N.Y. 1942) *settlement approved as modified,* 48 F. Supp. 500 (S.D.N.Y. 1942) ; Mann v. Luke, 82 N.Y.S.2d 725, 730 (Sup. Ct. 1948). The text above, beginning with "A similar problem," was quoted with approval in Heller v. Boylan, *supra* note 66, at 693, which, however, arrived on its facts at a contrary solution. *Cf.* Diamond v. Davis, *supra* note 58; Singer v. Adams (Sup. Ct. 1946) (unreported) referred to in Proxy Statement dated Mar. 22, 1948 of Colgate-Palmolive-Peet Co. (agreement, in settlement of stockholders' action, to deduct bonus fund in computing profit-sharing compensation. For details of cases, see Volume II, Chapter 19.

[71] See text to note 63 *supra.*

ring gains and losses)." [72] These are good precedents for the avoidance of problems and controversies, but they are probably not followed as frequently as they should be. The average bonus contract no doubt still provides in general terms that the executive is to share in "net earnings." [73]

Quite apart from any express clause on the subject, a strong argument can be made for interpreting a general reference to "net earnings" in bonus contracts as applying only to operating earnings.[74] The purpose of the contract is to give the executive a share in earnings produced by his own efforts, and it may well be urged that any intention to give him a share in capital gains or other income not derived from the normal operation of the business must be stated in explicit terms. Suppose, for example, that the corporation receives an attractive offer for the purchase of its interest in an important

[72] For a provision "excluding capital payments and capital losses," see NEW ENGLAND, App. Q, ¶ 2(c)(13)(iii); as to deduction of pro-rata share of net operating losses of subsidiaries, see *id.* at (iv).

Likewise, a plan adopted by the Continental Oil Company in Jan. 1937, provided that "Net nonrecurring gains and profits will not be included in the computation of earnings except to the extent authorized by the Board of Directors," excerpt from report of the Continental Oil Co. to the SEC, Form 10K, Item 5, as quoted in BAKER, *op. cit. supra* note 1, at 212.

The Bonus Plan of du Pont is based on "surplus net receipts . . . on the capital employed by the company and its substantially wholly owned subsidiaries, which capital is primarily of an operative as distinguished from an investment character." See DU PONT, App. X. Other portions of the du Pont plan indicate that it was not intended to distribute under the plan earnings derived from investments, such as the company's investment in the stock of General Motors Corporation. As to adjustment of the company's net income for the General Motors investment, see *id.*, ¶ IV, 3(a).

In a survey of 125 plans published in 1959, only 17 specifically excluded capital gains and losses from the income figure used in computing the bonus. Simons, *supra* note 9, at 50 (arguing against such exclusion but favoring a clause, found in the plans of 18 companies, excluding "unusual items of income or loss" in the discretion of the board of directors).

In favor of inclusion of capital gains in the profit-participation base, it can be argued that at least part of capital gains may result from previously deducted depreciation on the assets sold. On this theory, capital gains on such assets should be included in profit participation to the extent that the assets were depreciated at the time sold and profit-participation income had thereby been reduced in prior years. However, the executives in such prior years may not have been the same as those in the year of sale.

[73] See SALARY ADMINISTRATION PLANS, *supra* note 59. However, determination of "net earnings" is usually to be made by the company's independent accountants or auditors "in accordance with sound accounting practice." FAIRBANKS, App. M, ¶ (c); Curtiss-Wright, Executive Compensation Plan, ¶ 2(a), Proxy Statement, Mar. 10, 1950, ¶ 9. This provision would probably assure full consideration of factors affecting "net earnings" discussed in the text.

[74] *Cf.* discussion in text to note 64 *supra*. In Smith v. Dunlap, 269 Ala. 97, 111 So.2d 1 (1959), the court held that the plan there under consideration could not be interpreted to include profits from the sale of the stock of another corporation.

subsidiary. If the executive has a significant role in determining whether the offer should be accepted and is to share in whatever capital gain is realized by the corporation upon the sale, he will be strongly tempted to approve the proposition, even though the corporation would then be faced with the problem of finding an equally advantageous investment for its funds. As the corporation is not in the business of buying and selling its investments in subsidiaries, there appears no compelling reason for allowing the executive to share in any profit so derived.[75]

On the other hand, if the executive is not to share in non-recurring profits, he will argue that he should not have to take the burden of non-recurring losses. There is merit in this contention, and provisions such as the one set forth in the form contract [3(b)(iii)] are occasionally inserted so that the executive will neither benefit from non-recurring profits nor share the burden of non-recurring losses.[76] It is evident, however, that if the corporation sells an asset —for example, its investment in a subsidiary—at a considerable loss, resulting in an over-all balance sheet loss for the year, the stockholders will be disgruntled if the executive receives a substantial bonus for the very year in which the loss was incurred. This situation may be prevented by the type of clause, heretofore discussed, limiting incentive compensation by requiring a minimum return on invested capital. In the absence of such a limitation, it may not be good judgment for a top executive to seek to have his bonus computed on a basis more advantageous than that used to report the income to the stockholders. Yet such special methods of computation are frequently provided for. The parties may agree, for example, that losses due to events occurring before the executive became connected with the company, but actually charged off on the books after his employment began, should not be deducted from income in determining his bonus.

[75] The above passage, beginning "Quite apart," etc., as it appeared in an article by Judge Washington (*supra* note 67, at 52–53) and in the first edition of this volume, was quoted with approval and followed in Heller v. Boylan, *supra* note 66. In that case, the quoted view was strongly supported by the fact that under the contract there involved the subsidiary's profits were excluded in computing percentage compensation. See also Winkelman v. General Motors Corp., *supra* note 70, at 985–86 (non-operating profit from sale by corporation of its own stock to Managers Securities Plan and to Management Corporation excluded from bonus base) ; but see *id.* at 997 (interest on same affiliates' debt to parent included as part of bonus base). It would seem that bonus contracts, even though usually drafted by the corporation's attorneys, should be strictly construed in favor of the corporation. But see Flannery Bolt Co. v. Flannery, 16 F. Supp. 803 (W.D. Pa. 1935), *rev'd*, 86 F.2d 43 (3d Cir. 1936). *Cf.* Bookman v. Reynolds Tobacco Co., *supra* note 50.

[76] See NEW ENGLAND, App. Q, *supra* note 72.

Little is to be found in the cases bearing upon the validity of such an arrangement.[77]

An extreme case is conceivable in which a company reports a loss to its stockholders but nevertheless pays a bonus based on a special formula which shows earnings available for executive compensation. In such a case, are stockholders entitled to complain? It would seem that they are not. The distribution to the executive is not in the nature of a dividend, but rather in the nature of the discharge of an obligation to pay compensation based on application of a particular formula. Assuming always that the incentive compensation plan was properly adopted and reasonable, the mere use of a formula different from that used to determine net earnings constituting the basis for dividends should not in itself render the compensation improper or unreasonable. An incentive compensation formula is simply a measure of additional compensation without any necessary relationship to the measure used for the purpose of dividends. Thus, as we have noticed, sales managers often receive bonus compensation based on a percentage of sales; [78] it is arguable that if sales increase, the sales manager is entitled to increased compensation even though the earnings of the corporation as a whole were materially reduced by poor management in other departments or factors otherwise beyond the sales manager's control.[79] However, the use of gross receipts as a compensation base would not be proper in the case of a top executive charged with responsibility for the operations of the enterprise as a whole, since he might be able to cause an increase in gross receipts by means that would reduce net profits.[80]

[77] Where a salesman's contract provided that he was to receive a percentage of the "net profits" of the business for a given year, and there was no express provision that the company's normal accounting methods should be followed, it was held that losses due to bad debts previously on the books and not charged off until the year in question should not be considered in computing the salesman's compensation. See Stein v. Strathmore Worsted Mills, *supra* note 58 at 92, 108 N.E. at 1031; *cf.* Hubbard v. New York, N.E. & W. Investment Co., 14 Fed. 675 (C.C.D. Mass. 1882). It has been suggested that the same result can be attained by a clause giving the board of directors power to exclude unusual items. See Simons, *supra* note 9, at 51.

[78] See *supra* note 11.

[79] In Bettendorf v. Bettendorf, 190 Iowa 83, 179 N.W. 444 (1920), the court was called upon to construe a contract giving the executive a percentage of the net earnings of the Bettendorf Axle Company "which may have accrued exclusively from the railway department [of the Axle Company]." This provision was enforced literally, the court stating that the intention was to "eliminate deductions owing to loss in other departments." See reference *supra* note 49 to Loew's stockholder meeting.

[80] See SAMUEL, *supra* note 51, at 164–66.

A question also arises as to whether creditors can complain of these special formulae for determining earnings. Probably not, provided the formulae have been adopted in advance of the rendition of the services and not as a means of defeating creditors' claims. In any event, actual injury to creditors would have to be shown—and it would be an unusual case in which such injury could be proved.

Apart from capital gains and losses, dividends received on stock of subsidiary or affiliated corporations,[81] and the like, questions relating to the computation of profits for incentive compensation purposes should generally, and in the absence of a specific provision in the formula, be resolved in the same way as they are resolved in computing earnings reported to stockholders. In the *Epstein* case,[82] for example, a subsidiary had been reorganized as the result of a foreclosure; bondholders received new securities carrying a lower interest rate, and the parent company had maintained its stock interest only after putting in additional capital. A loss was taken in the published balance sheet, but was not reflected in computing the bonus fund. The justification offered was that the parent company's asset was of substantially the same value, because carrying charges had been reduced. The court rejected this argument without much discussion, apparently on the ground that all losses reported to the stockholders should be taken by the bonus fund.[83]

A similar view was expressed in *Heller v. Boylan*,[84] where a "loss" on the retirement of the preferred stock of a subsidiary was treated by the company as not being an actual loss for percentage compensation purposes: [85]

• Of course, if this was a real loss, it should have been deducted from the bonus computation. And if there was—or will be—an ultimate actual loss to the stockholders, there was—or will be—corresponding loss for bonus-computing purposes. As already observed, our concern is not with matters of accounting. Unless and until a loss is actually

[81] Heller v. Boylan, *supra* note 66. See text to note 92 *infra*.

[82] Epstein v. Schenck, *supra* note 24, at 982. For deduction of operating losses of subsidiaries by express provision see NEW ENGLAND, App. Q, ¶ 2(c)(B)(iv).

[83] Similarly, the corporation in the *Epstein* case, *supra* note 24, had made substantial payments to the estate of Irving Thalberg in settlement of a dispute, taking the amount of the payment as a business expense deduction for income tax purposes. The payment was not deducted, however, in the computation of the bonus fund, apparently because it was regarded as in the nature of bonus compensation (Mr. Thalberg having been one of the bonus recipients in past years). The court pointed out that this payment was not in fact a bonus, but was rather in the nature of a "general appeasement." Recomputation was directed.

[84] *Supra* note 66.

[85] *Id.* at 692.

sustained, no deduction should be made. However, stockholders and officers should occupy a parity; there is to be no discrimination. The Company cannot simultaneously blow hot for its officers and cold for its stockholders.

A further point as to the deduction of losses was raised in the *Gallin* case, where the referee found that certain losses should have been (but were not) deducted from the bonus fund.[86] The referee stated the amount of each such loss and then deducted from each loss the amount of the "tax saving" it produced for the company; the bonus fund was then recomputed on the basis of this net loss. The referee made this deduction for "tax saving" without discussion, and no facts appear from which one can form a definite opinion as to the justification for this procedure in the *Gallin* case. It would seem, however, that such a procedure is justified only where the "tax saving" is not already reflected in the bonus computation; in many cases, it will be so reflected.

Computation: Additional Problems. If the contract provides that, in computing incentive compensation, earnings shall be subject to a deduction of a stated amount in respect of each issued share, does this apply to shares issued as stock dividends, as well as to other shares? Much will depend on the language of the contract. In the *Epstein* case,[87] the contract provided that "additional shares sold for bona fide consideration in cash or property approximately equal to the then market value of such stock" should be counted in the number of shares on which $2 per share was deductible in arriving at the bonus fund. The court held that shares issued as a stock dividend did not come within this category, and that no deduction need be taken for them.

Should profits available for bonus be deemed to include income earned by foreign subsidiaries or other foreign income when such income cannot be transmitted to the United States by reason of currency restrictions? The few cases which have passed on this subject indicate that a decision by a disinterested board, favoring the inclusion of such income, will not be upset, but that the executives should in fairness make some concession, and not insist on receiving rewards based on income which is of doubtful collectibility. In the *Epstein*

---

[86] Gallin v. Nat'l City Bank, 155 Misc. 880, 281 N.Y. Supp. 795 (Referee's Report, 1935). The referee divided his discussion between (1) losses charged by the company against capital surplus and (2) losses charged by the company against surplus. This division was evidently for convenience, as it seemed to have made no difference in the result.

[87] *Supra* note 24.

case,[88] Judge Valente held that under the contract language it was technically immaterial whether foreign profits were transmitted. He pointed out, however, that the contract included a saving clause permitting either party to claim adjustments, and added : [89]

• The directors might find it advisable in their discretion to make a final adjustment by way of compromise so as to introduce finality and avoid future conflicts. On this point, however, the court can only advise—it cannot command.

Similarly, in *Schwab v. Kirby*,[90] the directors of the Woolworth Company allowed German profits to be included in bonus income during the years 1933–38, complying with the contract terms. In 1938 an agreement was made with the executives discontinuing this inclusion. Judge Schmuck dismissed the complaint, which challenged the 1933–38 payments as against the directors and the employees. The court held that the board had acted fairly and without self-interest or negligence.[91]

Should dividends received by the company on its own stock, held in its treasury or owned by subsidiaries, be included in bonus income? Quite clearly, they should not.[92]

The propriety of other common practices tending to increase the bonus fund has been recognized by the courts in specific situations. The idle plant account may be excluded from capital employed,[93] as may good will, at least where largely fictitious.[94] The courts have refused to interfere with the determination of depreciation rates or to compel depreciation of idle plant.[95] Calculation of the bonus before

[88] *Ibid.*

[89] *Id.* at 984.

[90] 21 N.Y.S.2d 991 (Sup. Ct. 1940).

[91] See *supra* note 24. For a contractual provision that blocked foreign earnings are not to be included until received, but are then to be treated as earnings for the year of original accrual, see UNIVERSAL, App. O, ¶ 3; AMERICAN OPTICAL, App. T (exclusion of income "not realized or readily convertible into dollars at an exchange rate deemed favorable by the Board at the time"). *Cf.* Loew's, Inc., Proxy Statement, *supra* note 36, at p. 5 (contract with Louis B. Mayer providing for exclusion of foreign receipts unless transmitted to the United States or used abroad). As to when a loss on foreign exchange should be reflected, consult The Foundation Co., 14 T.C. 1333 (1952).

[92] Heller v. Boylan, *supra* note 66; Winkelman v. General Motors Corp., *supra* note 70, at 997–98 (dividends from subsidiaries, as distinguished from dividends from affiliates, excluded), and *id.* at 994 (exclusion of dividends from treasury stock).

[93] Winkelman v. General Motors Corp., *supra* note 70, at 998–99; Meyers v. Cowdin, *supra* note 24.

[94] Diamond v. Davis, *supra* note 58.

[95] Cases *supra* note 93. *Cf.* Gottlieb v. Schenck, *supra* note 70 (valuation of inventories).

taxes has been upheld when the bonus plan so provides.[96] When the bonus is payable only after taxes, tax deductions have been limited to taxes actually paid, with the bonus treated as an expense in computing the tax.[97] As a consequence of decisions of this nature, settlements in stockholder litigation today, while giving some relief from practices flagrantly disadvantageous to stockholders, no longer produce the large amounts once obtained.[98]

Special Clauses on Proration and Merger. If the executive's employment terminates during a bonus year, the problem of proration arises. This may be treated in the manner indicated in the footnotes to clause 5 of the form contract set forth in Chapter 2.[99]

The merger provisions (clause 6 of the form contract)[100] may be clarified, in an incentive compensation plan or contract, by addition of the following:

• 6. (b) In the event of such a consolidation, merger or sale, the Executive's contingent compensation shall, as to subsequent opera-

[96] Mann v. Luke, 272 App. Div. 19, 68 N.Y.S.2d 313 (1st Dep't 1947) (involving West Virginia Pulp & Paper Co.). See Mencher v. Alden, *supra* note 64.

[97] Meyers v. Cowdin, *supra* note 24 (holding also that, in computing consolidated net earnings, the intercorporate dividends tax need not be deducted unless the dividends had actually been paid to the parent and the tax thus made payable). See discussion in text to notes 64–65, *supra*.

[98] See, e.g., Diamond v. Davis, *supra* note 58 (refusing to impose liability in the amount of $50,000 for current year and making changes in accounting practices prospective only) ; Mann v. Luke, *supra* note 70 (finding that corporation was prepared to make certain accounting changes and to retransfer undistributed bonus funds on abandonment of plan to surplus). See also same case, 83 N.Y.S.2d 387 (Sup. Ct. 1948) (denying attorney's fee to plaintiffs for failure to show benefit brought about by their lawsuit).

[99] See Chapter 2, text to notes 32 and 33. The following clause has been used:

If, while in the employ of the Corporation or of any of its subsidiary companies, [the Executive] should die before the last day of any calendar or fiscal year, or if this contract should be terminated by the Corporation for cause before the last day of any calendar or fiscal year, said additional compensation shall be computed as follows: The total amount of additional compensation for the calendar or fiscal year which would have been payable to [the Executive] in the event that he had lived or continued in the employ of the Corporation during such calendar or fiscal year shall first be computed. This sum shall be divided into as many equal parts as there are months in such fiscal period, and [the Executive], or his personal representative, shall receive one of such parts for each month from the first day of said fiscal period to the last day of the third calendar month following the date of his death, or termination of employment as aforesaid. In no event, however, shall the additional compensation be computed upon a period beyond the last day of the calendar or fiscal year in which such death occurs or in which such employment is terminated as aforesaid.

See also for a very simple provision, SAFEWAY, App. P; LERNER STORES, App. F, § 4.

[100] See merger clause, Chapter 2, text to note 38.

tions, be based as nearly as may be upon the earnings attributable to the assets owned by the Corporation at the time of any such consolidation, merger or sale, and shall be determined by the independent accounting firm employed by the Successor Corporation as its auditors, the determination of such accounting firm to be final and binding upon the Successor Corporation and upon the Executive.

It should be observed that such a clause would not apply by its terms to the acquisition of all the capital stock of another corporation, although the subsequent profits of the new subsidiary would probably be included in computing incentive compensation, at least under the usual provision basing such compensation upon consolidated net earnings.[101] If so intended, provision may be made for this contingency.[102]

Payment Date: Deferred Profit Sharing; Advance Payments. Many plans today provide for payment of incentive compensation awards in instalments, either in successive years after the awards have been made or following retirement or other termination of employment. Such arrangements are discussed in a later chapter.[103]

Occasionally, corporations make a payment or payments on account of incentive compensation in the course of the year during which it is being earned rather than at or after the close of the year.[104] Unless such advance payments are authorized by the plan, they should be regarded with suspicion. State legislation may forbid

[101] See the computation clause in text to note 54 *supra*.

[102] If the stock of the new subsidiary is exchanged for physical assets of the parent, the operations of the new subsidiary should in fairness be added to the profit-sharing base, since earnings from the assets thus transferred will no longer be available for the purpose of profit-sharing. On the other hand, the stock of a new subsidiary or the assets of another corporation may be acquired with treasury stock of the parent in respect of which dividends have been excluded for the purpose of profit-sharing computation.

[103] See Chapter 6, text to notes 35 ff.

[104] See profit-sharing plans of Walter Kidde and Co. and American District Telegraph Co., CASEY AND ROTHSCHILD, PAY CONTRACTS WITH KEY MEN (1953), Exs. 140, 139. Periodic payments on account of profit participation are found with some frequency in plans in which lower-ranking personnel participate. BROWER, *op. cit. supra* note 1, at 15. Of the plans examined in this study, 6% provided for semiannual payments, 12.1% for quarterly payments, and 4.8% for monthly payments.

In the AMA Survey of fifty representative plans, slightly more than 10% paid more often than once a year; usually about 75% was paid on estimated profits and the balance after the year's audited profits were determined. AMA, INCENTIVE COMPENSATION, *supra* note 1, at 33.

loans to officers.[105] Also, serious difficulties may arise if the profits for the year are less than were anticipated.[106] The tax consequences of such advance payments are discussed in the following chapter.[107]

[105] CAL. GEN. CORP. L., § 823; CONN. GEN. CORP. L., § 33–321(c) ; DEL. GEN. CORP. L., § 143; MICH. GEN. CORP. L., § 450.46; N.J. STAT. ANN. § 14 :8–10; N. Y. STOCK CORP. L. § 59 and N. Y. BUS. CORP. L., §714 (eff. April 1, 1963) ; OHIO REV. CODE, § 1701.95(A)(3) ; cf. VA. STOCK CORP. L., § 13.1–3(f) (corporation authorized to lend money to its employees, officers, and directors, and otherwise assist them). Consult Model Business Corporation Act, §§ 4(f), 42, 43(d) (authorizing corporation "to lend money to its employees other than its officers and directors, and otherwise assist its employees, officers and directors," but prohibiting loans to officers or directors).

Such loans appear permissible in the absence of a prohibiting statute, the statute being considered in derogation of common law. Flexner v. B. T. Babbitt, Inc., 290 N.Y. 604 (1943).

Since executives often own some shares of stock, a statute confined to stockholders, such as that in Michigan or New York, would be applicable. Consult Nat'l Lock Co. v. Hoagland, 101 F.2d 576 (7th Cir. 1938).

[106] See Gallin v. Nat'l City Bank, supra note 52, at 700.

[107] See Chapter 4, text to notes 50 ff.

CHAPTER 4

PROFIT PARTICIPATION:
CORPORATE, TAX, AND POLICY QUESTIONS

CORPORATE AND POLICY QUESTIONS

Corporate Power to Grant Incentive Compensation. We have seen that profit participation or incentive compensation arrangements are a well-recognized means of compensating executives. When properly adopted they have received judicial approval.[1] Amounts granted as profit-sharing compensation, because of their relative size, have perhaps been subject to greater attack than salary compensation. But attacks based upon alleged excessiveness have not been as successful as attacks based upon miscomputation.[2] As a matter of

---

[1] With the power to establish incentive compensation plans undoubted, questions as to the proper manner of adoption—sanction by directors or by stockholders or both jointly—the scope of the plan and its desirability have occupied the courts. Ransome Concrete Machinery Co. v. Moody, 282 Fed. 29 (2d Cir. 1922); Joy v. Ditto, 356 Ill. 348, 190 N.E. 671 (1934); *In re* Estate of Wood, 299 Mich. 635, 1 N.W.2d 19 (1941) (salary payable for one year after death); Roberts v. Mays Mills, 184 N.C. 406, 114 S.E. 530 (1922); Wachovia Bank & Trust Co. v. Steele's Mills, 225 N.C. 302, 34 S.E.2d 425 (1945); Booth v. Beattie, 95 N.J. Eq. 776, 118 Atl. 257 (1922), *aff'd per curiam,* 123 Atl. 925 (1924); Smith v. Bedell Bros., 84 N.J. Eq. 268, 96 Atl. 898 (1915); Bennett v. Millville Imp. Co., 67 N.J. 320, 51 Atl. 706 (1902); Gallin v. Nat'l City Bank of N.Y., 152 Misc. 679, 273 N. Y. Supp. 87 (Sup. Ct. 1934), 155 Misc. 880, 281 N. Y. Supp. 795 (confirmed, Referee's Report, 1935); Bull & Co., Inc. v. Morris, 132 Misc. 509, 230 N.Y. Supp. 122 (Sup. Ct. 1928), *aff'd mem.,* 226 App. Div. 868 (1st Dep't 1929); Young v. United States Mortgage & Trust Co., 214 N.Y. 279, 108 N.E. 418 (1915); Warner v. Morgan, 81 Misc. 685, 143 N.Y. Supp. 516 (Sup. Ct. 1913), *aff'd mem.,* 165 App. Div. 903, 148 N.Y. Supp. 1149 (1st Dep't 1914); Giveen v. Gans, 91 App. Div. 37, 86 N.Y. Supp. 450 (1st Dep't 1904), *aff'd per curiam,* 181 N.Y. 538, 73 N.E. 1124 (1905); Putnam v. Juvenile Shoe Corp., 307 Mo. 74, 269 S.W. 593, 596 (1925). See also Note, 164 A.L.R. 1125 (1946). For statutory authorization, see CONN. GEN. STAT. § 33–24 (1958); N.J. STAT. ANN., tit. 14, § 14:9–1 *et seq.* (1939). Tax decisions also recognize such plans as valid forms of compensation. See, e.g., William S. Gray & Co. v. United States, 35 F.2d 968, 974 (Ct. Cl. 1929). Of course the existence of corporate power does not of itself justify a tax deduction. *Cf.* Wachovia Bank & Trust Co. v. Steele's Mills, *supra,* with the tax decision relating to the same trust, disallowing the deduction, Robertson v. Steele's Mills, 172 F.2d 817 (4th Cir. 1949), *cert. denied,* 338 U.S. 848 (1949).

[2] See text *infra* to notes 31 ff. See Anglo-American Equities Corp. v. E. H. Rollins & Sons, 258 App. Div. 878, 16 N.Y.S.2d 105 (1st Dep't 1939), *aff'd w.o. op.,* 282 N.Y. 782, 27 N.E.2d 200 (1940); Diamond v. Davis, 38 N.Y.S.2d 93 (Sup.

corporate as well as tax law, incentive compensation, like salaries and other forms of remuneration, must be measured by the value of the services [3] and cannot be based on extraneous factors such as the size of the executive's stockholdings.[4] On the other hand, the fact that compensation will be contingent on profits may justify an amount

---

Ct. 1942), *aff'd w.o. op.*, 265 App. Div. 919, 39 N.Y.S.2d 412 (1st Dep't 1942), *aff'd w.o. op.*, 292 N.Y. 554, 54 N.E.2d 683 (1944), 62 N.Y.S.2d 181 (Sup. Ct. 1945). *Cf.* Mann v. Luke, 82 N.Y.S.2d 725 (Sup. Ct. 1948) (compromise approved); Auer v. Wm. Meyer Co., 322 Ill. App. 244, 54 N.E.2d 394 (1st Dep't 1944). Consult Volume II, Chapter 19.

For later litigation based on allegedly excessive compensation chiefly through profit participation plans, see Duane v. Menzies, 144 A.2d 229 (Del. Ch. 1958) (five-year employment contract made by Servel, Inc. with $75,000 salary and 5% of amount by which operating results each year exceeded those in 1954; proposed settlement of stockholder suit based on alleged excessive compensation substituting as formula 5% of net income before taxes disapproved on ground, *inter alia*, of lack of agreement to restore amounts for past years); Nadler v. Bethlehem Steel Corp., 154 A.2d 146 (Del. Ch. 1959) (proposed settlement of stockholder suit charging excessive incentive compensation which involved substitution of dividend unit plan disapproved because not reducing percentage payable); Yaeger v. Phillips. Referee's Report dated Nov. 2, 1953, N. Y. County Clerk's Index No. 18,308/1951 (Sup. Ct. 1953), *confirmed*, 128 N.Y.S.2d 376 (Sup. Ct. 1953), *app. dismissed*, 283 App. Div. 929 (1st Dep't 1954) (settlement of stockholders' action involving reduction of additional compensation fund for officers and key executives of Devoe and Raynolds Company, Inc. from 10% to 7% of net income approved); Smith v. Dunlap, 269 Ala. 97, 111 So.2d 1 (1959) (complaint charging that as a result of bonus or incentive plan officers and directors received excessive compensation held to state a cause of action); N. Y. Times, Jan. 25, 1961, p. 52, col. 6 (stockholder suit against Fruehauf Trailer Company executives based on payment of "alleged illegal bonuses").

Litigation has been instituted to preclude or seek reimbursement for incentive compensation payments to executives guilty of illegal price-fixing or other violations of the antitrust laws. See, e.g., N. Y. Times, Feb. 25, 1961, p. 24, col. 1. For a resolution proposed by a stockholder of General Electric Company to "recapture any incentive compensation paid to any officer or employee of the Company who pleaded guilty, or nolo contendere, to the 1960 anti-trust indictments for the entire period of time covered by those indictments," see Proxy Statement for Annual Meeting on Apr. 26, 1961, at p. 26. The ground of the resolution was that incentive compensation so paid constituted "unjust enrichment."

[3] Wiseman v. Musgrave, 309 Mich. 523, 16 N.W.2d 60 (1944). *Cf.* The Wall Street Journal, Apr. 27, 1961, p. 1, col. 6: "Stockholder suits spring from a variety of situations. Many are touched off by charges of excessive executive compensation . . ."; N. Y. Times, Jan. 25, 1961, p. 52, col. 6 (stockholder suit against Fruehauf Trailer Company based on payment of "alleged illegal bonuses").

[4] Scott v. P. Lorillard Co., 108 N.J. Eq. 153, 154 Atl. 515 (1931). But *cf.* Bookman v. R. J. Reynolds Tobacco Co., 138 N.J. Eq. 312, 48 A.2d 646 (1946), construing stock purchase statute. Compare Berkwitz v. Humphrey, 163 F. Supp. 78 (N.D. Ohio 1958) holding "shadow stock" plan invalid to the extent that amount of compensation depended upon the market price of stock, with Lieberman v. Becker, 155 A.2d 596 (Sup. Ct. Del. 1959) upholding validity of similar plan. See Chapter 6, text to notes 95–96.

larger than a salary fixed as a commitment payable irrespective of profits.[5]

While the power to grant incentive compensation is undoubted, the manner in which the power has been exercised may give rise to questions. Awards are sometimes made informally and without pre-arranged plan. As we shall see, informal awards of this nature may jeopardize the corporation's tax deduction for compensation thus paid.[6] In addition, they may give rise to a contention that profits distributable to stockholders are being appropriated.[7] Accordingly, a formal plan or agreement made well in advance of the end of the year is advisable, with the formula set forth and, preferably, designation made of the contemplated beneficiaries or at least the group among which selection is to be made. The agreement may be unilateral and terms may be added at the end of the year.[8] Looser practice is undesirable, particularly when there has been no established incentive compensation practice.[9]

Relationships Created by the Plan: Powers of Administering Agency. An incentive compensation plan may not only set forth the formula for computing the amount available as incentive compensation but may also designate the participants in the plan and state the share to be received by each.[10] Under such a plan, it is reasonably clear that each participant has a contractual right to re-

---

[5] Gottfried v. Gottfried, 112 N.Y.S.2d 431, 460–61 (Sup. Ct. 1952); Yaeger v. Phillips, 128 N.Y.S.2d 376, *supra* note 3. *Cf.* Rogers v. Hill, 289 U.S. 582 (1933).

[6] See text *infra* to notes 73 ff.

[7] Church v. Harnit, 35 F.2d 499 (6th Cir. 1929), *cert. denied*. 281 U.S. 732 (1929); Steeple v. Max Kuner Co., 121 Wash. 47, 208 Pac. 44 (1922); Young v. United States Mortgage & Trust Co., *supra* note 1; Holmes v. Republic Steel Corp., 84 Ohio App. 442, 84 N.E.2d 508 (1948), *affirming* 69 N.E.2d 396 (Ohio Com. Pleas 1946); Nat'l Loan & Investment Co. v. Rockland Co., 94 Fed. 335 (8th Cir. 1899); St. Louis, F.A. & W.R. Co. v. Tiernan, 37 Kan. 606, 15 Pac. 544, 553 (1867); Powell v. Republic Creosoting Co., 172 Wash. 155, 19 P.2d 919 (1933); Zwolanek v. Baker Mfg. Co., 150 Wis. 517, 137 N.W. 769 (1912).

[8] Zwolanek v. Baker Mfg. Co., *supra* note 7 (bylaw treated as offer accepted by rendition of services); Holmes v. Republic Steel Corp., *supra* note 7 (amount of bonus fixed at end of year).

[9] Loose practice is particularly undesirable in the case of the closely held corporation where the question is more likely to arise as to whether payments made informally constitute payments for personal services, or are distributions of profits to stockholders or other non-compensating payments. See text *infra* to notes 68 ff.; 4 MERTENS, LAW OF FEDERAL INCOME TAXATION § 25.65 (Zimet and Diamond Rev. 1954). *Cf.* Santarelli v. Katz, 270 F.2d 762, 765 (7th Cir. 1959): "The controlling fact is that there was no Board resolution, charter provision, bylaw, nor express contract which authorized the payment of corporate monies. . . ." For further discussion, consult Chapter 8.

[10] E.g., AMERICAN TOBACCO, App. U, § 1(B) (providing percentage share of profits for president and two senior vice presidents).

ceive his share of incentive compensation once it has been earned.[11] It would also seem that, unless there is a provision in the plan to the contrary, a participant who has been deprived of his right to earn his share of incentive compensation by the company's termination of his employment without cause may maintain a suit for damages, at least when he has a definite term of employment.[12]

Group incentive compensation plans usually provide, however, that awards shall be made annually to those selected by a designated agency—most frequently, the board of directors or a committee appointed by the board, perhaps on recommendation of the president or division heads. Questions may then arise as to the finality of the decisions of this agency.

There is little discussion in the cases of the agency's status or power as an arbitration board; the emphasis is rather on the legal effect of the terms and conditions of the plan under which the funds are segregated. The answer to any question as to the power of the agency to make a binding decision seems to depend upon the nature of the relationship between employer and employee as established under the plan. The courts ask: Are the provisions of the plan part of the contract of employment, so that by fulfilling certain conditions the employee has become indefeasibly entitled to a specific award? If so, the courts have refused to give to the agency—which is often merely a part of the management—a free hand in the settlement of what is in effect a dispute between employer and employee as to the

---

[11] See cases cited *infra* notes 21 and 22. For enforceability of rights under pension plans, see Bird v. Connecticut Power Co., 144 Conn. 456, 133 A.2d 894 (1957); Ball v. Victor Adding Machine Co., 236 F.2d 170 (5th Cir. 1956).

[12] See cases cited *infra* notes 21 and 22. However, if the plan provides that the company reserves the right to discharge the employee, his inchoate rights to benefits may be terminated by termination of his employment although without cause. Schneider v. McKesson & Robbins, 254 F.2d 827 (2d Cir. 1958) (pension); Hablas v. Armour & Co., 270 F.2d 71 (8th Cir. 1959) (*semble*); Bailey v. Rockwell Spring & Axle Co., 13 Misc.2d 29, 175 N.Y.S.2d 104 (Sup. Ct. 1958) (*semble*).

When the executive contends that a payment constitutes a gift rather than compensation in order to avoid a tax, however, this contention has met with little success. See Willkie v. Com'r, 127 F.2d 953 (6th Cir. 1942), *cert. denied,* 317 U.S. 659 (1942). But *cf.* Bogardus v. Com'r, 302 U.S. 34 (1937); Com'r v. Duberstein, 363 U.S. 278 (1960). Note, however, that if the corporation continues to pay compensation to employees called into military service or otherwise serving the government for nominal compensation and who plan to return to their civilian employment, such compensation will be allowed as a business expense. Berkshire Oil Co., 9 T.C. 903 (1947); Hemenway-Johnson Furniture Co., 7 CCH Tax Ct. Mem. 380 (1948), *aff'd* 174 F.2d 793 (5th Cir. 1949); I.T. 3414, 1940–2 Cum. Bull. 64; I.T. 3602, 1943–1 Cum. Bull. 64 (payments to dependents). But inquiry may still be made as to whether the compensation is excessive or is paid for family or other personal reasons. Bur. Int. Rev. letter, Mar. 8, 1945, 4 CCH 1945 Stand. Fed. Tax Rep., ¶ 6156. See N.B. Drew, 12 T.C. 5 (1949).

interpretation of a contract, and they have had little hesitancy in overruling the refusal of the agency to make the award.[13]

However, if it is determined that under the plan the employer was merely promising to confer benefits in the future upon undesignated employees, and that the power of conferring the benefits and the discretion as to who shall receive the benefits have merely been delegated to a selecting agency, the courts have not been sympathetic to employees who complain of decisions of the selecting board because they have been omitted from the list of recipients.[14]

These results are not materially varied in cases where the plan contains a provision that the right of the employee to participate in any benefits shall be determined conclusively by the administering board. Such a provision will be interpreted in the light of the purpose of the plan as a whole. Several cases indicate that the courts will not interfere if such a provision is coupled with other provisions [15] which show that the employer is not making an offer containing definite conditions for acceptance, but is promising to bestow special benefits on those employees who in the opinion of the selecting agency deserve them.[16] This is illustrated by the New York cases, beginning

[13] Fickling v. Pollard, 51 Ga. App. 54, 179 S.E. 582 (1935) ; Psutka v. Michigan Alkali Co., 274 Mich. 318, 264 N.W. 385 (1936) ; McLemore v. Western U. Teleg. Co., 88 Ore. 237, 171 Pac. 390 (1918) ; Jensen v. Bell Telephone Co., 29 Pa. D. & C. 476 (1937) ; see also Coats v. General Motors Corp., 11 Cal.2d 601, 81 P.2d 906 (1938). Consult Dix, *Retirement Allowance and Pension Plans*, 31 GEORGETOWN L.J. 22, 29 (1942). But *cf.* Doyle v. French Telegraph Cable Co., 244 App. Div. 586, 280 N.Y.Supp. 281 (1st Dep't 1935) (modification of pension plan by government decree binds employees covered by plan).

[14] Clark v. New England Tel. & Tel. Co., 229 Mass. 1, 118 N.E. 348 (1918) ; McCabe v. Consolidated Edison Co., 30 N.Y.S.2d 445 (City Ct. 1941) ; Korb v. Brooklyn Edison Co., 258 App. Div. 799, 15 N.Y.S.2d 557 (2d Dep't 1939) ; Burgess v. First Nat'l Bank, 219 App. Div. 361, 220 N.Y.Supp. 134 (2d Dep't 1927) ; McNevin v. Solvay Process Co., *infra* note 17; Magnolia Petroleum Co. v. Butler, 86 S.W.2d 258 (Tex. Civ. App. 1935) ; Spiner v. Western U. Teleg. Co., 73 S.W.2d 566 (Tex. Civ. App. 1934) ; see also Cowles v. Morris & Co., 330 Ill. 11, 161 N.E. 150 (1928). A specific provision that the employees shall have no rights under the plan has been held enforceable. Gearns v. Commercial Cable Co., 177 Misc. 1047, 33 N.Y.S.2d 856 (Mun. Ct. 1942).

[15] A provision reserving to the employer the power, without liability, to modify or revoke the plan, may have some weight in a court's decision that no contract was intended. See Wallace v. Northern Ohio Traction & Light Co., 57 Ohio App. 203, 13 N.E.2d 139 (1937) ; Magnolia Petroleum Co. v. Butler, *supra* note 14; Note, 34 MICH. L. REV. 129 (1935) ; Note, 34 MICH. L. REV. 700 (1936). So will a provision that no rights shall be enforceable by employees. Gearns v. Commercial Cable Co., *supra* note 14.

[16] Cases *supra* note 14. A different question arises when the employee seeks recovery of contributions which he himself has made to the fund. It seems clear that he can recover. *Cf.* Walters v. Pittsburgh & Lake Angeline Iron Co., 201 Mich. 379, 167 N.W. 834 (1918) ; Note, 53 HARV. L. REV. 1375, 1380 (1940). Where the plan is terminated, two states by statute provide for priority of these funds before

with *McNevin v. Solvay Process Co.*, decided in 1898.[17] There the company set aside a certain percentage of its profits for the purpose of maintaining a pension fund. The plan for administering the fund provided that it was "to remain under the sole control of the defendant's trustees, who are authorized to decide all questions concerning the rights of the employees in the fund without appeal." [18] Other provisions declared that the sums set aside were gifts which remained the property of the corporation until paid over to the employees and that the trustees had full discretion in deciding whether to set aside any profits in any year for the purpose of maintaining the fund. A discharged employee sued for a share of the fund, claiming that the company, by crediting him with certain amounts on a passbook, had become obligated to pay. The court, stating that "a person or a corporation proposing to give a sum for the benefit of any person or any set of persons has the right to fix the terms of his bounty, and provide under what circumstances the gift shall become vested and absolute," [19] decided that the provisions of the plan must control and that the employee was not entitled to recover. Later New York cases, and numerous cases in other jurisdictions, take a similar view.[20]

On the other hand, despite a provision giving full authority to a board or committee, if the plan also contains specific conditions the performance of which is to entitle an employee to benefits, a decision by the administering agency denying him benefits will be set aside if the court finds that the conditions had been met.[21] This result may be

---

any other obligations of the employer are satisfied. N.J. Rev. Stat., tit. 14, § 14:9–4 (1939); N.Y. Dr. and Cr. Law, § 21–a. However, the protection already received under sick-benefit plans may defeat recovery. *Cf.* Atlantic Coast Line R.R. v. Wright, 237 Ala. 410, 187 So. 475 (1939).

[17] 32 App. Div. 610, 53 N.Y. Supp. 98 (4th Dep't 1898), *aff'd*, 167 N.Y. 530, 60 N.E. 1115 (1898).

[18] 32 App. Div. at 611.

[19] *Id.* at 612.

[20] Cases *supra* note 14. The soundness of the New York cases has been questioned, on the ground that they are based on an incorrect view that promises to pay pensions are merely promises to make a gift. *Legal Status of Private Industrial Pension Plans*, 53 Harv. L. Rev. 1375 (1940). It is, however, difficult to see how the courts could have interpreted the plans before them in those cases in any other manner; their interpretation, indeed, is in line with that in other jurisdictions. *Supra* note 14. There seems to be nothing in the New York cases to prevent the courts from holding that pension and profit-sharing plans, if drawn on an offer-acceptance basis, constitute a contract between employer and employee. *Cf.* Roddy v. Valentine, 268 N.Y. 228, 197 N.E. 260 (1935); Zwolanek v. Baker Mfg. Co., *supra* note 7. But *cf.* cases cited *supra* note 13.

[21] Psutka v. Michigan Alkali Co., *supra* note 13; Jensen v. Bell Telephone Co., *supra* note 13; see also Schofield v. Zion's Co-Operative Mercantile Inst., 85 Utah 281, 39 P.2d 342 (1934). *Cf.* Zwolanek v. Baker Mfg. Co., *supra* note 7.

reached through a conclusion that the plan constituted a continuing offer, acceptance of which by fulfillment of the conditions gave rise to a contract, or, with the "gift" rationale employed, the result may be reached by a finding of "bad faith" or "fraud" on the part of the administering agency.[22]

The Accountant's Role. An incentive compensation contract or plan will usually provide that computation of the amount of incentive compensation shall be made by the corporation's regular public accountants,[23] that they shall follow accepted accounting practice in making the computation,[24] and that their determinations shall bind both the corporation and the executive.[25]

"Accepted accounting practice," however, is not quite the positive solution of all difficulties that lawyers would like to consider it. Accountants can differ in their views as frequently as lawyers; their craft is subject to almost as many variables and guesses as the law. Earnings, after all, are not something fixed and concrete; they are not to be computed by subtracting disbursements from cash receipts. Rather, they represent an informed estimate of income guided by accounting conventions which, although they may be valid in a majority of cases, may not bear a very direct relation to the realities of a particular business.[26] When the contract provides, then, that the computation of earnings shall be made according to accepted accounting practice and that the decision of the company's auditors shall be final, the parties have in fact entered into something very similar to an arbitration agreement. The honesty and good judgment of the arbitrators will be of real importance.

[22] Coats v. General Motors Corp., *supra* note 13; Hunston v. Sparling, 87 Cal. App. 2d 711, 197 P.2d 807 (1949); Robinson v. Standard Oil Co. of La., 180 So. 237 (La. App. 1938); Twiss v. Lincoln Tel. & Tel. Co., 136 Neb. 788, 287 N.W. 620 (1939); McLemore v. Western U. Teleg. Co., *supra* note 13; Jensen v. Bell Telephone Co., *supra* note 13; Grady v. Appalachian Electric Power Co., 126 W.Va. 546, 29 S.E.2d 878 (1944); see also Cowles v. Morris & Co., *supra* note 14.

[23] In addition to contracts cited *supra* Chapter 3, see, e.g., FAIRBANKS, App. M, ¶ (b); National Sugar Company plan set forth in DARTNELL PUBLICATIONS, INC., SALARY ADMINISTRATION PLANS, 31 (1945).

[24] ALLIED, App. N, ¶ 2 ("good accounting practice"); BLOOMINGDALE, App. R, ¶ 3D ("usual practice of the employer and accepted accounting methods").

[25] See contracts referred to *supra* note 23, and Chapter 3, text to note 53.

[26] See 1 BONBRIGHT, VALUATION OF PROPERTY 253 (1937). An honest failure to take sufficient depreciation may inflate purported earnings just as misleadingly as fraudulent misstatement. *Cf.* BAKER, EXECUTIVE SALARIES AND BONUS PLANS 16 *et seq.* (1938). The courts, on the other hand, sometimes seem a little too certain as to just what "net profits" are. See Orlando Orange Groves Co. v. Hale, 107 Fla. 304, 313, 144 So. 674, 677 (1932), 119 Fla. 159, 161 So. 284 (1935); Stein v. Strathmore Worsted Mills, 221 Mass. 86, 88, 108 N.E. 1029, 1030 (1915); *In re* The Spanish Prospecting Co., Ltd., [1911] 1 Ch. 92, 98–101. Consult Maguire v. Osborne, 384 Pa. 430, 121 A.2d 147 (1956).

In *Epstein v. Schenck,* Judge Valente had this to say as to the duties of accountants in making bonus computations: [27]

• Where there was an honest difference of opinion as to the application of alternative sound accounting methods, there can be no exception. Where, however, independent accountants have an opinion of their own which differs from that of the inside auditors, they should assert their views, and not merely proceed along the line of least resistance. Where they follow a certain precedent in a method of accounting approved and known by all parties, there can be no criticism. But where a new situation arises and the views of the independent auditors differ from those of the management, they should assert their views or at least submit their difference in point of view, for determination by the Board of Directors, so that the proper responsibility may be fixed.

Subsequent cases establish the rule that when the views of independent accountants are sought and followed in good faith, liability for miscomputation will not be imposed.[28] On the other hand, if there is evidence of coercion or bad faith, even a contract clause purporting to make the accountants' decisions binding in every instance will hardly be permitted to control.[29]

The Directors' Role. Subject to what has been said in the preceding chapter regarding special earnings formulae, it is ordinarily wise to have the incentive compensation arrangements expressly recognize the power of the directors to reduce the amount of the corporation's net earnings by setting up whatever reserves for losses and contingencies they, in the exercise of good business judgment, deem necessary. One of the criticisms of such arrangements is that the executive will be tempted to exercise his influence in the direction of keeping the corporation from adopting a conservative policy with respect to depreciation, writing off assets of doubtful value, making provision for contingencies, and similar matters. An independent and conscientious firm of accountants can, of course, be of great service in this connection. However, an accountant may be put in a very embarrassing position if the corporation president, a participant in

[27] Epstein v. Schenck, 35 N.Y.S.2d 969, 980 (Sup. Ct. 1939).

[28] Diamond v. Davis, 62 N.Y.S.2d 181 (Sup. Ct. 1945); Mann v. Luke, *supra* note 2, at 728–29 (Sup. Ct. 1948). This is especially true when the auditors have been approved by the stockholders. Meyers v. Cowdin, 47 N.Y.S.2d 471, 475–76 (Sup. Ct. 1944), *aff'd w.o. op.,* 270 App. Div. 827, 60 N.Y.S.2d 129 (2d Dep't 1946), *aff'd w.o. op.,* 296 N.Y. 755, 70 N.E.2d 555 (1946).

[29] Heller v. Boylan, 29 N.Y.S.2d 653 (Sup. Ct. 1941), *aff'd w.o. op.,* 263 App. Div. 815, 32 N.Y.S.2d 131 (1st Dep't 1941). For the tax aspects of erroneous computation see text *infra* to note 52.

incentive compensation, informs him that a questioned asset, such as an account receivable, should be carried on the books without write-down in view of its possible recovery in value, even though the accountant believes that the facts would justify a substantial write-down. The accountant knows that there can be a reasonable differ-ence of opinion on such matters, and that he is hardly justified in viewing the executive's stand as based entirely on personal motives. To relieve the accountant of the entire burden of responsibility in such a situation, it may be advisable for the board of directors to assign a committee of its members to supervise the completion of the annual audit and the computation of the amount available for incen-tive compensation.[30]

In the last analysis, the responsibility for bonus as well as other payments out of corporate assets rests with the board of directors. Directors have been held personally liable for overpayments. A num-ber of stockholders' actions have been brought in New York based both upon the charge that incentive compensation payments resulted in excessive compensation and upon the charge that compensation payable under the contract was computed by the bonus-receiving executives themselves, that the computation was incorrect, and that the directors were liable for negligence and waste in not having seen to it that the compensation was properly computed and confined to the correct amount. While the courts have given the directors broad discretion in respect of the amount of executive compensation paid, they have been relatively strict in holding directors to accountability for miscalculation.[31]

It is accordingly in the directors' own interest to exercise a real measure of supervision over the calculation of a profit-sharing bonus. Complete reliance upon figures prepared by unsupervised employees, particularly if they have an interest in the bonus plan, may expose the directors to liability. This is evident from the referee's report in *Gallin v. National City Bank,* which reads in part : [32]

[30] As to a somewhat similar committee, see Annual Report (1939) of E. I. du Pont de Nemours & Co., and Annual Report (1945) of General Motors Corp.

[31] Epstein v. Schenck, *supra* note 27; Heller v. Boylan, *supra* note 29; Gallin v. Nat'l City Bank, *supra* note 1; Winkelman v. General Motors Corp., 39 F. Supp. 826 (S.D.N.Y. 1940), 44 F. Supp. 485 (1942); Gottlieb v. Schenck, 82 N.Y.S.2d 917 (Sup. Ct. 1942); Neuberger v. Barrett, 180 Misc. 222 (Sup. Ct. 1942) (Union Carbide & Carbon Corp.). See also cases cited *supra* note 28. *Cf.* Singer v. Adams (Sup. Ct. 1946) (unreported) referred to in Proxy Statement dated Mar. 22, 1948 of Colgate-Palmolive-Peet Co. (agreement, in settlement of stockholders' action, to deduct bonus fund in computing profit participation). For details of cases, see Volume II, Chapter 19.

[32] 155 Misc. 880, at 892–93, 281 N.Y. Supp. 795 at 807, 808 (Sup. Ct. 1935). While the figures in this case were not prepared by independent public accountants,

• The only figures before the executive committee or the board of directors of the company with respect to the management fund when they authorized distribution of the fund was a statement prepared by the auditor or controller or someone in the controller's department "showing merely the net amount which was available for distribution." . . . The executive committee did not ascertain or know how the management fund was computed, or whether any current losses had not been eliminated or there had been any elimination from capital, surplus and undivided profits. . . .

. . . It was incumbent upon the directors to see to it that the formula was followed with strict impartiality and they could not delegate this duty to those who would participate in the fund or to others who acted under the supervision and guidance of the latter. The board of directors and executive committee of the company, to insure the proper computation of the management fund, should have intrusted that work to officers or employees in no manner interested in the management fund. Failure so to do constituted a breach of their duty as directors and subjects them to liability for the restoration of moneys improperly paid through such erroneous computations of the management fund.

The referee found that certain realized losses had not been deducted from net profits in the computation of the bonus fund, and held the directors liable.

In contrast, when directors in good faith and under an appropriate contract clause rely on the report of independent accountants, we have holdings such as the *Epstein* case,[33] in which the board was held to be under no liability, even though the accountants made several mistakes in computation. The court made it clear that once the directors have acted with due care in choosing an independent firm, they are under no duty to have the computation rechecked by still another firm, if no suspicious circumstances arise. A complaint by stockholders alleging that the executives were overpaid is not in itself enough to require the directors to make a recomputation, in the absence of specific charges that previous computations were incorrect.[34]

---

the principle that the board of directors or its executive committee should know something of the manner in which the bonus fund was computed would likewise appear applicable to figures prepared by independent accountants.

[33] *Supra* note 27. To the same effect, see Judge Leibell's opinion in Winkelman v. General Motors Corp., *supra* note 31 (independent accountants' report reviewed by non-participating directors on Finance Committee). See cases cited *supra* notes 28 and 31.

[34] *Cf.* Winkelman v. General Motors Corp., *supra* note 31.

In *Heller v. Boylan,* the second American Tobacco case,[35] the computations were made by the company's treasurer, the bonus being payable under a bylaw which stated that the treasurer's determinations should be "binding and conclusive." [36] The court found a number of miscomputations, and imposed liability on the bonus recipients. It did not, however, impose liability on the non-recipient directors, relying chiefly on the theory that under the bylaw the administration of the bonus plan was a matter for the stockholders and the treasurer, beyond the control of the directors. This reasoning, standing alone, seems somewhat doubtful. The directors, in the absence of express bylaw language relieving them, must still be responsible to the stockholders for the total welfare of the company.

The teaching of these cases, as a group, is plain. The directors should see to it that the computation is made by disinterested persons (preferably independent accountants). While reliance in good faith upon their computations will ordinarily relieve the directors of liability, as a matter of good practice and sound precaution the directors should also have some assurance that all material facts bearing upon a specific problem have been placed before the accountants. It would also appear advisable for the board as a whole to review the ultimate calculations of the accountants and their recommendations with respect to any problem involving a substantial amount so as to correct any patent errors, or, if none is found and the problem warrants, to adopt an appropriate resolution approving the accountants' recommended solution of the specific problem—perhaps even to authorize and adopt an amended contract to cover the point. One of the holdings in the *Gallin* case is important in this connection. The referee there stated: [37]

• The record shows clearly that whenever the executive committee and board of directors of the bank desired to modify the formula so as to eliminate a loss, whether charged to surplus or as a current operating loss, they effected such modification of the formula by an express resolution or action duly adopted at a regular or special meeting of the executive committee or the board.

The referee seems to have proceeded on the basis that any such modification of the formula by express action of the executive com-

[35] 29 N.Y.S.2d 653 (Sup. Ct. 1941), *aff'd w.o. op.,* 263 App. Div. 815, 32 N.Y.S.2d 131 (1st Dep't 1941).

[36] Subsequent cases, in which independent accountants were employed, distinguish Heller v. Boylan on this and other grounds. See Mann v. Luke, *supra* note 2, at 730, and other cases cited in notes 28 and 31. For the language of the American Tobacco bylaw in its present form, see App. U.

[37] *Supra* note 32, 155 Misc. at 895, 281 N.Y. Supp. at 810.

mittee or the board of directors would justify a corresponding change in the computation.[38] All of the adjustments made by the referee (with imposition of liability) seem to have been made on account of items which were not made the subject of express resolution—usually losses not properly charged against earnings available for compensation. Does this mean that any modification of a computation formula made by the executive committee or the board of directors in favor of an executive, so that his compensation can be figured on a more advantageous basis, is to be regarded as valid and proper? It would seem unsafe for counsel to rely on such a theory.[39] An amendatory contract, adopted with all the formality of the original agreement, seems advisable and perhaps even necessary.

TAX QUESTIONS

Current Distribution Plans. Plans providing for distribution of incentive compensation as earned present relatively few tax problems. If the award is paid in full in the same year in which it has been earned, the executive is of course taxable on the award for that year.[40] In the case of a group plan with awards conditioned on profits, the awards are generally not paid until the profits have been finally computed following audit after the close of the year in which the profits were earned. Under such a plan the executive will be taxed in the year of payment unless the award was actually made in the preceding year and the executive in effect chose not to receive payment in that year, or unless the executive is a controlling stockholder and could have directed payment in the preceding year.[41]

Awards by a corporation on an accrual basis paid in the year after they have been earned may be deducted in the year in which they were earned;[42] a different question is presented in the case of deferred

---

[38] *Cf.* Mann v. Luke, *supra* note 2, at 729.

[39] *Cf.* Winkelman v. General Motors Corp., *supra* note 31, at 1003.

[40] At least if he is on the cash basis. INT. REV. CODE OF 1954, § 451; Treas. Reg. § 1.451–1 (1960). See J. H. McEwen, 6 T.C. 1018 (1946). The usual provision is for payment after the close of the taxable year next following the computation of profits. For problems involving reasonableness, see text *infra* to note 64 ff.

[41] This involves the doctrine of constructive receipt. See Treas. Reg. § 1.451–2 (1960); C. E. Gullett, 31 B.T.A. 1067, 1069 (1935) (quoted in Rev. Rul. 60–31, 1960, 1960–1 CUM. BULL. 174, a comprehensive ruling dealing with deferred compensation arrangements discussed below in Chapter 5, text to notes 115 ff.). For a case of a closely held company in which the controlling stockholder rule was applied, see James J. Cooney, 18 T.C. 883 (1952); but *cf.* Basil F. Basila, 36 T.C. No. 7 (1961) (no constructive receipt though bonus earned, amount ascertained and paid in part).

[42] Willoughby Camera Stores v. Com'r, 125 F.2d 607 (2d Cir. 1942); Com'r v. Produce Reporter Co., 207 F.2d 586 (7th Cir. 1953), *affirming* 18 T.C. 69 (1952).

compensation, for which the deduction may be taken only in the year of payment.[43] For the corporation to be entitled to a deduction for current compensation in the year prior to the year of actual payment, the awards must have been fully earned and the amount therefore must have been ascertainable at the close of such year; also, there must be no conditions to payment of the awards other than final determination of their amount based upon facts and figures known or ascertainable as of the close of the year.[44] When incentive compensation is payable to executives who are controlling stockholders, the corporate deduction can be taken only if the compensation is paid or made available within two and one-half months of the close of the year in which the compensation was earned.[45]

If the total amount of incentive compensation to be awarded is ascertainable as of the close of the year during which the compensation was being earned, the company on an accrual basis may take the deduction for that year even though the amount of participation of the individuals who will receive the awards is not determined until after the close of the year.[46] On the other hand, if the total amount of incentive compensation awards that will be made for the preceding year is not ascertainable prior to the close of the year—for example, because incentive compensation awards for the total amount are not made or are made only in a subsequent year or years—the corporate deduction will be confined to that part of the incentive compensation,

[43] INT. REV. CODE OF 1954, § 404(a)(5). For the distinction between plans for current and deferred compensation, and the employer's right to a deduction in the case of deferred compensation plans, see Chapter 6, text to notes 1–12.

[44] Treas. Reg. § 1.461–1(a)(2) (1960). The leading case which established this rule for deductions by taxpayers on the accrual basis is United States v. Anderson, 269 U.S. 422 (1926). See also Anderson-Clayton Securities Corp., 35 B.T.A. 795 (1937), acq., 1937–2 CUM. BULL. 2.

However, it has been held that compensation may be deducted even though subject to an event which was not within the control of the company. Produce Reporter Co., 18 T.C. 69 (1952), supra note 42 (bonuses subject to approval of Wage Stabilization Board). In that case, the deduction was permitted though an individual employee might not receive his bonus if he failed to remain with the company throughout the year following that for which the bonus was awarded.

[45] INT. REV. CODE OF 1954, § 267(a)(2). In the case of a cash-basis taxpayer, the deduction is allowable if the compensation is taxable to him as constructively received. Treas. Reg. § 1.267(a)–1(b)(1)(ii) and (iii) (1960). The deduction is also allowable if payment is made in the form of a check or a negotiable promissory note (not necessarily payable on demand) which is the equivalent of cash. Rev. Rul. 55–437, 1955–2 CUM. BULL. 548. But see H & H Drilling Co., 15 T.C. 961 (1950) (no deduction for check issued and immediately endorsed by employee and returned to employer for deposit in its own account).

[46] Rev. Rul. 57–88, 1957–1 CUM. BULL. 88; Willoughby Camera Stores v. Com'r, supra note 42; Avco Mfg. Corp., 25 T.C. 975, 999–1001 (1956), acq. on this issue, 1957–1 CUM. BULL. 3, vacated and remanded by stipulation, 2d Cir., Aug. 5, 1957. Cf. Kershaw Mfg. Co., Tax Ct. Mem. 1961–98, CCH TAX CT. MEM. 443 (1961).

if any, which must in all events be paid promptly following its determination based upon facts and figures known or ascertainable as of the close of that year.[47] Similarly, no deduction is allowable when compensation based on profits is retained in the business and is subject to reduction by subsequent losses.[48]

Tax problems presented when payment of incentive compensation is made in the form of stock will be discussed in the second volume of this edition.

Advance Payment Plans and Overpayments. As we have seen,[49] an incentive compensation plan may occasionally provide for payments on account during the course of the year in which the profits that form the basis for the compensation are being earned. Will the executive be subject to tax on such interim payments in the year in which they are received or in the following year in which the final computation of the compensation is made? The answer will depend on whether the payment was treated merely as an advance against the compensation due or, on the contrary, was received under a claim of right as a payment on account.[50] When the executive has expressly agreed to repay any payments received in excess of the amount payable shown in the final computation, his right to the payments received will not be established until the final computation, and the advance payments should be taxed as income in the year of the computation rather than the year of receipt.[51] On the other hand,

[47] Bauer Bros. Co. v. Com'r, 46 F.2d 874 (6th Cir. 1931), *cert. denied*, 283 U.S. 850 (1931); Oakland California Towel Co., 9 B.T.A. 208 (1927); Powell Pressed Steel Co., 4 CCH Tax Ct. Mem. 455 (1945); Field & Start, Inc., 17 B.T.A. 1206 (1929), *aff'd per curiam*, 44 F.2d 1014 (1930), *cert. denied*, 283 U.S. 826 (1931); Fuller Brush Co., 8 B.T.A. 855 (1927); McCauley-Ward Motor Supply Co., 10 B.T.A. 394 (1928); Addressograph-Multigraph Corp., 4 CCH Tax Ct. Mem. 147, 180–81 (1945).

[48] S. Naitove & Co. v. Com'r, 32 F.2d 949 (App. D.C. 1929), *cert denied*, 280 U.S. 582 (1929).

[49] See Chapter 3, text to note 104.

[50] The leading case establishing the claim of right doctrine is North American Oil v. Burnet, 286 U.S. 417 (1932), in which the court stated (at 424): "If a taxpayer receives earnings under a claim of right and without restriction as to its disposition, he has received income which he is required to return, even though it may still be claimed that he is not entitled to retain the money, and even though he may still be adjudged liable to restore its equivalent." The decision has been applied by courts in numerous contexts. See 2 Mertens, Law of Federal Income Taxation § 12.103 (Zimet and Stanley rev. ed., 1955).

[51] Wells v. United States, 106 Ct. Cl. 378, 64 F. Supp. 476 (1946). In this case, the taxpayer had reported all advance payments on account of profits in the year of receipt and was awarded a refund of tax upon profits beyond those to which he was entitled under the final computation. The advance payments under the circumstances mentioned may be considered in the nature of loans. If so considered, the question of the legality of loans to officers must be kept in mind. See Chapter 3, note 105.

advance payments which are received under a claim of right because the executive is not expected to repay them are subject to tax in the year received, even though he is obliged in a subsequent year to repay a certain amount when it is established that the payment was based upon an erroneous computation.[52]

Similarly, the executive has been held taxable in the year of receipt even though he repays to the corporation a portion of his compensation following a determination by the Commissioner of Internal Revenue that the compensation was unreasonable, with a corresponding disallowance of the corporation's deduction as a result thereof.[53] An officer of a closely held corporation has been held taxable on the entire salary paid to him when the deduction by the corporation for his salary was reduced on the ground that the salary was excessive, and he was obliged in a subsequent year to pay the corporate income tax as a transferee.[54] Under such circumstances, the executive has been refused a refund of the tax upon the compensation repaid to the corporation; the repaid compensation is held to have been paid and received under a claim of right and to have constituted taxable income irrespective of any underlying equity between the executive and the employer in accordance with which the repayment was subsequently made.[55]

Although a refund of tax for a prior year has thus been denied, compensation repaid by an executive may be claimed by him as a business deduction for the later year in which such repayment was made, at least if repayment was made pursuant to a prior agreement with the corporation.[56] As to compensation, the result might have been different if the executive had been a controlling stockholder or if the transaction resulting in the refund had not been at arm's length. When a deduction is allowable due to the restoration of an amount received under a claim of right, a relief section incorporated in the

---

[52] United States v. Lewis, 340 U.S. 590 (1951) (repayment following state court judgment holding bonus contract misinterpreted), *disagreeing with* Greenwald v. United States, 102 Ct. Cl. 272, 57 F. Supp. 569 (1944), which had held to the contrary; Haberkorn v. United States, 173 F.2d 587 (6th Cir. 1949), *affirming,* 78 F. Supp. 192 (E.D. Mich. 1948).

[53] Ruben Simon, 11 T.C. 227 (1948); Fleischer v. Com'r, 158 F.2d 42 (8th Cir. 1946); Richard Downing, 43 B.T.A. 1147 (1941).

[54] Healy v. Com'r, 345 U.S. 278 (1953).

[55] Cases cited *supra* notes 52 and 54.

[56] Consult United States v. Lewis and Haberkorn v. United States, both *supra* note 52, and Richard Downing, *supra* note 53, at 1154. But *cf.* United States v. Simon, 281 F.2d 520 (6th Cir. 1960) (partnership denied deduction for voluntary return of rent to controlled corporation after rent questioned as excessive by Internal Revenue Service); Patrick v. United States, 186 F. Supp. 48 (W.D. S.C. 1960) (repayable advance by corporation not constructive dividend). Consult Dixon, *Planning Reasonable Compensation,* 19 INST. FED. TAX. 181, 192 (1961).

Internal Revenue Code of 1954 provides that the taxpayer may either take the deduction in the year of repayment or reduce his tax for that year by the amount of tax attributable to the inclusion of the item in the earlier year, whichever results in a lesser tax.[57]

How should the corporation treat compensation subsequently repaid to it? When the repayment by the executive represents an overpayment of incentive compensation which was in the nature of a provisional payment received without any claim of right, the entire transaction should be reflected by the corporation for the year in which the profits subject to incentive compensation were earned, so that the tax deduction will merely be that shown by the final computation.[58] A repayment by the executive in respect of compensation paid and received under a claim of right presents a more difficult question. To the extent that such repayment is deemed voluntary, it would appear to constitute a capital contribution or gift rather than either income or a decrease in the deduction for the year in which the compensation was paid.[59] On the other hand, if the corporation recovers the excess payment on the ground that the previous payment was one to which the executive was not entitled, it will be taxable on the amount recovered.[60]

When an executive both receives compensation and returns it in the same taxable year, he is not taxable on the amount refunded.[61]

Deferred Distribution Plans. As we shall see, many plans today provide that incentive compensation based on one year's profits shall be payable in instalments over a period of more than one year either during employment or following termination of employment.[62] The complex tax questions presented by this type of plan are discussed in a following chapter.[63]

"Reasonable" Profit-Sharing Compensation. The aim of the taxing authorities is to prevent the deduction as compensation of what in reality is or may be regarded as a distribution of profits in

[57] INT. REV. CODE OF 1954, § 1341. The section applies only when the deduction in the later year exceeds $3,000.

[58] Cf. Dixie Pine Products Co. v. Com'r, 320 U.S. 516 (1944); Harrington Co., 6 T.C. 720 (1946); Maggio Bros. Co., 6 T.C. 999 (1946).

[59] Schlaudt, *Returnable Compensation Arrangements,* 8 INST. FED. TAX. 724 (1950).

[60] Cf. Howard Paper Co., 43 B.T.A. 545 (1941).

[61] Albert W. Russel, 35 B.T.A. 602 (1937); Willis W. Clark, 11 T.C. 672 (1948).

[62] See e.g., James D. Mooney, 9 T.C. 713 (1947); Howard Veit, 8 T.C. 809 (1947); 8 Tax Ct. Mem. 919 (1949); E. T. Sproull, 16 T.C. 244 (1951), *aff'd per curiam,* 194 F.2d 541 (6th Cir. 1952).

[63] See Chapter 5, text to notes 46 ff.

the form of dividends to stockholders or their equivalent.[64] A deduction claimed for payments of compensation pursuant to an incentive plan may be reviewed with greater care by the tax authorities than ordinary compensation, particularly in the case of a closely held corporation, but the Treasury Regulations do not condemn profit-sharing or incentive compensation payments as such: [65]

• The form or method of fixing compensation is not decisive as to deductibility. While any form of contingent compensation invites scrutiny as a possible distribution of earnings of the enterprise, it does not follow that payments on a contingent basis are to be treated fundamentally on any basis different from that applying to compensation at a flat rate. Generally speaking, if contingent compensation is paid pursuant to a free bargain between the employer and the individual made before the services are rendered, not influenced by any consideration on the part of the employer other than that of securing on fair and advantageous terms the services of the individual, it should be allowed as a deduction even though in the actual working out of the contract it may prove to be greater than the amount which would ordinarily be paid.

In substance, the Regulations thus adopt the view that, although the reasonableness of all compensation, including contingent or incentive compensation, must be judged by the same standards, amounts paid pursuant to a contingent arrangement may be greater than flat amounts fixed in advance as a salary if the arrangement is reasonable in the light of the facts known when the arrangement is made. The cases also give some significance to the contingent character of a compensation arrangement. In *Botany Worsted Mills v. United States,*[66] an early important case on the deductibility of compensation con-

---

[64] See Volume II, Chapter 16 as to this point and for a detailed discussion of the requirement that compensation be reasonable in order to be deductible as a business expense.

[65] Treas. Reg. § 1.162–7(b)(2) (1958). The language is the same as that used in prior Regulations. See, e.g., Treas. Reg. 111, § 29.23(a)–6(2) (1943). Consult Austin v. United States, 28 F.2d 677 (5th Cir. 1928) construing an earlier version of the Regulations and stating (at 678): "It is immaterial that in the actual working out of the contract contingent compensation may prove to be greater than the amount which ordinarily would be paid."

[66] 278 U.S. 282 (1929). See Thomas N. Perkins, 33 B.T.A. 606, 622–23 (1935) (quoting Austin v. United States, note 65 *supra*); Howard Sole, Inc., 12 CCH TAX CT. MEM. 238 (1952); Midland Ford Tractor Co., Tax Ct. Mem. 1958–23, 17 CCH TAX CT. MEM. 1060, *aff'd,* 277 F.2d 111 (8th Cir. 1960). *Cf.* Patton v. Com'r, 168 F.2d 28 (6th Cir. 1948) (deduction for compensation paid non-stockholder bookkeeper reduced from $46,000 to $13,000 although compensation based on profit-sharing formula).

tingent on profits, the United States Supreme Court, without emphasizing that payments were made on the basis of a percentage of the net profits, merely decided that the taxpayer had not produced any evidence from which it could be determined whether the payments bore any relation to the value of the services. An important factor in such cases has been the presence or absence of an arm's length relationship when the incentive compensation formula was fixed.[67]

Percentage of profit formulae can obviously be contrived to absorb all profits, and this objective may often be present in a closely held company in which all the stockholders are executives. When the percentages have been so high as to absorb all or substantially all of the profits, with little or nothing being paid to stockholders, deductions have been denied.[68] Provision for the payment of dividends to stockholders before any percentage payments to officers and employees has weight in the allowance of a deduction.[69] When the taxpayer has shown that the success of the business depended largely upon the personal efforts and ability of its officers and employees, deductions for percentage payments amounting to a very high proportion of the net profits have been allowed.[70] If the officers and employees own most of the stock of the corporation and their percentage payments are figured on the basis of their stockholdings, the

[67] See James J. McHale Co. v. United States, 151 F. Supp. 115 (N.D. Ohio 1957) and Hyman Friednash, 11 CCH Tax Ct. Mem. 96 (instances of arm's length bargaining). But cf. University Chevrolet Co., 16 T.C. 1452 (1951), aff'd, 199 F.2d 629 (5th Cir. 1952) in which compensation received under a profit participation plan applicable to General Motors agency managers, although considered reasonable when not coupled with stock ownership, was held unreasonable when the manager became the sole stockholder of the automobile agency. The Tax Court stated (16 T.C. at 1455): "The circumstances differed vitally once Davis [the employee] became sole owner of the petitioner corporation. For a sole owner to pay himself a bonus as an incentive to do his best in managing his own business is nonsense." This decision was followed in Mullen Chevrolet Co., 10 CCH Tax Ct. Mem. 682 (1955) and City Chevrolet Co., Tax Ct. Mem. 1954-155, 13 CCH Tax Ct. Mem. 874 (1954), aff'd per curiam, 228 F.2d 894 (4th Cir. 1956). Cf. Howard Sole, Inc., supra note 66. See also Adams Tooling, Inc., 33 T.C. 65 (1959). Cf. Irby Construction Co. v. United States, 61-2 CCH U.S.T.C. ¶ 9497 (Ct. Cl. 1961).

[68] Long Island Drug Co. v. Com'r, 35 B.T.A. 328 (1937), aff'd, 111 F.2d 593 (2d Cir. 1940); Am-Plus Storage Battery Co. v. Com'r, 35 F.2d 167 (7th Cir. 1929); see also H. L. Trimyer & Co. v. Noel, 28 F.2d 781 (E.D. Va. 1928).

[69] Mayson Mfg. Co. v. Com'r, 178 F.2d 115 (6th Cir. 1949); cf. Com'r v. R. J. Reynolds Tobacco Co., 260 F.2d 9 (4th Cir. 1958). See Long Island Drug Co. v. Com'r, supra note 68.

[70] William S. Gray & Co. v. United States, supra note 1; Crucible Steel Casting Co., 5 CCH Tax Ct. Mem. 284 (1946); California Vegetable Concentrates, Inc., 10 T.C. 1158 (1948); Federal Machine & Welder Co., 11 T.C. 952 (1948). Cf. General Water Heater Corp. v. Com'r, 42 F.2d 419 (9th Cir. 1930); Robert Rogers, Inc. v. United States, 93 F. Supp. 1014 (Ct. Cl. 1950).

courts frequently regard the result as merely a disguised method of paying dividends which does not entitle the corporation to a deduction.[71]

Incentive compensation practices have proved particularly advantageous to a corporation when an officer has been paid for a period of years under a percentage contract and in a particular year, because of increased trade or a fortunate business deal, the payments were correspondingly increased; the courts, in allowing deductions, have considered the reasonableness of the compensation in the light of the expected value of the recipient's services at the time the contract was made.[72]

Part of this not unfavorable attitude toward incentive compensation contracts is evidently due to the respect shown toward formal arrangements made in advance of the taxable year: the good faith of the taxpayer is thus relevant; a share of the profits granted after the year's earnings is considerably more questionable.[73] From a practical viewpoint, therefore, advance arrangements of a formal nature are particularly important for incentive compensation. Some corporations have made formal bonus arrangements in advance, but have provided that the stated percentage shall be regarded as a bonus fund, which the directors may distribute in whole or in part solely to those officers and employees who are deemed to merit additional compensa-

[71] L. E. Pinkham Co. v. Com'r, 128 F.2d 986 (1st Cir. 1942); Gilman Paper Co. v. Com'r, 284 F.2d 997 (2d Cir. 1960); General Water Heater Corp. v. Com'r, *supra* note 70; Am-Plus Storage Battery Co. v. Com'r, *supra* note 68; see also Tumwater Lumber Mills v. Com'r, 65 F.2d 675 (9th Cir. 1933); H. L. Trimyer & Co. v. Noel, *supra* note 68. But *compare* Crucible Steel Casting Co., *supra* note 70. For an instance of a publicly held corporation in which a bylaw provided for a distribution of a portion of the profits among employees holding a special class of stock in proportion to stockholdings, *compare* R. J. Reynolds Tobacco Co. v. United States, 138 Ct. Cl. 1, 149 F. Supp. 889 (1957), *cert. denied,* 355 U.S. 893 (1957), disallowing deductions for such profit distributions, with Com'r v. R. J. Reynolds Tobacco Co., *supra* note 69, affirming Tax Court decision which evolved a formula allowing the deduction in other years of a portion of such distribution.

[72] Austin v. United States, *supra* note 65; Thomas N. Perkins, *supra* note 66; California Vegetable Concentrates, Inc., *supra* note 70. *Cf.* Am-Plus Storage Battery Co. v. Com'r, *supra* note 68; James J. McHale Co. v. United States, *supra* note 67 (payment of over $80,000 to a 50% stockholder approved although corporate net income before taxes was only about $12,000, since arrangement was arm's length and not tax-motivated). But *compare* Hoffman Radio Corp. v. Com'r, 177 F.2d 264 (9th Cir. 1949) (abnormal earnings because of war conditions resulted in disallowance of percentage compensation originally fair and equitable) with Robert Rogers, Inc. v. United States, *supra* note 70.

[73] See, e.g., Toledo Grain & Milling Co. v. Com'r, 62 F.2d 171 (6th Cir. 1932); Crucible Steel Casting Co., *supra* note 70. Bonuses voted near the year-end will be regarded with suspicion. Wenatchee Bottling Works v. Hendricksen, 31 F. Supp. 763 (W.D. Wash. 1940).

tion. Such provisions permit flexibility in the distributions made without adversely affecting the tax problem.[74]

From the accounting standpoint, also, formal action in advance may be important. It is desirable, for example, to set up reserves on the company's books during 1962 with respect to bonuses payable for 1962, even though the ultimate amount will not be determined until 1963. Such reserves are commonly established each quarter, based on estimated quarterly earnings. When the books are closed for 1962, adjusting entries can be made, reconciling the reserved amounts with the actual amounts payable. Unless advance authorization in the current year has been obtained, the deduction cannot be taken for that year, notwithstanding current reserves, because no liability to pay additional compensation was incurred in the year in which the profits were earned.[75]

To avoid the necessity of justifying profit-sharing payments as "reasonable" compensation, the contention has been advanced that such payments represent an ordinary business expense necessary to maintain high production standards and to preserve the good will of employees under the modern viewpoint of management-labor relations. According to this contention, such payments should hence be deductible without proof of reasonableness. The contention has not met with notable success. Rejected by the Tax Court,[76] it has to date been upheld only by the Federal Court of Appeals for the Sixth Circuit on the theory that profit-participation payments may be deductible not as compensation but as ordinary business expenses.[77] But even that court has held that such profit-sharing payments, though considered a general business expense, must be justified as "reasonable,"

[74] However, the case of Botany Worsted Mills v. United States, *supra* note 66, where the corporation had adopted such an arrangement, shows that if the payments are questioned, the taxpayer must be prepared to prove that the payments had been earned.

[75] Desco Corp. v. United States, 55 F.2d 411 (D. Del. 1932). See also Bauer Bros. Co. v. Com'r, *supra* note 47; Ox Fibre Brush Co. v. Blair, 32 F.2d 42 (4th Cir. 1929), *aff'd sub nom.* Lucas v. Ox Fibre Brush Co., 281 U.S. 115 (1930); Southern Tire & Rubber Co., 18 B.T.A. 210 (1929); Southland Coal Co., 16 B.T.A. 50 (1929); Oakland California Towel Co., *supra* note 47; *cf.* American Snuff Co. v. Com'r, 93 F.2d 201 (6th Cir. 1937), *cert. denied,* 303 U.S. 662 (1938); Helvering v. J. L. Brandeis & Sons, 75 F.2d 487 (8th Cir. 1935).

[76] Roberts Filter Mfg. Co., 10 T.C. 26 (1948), *aff'd,* 174 F.2d 79 (3d Cir. 1949). *In accord:* Robertson v. Steele's Mills, *supra* note 1. *Cf.* provisions of the Sears Roebuck plan referred to in Leslie, *Trusteed Profit-Sharing,* 9 MGMT. REC. 392 (1947). See Magill, *The Lincoln Electric Co. Decision in the Light of Roberts Filter Manufacturing Co.,* 7 INST. FED. TAX. 80 (1949).

[77] Lincoln Electric Co. v. Com'r, 162 F.2d 379 (6th Cir. 1947), *reversing* 6 T.C. 37 (1946). See Magill, *supra* note 76, and Note, *The Lincoln Electric Co. Case,* 4 MIAMI L.Q. 12 (1949).

since reasonableness is implicit in the statutory requirement that a deductible business expense must be both "ordinary" and "necessary." [78] This decision thus represents a hollow victory for the taxpayer.

Concluding Remarks. Profit participation is said by its proponents to offer a powerful inducement to management to increase the company's earnings. It is argued that the corporation can cut its fixed expenses by offering salaries of only moderate size, holding out as bait the prospect of substantial bonuses dependent on the future success of the business. Stockholders, it is claimed, should be willing to pay a higher rate of compensation if and when the corporation makes increased earnings. It has even been argued that in corporations in which ownership and active management are in different hands the stockholders should receive only that portion of the profits which is "sufficient to insure the continued supplying of capital and taking of risk," [79] granting to management the remaining profits as a reward for efficiency, on the premise that the general good is best served by encouraging profitable and efficient business enterprise.

That, at least, is one side of the picture. On the other side, there is the fact that, with the acquiescence of an indifferent or controlled board of directors, executives sometimes ask and obtain a "minimum" salary that is unconscionably high, and secure in addition an unduly large percentage of the profits. [80] And, contrary to the argument that profit-sharing results in lower fixed salaries, there is evidence that companies with profit-sharing plans often pay fixed salaries as high as or even higher than average. [81] It is also true that business leaders often credit themselves with having produced the large earnings of periods of prosperity, without accepting responsibility for the falling-off of earnings during periods of depression. [82]

---

[78] Lincoln Electric Co. v. Com'r, 176 F.2d 815 (6th Cir. 1949), *cert. denied*, 338 U.S. 949 (1950). *Cf.* Botany Worsted Mills v. United States, *supra* note 66; Com'r v. Flowers, 326 U.S. 465 (1946); Limericks, Inc. v. Com'r, 165 F.2d 483 (5th Cir. 1948). See also Lincoln Electric Co. Employees Profit-Sharing Trust v. Com'r, 190 F.2d 326 (6th Cir. 1951), *reversing* 14 T.C. 598 (1950). As to the general concept of ordinary and necessary expenditures, see Deputy v. du Pont, 308 U.S. 488 (1940).

[79] See BERLE AND MEANS, THE MODERN CORPORATION AND PRIVATE PROPERTY 342–43, 350 (1932); O'LEARY, CORPORATE ENTERPRISE IN MODERN ECONOMIC LIFE 37 (1933). See also Chapter 1, note 86.

[80] See WORMSER, FRANKENSTEIN, INCORPORATED 115–23 (1931); REIS, FALSE SECURITY 2–23 (1937). See also the discussion of the bonus problem in *Bureaucracy and Trusteeship in Large Corporations* (TNEC Monograph 11, 1940), at 90, 91, 114, 115.

[81] See Chapter 3, text to notes 5 ff.

[82] There is some evidence that bonus-paying companies had a somewhat smaller decline in earnings in the 1928–32 period than did non-bonus-paying companies. See

Be that as it may, prevailing business opinion awards to management credit for earnings, however produced, and management is likely to demand a share.[83]

There is no doubt that a change of executives can make all the difference between a surplus and a deficit for an individual enterprise. Real managerial ability is something worth paying for and paying for well, even though the executive may in fact be receiving a portion of an earnings increase due rather to general business conditions (or to government contracts awarded under a defense program) than to his own efforts.[84] If an attempt is made to limit the executive to a share of those profits which he himself has helped to produce, the discussion in the preceding chapter indicates the variety of ways in which contractual limitations may be imposed.

We have seen that incentive compensation arrangements may offer a temptation to set up systems of accounting which will show an unduly high margin of profit, and methods of computation which will enlarge the bonus, and may lead to the adoption of corporate policies which will increase current profits at the expense of the company's future. Contracts under which executives are paid on the basis of profits, without any limitation on total amounts payable or any provision for the prior payment of dividends, place a premium on increasing the gross profits of the company by any possible means.[85] We have discussed certain provisions which may protect stockholders under these circumstances,[86] but in the last analysis it is the honesty

---

BAKER, EXECUTIVE SALARIES AND BONUS PLANS, 40–41, 44, 69, 107 (1938). But it seems doubtful that any significant trend is shown. For views as to the effectiveness of profit participation in creating extra profits, see Chapter 3, note 4.

[83] See Chapter 1, text to notes 85 and 86. It has been suggested that even when compensation to management is confined to payment of large flat salaries, these rewards "should probably be looked upon as a form of commuted profits. . . ." O'LEARY, op. cit. supra note 79, at 29. See also Taussig and Barker, American Corporations and Their Executives, 40 Q.J. ECON. 1, 40 (1925); AMERICAN MANAGEMENT ASSOCIATION, EXECUTIVE COMPENSATION SURVEY 1950–51, especially pp. 24–25.

[84] BAKER, op. cit. supra note 82, at 227, lists numerous causes for increases in earnings beyond the control of management. See also O'LEARY, op. cit. supra note 79, at 36; KENNEDY, DIVIDENDS TO PAY 114–35 (1939). For a contrary view, see PATTON, MEN, MONEY AND MOTIVATION 38 ff. (1961). Consult Madden, A Yardstick for Executive Incentive Plans, 9 NICB MGMT. REC. 393 (1947), for suggestions as to measuring executives' contribution to successful management at various levels.

[85] See Raynolds v. Diamond Mills Paper Co., 69 N.J. Eq. 299, 315, 316, 60 Atl. 941, 948 (1905); Berendt v. Bethlehem Steel Corp., 108 N.J. Eq. 148, 149, 154 Atl. 321 (1931); cf. Summers, A Comparison of the Rates of Earnings of Large-Scale and Small-Scale Industries, 46 Q.J. ECON. 465, 479 (1932); Livermore, The Success of Industrial Mergers, 50 Q.J. ECON. 68 (1935); The Relative Efficiency of Large, Medium-Sized and Small Business (TNEC Monograph 13, 1941).

[86] See Chapter 3, text to notes 52 ff.

and diligence of the board of directors upon which reliance must chiefly be placed.

The existence, particularly in the post-1929 period, of a substantial public sentiment against the use of bonus arrangements cannot be denied. Part of this sentiment is undoubtedly due to the feeling that corporation executives are already sufficiently well paid, and that the development of the company's earning power is exactly the thing for which they receive salaries. Anything additional, it is felt, is in the nature of a gratuity or windfall.

Another reason for this attitude perhaps lies in the fact that we customarily think of profit-sharing as being coupled with responsibility for losses. A partnership, after all, is not a one-sided arrangement; profits are shared, but so are the risks of the enterprise. The executive's bonus arrangement looks very much like an attempt to obtain all the advantages of a partnership without its disadvantages. A parallel is to be found in the law's treatment of hybrid securities: if we try to give a bondholder voting rights and a share in the profits, or if we try to give a stockholder a mortgage on the assets in order to secure his stock investment, our efforts are not likely to meet with much success.[87] Profits, most of us are still inclined to feel, should go to those who risk their capital and subject themselves to the possibility of standing a loss. The answer can, of course, be made that the executive is risking his own talents and earning power. Technically, also, the mere fact that an employee takes part of his wages in the form of a share of the profits of the enterprise will not of itself make him a partner.[88] Nevertheless, this underlying feeling persists, and constitutes one of the reasons why incentive compensation arrangements must be carefully and fairly drawn with both the interests of stockholders and good public relations at all times in mind.

Protection of the corporation and its stockholders will often result also from the executive's own self-interest. Today, the executive of at least our larger corporations will usually identify his future with that of the corporation which employs him. He may be a beneficiary of one or more plans conferring benefits in the event of his death or retirement which are far more substantial than those he would receive if he should leave the corporation's employ prior to that time. He may be the owner of a stock interest acquired under a stock bonus

---

[87] See Stephenson v. Go-Gas Co., 268 N.Y. 372, 380, 197 N.E. 317, 320 (1935); Uhlman, *The Law of Hybrid Securities*, 23 WASH. U.L.Q. 182 (1938); Comment, 45 YALE L.J. 907 (1936).

[88] See UNIFORM PARTNERSHIP ACT, § 7(4a).

or stock option or stock purchase plan. But whether or not he is the holder of stock, his interests are in many respects similar to those of a stockholder.[89] Incentive compensation arrangements properly conceived can still further identify his interests with those of the stockholders.

[89] Balderson, *Profit Sharing for Employees and Executives,* 9 NICB MGMT. REC. 388 *et seq.* (1947).

CHAPTER 5

DEFERRED COMPENSATION:
THE CONTRACT AND THE EXECUTIVE'S TAX

THE CONTRACT

The deferred compensation plan, upon an individual or group basis, constitutes a usual method of compensating the executive, and most large companies today have such plans in effect in one form or another.[1] Plans of this nature have in common a provision for payments to the executive to begin in the future in consideration chiefly of services rendered or to be rendered prior to commencement of the future payments. Group pension, profit-sharing, and thrift plans, as well as insurance and stock option and stock purchase plans, all have aspects of deferred compensation, and even the annual year-end bonus is a deferred payment for past services. In this chapter, we are primarily concerned with an unsecured, unfunded obligation of the corporate employer to make payments to the executive over a period of time in the future. Such an obligation may arise as the result of an individual arrangement with an executive or a plan for a group of executives.

[1] Lasser and Rothschild, *Deferred Compensation for Executives,* 33 HARV. BUS. REV. 89 (Jan.–Feb., 1955), (estimating that out of 1,087 companies with stock listed on the New York Stock Exchange as of July 31, 1954, over 900 had in effect some form of arrangement for deferred benefits to designated executives individually or as a group). *Cf.* Patton, *Annual Report on Executive Compensation,* 36 HARV. BUS. REV. 129, 131 (Sept.–Oct., 1958) (stating that of some 600 companies listed on major stock exchanges covering major fields of business, 33% employed some form of deferred compensation in compensating top executives during the year 1957 as against 26% in 1956 and 17% in 1955; 90% had pension plans, 60% had granted stock options, 11% had deferred profit-sharing plans and 5%, principally in the oil industry, had savings or thrift plans which included executives). A similar survey for 1955 showed that 50% of all department stores surveyed provided deferred compensation for their executives, and that group or individual deferred compensation arrangements were also important in steel, textile, and rubber industries; as to company size, 40% of the large companies were found to have deferred compensation arrangements for executives. Patton, *Annual Report on Executive Compensation,* 34 HARV. BUS. REV. 124, 126 (Nov.–Dec., 1956). Consult Rosensteel, *Executive Compensation: A Balanced Program,* 45 MGMT. REV. 388, 396 (1956) (15% of publicly held corporations make use of deferred compensation in paying top executives). The discrepancy in percentage estimates among the surveys may arise from differences in the type of arrangements considered within the category of deferred compensation.

In considering each type of arrangement, we must keep in mind the purpose of the arrangement. The deferred benefit type of plan antedates the current high income tax.[2] Many of such plans have been adopted without reference to tax considerations and have business justification independent of tax considerations.[3] On the other hand, the tax factor, as in many other fields, has played an important and often decisive role.[4] Tax problems are discussed later. It is sufficient to say here that a primary tax objective is to defer the executive's receipt of benefits and his payment of income tax thereon until a time when it is expected that he will have less income and, with a lower tax bracket, be permitted to retain a greater share of the benefits than if such benefits were paid currently. A corollary tax objective is to preserve the company's tax deduction for its payments to the executive, at least to the extent that the deduction will be available when the payments are actually made.

In the preparation of such contracts, the draftsman should not lose sight of corporate problems, the need of adequate consideration for future payments, and other matters discussed in the chapter that follows.

Amount and Method of Payment. A typical contract might provide:

• 3. For all services to be rendered by him in any capacity hereunder, the Company agrees to pay the executive (a) so long as he shall be employed hereunder, a fixed salary at the rate of $...... per annum, payable in equal monthly instalments at the end of each month; and (b) upon the termination of his employment, except as otherwise provided and subject to the conditions set forth in paragraph 7 below,

---

[2] Thus, the du Pont Bonus Plan has been in existence in one form or another since 1904—nine years before a federal income tax was authorized by constitutional amendment.

[3] See Lasser and Rothschild, *supra* note 1, at 94.

[4] Schulman, *Effect of Taxation on Methods of Remuneration for Personal Services,* and Biegel, *Equity of Tax Treatment of Retirement Allowances,* in Joint Committee on the Economic Report, *Tax Policy for Economic Growth and Stability,* 84th Cong., 1st Sess., 167, 763 (1955). See also Holzschaeber, *Tax Thoughts on Deferred Compensation Plans,* 26 N.Y. CERT. PUB. ACCT. 41 (1956); Freedman, *A Restatement of Tax Incentives in Compensating High-Salaried Executives,* 4 RUTGERS L. REV. 617 (1950). Consult also, for example, Cox, *Aspects of the du Pont Bonus Program,* 17 INST. FED. TAX. 905, 927 ff. (1959). For a bibliography of articles on deferred compensation that have been published as part of the proceedings of the Annual Institute on Federal Taxation of New York University, see Fillman, *Ford Motor Company Employee Benefit Plan,* 17 INST. FED. TAX. 883, 893, n. 20 (1959). Consult the articles assembled and edited by SELLIN, TAXATION OF DEFERRED EMPLOYEE AND EXECUTIVE COMPENSATION (1960); TAX MANAGEMENT PORTFOLIO FOR EXECUTIVES, LEFEVRE, DEFERRED COMPENSATION ARRANGEMENTS (1960).

contingent compensation equal to the sum of $. . . . . . for each period of twelve (12) months that the Executive shall have been employed hereunder, each such sum, if and to the extent payable, to be paid in 120 equal monthly instalments at the end of each month commencing in January of the calendar year next following termination of the Executive's employment.

This provision represents a readily apparent method of providing for payment in the future of a portion of the stipulated annual remuneration for current services. Although a number of companies have adopted this direct approach,[5] a more popular method in the past has been a provision separate from the compensation clause under which the executive, as part of his employment contract, is engaged for a stipulated annual sum to render consultative and advisory services for a period of years following termination of his active employment.[6] The latter type of provision is not so directly related to current services in the employment contract itself, but in most cases the difference has been one of form rather than substance since, irrespective of the terms of the contract, the payments following termination of employment are based chiefly on services rendered and to be rendered during active or full-time employment rather than on services to be rendered thereafter, the value of which may be problematical. In fact, if the contract bases future payments entirely or too largely on services following termination of active employment, a question may arise as to whether such future payments are supported by adequate consideration.[7]

The clause set forth above bases the amount of future compensation on years of service.[8] It is more usual to fix the specific annual

[5] See, e.g., AMERICAN HOME PRODUCTS, App. OO; LERNER STORES, App. F, § II(b); GENERAL BAKING, App. H.; CASEY AND ROTHSCHILD, PAY CONTRACTS WITH KEY MEN (1953) (hereafter referred to as CASEY AND ROTHSCHILD), Ex. 87 (White Motor Co. and Robert F. Black), Ex. 88 (Hiram Walker-Gooderham & Worts, Ltd. and Howard R. Walton).

[6] See CHRYSLER, App. HH; FEDERATED, App. NN.

[7] Consult Fidanque v. American Maracaibo Co., 33 Del. Ch. 262, 92 A.2d 311 (1952); Chapter 6, text to notes 91 ff. and, in particular, note 92. A provision requiring postemployment services is no longer so popular, since it may jeopardize social security benefits and capital gains treatment of lump-sum payments under pension and profit-sharing plans. See Chapter 6, text to notes 99, 111.

[8] GOODYEAR, App. JJ. See AMERICAN HOME PRODUCTS, App. OO and that company's Proxy Statement dated Mar. 27, 1950, p. 4 (chairman and president, upon leaving employment, to receive respectively $15,000 and $12,500 a year for as many years as each has been employed). Consult the plan of Gimbel Bros. Inc., outlined in Allison, *Incentive Compensation Plans*, FORTUNE, May 1949, p. 143, at p. 144; see CASEY AND ROTHSCHILD, Ex. 108. *Cf.* MANUFACTURERS TRUST, App. PP ($25,000 for each year of full-time and of consulting employment).

payment that the company will be required to make,[9] or it may be provided that the future payment shall be a percentage of the salary that is being paid prior to retirement.[10] As an alternative to a flat sum, the future payments may be based on a share of the company's current profits during employment,[11] a method more popular in group plans for executives.[12] When the future payments are in consideration of consultative or advisory services, the amount may be reduced if the executive is unable to perform such services because of disability, but such a provision is rare; [13] it is more usual to provide that the payments will not be reduced if the executive is unable to perform the services required following termination of employment.[14] Future payments, though fixed in amount, may be made subject to adjustment to reflect inflation.[15]

[9] E.g., FEDERATED, App. NN; CASEY AND ROTHSCHILD, Ex. 87 (White Motor Co. and Robert F. Black—monthly payments).

[10] CASEY AND ROTHSCHILD, Ex. 86 (American Shipbuilding Corp. and W. H. Gerhauser) ; Vanadium Corp. of America, Proxy Statement dated Mar. 25, 1959, p. 27 (30% of annual rate of regular compensation paid prior to retirement) ; William M. Wrigley, Jr. Co., Proxy Statement dated Mar. 20, 1959, p. 2 (monthly retirement pay of $\frac{1}{12}$ of 1% of yearly salary at age 65 and in excess of $10,000). The deferred compensation plan of Standard Oil Company of California was intended to provide executives with amounts which, when added to their retirement annuities, would bring the total amount received through the company to 50% of salary at time of retirement. See CASEY AND ROTHSCHILD, Ex. 93.

[11] See CASEY AND ROTHSCHILD, Ex. 105 (Lerner Stores Corp. and Russell N. Levin—reduction of payments under deferred compensation contract to employee's widow and children, if consolidated earnings under $3,000,000), and cf. Ex. 104 (payments subject to unilateral cancellation if company fails to earn operating profit for two preceding years). Cf. FEDERATED, App. DD; TEXAS, App. II (deferred compensation payable in stock).

[12] E.g., GENERAL ELECTRIC, App. AA. See Chapter 6, text to notes 47 ff.

[13] For examples, see Kuhn v. United States, 258 F.2d 840 (3d Cir. 1958), reversing 157 F. Supp. 331 (D. N.J. 1958) (Kuhn, a retired vice-president of Botany Mills, Inc., agreed to serve the company in an advisory capacity for $25,000, the payments to "be continued during the lifetime of Kuhn but at the reduced rate of $15,000 per annum, if Kuhn is unable to perform the [advisory] services . . . because of permanent ailment and incapacity if such condition is attested by competent medical certificate submitted to the corporation") ; TEXAS, App. II (deferred compensation payments to cease in the event of total disability) ; CASEY AND ROTHSCHILD, Ex. 111 (Ward Baking Co. and Faris R. Russell—providing for a reduction in payments on disability).

[14] See LERNER STORES, App. F; CASEY AND ROTHSCHILD, Ex. 112 (Mojud Hosiery Co. and John K. Voehringer) ; Ex. 88 (Hiram Walker–Gooderham & Worts, Ltd. and Howard R. Walton).

[15] See DEVOE AND RAYNOLDS, App. L; CASEY AND ROTHSCHILD, Ex. 106 (Continental Oil Co. and Leonard F. McCollum—inflation adjustment in salary up to $50,000 based on "All Commodities" index of Bureau of Labor Statistics). Protection against inflation may be sought through a provision increasing deferred pay as active executives receive salary increases. See CASEY AND ROTHSCHILD, at 119 (*Foote Brothers Gear Co.*).

The effect of inflation on dollar content of future payments may be somewhat mitigated if such payments are made in common stock of the company rather than in cash,[16] but this form of payment is more frequently found in group plans than under individual arrangements.[17]

The payments contemplated by a deferred compensation arrangement will usually commence following termination of employment, since a primary purpose of such arrangements is to provide the executive with income when he is no longer earning a salary as a full-time employee.[18] Most frequently, the annual instalments will extend over a ten-year period,[19] but if the total is expected to be relatively small, it may be payable over perhaps five or six years.[20] Larger amounts have been made payable over fifteen to twenty years.[21] In the case particularly of chief executives, some contracts provide, in lieu of a fixed period, that the payments shall continue for the life of the executive,[22] sometimes with provision for a lesser annual payment to his widow during her life, if she survives the executive.[23] Or provi-

[16] See TEXAS, App. II.

[17] See TEXAS, App. KK; and Chapter 6, text to notes 47 ff.

[18] See Lasser and Rothschild, *supra* note 1, at 96; Patton, *Executive Compensation: Tax Gimmicks v. Incentives*, 31 HARV. BUS. REV. 113 (1953); Blake, *Current Trends in Fringe Benefits*, 106 J. ACCOUNTANCY 33 (1958). The contract may preclude payment of deferred compensation if and when outside earnings of retired executives exceed designated amounts. See LERNER STORES, App. F; FEDERATED, App. NN; CASEY AND ROTHSCHILD, Ex. 102 (Gimbel Bros.), and Ex. 103 (Lerner Stores Corp. and Russell N. Levin). For a group plan expressing this purpose see TEXAS, App. KK, conditioning the maturity of the deferred compensation payments upon retirement for age or disability. A purpose of such provision may be to impose a condition so as to avoid immediate tax. See text to note 124, *infra*.

[19] CASEY AND ROTHSCHILD, Ex. 86 (American Shipbuilding Corp. and W. H. Gerhauser), and Ex. 85 (Endicott-Johnson Corp. and Charles F. Johnson).

[20] See TEXAS, App. II (five years); CASEY AND ROTHSCHILD, Ex. 87 (White Motor Co. and Robert F. Black—$1,500 per month for six years).

[21] The General Electric Incentive Compensation Plan (App. AA) originally provided for ten to fifteen years of payments, depending on the year in which employment terminated. It was subsequently amended to provide for payments of from fifteen to twenty years. The pay-out period under the Additional Compensation Plan of American Smelting and Refining Company was similarly extended.

[22] CHRYSLER, App. HH; FEDERATED, App. NN; CASEY AND ROTHSCHILD, Ex. 91 (North American Co. and Herbert C. Freeman).

[23] E.g., CASEY AND ROTHSCHILD, Ex. 109 (Noma Electric Co. and Henry Sadacca—same payments to widow for five years), Ex. 115 (Safeway Stores, Inc. and L. A. Warren—surviving widow to receive for life one-half of amount paid to her husband as deferred compensation), Ex. 110 [American Maracaibo Co. and Frederick R. Ryan—one-fifth of payments to widow for five years, or until earlier death but held, on the facts, to be an invalid gift of corporate assets because paid for past services in Fidanque v. American Maracaibo Co., 33 Del. Ch. 262, 92 A.2d 311 (1952)], but *cf.* Ex. 86 (American Shipbuilding Corp. and W. H. Gerhauser—payments to continue for named widow's life though deferred payments to executive limited to ten-year period). *Cf.* Moore v. Keystone Macaroni Mfg. Co., 370 Pa. 172, 87 A.2d 295 (1952).

sion may be made for payment of an aggregate sum, in instalments or otherwise, on the death of the executive to his estate or beneficiaries whom he designates.[24] The sum thus to be paid is often fixed as the total of the remaining payments that the executive would have received had he lived.[25]

Provisions of this nature make such future payments similar to pensions and annuities. Indeed, such arrangements may be indistinguishable in substance from the unfunded pension plan that was once general, and which is still used in a few industries and by smaller companies, which cannot afford a funded pension plan.[26] In fact, deferred compensation is often intended to substitute for or to supplement pensions deemed inadequate, where it would be too expensive to provide adequate pensions as part of a general pension plan.[27] Thus, it is not unusual for the arrangement to stipulate that the executive receiving such compensation shall not participate in the company's pension plan,[28] or, if he does so participate, that his compensation following retirement shall be reduced in amount for any year in which, when added to the amount received under the pension or

[24] CASEY AND ROTHSCHILD, Ex. 108 (Gimbel Bros.—fifteen annual instalments payable to person designated under executive's will or to the representative of his estate), Ex. 88 (Hiram Walker-Gooderham & Worts, Ltd. and Howard R. Walton —transfer of annuity, except right to claim surrender value, to designated representative, but only if executive dies within first ten years of deferred compensation period). See LERNER STORES, App. F (unpaid instalments of deferred compensation to become due). See WASHINGTON AND ROTHSCHILD, COMPENSATING THE CORPORATE EXECUTIVE (rev. ed. 1951) App. HH (sum equal to ¼ of annual deferred compensation instalment for each year of full service payable to estate representative in three equal annual instalments).

[25] See CASEY AND ROTHSCHILD, Ex. 85 (Endicott-Johnson Corp. and Charles F. Johnson—on death of executive during ten-year period of receipt of deferred compensation, unpaid instalments continue until paid, or their present value commuted on the basis of a compounded interest rate of 2¾% is payable in a lump sum).

[26] E.g., CASEY AND ROTHSCHILD, Ex. 94 (Brown Shoe Co.—provision for payment by company of life annuities to executives with 36 to 50 years of service and having salaries of from $15,000 to $40,000 per annum).

[27] See Lasser and Rothschild, *supra* note 1, at 100; Rosensteel, *supra* note 1, at 397; Young, *Individual Deferred Compensation,* 95 TRUSTS AND ESTATES 705 (1956). Deferred group profit-sharing plans are often used as substitutes for pension plans by smaller enterprises because they are believed to entail less of a fixed commitment. Lurie, *Plastic Contributions for Pensions and Profit-Sharing,* 67 YALE L.J. 1003 (1958). See also CASEY AND ROTHSCHILD, Ex. 91 (North American Co. and Herbert C. Freeman—executive entitled to annuity of $10,417 per year under pension plan granted "supplemental pension" of $15,000 upon future retirement as chairman of the executive committee).

[28] *Cf.* CASEY AND ROTHSCHILD, Ex. 114 (Lerner Stores Corp. and Russell N. Levin—all benefits under retirement plan to be deducted from deferred compensation payments, but deduction for beneficiaries limited to 11³⁄₁₀%); AMERICAN TOBACCO, App. U, § 8 (incentive compensation award to be reduced by annual credits under profit-sharing plan).

retirement plans, it exceeds a stated annual total.[29] A tie-in of the deferred compensation agreement with the pension plan in this manner could conceivably be held to render the contract a part of the pension plan and hence disqualify the pension plan under Section 401 of the Internal Revenue Code because of discrimination in favor of the executive with whom the contract is made. However, no reported instance has been found in which the Treasury Department has taken this position and, in at least one private ruling, the Commissioner of Internal Revenue has held to the contrary.[30]

Conditions As To Payment. Another provision of our typical contract might be:

• 7. The contingent compensation provided for in paragraph 3(b) above shall be payable if and when but not unless:

    (a) The employment of the Executive shall have been terminated

        (i) by retirement of the Executive in accordance with any provision of the Employees' Retirement Plan of the Corporation, as in effect at the time of such retirement; or

       (ii) by the death or disability of the Executive; or

      (iii) by the Corporation for any reason other than dishonesty or wrongful conduct on the part of the Executive; or

      (iv) as the result of circumstances not deemed by the Board of Directors of the Corporation in its sole judgment to be prejudicial to the interests of the Corporation; and

    (b) The Executive shall, if and as long as such contingent compensation shall be paid and without additional compensation, fee, or other payment by the Corporation (other than payment or reimbursement of reasonable actual out-of-pocket travel and other disbursements)

        (i) render such consulting and advisory services as the Corporation may from time to time reasonably request, having in mind the Executive's health, residence, and personal circumstances, in connection with any matter on which the Executive was working at the time of the termination of his employment or with

---

[29] *Cf.* Plan of Standard Oil Company of California, *supra* note 10; AMERICAN TOBACCO, App. U, § 8. On the other hand, a deferred compensation agreement may provide that it shall not affect the executive's pension rights. *Cf.* MANUFACTURERS TRUST, App. PP.

[30] Private Ruling letter to J. K. Lasser and Co., dated May 12, 1952.

respect to which the Executive might be expected to have special competence by reason of his former employment by the Corporation or otherwise;

(ii) continue to serve on the Board of Directors of the Corporation if elected, provided that the Executive shall not be under obligation to serve on any committee of the Board;

(iii) refrain, after the expiration of a period of thirty (30) days from the mailing to him of written notice by the Secretary of the Corporation of a direction to do so, from engaging in the operation or management of a business, whether as owner, stockholder, partner, officer, employee or otherwise, which at the time of the termination of the Executive's employment shall be in competition with the Corporation or any of its subsidiaries, provided that ownership as an investor of not more than five per cent (5%) of the outstanding shares of stock of any company listed on a national securities exchange or having at least one hundred (100) shareholders shall not in itself constitute a violation of these provisions;

(iv) refrain from disclosing to unauthorized persons information relative to the business of the Corporation or any of its subsidiaries which he shall have reason to believe is confidential; and

(v) refrain from otherwise acting or conducting himself in a manner which he shall have reason to believe is inimical or contrary to the best interests of the Corporation.

In the event that the Executive shall fail to comply with any provision of this paragraph 7(b) the Corporation's obligation to make any further payment of the contingent compensation provided for in paragraph 3(b) above shall forthwith terminate, but the Executive shall not have any obligation to repay to the Corporation any payments theretofore made to him.

In the clause set forth above, the provisions relating to deferred compensation are simply made conditions to the receipt of deferred compensation. Such conditions are sometimes in the form of agreements by the executive; if they are so worded, the executive's failure to observe his agreement may not only terminate his right to future payment but subject him to a claim for damages as well.

The provisions conditioning receipt of the deferred payments in the clause under consideration fall into two categories: a pre-retirement set of conditions based on continuous employment until retirement without either voluntary resignation by the executive or discharge for cause by the company, and a post-retirement set of conditions based on requirements during the period in which the payments are being received by the executive. General agreement exists as to the desirability of the first set of conditions, both as a corporate and as a tax matter. With regard to the second set of conditions, a respectable body of opinion holds that such conditions are unnecessary and, more often than not, meaningless and undesirable.[31]

The requirement that the executive render consultative and advisory services [32] may be held to continue the employment relationship notwithstanding formal retirement under the company's pension plan,[33] to the prejudice of the executive and at least the bookkeeping

---

[31] Schulman, *supra* note 4, at 173; Rudick, *Compensation of Executives Under the 1954 Code,* 33 TAXES 7 (1955): "Even where they [future payments] are non-forfeitable, it is almost equally clear that he (the executive) will not be taxed until the maturity of the payment." See Oreste Casale, 26 T.C. 1020, 1026 (1956), *rev'd on other grounds,* 247 F.2d 440 (2d Cir. 1957); Drucker, *Keep the Carrot Dangling,* FORTUNE, Oct. 1949, p. 81, decrying deferred compensation as a threat to executive mobility. Consult Chapter 6, text to note 116.

[32] See Young, *supra* note 27. For individual examples, see TEXAS, App. II ("faithfully to serve the Company in an advisory and consulting capacity and will render advice and assistance to the Company in connection with its business affairs and with respect to any proposed legislation or litigation affecting the Company's interest"); FEDERATED, App. NN, ¶ 9; CASEY AND ROTHSCHILD, Ex. 86 (American Shipbuilding Corp. and W. H. Gerhauser—"give and devote to the Company the full benefit of his advice, skill, knowledge and counsel"), Ex. 88 (Hiram Walker-Gooderham & Worts, Ltd. and Howard R. Walton—during the "secondary term of employment" executive agrees to serve on Board of Directors, if elected, and to attend its meetings), also Exs. 85, 87, 89, and 97; *cf.* Exs. 96 and 98 (expressly barring the return to full-time duty). For deferred compensation agreements which do not require the rendering of consultative and advisory services, see LERNER STORES, App. F and CASEY AND ROTHSCHILD, Ex. 91 (North American Co. and Herbert C. Freeman). It should be pointed out that all of these contracts were executed before Revenue Ruling 60–31, discussed in the text to notes 52 and 115 *infra.*

[33] A continued employment relationship during the term of deferred compensation is often implied in the language used in the agreement. E.g., CASEY AND ROTHSCHILD, Ex. 88 (Hiram Walker-Gooderham & Worts, Ltd. and Howard R. Walton—speaking of termination of the executive's employment during the secondary term thereof); MANUFACTURERS TRUST, App. PP (executive eligible for employee benefits during advisory period). *Cf.* General American Transportation Co., Proxy Statement dated Mar. 27, 1959 (directors and officers resign as such after age 65 but remain in company's employ at reduced annual compensation). On the other hand, some contracts expressly deny that the deferred compensation payments create an employment relationship. CASEY AND ROTHSCHILD, Ex. 91 (North Ameri-

annoyance of the company.[34] A requirement that the executive simply hold himself available for services, with a provision that he receive additional payment for such services as he may actually render, may substantiate an argument that the provision is an empty one.[35] Also, a requirement that consultative and advisory services be rendered may, in the hands of an unfriendly board, bring into jeopardy the executive's continued right to payments.

The significance of an agreement not to compete [36] must be determined by reference to conditions in the industry and the position of the executive giving the agreement. In certain situations such agreements undoubtedly have real value.[37] To the extent that such an

can Co. and Herbert C. Freeman). See also GOODYEAR, App. JJ (defining cessation of employment as the termination of full-time employment relationship).

For adverse effect on tax treatment of pension, see Chapter 6, text to note 111.

[34] See Chapter 6, text to note 111.

[35] However: "They also serve who only stand and wait." Milton, "On His Blindness," line 14, cited in Miller, *Executive Estate Planning*, 17 INST. FED. TAX. 1171, 1194 (1959).

[36] For examples of such agreements, see FEDERATED, App. NN (barring Mr. Lazarus from being an officer, director, or employee or having an economic interest, by way of loans, stockholdings, or in any other form of more than $500,000 in a competing business, defined as one substantially similar to the whole or any substantial part of the business now or at the end of the period of active service conducted by the employer or any of its subsidiaries and affiliates within 25 miles of the outer limits of any city where at the time of the executive's engaging in such competing business, the employer, or any of its subsidiaries or affiliates are conducting a retail store). For a similar provision, see the contract between Lerner Stores Corp. and Russel N. Levin, CASEY AND ROTHSCHILD, Ex. 101. Other contracts for deferred compensation have simpler clauses, e.g., CASEY AND ROTHSCHILD, Ex. 87 (White Motor Co. and Robert F. Black—prohibiting "services to any other motor vehicle company or to any business which competes with" the White Motor Company), Ex. 89 (General Baking Co. and George L. Morrison—"not to engage or have any financial interest in any business competing with or of a character similar to the business conducted by" the Company), Ex. 94 (Brown Shoe Co.— executive will neither directly nor indirectly engage for five years in any business which is in competition with that conducted by the Company), and Ex. 100 (Ekco Products Co. and Arthur Keating—prohibiting engaging in a competing business but permitting Mr. Keating to hold a minority interest therein upon disclosure to Ekco's Board of Directors, with Mr. Keating also permitted to continue as an officer and director of a named corporation). For a broader clause barring the executive from any business activity (except as the administration of his personal investments may require), unless the business is non-competing and the activity limited to service as a director and approved by the Company's Board, see the contract between Ward Baking Co. and Faris R. Russell, CASEY AND ROTHSCHILD, Ex. 99.

[37] Consult John Roane, Inc. v. Tweed, 33 Del. Ch. 4, 89 A.2d 548, 41 A.L.R.2d 1 (1952) (covenant not to compete made by manager of insurance agency branch office enforced so as to give former employer adequate protection). Cases involving managerial personnel are collected in Annotation, 41 A.L.R.2d 15, 96–98. Only one of these cases—Wahlgren v. Bausch & Lomb Optical Co., 68 F.2d 660 (7th Cir. 1934), *cert. denied,* 292 U.S. 639, *rehearing denied,* 292 U.S. 615 (1934)— appears

agreement has value, thought should be given to whether the agreement not to compete may be invalid as in restraint of trade.[38]

To be fully effective, a condition reducing or eliminating the future payments for any year in which the executive's income exceeds a stated sum [39] may require provisions for verifying his income and possibly examining his income tax returns—stipulations which the executive may find offensive. A condition reducing or eliminating payments in the absence of company profits in a given figure [40] should properly involve elaborate provisions and definitions for the determination of profits under manifold and varying circumstances over the long period of time contemplated. Such provisions may be unacceptable to an executive unwilling to have his livelihood following retirement depend on the fortunes of a company years after he has severed connections with it.

On the other hand, conditions tailored to the individual case may be logical and proper, to the real advantage of the company and without exposing the executive to unfair risk. Thus, a company engaged in an industry in which confidential methods and processes are important might properly ask executives familiar with such methods and processes to continue to keep them confidential and might make future payments after retirement contingent on non-disclosure.[41] A requirement that an engineer, physicist, or other technician respon-

---

to involve a covenant not to compete entered into by a top-level executive; the case did not involve a deferred compensation agreement. See note 38 *infra*.

[38] See WILLISTON, CONTRACTS, § 1643 (rev. ed. 1937), and cases cited *supra* note 37. Consult Chapter 2, text to notes 30 and 31. Considerations as to the scope of the restraint in regard to time and place and the threat of depriving an employee of his livelihood [see May v. Young, 125 Conn. 1, 2 A.2d 385, 119 A.L.R. 1445 (1938)] may not have application to the usual deferred compensation agreement, under which the payments of deferred compensation commence on retirement or disability and continue for an extended period, for the executive is usually given a livelihood by the very agreement which imposes the restraint. Nor may such considerations apply to the retired executive who receives deferred compensation since the public is not being deprived of his active services to the same extent as in the case of a younger man.

[39] See FEDERATED, App. NN (deferred compensation need not be paid in any year in which executive's income from permitted employment or a proprietary interest in business exceeds $55,000) ; CASEY AND ROTHSCHILD, Ex. 103 (Lerner Stores Corp. and Russell N. Levin—limit set at $25,000), and Ex. 102 (Gimbel Bros.—executive's earnings cannot exceed 75% of base salary).

[40] E.g., CASEY AND ROTHSCHILD, Ex. 86 (American Shipbuilding Corp. and W. H. Gerhauser—enabling the company to reduce or cancel deferred compensation payments for any year if, in the two preceding years, the company has failed to earn an operating profit), and Ex. 105 (Lerner Stores Corp. and Russell N. Levin—conditioning continuing payments to widow or children of executive on the company's having in the preceding fiscal year before-tax earnings of $3,000,000).

[41] *Cf.* AMERICAN CYANAMID, App. K (non-disclosure clauses in employment contracts).

sible for an invention is to continue to advise concerning its possible improvement, to assist in obtaining further patents, and to defend those already obtained could be a logical condition to payments following termination of employment. An executive of a real estate company could well be asked, as a condition to receiving deferred payments, to release any and all right to the commissions which he might otherwise claim from the company after retirement. A top executive who has been serving on the board of directors might be asked to continue to serve on the board and its committees without fee or other compensation while he is being paid deferred benefits.[42] To the extent that the continued payment of deferred compensation is based on conditions which are logical and proper, conservative corporate and tax thinking favor such conditions.

Finally, the right to receive deferred payments may be made non-assignable (except in the event of death),[43] a provision which (it has been thought) may deprive the right of any ascertainable value for tax purposes.[44] The point may be open to question,[45] but a prohibition against assignment is obviously in the interests of the company, which would not wish to have corporate obligations of this nature in the hands of outsiders.

TAX PROBLEMS

The Income Tax Treatment of the Executive. As we have just seen, deferred compensation may be contingent upon continued employment for a prescribed period. When this is the case, possible loss of a bonus as the result of prior termination of employment has been held to prevent taxability of the deferred bonus until the bonus has been fully "earned out." *James D. Mooney*[46] was a Tax Court decision involving the General Motors Bonus Plan, in accordance with which bonuses declared in one year were paid in instalments

[42] CASEY AND ROTHSCHILD, Ex. 87 (White Motor Co. and Robert F. Black), and Ex. 88 (Hiram Walker-Gooderham & Worts, Ltd. and Howard R. Walton).

[43] See LERNER STORES, App. F, § 7 (assignable only with company's consent); CASEY AND ROTHSCHILD, Ex. 85 (Endicott-Johnson Corp. and Charles F. Johnson). As to non-assignability of rights under deferred compensation group plans, see FEDERATED, App. DD, § 7.3.

[44] See discussion of this point and authorities cited in Miller, *supra* note 35, at 1176, n. 13.

[45] Thus, on the economic benefit theory, hereafter discussed, an annuity has been held taxable to an employee even though the annuity was not assignable and had no cash surrender or market value. Renton K. Brodie, 1 T.C. 275 (1942); United States v. Drescher, 179 F.2d 863 (2d Cir. 1950), *cert. denied*, 340 U.S. 821 (1950).

[46] 9 T.C. 713 (1947).

over a four-year period.[47] The taxpayer there took the position that he was taxable on these bonus instalments only when he received them, and claimed specifically that the fourth instalment of his 1936 bonus, the third instalment of his 1937 bonus, and the second instalment of his 1938 bonus, all received in 1939, were subject to tax in 1939 rather than in the respective years in which the bonuses had been declared. The Tax Court sustained his position, holding upon the facts that the bonus was not earned solely in the year in which it had been declared, but over the entire four-year period in which it was being paid.[48] It pointed out that if the executive had left the company or had been dismissed before the end of the four-year period, he would have lost his right to the bonus to the extent that it had not been paid.[49] As a result of this and other provisions,[50] the Tax Court found that the bonus had not been paid solely for the one year of employment preceding the declaration of the bonus.

Uncertainty has arisen primarily when compensation has been fully earned by services during employment but payment has been deferred until some future time, such as termination of employment. The expectation of the executive who earned the compensation has been that he, as a cash-basis taxpayer, would be taxable on such compensation only in the year in which it was paid to him.[51] Whether his expectation was justified was a matter of uncertainty for many years. Finally, the Treasury Department clarified its position in a comprehensive Revenue Ruling dealing with deferred compensation arrangements,[52] a ruling regarded by tax practitioners as of unusual importance since it represents a definitive position, taken after much deliberation, on what had become a well-established corporate practice. Until this ruling, which will be discussed below, was issued, the advice of many tax practitioners had been that the executive could not safely assume that he would be taxed only on receipt of his deferred compensation unless his rights to such compensation following termination of employment were subject to post-employment

---

[47] For the present plan, see App. V.

[48] *Supra* note 46, at 718. The plan (¶ 6) required the remaining instalments to be "earned out" by "continuing service."

[49] *Ibid.* In effect, the Commissioner conceded that Mr. Mooney had not received title until 1939 to the stock which constituted the bonus award and could not be taxed thereon until then. *Id* at 719. Conversely, the taxpayer has no deductible loss if he fails to earn out the bonus. John L. Seymour, 14 T.C. 1111 (1950).

[50] *Supra* note 46, at 715–16.

[51] *Cf.* Freeman v. United States, 71 F.2d 969 (3d Cir. 1934), *cert. denied,* 293 U.S. 621 (1934); Jackson v. Smietanka, 272 Fed. 970 (7th Cir. 1921) (a leading case); consult MAGILL, TAXABLE INCOME 182, 186–87 (rev. ed. 1945).

[52] Rev. Rul. 60–31, 1960–1 CUM. BULL. 174.

conditions such as the rendition of consultative services or compliance with a covenant against competition with the employer company.

The basis of advice as to the necessity for such conditions was found in two legal concepts which have been invoked by the tax authorities to require the inclusion of certain amounts, prior to their actual receipt in cash, in the gross income of cash-basis taxpayers. These concepts are usually referred to as the *economic benefit doctrine* and the *constructive receipt doctrine*. The economic benefit doctrine deals with the question of *what,* beyond amounts received in cash, is taxable to a cash-basis taxpayer. The constructive receipt doctrine deals with *when* a taxable item must be included in the gross income of a cash-basis taxpayer.[53] Stated simply, the economic benefit doctrine is an application of the rule that a cash-basis taxpayer is taxable not only on the receipt of cash but also on the transfer to him of other property having a fair market value.[54] The constructive receipt doctrine imposes a tax on a cash-basis taxpayer as to an item which he has at his disposal, even though he has elected not to receive it.[55]

Analytically, the applicability of the economic benefit doctrine arises first: if what the taxpayer actually receives is a kind of property taxable to him on the cash basis, it is not necessary to consider whether he is in constructive receipt of income. It must be observed, however, that both the courts [56] and the tax authorities have tended

[53] See Note, *Contract Right Income to Cash Method Taxpayer Who Refused Cash Offer,* 58 MICH. L. REV. 480 (1960).

[54] See, generally, 2 MERTENS, LAW OF FEDERAL INCOME TAXATION (1955), Chapter 11; MAGILL, *op. cit. supra* note 51.

[55] A statement which is frequently quoted as an expression of this doctrine is that of Mr. Justice Holmes in Corliss v. Bowers, 281 U.S. 376, 378 (1930): "The income that is subject to a man's unfettered command and that he is free to enjoy at his own option may be taxed to him as his income, whether he sees fit to enjoy it or not." See, generally, MERTENS, *op. cit. supra* note 54, Chapter 10; Zarky, *Problems in Constructive Receipt and Deferral of Income,* 13 INST. FED. TAX. 53 (1955). The statement by the Treasury Department of the doctrine is set forth in Treas. Reg. § 1.451–2, (1957), quoted in text to footnote 79, *infra.* Cases indicating the scope of the doctrine are Loose v. United States, 74 F.2d 147 (8th Cir. 1934); Richards' Estate v. Com'r, 150 F.2d 837 (2d Cir. 1945); Weil v. Com'r, 173 F.2d 805 (2d Cir. 1949); Richard v. Hyland, 7 CCH TAX CT. MEM. 236 (1948), *aff'd,* Hyland v. Com'r, 175 F.2d 422 (2d Cir. 1949); Hamilton Nat'l Bank of Chattanooga, 29 B.T.A. 63, 67 (1933); Adolph Zukor, 33 B.T.A. 324 (1935); Richard R. Deupree, 1 T.C. 113 (1942), discussed in text to note 81 *infra;* J. A. Steur, 7 T.C. 1075 (1947). A similar problem exists with respect to qualified pension and profit-sharing plans as to when the benefits become "available" to the employee participants. INT. REV. CODE OF 1954, § 402(a); see Rev. Rul. 55–423–25, 1955–1 CUM. BULL. 41–44.

[56] See, e.g., Frank Cowden, Sr., 32 T.C. 853 (1959), *rev'd,* Com'r v. Cowden, *infra* note 71, discussed in 58 MICH. L. REV. 480 (1960) and in 73 HARV. L. REV. 1199, 1209–10 (1960).

to obscure the distinction between the two doctrines and have some-times used reasons germane to one for supporting a conclusion under the other. Thus, as we shall see, when the Treasury Department considered the problems raised in the Revenue Ruling referred to above,[57] its conclusions were based in part on the applicability of the economic benefit doctrine, although it purported to deal only with the problem of constructive receipt. In reaching their conclusions in cases involving these questions, apart from their articulation of the result, courts have undoubtedly been influenced by their views as to the desirability of permitting cash-basis taxpayers to determine when they will receive income and be subject to tax.[58]

The Economic Benefit Doctrine. A cash-basis taxpayer is clearly required to include in gross income, when received by him, not only items of cash but the value of any property or services which he receives.[59] The broad sweep of the gross income concept has been noted by the Supreme Court.[60] In cases dealing with compensation arrangements providing for the deferred receipt of cash, courts have held that rights received by the executive may be taxable prior to their realization in cash, on the ground that they constitute a cash equivalent.[61] A case which clearly states the economic benefit doctrine is *Renton K. Brodie*,[62] involving an officer of Procter and Gamble Company who received as compensation for services in the taxable year a paid-up retirement annuity contract, issued in his name with no conditions attached. The annuity contract was non-assignable and had no cash surrender value. The Tax Court recognized that in

[57] Rev. Rul. 60–31, 1960–1 CUM. BULL. 174.

[58] For example, J. D. Amend, 13 T.C. 178, 184 (1949) involved the question whether payment was constructively received by a farmer who sold his wheat in August 1944 and 1945 under contracts providing for delivery and payment in January 1945 and 1946. The Tax Court held the doctrine inapplicable, pointing out that this was a method of marketing which Amend had followed for a number of years and indicating that if the year in question had been the first in which such a contract had been made by him, the result might have been different. *But cf.* Cowden v. Com'r, *infra* note 71.

[59] INT. REV. CODE OF 1954, § 61; Treas. Reg. § 1.61–1 (1957).

[60] Helvering v. Clifford, 309 U.S. 331 (1940); Com'r v. Smith, 324 U.S. 177, 180–81 (1945); Com'r v. LoBue, 351 U.S. 243 (1956); see Old Colony Trust Company v. Com'r, 279 U.S. 716, 729 (1929) (employee held taxable on income tax paid on his behalf by his employer).

[61] One such situation relates to annuity policies purchased by the employer for the executive. United States v. Drescher, *supra* note 45; Tom Girdler, 2 CCH TAX CT. MEM. 482 (1943); W. A. Shannon, 4 CCH TAX CT. MEM. 350 (1945); Miller v. Com'r, 144 F.2d 287 (4th Cir. 1944) (civil service pension); Oberwinder v. Com'r, 147 F.2d 235 (8th Cir. 1945) (annuity assignable, but without cash surrender value); *cf.* Richard R. Deupree, *supra* note 55 (constructive receipt). Another such situation relates to stock acquired by the executive from the employer subject to restrictions which may render the stock unmarketable.

[62] *Supra* note 45.

his case, in contrast to a related case, there was no problem of constructive receipt, since the failure of the executive to receive cash rather than the annuity contract was not due to his own volition.[63] It held, nevertheless, that the taxpayer was required to include in gross income the amount paid by the company for the annuity contract, because the taxpayer received unconditionally the benefit of the provisions of the contract.

A type of arrangement clearly calling for the application of the economic benefit doctrine is that in which the deferred payments are placed irrevocably in trust for the benefit of the executive. *E. T. Sproull*[64] involved the question of the taxability to an executive of an amount transferred to a trust for his benefit at the end of December, 1945. Under the terms of the trust instrument, one-half of the amount transferred was payable to the executive in December, 1946, and the balance in December, 1947. Here, too, the Tax Court agreed that the doctrine of constructive receipt was not applicable, finding that the action of the company in setting up the trust was not initiated by the taxpayer or taken pursuant to his direction. It stated: [65]

• . . . Here, we think it must be held that the expenditure of [the amount] in setting up the trust conferred an economic or financial benefit on petitioner properly taxable to him in 1945. The fund was ascertained and paid over by petitioner's employer for his benefit in that year. Petitioner had to do nothing further to earn it or establish his rights therein. The only duties of the trustee were to hold, invest, accumulate, and very shortly pay over the fund and its increase to petitioner or his estate in the event of his prior death. No one else had any interest in or control over the monies. The trust agreement contained no restriction whatever on petitioner's right to assign or otherwise dispose of the interest thus created in him. . . .

The economic benefit doctrine was an alternative ground of decision in *Miller v. Commissioner,*[66] a case involving annuities purchased for a civil service employee under the Federal Civil Service Retirement Act.[67] The amounts involved were sums deducted from

---

[63] The related case which involved an executive of the same company who participated in the same plan in which the Tax Court held the doctrine of constructive receipt applicable was Richard R. Deupree, *supra* note 55.

[64] 16 T.C. 244 (1951), *aff'd per curiam,* 194 F.2d 541 (6th Cir. 1952). For earlier cases involving the question whether a taxpayer had received a taxable economic benefit under a compensation contract, see Rodrigues v. Edwards, 40 F.2d 408 (2d Cir. 1930) and Schneider v. Duffy, 43 F.2d 642 (D.N.J. 1930).

[65] 16 T.C. at 247–48.

[66] *Supra* note 61.

[67] Act of May 29, 1930, ch. 349, 46 Stat. 468, as amended by the Act of Aug. 4, 1939, ch. 426, 53 Stat. 1201, § 2.

the basic compensation of federal civil service employees, entitling them to annuities on retirement. The court pointed out that the employee

• . . . under any view of the transaction, as a result thereof, received additional compensation in the form of economic benefits under the Retirement Act. . . . The decisions in cases where an employer has paid premiums on life insurance policies issued for the benefit of an employee are in point.[68]

It has been suggested that the economic benefit doctrine might be extended to tax the value of an employer's unfunded obligation to make future payments to the employee; with an amply solvent employer, it has been argued, the rights of the employee are not very different from those of an annuitant under an annuity contract issued by a life insurance company.[69] No decided case involving a deferred compensation contract has gone this far,[70] although in at least one case,[71] a Federal Court of Appeals has declared that an obligation to pay in future years may be taxable in the year in which the obligation was received if all necessary elements are present to render the obligation marketable.[72]

[68] *Supra* note 61, at 289.

[69] See Eisenstein, *A Case of Deferred Compensation,* 4 TAX L. REV. 391 (1949) ; Blodgett, *Deferred Compensation of Executives,* 6 INST. FED. TAX. 764, 806 (1948) ; Allison, *Executives' Pensions Without Section 165,* 8 INST. FED. TAX. 451, 453 (1950) ; Rudick, *Income Taxes and Deferred Compensation Arrangements,* PROC. U. SO. CAL. TAX INST. (1948). *Cf.* Note, 1 LABOR L.J. 945 (1950). See Lasser, *How to Defer Compensation to Obtain Minimum Taxes,* 89 J. ACCOUNTANCY 42, 45–46 (1950) (suggesting that the Treasury might make a test case when (a) the corporate obligation to make payments in the future is accompanied by a reduction in salary, (b) when the executive is close to retirement and either foregoes an increase in salary or accepts a reduction in salary, (c) when the executive is the controlling stockholder of a closely held corporation). See also Note, 60 YALE L.J. 169 (1951) (suggesting that the employer's unfunded obligation to make future payments be taxed to the executive as if the employer had purchased an equivalent annuity). Consult Olmsted Inc. Life Ins. Agency, *infra* note 91 (rejecting tax on unfunded obligation of insurance company).

[70] But *cf.* Mertens v. Rogan, 153 F.2d 937 (9th Cir. 1946) (unsuccessful attempt by Commissioner to tax motion picture actor on company's obligation to reimburse him for future income taxes on compensation earned in the current year). The courts have refused to sustain contentions by corporate taxpayers that their obligation to pay pensions upon retirement should be treated for tax purposes in the same way as the delivery of an annuity contract. Frederick J. Wolfe, 8 T.C. 689 (1947), *aff'd,* 170 F.2d 73 (9th Cir. 1948), *cert. denied,* 336 U.S. 914 (1949) ; Perry v. Com'r, 152 F.2d 183 (8th Cir. 1945) ; Hill's Estate v. Maloney, 58 F. Supp. 164 (D.N.J. 1944).

[71] Cowden v. Com'r, 289 F.2d 20 (5th Cir. 1961), *rev'ing* Frank Cowden, Sr., *supra* note 56 (lump-sum advance oil royalty made payable over a three-year period solely to accommodate payees).

[72] "We are convinced that if a promise to pay of a solvent obligor is unconditional and assignable, not subject to set-offs, and is of a kind that is frequently trans-

Such a decision would seem to be of limited application to the usual deferred compensation agreement with an employee, which will typically prohibit assignment by the employee and will often impose conditions to payment.[73] Even without such a prohibition and without any such conditions, an unfunded obligation of an employer under a deferred compensation contract with an employee cannot properly be compared to an annuity contract issued by an insurance company and delivered to an employee by his employer. In the case of an annuity contract, the delivery of the annuity contract is the compensation bargained for, whereas in the case of a deferred compensation agreement, it is the payments by the employer pursuant to the agreement that constitute the intended compensation.[74]

There is understandable reluctance on the part of the courts to tax as current income the receipt by a cash-basis taxpayer of a mere obligation to pay, since to do so tends to obliterate the distinction between the cash and the accrual basis and to render liable to immediate tax individuals who may be without resources to pay the tax until they receive the funds on which the tax is levied.[75]

But in all events, the Treasury Department in its Revenue Ruling on deferred compensation adopted the view that the economic benefit doctrine does not apply to a mere unfunded promise by an employer to make future payments to an employee.[76] On the other hand, it has

---

ferred to lenders or investors at a discount not substantially greater than the generally prevailing premium for the use of money, such promise is the equivalent of cash and taxable in like manner as cash would have been taxable had it been received by the taxpayer rather than the obligation." *Id.,* at 24.

[73] See text *supra* to notes 31 ff.

[74] Mertens v. Rogan, *supra* note 70 (agreement to reimburse taxes). Such an obligation is a mere promise to make future periodic payments. Promises of this nature have been treated by the courts as being without ascertainable value for tax purposes and incapable of taxation, evidence of their market value being "no more than an opinion as to the value of a unique right of action for which there were no known buyers, nor any but an imaginary demand." Helvering v. Walbridge, 70 F.2d 683, 685 (2d Cir. 1934), *cert. denied,* 293 U.S. 594 (1934); Perry v. Com'r, *supra* note 70; Frederick J. Wolfe, *supra* note 70; Hooker v. Hoey, 27 F. Supp. 489 (S.D.N.Y. 1939), *aff'd on op. below,* 107 F.2d 1016 (2d Cir. 1939); William E. Freeman, 4 T.C. 582 (1945). See also Com'r v. Kann's Estate, 174 F.2d 357 (3d Cir. 1949); Bella Hommel, 7 T.C. 992 (1946); Frank C. Deering, 40 B.T.A. 984 (1939). *Cf.* Schaefer v. Bowers, 50 F.2d 689 (2d Cir. 1931), *cert. denied,* 284 U.S. 668 (1931); Richards' Estate v. Com'r, *supra* note 55 (Learned Hand, C.J.: "high expectations" are not the equivalent of "actual command" of income); Bedell v. Com'r, 30 F.2d 622 (2d Cir. 1929) (vendee's promise to pay purchase price on passage of title held without taxable value as such).

[75] See, e.g., Harold W. Johnston, 14 T.C. 560, 566 (1950); Nina J. Ennis, 17 T.C. 465 (1951). Even items such as promissory notes have been taxed reluctantly. See Note, *Checks and Notes as Income When Received by Cash-Basis Taxpayer,* 73 HARV. L. REV. 1199 (1960).

[76] *Supra* note 57, at 177.

taken the position that the payment of money to an escrow agent under an irrevocable escrow agreement, with provision for payments out of the fund in the future, will be treated as conferring an immediately taxable economic benefit.[77]

The Constructive Receipt Doctrine. It has been said that the doctrine of constructive receipt, developed by the tax authorities to defeat manipulation of the receipt of taxable income by cash-basis taxpayers, has achieved the status of a test as to the realization of income under the Code.[78] The scope of the doctrine is thus stated in the Treasury Regulations : [79]

• Income although not actually reduced to a taxpayer's possession is constructively received by him in the taxable year during which it is credited to his account or set apart for him so that he may draw upon it at any time. However, income is not constructively received if the taxpayer's control of its receipt is subject to substantial limitations or restrictions. Thus, if a corporation credits its employees with bonus stock, but the stock is not available to such employees until some future date, the mere crediting on the books of the corporation does not constitute receipt.

Although the doctrine was originally one of rather limited application,[80] it has been the crucial issue in a number of cases in the field of deferred compensation.

An instance of a corporation-executive relationship in which the doctrine of constructive receipt was applied is *Richard R. Deupree.*[81] This case, a companion to the *Brodie* case,[82] involved the president of Procter and Gamble Company, to whom the board of directors had awarded a 15% interest in an additional compensation fund. In the years 1935, 1936, and 1937 Mr. Deupree received bonuses out of this fund in cash. In 1938, the company at his direction purchased a single premium annuity for his benefit out of the fund. The annuity was non-assignable and had no cash surrender value. The Tax Court held that under these circumstances the premium paid by the company for the policy was taxable to Mr. Deupree through constructive receipt, since his failure to receive the sum involved in cash was due entirely to his own volition.

[77] *Id.* at 22.
[78] Ross v. Com'r, 169 F.2d 483, 491 (1st Cir. 1948), opinion by Mr. Justice Frankfurter.
[79] Treas. Reg. § 1.451–2(a) (1957).
[80] *Supra* note 53, at 481–82.
[81] *Supra* note 55.
[82] *Supra* note 45.

Against the thrust of the constructive receipt argument, taxpayers have prevailed in a number of cases involving amendments to existing contracts deferring income to a subsequent year. Such cases suggest strongly that the amending contract must have substance and reality. An amendment generally is deemed to have substance for tax purposes where both parties were mutually interested in, or benefited by, making the amendment, and it was not motivated solely to enable the executive to postpone his tax, although it is not clear that this dual interest is always essential. Where the amendments are made before the date originally fixed for payment has arrived, they frequently are regarded as effective so as not to entail taxability on the basis of the original contract.

Kay Kimbell [83] is a decision of the Board of Tax Appeals which attributed great significance to the reality of the contractual arrangements. Although it did not involve deferred compensation, it is important because it has influenced subsequent decisions in the field of deferred compensation. In the *Kimbell* case, involving oil payments based on production, the original agreement was amended prior to the date when the first payments were due so as to defer the commencement of such payments. In holding that the taxpayer was not taxable on the payments on the basis of constructive receipt before he actually received them, the Board stated: [84]

• If the parties had a right to make the first oral agreement, they had a right to make the second, and our only concern is whether these agreements actually existed and were intended as real, genuine, bona fide agreements between the parties . . . we know of no reason why from a tax standpoint full legal effect should not be accorded the second oral agreement . . . , which was entered into prior to the date that any of the oil payments in question were to begin. . . .

Subsequently, in *Howard Veit* [85] an executive successfully defeated the attempt of the Commissioner to ignore an amendment to an existing contract and to tax him under the doctrine of constructive receipt on the basis of the original contract. The taxpayer was employed as a sales executive by M. Lowenstein & Sons, Inc. for the years 1939 and 1940 pursuant to a written contract dated January 2, 1939, at an agreed fixed annual compensation and, in addition, a percentage of the net profits of the corporation for 1939 and 1940.

[83] 41 B.T.A. 940 (1940).
[84] *Id.* at 948.
[85] 8 T.C. 809 (1947), *acq.* 1947–2 CUM. BULL. 4. A companion memorandum decision applying the same principle to a subsequent year is Howard Veit, 8 CCH TAX CT. MEM. 919 (1949), *infra* note 90.

Under the original contract Mr. Veit's share in the profits was to be determined not later than May 1, 1941, and was to be paid in 1941. On November 1, 1940 the parties entered into a further contract of employment for the year 1941 at a fixed salary plus a percentage of certain sales. "At the request of the corporation" [86] it was provided that as additional consideration for the execution of the contract, the profit participation applicable to the year 1940 should be paid in 1942.

The Tax Court rejected the Commissioner's contention that the executive had constructively received the 1940 bonus in 1941 pursuant to the original contract. It concluded that the agreement to defer payment was a bona fide business transaction mutually profitable to both and not motivated solely by the executive's desire to postpone his tax. In support of this view, the facts showed that the company needed to retain and utilize the funds because of the extreme fluctuations in its business, that it was the company's custom to delay payment of percentage participations, that the suggestion for deferring payment emanated from the employer, and that the executive became entitled to receive interest on the amount deferred.[87] The Tax Court's conclusion was stated in the following terms: [88]

• The whole agreement of November 1, 1940, was an arm's-length business transaction entered into by petitioner and the corporation which was regarded as mutually profitable to both. The only way we should be justified in holding that petitioner constructively received the [amount] in 1941 would be to hold that the agreement to defer the payment of such [amount] until 1942 was a mere subterfuge and sham for the purpose of enabling petitioner to postpone his income tax on the amounts involved to another year. The evidence does not justify such a holding, but, on the contrary, seems to establish that the agreement to defer the payments until 1942 was an arm's-length contract arrived at in the ordinary course of business.

In finding that the case was similar to that of *Kay Kimbell,* the Tax Court stated: [89]

• In both cases there was an agreement to pay at a particular time indefinite amounts, and, prior to the date on which those amounts were due or could be determined, payment was deferred.

A subsequent memorandum decision of the Tax Court was concerned with a second amendment to the same taxpayer's compensa-

[86] 8 T.C. at 812.
[87] *Id.* at 812, 813, 814.
[88] *Id.* at 816.
[89] *Id.* at 818.

tion contract, further postponing the payment of his profit participation for the year 1940. The Tax Court once again refused to sustain the Commissioner's claim that the amount had been constructively received, although the case was more difficult for the taxpayer. The ground of the decision was that the amount involved was not yet payable when the second amendment was made and that the deferment was an arm's-length transaction.[90]

The possibility of deferring compensation by a novation made prior to the time the compensation is payable, although the services have already been rendered, was buttressed by the decision in *Commissioner v. Oates*.[91] Although the Commissioner of Internal Revenue originally refused to acquiesce in this decision,[92] the Treasury Department as part of its general ruling on deferred compensation substituted an acquiescence for its prior non-acquiescence.[93] The case therefore merits careful study.

Mr. Oates, as a general agent in Chicago for Northwestern Mutual Life Insurance Company, was entitled under his general agency contract to receive, upon retirement, commissions on renewal premiums as they were collected during the nine-year period following the date of retirement. This arrangement would have resulted in a comparatively large amount of commissions during the first year, progressively decreasing until nothing at all was payable after the ninth year. In order to "give the greatest stability and security of income by leveling the potential payments of terminal commissions over a period more nearly in accord with the life expectancy of the retired general agent," [94] the insurance company and the general agents, through their association, adopted a plan under which a retiring general agent could elect to receive his renewal commissions either under the old contract or, as provided in a new or amended contract, in equal monthly instalments over a period of years not to exceed fifteen in number. Once made, the election could not be

---

[90] The Tax Court said: "Respondent stresses that the amount of petitioner's share of 1940 profits had not been ascertained when the contract of November 1, 1940, was made, while on December 26, 1941, it had been computed, credited on the corporate books, and the full amount deducted on the corporation's 1940 tax return. We do not deem these differences material. Under existing contracts there was never a time when the $87,076.40 was unqualifiedly subject to petitioner's demand or withdrawal. He did not voluntarily refrain from collecting money available for him, nor did he agree to the debtor's deferred payment of money available when the agreements were made . . . ." 8 CCH Tax Ct. Mem. 919, 922 (1949).

[91] 207 F.2d 711 (7th Cir. 1953). See also Olmsted Inc. Life Ins. Agency, 35 T.C. No. 51 (1960).

[92] 1952-2 Cum. Bull. 5.

[93] *Supra* note 52, at 180.

[94] 18 T.C. 570, 574.

changed. Pursuant to this option Oates elected to receive his renewal payments over a period not to exceed 180 months. On its books the company credited him with commissions as the renewal premiums were collected, but paid him only the monthly instalments which he had elected to receive under the amended contract. The Commissioner sought to tax him as the commissions were credited to his account rather than as the amounts were received in cash. Notwithstanding that the new arrangement for payment arose solely from Oates' election and appears to have benefited him exclusively, both taxwise and in the sense of giving him a more nearly equal annualization of his retirement income,[95] the Court of Appeals, affirming the Tax Court, took the view that the amended contract "was in the nature of a novation, that is, a substitution of a new agreement or obligation for an old one which was thereby extinguished," [96] and that Oates' rights were to be determined entirely under the new election. It rejected the Commissioner's argument that the position of Oates was in all essentials analogous to that of the taxpayer in such cases as *Helvering v. Eubank* [97] and *Helvering v. Horst*,[98] holding that a taxpayer who has a right to receive income in the future and, in advance of the time he becomes entitled to receive it, assigns his right to receive it to another, is nevertheless taxable on the income in the year it is paid to his assignee. Since the question in those cases was one of whether income previously assigned by the taxpayer was taxable to him, and not, as in the *Oates* case, one of in which particular year income admittedly taxable to the taxpayer was to be taxed, the Court of Appeals was justified in rejecting the applicability of such authorities.

In other cases involving amendments to contracts, the question whether the deferment was regarded by the parties as having contractual significance or was arranged solely to suit the payee's tax interests has likewise been important to the ultimate decision.

A case illustrating the importance of these elements is *Drysdale v. Commissioner*.[99] The case was decided adversely to the taxpayer in the Tax Court,[100] but its decision was reversed on appeal on the basis of a different interpretation of the employment contract and of

---

[95] But *cf.* the Tax Court's statement with respect to the *Oates* case in George W. Drysdale, 32 T.C. 378, 384 (1959).

[96] *Supra* note 91, at 712.

[97] 311 U.S. 122 (1940) (assignment by retired insurance agent of right to receive renewal commissions when they became payable to him in the future).

[98] 311 U.S. 112 (1940) (assignment prior to maturity of detached bond coupon).

[99] 277 F.2d 413 (6th Cir. 1960).

[100] *Supra* note 95.

the facts. Mr. Drysdale, an engineer employed by the Briggs Manufacturing Company, had an unfunded deferred compensation contract made in 1952 providing for payment of $18,000 annually for ten years following termination of his full-time activities, or upon his reaching the age of 65. During the ten-year period in which the deferred payments were to be made, Mr. Drysdale was required to render consultative and advisory services and to refrain from accepting employment with, or acquiring an interest in, any activity inconsistent with, and adverse to, the interests of Briggs. His rights under the contract were subject to forfeiture upon his failure to comply with these requirements. The contract further provided that the rights of the taxpayer were non-assignable and that any attempt to assign such rights would immediately terminate the liability of Briggs.

On December 29, 1953, while the taxpayer was employed as an executive in the Briggs automotive and aircraft division, the division was sold to the Chrysler Corporation. Just prior thereto, on December 28, 1953, the taxpayer and Briggs amended the 1952 contract to allow the taxpayer to accept full-time employment with Chrysler. The amended contract reduced the amount to be paid to the taxpayer by Briggs from $180,000 to $90,000 and provided for its payment to a trust in five annual instalments of not less than $18,000 commencing one month after the sale by Briggs of its division to Chrysler; while the trustee was receiving the payments, the taxpayer was required to perform the advisory and consultative services provided for in the original contract. The trustee was to pay to taxpayer the amount of $1,500 monthly ($18,000 annually) until the fund was exhausted, commencing at age 65 or upon retirement from full-time employment, or if taxpayer died before reaching 65, the payments were to be made to his wife or estate. In all other respects, the 1952 contract was continued in full force and effect.

Following the sale to Chrysler the taxpayer became a full-time executive of Chrysler, receiving the approximate salary he had formerly received from Briggs. He continued to work for Chrysler until his retirement in 1957.

The issue in the case was whether the amounts paid by Briggs in 1954 and 1955 to the trustee pursuant to the terms of the amended contract were taxable income of the taxpayer in those years, even though he was not entitled to receive any part thereof until his retirement in 1957.

The Tax Court rejected the taxpayer's contention that he did not constructively receive the amounts in 1954 and 1955. It took the view that, although the case under consideration was similar to *Commissioner v. Oates* [101] in that the amended employment contract was made before the right to receive the deferred payments had accrued, it nevertheless fell on the other side of the line as to constructive receipt. The Tax Court noted that an officer of Briggs had testified that Briggs was willing and ready to pay the money directly to the taxpayer. It therefore concluded that, under the amended contract, the payments to the trustee were compensation for the advisory services rendered by the taxpayer during the years in issue and the taxpayer "apparently of his own volition and for no purpose other than to defer the reporting of income, effected a self-imposed limitation on his right to receive the payments direct." [102] To support its conclusion, the Tax Court relied on *Williams v. United States,*[103] a case in which a purchaser of timber desired and was able to pay the purchase price immediately but the seller declined to consummate the sale without first arranging an irrevocable escrow agreement whereby he would receive the purchase price over a five-year period.

In reversing, the Court of Appeals disagreed with the factual inference of the Tax Court that the sole purpose of the trustee arrangement under the amended contract was to defer Drysdale's taxes. It pointed out that under the original contract, Briggs was not obligated to pay Drysdale anything until he retired or reached the age of 65, that the amended contract was the result of negotiation, that in it the employer's obligation under the original contract was reduced, and that the right of Drysdale to accept employment with Chrysler was granted. It also pointed out that the testimony of the Briggs officer, relied on by the Tax Court, indicated a willingness to pay taxpayer directly, instead of the trustee, only if Briggs could control taxpayer's services, and that the use of the trust arrangement gave Briggs control, through the trustee, of those services during the term of the amended agreement. It therefore concluded that since Drysdale never, either under the original contract or as amended, had the right to receive or to demand any payment prior to retirement or reaching the age of 65, he did not constructively receive the amounts paid to the trustee in the taxable years. The appellate court disposed briefly of the alternative contention that the economic benefit doctrine required Drysdale to be taxed. In stating that the *Sproull* case [104] was not applicable, the court said: [105]

[101] *Supra* note 91.
[102] *Supra* note 95.
[103] 219 F.2d 523 (5th Cir. 1955).
[104] *Supra* note 64.
[105] *Supra* note 99, at 418.

• In that case, the trust agreement contained no restriction whatever on petitioner's right to assign or otherwise dispose of the interest created in him. In the present case, the taxpayer is restricted by the terms of both contracts from exercising any dominion over the funds in possession of the trustee. This is a crucial distinction. See *Commissioner v. LoBue,* 351 U.S. 243. . . .

In making this statement, the court doubtless was referring to the facts that under neither contract could Drysdale demand or receive any amount prior to his retirement in 1957, that his rights to receive after retirement were not assignable prior thereto, and that his rights to receive were forfeitable if he did not render the required consultative services.[106] As previously noted, however, it has been held that non-assignability is not, in itself, a basis for avoiding the application of the economic benefit doctrine.[107]

It is difficult to quarrel with the decision of the Court of Appeals in view of the taxpayer's rights under the particular contracts involved and the *Oates* decision,[108] which was thought to be analogous. But the approach of the Tax Court to constructive receipt, with its emphasis on the need for arm's-length bargaining and some purpose other than mere postponement of tax, cannot be disregarded. Thus, when no real agreement to defer is made in advance and the documents have no integrity, deferment will not be respected.[109] On the other hand, it has in effect been held that when provision has been made for deferment prior to the execution of an agreement, constructive receipt should not be applied to tax the payee simply because the payor was willing to make immediate or current payment and it was the payee at whose instance the deferment took place.[110] Upon similar principles, when deferment is agreed to before com-

---

[106] Counsel for the taxpayer has said that, in the argument before the Court of Appeals, the Government virtually conceded that the Tax Court was in error in construing the amended agreement as providing that the taxpayer acquired a non-forfeitable right to amounts paid to the trustee (see 9 U.S.L. WEEK, July 15, 1960, pp. 1059–60).

[107] See cases note 61, *supra.*

[108] *Supra* note 91.

[109] *Cf.* Morris Zeltzerman, 34 T.C. 73 (1960), *aff'd per curiam,* 283 F.2d 514 (1st Cir. 1960) (doctor held taxable on deferred portion of compensation from hospital, on the ground that there was no real or binding agreement for such deferment); Maxwell B. Llewellyn, Tax Ct. Mem. 1960–197, 19 CCH TAX CT. MEM. 1023 (1960).

[110] *Cf.* Cowden v. Com'r, *supra* note 71. *Cf.* J. D. Amend, *supra* note 58; *cf.* also Glenn v. Penn, 250 F.2d 507 (6th Cir. 1958) and Williams v. United States, *supra* note 103, both involving sales transactions in which the availability to the seller of full payment of the purchase price was the crucial issue. Consult Casale v. Com'r, *infra* note 120 and text to note 123, Chapter 6, text to notes 72 ff.

pensation has been earned, the compensation should not be taxable prior to its receipt simply because there was a prior agreement for current payment.[111]

The case of *Miller v. Commissioner*,[112] involving the taxability of amounts deducted from the salary of a federal civil service employee under the Civil Service Retirement Act, has previously been mentioned [113] in connection with the economic benefit doctrine. It is notable, however, that the court also stated, as the first ground of its decision in favor of the Commissioner, that the amounts deducted were in effect received by the employee in cash and then expended to purchase the annuity. On the basis of constructive receipt, the decision is difficult to reconcile with decisions such as the *Veit* and *Oates* cases. However, the alternative ground of decision, namely that the employee acquired a vested interest in a fund representing an economic benefit to him, appears to be the essential reason for the decision that the amounts deducted were taxable to the employee.

The continued lack of clarity in the tax law did not prevent a large number of companies from entering into contracts and plans for deferred compensation.[114] A policy statement on the part of the Treasury Department was badly needed. In response to this need, the Treasury Department finally issued in 1960 the deferred compensation ruling previously mentioned.[115]

We have previously mentioned the ruling's clarification of the Treasury Department's position as to the economic benefit doctrine. Essentially, the positions taken by the Treasury Department with respect to constructive receipt were the following:

1. The Treasury Department recognized that the absence of conditions attached to the right to receive compensation following the termination of employment will not necessarily require the inclusion of instalments in gross income prior to their receipt in cash. Although the Treasury Department did not lay down any broad principles in this respect, it gave two examples. In one, the right to payments, following termination of employment, was conditioned upon noncompetition, the rendition of consultative services, and the non-assignment of the rights of the executive; in the other, no conditions were

---

[111] Cf. Com'r v. Oates, *supra* note 91; Wilfred Weathers, 12 CCH TAX CT. MEM. 314 (1953) (". . . these contract amendments were made before the date on which the definite right for payment had come into being under the prior contract.").

[112] *Supra* note 61. See also Rev. Rul. 56–473, 1956–2 CUM. BULL. 22.

[113] See text to note 66 *supra*.

[114] See note 1 *supra*.

[115] *Supra* note 57.

imposed. In neither example was the executive held to be taxable prior to the receipt in cash of the instalment payments provided for in the respective contracts.

2. The breadth of the Treasury's concession in this respect was left deliberately vague. In connection with the doctrine of constructive receipt in its application to the cases under consideration, it was stated: [116]

• However, the statute cannot be administered by speculating whether the payor would have been willing to agree to an earlier payment.

The Treasury, moreover, left room for the application of the doctrine of constructive receipt in particular cases by saying: [117]

• Consequently, it seems clear that in each case involving a deferral of compensation a determination of whether the doctrine of constructive receipt is applicable must be made upon the basis of the specific factual situation involved.

There was, therefore, left open for a contrary result a situation in which the stimulus for deferment comes entirely from the taxpayer, and one in which the willingness of the payor to agree to immediate payment is not a matter of speculation but an established fact. Moreover, it was made clear that advance rulings will not be issued in specific cases involving deferred compensation arrangements.

The doubt as to the relevance of the deliberate postponement of income at the request of the payee, even though the payor is willing to make earlier payment, is further increased by an examination of the specific cases dealt with in the ruling. Two of the five cases under consideration were decided unfavorably to the taxpayer. In one of these cases, the ruling states as a fact that the taxpayer could have demanded receipt of payment of an escrowed bonus at the time of signing the contract. In the second of these cases, the ruling states that the contract providing for deferment of payment was not customary and was executed at the demand of the taxpayer. In the first of these cases, however, the ruling adverse to the taxpayer is based upon the fact that the bonus was escrowed, thereby bringing into play the economic benefit doctrine. In the second of these cases, the ruling is adverse to the taxpayer on the ground that he was a member of a joint venture and, therefore, entitled to his share of the income when

[116] *Id.* at 20.
[117] *Id.* at 21.

earned. In neither case, therefore, does the statement as to the attitude of the taxpayer seem relevant.

Moreover, in another case dealt with in the ruling, involving two contracts between an author and publisher—one, the usual royalty contract, providing for current payment, and the other, signed at the same time, placing a dollar limit on the amount payable to the author during any particular year—the Treasury Department, although taking the position that the author was taxable only on his receipt of payment, was silent as to which party was responsible for the arrangements. It seems clear, however, that the author could have had current payment of his royalties by simply not executing the second contract. The case of the author, moreover, is stated to be similar to the cases involving deferred compensation contracts for executives. If this case stood alone, it could be argued that when a cash-basis taxpayer, prior to the time that he has earned income which the payor is willing to pay currently, enters into an agreement in which he deliberately defers the receipt of such income, the deferment is effective for income tax purposes. But in view of the reservation of the Treasury Department of the right to examine the facts of each situation in relation to the doctrine of constructive receipt, such a broad statement of the Treasury's position would be unjustified.

3. The Treasury Department did not deal in its ruling with amendments to existing contracts which defer the right to receive income, such as was exemplified in the *Oates* case.[118] On the other hand, the Treasury Department approved the result of the *Oates* case itself.[119]

The Closely Held Corporation. The application of the doctrine of constructive receipt to deferred compensation under arrangements between an executive and a corporation which he controls involves a different set of problems.

A taxpayer who controls a company controls the receipt of his compensation. The doctrine of constructive receipt would thus appear applicable to impose an immediate tax on compensation that is deferred, since the executive is in effect responsible for the deferment. Logically extended, this approach could render an employee who is a controlling stockholder taxable on compensation that is not even voted to him, on the ground that his compensation was less than he should have caused the company to pay. No reported case has gone this far, and in fact there has been a strong judicial trend towards respecting the corporate identity when the Commissioner of

---

[118] *Supra* note 91.
[119] *Supra* note 57, at 180.

Internal Revenue has sought to tax income to a shareholder-executive by combining his tax position with that of the corporation.[120] Thus, in *Casale v. Commissioner*,[121] the Commissioner included in the gross income of the taxpayer, who was a chief officer and virtually the sole shareholder of a corporation, the amount of the premium on a life insurance policy on his life purchased by the corporation. The policy provided for monthly payments to Mr. Casale when he became 65. These payments were required by a deferred compensation agreement entered into between the corporation and the taxpayer, creating an unfunded obligation on the part of the taxpayer to pay a pension to him at age 65 in consideration of past services but subject to forfeiture if the executive, against the wishes of the corporation, left its employ before reaching 65. The pension was payable, however, if the taxpayer's employment was terminated before 65 (1) by the corporation without the taxpayer's fault, (2) by the insolvency of the corporation, and (3) by a wrongful act or default of the corporation. It was forfeitable after retirement if the taxpayer accepted employment with any competitor of the corporation without the consent of the corporation.

The Tax Court held that the taxpayer was required to include in his gross income the amount expended by the corporation as a premium on the life insurance policy. It stated: [122]

• Hence the pivotal point for decision in the case before us is whether or not the transaction, whereby the compensation agreement was executed and the insurance contract purchased, was a sham for tax purposes.

* * *

To sustain petitioner's argument of forfeitability in the light of the record would be a gross distortion of fact. As he controlled the corporation by virtue of his stock ownership, his assent was the corporation's assent, his wishes the corporation's wishes.

The decision of the Tax Court was reversed by the Second Circuit Court of Appeals, on the ground that the corporation was not a sham and that its ownership of the insurance policy could not be treated as

---

[120] See Casale v. Com'r, 247 F.2d 440 (2d Cir. 1957) ; consult Prunier v. Com'r, 248 F.2d 818 (1st Cir. 1957) and Sanders v. Fox, 253 F.2d 855 (10th Cir. 1958) denying the taxability of shareholders of closely held corporations on insurance arrangements. See also Rev. Rul. 59–79, 1959–1 CUM. BULL. 15, in which the Treasury Department announced its acquiescence in these decisions.

Cf. Com'r v. Gross, 236 F.2d 612, 618 (2d Cir. 1956) ("The officers of a corporation are not compelled to take salaries for the services they render").

[121] *Supra* note 120.

[122] Oreste Casale, 26 T.C. 1020, 1025, 1026.

ownership by the taxpayer. The court pointed out that apart from any question as to the reality of the conditions attached to the right to receive a pension, the petitioner had the economic risk of the insolvency of the corporation.

The holding of the appellate court in the *Casale* case that the corporation should not be ignored for tax purposes does not dispose of the question of the applicability to the pension of the doctrine of constructive receipt. To say that the premiums paid by the corporation in such a situation did not represent a realization of income by the stockholder-executive is not necessarily to recognize the efficacy for income tax purposes of the agreement of his controlled corporation to pay him only in the future for his present services. Even if the legal personality of the corporation may be respected, this does not necessarily mean that there should be imputed to the corporation an attitude or an interest with respect to the payment of deferred compensation which is different from that of its controlling stockholder. This situation, therefore, presents in its starkest form the question of the relevance of the attitude of the parties in a deferred compensation contract. For, clearly, conditions imposed upon an executive who is the controlling stockholder cannot be held to restrict realistically his power to obtain his deferred compensation currently. Moreover, the Treasury Department's ruling on deferred compensation did not say that the attitude of the payor was immaterial, but merely that, as a matter of tax administration, it would not speculate about the payor's attitude.

Although the point was not considered by the court, the *Casale* decision in effect sanctioned deferment of income without any demonstrable business purpose. Taxpayers have been permitted to postpone the receipt of income in other situations, but in a case such as *J. D. Amend,* for example, in which the Tax Court did not find a business purpose, there was an independent party not subject to the taxpayer's control and the Tax Court stressed that the contracts were "bona fide arm's lengh transactions." [123] Of course, even in a closely held company there may be an independent party when a block of stock owned by another person or group can bring about what is tantamount to an arm's-length transaction.

[123] *Supra* note 58, at 185.

CHAPTER 6

DEFERRED COMPENSATION:
THE COMPANY'S DEDUCTION
AND OTHER ASPECTS

THE COMPANY'S TAX POSITION IN THE CASE
OF AN UNFUNDED PLAN

Most corporations keep their accounts on an accrual basis and, prior to the Revenue Act of 1942, their right to accrue deferred compensation as a liability for services rendered during the taxable year depended upon the principles applicable to accrual accounting generally.[1] If payment of the deferred compensation was contingent upon performance by the executive, no immediate deduction was permitted even though the employer set up a reserve on its books in anticipation of future payments.[2] On the other hand, if the liability to pay deferred compensation was not thus contingent, the corporation was permitted to deduct the full extent of the liability in the year incurred even though payment of the compensation took place in subsequent years.[3]

The Revenue Act of 1942 sharply curtailed this right of the employing company,[4] and the Internal Revenue Code of 1954 now

[1] See Com'r v. Brooklyn Radio Service Corp., 79 F.2d 833 (2d Cir. 1935). INT. REV. CODE OF 1954, §§ 441, 446, and 451 set forth the statutory provisions generally applicable.

[2] I.T. 1891, III-1 CUM. BULL. 132 (1924); O.D. 124, 1 CUM. BULL. 107 (1919). The Commissioner's position in James D. Mooney, 9 T.C. 713, 719 (1947) is in accord. See also S. Naitove & Co., 8 B.T.A. 589 (1927), aff'd, 32 F.2d 949 (App. D.C. 1929), cert. denied, 280 U.S. 582 (1929); Field & Start, Inc., 17 B.T.A. 1206 (1929), aff'd, 44 F.2d 1014 (2d Cir. 1930), cert. denied, 283 U.S. 826 (1931). However, failure to set up a book reserve in the amount of estimated actual loss has been accorded some weight in connection with a claim for a deduction. Lucas v. American Code Co., 280 U.S. 445, 451–52 (1930); Lucas v. Providence Coal Mining Co., 60 F.2d 86, 87 (6th Cir. 1932). As to the treatment of dividends on awarded but undelivered bonus stock, see I.T. 1891, supra. State legislation should be consulted for provisions prohibiting the issuance of shares for services to be rendered. E.g., DEL. CONST., art. IX, § 3.

[3] E.g., Oxford Institute, 33 B.T.A. 1136 (1936) (employees' trust); Thurman v. Studebaker Corp., 88 F.2d 984 (7th Cir. 1937) (employees' stock purchases); Gen. Outdoor Advertising Co. v. Helvering, 89 F.2d 882 (2d Cir. 1937).

[4] Act of Oct. 21, 1942, ch. 619, 56 Stat. 798, § 165(b).

permits a deduction for deferred compensation only in the year in which the compensation is actually paid, and then only if the executive's right to such compensation was non-forfeitable at the time it was paid.[5] Although this limitation was primarily intended to apply to a "trust" or "plan," Section 404 of the Code, in which the limitation is now found, makes it applicable to a "method of employer contributions or compensation" which "has the effect of" a plan deferring the receipt of compensation;[6] under the Treasury Regulations any corporate obligation, whether funded or unfunded, to pay deferred compensation to an employee is declared to be a "method" having the effect of such a deferring plan.[7] Accordingly, the employing company, despite its accrual system of accounting, will generally be permitted to take its deduction for compensation payable to an executive only in the year in which the compensation is paid, if at all.[8] This appears to be true even if the company's obligation to make future payments to an executive is unconditional and the executive's rights to such future payments are non-forfeitable; in such a situation, even though the executive might conceivably be subject to tax, the company must postpone its tax deduction to the years in which the payments are actually made.[9]

[5] INT. REV. CODE OF 1954, § 404(a)(5). This applies to plans which do not qualify as pension trusts, employees' annuities, or stock bonus or profit-sharing trusts under § 404(a)(1), (2), or (3).

The 1954 Code (§ 462) originally contained a provision which sought to conform tax accounting with accounting principles generally, and which might have been construed to restore the company's right to accrue and deduct currently compensation deferred for future payment. However the provision was retroactively repealed. Act of June 15, 1955, ch. 143, 69 Stat. 134, § 1(b).

[6] INT. REV. CODE OF 1954, § 404(b).

[7] Treas. Reg. § 1.404(b)–1 (1956).

[8] It has been suggested that if compensation is payable only on condition that it be earned out in subsequent years, there is no plan deferring the receipt of compensation within the meaning of § 404 of the 1954 Code; since the compensation is, in effect, being paid currently as it is earned out, it should be deductible without reference to § 404. See Fillman, *Ford Motor Company Employee Benefit Plans,* 17 INST. FED. TAX, 883, 889 ff. (1959). This construction would, among other things, permit deduction of the entire amount of deferred compensation in a year in which the executive died, even though the compensation was still payable over a period of years. The construction was consistent with Rev. Rul. 54–625, 1954–2 CUM. BULL. 85, but the latter ruling was modified by Rev. Rul. 55–212, 1955–1 CUM. BULL. 299, which took the view that such amounts are deductible only when paid even though unconditionally payable following the death of the executive.

In one case, a company was permitted to take a deduction both for amounts paid to a trustee for a bonus to employees and for an unsecured commitment to pay a bonus to employees, even though in both cases each employee was required to earn out his bonus in the year following that of the award; any amount forfeited by an employee was to be added to payments to be made to the others, with the company having no right to repayment. Produce Reporter Co., *infra* note 11.

[9] But *cf.* Rev. Rul. 54–625, *supra* note 8.

A slight inroad on the foregoing rule has been made for incentive compensation or bonus plans under which awards earned in one year are not paid until the following year. Under such plans, the awards are presumably taxable to the recipients only in the year in which received,[10] but it has been held that the company may take its deduction in the year in which the awards were earned provided the amounts were ascertainable or communicated to the recipients prior to the end of that year.[11] Apart from this type of case, the company's tax deduction will, as a general rule, coincide in point of time with the year in which the executive is subject to tax under the usual conditional deferred compensation arrangement. This was the objective of a provision of the Internal Revenue Code of 1954 in the form in which it passed the House of Representatives.[12]

A company which has established its right to a tax deduction for deferred compensation so far as the appropriate period is concerned may still be called upon to justify such payments as reasonable.[13] If the deferred compensation clause is phrased in terms of payment for consultative and advisory services, the taxing authorities could conceivably take the position that such payments represent excessive compensation for the services actually rendered. The draftsman of such a clause must bear in mind that some day the company may be called on to justify the amount of its deferred compensation payments in terms of services rendered during active employment, as well as

---

[10] See discussion in Chapter 4, text to notes 40 ff.

[11] Consult Produce Reporter Co., 18 T.C. 69 (1952), aff'd on other points, 207 F.2d 586 (7th Cir. 1953); Avco Manufacturing Corporation, 25 T.C. 975, 1000 (1956); Rev. Rul. 57–88, 1957–1 Cum. Bull. 88; Rev. Rul. 55–446, 1955–2 Cum. Bull. 531. See Chapter 4, text to notes 42 ff.

The 1957 Revenue Ruling, *supra*, suggests that for the company to be entitled to a tax deduction the amounts must have been both ascertainable and communicated to the individual employees before the end of the taxable year. However, in the case of Avco Manufacturing Corporation, *supra*, only the fact that bonuses were to be paid pursuant to specific formula was communicated and in the case of "Produce Reporter Company, *supra*, although the specific amount of his bonus was communicated to each employee before the end of the taxable year, the bonus was forfeitable until paid. The proper rule should be that, in the case of a completely discretionary plan, the bonus to be deductible must be authorized and each employee must be informed prior to the end of the year of the specific amount he is to receive, but no communication of specific amounts to individual employees is necessary when the total bonuses to be paid are calculated by formula in effect before the end of the year.

[12] H.R. 8300, § 403(a)(5). See H.R. Rep. No. 1337, 83d Cong. 2d Sess., printed in 3 U.S. Cong. News 4025, 4069, 4290 (1954).

[13] Int. Rev. Code of 1954, § 162(a)(1). Under § 404(a), to have a tax deduction the company must also satisfy the conditions of § 162, including, presumably, the requirement of reasonableness.

services and other consideration supplied during the post-employment period while the payments are being made.

Plans under which compensation is payable in or measured by the value of stock present additional questions based, for example, on a possible argument as to a lack of relationship between services rendered and compensation payable, a point discussed hereafter in connection with corporate power to pay deferred compensation.[14] Further, to the extent that such a plan provides for the payment of dividend equivalents, or that dividend units entitle the holder to payments at the rate declared on shares of outstanding stock, the corporate deduction may be questioned on the ground that neither shares of stock nor dividends constitute a proper measure of compensation. However, cases that suggest the possibility of questioning the corporate deduction on these grounds are distinguishable,[15] and it would seem that dividend equivalent payments are as much a form of compensation as are other types of bonuses and plans for profit participation. Therefore, dividend equivalent payments should be just as deductible by the company as any bonus or plan for profit participation, the only qualification being that when these payments are added to salary and other payments, total compensation is reasonable.

Funding

A transfer to a trust of amounts representing deferred compensation credited but not yet payable presents a serious dilemma for the company and the executive. If the transfer to the trust is un-

---

[14] See text *infra* to notes 88 to 98. For a valuable discussion of tax problems presented by plans providing for payment in stock, see Lentz, *Different Kinds of Stock Bonus Plans,* SELLIN, TAXATION OF DEFERRED EMPLOYEE AND EXECUTIVE COMPENSATION (1960).

[15] *Cf.* R. J. Reynolds Tobacco Co. v. United States, 138 Ct. Cl. 1, 149 F. Supp. 889 (1957), *cert. denied,* 335 U.S. 93 (1957) (disallowing deductions as compensation of distribution of a portion of the profits of a company among employees holding a special class of stock) with Com'r v. R. J. Reynolds Tobacco Co., 260 F.2d 9 (4th Cir. 1958), *affirming* TAX CT. MEM. 1956–161, 15 CCH TAX CT. MEM. 810 (allowing a partial deduction for such distributions). Consult Cox, *Aspects of the du Pont Bonus Problem,* 17 INST. FED. TAX. 905, 923 (1959).

A private ruling that the company was entitled to a tax deduction for its payments in respect of dividend units was issued to Union Carbide Corporation upon its dividend unit plan, App. GG. *Cf.* Graybar Electric Co., Inc., 29 T.C. 818 (1958), *aff'd,* 267 F.2d 403 (2d Cir. 1959), *cert. denied,* 361 U.S. 822 (1959) (payments to estates or beneficiaries of employees, on termination of employment through death, of purchase price of stock plus interest plus increase in book value of stock, held payments "in respect of the stock and not in respect of services rendered," and hence not deductible as compensation) with National Clothing Co., 23 T.C. 944 (1955) (payments on repurchase of stock on termination of employment at then book value held deductible as compensation, employees not having been required to pay for stock except through application of dividends).

conditional and the executive's rights to future payment are non-forfeitable, the company is entitled to a deduction for the year when the transfer to the trust is made.[16] However, the executive will be taxable immediately on the amounts transferred to the trust for his benefit, thereby defeating the intended deferment of tax.[17] On the other hand, if the rights of the executive are forfeitable when the transfer to the trust is made, the executive will not be subject to tax on the transfer or when his rights become non-forfeitable,[18] but, under a specific provision of the Treasury Regulations, the company may never be entitled to a deduction for such payment. This inability of the employer to obtain a deduction, which is quite surprising as a matter of principle, results from interpretation by the Treasury of the provision of the Code [19] permitting a deduction under an unqualified deferred compensation plan "if the employees' rights to or derived from such employer's contribution or such compensation are non-forfeitable at the time the contribution or compensation is paid." The Regulations [20] construe this statutory provision to mean that: "If an amount is paid during the taxable year to a trust or under a plan and the employee's rights to such amounts are forfeitable at the

[16] INT. REV. CODE OF 1954, § 404(a)(5).

[17] J. H. McEwen, 6 T.C. 1018 (1946); David Watson Anderson, 5 T.C. 1317 (1945). Cf. Rodrigues v. Edwards, 40 F.2d 408 (2d Cir. 1930) (stock held in trust during term of employment held income as set aside); Hackett v. Com'r, 159 F.2d 121 (1st Cir. 1946), affirming 5 T.C. 1325 (1945); E. T. Sproull, 16 T.C. 244 (1951), aff'd per curiam, 194 F.2d 541 (6th Cir. 1952). Consult INT. REV. CODE OF 1954, §§ 402(b), 403(c); Treas. Reg. §§ 1.402(b)-1(a)(1) and 1.403(b)-1(a) (1956).

[18] Julian Robertson, 6 T.C. 1060 (1946); Harold G. Perkins, 8 T.C. 1051 (1947); James D. Mooney, supra note 2. The leading cases prior to the amendments made by the Revenue Act of 1942 are Adolph Zukor, 33 B.T.A. 324 (1935), and Schaefer v. Bowers, 50 F.2d 689 (2d Cir. 1931), cert. denied, 284 U.S. 668 (1931) (employees' stock purchase plan; not taxable income to employee until received, since final receipt of stock was conditional on continued service and company's continued operation of plan); Reginald Denny, 33 B.T.A. 738 (1935) (loan to be repaid if motion picture corporation did not exercise option to continue to employ him; held taxable income in the year corporation exercised option); K. R. Kingsbury, 31 B.T.A. 1126 (1935) (company contracted to set up trust fund for officers; first five years the officers received the trust income; upon completion of five years' service, life estate in the income with limited power of appointment vested in them; held vesting of life estate and power of appointment is taxable event). As to partly forfeitable payments, such as annuity premiums paid both currently and in advance and for which repayment may be demanded on death of employee prior to time for which premiums are prepaid, cf. Paul A. Draper, 6 T.C. 209 (1946).

[19] Supra note 16.

[20] Treas. Reg. § 1.404(a)-12 (1956). See Draper & Co., 5 T.C. 822, 841 (1945). In Produce Reporter Co., supra note 11, the company was held to be entitled to a tax deduction for amounts paid to a bank for distribution to employees, although the rights of individual employees were forfeitable. However, this was a special situation involving what was considered to be current bonus awards paid after the year end.

time the amount is paid, no deduction is allowable for such amount for any taxable year."

The United States Court of Claims, in a case [21] involving the construction of the corresponding and substantially identical provision of the Internal Revenue Code of 1939, held the Regulation invalid as an incorrect construction of the statute. The Court took the view that when the rights of employees under a non-qualified plan are forfeitable at the time of payment to a trust, the employer is entitled to a tax deduction at the time that payment is made by the trustees to the employees. The Treasury Department has announced [22] that it will not follow this decision, taking the position that its Regulation is a long-standing interpretation of the Code supported by legislative history.

Because of these onerous tax consequences, deferred compensation under non-qualified arrangements is rarely funded.[23] On the other hand, some tax attorneys have approved arrangements under which corporate funds or other property are deposited with a bank under an escrow agreement requiring the bank to hold the property for the company and to pay the executive from the property only if and when the company should fail to make a payment called for by the company's agreement with the executive. The thinking behind this type of arrangement is that it results in no "trust" within the meaning of the statute and that the executive has no vested interest in any fund or property; it is accordingly expected that the tax consequences will not be affected by the escrow agreement. It may be mentioned that in one of the cases decided adversely to the taxpayer in Revenue Ruling 60-31 the deferred compensation was placed in escrow; [24] the only difference from the arrangement just mentioned was that the escrow fund was the source of the deferred payments rather than security for the payments by the employer.

Although funding of deferred compensation arrangements involves tax risks, some arrangement short of actual funding may be made without incurring these risks. The essential distinction in all of these alternative arrangements is that the company continues to retain the amounts credited to the deferred compensation account and the

---

[21] Russell Mfg. Co. v. United States, 175 F. Supp. 159 (Ct. Cl. 1959). *But cf.* Wesley Heat Treating Co. v. Com'r, 267 F.2d 853 (7th Cir. 1959) which seems contrary to the *Russell Manufacturing* case, although it is described by the Court of Claims as "clearly distinguishable." See 175 F. Supp. 159, 163, n. 4.

[22] Rev. Rul. 59–383, 1959–2 Cum. Bull. 456.

[23] Rothschild, Compensation and Incentives for Executives, Encyclopedia of Tax Procedures 965, 985–86 (rev. ed. 1960).

[24] Rev. Rul. 60–31, 1960–1 Cum. Bull. 174.

executive is not given an interest in any specific assets. Thus, the Treasury Department has recognized that the company may set aside amounts credited to an account for deferred compensation and invest these amounts, crediting the deferred compensation accounts with the income.[25] In such a case, the executive has no interest in the securities constituting the investments and the company has no obligation to invest the reserves. While it is conceivable that a question may arise as to whether the investment constitutes an unreasonable accumulation of surplus giving rise to a liability for the surtax imposed by Sections 531 and 532 of the Internal Revenue Code, in the normal case this risk would not seem to be substantial.[26] Similarly, there would seem to be no reason why interest could not be credited to deferred compensation accounts by the company.[27]

A method of financing deferred compensation payments in frequent use is the purchase by the company of an insurance or annuity policy of which the company is the sole beneficiary and owner.[28] Even though it may be contemplated that the proceeds of the policy will be used to pay the executive's deferred compensation, the tax consequences of such an arrangement for an executive should not differ from those attaching to unsecured arrangements generally.[29] The premiums paid by the company for such policies will not consti-

---

[25] *Id.* at 175, 178–79.

[26] For smaller, closely held companies, the accumulation of $100,000 now permitted under § 535(c)(2) of the 1954 Code should be of material assistance. Even a reserve for deferred compensation payments to a controlling stockholder may be held to justify accumulations, particularly if used to purchase life insurance in favor of the company. *Cf.* Emeloid Co. v. Com'r, 189 F.2d 230 (3d Cir. 1951). On the other hand, deferring payment of salary may not justify a cash reserve when the company's duty to pay is indefinite as to time. Consult Smoot Sand & Gravel Corp. v. Com'r, 241 F.2d 197 (4th Cir. 1957), *cert. denied,* 354 U.S. 922, *rehearing denied,* 354 U.S. 943 (1957) (involving interest on bonds payable to controlling stockholder where payment could be postponed indefinitely in his discretion). When the compensation agreement is made with an executive who is not a stockholder, the possibility that §§ 531 and 532 would apply would seem to be slight; at least in publicly held companies it could hardly be said that the purpose penalized by these sections is present even if the executive should be a minor stockholder.

[27] See Appert, *Contingencies in Deferred Compensation May Still Be a Wise Precaution,* 13 J. TAXATION, July 1960, pp. 12, 13.

[28] *Cf.* CASEY AND ROTHSCHILD, PAY CONTRACTS WITH KEY MEN (1953), Ex. 88 (Hiram Walker-Gooderham & Worts, Ltd. and Howard R. Walton—agreement to endorse to executive monthly checks received by company under annuity policy).

[29] Casale v. Com'r, 247 F.2d 440 (2d Cir. 1957); *cf.* Prunier v. Com'r, 248 F.2d 818 (1st Cir. 1957); Sanders v. Fox, 253 F.2d 855 (10th Cir. 1958) (involving stock redemption agreements in closely held corporations rather than deferred compensation). The Treasury has acquiesced in these decisions. Rev. Rul. 59–79, 1959–1 CUM. BULL. 15.

tute a tax deduction,[30] but the proceeds from the insurance or annuity will not be subject to taxation.[31] Further, as and when it receives such proceeds, the company will be entitled to a deduction for any payments made to the executive.[32]

GROUP PLANS

As we have seen, individual arrangements chiefly call for deferred compensation fixed in amount at the time the arrangements are made,[33] and usually provide that payment is to commence only on retirement or other termination of employment [34] with the compensation thus deferred being in the nature of a pension. Compensation deferred under group plans, on the other hand, is generally based on current profits, representing incentive compensation currently awarded with payment deferred to a later date.[35] Such deferment may be on a short-term or a long-term basis. Also, as distinguished from individual arrangements, group plans may provide for payment to be made in shares of the stock of the company, or measured by the increase (or decrease) in the value of such shares. Such plans, sometimes referred to as phantom or shadow stock plans, will be outlined hereafter.[36]

Short-Term Deferment. Short-term deferment contemplates that the compensation that is being deferred shall be paid during active employment rather than on retirement.[37] The prototype of

[30] INT. REV. CODE OF 1954, § 264(a)(1).

[31] *Id.,* § 101(a)(1).

[32] See cases cited note 29 *supra.*

[33] See Chapter 5, text to notes 8–10.

[34] See Chapter 5, text to notes 18–25.

[35] "Phantom stock" units under a deferred compensation plan, on the other hand, may be awarded annually or at other intervals without reference to company profits. See note 47 *infra.* But *cf.* BETHLEHEM STEEL, App. FF (ceiling based on percentage of dividends declared).

[36] *Cf.* KOPPERS, App. LL. See text to notes 76 ff. *infra.*

[37] In addition to plans referred to in footnotes to this and succeeding sections of this chapter, reference is made to plans of the following companies as examples of short-term deferment: Bigelow-Sanford Carpet Company, Inc. (incentive compensation plans adopted annually by board of directors); Colgate-Palmolive Company (Profit Incentive Plan); Crucible Steel Company; General Aniline & Film Corporation (Executive Incentive Compensation Plan); General Foods Corporation (Management Incentive Plan); International Telephone and Telegraph Corporation (Bonus Plan); Lear, Inc. (Incentive Bonus Plan); McKesson & Robbins, Inc. (Management Incentive Plan); Monsanto Chemical Company (Bonus Plan); North American Aviation, Inc. (Incentive Compensation Plan); United States Rubber Company (Bonus Plan); Radio Corporation of America (Bonus Plan).

No effort was made to ascertain the status of the cited plans at the time this volume went to press.

such plans is the General Motors Bonus Plan, first adopted in 1918.[38] Under that Plan, a bonus award for a particular year may be paid in five instalments, the first currently when the award is made and the subsequent instalments at yearly intervals thereafter.[39] The plan contains both sets of conditions discussed above in connection with individual arrangements.[40] The continued services condition is expressed in a requirement that each instalment other than the first be earned out over the four-year period following the making of the award; unless otherwise determined by the Bonus and Salary Committee appointed under the plan, an employee who resigns or whose employment is terminated for cause loses any right to earn out the unearned portions of his past bonus awards.[41] If employment should be terminated under circumstances not resulting in a forfeiture of bonus awards, continued payment of instalments is made conditional upon the beneficiary's not engaging in competitive activities and not acting or conducting himself "in a manner inimical or in any way contrary to the best interests" of the company.[42] These have not been paper conditions; over the years they have resulted in an impressive total of forfeitures.[43]

These short-term deferment features of the General Motors Bonus Plan were supplemented in 1957 by a stock option plan under which not more than 25% of any bonus award may be in the form of contingent credits payable not during employment but following its termination.[44]

Short-term deferment provisions such as those in the General Motors Bonus Plan are intended to retain executives against opportunities that may be offered elsewhere. An executive will not be as tempted by an offer from a competitor if its acceptance will result in the loss of substantial bonuses payable over future years. A second purpose of the short-term deferred plan is to spread incentive com-

---

[38] The present modified plan was approved by stockholders on May 24, 1957, and is reproduced as Appendix W.

[39] App. V, ¶ 6.

[40] Ibid. (earning out by continuing service); ¶ 8 (competition or conduct inimical or contrary to the best interests of the corporation). See Chapter 5, text to notes 31–42.

[41] Id. ¶ 8(a).

[42] Ibid.

[43] Thus, the portions of prior years' bonus awards to which bonus beneficiaries under the General Motors Bonus Plan lost their rights amounted to $377,511 in 1957 and $199,627 in 1956. See General Motors Corp., Annual Report for 1957, p. 44.

[44] See App. V, ¶ 6, and App. W, ¶ 5. The provisions were adopted at the Annual Meeting of Stockholders on May 24, 1957. See Proxy Statement dated Apr. 16, 1957.

pensation awards from good years, to reduce fluctuations in income and cushion the shock of lower bonuses in lean years. As a consequence of receiving instalments from bonus awards of prior years the executive, in a year in which no bonus is awarded, will not be as drastically affected as the executive of a company on a current payment basis.[45]

To the executive, such plans may offer tax advantages chiefly (1) for the first few years of increasing annual compensation after the executive has been admitted to the bonus plan and (2) for the first few years of decreasing annual income following termination of employment while instalments are still being paid. During the intervening period, assuming a bonus award greater or similar in size, cumulative bonus instalments will each year swell the executive's total income and bring him into higher tax brackets. In this respect, the short-term plan is less favorable than the long-term plan, which results in payment when taxable income may be considerably lower than during active employment.

The short-term deferred plan is nevertheless more advantageous as a tax matter than the current incentive compensation payment without deferment. It is simpler in operation than the long-term plan, is more easily explained, has more appeal to younger executives, and does not impose the substantial, long-range obligations that may have to be reflected in the balance sheet.[46]

Long-Term Deferment. A number of companies make provision for a portion of the incentive compensation awards to be paid on retirement or other termination of employment.[47] The prototype of

[45] The General Motors Plan, in operation for forty years, has failed to provide a bonus in only three years. Thus, in 1946 net earnings were $87,526,311, as against the $95,121,691 required for a 7% return on net capital, prerequisite to the bonus being paid. See General Motors Corp., Annual Report for 1946, p. 49; General Motors Corp., Proxy Statement dated Apr. 21, 1947, pp. 5–7. It was in the following year that the substantial increase in the bonus reserve was made, both through reducing the return on net capital from 7% to 5% and increasing the Bonus Fund's share of net profits from 10% to 20%. The increase was explained on the grounds (a) that increased taxes, in particular, required larger earnings and volume of business, and (b) that failure to increase the bonus reserve would result in lower bonuses in relation to salary than in pre-war years. General Motors Corp., Proxy Statement *supra,* pp. 10–12. Further, the increase in the capital of the corporation meant that a return of 7% on capital would have required earnings of $1.97 a share in 1947 as compared to $1.40 under the adjusted formula and $1.36 before the war. *Id., * p. 11.

[46] See text to note 112 *infra.*

[47] GENERAL ELECTRIC, App. AA (providing for deferment of stock allotments to termination of employment and for immediate payment of cash balance of allotment); Schenley Distillers Corp. (immediate cash payment limited to first $5,000).

this form of deferred compensation is the General Electric Incentive Compensation Plan adopted in 1951.[48] The GE plan also contains the two sets of conditions previously mentioned in connection with individual arrangements.[49] The continued employment condition is a requirement that the executive earn out the deferred or contingent portion of his annual award by remaining in the company's employ for three more years; this portion of the award will be forfeited pro rata if employment should be terminated prior to the end of the three-year period for any reason other than death, disability, retirement under the pension plan, or circumstances deemed by the administering committee "not to be contrary to the interests" of the company.[50] The condition to payment after termination of employment consists of a prohibition against engaging, without the consent of the administering committee, in the operation or management of a busi-

---

In addition to plans referred to in footnotes to this and succeeding sections of this chapter, reference is made to plans of the following companies as examples of long-term deferment: American Smelting and Refining Company (Additional Compensation Plan); AMERICAN SUGAR REFINING, App. Z; Clinchfield Coal Corporation (Incentive Retirement Plan); Eastman Kodak Company (Deferred and Incentive Compensation Plan); The Goodyear Tire & Rubber Company (Profit-Sharing Plan); W. R. Grace & Co. (Bylaw); Jones & Laughlin Steel Corporation (Deferred Rewards Fund); Marshall Field & Company (Contingent Allotment Plan); National Distillers Products Corporation (Extra Compensation Plan); Norfolk & Western Railway Company (Executives' Contingent Compensation Plan); Otis Elevator Company (Incentive Compensation Plan); Merck & Co., Inc. (Executive Incentive Plan); The Pennsylvania Railroad Company (Contingent Compensation Plan); Pittsburgh Plate Glass Company (Plan for Incentive Compensation to Key Employees); The Pittston Company (Incentive Retirement Plan); The Standard Oil Company, an Ohio Corporation (Incentive Compensation Plan).

Long-term deferment is usually the feature of phantom stock and unit plans, under which units are allocated to executives based on the value of shares of stock and, on termination of employment, either the increment in value of the shares represented by the units, or a corresponding number of shares, is paid to the executive in instalments over a period of years. For examples of phantom stock plans, see KOPPERS, App. LL, and Pittsburgh-Consolidation Coal Company (Management Unit Plan), both of which were challenged in stockholder litigation, the first successfully, *infra* note 95, and the second unsuccessfully, *infra* note 96. See also BETHLEHEM STEEL, App. FF and Vick Chemical Company (Management Incentive Compensation Plan). For examples of unit plans, see TEXAS, App. KK; Gulf Oil Company (Incentive Compensation Plan); Continental Can Company, Inc. (annual employment contracts: see Proxy Statement for Special Meeting of Common and Preferred Stockholders, Oct. 26, 1956, p. 34).

No effort was made to ascertain the status of the cited plans at the time this volume went to press.

[48] Proxy Statement of Annual Meeting, Apr. 17, 1951. The plan (App. AA) was not adopted by the Board of Directors until Dec. 21, 1951.

[49] See Chapter 5, text to note 31.

[50] App. AA, § IV (3)(a).

ness having a net worth in excess of $5,000,000 which is, at the time, in competition with the company.[51]

As distinguished from the General Motors Plan, which defers payment of 80% of all bonus awards of over $1,000,[52] the General Electric Plan defers payment of 50% of incentive compensation awards in the case of awards to officers and executives selected by the committee administering the Plan;[53] incentive compensation awards to all others continue to be paid in full.[54] Other long-term deferred plans similarly distinguish between groups of executives for purposes of deferment.[55]

Combined Short-Term and Long-Term Deferment. Distinctions between groups of executives for purposes of deferment of incentive compensation awards are usually based on the differing situations of the several executive groups. Speaking generally, the junior executive is in an expensive period of life in terms of his annual income; he may be completing the purchase of his home and the accessories that go with it, sending his children to school or college, or supporting parents or older relatives. As a result, the junior executive has cash needs, and a deferred compensation plan may seem to him a threat to an increase in current compensation which he might otherwise receive and which would be far more welcome.[56] To middle management also a long-term deferred plan may not provide as direct and significant an incentive as a currently payable award. Again, speaking generally, this group will be more willing to accept short-term deferment and, for this group, the company may wish to spread payment of each annual award, both to level out income and to provide holding power. For the top executive group, high tax brackets may have greatly impaired any incentive value of awards currently paid; for members of this group, some of whom may be close to retirement, deferment would be welcome to supplement retirement pay.[57]

[51] *Id.* § IV(3)(b). *Cf.* CASEY AND ROTHSCHILD, Ex. 92 (Federated Department Stores, Inc.) ¶¶ 5.2 and 5.3 for a similar provision, with a definition of competing business dependent upon the division of the employer's business with which it competes.

[52] App. W, ¶ 6.

[53] App. AA, § III(1).

[54] *Id.,* § III(2).

[55] E.g., KENNECOTT, App. EE.

[56] See Patton, *Executive Compensation: Tax Gimmicks v. Incentives,* 31 HARV. BUS. REV. 113 (Nov.–Dec., 1953), criticized in Lasser and Rothschild, *Deferred Compensation for Executives,* 33 *id.* 89, 102 (Jan.–Feb., 1955).

[57] Holzschaeber, *Tax Thoughts on Deferred Compensation Plans,* 26 N.Y. CERT. PUB. ACCT. 41 (1956); Blake, *Current Trends in Fringe Benefits,* 106 J. Ac-

To meet the diverse needs of these groups, several companies have adopted or amended incentive compensation plans to authorize current payment, short-term deferment, or long-term deferment, depending on the group to which the award is to be made.[58] The 1957 amendments of the General Motors Bonus Plan heretofore mentioned,[59] as well as those of the du Pont Bonus Plan in the same year,[60] were, in effect, intended to permit both short-term deferment for middle management and long-term deferment for top executives.

Special Tax Problems of Group Plans. The tax consequences of group deferred plans, both short-term and long-term, are in general similar to those presented by individual deferred arrangements.[61] The executive under a group plan should be subject to tax not in the year in which the bonus award is made but in the respective years in which he receives payment of the instalments of the award.[62] The company should receive its tax deduction in the years in which the award is being paid,[63] even though the amount of the award when made may have been irrevocably charged to a bonus reserve or fund.

COUNTANCY, Sept. 1958, p. 33. *Cf.* Minneapolis-Honeywell Regulator Co., Proxy Statement for Annual Meeting of Apr. 30, 1957, seeking stockholder approval for extending commencement of deferment, chiefly for "a relatively small number of older officers" (pp. 4–5): "In the case of a senior officer in the higher tax brackets, income taxes may eliminate a large part of the incentive which the By-law was intended to afford, if an award must be paid while the officer is in active service receiving his regular compensation currently."

[58] Gulf Oil Company, Incentive Compensation Plan; KENNECOTT, App. EE ("A" awards contingently payable following termination of employment, "B" awards payable over five-year period following year for which award made); Minneapolis-Honeywell Regulator Co., Proxy Statement for Annual Meeting of Apr. 30, 1957 (change in bylaw from short-term deferment to authorize deferment by Committee commencing not later than tenth year after year for which award made); Bell Aircraft Corporation, Deferred Incentive Compensation Plan for Officers and Key Employees, ¶ 3 (first deferred instalment to be paid not earlier than January 15 of year following year for which allotment made and not later than January 15 of year following year of termination of employment); The New York Central Railroad Co., Proxy Statement for Annual Meeting on May 24, 1956, p. 5 (two instalments under incentive bonus plan currently payable, with balance on retirement). But *cf.* The Pittston Co., Proxy Statement for Annual Meeting on May 4, 1954, pp. 5–6 (deferment changed from short-term to retirement, with no discretion).

[59] *Supra* note 38.

[60] See App. X and Y.

[61] See discussion in Chapter 5, text to notes 46 ff.

[62] *Ibid.*

[63] See discussion *supra*, text to notes 4 to 12. For a statement of the expected tax consequences of its plan, see Bell Aircraft Corporation, Proxy Statement for Special Meeting of Stockholders, July 31, 1956, p. 6: "Payments made in cash or stock under the Deferred Incentive Compensation Plan give no income tax advan-

As we have seen,[64] the short-term deferred plan may effect less of a tax saving to the executive than the long-term plan; by that very token, it may perhaps be less subject to attack based on tax motivation. Also, in the case of the short-term plan, the deferred compensation becomes payable when earned out, whereas under the usual long-term plan, the deferred compensation may be fully earned out years before termination of employment makes it payable.[65] Unless other factors are involved, however, the differences between short-term and long-term plans do not in principle appear to be of sufficient substance to warrant different tax treatment.

On the other hand, when there is deferment for some executives and not for others or a difference in deferment between executives, group plans present special problems. For example, if executives to whom awards are made constitute a majority of the board of directors or even a significant fraction of the board, it may perhaps be contended that such executives control the manner in which their awards are to be paid.[66] Under such circumstances, if an award to one executive is paid currently and an award to another is deferred, the latter may be held to have had an individual choice as to time of payment and be currently taxed on his award notwithstanding that payment has been deferred.[67] Even when executives are not directors, deferment of awards on an individual, case-by-case basis, and without reference to any rule, may make it appear that it was the executive who determined when his award was to be paid and this may render him subject to tax under constructive receipt principles. To forestall

---

tage to employees receiving such payments other than that which may accrue through spreading of deferred compensation over several tax years of such employee [sic] since the full amount of such cash payments and the fair market value of stock will be taxed to the employee as ordinary income in the year in which received. The Corporation, in turn, expects to receive the benefit of a Federal income tax deduction for such cash payments and for the fair market value of such stock in the year in which the cash is paid or the stock distributed and will incur a capital gain or loss on the difference between the fair market value of such stock when so distributed and the acquisition cost to the Corporation."

Contrary to the last statement, while the company may deduct the fair market value of the stock at the time it is distributed [Package Machinery Co., 28 B.T.A. 980 (1933)], there is no gain or loss to the company, for federal income tax purposes, based on a value at that time higher or lower than when the stock was acquired by the company. Consult Reg. § 1.1032–1 (1956); Hercules Powder Co. v. United States, 180 F. Supp. 363 (Ct. Cl. 1960).

[64] See text to notes 45 and 46 *supra*.

[65] As to the effect of a forfeitable right becoming non-forfeitable, see Chapter 5, note 52.

[66] Compare problems incident to closely held corporations, discussed in Chapter 5, text to notes 120–23.

[67] See Chapter 5, text to notes 78–123, and particularly to note 81.

such a contention, one or more, or all, of the following steps have been considered desirable:

1. The plan should itself contain the specific formula for deferring payment [68] or, in the interests of flexibility, should permit a committee to prescribe the formula. It should provide that no member of the committee may, while serving on the committee, be eligible to receive an award or, perhaps, to receive payment of an instalment of any awards theretofore granted, a provision desirable apart from tax considerations to avoid criticism based on self-dealing.[69]

2. The plan should preclude deferment on an individual basis and should provide that deferment must be pursuant to a rule of general application.[70]

[68] It is conventional for the plan to stipulate the specific percentage of the award that is to be deferred. E.g., AMERICAN TOBACCO, APP. U (50% of award); cf. Pittsburgh Plate Glass Company, Plan for Incentive Compensation to Key Employees, as amended on Nov. 7, 1956, ¶ 9A (for key employees whose incentive compensation is $10,000 or more or whose total compensation is $50,000 or more, not in excess of 75% nor less than 50% of total incentive compensation for group to be paid in cash, with remainder utilized as a measure for contingent allotment of common stock).

[69] Thus, under the "profit-sharing plan" of Goodyear Tire and Rubber Company, a committee consisting of all directors who do not participate in the plan establishes a classification of participants to whom distribution is deferred. See 55th Annual Report to Shareholders for 1953, p. 22. See The American Sugar Refining Company, Incentive Compensation Plan (1958), §§ 2(a) and 4 (committee defined as all directors who are not employees); Clinchfield Coal Corporation, Incentive Retirement Plan (1953), ¶¶ 3 and 4(b) ("No participant in the Plan shall at any time be a member of the Directors' Committee . . . No award shall be made to any person while he is a member of the Directors' Committee nor within three years thereafter"); General Foods Corporation, Proxy Statement dated June 15, 1956, p. 15 (intent declared not to amend Management Incentive Plan without stockholder approval so as to alter powers of the committee or qualification of its members—viz., ineligibility to participate). Cf. General Aniline & Film Corporation, Executive Incentive Compensation Plan, §§ VIII (3) and IV (3) (board of directors can delegate authority to administer plan to a compensation committee, provided no member shall be eligible for an award while serving and "No employee who is also a member of the Board of Directors shall participate in any deliberations or decisions of the Board of Directors concerning consideration of an award or payment under the Plan to himself"); Marshall Field & Company, Proxy Statement dated Mar. 22, 1956, p. 3 (action of independent committee of directors subject to approval of board).

[70] Cf. Norfolk & Western Railway Co., Proxy Statement dated Apr. 4, 1956, p. 4 (contingent monthly allotments under Executives' Contingent Compensation Plan equal to a flat percentage of monthly salaries of officers with annual salaries of $30,000 or more); Pennsylvania Railroad Co., Proxy Statement for Annual Meeting, Mar. 8, 1956, p. 4 (contingent allottments to "officers in key positions" are in lieu of and in the same percentage as cash increases in salaries to officers and supervisory employees not participating in plan); Gulf Oil Co., Proxy Statement for Annual Meeting, Apr. 22, 1958, p. 2 (ten instalments for those 63 or over, as against five instalments for those under 63); Calumet & Hecla, Inc., Proxy Statement dated March 9, 1956, p. 5 (amount deferred depends on age).

3. The deferment plan should be submitted to stockholders for their approval.[71]

4. If the formula for deferment may be changed from year to year, by amendment of the plan or otherwise, the plan should require that both the group whose awards will be deferred and the formula for deferment be established well before the end of the year for which the awards are to be made; at least six weeks, and prudence would dictate a period of several months, before the year's end.

This last provision may itself be sufficient to defeat a contention of constructive receipt, for the constructive receipt rule should be inapplicable to a payment deferred before it has been earned.[72] In reliance on the belief that the Commissioner of Internal Revenue cannot disregard provisions for future payment made before benefits are payable, some companies have given employees an election as to the time when they wish to receive benefits, requiring only that the election be exercised before the benefits have been earned.[73] The

[71] See GENERAL ELECTRIC, App. AA; GENERAL MOTORS, App. V. Cf. CASEY AND ROTHSCHILD, op. cit. supra note 28, Ex. 116 (Lerner Stores Corp. and Russell N. Levin), and Ex. 118 (Ward Baking Co. and Faris R. Russell), for examples of ratification by stockholders of individual deferred compensation agreement. For the weight given stockholder approval, see Koster v. Warren, infra note 91. The company will usually take the position that stockholder approval, though sought, is not necessary. E.g., Bell Aircraft Corp., Proxy Statement for Special Meeting of Stockholders, July 31, 1956, p. 5 ("While, in the opinion of counsel, approval of such plans by stockholders is not required, the Directors believe that as a matter of policy the stockholders should be fully informed as to the provisions of the plans and be given an opportunity to express their approval or disapproval"); General Foods Corp., Proxy Statement for Annual Meeting, July 25, 1956, p. 15 (plan adopted by board of directors subject to approval of stockholders and if majority of all stock voted is voted against approval, "the plan will not become effective"); The Pittston Co., Proxy Statement dated Apr. 16, 1954, pp. 6–7 ("In the belief that agreements of this type should be submitted to stockholders, the Plan was adopted by the Board of Directors of the Company subject to approval by the stockholders at this annual meeting").
Plans in existence for a long period of time may not have been submitted to stockholders for approval. Thus, the "profit-sharing plan" of The Goodyear Tire and Rubber Company, in effect since 1937, does not appear to have been so submitted. Cf. Bigelow-Sanford Carpet Co., Inc., Proxy Statement dated Mar. 29, 1956 ("Since 1946 the Board of Directors each year has adopted incentive compensation plans for officers and key employees"); W. R. Grace & Co., Proxy Statement dated Apr. 17, 1956, p. 5 (deferment under 1923 Bylaw a "practice" of the board of directors). As to the necessity of stockholder approval, see Chapter 8.
[72] See discussion in Chapter 5, text to notes 83 ff.
[73] Cf. Profit-Sharing and Savings Plan for the Employees of The Hanover Bank, under which employees may elect on or before December 15 of each year to take their profit-sharing distribution in cash, or to place it in a qualified profit-sharing trust, or to take one-half in cash and place one-half in the trust; Supplementary Compensation Plan of Irving Trust Company, as Amended as of January 1, 1956 (providing for election as to each year's contributions prior to October 1 of such year). Consult Rev. Rul. 56–497, 1956–2 CUM. BULL. 284.

conservative practice is to require the election to be exercised before the beginning of the year to which it is to apply, but the underlying reasoning should apply equally to permit exercise of the election during the year itself, so long as no part of the payment is due until the end of the year, or may never be due, as in the case of an award wholly dependent on the operations for the entire year.

The Treasury Department, in a related situation, has apparently concurred in the thinking behind plans conferring these employee elections; it has ruled that under the statute taxing benefits from qualified pension and profit-sharing plans in the year when such benefits are "made available," [74] an election to defer payment of the benefits falling due does not result in such benefits having been "made available" if the plan requires the election to be exercised in advance of the time of payment of the benefits. [75]

Phantom or Shadow Stock Plans. A special type of long-term deferred compensation plan involves use of the company's stock as a measuring rod for ultimate compensation, usually coupled with credits for amounts equivalent to dividends. [76] Typically, units corresponding to shares of stock, but not representing any proprietary interest, are allocated to designated executives and credited on the books of the corporation to the account of the executives; the credits are equal to the then market price of a number of shares of stock corresponding to the units credited. [77] The account of each executive to whom units are awarded may be credited during his employment with dividends declared on an equivalent number of shares of stock [78] and the units in his account are adjusted for changes in the number of outstanding shares of stock as the result of capital readjustments, such as stock splits and possibly stock dividends over a certain size. [79] When the executive becomes entitled to benefits under the plan upon retirement or termination of employment, a revaluation of his units is made to reflect the current market price of the stock; [80] to avoid a low valuation caused by a temporary decline in the price of the stock at the time employment terminates, the plan may give the executive

[74] Int. Rev. Code of 1954, § 402(a).

[75] Rev. Rul. 55–423, 55–424, 55–425, 1955–1 Cum. Bull. 41, 42, 43.

[76] See Lieberman v. Becker, 155 A.2d 596 (Sup. Ct. Del. 1959) (upholding the validity of the unit plan of The Koppers Company, Inc. (App. LL)). But see Berkwitz v. Humphrey, 163 F. Supp. 78 (N.D. Ohio 1958) (holding invalid the feature of the unit plan of Pittsburgh-Consolidation Coal Company providing for valuing units on retirement on the basis of the market price of the stock).

[77] See Lieberman v. Becker, *supra* note 76, at 597.

[78] *Ibid.*

[79] See Berkwitz v. Humphrey, *supra* note 76, at 84.

[80] See Lieberman v. Becker, *supra* note 76, at 597.

(or his beneficiary) the option of selecting a later valuation date.[81] The total amount, consisting of the units valued in this manner plus dividend equivalents credited during employment, will then be made payable over a period of years following termination of employment to the executive or, if he should die prior to receiving all payments, to his designated beneficiary.[82] To cover its liability based on increased valuation of units at the time the obligation to make payments matures, the company may set aside a number of its unissued shares for subsequent issue and sale.[83]

The precedent for this type of plan may be found, as a current substitute for stock options, in the closely held company and, in particular, in service organizations such as advertising and engineering firms, which sell stock to key personnel at book value with an agreement to repurchase on termination of employment at book value at that time. An early plan of this nature provided for allocation of units on the basis of book value of shares of stock, with payment on termination of employment of the increase in book value from the time of allocation.[84]

From the phantom or shadow stock plan there has evolved the dividend unit allocation, which E. I. du Pont de Nemours Company has now made part of its bonus plan system.[85] The holder of a dividend unit awarded during employment in lieu of a portion of a current bonus is entitled to receive payments equivalent to dividends on outstanding stock until his death or age 85.[86] Instead of receiving a cash bonus or a bonus of a specified number of shares of stock, the executive thus receives the right for a fixed period of years to be paid the income that he would have received on such shares.[87]

The propriety of plans of this sort will be discussed in the section which follows.

QUESTIONS OF CORPORATE POWER

In the case of an executive who has been receiving an annual salary of $50,000 from Company A, the power of Company B to employ the executive for five years and to pay him for his services $25,000 a year for ten years seems scarcely open to question. Instead of disbursing a total of $250,000 over five years, the company will be

---

[81] *Ibid.*
[82] *Id.* at 598.
[83] *Ibid.*
[84] See note 98 *infra.*
[85] Consult Cox, *supra note* 15. APP. x.
[86] *Id.* at 912–13.
[87] *Id.* at 917.

paying the same total over ten years and over the intervening period will gain the use of the money. In the absence of an unanticipated tax factor, the deferred compensation arrangement will thus result in no added cost.

There will, of course, be the ever-present possibility of a change in the tax law or in tax rates, as well as the possibility of drastically reduced corporate profits, which may cause compensation paid in the future to cost the company more after taxes than would compensation paid currently. These possibilities must be weighed against the tangible advantage gained by the company's use of the money during the intervening period and the intangible advantage of securing the executive's services on a basis satisfactory to him. The possibility that deferred compensation may result in a loss in tax advantages constitutes one of the cost factors that must be weighed by the board of directors in determining the reasonableness of the compensation. Because of possible tax disadvantages, however, and because of the substantial amounts that may be involved, many companies seek stockholder approval of deferred compensation arrangements, sometimes explaining the tax factors when they do so.[88]

In the type of situation just discussed, involving the original employment of an executive, the deferred compensation is clearly based on future services to be rendered after the arrangement for such compensation is made. More difficult questions of corporate power arise when deferred compensation is based on services rendered over a period of years before the arrangement for such compensation. Arrangements of this nature are by no means unusual. They may involve, for example, a chief executive who has devoted his business life to the company and is approaching retirement with an inadequate pension.[89] Although the arrangement may call for future services and prohibit competitive activity, the value to the company of these provisions may be so self-evidently small as to make it apparent that the company is seeking to compensate the executive for past services. The question then presented is the same question of corporate power to compensate for past services that arises in connection with the validity of past service pensions.[90]

[88] *Supra* note 71.

[89] Consult Lasser and Rothschild, *supra* note 56. See CASEY AND ROTHSCHILD, *op. cit. supra* note 28, Ex. 91 (North American Co. and Herbert C. Freeman—reciting as basis for agreement for deferred compensation that president's salary had not been increased when he was promoted from vice-president and that his annuity under the company's retirement plan was $10,417 per annum).

[90] See Chapter 8, text to notes 182 ff. and discussion and authorities cited in Volume II, Chapter 13.

It is sufficient here to suggest the following:

1. Whereas a pension plan today calls for no justification as a matter of social policy, a deferred compensation agreement with an individual executive, even though intended to provide a retirement allowance, may not find so ready an acceptance.

2. The conditions to payment of deferred compensation so frequently imposed—such as the rendition of consulting services and the restraint on competitive activity—may add nothing to justify the future payments [91] and may in fact seem so insubstantial as to lead to a conclusion that corporate assets are being wasted.

3. This is not to suggest that conditions to payment, which the executive is willing to accept, should be omitted. On the contrary, such conditions, at the very least, represent an additional consideration which the company would not otherwise have secured, and which may prove, dependent on circumstances, to be of value far beyond that expected when the agreement was made. But if such conditions are not the real consideration for the payments, the payments should not be tied to the conditions too closely.

4. Frequently, when there are payments which are based in large part on prior services, the rule prohibiting compensation for past services may be found inapplicable. That rule was intended to apply when the past services were being rendered without expectation of additional compensation.[92] The arrangement for a retirement allowance or other compensation following termination of employment is often made against the background of a commitment of long standing that some provision for additional compensation for the services

[91] See Chapter 5, text to note 31. Consult Koster v. Warren, 176 F. Supp. 459 (N.D. Cal. 1959) (no reasonable probability that minority stockholder could successfully attack long-term consultation contracts made by Safeway Stores, Inc. with former officers and directors).

[92] *Cf.* 6A FLETCHER, CYC. CORP. (perm. ed., 1954) § 2939: "It seems to be the rule that a private corporation has no power voluntarily to pay a former officer or employee a sum of money for past services, which it is under no legal duty to pay, and which would not constitute a legal consideration for a promise to pay." See Chapter 8, text to notes 180 ff. See also Fidanque v. American Maracaibo Co., 33 Del. Ch. 262, 92 A.2d 311 (1952); Moore v. Keystone Macaroni Mfg. Co., 370 Pa. 172, 87 A.2d 295 (1952). For an analysis of earlier cases, consult Volume II, Chapter 13.

Cf. Willoughby Camera Stores v. Com'r, 125 F.2d 607 (2d Cir. 1942) (promise of some bonus may, on breach, entitle employee only to nominal damages but is adequate consideration for substantial bonus). Consult Rosen v. Guaranteed Sanitations, Inc., N.Y.L.J., Feb. 14, 1961, p. 14, col. 5 (Aurelio, J., Sup. Ct.) (resignation as officer and director at age 67, on sale by founder of his stock, relinquishment of annual salary of $25,000, covenant not to compete, and occasional advice as called for, held adequate consideration for lifetime payment of $7,500 a year). Consult Chapter 8, text to notes 47, 180.

being rendered will be made.[93] To such a case the past service rule should not be applicable.[94]

5. A separate problem will arise if the amount of deferred compensation is not determinable when the agreement to pay such compensation is made, because the deferred compensation is payable in shares of stock as under the shadow or phantom stock type plan or is measured by the market value of shares of stock, or, as in the case of the dividend unit plan, is payable in amounts measured by dividends. As a result of such arrangements, the amount of the compensation ultimately to be paid will not be known until the payments are to be made, and, in the case of shadow plans, will depend on all the fortuitous circumstances that determine the market price of stock at any particular time. It has accordingly been contended that there is no sufficient relationship between the amounts to be paid and the services rendered, and that compensation depends on fluctuations in the market price of shares of stock and other factors extraneous to the value of the executive's services. In one case, this contention was upheld and the deferred compensation plan enjoined.[95] In Delaware, the contention has been rejected and a similar plan has been upheld.[96]

Compensation that is payable in stock or measured by the value of stock has many similarities to a stock bonus, a qualified group retirement plan providing for payment or measurement of retirement allowances in terms of stock of the employing company, or a stock option. Recognition of this similarity was a ground for upholding such plans in Delaware. An outstanding difference is that in the phantom or shadow stock plan (just as in the General Electric type of plan) the obligation of the corporation is not measurable at the time of the allocation or award unless the corporation at that time purchases or sets aside the number of shares that measures its obligation and retains such shares until the obligation matures. If the corporation fails to do so, a non-measurable obligation will hang as a Damoclean sword and the amount ultimately paid may be deemed a waste of assets, with the board of directors chargeable with failure to exercise discretion in fixing liability at the time of award.[97] The usual type of plan employed by closely held companies is subject to

[93] See Lasser and Rothschild, *supra* note 56, at 100.

[94] See Volume II, Chapter 13.

[95] See Berkwitz v. Humphrey, *supra* note 76.

[96] See Lieberman v. Becker, *supra* note 76. *Cf.* Nadler v. Bethlehem Steel Corporation, 154 A.2d 146 (Del. Ct. Ch. 1959) (disapproving settlement involving new dividend unit plan).

[97] *Cf.* Rogers v. Hill, 289 U.S. 582 (1933).

less criticism in that it provides for ultimate payment in terms of book rather than market value.[98]

OTHER PROBLEMS: STATUS OF RETIRED EXECUTIVE

The status of a retired executive whose active employment has terminated and who is receiving payments under a deferred compensation agreement may become important in a variety of contexts.

Effect on Social Security Benefits. Even to an executive who retires with a substantial pension, monthly social security payments may be important, since they will be exempt from income tax.[99] The executive's right to such benefits may be affected by the existence of an obligation to render consultative services after retirement, so long as he is under the age of 72, and may also vary depending upon whether he renders such services as an independent contractor or as a part-time employee.

When an individual under the age of 72, who is entitled to social security benefits, has earnings in excess of $1,200 per taxable year, the excess is charged under the Social Security Act against his social security benefits beginning with the first month of the taxable year, except that the first $500 of the excess over $1,200 is charged against social security benefits only at the rate of one-half that charged for all of such excess.[100] It is provided, however, that no part of the excess is chargeable for any month "in which such individual did not engage in self-employment and did not render services for wages . . . for more than $100." [101]

If the deferred compensation is made conditional on the rendition of consultative services, the reduction of social security benefits would be operative unless the executive can bring himself within the exception quoted. If his status is that of an independent contractor, his task is easier than if he is considered an employee. To avoid the loss of social security benefits in a particular month, an independent contractor who receives payments which might be considered earnings need only show that he rendered no substantial services in that

---

[98] See Berkwitz v. Humphrey, *supra* note 76, at 94, in which the court indicated that a unit plan which used book value as a basis of measuring compensation "differed significantly" from a plan which used market price as the measuring rod, and held the latter type invalid.

[99] I.T. 3447, 1941–1 CUM. BULL. 191.

[100] Social Security Act, §§ 203(b), 203(f), as amended by PUB. L. 87–64 approved June 30, 1961, effective as to benefits for months after December 1961.

[101] Social Security Act, § 203(f)(1), *supra* note 100.

month.[102] An employee, on the other hand, must show not only that he did not render services for wages of more than $100 during the month of payment but also that payments made during a particular year were made for services rendered in a different year.[103]

When there is no requirement of consultative services, the payments will be regarded as made "on account of retirement" for social security benefit purposes and such payments will not reduce social security benefits.[104]

Liability for Employment Taxes. The Internal Revenue Code requires federal income tax withholding for all payments to an executive under a deferred compensation arrangement, including payments for past as well as present services.[105] No withholding is required for deferred compensation payments made to the estate or a beneficiary of a deceased executive.[106]

When payments after retirement are made for current consultative services, the company has an obligation (whether or not the executive has attained the age of 72) to withhold and pay social security tax, if the status of the executive is considered to be that of an employee.[107] Or, if his status is considered to be that of an independent contractor, the executive must pay the tax on his self-employment income.[108] In either event, such payments, to the extent that they are made for current consultative services, will be applicable to reduce the retirement income credit under Section 37 of the Code.[109]

Capital Gains Treatment under Qualified Plans. Far more important to the executive than social security and withholding ques-

---

[102] Social Security Act, § 203(f)(4)(A), *supra* note 100. As to what constitutes substantial services, see 20 C.F.R. 404.416, 404.416a (1960) (normally, services will not be considered substantial if they amount to less than 45 hours during any calendar month).

[103] Social Security Act, § 203(f)(6), *supra* note 100.

[104] Social Security Act, § 209(c), 42 U.S.C. § 409(c) (1958).

[105] INT. REV. CODE OF 1954, § 3401; Treas. Reg. §§ 3401(a)-2, 3401(b)-1.

[106] Rev. Rul. 59–64, 1959–1 CUM. BULL. 31.

[107] INT. REV. CODE OF 1954, § 3402. Payments made "on account of retirement" are excluded from "wages" subject to tax for Social Security and Unemployment Insurance purposes. INT. REV. CODE OF 1954, §§ 312(a)(3), 3306(b).

[108] INT. REV. CODE OF 1954, §§ 1401, 1402(a) and (b); Rev. Rul. 54–586, 1954–2 CUM. BULL. 345.

[109] INT. REV. CODE OF 1954, § 37(d). Since the maximum retirement income under § 37(a) is $1,200 and this is reduced by Social Security benefit payments, this question will usually not have any importance except in community property states where each spouse is entitled to the credit as to income earned by either of them prior to retirement. See Treas. Reg. § 1.37–2(a) (1956).

tions may be his right to capital gains treatment on a lump-sum payment from the company's pension or profit-sharing plan following retirement.[110] This right is threatened for an executive under a deferred compensation plan calling for consultative or advisory services. It has been held that the "separation from the service" of the employer requisite for capital gains treatment of a lump-sum payment has not taken place if the executive continues to be subject to call for services.[111] The capital gains treatment may be jeopardized whether the services are rendered as an employee or as an independent contractor.

ACCOUNTING QUESTIONS

As we have seen, the company's tax deduction for contingent compensation payable under the usual deferred compensation agreement or plan must await the year when such compensation is actually paid to the executive. By agreeing to pay such compensation, however, the company has incurred an obligation which may be substantial in nature and which should be reflected or disclosed in current financial statements.

The method of reflecting or disclosing deferred compensation is not uniform. Some companies may merely refer to the existence of the arrangement in a footnote to their financial statements, the more conservative practice being to provide a reserve for the payments to be made in the future, often with an adjustment in amount to reflect the net cost of such payments after taxes computed at current rates.[112]

To the extent that deferred payments are regarded as compensation for current services, they will be charged to current operating

---

[110] Id., §§ 402(a)(2), 403(a)(2).

[111] Rev. Rul. 57-115, 1957-1 CUM. BULL. 160. For discussion, see Chapter 5, note 34. If services are in fact called for during the deferred compensation period, it may not suffice to incorporate a provision into the contract denying the existence of an employment relationship. Cf. CASEY AND ROTHSCHILD, Ex. 91 (North American Co. and Herbert C. Freeman—contains such a provision but does not call for consultative services during the deferred compensation period). In a pending Tax Court case, Sam D. Traub, Docket #89,662, filed Oct. 24, 1960, the Commissioner of Internal Revenue has taken the position that a former executive who agreed to perform services as an independent consultant is not entitled to capital gains treatment. Cf. Estate of Frank B. Fry, 19 T.C. 461 (1952), aff'd per curiam, 205 F.2d 517 (3d Cir. 1953). But cf. Letter Ruling, 1961 P-H FED. TAX SERV. ¶ 54, 802 (retired executive continued on retainer as consultant entitled to capital gains).

[112] E.g., Pittsburgh Consolidation Coal Co., Proxy Statement for Annual Meeting, Apr. 18, 1956, p. 4 (reserve after applicable taxes on income); cf. Gulf Oil Co., Annual Report for 1953, p. 31 (total award charged against current income). Consult Briloff, Accounting Problems of Pension and Profit-Sharing Plans, SELLIN, op. cit. supra note 14, at 313, 326.

expense and reflected in profit and loss; to the extent that such payments are regarded as compensation for past services, they will generally be charged to surplus. There is, however, no hard and fast rule. The company's method of accounting for deferred compensation will not necessarily be known to the executive, much less be approved by him, and should not be held conclusive as to the intention of the parties.

Some companies consider that contingent compensation represents payment for future consultation services or an agreement not to compete, or both, and make no charge against income during the executive's full-time employment, contemplating that such contingent compensation will be charged against income in the future as and when earned and paid.

Accounting for deferred compensation for cost purposes under contracts with the Federal Government or, in the case of public utilities, for rate-making or other special purposes, will depend on statutory and contractual provisions applicable to the specific situation.[113]

Policy Considerations

Critics of deferred compensation arrangements have argued along the following lines:

1. The executive who obtains the benefit of a deferred compensation arrangement is seeking to pay a smaller tax than those outside the corporate sphere and to shift to others the cost of his tax savings.[114]
2. The company, through such an arrangement, is paternalistically guaranteeing the executive the estate which others must create for themselves through their own thrift.[115]

[113] E.g., Armed Services Procurement Regulation (ASPR), § XV, on cost principles applicable to cost-plus-fixed-fee contracts, and § VIII, applicable to termination of defense contracts for the convenience of the Government. Both sections make allowance for reasonable compensation for executives of the contractor. It does not appear, however, that the allowability of deferred compensation has given rise to disputes under formal contract dispute procedures. Pension costs are held a proper cost provided that the employee's contribution covers services rendered for the performance of the contract under which recovery is sought. Appeal of American Bridge Co., ASBCA No. 126 (1958).

[114] For examples of the criticism summarized in this and the following paragraphs of the text, see LIVINGSTON, THE AMERICAN STOCKHOLDER 230 *passim* (1958) (". . . executives have made themselves into a preferred group, a tax-protected elite"); GILBERT, DIVIDENDS AND DEMOCRACY (1956), and annual reports of Gilbert and Gilbert on stockholders meetings.

[115] "I find that in all cases in my diversified, though skinny, 'portfolio,' I am under contract to pay enormous pensions to a lot of fat cats who have been drawing

3. Through such an arrangement, the executive is endeavoring to have the company provide him with an income after retirement, not on the relatively modest basis available to employees generally under a qualified pension program, but on the basis of his highest earnings during employment.

4. Conditions attached to deferred compensation which tie the executive to his company, to the extent that they have meaning at all, freeze men in jobs and discourage initiative.[116]

5. As they multiply, such arrangements saddle the company with a sizable future burden and may perhaps render the company unsalable and unmergeable and leave it with its credit impaired and its future constricted.[117]

6. As a conclusion from the sum of the foregoing contentions, deferred compensation arrangements unfairly burden the company and its stockholders and mortgage the company's future for the "personal" and unjustifiable advantage of one or a few.

As against these contentions, it should be pointed out that deferred benefit plans were first adopted long before federal income taxes became a matter of consequence.[118] Their business justification in individual situations derives from factors such as the following:

---

big salaries from me and millions of other faceless suckers for many years and, by all rights, should have saved money for their old age just as we have tried to do." Westbrook Pegler, nationally syndicated column released May 12, 1953 and published in Hearst publications, including N. Y. Journal American. *Cf. id.,* May 14, 1953 (speaking of company thrift plans for employees as "coddling paternalism").

[116] "Deferred compensation schemes have degenerated into a grossly anti-social conspiracy to cut down and inhibit social mobility and competition for talent. All these plans have become schemes to tie executives to a corporation with golden chains, to make it financially almost impossible for a man to leave, no matter how unhappy, how frustrated or how futile his work, and to make it equally impossible for a corporation to fire him, no matter how poorly he does his work. As a result these schemes, instead of promoting executive morale, have destroyed it. In every company I know there are dozens of people who should have left the company—or should have been fired—but who stay on because the penalty of leaving is simply too great. These people spread malaise, disaffection and low morale like Typhus Mary. And let me say that I am not terribly worried about what the economists call 'monopoly.' But I am in the name of the 'Open Society' going to wage unceasing warfare against any attempt to establish a monopoly on talent—and every one of these deferred compensation plans is such a monopolistic conspiracy." Letter from Peter Drucker to one of the authors, dated March 4, 1955. *Cf.* MASON, *Introduction,* THE CORPORATION IN MODERN SOCIETY 1, 14 (1960) (criticizing "the increasing drag of pension rights and other endowments which ordinarily cannot be transferred"); Schulman, *Tax Differentials in Executive Compensation,* INCOME TAX DIFFERENTIALS 67, 81 ("it is perhaps questionable whether practices which tend to immobilize the executive are ultimately of benefit to the national economy.").

[117] E.g., Mann, *Deferred Compensation and Stock Option Plans may be Legal; but are they Ethical?,* 53 J. ACCOUNTANCY 324 (1952).

[118] See Chapter 5, notes 2 and 3.

1. A deferred compensation arrangement may serve to provide a retirement allowance that could not have been paid as part of a general pension plan; and it may be the sole means at the disposal of the smaller company of securing the employment (or sometimes the retention) of an executive whose services might otherwise be beyond the company's financial resources.

2. Postponement of compensation, and its payment on a conditional basis, may serve as a powerful inducement to continued services and, at least when based on profits, as a stimulus to greater efforts which is more potent than a currently paid bonus.

3. Deferred pay arrangements operate to spread income more or less evenly over a period of years, reduce fluctuations in earnings, and assure a minimum flow of income.[119]

4. Deferred benefit plans store a part of the executive's earnings for the future, serving thus as a valuable thrift measure and relieving the company of possible future obligations to employees with long service or to their families.

5. Deferred pay arrangements may represent one of the few methods available today to restore pay differentials between higher and lower paid personnel in a period in which high taxes, coupled with inflation, make it difficult if not impossible for the company to provide adequate salary increases.[120]

To sum up, the tax factor has undoubtedly played a major role in the development of deferred compensation arrangements. The urge for these arrangements stems from the treatment by the federal tax laws of all income—dividends, interest, wages, salaries—as taxable on the same basis, and from the absence of real recognition of the need for averaging-out. Opinions may vary as to the justice of this result.[121] It is fair to point out that the executive's income, like that of the professional man, represents in large part something akin to a return of capital. The income of one who lives by selling his services reaches a peak during a limited number of years, and under

[119] *Cf.* Com'r v. Oates, 207 F.2d 711 (7th Cir. 1953).

[120] Lasser and Rothschild, *supra* note 56, at 101.

[121] It is sometimes argued that income tax laws should distinguish between earned and unearned income, favoring the former. The Commonwealth of Massachusetts, for example, makes such a distinction. MASS. ANN. LAWS, 1945, C. 62, §§ 1, 5 (taxing income from dividends and interest at 6%, as contrasted with earned income, which is taxed at 1½%). The federal income tax laws formerly granted a preferential treatment to earned income. See Revenue Act of 1924, § 209(d); Revenue Act of 1934, § 25(a)(4) and (5). Since 1944, however, earned and unearned income are taxed alike. See Revenue Act of 1943, § 107(a), 58 STAT. 31 (1944); Silverson, *Earned Income and Ability to Pay*, 3 TAX L. REV. 299 (1948) (discussing discriminations against earned income, with a suggested solution); Bravman, *Equalization of Tax,* 50 COLUM. L. REV. 1 (1950).

traditional ideas of thrift the earnings of those years should be largely put aside to provide a fund for the future. But under present rates of taxation that is not possible, for earnings during the peak years must in large part be turned over to the government. The result is that many an executive, unable himself to build resources out of his current compensation, welcomes arrangements under which a portion of his earnings will be set aside and paid to him or his family in the future.

CHAPTER 7

EXPENSE ACCOUNTS, PERQUISITES, AND FRINGE BENEFITS *

THE EXPENSE ACCOUNT

Corporate Practice. Except for personnel directly connected with sales, the large, publicly held company employs the expense account primarily for its top executives.[1] Its use to provide for payment or reimbursement of travel and entertainment expenses is also widespread among closely held companies whose affairs are often interwoven with those of their stockholder-executives.[2]

Corporate practice recognizes as properly reimbursable those expenses coming within the two major categories of travel and entertainment.[3] Travel on company business includes the cost of baggage

* The substance of the expense account section of this chapter, before revision to reflect subsequent developments, was first published in 67 YALE L.J. 1363 (1958) and was republished, without the footnotes, in U. S. NEWS AND WORLD REPORT, Jan. 23, 1959, p. 82 et seq. The article was cited in 1959 in the United States Senate and in hearings before the Senate Finance Committee and was made part of the record of panel discussions held later in that year by the Ways and Means Committee of the House of Representatives. See *Hearing on H.R. 7523 Before the Senate Committee on Finance,* 86th Cong., 1st Sess. 90, 101 (June 23, 1959); CONG. REC. 10807 (daily ed. June 25, 1959).

Legislation in the area was under consideration as this book went to press.

[1] However, the expense account may be found at all management levels in advertising, motion picture, television, and related industries.

[2] SANDERS, EFFECTS OF TAXATION ON EXECUTIVES 144 (1951). *Cf. id.* at 143: "Whether a particular item of expense is a personal expense or an expense of the business is in many cases impossible of categorical answer because it is both"; *id.* at 152: "[F]or all executives in positions of great importance, their business, social, and personal affairs are so much intermingled that it is not easy to draw the line between them. . . ."

[3] The reference here is to general corporate practice, not the tax results of such practice, which are discussed in the following sections. Specific items mentioned are based on evidence of corporate practice and on various surveys. See NEUHOFF, EXECUTIVE EXPENSE ACCOUNTS, NICB Studies in Business Policy No. 67 (1954); *Executive Expense Practices,* AM. BUSINESS, Jan. 1957, p. 29; *Executive Expenses Viewed Morosely,* BUSINESS WEEK, Apr. 10, 1954, p. 47; *What Goes and What Won't Go on Expense Accounts,* CHANGING TIMES, Sept. 1954, p. 39; *Reducing Your Expense Account Headaches,* 43 MGMT. REV. 305 (1954); Furash, *Expense Accounts,* 38 HARV. BUS. REV. 6 (Mar.-Apr., 1960); PFLOMM, ADMINISTRATION OF EXECUTIVE EXPENSE ACCOUNTS, NICB Studies in Business Policy No. 96 (1960); Hoffman, *Control of the Executive's Expense Account,* THE TAX EXECUTIVE, Oct. 1960, 23.

handling, tips, hotel accommodations and food, and of telephone, telegraph, stenographic, and other special services. Entertainment, both of the company's customers and, less frequently, of the executive's employees and business associates, includes the cost of restaurants, theaters, sporting events, gifts, and, occasionally, the incidental expenses of home entertainment.[4] Other expenses often reimbursed by the corporation are subscription costs for business journals and periodicals, dues of trade and professional associations, dues and charges of town and lunch clubs—occasionally of country clubs as well[5]— and operating costs of automobiles and airplanes.[6] On the borderline between proper and improper expenses are laundry and valet charges,[7] maintenance fees for yachts used primarily in entertaining company personnel, and the costs of attending a convention, especially when it is incidental to a vacation trip or when the executive seeks to deduct the traveling expenses of his wife.[8] Frequently outside the sphere of reimbursable items are the costs of hunting, fishing, and other sports.

Corporate practice generally refuses to recognize entertainment, telephone and other charges considered personal, barber services, shoeshines, excessive taxi fares, cocktails, movies, tobacco, and magazines for self-entertainment away from home, valet and laundry

[4] At-home entertainment, not found as a common occurrence, was reimbursed by about half the companies surveyed by the Conference Board. NEUHOFF, *op. cit. supra* note 3, at 14.

[5] Two out of three companies surveyed by the Conference Board paid club dues, but only in the case of top executives. *Id.* at 15. An increasing number of companies have adopted policies designed to encourage membership in technical societies by engineers, chemists, and other professional employees. See *Company Payment of Membership Expenses,* 22 NICB MGMT. REC. 19 (1960).

[6] In the Conference Board survey, mileage allowances were found to range from 6¢ to 10¢ a mile, with the usual allowance being 7¢ or 8¢. NEUHOFF, *op. cit. supra* note 3, at 10. This survey was published in 1954. In 1955, the mileage allowance for government employees using their own cars on official business was increased from 7¢ to 10¢ a mile. 69 Stat. 394 (1955), 5 U.S.C. § 837 (Supp. V, 1958). For the cost of airplane operation, see *Management's 10,000 Plane Air Fleet,* FORTUNE, Nov. 1953, p. 117. (Piper Tri-Pacer costs 6.4¢ per mile; DC-3 about ten times that).

[7] The Conference Board found that most of the companies in its survey paid laundry expenses during trips of over a week and valet expenses during trips of over three days. NEUHOFF, *op. cit. supra* note 3, at 10. Compare *Executive Expense Practices, supra* note 3 (trips of 7–10 days and 4–7 days, respectively).

[8] The Conference Board found that few companies pay the expenses of the wife of a top executive on an extended trip even when the wife's presence "is considered a business asset." NEUHOFF, *op. cit. supra* note 3, at 12. On the other hand, the HARVARD BUSINESS REVIEW survey found that 73.1% of executives in top management were accompanied by their wives; only 17.17% were with companies that never paid for the wife's expenses. Furash, *supra* note 3, Ex. II. For an example of a contractual provision for such payment, see note 10, *infra.* For tax treatment, see note 77 *infra* and accompanying text.

charges for short trips, and, generally, overspending for meals, tips, and similar items.

Some corporations have recognized the desirability of an expense clause in the employment contract when substantial expenses are contemplated. The clause serves not only to avoid the possibility of future controversy and to protect the directors from stockholder criticism, but also to simplify the tax position of both corporation and executive. A typical clause reads:

• 8. It is contemplated that in performing services hereunder the Executive will be required to incur entertainment expense in the interests and on behalf of the Corporation and in furtherance of its business. To defray such expense the Corporation agrees to make available to the Executive sums not to exceed a total of $.... per annum. Subject to such limitation in amount, the Corporation at the end of each month during the period of this agreement will, upon submission of appropriate bills or vouchers, pay all such expense incurred by the Executive during such month, such payment to be made either directly to the payee named in such bills or vouchers, or, to the extent paid by the Executive, by reimbursement of the Executive. The Executive agrees to maintain adequate records, in such detail as the Corporation may reasonably request, of all expenses to be reimbursed by the Corporation hereunder and to make such records available for inspection as and when reasonably requested by the Corporation. The provisions of this paragraph are not intended to apply to traveling expense or to business expense (other than entertainment) incurred by the Executive with the specific approval of the Corporation and such expense, as and when incurred, shall be separately paid, or reimbursed to the Executive, by the Corporation, upon submission of appropriate bills or vouchers and upon his maintenance of adequate records, but otherwise without reference to the provisions of this paragraph.

By way of variation, the expense clause may provide for reimbursement of all actual expenses of a generally designated nature,[9] or

[9] See UNIVERSAL, App. O, ¶ 2; CASEY AND ROTHSCHILD, PAY CONTRACTS WITH KEY MEN (1953) (hereinafter cited as CASEY AND ROTHSCHILD) Ex. 165 (Pepsi-Cola contract with Alfred N. Steele—"All travel and other expenses incident to the rendering of services by the Executive hereunder"); *id.* Ex. 166 (Universal contract with N. J. Blumberg—"All reasonable entertainment and other expenses incurred or expended by him in the performance of his duties hereunder for Universal"); *id.* Ex. 169 (Loew's, Inc. contract with William F. Rodgers—"All reasonable and necessary expenses incurred, including living and traveling expenses of such official travel"). In *Executive Expense Practices, supra* note 3, the survey found that 55% of the companies surveyed reimbursed executives for their expendi-

for payment of expenses up to a maximum figure,[10] with or without a requirement for vouchers or other detail.[11] Or the clause may stipulate payment of a fixed weekly, monthly, or annual sum.[12] Separate provision may be made for specific facilities which the executive is to keep at the disposal of the corporation, and for the business use of which he is to be paid.[13] And though the type of clause set forth above contemplates separate payment of business expenses outside the category of entertainment, such a clause may of course limit payment or reimbursement to non-entertainment expense.[14] In most cases, payment or reimbursement for travel and similar non-entertainment expense is company practice without specific provisions in the employment contract.

As an alternative to paying or reimbursing expenses, the corporation may fix the executive's salary with a view to his assuming the payment of entertainment and similar costs. If the executive is to pay such bills himself, a clause in the employment contract to that effect, along the following lines, may be helpful from a corporate as well as a tax viewpoint:

---

tures, 37% combined reimbursement with direct payment of expenses incurred by executives, and only 7% had flat expense allowances; of the companies with flat expense allowances, over one-half had fewer than 1,000 employees.

[10] See, e.g., CASEY AND ROTHSCHILD, Ex. 167 (Loew's, Inc. contract with Louis B. Mayer—expenditures for meetings and entertainment, whether at home or elsewhere, and for appropriate gifts up to $20,000); WASHINGTON AND ROTHSCHILD, COMPENSATING THE CORPORATE EXECUTIVE (rev. ed. 1951) (hereinafter cited as WASHINGTON AND ROTHSCHILD), App. E (Burlington Mills contract with Herbert M. Kaiser, providing up to $20,000 annually for cost of entertainment and incidental expenses). When the contract contemplates long periods of travel away from home, the executive is sometimes reimbursed for his wife's travel expenses. See UNIVERSAL, App. O, ¶ 2 (travel in excess of two weeks); see CASEY AND ROTHSCHILD, Ex. 166. For discussion of deductibility by the executive of his wife's travel expenses, see notes 77 and 78 *infra* and accompanying text.

[11] CASEY AND ROTHSCHILD, Ex. 165 ("The Company will reimburse the Executive on presentation of expense accounts for any such entertainment expenses, which are adaptable to the usual accounting procedures of the Company"); *id.* Ex. 166 ("expenses shall be paid promptly as vouchers therefor are presented by Blumberg"); *id.* Ex. 167 (Loew's will promptly reimburse Mr. Mayer for such expenditures upon the submission from time to time of statements therefor"); see U. S. RUBBER, App. B (bills required for traveling expenses only).

[12] See, e.g., CASEY AND ROTHSCHILD, Ex. 168 (Panhandle Producing & Refining Co. contract with Roger Gilbert—$250 per month for entertainment expenses); *id.* Ex. 169 (Loew's, Inc. contract with William F. Rodgers—"$200 per week (in addition to the traveling expenses, if any, hereinbefore provided), for unusual expenses incurred in behalf of the Corporation for which it is difficult or impossible for Rodgers to account in detail"); see also Paramount Pictures, Inc. contract with Reuben B. Bolstad, Dec. 31, 1945, SEC Rep. Form 8K (Mar. 1946) ($75 per week from a subsidiary of the employing corporation).

[13] WASHINGTON AND ROTHSCHILD, App. J, ¶ 7.

[14] See CASEY AND ROTHSCHILD, Ex. 169 (reimbursement for expenses incurred in "official travel" and $200 weekly allowance for "unusual expenses").

• 8. The Company acknowledges that the successful operation and management of its business has required and will continue to require the Executive to expend, in the discharge of his duties as general manager and in the interests and on behalf of the Company and its business, substantial sums for traveling, board, meals and other usual business costs incident to relations with company personnel and with persons and representatives of companies with whom the Company has or might expect to conduct business. For such costs as are readily susceptible to the usual accounting, the Executive shall be reimbursed by the Company upon presentation of statements in the manner required by Company policy. For any other such costs as are not readily susceptible to the usual accounting, the Executive shall not be entitled to reimbursement, it being understood and agreed that his compensation has been determined with a view to enabling him to incur and pay costs of this nature on behalf of the Company out of such compensation.

For the controlling stockholder-executive of a closely held company, this clause may not be desirable. By failing to identify the exact portion of over-all payment representing salary, it leaves unfixed the amount of salary which the company can claim as a deduction for reasonable compensation. This uncertainty, coupled with the general absence of an arm's length relationship, renders an expense clause less useful to a controlling stockholder-executive than records properly substantiating the nature of payments or reimbursements made from time to time for specific expenses.[15]

Questions relating to the expense clause have arisen primarily in tax cases involving either the company's tax deduction or the executive's income tax or tax deductions. Stockholder litigation has been infrequent.[16] It should be noted, however, that the expense allowance,

[15] *Cf.* ROTHSCHILD, COMPENSATION AND INCENTIVES FOR EXECUTIVES, ENCYCLO-PEDIA OF TAX PROCEDURES 965, 974 (1960).

[16] In Cohn v. Columbia Pictures Corp., N.Y. County Clerk's Index No. 9038/1950 (Sup. Ct. 1950), a stockholder's action against a corporation and its directors was based, among other things, on alleged payment by the corporation of: (1) the expense, including personnel, food, and operation, of a yacht used one summer by the president of the corporation; (2) the cost of building and maintaining a projection theater at the home of the president; (3) the expense of New Year's Eve parties at the president's home; and (4) the price of clothes for the president's wife. In recommending approval of a settlement of the action, the Referee reported that: (1) "the corporation had a good business purpose in chartering the yacht for Mr. Cohn that summer. For the cost of charter and maintenance they had him available throughout the summer at a time when he otherwise would have gone on vacation"; (2) the president's personal use of the projection theater to entertain some of his personal guests was "inconsequential when compared with the use to which it has been put for the benefit of" the corporation, and the $129,000 cost of the theater, and the subsequent cost of its maintenance, were "a small enough consideration to pay for the extra services rendered by Mr. Cohn in this manner"; (3) three New

like any other corporate expense, can be criticized as either excessive in amount or wholly improper.[17]

Income Tax Treatment of Expense Account Items.

THE CORPORATION'S DEDUCTION. If a corporate executive entertains customers of the company in the interest of advancing its business relations, if he travels on company business away from the place where his office is located, or if he otherwise properly incurs expenses on behalf of his employer, payment of the executive's bills, either directly or by way of reimbursement, is normally deductible by the corporation as an ordinary and necessary business expense.[18]

Year's Eve parties, together costing about $9,000, were "necessary and proper in order to foster a good relationship between the motion picture companies, the stars, and other persons in the industry"; and (4) the garments made for the president's wife by the company's wardrobe department were paid for on a cost plus 10% basis, and since they were made only "during the slack period . . . idle personnel of the corporation were being used to good advantage." Referee's Report Pursuant to Order Dated March 13, 1952, pp. 26–29 (July 8, 1952), *approved,* 117 N.Y.S.2d 809 (Sup. Ct. 1952). The settlement involved the president's payment to the corporation of $20,000 toward a $40,000 bill which had been paid by the corporation to attorneys employed for the president in connection with the negotiation of his employment contract. It also authorized the board of directors to increase the president's expense allowance to $600 a week from the $300 figure which had been paid since 1932. *Cf.* Heddendorff v. East Boston Corp. (D. Mass. 1958), reported in N.Y. Times, June 19, 1958, § 1, p. 22, col. 4 (stockholder action challenging, *inter alia,* $106,000 of expenses, including $1,868 for liquor, paid by the corporation for its president, Bernard Goldfine). See also Abramson v. Blakeley, Civ. Action 1210 (Del. Ch. 1960) (executive of Schenley Industries, Inc. required under compromise and settlement to reimburse company for $38,423 for allegedly excessive business expenses). For a suit by stockholders against executives of Canadian Javelin, Ltd. charging "lavish living at company expense," see Wall Street Journal, Apr. 27, 1961, p. 1, col. 6 at p. 20, col. 1 (alleged pleasure trips in company aircraft, including transportation "for the sole purpose of attending a wine festival in France").

[17] Charges of extravagant expense account spending have been involved in proxy contests. See, e.g., N. Y. Times, Mar. 14, 1954, § 3, p. 1, col. 3, p. 10, cols. 3–4 (New Haven R.R.). See also *id.,* Apr. 9, 1954, p. 38, col. 1; Edwards, *Life on the Cuff,* TODAY'S LIVING, Mar. 17, 1957, p. 5 (both reporting stockholder charges against Lucian W. Sprague, chairman of the Minneapolis & St. Louis Railroad, based on alleged corporate payment for "two big, powerful autos, a super first-class trip to Europe with Mrs. Sprague, and the cost of a private island retreat, not to mention occasional bills for groceries and flowers").

Corporations subject to regulation may also have expense items questioned by regulatory commissions. Thus, in fixing the operating expenses for fare-setting purposes, the District of Columbia Public Utilities Commission has disallowed travel and entertainment expenses of D. C. Transit, Inc., including the cost of a hotel apartment and long-distance telephone calls of the company's president. See *Hearings Before the House Select Committee on Small Business on Complaints of Small- and Independent-Business Men Operating Sightseeing Businesses in the District of Columbia,* 85th Cong., 2d Sess. 91–106 (1958).

[18] Sanitary Farms Dairy, Inc., 25 T.C. 463 (1955) (deduction for safari expenses held legitimate).

The corporation may likewise take a deduction if, instead of paying or reimbursing specific expenses, it grants the executive a fixed expense or per diem allowance for travel and related costs, provided, of course, that the allowance is reasonable. The large, publicly held corporation appears to have encountered little difficulty in taking deductions for its employees' entertainment and travel expenses,[19] and those relatively few problems which have arisen have usually been resolved at the field-audit level.[20]

In the context of the closely held corporation, on the other hand, the corporate deduction is frequently and successfully challenged by the Commissioner.[21] A challenge is made and generally sustained, in whole or in part, whenever the expenditure appears primarily to serve a personal rather than a business purpose,[22] as when the cor-

[19] Few decisions have been found involving litigated deductions by large, publicly held companies or their executives. For an exceptional case, see Penn v. Robertson, 29 F. Supp. 386 (M.D.N.C. 1939), aff'd, 115 F.2d 167 (4th Cir. 1940) (allowing expenses of vice-president of American Tobacco Company).

[20] Company payment or reimbursement of an executive's personal expenses (for example, of rent for an apartment used by the executive apart from his work) would appear tantamount to additional compensation taxable to the executive and deductible by the company. See note 13 supra and accompanying text. As a practical matter, in the case of publicly held companies, some field agents have disallowed the corporate deduction of personal items without seeking to tax the executive upon the company's payments. Their analysis appears to end with the statement that the payments were not normal or necessary expenses of the corporate business.

In the case of the closely held company, improper payments by the company for the benefit of a stockholder-executive may be held dividends and hence non-deductible by the company. See cases cited note 31 infra. Moreover, when an executive is unable to prove the expense item, a close corporation with no independent records will often find it difficult to substantiate the contention that the payment is deductible as compensation. See P. S. Thorsen & Co., 15 B.T.A. 1281 (1929); Frishkorn Real Estate Co., 15 B.T.A. 463, 466 (1929). See also Donald V. Smith, 6 CCH Tax Ct. Mem. 548, 561 (1947) (fixed expense allowance fund not "reasonably equivalent" to unitemized but estimated expenses).

[21] Expense deductions claimed by closely held corporations are considered the main source of abuse. Expense Accounts: A $5 Billion Tax Deduction and Growing, U. S. News and World Report, Aug. 16, 1957, p. 83, at 88 (quoting Under-Secretary of the Treasury Fred C. Scribner, Jr.). See also note 20 supra.

[22] See, e.g., Wm. T. Stover Co., 27 T.C. 434, 440–41 (1956) (yacht used for personal pleasure of company's principal stockholder-executive, as well as for business entertainment); C. & C. Beverage, Inc., 13 CCH Tax Ct. Mem. 649, 652–53 (1954) (country club dues of president when desire to play golf was main motivation of membership, even though some company customers belonged to the club and others were entertained there); Friedlander Corp., 19 T.C. 1197, 1210–11 (1953), rev'd on other grounds, 216 F.2d 757 (5th Cir. 1954) (Rotary Club membership dues of company president which he had previously paid for twenty years out of his personal funds); James Schulz, 16 T.C. 401, 406 (1951) (entertainment held to exceed business needs since company had more orders than it could fill); Fred W. Leadbetter, 39 B.T.A. 629, 634 (1939) (cost of five automobiles maintained for personal use of executive and his family); cf. Sam Rosania, Sr., 15 CCH Tax Ct. Mem. 580, 586 (1956) (use of corporate auto for president's personal needs

poration pays for a yacht,[23] expensive residence,[24] hunting expedition,[25] or similar luxury.[26] In special circumstances, however, the corporation may establish that all or part of a luxury expenditure serves an exclusive corporate purpose.[27] Even when the corporation is entitled to some deduction—when there are no exact accounts distinguishing between personal and business costs—the Tax Court is free to substitute its judgment for the taxpayer's in apportioning the expenditure between deductible and non-deductible amounts.[28]

When a corporate disbursement is disallowed as a business expense deduction, complete loss of the deduction is possible whether the corporation is publicly or closely held. Theoretically, a company's direct payment or reimbursement of an executive's personal expenses would appear to be tantamount to additional compensation taxable to the executive and deductible by the company. In one case involving

---

treated as giving president $500 additional taxable income). Decisions involving the right of a sole proprietor, a partner, or one engaged in professional practice to deduct entertainment expenses are relevant to the closed corporation's right to deduct. See Richard A. Sutter, 21 T.C. 170 (1953) (various categories of physician's entertainment expenses disallowed in whole or in part). *But see* Olivia de Havilland Goodrich, 20 T.C. 323, 331–32 (1953) (actress's gifts to business associates who would not accept compensation for services held deductible business expenses).

[23] American Properties, Inc., 28 T.C. 1100 (1957) (expense of racing boats found sole stockholder's personal hobby); Wm. T. Stover Co., *supra* note 22, at 440-41 (cabin cruiser); Thomas W. Briggs, 15 CCH TAX CT. MEM. 440, 447–48 (1956) (yacht maintained by taxpayer and his corporation); Richard A. Sutter, *supra* note 22, at 174 (yacht); Hal E. Roach Studios, 20 B.T.A. 917 (1930) (yacht used partly for business and partly for pleasure).

[24] Lanteen Medical Laboratories, Inc., 10 T.C. 279, 288–90 (1948) (ranch with landscaping, imposing dwellings, and golf course).

[25] Richard A. Sutter, *supra* note 22. But *cf.* Sanitary Farms Dairy, Inc., *supra* note 18 (cost of safari allowed as advertising expense).

[26] E.g., Paul E. Jackson, 13 CCH TAX CT. MEM. 1175, 1178 (1954) (mink coat for advertising executive's wife); Haverhill Shoe Novelty Co., 15 T.C. 517 (1950) (wedding of treasurer's daughter); see Jacobs, *Glamorous Fringe Benefits*, 36 B.U.L. REV. 151 (1956).

[27] E. E. Dickinson, 8 B.T.A. 722 (1927) (yacht used for entertainment of business customers held a business asset); *cf.* Sanitary Farms Dairy, Inc., *supra* note 18. Proof of the executive's dislike of the specific luxury involved may help convince a court that it serves an exclusive business purpose. See Johnson v. United States, 45 F. Supp. 377 (S.D. Cal. 1941), *rev'd on other grounds,* 135 F.2d 125 (9th Cir. 1943) (membership in Los Angeles country club).

[28] One-half of the deductions claimed for the use of yachts was allowed in Wm. T. Stover Co., *supra* note 22; Thomas W. Briggs, *supra* note 23. In Richard A. Sutter, *supra* note 22, one-fourth of the deductions was allowed on facts deemed less favorable to the taxpayer. See also George A. Searight, 9 CCH TAX CT. MEM. 731 (1950) (deduction reduced from $10,301 to $444.42). In Al J. Smith, 33 T.C. 861 (1960) the Tax Court found that taxpayer did not consume less than his guests in apportioning deductible portion of cost of meals. Compare authorities cited note 93 *infra.*

a closely held company, the court so held with respect to the disallowed portion of a reimbursement for entertainment and travel expenses.[29] As a practical matter, however, a disallowed expense deduction will usually not be allowed as a deduction for additional compensation; [30] in the case of a closely held company, it more often is considered a distribution in the nature of a dividend—taxable to the executive but not deductible by the corporation.[31]

THE EXECUTIVE'S TAX STATUS. *Receipt of Income.* If expenses incurred by an executive are proper business expenses of his corporation, their payment by the corporation clearly does not constitute compensation to the executive, whether corporate payment is made directly or is reimbursed to the executive who initially made the payment.[32] To qualify for this treatment, however, the executive must be able to demonstrate that the expense paid or reimbursed was a business expense of the corporation—not an expense of his own. Adequate recording of expenses by the corporation indicating amounts and corporate purposes, and reimbursement based upon the presentation of adequate bills or vouchers, will of course facilitate this aim. If the executive is to be reimbursed for the partial use in

[29] W. Horace Williams Co. v. Lambert, 56–2 U.S.T.C. ¶ 9839 (E.D. La. 1956), *aff'd sub nom.* Williams v. United States, 245 F.2d 559 (5th Cir. 1957) (disallowing executive's deduction claimed for travel and entertainment equal to his expense allowance but unsubstantiated by detailed records, and charging amount to him as income).

[30] See Joseph Morgenstern, P-H 1955 T.C. MEM. DEC. ¶ 55086 (depreciation of automobile maintained by corporation for benefit of principal stockholder-executive held not intended or treated by corporation as compensation to executive) ; *cf.* Marvin T. Blackwell, 15 CCH TAX CT. MEM. 962, 968–71 (1956) (corporation failing to raise argument that disallowed expenses were additional compensation) ; Hal E. Roach Studios, *supra* note 23 (same). *But see* Rodgers Dairy Co., 14 T.C. 66, 73 (1950) (amount disallowed as automobile expense would represent additional compensation to executive who had personal use of automobile).

[31] See B. F. Crabbe, 14 CCH TAX CT. MEM. 1305, 1308–10 (1955) (disallowed travel expense reimbursement held dividend to president of closely held corporation) ; Louis Greenspon, 23 T.C. 138, 148–52 (1954), *aff'd,* 229 F.2d 947 (8th Cir. 1956) (corporate expenses in improving stockholder-executive's farm, which was his home but little used for business entertainment, held non-deductible by corporation and in nature of corporate distribution taxable to executive as income) ; *cf.* Byers v. Com'r, 199 F.2d 273, 275 (8th Cir. 1952) ; 58th St. Plaza Theatre, Inc. v. Com'r, 195 F.2d 724 (2d Cir. 1952) ; Flora Regensburg, 1 CCH TAX CT .MEM. 925 (1943), *aff'd,* 144 F.2d 41 (2d Cir.), *cert. denied,* 323 U.S. 783 (1944). *But cf.* Joseph Morgenstern, *supra* note 30 (non-deductible payment by corporation not treated as dividend to stockholder-executive). See also note 20 *supra.*

[32] The amounts so paid or reimbursed to the executive need not be included in his gross income, if he is required to and does account to the company. Treas. Reg. § 1.167(a)–17(b) (1958). As to what constitutes such an account, see *infra* note 97. Eitingon-Schild Co., 21 B.T.A. 1163, 1175–76 (1931) ; Julius Forstmann, 6 B.T.A. 21 (1927).

company business of a home, club, automobile, or airplane, an appropriate formula should be evolved to substantiate the cost attributable to such use.[33] If verifying records of this nature cannot be produced, expenses reimbursed to the executive may be taxed to him wholly or partially as income.[34]

As distinguished from payment or reimbursement of specific expenses, a flat expense allowance must be reported as gross income in the executive's income tax return; business expenses paid by him from the allowance may then be deducted in computing adjusted gross income.[35] Although such expenses might reasonably be considered unreimbursed employee expenses deductible only from adjusted gross income on the theory that the corporation, having designated an enlarged area of executive responsibility, is merely providing additional salary with which the executive may perform his expanded function, the Tax Court has preferred to view the transaction as a prepayment for corporate expenses that the executive is expected to incur. Again, the burden rests with the executive as taxpayer to prove that he incurred the expenses in the company's interest and that the amount deducted corresponds to his actual disbursements.[36]

[33] The difficulties involved in allocating business and personal costs without ascertainable formulas leave the courts with little evidence on which to base their decision. See Willard I. Thompson, 15 T.C. 609 (1950); *McDonald, Travel and Entertainment Expenses,* ENCYCLOPEDIA OF TAX PROCEDURES 1038, 1049, n. 26 (1960) (collecting cases). See also the contract clause cited note 13 *supra.* For suggestions about records that should be kept and workable formulas, see Dendy, *How To Get the Maximum Deductions From Compensation,* 8 INST. FED. TAX. 1052, 1055 (1950); Green, *How To Handle Expense Accounts of Corporate Executives, id.* at 564, 566–68; Hayes, *Deductions for Travel and Entertainment Expense,* 4 ARTHUR YOUNG J. 1 (1957); Hemmings, *Technical Rules Underlying Current Furor Over Deductibility of T & E Expenses,* 8 J. TAXATION 2 (1958); Osmond, *The Corporate Executive and the Business Expense Deduction,* 33 TAXES 68 (1955); Perkins, *Recommendations for Preventing Disallowance of Expenses for Travel and Entertainment,* 4 J. TAXATION 10 (1956); Stuart, *Social Club Dues and Expenses,* 31 TAXES 69, 71–72 (1953). When the use of facilities is contemplated and no formula for payment is feasible, payment for the facilities has been combined with reimbursement for entertainment expense. See BURLINGTON, App. J, ¶ 7; *cf.* Parker, *A Check List of Deductions for the Professional Taxpayer,* 29 N.Y.S.B. BULL. 141 (1957).

[34] B. F. Crabbe, 15 CCH TAX CT. MEM. 216, 219–21 (1956); B. F. Crabbe, *supra* note 31 (same for different years); Victor Cooper, 8 CCH TAX CT. MEM. 689, 697 (1949). See Joseph L. Weinfeld, 20 CCH TAX CT. MEM. 70 (1961) (salesman allowed deduction of $7,000 as traveling expenses on the basis solely of daily diary entries).

[35] See Treas. Reg. § 1.162–17(c) (1958); *cf.* Walter I. Geer, 28 T.C. 994 (1957) (Georgia state court judge's contingent travel allowance of $200 per month held income). See also Treas. Reg. 118, § 39.23(a)(2) (1953).

[36] Walter I. Geer, *supra* note 35; Ned Wayburn, 32 B.T.A. 813 (1935); Green, *supra* note 33, at 566. An unqualified commitment to pay a specific expense allow-

Expenditures involving transactions that are illegal, improper, or otherwise against public policy should not be deemed "ordinary and necessary" business expenses.[37] Entertainment of or gifts to a public official should thus be disallowed as a tax deduction, whether claimed by the executive making the disbursement or by his employer.

Deductions from Income. Individual or Corporate Deduction? An executive, by virtue of his position, may make expenditures which he considers to be ordinary requirements of his occupation and for which no reimbursement is contemplated or received. Since a corporate executive is usually deemed in the "trade or business" of being an executive,[38] compensation received from his employment is income

---

ance with no requirement of an accounting makes it necessary for the corporation to include the expense allowance in its information returns, Forms 1096 and 1099. Treas. Reg. §§ 1.6041–2a, 1.6041–3(i) (1958). There is, however, no requirement for withholding of Federal income tax [Treas. Reg. § 1.3401(b)(2) (1957)], nor is such an allowance subject to social security tax [C.F.R. 26 § 31.3121(a)–1(H) (1956)] or to the federal unemployment tax [C.F.R. 26 § 31.3306(b)–1(h) (1956)]. The former requirement of an accounting by the employee to the employer, to avoid social security and unemployment taxes, has been eliminated. See Mim. 6547, 1950–2 CUM. BULL. 113.

[37] For cases disallowing expenditures as per se illegal, see R. E. L. Finley, 27 T.C. 413, 423–24 (1956) (liquor purchased for business entertainment in prohibition state); Fred D. Newman, P-H 1952 T.C. MEM. DEC. ¶ 52267 (cost of whisky samples given to employees of state liquor store in violation of state law); Lorraine Corp., 33 B.T.A. 1158, 1166 (1936) (liquor purchased for entertainment purposes during Prohibition). Expenditures not illegal in themselves are generally disallowed when their deduction would frustrate national or state policies. See Com'r v. Heininger, 320 U.S. 467, 473, n. 8 (1943) (citing cases). For applications of this rule in particular contexts, see Wm. T. Stover Co., *supra* note 22, at 443–45 (disallowing deduction for compensation paid state hospital director as consultant by taxpayer who sold supplies to the hospital); see also Duval Motor Co., 28 T.C. 42, 54 (1957) (disallowing cost of gift certificate given to state highway patrol director by dealer selling cars to the highway patrol); Cecil I. Haas, P-H 1953 T.C. MEM. DEC. ¶ 53322, at 1007 (holding expenditures for the entertainment of public officials to be contrary to public policy and therefore non-deductible). In order for expenditures to be disallowed as against public policy, the federal or state policy must be sharply defined. *Compare* Lilly v. Com'r, 343 U.S. 90 (1952) (allowing optometrist's deduction of payments to physicians referring their patients to the optometrist, where state statute enacted after payments had been made prohibited such conduct), *with* Textile Mills Securities Corp. v. Com'r, 314 U.S. 326 (1941) (upholding Treasury Regulation disallowing deduction of lobbying expenses although Congress had not declared such expenditures illegal). When federal tax law recognizes as a "business" an activity illegal under state law, legitimate expenses of that business are deductible. See Com'r v. Sullivan, 356 U.S. 27 (1958), *affirming* 241 F.2d 46 (7th Cir. 1957) (rent and wages of bookmaker). On the relationship of deductibility and public policy generally, see Comment, *The Effect of Lilly on the Disallowance of Expense and Loss Deductions Deemed Contrary to Public Policy,* 41 MARQ. L. REV. 305 (1957); Notes, 51 COLUM. L. REV. 752 (1951), 38 VA. L. REV. 771 (1952).

[38] See Folker v. Johnson, 230 F.2d 906 (2d Cir. 1956) (corporate executive held in "trade or business" for loss-carryback purposes); Samuel H. Ranson, Jr., 11

from a trade or business, and ordinary and necessary expenses required by his employment are deductible as business expenses.[39] Educational courses which he undertakes for the purpose of maintaining the skills required in his work are deductible,[40] but courses taken with a view to obtaining a promotion are not.[41] It is equally well-established that the executive as taxpayer may not take deductions belonging to another taxpayer—the corporation which employs

---

CCH TAX CT. MEM. 699, 701 (1952) (same); see also Schmidlapp v. Com'r, 96 F.2d 680, 681–82 (2d Cir. 1938); cf. Anders J. Lagreide, 23 T.C. 508, 512–13 (1954) (teacher held engaged in "trade or business" for loss-carryback purposes).

A corporate executive has been allowed to deduct compensation paid for legal or other professional services on the ground that he is engaged in a trade or business. Hochschild v. Com'r, 161 F.2d 817 (2d Cir. 1947); Foss v. Com'r, 75 F.2d 326, 327–28 (1st Cir. 1935). See Lillian M. Goldsmith, 7 B.T.A. 151 (1927) (allowance of deduction to corporate officer owning half the stock of corporation for salary paid to a substitute hired to look after interests of officer during absence). See also Cohn v. Columbia Pictures Corp., supra note 16 (allegedly improper payment by corporation of executives' legal expenses). But cf. Fred F. Fischer, P-H 1947 T.C. MEM. DEC. ¶ 47131 (expenses held those of corporation, not of executive); Hal E. Roach, 20 B.T.A. 919 (1930) (same).

For a carefully reasoned discussion, see Trent v. Com'r, 61–2 CCH U.S.T.C. ¶ 9506 (2d Cir. 1961) (loan to company by executive held to result in business bad debt).

[39] Schmidlapp v. Com'r, supra note 38. However, expenses incurred in organizing a business by one who later becomes an executive in that business are not deductible. Frank B. Polachek, 22 T.C. 858, 862–63 (1954); Morton Frank, 20 T.C. 511 (1953); Dwight A. Ward, 20 T.C. 332, 343–44 (1953).

Amounts paid as employment agency fees are deductible. In 1960 the Treasury Department revoked a forty-year-old ruling which had permitted the deduction. O.D. 579, 3 CUM. BULL. 130 (1920); see Rev. Rul. 60–158, 1960–1 CUM. BULL. 140. As a result of protest, it reinstated its former ruling. See Rev. Rul. 60–223, 1960–1 CUM. BULL. 57. Other expenditures incurred in seeking a change of employment have been held non-deductible. I.T. 1397, 1–2 CUM. BULL. 145 (1922); T. W. Ryan, Tax Ct. Mem. 1959–131, 18 CCH TAX CT. MEM. 580 (1959).

[40] Treas. Reg. § 1.162–5 (1958). In Rev. Rul. 60–97, 1960–11 INT. REV. BULL. 9, the Treasury Department elaborated upon provisions of the Regulations distinguishing deductible from non-deductible educational expenses. The leading case is Coughlin v. Com'r, 202 F.2d 307 (2d Cir. 1953) (travel and other expenses of a lawyer specializing in taxation who attended the Institute on Federal Taxation of New York University).

[41] Treas. Reg. § 1.162–6 (1958). See Rev. Rul. 60–97 supra note 40. For an example, see Knut F. Larson, 15 T.C. 956 (1950) (tuition, books, and other expenses for evening engineering courses). Compare John S. Watson, 31 T.C. 1014 (1959) (a doctor specializing in internal medicine may deduct the cost of psychoanalysis since it improves his skills in internal medicine) with Namrow v. Com'r, 288 F.2d 648 (4th Cir. 1961), affirming Arnold Namrow, 33 T.C. 419 (1959) (a psychiatrist analyzed with a view to becoming a member of a psychoanalytical group could not deduct the cost of his analysis since it was undertaken to qualify him for a different branch of practice). See also Joseph T. Booth III, 35 T.C. No. 119 (1961) (expenses of lawyer who took graduate courses in taxation not deductible). Consult Hagendorf, IRS and Tax Court Are Unclear on Tax Treatment of Costs of Education Related to Job, 12 J. TAXATION 353 (1960).

him.[42] What will ultimately be held to be the executive's business expense and what will be considered the corporation's cannot always be known in advance, and a shadowy borderland remains in which a business expense deduction may be lost both by the corporation and the executive. The corporation cannot take the deduction upon its income tax return for the obvious reason that it did not incur the expense. The executive may be denied the deduction if he cannot persuade the tax authorities or the courts that the expense was one which he was required or expected to bear by reason of his position as a corporate officer.[43]

When the executive receives a fixed expense allowance to cover a stipulated type of expenditure, he can more readily prove the expenditure to have been on behalf of the corporation. Here, clearly, the corporation expects, if it does not require, that the executive make the stipulated expenditure in discharging the duties of his office. Although expenditures like luncheons purchased by a sales executive for customers may be in the corporation's interest, the corporation has relieved itself from incurring them by asking the executive to do so. Such payments will in appropriate circumstances be deductible by the executive as necessary and ordinary expenses.[44] In the absence of a flat expense arrangement, a corporate resolution [45] or policy

[42] E.g., *compare* Hal E. Roach Studios, *supra* note 23, *with* Hal E. Roach, *supra* note 38. *Cf.* authorities cited note 43 *infra*.

[43] Rev. Rul. 502, 57–2 Cum. Bull. 118; see Penn v. Robertson, *supra* note 19 (annual travel and entertainment expenses of vice-president of American Tobacco Company, averaging $13,500, held deductible since in proper relationship to salary average of over $450,000); Hal E. Roach, *supra* note 38. See also Schmidlapp v. Com'r, *supra* note 38; Cohan v. Com'r, 39 F.2d 540 (2d Cir. 1930); Lempert, *Who Can Deduct a Business Expense?*, 11 Tax L. Rev. 433, 436–41 (1956); Note, 66 Harv. L. Rev. 1508, 1509–11 (1953).

[44] "Reimbursement for such expenses to the corporation officer . . . would tend to indicate that they are a necessary expense of his office." But "the presence of such evidence does not conclusively determine that the expenses are deductible. . . ." Rev. Rul. 502, 1957–2 Cum. Bull. 118. See Arthur Brookfield, 15 CCH Tax Ct. Mem. 247 (1956) (deduction allowed to extent of entertainment expense reimbursement but denied for expenses in excess thereof); Green, *supra* note 33, at 565–66; Lempert, *supra* note 43, at 437. It has been said in justification of denying the deduction that the government should not reimburse the executive indirectly, when the employing corporation has refused to do so directly. Nathaniel J. Hess, 24 B.T.A. 475, 479–80 (1931). *Cf.* Harry Boverman, 10 T.C. 476, 477–81 (1948) (insurance manager denied deduction for prizes awarded agents because prohibited by his employment contract).

[45] An example of such a provision, in the form of a resolution of the Board of Directors, follows:

Resolved, that the Board recognizes that the successful operation and management of the Company's business has required and will continue to require [name] to expend, in the discharge of his duties as [position], substantial sums for the entertainment of various persons and representatives of com-

statement [46] will go far toward meeting the executive's burden of proof.[47] Without such corporate expressions of executive responsibility, the executive may find that expenses which he considered incidental to his employment are not deductible on his income tax return.[48] Moreover, if the employing corporation has a reimburse-

---

panies with whom the Company has or might expect to have business relationships. For any such entertainment expenses which are not susceptible to the usual accounting, [name] shall not be entitled to reimbursement, it being understood that his compensation has been determined with a view to enabling him to incur such type of expense on behalf of the Company out of such compensation.

[46] See CASEY AND ROTHSCHILD, Ex. 170 (Time, Inc. memorandum to salesmen —"Time salesmen are paid high salaries because selling is not a routine job. . . . There are many expenses incidental to selling which the salesman is not expected to recover from the Company on top of his salary").

[47] Rev. Rul. 502, 1957–2 CUM. BULL. 118, was issued in response to a request for advice as to whether a corporate resolution or other statement embodied in the minutes would meet the executive's burden of proving travel or entertainment expenses to have been necessary and ordinary expenses of his business as a corporation executive. The quotation therefrom in note 44 *supra* applies to a "resolution requiring the assumption of such expenses by" the executive. However, the absence of such evidence is not conclusive. For other acceptable evidence of a corporate policy requiring executives to meet entertainment expenses from their own pockets as a function of their corporate office, see Albert L. Sanderson, 16 CCH TAX CT. MEM. 105 (1957) (salary of vice-president increased to enable him to pay club dues in accordance with trust company's personnel policy).

[48] Samuel Saffan, 16 CCH TAX CT. MEM. 822 (1957) (cost of using own automobile in corporate business by officer-stockholder disallowed); William and Jeanne Auerbacher, 15 CCH TAX CT. MEM. 1147, 1150 (1956) (incidental effect on morale of department store buyer's gifts to employees working under her, not required by store policy, was insufficient business reason to constitute gifts a business deduction); Harry Kahn, 26 T.C. 273 (1956) (travel and entertainment expenses incurred by substantial stockholder in year when corporation had a loss); Arthur Brookfield, *supra* note 44, at 253 (club dues); Charles N. Kimball, 14 CCH TAX CT. MEM. 1011 (1955) (disallowing office and travel expenses of president of gold mining company); Jacob M. Kaplan, 21 T.C. 134, 145–46 (1953); James M. Hawkins, 20 T.C. 1069, 1075 (1953); Andrew Jergens, 17 T.C. 806, 811 (1951); Wilbur H. Clayton, 7 CCH TAX CT. MEM. 349 (1948) (cost of entertaining employees to allay their discontent disallowed); Cecil P. Stewart, 5 CCH TAX CT. MEM. 229, 233–34 (1946) (entertainment expenses incurred by corporation's president disallowed); Hal E. Roach Studios, *supra* note 23; Abraham W. Ast, 9 B.T.A. 694 (1927); Ralph C. Holmes, 37 B.T.A. 865 (1938), taxpayer's appeal to 2d Cir. dismissed on taxpayer's motion, Mar. 15, 1939 (expense of corporate director in preparing and mailing recommendations to shareholders as to action to be taken upon his resignation as chairman of the board of directors held personal and disallowed); Franklin M. Magill, 4 B.T.A. 272 (1926). See also A. Augustus Low, 3 CCH TAX CT. MEM. 859 (1944), *aff'd sub nom.* Low v. Nunan, 154 F.2d 261 (2d Cir. 1946) (unpaid corporate officer held not engaged in business and hence not entitled to business deductions).

When the expense is incurred by the executive of his own accord to maintain good relations with his subordinates or to hire a personal assistant to render business services directly to him, not the corporation, the executive may take a business expense deduction for the amount thus spent. William and Jeanne Auerbacher, *supra;* Harold A. Christensen, 17 T.C. 1456 (1952) (field manager entertained

ment policy for the particular kind of expense which the executive has incurred, a deduction by the executive may be barred if he has failed to seek reimbursement. By providing for reimbursement, the employing corporation has assumed responsibility for the expenditure and has, in effect, denied that the executive was required to bear it out of his own pocket.[49]

Personal or Business Expense? As a general rule, the expenses of an executive for travel, for entertainment, or for services which are necessary and ordinary incidents of his "business" as a corporate executive, are considered business rather than personal expenses and hence are deductible by him.

Expenses for *travel* and *transportation* include not only unreimbursed amounts spent in connection with trips away from home [50]

---

salesmen supervised by him) ; John Sidney Thompson, 9 CCH Tax Ct. Mem. 694 (1950) (salary of assistant employed and paid by president whose compensation consisted of commissions). *Cf* Arthur Brookfield, *supra* (district sales manager denied deduction since, contrary to *Christensen,* he could not show dependence of his compensation, including participation in bonus plan, upon efforts of sales force he supervised). *But see* James D. Robinson, 45 B.T.A. 39 (1941) (employee's service rendered to corporation).

[49] See Heidt v. Com'r, 274 F.2d 25 (7th Cir. 1959) (corporate officer, charged with responsibility for setting for himself and other employees reasonable standards for the use of expense accounts, denied deduction for use of personal automobile on company business, having promulgated rule that he would not claim reimbursement for expenses incurred in the use of his own automobile while engaged in company business) ; Coplon v. Com'r, 257 F.2d 535 (6th Cir. 1958) (sales manager denied deduction for his expenses in entertaining and providing gifts for various local managers and their families, on the ground that he could have obtained reimbursement from the company for such expenses) ; Horace E. Podems, 24 T.C. 21 (1955) (Internal Revenue agent denied deduction for automobile expense for which the government would have reimbursed him on submission of appropriate request; difference between the actual cost of his travel and the reimbursement which he could have received allowed) ; Harry A. Worth, 20 CCH Tax Ct. Mem. 216 (1961) (corporate officer entitled to but not able to collect reimbursement because of company's financial condition could not deduct expenses).

[50] E.g., Mary Sachs, 11 CCH Tax Ct. Mem. 882, 885, 889 (1952), *rev'd on another issue,* 208 F.2d 313 (3d Cir. 1953) (expenses allowed in full) ; see Frank L. Kluckhohn, 18 T.C. 892 (1952) (expenses allowed in part, taxpayer having lost his records) ; Wallace L. Chessire, 11 CCH Tax Ct. Mem. 146 (1952) (rent of New York City apartment occupied when taxpayer's business required his presence in that city). The executive's traveling expense to and from his place of business is generally not deductible, even though his home may be in a suburb or in another city. Com'r v. Flowers, 326 U.S. 465 (1946). The expenses of a suburbanite staying in town overnight because of work are not deductible. See John S. Martin, 3 CCH Tax Ct. Mem. 626 (1944).

When the employing corporation has two or more places of business and the executive travels between the one where his home is located and another, his traveling expenses may be deductible. Joseph H. Sherman, Jr., 16 T.C. 332 (1951). As to whether such travel "while away from home," Int. Rev. Code of 1954, § 162(a)(2), is limited to overnight travel, *compare* the Commissioner's view in Your Federal Income Tax 49 (1961), *with* Chandler v. Com'r, 226 F.2d 467 (1st Cir. 1955), *reversing* Douglas A. Chandler, 23 T.C. 653 (1955). For a similar deci-

but also local business transportation costs; both are deductible from the executive's gross income and are thus available to him in addition to the standard deduction.[51] Such expenses are deductible, furthermore, whether public transportation facilities or the executive's own automobile or airplane are used.[52] Hence, so long as disbursements are made only for items which are reasonably necessary to fulfillment of business purposes,[53] the executive will be relieved from tax on all amounts expended during travel. Within this rule are travel expenses of the executive incurred in attending business conventions and meetings of professional groups.[54] However, when

---

sion, see Emmert v. United States, 146 F. Supp. 322 (S.D. Ind. 1955). See also Carroll B. Mershon, 17 T.C. 861 (1951); Kenneth Waters, 12 T.C. 414 (1949), both decided under the 1939 Code. The Commissioner, contrary to the foregoing decisions, adheres to the view that travel "while away from home" means travel overnight. See Comment, 36 B.U.L. REV. 139 (1956). The actual cost of local business transportation, whether by public or private facilities, is deductible by the executive from his gross income. INT. REV. CODE OF 1954, § 62(2)(B). Rev. Rul. 60–16, 1960–1 CUM. BULL. 58. The courts are in some disagreement as to when a taxpayer's stay in a particular location for a job has the effect of changing his tax "home," so that his expenses while at that location are non-deductible. For the Treasury Department test as to what is a temporary or indefinite stay, see Rev. Rul. 60–189, 1960–1 CUM. BULL. 60. See Com'r v. Peurifoy, 254 F.2d 483 (4th Cir. 1957), aff'd, 358 U.S. 59 (1958); Claunch v. Com'r, 264 F.2d 309 (5th Cir. 1959); Harvey v. Com'r, 283 F.2d 491 (9th Cir. 1961) (rejecting Treasury test); T.I.R. No. 314, Apr. 18, 1961 (announcing disagreement with the *Harvey* decision); Burns v. Gray, 284 F.2d 436 (6th Cir. 1961) (also contrary to Treasury view).

[51] INT. REV. CODE OF 1954, § 62(2); Rev. Rul. 60–16, *supra* note 50; Rev. Rul. 502, 1957–2 CUM. BULL. 118. Examples of local transportation costs are cabs to and from an airport and expenses of the executive's automobile to the extent used in connection with local business calls. Business expenses of the executive, other than travel, meals, and lodging while away from home and local transportation expenses, are deductible only from adjusted gross income and therefore cannot be deducted if the executive uses the optional standard deduction. INT. REV. CODE OF 1954, § 62. Examples of items which are not deductible in arriving at adjusted gross income are club dues and business gifts for which the executive is not entitled to reimbursement. See Schwanbeck, *Tax Aspects of Employee Expense Accounts,* 37 TAXES 1131 (1959).

[52] Lang v. United States, 134 F. Supp. 214 (N.D. Ga. 1955); John A. Lovelady, 15 CCH TAX CT. MEM. 1498 (1956); William and Jeanne Auerbacher, *supra* note 48, at 1151–52 (*semble*); Marvin T. Blackwell, *supra* note 30 (automobile expense, including insurance, allowed in part); Seymour Wetzler, 11 CCH TAX CT. MEM. 1001 (1952). Many of these cases involve partial disallowances of deductions claimed for automobile expenses based on findings that personal use was greater than that claimed by the executive.

[53] For a discussion of the requirement of "reasonableness" as applied to travel, see MCDONALD, *op. cit. supra* note 33, at 455–57.

[54] Rev. Rul. 60–16, 1960–3 CUM. BULL. 10; Rita M. Callinan, 12 CCH TAX CT. MEM. 170 (1953); L. F. Ratterman, 7 CCH TAX CT. MEM. 476 (1948), aff'd w.o. op., 177 F.2d 204 (6th Cir. 1949). See also Wage v. Burnet, 50 F.2d 343 (D.C. Cir. 1931). With respect to travel expenses of the executive's wife, see text to note 78 *infra*. But cf. Rev. Rul. 59–16, 1959–3 INT. REV. BULL. 7 (expense of travel to convention required of delegate not deductible).

some of the expenses incurred during business travel are traceable to non-business motives, the Commissioner will deny a deduction for at least those expenses. Costs of business travel will not be held non-deductible simply because some opportunity for recreation, such as sightseeing or non-business entertainment, exists in connection with the trip; but the cost of these incidental personal activities should be separately allocated and will be non-deductible. On the other hand, if the primary purpose of the trip is personal—for example, a vacation—the travel expenses will be non-deductible except to the extent of specific expenses relating solely to business activities.[55]

In large companies, key personnel may be moved from one company location to another, and their *moving expenses* may present an important element of personnel policy. Many companies pay moving expenses,[56] but the significance of such payments is, of course, vitally affected by their treatment for income tax purposes. For the company, the payments, if reasonable in amount, are deductible business expenses. For the executive who moves to a new location on a *permanent* assignment, his tax treatment will depend on whether he is moved by his present employer or by a new employer. The Treasury Department has ruled [57] that when an employee is transferred in the interest of his employer from one position to another for permanent duty, the allowance or reimbursement received for moving himself, his immediate family, household goods, and personal effects is not taxable to the employee, since it is "primarily for the benefit of the employer and not compensatory in nature." [58] The result is

---

[55] Treas. Reg. § 1.162–2(b)(1) (1958). The Regulations represent a change from the position taken by the Commissioner in Rev. Rul. 56–168, 1956–1 Cum. Bull. 93, 94, under which business expenses on a trip primarily for pleasure were non-deductible. See also R. E. Duncan, 30 T.C. 386 (1958). When the executive travels on business but is accompanied by his family, he can charge hotel accommodations to business expense at the rate for a single person. Treas. Reg. § 1.162–2 (b)(1) (1958). See McDonald, *supra* note 33, at 1048. For deductibility of the travel costs of a wife accompanying her husband-executive to conventions or on business trips for the purpose of rendering business services to him, see notes 77

[56] See COMPANY PAYMENT OF EMPLOYEES' MOVING EXPENSES, NICB Studies and 78 *infra* and accompanying text. in Personnel Policy No. 154 (1956). The survey does not show statistically the percentage of companies which pay moving expenses, but shows the pay practices among companies which pay some portion of moving expenses. It covers companies in a number of different industries distributed throughout the United States. Of these companies, practically all pay such expenses for top management and supervisory personnel; 95% contribute toward expenses of technical and professional workers; 89% assist salesmen; 72% help rank-and-file clerical workers; and nearly 70% help rank-and-file production or operating workers. About 75% pay expenses only if the transfer is initiated by the company. For a contract clause relating to moving expenses, see AMERICAN CYANAMID, App. K, ¶ 3.

[57] Rev. Rul. 54–429, 1954–2 Cum. Bull. 53.

[58] *Ibid.*

otherwise if the allowance or reimbursement is received from a new employer to pay or reimburse for moving to another locality. Such an allowance or reimbursement is taxable compensation.[59] Moving expenses paid or reimbursed by the employer to a new employee likewise constitute wages for the purposes of income tax withholding, the social security tax, and the federal unemployment tax.[60]

In the case of any relocation, whether in continuing or new employment, the paid or reimbursed living expenses of an executive and his family in the new locality before they have settled in their new home constitutes taxable income; if not reimbursed, the expenses are personal and non-deductible.[61] This hardly seems a fair result when the executive must continue temporarily to maintain his former residence, but the result may perhaps be obviated, at least as to the executive himself, if his stay in the new locality can be regarded as in the nature of a travel status.

In order to induce an executive to move from one locality to another, the company may guarantee the executive against loss on the sale of his former home. In one case, it was held that when a house was sold at a loss, the employer's payment was not compensation taxable as ordinary income but was a part of the amount realized on the sale of the house. In that particular case, the employee had no gain for tax purposes; the court indicated, however, that any gain (i.e., the excess of the amount realized over the tax basis) would have been taxed as a capital gain.[62] On the other hand, the executive may be transferred to a new locality where the cost of housing is higher than at his former post. In such a case, if the employer makes

---

[59] Rev. Rul. 55–140, 1955–2 CUM. BULL. 317; *accord,* United States v. Woodale, 255 F.2d 370 (10th Cir. 1958), *cert. denied,* 358 U.S. 824 (1958).

But *cf.* John E. Cavanagh, 36 T.C. No. 32 (1961) (temporary employment rendered moving expenses non-taxable).

[60] Rev. Rul. 59–236, 1959–2 CUM. BULL. 234.

[61] Rev. Rul. 54–429, 1954–2 CUM. BULL. 53. A study of the practices of companies which pay moving expenses indicates that about 66% of these companies pay the major temporary living expenses of a top management executive prior to his settling in the new location, about 47% of these companies pay for trips of such executives to visit their families, and about 40% pay the major temporary living expenses of the families. See COMPANY PAYMENT OF EMPLOYEES' MOVING EXPENSES, *supra* note 56, at 34–39.

In John E. Cavanagh, *supra* note 59, family living expenses were held non-taxable.

[62] O. S. Schairer, 9 T.C. 549 (1947). The Conference Board survey, *supra* note 56, indicates that of 151 reporting companies that pay some portion of employees' moving expenses, about 18% afford protection from loss, as a matter of general policy or occasionally in the case of top management.

up the difference, the payment is taxable as compensation to the employee.[63]

If the employee moves his family in connection with a temporary change of assignment, any expense incurred for his family would be personal expense and non-deductible,[64] and would be taxable as ordinary income if paid by the employer.

With regard to *business entertainment,* deductible expenses have included the cost of food and liquor,[65] tickets for theater performances and other public entertainment,[66] and gifts to business associates or employees.[67] Also held deductible have been the cost of dining clubs, payments made for country club memberships,[68] and expenses of maintaining seasonal residences, yachts,[69] hunting lodges,[70]

---

[63] Le Grand v. United States, 105 F. Supp. 177 (N.D. Ohio 1952).

[64] George B. Lester, 19 B.T.A. 549 (1930).

[65] *Cf.* Louis Reinheimer, 16 CCH Tax Ct. Mem. 56, 60 (1957) ; Richard A. Sutter, *supra* note 22; Charles S. Guggenheimer, 18 T.C. 81, 85–86 (1952) ; Harold A. Christensen, *supra* note 48; Osmond, *supra* note 33, at 70, nn. 19–20 (collecting cases). *But cf.* R. E. L. Finley, *supra* note 37 (illegal liquor purchase disallowed as deduction) ; Rev. Rul. 307, 1955–1 Cum. Bull. 22 (same; citing Lilly v. Com'r, *supra* note 37).

[66] Maurice E. Harvey, 12 CCH Tax Ct. Mem. 1358, 1362–63 (1953) (Kentucky Derby, football games, Mardi Gras in Mobile, Alabama) ; Harold A. Christensen, *supra* note 48.

[67] Marvin T. Blackwell, *supra* note 30, at 972–73; Olivia de Havilland Goodrich, *supra* note 22; Harold A. Christensen, *supra* note 48.

[68] Johnson v. United States, *supra* note 27; Charles S. Guggenheimer, *supra* note 65 (both involving lawyers) ; see also Albert L. Sanderson, *supra* note 47 (trust company vice-president) ; Kenneth Blanchard, 12 CCH Tax Ct. Mem. 550, 557–58 (1953) (physician). The Tax Court tends to disallow a deduction for club dues unless a demonstrably successful business purpose or a requirement of membership imposed by the employing corporation is shown. *Ibid.* (physician's club dues deductible only to the extent that business use of club specifically shown) ; Norman M. Hussey, 11 CCH Tax Ct. Mem. 141 (1952) (partial deduction allowed to lawyer demonstrating use of club to build practice). See William and Jeanne Auerbacher, *supra* note 48 at 1151 (holding that petitioner cannot argue generally, but must show whom he entertained at club) ; Arthur Brookfield, *supra* note 44, at 253; Mary Sachs, *supra* note 50, at 890 (initiation fee paid to club may also be held non-deductible as in the nature of capital expense). Dues to business organizations, such as Chambers of Commerce, are generally deductible. See, e.g., Smith-Bridgman & Co., 16 T.C. 287 (1951) ; see also Mary Sachs, *supra* at 890. *But see* Arthur S. McKenzie, 11 CCH Tax Ct. Mem. 437, 438 (1952) (Chamber of Commerce dues not considered a proper business expense of a Veterans Administration clerk-typist). See also Osmond, *supra* note 33, at 70–71, n. 23; Stuart, *supra* note 33.

[69] Wm. T. Stover Co., *supra* note 22; Thomas W. Briggs, *supra* note 23; Richard A. Sutter, *supra* note 22; Charles J. McLannan, 4 CCH Tax Ct. Mem. 672 (1945).

[70] S. P. McCall, 13 CCH Tax Ct. Mem. 446, 450 (1954) ; Walter O. Kraft, 8 CCH Tax Ct. Mem. 606 (1949).

and other facilities used for business entertainment.[71] Sustaining the latter category of deductions has, however, proved difficult, since facilities such as clubs, yachts, and summer homes are not often exclusively maintained for business use. Executives involved in such cases have tended to disregard their personal use in preparing their returns or have overestimated their business use.[72] From the difficulty of determining the relative quanta of business and personal use, especially in instances where the taxpayer's ownership of the facility appears dependent on the indirect public subsidy inherent in a tax deduction, arise many of the contested, often sensational, tax cases.

The personal-business dichotomy, epitomized by the yacht cases, has been the basis of controversy in homelier contexts. Thus, the Tax Court has questioned the extent to which ordinary living expenses incurred in connection with business entertainment or travel can be deducted.[73] Here, it is apparent that the business deduction

[71] Thomas W. Briggs, *supra* note 23, at 448, 452 (corporation with headquarters in Tennessee allowed 50% of deduction claimed for rent of New York City apartment used for entertainment of customers and press, and for employees). *But see* Estate of Edwin Raymond Fisher, 11 CCH Tax Ct. Mem. 607, 610 (1952) (disallowing, as personal expense, deduction for additional rental of higher-priced apartment to which corporation's customer-relations man moved, ostensibly to better entertain actual and prospective customers, notwithstanding taxpayer's motive); Cecil P. Stewart, *supra* note 48, at 232–33 (disallowing expense deduction for loss on stock in co-operative apartment building claimed to be used for entertaining customers).

Other deductions of varied character arising from the variety of business life have been allowed from time to time. See, e.g., Arthur Brookfield, *supra* note 44, at 254 (subscription to technical journals). To deduct the cost of clothing, a clear business purpose for its purchase must be shown. Wilson John Fisher, 23 T.C. 219, 225 (1954) (musician playing at hotels); Olivia de Havilland Goodrich, *supra* note 22, at 329 (motion picture actress). A taste for expensive clothing cannot be indulged. William and Jeanne Auerbacher, *supra* note 48, at 1150–51; Paul E. Jackson, *supra* note 26. Office expenses, which clearly are deductible, seem to have caused little litigation. See Parker, *supra* note 33. *But see* Paul Bakewell, Jr., 23 T.C. 803 (1955) (lawyer's hearing aid not a deductible business expense).

[72] See, generally, cases cited notes 68–70 *supra*.

[73] Richard A. Sutter, *supra* note 22. Emphasizing the presumption that personal living expenses apparently remain non-deductible under the Internal Revenue Code of 1954, § 262, so as to prevent taxpayers from shifting their burden of paying personal expenses to the public, the Tax Court said: "Running through most of the contested items is the stubborn thread of a single problem which has never apparently been squarely and expressly passed upon. . . . When a taxpayer in the course of supplying food or entertainment or making other outlays customarily regarded as ordinary and necessary includes an amount attributable to himself or his family, such as the payment for his own meals, is that portion of the expenditure an ordinary and necessary business expense on the one hand or a nondeductible personal item on the other?" *Id.* at 173. The Tax Court concluded that meals at home for oneself and one's dependents remain a non-deductible personal expense, notwithstanding the presence of business guests. The entire cost of luncheons at Chamber of Commerce meetings was disallowed in *Sutter*.

reduces the burden of expenses, all or part of which must otherwise have been incurred by the taxpayer as a personal expense. Every executive and his family must eat; but should the entire cost of a dinner, often more elaborate than usual, become a tax deduction because a business guest is entertained at the table? Or should the deduction be limited to the amount attributable to the guest's share of the meal or to the shares of both the guest and the executive? Or should a deduction for the host be limited to the difference between the cost of his ordinary dinner and the more elaborate dinner of which he partakes because of the business guest?[74] As a practical matter, a Tax Court decision raising these questions has remained more of a warning than a real limitation on deductions.[75]

The final category of business deductions involves *services* for which the taxpayer is required to pay out of his own pocket. Examples are telephone calls, telegrams,[76] and stenographic assistance on a business trip. Since secretarial services are costly, the executive may prefer to have his wife accompany him on the trip in order to serve as a stenographer, typist, or social secretary. If bona fide business services of this kind are rendered by the executive's wife, the cost of her travel may be deducted as a business expense.[77] The wife's serv-

---

[74] See MORGAN, EXPENSE ACCOUNT *passim* (1958). *But cf.* BRYSON AND LEFEVRE, TAX ASPECTS OF EXECUTIVES' COMPENSATION 16 (1955).

[75] For an application of the principles in Richard A. Sutter, *supra* note 22, see Charles O. Gunther, Jr., 13 CCH TAX CT. MEM. 984, 991 (1954).
See also Al J. Smith, *supra* note 28.

[76] Ernest Huddleston, 13 CCH TAX CT. MEM. 395 (1954) (allowing a truck driver deduction for one-half of the cost of a telephone which his employer required him to have in his home); Julius C. Hendricks, 8 CCH TAX CT. MEM. 993 (1949) (cost of telephone calls and telegrams of an advertising solicitor held deductible). The Treasury Department has ruled against deductibility of laundry and cleaning services while traveling; see YOUR FEDERAL INCOME TAX 49 (1961). To the same effect is David Sonenblick, 4 B.T.A. 986 (1926).

[77] "Where a taxpayer's wife accompanies him on a business trip, expenses attributable to her travel are not deductible unless it can be adequately shown that the wife's presence on the trip has a bona fide business purpose. The wife's performance of some incidental service does not cause her expenses to qualify as deductible business expenses. The same rules apply to any other members of the taxpayer's family who accompany him on such a trip." Treas. Reg. § 1.162-2(c) (1958). This Regulation provision was cited as a basis of disallowing the deduction of the expenses of a wife who accompanied her husband to an annual convention of agents of an insurance company, even though the company encouraged such participation by wives as a matter of business policy, in Patterson v. Thomas, 289 F.2d 108 (5th Cir. 1961). Reaching the same result on similar facts is Rudolph v. United States, 189 F. Supp. 2 (N.D. Tex. 1960). See also Rev. Rul. 168, 1956–1 CUM. BULL. 93; Rev. Rul. 57, 1955–1 CUM. BULL. 315; *cf.* Walkup Drayage & Warehouse Co., 4 CCH TAX CT. MEM. 695, 703 (1945) (corporation allowed to deduct expenses of president's wife, formerly his secretary, who accompanied him on business trip). "There was a time when a man took along his secretary on a business trip and said she was his wife. . . . Nowadays, for income tax expense

ices, however, are usually nominal, and expenditures incurred by the executive in taking her on a business trip are ordinarily held to be personal and non-deductible, even though the wife helps to entertain business customers or otherwise proves incidentally useful.[78] The test appears to be whether the wife has discharged a function for which the executive would otherwise have had to employ and pay other help.

Questions of Proof. Assuming that the executive has incurred business rather than personal expenses for which he can claim a deduction on his income tax return, he still must be prepared to prove the actual amount of the expenses and their payment in the tax year for which the deduction is claimed. Especially in closely held corporations, where absence of effective corporate control over the taxpayer's expenditures casts suspicion on claimed deductions, proof of business travel or entertainment is often so vague as to raise a serious question whether the claimed expense was actually incurred or, if incurred, whether it served a business purpose. When only

---

reasons, he takes his wife and says she's his secretary." N. Y. Times, Feb. 16, 1958, p. 9, col. 6 (quoting the JOURNAL OF THE BRITISH INCOME TAXPAYERS' SOCIETY) ; see Bougher, *Deductibility of Expenses of Wife on Business Trip,* 10 BUS. LAW. 54 (1955) ; Livingston, *Wives Can Be Deductible,* Washington Post, May 2, 1956, p. 27, cols. 3–4. The Treasury Department is requiring information on employer tax returns as to payment of expenses of executives and their wives at business conventions and meetings. Consult Treasury Dep't Announcement 60–35, 1960–16 INT. REV. BULL. 56.

The *Rudolph* case, *supra,* was affirmed *per curiam* with a dissenting opinion 61–2 CCH U.S.T.C. ¶ 9539 (5th Cir. 1961).

[78] Mere typing of an occasional business letter or attendance at business luncheons and receptions with her husband is not sufficient business purpose to justify a deduction. These incidental services do not establish a business need for her presence at conventions or other business engagements of her husband away from home. See Rev. Rul. 168, 1956–1 CUM. BULL. 93; Rev. Rul. 57, 1955–1 CUM. BULL. 315. For Tax Court decisions disallowing a wife's travel expenses on the same theory expounded by these rulings, see B. F. Crabbe, *supra* note 34; Axel S. Stokby, 12 CCH TAX CT. MEM. 761, 766 (1953) ; L. L. Moorman, 26 T.C. 666 (1956) ; Walter M. Sheldon, Tax Ct. Mem. 1961–44, 20 CCH TAX CT. MEM. 241 (1961). *Cf.* Allenberg Cotton Co. v. United States, 61–1 CCH U.S.T.C. ¶ 9131 (W.D. Tenn. 1960). *Compare Stokby with* John C. Thomas, CCH B.T.A. MEM. DEC. 10622-A (1939) (allowing travel expense deduction for wife acting as husband's singing coach and foreign language elocution teacher on tours). See Andrews, *Whose Income Tax Are You Paying?,* AMERICAN, Feb. 1954, pp. 21, 105 (former Commissioner of Internal Revenue writes that wives may be included as part of a business expense at "a dinner for promotional purposes to which other wives are invited" but that clothes for such a dinner would not be deductible). Consult Rev. Rul. 1960–348, 1960–40 INT. REV. BULL. 9 (value of meals and lodging furnished wives and children of faculty members required to live on school premises as condition of employment not taxable to faculty members) withdrawing contrary ruling in Rev. Rul. 59–409, 1959–2 CUM. BULL. 48. For corporate practice see *supra* note 8.

nebulous taxpayer records indicate the business purpose supporting the deduction, it will be disallowed on audit and the disallowance will be sustained on appeal.[79] In the case of the closed corporation, if there are no carefully prepared records, only the general testimony of the stockholder-executive will normally be available to substantiate the facts on which the deduction is based, and evidence insufficient to establish the executive's deduction is also insufficient to sustain a corporate deduction.[80]

The quantum of evidence that will be required to sustain the taxpayer's burden of proof cannot always be anticipated, but the executive can follow simple practices which will aid his case before the taxing authorities.[81] From a travel itinerary showing places visited and modes of travel, transportation costs can be reconstructed. Hotel bills, if preserved, will indicate not only the cost of the lodging but also incidental charges for telephone calls, room service, and, in many instances, the hotel's restaurant charges.[82] If credit and "club" cards are used in charging expenses, bills rendered by the "clubs" may show the amounts spent by the executive as well as the time and place of the expenditure. The cost of gas and oil consumed in travel by private automobile can be calculated with reasonable accuracy from records of mileage traveled.[83]

While documentary evidence of this type will provide the strongest support for claimed deductions, the Commissioner has recognized that absolute certainty is unattainable and that a taxpayer cannot be "required to secure, retain, and produce receipts for each meal and for each night's lodging." Accordingly, the "Revenue Service allows considerable latitude with respect to recordkeeping or evidence tending to prove [travel and entertainment] . . . expenses." [84] For example, the Commissioner will consider a diary-type expense log as probative of travel and entertainment expenses incurred by the execu-

[79] E.g., Dave Rubin, 26 T.C. 1076, 1081–82 (1956) ; M. L. Cottingham, 15 CCH TAX. CT. MEM. 987, 991 (1956) ; Gordon Pascal, 15 CCH TAX CT. MEM. 434 (1956) ; B. F. Crabbe, *supra* note 34.

[80] See M. L. Cottingham, *supra* note 79, at 991–92; B. F. Crabbe, *supra* note 34; Oscar J. Cahn Corp., 13 CCH TAX CT. MEM. 195 (1954) (taxpayer claimed deduction of $73,798.51; Commissioner allowed $19,164.51 which the Tax Court increased to $36,000) ; *cf.* Treas. Reg. § 162.17(d)(3) (1958) (calling for "approximations based upon reliable secondary sources").

[81] In 1958, the Treasury Department adopted regulations setting forth acceptable methods of expense account record-keeping by employees. Treas. Reg. § 1.162–17(d) (1958). See U. S. Income Tax Form 2106 (Official Worksheet) (rev. 1959) ; LASSER, TAX AID RECORDS AND APPOINTMENT BOOK (1958).

[82] Treas. Reg. § 1.162–17(a)(3) (1958).

[83] *Ibid.*

[84] Rev. Rul. 497, 1954–2 CUM. BULL. 75, 76.

tive.[85] Details of engagements noted in business diaries or desk calendars, and memoranda dictated while facts are fresh in mind will also help to substantiate the deduction and its amount. Credible oral evidence of expenses will be accepted and, if the amounts appear reasonable, the deduction will be considered established.[86]

Besides offering testimony of particular expenditures, moreover, the executive may be able to establish a deduction based on his average travel costs over a period of time or the average cost of entertaining in an ordinary manner.[87] Testimony as to business travel costs generally, however, will not be accepted by the Tax Court, even in statistical form.[88] Nor will the Tax Court view as adequate evidence checks drawn by the executive of a close corporation against the corporate treasury in round amounts, with a cryptic notation on the stubs such as "travel expenses." [89] Here, the executive can at least seek to establish total expenditures by returning the amount drawn from the corporation but not spent, or by obtaining reimbursement for expenditures in excess of the amount advanced by the corporation.[90]

When travel or entertainment involves use of facilities owned by the executive or maintained by him for general use, records should indicate not only the total expenditure but also the facts which support apportionment between business and personal use.[91] Under the rule of *Cohan v. Commissioner*,[92] a deduction for business expenses which have unquestionably been incurred will not be entirely lost for failure to prove their exact amount. But the deduction may be lost to a large extent since the taxing authorities tend to allow less to the taxpayer than the amount claimed by him.[93]

[85] Treas. Reg. § 162–17(d)(2) (1958). See Rev. Rul. 195, 1954–1 CUM. BULL. 47; Hayes, *supra* note 33; Perkins, *supra* note 33.

[86] Rev. Rul. 195, 1954–1 CUM. BULL. 47.

[87] John A. Lovelady, *supra* note 52; Charles O. Gunther, Jr., *supra* note 75, (daily total travel cost).

[88] Charles O. Gunther, Jr., *id.* at 990 (estimate of $16.50 per day based on article in Baltimore Sun about average daily travel cost of executives held no substitute for cost records or estimate of taxpayer's actual expenses).

[89] E.g., B. F. Crabbe, *supra* note 34, at 220–21.

[90] See Siegfried v. United States, 55–2 U.S.T.C. ¶ 9531 (N.D. Okla. 1955) (reimbursement received by insurance executive reporting travel cost to corporate employer on monthly vouchers specifying categories of transportation, hotel, food, and miscellaneous held not to constitute income). See also Perkins, *supra* note 33, at 11–13.

[91] See Richard A. Sutter, *supra* note 22; *cf.* Thomas W. Briggs, *supra* note 23.

[92] *Supra* note 43.

[93] For a table illustrating application of the *Cohan* rule by the Commissioner and the Tax Court in twenty-nine decisions, see INSTITUTE FOR BUSINESS PLANNING, ACCOUNTING FOR TRAVEL AND ENTERTAINMENT EXPENSES § 2 (1958). For decisions affirming the Commissioner's allocation of expenses, see Wm. T. Stover Co., *supra*

Accounting to the Employer. In 1957, the Treasury Department proposed expansion of its Regulations to include reporting of all payments received by an employee as reimbursement of expenses; in conjunction with the new Regulation, the Department published an income tax form which would have required total reimbursed expenses to be reported in the employee's gross income and claimed business expenses to be deducted with appropriate itemization.[94] Strong protests from many quarters led to abandonment of this requirement and to a subsequent Treasury Regulation which distinguishes between expense account arrangements under which the employee is required to account to his employer and those in which no accounting is required.[95]

The Regulations state that accounting means submitting "an expense account or other required written statement to the employer showing the business nature and the amount of all of the employee's expenses (including those charged directly or indirectly to the employer through credit cards [96] or otherwise) broken down into such

---

note 22, at 436–37, 440–41 (upholding Commissioner's 50% disallowance of cabin cruiser expenses); Richard A. Sutter, *supra* note 22 (affirming Commissioner's 75% disallowance of claimed operational expenditures for boat); Charles S. Guggenheimer, *supra* note 65 (20% of claimed deduction for travel and entertainment expenses allowed by Commissioner and affirmed by Tax Court); see also B. F. Crabbe, *supra* note 34; Anne Klein Ansley, 12 CCH Tax Ct. Mem. 1110, 1114, 1116 (1953). For decisions taking an intermediate position between the minimum allowed by the Commissioner and taxpayer's claimed deduction, see Frank L. Kluckhohn, *supra* note 50 (Commissioner's allowance of one-half of general travel expenses in connection with lectures and disallowance of entire cost of trip to Australia; modified by Tax Court under the *Cohan* rule to allow as deductions two-thirds of general travel costs and 70% of expense of Australian trip); see also Albert L. Sanderson, *supra* note 47; Louis Reinheimer, *supra* note 65; William and Jeanne Auerbacher, *supra* note 48, at 1151 (Tax Court allowed in lieu of $2,303.36 claimed, nominal $100 deduction for unspecified business entertaining at club); Arthur Brookfield, *supra* note 44, at 254 (*Cohan* rule applied to deduction claimed for cost of technical magazines); Norman M. Hussey, *supra* note 68 (Tax Court allowing $600 of $895 claimed by taxpayer as deduction for club expenses).

[94] 1957 U. S. Income Tax Form 1040, line 6(a); General Instructions, Publication 3, at 6 (1957); see Int. Rev. News Release IR-204, in 5 CCH 1957 Stand. Fed. Tax Rep. ¶ 6932: "The new line will enable the Service to give attention to those returns where deductions for expenses appear to be disproportionate in relation to the employee's income and occupation, and thus aid in detection of abuses that have arisen in this area." After the form was distributed, the Internal Revenue Service announced that it would not be applied "retroactively" to 1957. 1957–48 Int. Rev. Bull. 83; see U. S. News and World Report, Dec. 6, 1957, p. 97. Consult, generally, Hoffman, *Control of the Corporate Executive's Expense Account,* Tax Executive, Oct. 1960, p. 23.

[95] Treas. Reg. § 1.162–17 (1958).

[96] Charging items to the employer does not constitute an accounting, since the charge does not show the business nature of the expense. Rev. Rul. 59–410, 1959–2 Cum. Bull. 64.

broad categories as transportation, meals and lodging while away from home overnight, entertainment expenses, and other business expenses." [97] The Commissioner of Internal Revenue is given discretion in the Regulations to approve, as equivalent to an accounting, reasonable business practices providing for mileage and per diem allowances in lieu of subsistence and for similar allowances, in accordance with a fixed scale.[98]

If no adequate accounting is required by his employer, the employee is required to submit as part of his tax return information as to the total amounts of advances and disbursements received by him,

[97] The Treasury Department subsequently spelled out in detail the type of information that would be considered an accounting for the purpose of Treas. Reg. § 1.162–17(b)(4) (1958). See Rev. Rul. 60–120, 1960–1 CUM. BULL. 83. At the same time, it sought to emphasize the importance of the controls that the employer should maintain to insure that the employee is paid for advances or reimbursements for proper business expenses only, stating: "For example, one important control is present if the employer requires that an expense account must be examined and approved by a person responsible directly or indirectly to him for a proper audit of the account, except that the person incurring the expense should not audit his own account." Id. at 84. The Department has announced that on audit of the employer's tax returns, an examination will be made of the adequacy of the methods employed in requiring an accounting as to business expenses; if found to be inadequate, a list of employees and expense allowances will be required for further action. T.I.R. 198, Dec. 29, 1959.

[98] Treas. Reg. § 1.162–17(b)(4) (1958). Following the issuance of the Regulations, a ruling was issued that when an employee is paid or reimbursed for travel expense, including meals and lodging, at a rate not in excess of 125% of the rates authorized to be paid by the Federal Government in the locality in which the travel takes place, the employee would be deemed to have accounted to his employer for the purposes of the Regulations. Rev. Rul. 58–453, 1958–2 CUM. BULL. 67. It was stated that the maximum amount allowable at that time as 125% of the Federal Government allowance was 12½¢ per mile for traveling and a per diem allowance of $15.00 for subsistence while traveling within the continental United States, and that these amounts would be adjusted whenever the Federal Government allowances were changed. With respect to travel outside the continental United States, the per diem allowance for subsistence was to be based on Standard Government Travel Regulations for different foreign localities. In accordance with the ruling, Supplement I, incorporated by reference, consisted of the per diem allowance in various foreign locations as of Nov. 8, 1957 according to the Standardized Government Travel Regulations. This supplement has been re-issued from time to time thereafter. See, e.g., Supplement VIII giving the rates effective Dec. 1, 1960. 1960–52 INT. REV. BULL. 11.

The ruling provided that if per diem allowances and mileage allowances of a particular employer did not fall within the scope of the ruling "the presence of unusual circumstances which account for the variation" might be grounds for considering the employees as having accounted to the employer and that in such cases the employer should apply for a ruling. A request for a different per diem subsistence allowance for different groups of executives, depending on the grade or salary of the executive, was denied. See Rev. Rul. 60–282, 1960–35 INT. REV. BULL. 15. However, a difference of allowances based on differences in traveling costs in various parts of the United States and a system of minimum mileage allowances was approved. Ibid.

and information as to business expenses incurred by him, broken down into the same broad categories that are required for an accounting to the employer.[99] Although reserving the right to require any taxpayer to furnish substantiation for expense account items, the Regulations state [100] that this will normally be required in the case of an employee (1) who is not required to or does not account to his employer, or (2) who claims a deduction for business expenses in excess of advances or reimbursements, or (3) whose family owns more than 50% of the corporate employer, or (4) whose employer, according to the determination of the Treasury Department, does not have adequate accounting procedures as to expense accounts. Thus, it will be seen that the Regulations bear most heavily against the controlling stockholders of closely held corporations and executives who either have flat expense account arrangements or, even if they have a reimbursement arrangement for certain expenses, also claim a deduction for additional expenses.

LEGISLATIVE ACTION. The problems posed by expense accounts have led toward Congressional action intended to prevent abuses.[101]

[99] Treas. Reg. § 1.162–17(c)(2) (1958).
[100] Treas. Reg. § 1.162–17(d) (1958).
[101] Section 301 of the Public Debt and Tax Rate Extension Act of 1960 (P.L. 86–564, 86th Cong., 74 Stat. 290, June 30, 1960) provided [§ 301(a)] that the Joint Committee on Internal Revenue Taxation should make an investigation "of present law, regulations, and practices relating to the deduction, as ordinary and necessary business expenses, of expenses for entertainment, gifts, dues or initiation fees in social, athletic or sporting clubs or organizations, and similar and related items," and called on the Joint Committee to report the results of its investigation to Congress as soon as practicable during the 87th Congress, together with any recommended changes in law or administrative practices. This section further required [§ 301(b)] the Secretary of the Treasury to report as soon as practicable during the 87th Congress as to the results of the enforcement program of the Internal Revenue Service, together with such recommendations with respect thereto as he might consider necessary or appropriate to avoid the misuse of the business expense deduction. This action was the result of a compromise reached by a Conference Committee of both houses of Congress, rejecting an amendment to § 162(a) of the Internal Revenue Code of 1954 proposed by Senator Clark of Pennsylvania and adopted by the Senate which would have denied a tax deduction for any business entertainment (except for expenses for food or beverages incurred for the primary purpose of advancing the trade or business of the taxpayer) and for business gifts other than those not exceeding $10 per person per year. For the discussion on the floor of the Senate, see 106 CONG. REC. 13132–42 (daily ed. June 24, 1960), 13459, 13460–65, 13476–81, 13487–92 (daily ed. June 27, 1960), 13639–49 (daily ed. June 28, 1960); for the discussion on the floor of the House of Representatives, see 106 CONG. REC. 13639–49 (daily ed. June 27, 1960).

In 1959, Senator Clark of Pennsylvania had proposed statutory amendments which would have limited to $1,000 the entertainment deduction of any taxpayer and denied any deduction for maintenance of yachts or vacation lodges, gifts, dues of social organizations, and expenses of travel outside the United States. See 105

Prior to 1961, the legislative approach was not supported by the Treasury Department, which instead favored improved enforcement measures,[102] with the more detailed reporting on the part of the employee to his employer described above [103] and specific information from employers concerning expense account practices.[104]

PERQUISITES AND FRINGE BENEFITS

The terms "perquisites" and "fringe benefits" have been variously defined. The dictionary definition of a perquisite is "a gain or profit incidentally made from employment in addition to regular salary." [105] The term "fringe benefits" has also been used to include any benefit other than the employee's fixed wage or salary; within its ambit has fallen anything from overtime and the coffee break on the one hand, to pensions and stock options on the other.[106]

The term "perquisite" has an invidious caste content in some quarters and may be falling into disuse; we use it in the course of the ensuing discussion to connote a benefit, such as a luncheon or club membership,[107] that is incidental to an executive position and is un-

CONG. REC. 10804–26 (daily ed. June 25, 1959). These amendments were defeated by a vote of 44 to 34. *Id.* at 10826.

Panel discussions of expense account abuses were held by the House Ways and Means Committee at the end of 1959 in connection with its general study of income tax revision. House of Representatives Committee on Ways and Means, *Income Tax Revision,* 86th Cong., 1st Sess. 555 ff. (Dec. 12, 1959).

[102] See letter of Dana Latham, Commissioner of Internal Revenue, to Senator Byrd of Virginia, dated June 27, 1960, reprinted in 106 CONG. REC. 13639–40 (daily ed. June 28, 1960) ; letter of Jay W. Glassman, Assistant to the Secretary of the Treasury, to Senator Williams of Delaware, dated June 24, 1960, reprinted in 106 CONG. REC. 13139–40 (daily ed. June 24, 1960) (opposing legislation because of problems of "equity, administration, and statutory construction").

[103] See text to notes 94 ff. *supra.*

[104] As part of the 1960 Corporation Tax Return, Form 1120, information is required as to the twenty-five officers of the corporation with the highest aggregate salary and expense account allowances; however, this requirement does not apply to any officer whose total compensation, including expense account allowances, totals less than $10,000. The form also requires information as to the maintenance by the corporation of resort facilities, yachts for employees and their families, payments for attendance at business conventions, and paid vacations. The requirement for this information was first announced in T.I.R. 198, Dec. 29, 1959. As part of this release, Commissioner Latham stated that if the revenue laws could not be made effective by means of more rigorous enforcement, the Internal Revenue Service would propose changes in the laws. See also T.I.R. 221, Apr. 4, 1960 (Announcement 60–35, 1960–16 INT. REV. BULL. 56).

[105] WEBSTER'S NEW INTERNATIONAL DICTIONARY 1826 (2d ed. 1959).

[106] See MACAULAY, FRINGE BENEFITS AND THEIR FEDERAL TAX TREATMENT 4–8 (1959).

[107] For a discussion of such arrangements, see Wilson John Fisher, *supra* note 71; CANARY, FRINGE BENEFITS TO EMPLOYEES, ENCYCLOPEDIA OF TAX PROCEDURES

available to employees generally. We shall confine the term "fringe benefit" to a benefit, such as a membership in a company-sponsored Blue Cross hospital plan,[108] which is available to an executive only as one of a group of employees. As distinguished from a major benefit such as a pension plan, we shall use the term "fringe benefit" to connote a benefit that is relatively small in terms of salary.[109]

The common characteristic of both perquisites and fringe benefits is that they have an economic value to the employee in replacing what might otherwise be a personal expenditure. Despite the relatively small dollar value of any particular benefit, this economic value can become especially significant to the highly paid executive, to the extent that the perquisite or fringe benefit is tax-free.

Corporate Practice. With the distinction between perquisites and fringe benefits in mind, perquisites include such items as a company automobile, with or without chauffeur, an airplane,[110] a membership in a social or business club or organization,[111] medical examinations,[112] legal services,[113] payment of expenses at resort hotels during conventions,[114] the use of an apartment or suite maintained by

---

465, 466–67 (1956 ed) ; *cf.* Everett Doak, 24 T.C. 569 (1955), *rev'd*, 234 F.2d 704 (4th Cir. 1956) (involving a self-employed person rather than an employee). "The Hanover [Bank] provides [free] meals for its employees because of the crowded conditions in public restaurants and the unsatisfactory consequences to both the bank and its staff, and in the interests of health." N. Y. Times, July 8, 1957, p. 35, col. 2–3. If meals and lodging are furnished solely for the convenience of the employer, their value is not taxable to the employee. INT. REV. CODE OF 1954, § 119. See Note, 42 CORN. L.Q. 433 (1957) ; Comment, 53 MICH. L. REV. 871 (1955) ; text *infra* to note 130 ff.

[108] See note 138 *infra* and accompanying text.

[109] The Regulations under the Federal Insurance Contributions Act [26 C.F.R. § 402.227(a)(6) (1949)] and the Federal Unemployment Tax Act [26 C.F.R. § 403.227(a)(6) (1949)] provide that for the purpose of these taxes "ordinarily, facilities or privileges (such as entertainment, medical services, or so-called 'courtesy' discounts on purchases) furnished or offered by an employer to his employees generally are not remuneration for employment if such facilities are of relatively small value and are offered or furnished by the employer as a means of promoting the health, good will, contentment or efficiency of his employees."

[110] As early as 1953, company-owned airplanes outnumbered those of scheduled airlines seven to one. N. Y. Times, July 19, 1953, § 3, p. 1, col. 6–7, p. 5, col. 1. See *id.*, Aug. 1, 1954, § 1, p. 87, col. 7 (business planes numbered 21,500, almost seventeen times those operated by domestic airlines) ; BURGESS AND NEUHOFF, MANAGING COMPANY AIRPLANES, NICB Studies in Business Policy No. 65, at 3 (1954). See also N. Y. Times, July 6, 1952, p. 5, col. 2, describing plane fleet of Parker Pen Co.

[111] See note 5 *supra* and accompanying text.

[112] Company health programs for executives received their impetus after the end of World War II and especially in the decade beginning in 1950. See COMPANY HEALTH PROGRAMS FOR EXECUTIVES, NICB Studies in Personnel Policy No. 147 (1955), covering 120 companies, ranging from those having less than 500 employees to those having more than 50,000. Of these companies, 70% instituted such pro-

grams between 1945 and the early part of 1953. According to the Life Extension Examiners of New York, which examines executives for industry, the number of examinations increased 450% between 1946 and 1953 (*id.* at 5). About 75% of the companies studied by the Conference Board provide such programs on a voluntary basis, while the remaining companies have mandatory programs (*id.* at 13). When participations are voluntary, three-fourths of the companies report participation of 90% or higher (*id.* at 13). Almost 90% of the companies studied extend the medical examination program to middle management; slightly less than 50% include first-line supervisors, and about the same percentage cover key non-supervisory personnel such as chemists, engineers, attorneys, salesmen, and editors (*id.* at 45–46).

Many examples of programs for periodic medical examinations of executives are to be found in newspaper articles, magazines, and annual reports to stockholders. See *Bosses' Health,* BUSINESS WEEK, Oct. 17, 1953, p. 135. Socony-Vacuum Company, for instance, provides for semiannual examination for all top executives over sixty, with more widely spaced examinations for younger executives. *Ibid.* See Southern Natural Gas Co., 1956 Annual Report, p. 24. Lukens Steel Corporation requires a medical examination as an incident of promotion to a top position. FORTUNE, Aug. 1957, p. 92. See also Wall Street Journal, Apr. 2, 1956, p. 1, col. 6 (describing spread of executive health plans); *Symposium, Safeguarding Executive Health,* 46 MGMT. REV., May 1957, p. 58.

An important problem raised by these medical examination plans is disclosure of results to the employing corporation. In the normal doctor-patient relationship, such disclosure would appear in violation of professional ethics. However, until recently at least, executives seem to have been willing to have their physical condition disclosed to their superiors. *Bosses' Health, supra.*

Many companies have broad medical health programs that go far beyond periodic medical examinations for executives. Starting with programs aimed at occupational health hazards and on-the-job injuries under the impetus of the workmen's compensation laws, these companies now have programs aimed at keeping the individual worker fit. See COMPANY MEDICAL AND HEALTH PROGRAMS, NICB Studies in Personnel Policy No. 171 (1959).

In Estate of M. K. Kartsen, CCH TAX CT. MEM. 1042 (1954), medical and hospital expenses of the president and minority stockholder which had been paid by the corporation were held income to him; the corporate deduction therefor had previously been disallowed.

[113] In Cohn v. Columbia Pictures Corp., *supra* note 16, the company's president agreed, in settlement of a stockholder's action, to pay the company one-half of the counsel fees paid by the company to attorneys employed by the company to represent its president in the negotiation and preparation of a deferred compensation contract; in approving the settlement, the Referee stated that there was "scant likelihood of any recovery" on the company's behalf in respect of this matter.

Consult Rev. Rul. 60–14, 1960–1 CUM. BULL. 16 (payment of personal legal expenses of organization official by committee of organization held income to official); but *cf.* Cox v. Kraemer, 88 Fed. Supp. 835 (D. Conn. 1948) (reimbursement of legal expenses in defending against charges of misconduct held not taxable).

[114] Large-scale advertising by health resorts and hotels, emphasizing the alleged tax benefits of their use by executives at company expense, prompted the Internal Revenue Service in 1957 to issue a ruling explaining that no business or medical expense deductions for such expenditures were allowable, either to the company or the executive. Rev. Rul. 130, 1957–1 CUM. BULL. 108. Conventions are often held at resort hotels and sometimes on cruises. See N. Y. Times, Oct. 18, 1953, § 3, p. 1, col. 6; see also *id.,* Oct. 23, 1953, p. 36, col. 2–3, p. 38, col. 4–5; *id.,* Oct. 20, 1953, p. 41, col. 6–7, p. 44, col. 3 (annual convention of Savings Bank Association of New York held on cruise to Havana). In 1957, Commissioner Harrington directed agents to give attention to "the use of alleged branch offices established

the company,[115] hunting lodges, fishing camps, or yachts owned or to a large extent maintained by the company.[116] Also classified as perquisites are provisions sometimes included in employment contracts [117] for vacations,[118] absences during illness, management training courses at colleges and universities,[119] and, of course, expense allowances.[120] The term is also extended to include those non-pecuniary advantages which constitute the badge of status—the size and

in resort cities for the sole purpose of sending business executives to such cities for vacations." *What's Happening in Washington,* P-H ACCOUNTANT's WEEKLY REP., July 8, 1957, § 2, p. 2. See Patterson v. Thomas, *supra* note 77 (amounts expended by employer of insurance agent to pay for cost of his attending convention at resort hotel includible in his gross income and not deductible except to extent of time spent on business because the trip was primarily a pleasure trip for the agent). See Rudolph v. United States, *supra* note 77 (payment of expenses of trip by Dallas agency to New York convention held to be income on the ground that it was awarded as a reward for services). See also note 77 *supra* as to amounts paid for expenses of wives.

[115] See Chandler v. Com'r, 119 F.2d 623, 626–28 (3d Cir. 1941) (executive occupying with his family a rent-free lodge owned by corporation of which he was the sole stockholder held to have received compensation in an amount equal to the lodge's rental value). *But see* Richards v. Com'r, 111 F.2d 376 (5th Cir. 1940) (rental value of corporate premises occupied by chief executive and his wife who together were the sole shareholders held to constitute a gift from the corporation to the husband, the court emphasizing that under Louisiana law families often place title to property in a corporation to facilitate transfer to children after parents' death). See discussion of the employer-convenience rule, text to note 132 *infra.*

[116] The 1960 Corporation Income Tax Return, Form 1120, requires information from the company as to the maintenance for executives of facilities of these types. See note 104 *supra.*

[117] For examples of such clauses, see Chapter 2, note 50. As to provisions for continued salary payments during illness or disability, see CASEY AND ROTHSCHILD, Ex. 176 (Noma Electric Corp. contract with Henri Sadacca—providing for continuance of salary during sickness or partial disability) ; *id.,* Ex. 186 (Deep Rock Oil Corp. contract with W. H. Garbade—providing for $15,000 per annum for ten years payable to executive if disabled while employed).

[118] *Cf.* McCoy-Brandt Mach. Co., 8 B.T.A. 909 (1927) (allowing vacation expenses paid to skilled labor in short supply as an ordinary and necessary expense). For the view that the payment of such expenses would not have been held taxable to the employees in that case, see CANARY, *op. cit. supra* note 107, at 473.

In Abramson v. Blakeley, *supra* note 16, the settlement included a waiver by the president and chairman of the board of five months of accumulated vacation time.

[119] Thirty-two colleges and universities in all sections of the United States were giving executive development courses in 1957. EXECUTIVE DEVELOPMENT COURSES IN UNIVERSITIES, NICB Studies in Personnel Policy No. 160 (rev. 1957). The courses ranged in duration from two weeks at the University of Pennsylvania to seven and one-half months for middle management at Harvard University (*id.* summary). Companies usually limit participation in such courses to those who are already in middle-management and top-management positions (*id.* at 13).

[120] "In the process of liberalizing expense handling, several companies tell us that they have reached the point where they catalog expense accounts with other fringe benefits." *Executive Expense Practices, supra* note 3, at 30.

location of the office, its furniture and furnishings, the private secretary, the number of telephones.

Fringe benefits include many items that are not exclusively executive compensation and in a number of these benefits, such as overtime pay, the executive does not participate. Fringe benefits range from discounts on company products (or sometimes on products purchased by the company in bulk),[121] recreational facilities,[122] special rewards for length of service,[123] tuition-aid programs,[124] and

[121] "In practice, cash discounts to employees, even though they are sufficiently large to form a part of the wage pattern, are not reported as taxable income. However, in theory they probably are taxable and there are, of course, many other fringe benefits that would meet the same standards." *Employee and Executive Compensation Arrangements*, TAX PLANNING IN BUSINESS POLICY 28–29 (Proceedings of the Am. Inst. of Accountants 1955 Tax Conf. for Executives) (1956). The Regulations provide that bargain purchases by employees are to be treated as involving compensation to the extent that the price is less than the fair market value of the property purchased. Treas. Reg. § 1.161–2(d) (1958). In the case of a transaction with a single employee involving a substantial amount, this rule would be applicable. *Cf.* T.D. 2137, Jan. 30, 1915, holding that commission not paid by life insurance agent on policy written on his own life is taxable income to him. For application of this ruling, see Com'r v. Minzer, 279 F.2d 338 (6th Cir. 1960), and Com'r v. Daehler, 281 F.2d 823 (5th Cir. 1960). But see J. Simpson Dean, 35 T.C. 113 (1961), involving interest-free loans by a corporation to its stockholders in which the Tax Court rejected the Commissioner's contention that the stockholders received income equal to the value of the tax-free use of the money. See Harmony Dairy Co., Tax Ct. Mem. 1960–109, 19 CCH TAX CT. MEM. 582 (1960) in which a closely held milk company attempted unsuccessfully to justify the deduction as a business expense of free milk delivered to its officer-stockholders on the ground that this was a "fringe benefit"; the ground of the decision was that the company had failed to prove whether the products were received free of charge because of the recipient's executive position or because of his status as a stockholder.

[122] See N. Y. Times, Oct. 2, 1955, § 3, p. 1, col. 8, p. 9, col. 2 (describing Union Carbide's many company-sponsored activities). In 1955, company and employee outlays for company-sponsored recreational programs amounted to one billion dollars. *Id.,* Apr. 17, 1955, § 3, p. 4, col. 3; *see id.,* Nov. 12, 1956, p. 47, col. 3, p. 48, col. 2 ("Today there is hardly a large concern that doesn't have [an industrial recreation program] . . ."). See also Slaymaker Lock Co., 18 T.C. 1001 (1952), *rev'd on other issues,* 208 F.2d 313 (3d Cir. 1953) (allowing deduction for cost of improving land and buildings donated by the company to foremen's association, to be maintained by the association as recreational facility for all employees of the company).

[123] Recognition for length of service takes the form of (a) non-monetary service awards, such as service insignia, watches, and service clubs, (b) extra privileges, such as extra paid vacations, (c) monetary awards, and (d) increased job security. See STIGLITZ, RECOGNITION FOR LONG SERVICE, NICB Studies in Personnel Policy No. 106 (1950). Of 301 companies covered in the Conference Board survey, 94.7% gave non-monetary awards and 52.5% gave extra privileges whereas only 13% gave monetary awards and 11.6% gave increased job security. *Id.* at 3, Table 1. Most of the companies gave more than one type of recognition although 36.5% gave non-monetary service awards only. *Id.* at 3, Table 2.

[124] A study of the tuition-aid programs of 166 companies made by the National Industrial Conference Board contains valuable data as to the scope and cost of such

group health and medical programs,[125] to interest-free or low-interest loans for financing the purchase of a home,[126] and various insurance programs.

Fringe benefits may extend to the spouse and children of the employee, who may be covered by hospital and medical insurance, may participate in recreational programs, and may be eligible for company-financed scholarships at colleges and universities.[127] Benefits may be conferred on the employee after he has retired, through continued group insurance and medical benefits,[128] and on his family after his death.

---

programs. See TUITION-AID FOR EMPLOYEES, NICB Studies in Personnel Policy No. 151 (1956). The study shows that there are various requirements for eligibility such as occupation, length of service (a requirement of 40% of the companies), and approval of supervisors (*id.* at 11–12) ; only 24% of the companies require that the courses pertain to the eligible employees' present or future employment with the company, while 46% include cultural subjects such as English and foreign languages (*id.* at 9) ; 18% of the companies pay tuition costs at the end of a course and 90% of the companies require that the employee, to be eligible for financial aid, receive a passing grade (*id.* at 12–13) ; 47% of the companies pay the entire tuition, while 40% pay one-half of the cost (*id.* at 14) ; the median cost per participant was $48 with the greatest single group of companies falling into the $40–$60 range (*id.* at 31–32). Also included in the study are the individual plans of leading financial institutions, public utilities, and industrial concerns (*id.* at 36–67).

[125] For a discussion of such programs, see note 112 *supra.*

[126] In a survey in 1956 by the National Industrial Conference Board of employer assistance to employees moving to new locations (COMPANY PAYMENT OF EMPLOYEES' MOVING EXPENSES, *supra* note 56), of 151 companies furnishing some form of financial assistance, more than 25% made loans to assist with the purchase of a new home. More than one-fourth of companies making such loans made them without interest, usually on a short-term basis; another one-fourth charged interest at rates between 2% and 4%, while the balance charged interest rates up to 6%. In a ruling relating to interest-free loans for the purpose of split-dollar insurance, the Treasury Department stated: "The mere making available of money does not result in realized income to the payee or a deduction to the payor." Rev. Rul. 55–713, 1955–2 CUM. BULL. 23. *Cf.* J. Simpson Dean, *supra* note 121.

[127] Many companies have scholarship programs which are operated either directly or through company-financed charitable foundations; these programs frequently include scholarships for children of company employees satisfying prescribed eligibility standards. See 22 NICB MGMT. REC., June 1960, p. 20, describing a program of the Lockheed Aircraft Corporation under which twenty scholarships for four years of college are given annually; of these, five are given to children of company employees.

[128] A study made in 1957 by the National Industrial Conference Board showed that of 137 companies surveyed who had group health insurance, about one-fourth extended such insurance to retired employees. Because of the higher cost involved, most of these companies reduced the amount of protection available to retired employees. See FOX, TRENDS IN COMPANY GROUP INSURANCE PROGRAMS, NICB Studies in Personnel Policy No. 159, at 25 (1957). According to this study, the most common benefit extended to the retired employee (other than pensions) was group life insurance. Of over 200 companies surveyed in 1957, 55% extended death benefits to their retired employees. Of the companies with such a practice, almost

A steadily increasing percentage of the payroll dollar is represented by fringe benefits of various kinds [129] and fringe benefits are currently an important issue in collective bargaining negotiations.

Tax Aspects. In the absence of Tax Code provisions, perquisites and fringe benefits should in theory receive similar income tax treatment. In practice, however, the environment is less favorable for perquisites than for fringe benefits that are accorded a group which includes less highly paid employees.

Undoubtedly, a vital reason for the popularity of fringe benefits is their favored tax treatment. Over the years, these benefits have become industrial practices and, at least initially because of objectives deemed socially desirable, have on the whole been viewed benevolently by the Treasury Department in its tax administration. Favorable tax treatment commenced with rulings in 1919 and 1920. The 1919 ruling held tax-free to the employee the value of meals and lodging when furnished solely for the convenience of the employer; the employee benefit was thought to be merely a condition of employment which the employee could not reject.[130] The 1920 ruling held tax-free to employees premiums paid by a company for group term insurance on their lives.[131]

The convenience-of-the-employer rule adopted in 1919 was curtailed by the Treasury Department in 1950, when it took the view that the rule should be inapplicable if compensation was intended.[132] However, the Department's earlier position was largely reaffirmed and given legislative status in the Internal Revenue Code of 1954.[133]

---

all provided insurance protection by allowing retired employees to continue in the group insurance program. In most instances, the retired employee was found to be entitled to smaller benefits than those in effect prior to retirement. *Id.* at 40–42.

[129] The Chamber of Commerce of the United States, in a biennial study of fringe benefits (comprehensively defined), found that for 108 identical companies such benefits constituted 24.6% of the payroll dollar in 1959, as against 23.8% in 1958, 21.9% in 1955, and 20% in 1953. Going back to 1947, the percentage was only 14.7%. See U.S. CHAMBER OF COMMERCE, FRINGE BENEFITS 1959, at 5 (1960). The mean or average payment for fringe benefits in 1959 for a group of 1,064 reporting employers was $1,132 per employee or 54.8¢ per hour. *Id.* at 7, Table 2.

[130] O.D. 265, 1 CUM. BULL. 71.

[131] L.O. 1014, 2 CUM. BULL. 88.

[132] Mim. 6477, 1950–1 CUM. BULL. 16.

[133] INT. REV. CODE OF 1954, § 119, provides for the exclusion from the gross income of an employee of meals and lodging furnished for the convenience of the employer on the business premises of the employer and, with respect to lodging, as a condition of employment. The Treasury Regulations recognize § 119 to be applicable to meals and lodging meeting the tests of that section, even when such meals and lodging were treated as part of the compensation of an employee in an employment contract or statute fixing the terms of his employment. See Treas. Reg. § 1.119–1 (1956). On the other hand, when the employee has the option to

In the convenience-of-the-employer rule can be found the basis for the current practice of treating as tax-free such items as food in employee dining-rooms and cafeterias, employee use of apartments and hotel rooms at or near the company's place of business, and educational programs for employees.

The 1920 ruling on group term insurance was based upon grounds that may not square with income tax principles evolved over the years, but this ruling, with its implicit rejection of tax on *de minimis* individual benefits, today has the sanction of Treasury Regulation and, as part of a long-recognized position, is in the web and woof of industrial relations.[134] To this ruling also may be traced the tax immunity attaching to various fringe benefits, such as health and accident programs, which now have Congressional recognition.

HEALTH AND ACCIDENT INSURANCE PREMIUMS. Prior to the Internal Revenue Code of 1954, payments by a company of premiums under health and accident plans were held by the Treasury Depart-

---

receive additional compensation in lieu of meals and lodgings in kind, § 119 is not applicable. Treas. Reg. § 1.119–1(c)(2) (1956). The fact that the employer has a right to be reimbursed by the employee for the value of meals and lodging furnished to the employee will not prevent the application of § 119 to such meals and lodging. See Rev. Rul. 59–307, 1959–2 CUM. BULL. 48, announcing agreement with the decision of Boykin v. Com'r, 260 F.2d 249 (8th Cir. 1958) which decided a case contrary to the provisions of the Regulations issued in 1956. See Treas. Reg. § 1.119(c)(2) (1956).

[134] Leading Supreme Court cases that have considered the statutory concept of gross income in employer-employee relationships have taken a sweeping view of the scope of the concept in this area. See Com'r v. Smith, 324 U.S. 177 (1950); Com'r. v. LoBue, 351 U.S. 243 (1956). In the *LoBue* case, the court stated as to the meaning of the term "gross income" under § 22(a) of the Internal Revenue Code of 1939 in connection with a stock purchase agreement of an executive: "We have repeatedly held that defining 'gross income' as broadly as it did in Section 22(a) Congress intended to 'tax all gains except those specifically exempted.' See *e.g., Com'r v. Glenshaw Glass Co.,* 346 U.S. 426, 429–30. The only exemption Congress provided from this very comprehensive definition that could possibly have application here is the gift exemption of Section 22(b)(3). But there was not the slightest indication of the kind of detached and disinterested generosity which might evidence a 'gift in the statutory sense. . . .' The company was not giving something away for nothing." 351 U.S. at 246.

As to the difficulties of working out the delineation between gross income and gifts for income tax purposes, see Com'r v. Duberstein, 363 U.S. 278 (1960) and United States v. Kaiser, 363 U.S. 299 (1960), discussed in Rothschild, *Business Gifts as Income,* 19 INST. FED. TAX. 147, 155 ff. (1961). Cf. Rev. Rul. 59–58, 1959–1 CUM. BULL. 17 (holding that the value of turkeys and hams given by an employer to employees at Christmas or another holiday need not be reported as income); Rev. Rul. 131, 1953–2 CUM. BULL. 112 (rehabilitation payments to employees or their families who were injured or sustained damage as a result of a tornado not taxable to them since the size of such payments did not depend upon the length of service or the nature of the employment of the employees receiving such payments).

ment to be tax-exempt to the employee only in the case of group plans.[135] The 1954 Code both gave the Treasury Department rulings legislative sanction and eliminated the requirement that the premium or contribution be paid under a group plan.[136] The tax exemption thus applies to an individual policy protecting a single corporate officer from loss of income in case of accident or disability.[137]

Usually, such protection is provided either through group membership in the local Blue Cross organization, supplemented by the Blue Shield plan,[138] or through group health insurance purchased from an insurance company.[139] In either event, all or a portion of the cost of hospitalization, operations, and incidental medical and technical services is received by the employee without cost to himself or by paying only a part of the premium when such a plan is on a contributory basis.[140] Even in the latter case the employee benefits from the lower group rate as well as from his company's contribution.

Group disability insurance is another form of group insurance plan increasingly available to employees. For example, Ford Motor Company has had a plan providing for payment, after three months of total and continuous disability, of one-third of salary up to $10,000 a year, continuing for ten years if the disability is due to sickness and until age 65 if due to accident.

Group insurance against catastrophic illness is another current variation of employee health insurance benefit.[141] Many insurance

[135] Rev. Rul. 56–632, 1956–2 Cum. Bull. 101; Letter Ruling, Oct. 26, 1943, 3 CCH Stand. Fed. Tax. Rep. ¶ 6587. Premiums paid on individual policies were, however, held taxable to employees. See Rev. Rul. 210, 1953–2 Cum. Bull. 114; Rev. Rul. 58–90, 1958–1 Cum. Bull. 88.

[136] Int. Rev. Code of 1954, § 106.

[137] Rev. Rul. 58–90, 1958–1 Cum. Bull. 88. The Treasury Department announced, however, that it will not issue advance rulings as to whether an employee-stockholder may exclude from gross income amounts paid by the company to provide accident or health benefits. See T.I.R. 313, Mar. 23, 1961.

[138] In 1956, fifty million Americans were covered by Blue Cross, primarily through a company group. See Fox, op. cit. supra note 128, at 3.

[139] Forty million employees were covered in 1956 by commercial group hospital insurance under a company plan. Ibid.

[140] The basic trend has been for more companies to help pay for medical insurance protection. A study comparing the funding of medical expense insurance in 1949 and 1956 shows important increases in the proportion of company plans, both under Blue Cross and commercial insurance, in which the company pays all of the cost, and a corresponding decrease in plans where the entire cost is borne by the employee. Id at 11–12.

[141] Although the first major medical insurance plan was offered about 1949, the growth of this type of insurance has been dramatic. The Health Insurance Council reports that about 5,250,000 had such insurance at the end of 1955 and that during that year there was an increase of 138% over the number protected at the end of 1954. About 20% of a group of companies surveyed by the National Industrial Conference Board in 1956 had such plans and another 5% expected to have such a plan soon; of the companies having such plans at that time, a preponderance em-

companies issue policies providing for reimbursement of hospital and medical payments from $5,000 to $7,500 per employee for each accident or illness. Such policies usually have co-insurance clauses requiring the employee to pay a percentage, say 20% to 25%, or a minimum of perhaps $100 to $250 of his medical costs, with the insurance company paying or reimbursing the balance.

HEALTH AND ACCIDENT PAYMENTS AND SICK PAY. In addition to tax exemption for premiums or contributions paid by the company, the Internal Revenue Code of 1954 [142] makes the proceeds of health and accident plans tax-free in three categories: [143]

1. Payment or reimbursement of medical expenses of the employee, his spouse, and his dependents.[144]
2. Payments to compensate for the permanent loss or loss of use of a member or function of the body, or permanent disfigurement of the employee, his spouse, and dependents, provided the payments are computed with reference to the nature of the injury and without regard to the employee's absence from work (when he is the injured party).
3. Payments not in excess of $100 per week [145] to compensate for the loss of wages due to sickness or injury made pursuant to a wage continuation plan. Such payments are given tax-free status only after the first week unless the employee is hospitalized during at least one day of the sickness period or unless the absence is due to injury (as distinguished from sickness).[146]

---

ployed a large number of employees. Most of the plans reported were contributory. When major medical insurance was first sold on a group basis, it was usually offered only to high salaried groups, but this study shows a distinct trend toward the inclusion of lower salaried people as well. *Id.* at 17–18.

[142] INT. REV. CODE OF 1954, § 105.

[143] In the case of contributory plans, whether or not insured, the portion of the payments attributable to the employee's contribution is received tax-free. INT. REV. CODE OF 1954, § 105(a). For the determination of the portion of the payments attributable to employee contributions, see Treas. Reg. § 1.105–1(c),(d),(e) (1956).

[144] However, such payment or reimbursement is taxable to the extent of amounts attributable to deductions allowed for medical expenses under § 213. INT. REV. CODE OF 1954, § 105(b).

[145] This amount is considerably higher than the average amount payable under insured plans in 1956, according to a study of wage continuation plans covering employees earning salaries up to $150 per week. According to this study, the median amount payable to employees earning $80 or more per week was $40. See Fox, *op. cit. supra* note 129, at 30–31.

[146] The tax law in this respect corresponds roughly to industrial practice. A study of companies with insured disability plans showed that 60% of such plans start disability pay in the case of an accident on the first day of disability, while one-third start such benefits upon the eighth day. If an employee is home because of illness, 85% of the plans begin to pay after seven days, while 9% begin payments for illness after 3 days. Other plans have differing waiting periods. *Id.* at 29.

This treatment of sickness and accident proceeds is applicable to payments under any plan, whether insured or uninsured.[147] The requirement of a "plan" is liberally construed to include any policy regularly followed.[148] There is no requirement against discrimination in favor of highly compensated employees. A salary continuation plan can cover any group of employees, and separate plans may apply to different groups of employees; there is no statutory limit on the length of time during which salary continuation payments to an employee during sickness or injury continue to be tax-exempt.[149] As to reimbursement of medical expenses and payments for permanent bodily injury there is no dollar limit.

THE COMPANY'S DEDUCTION. The company's deduction for the expense of benefit programs should be allowable either as compensation or as ordinary and business expense. In the case of the closely held company, the disguised dividend problem may be present.[150] For companies generally, any unusual or costly benefit may be subject to challenge on the ground that the benefit brings total compensation to an unreasonable amount or that the program cannot be justified as "ordinary and necessary." [151] When the position is taken that a particular benefit is not compensation, the right to a deduction may depend on proving that the expense is a normal one in the light of prevailing business customs.[152]

[147] INT. REV. CODE OF 1954, § 105(e) ; Treas. Reg. § 1.105–5 (1956). For a description of the laws of New York, New Jersey, California, and Rhode Island which have non-occupational disability statutes, see U.S. DEPARTMENT OF LABOR, BUREAU OF EMPLOYMENT SECURITY, COMPARISON OF STATE UNEMPLOYMENT INSURANCE LAWS OF DECEMBER, 1955, at 126–38 (1956).

[148] Treas. Reg. § 1.105–5 (1956). But see Estate of Leo P. Kaufman, 35 T.C. No. 71 (1961) (finding that payments were merely made in the discretion of the employer, so that there was no plan).

[149] Treas. Reg. § 1.105–5 (1956). Cf. William L. Winter, 36 T.C. No. 2 (1961) (disability pay under pension plan held non-taxable).

[150] E.g., Harmony Dairy Co., supra note 121; cf. Rev. Rul. 58–1, 1958–1 CUM. BULL. 173 (facilities occupied by stockholder-employees at lesser rental than rentals charged to others) ; consult also cases supra note 115.

[151] Slaymaker Lock Co., supra note 122 (company expenditures for purchase and improvement of farm land and house conveyed to foremen's union for the recreation of all employees held a reasonable and necessary expense) ; Rev. Rul. 160, 1953–2 CUM. BULL. 114 (company contributions to employees' hospital association for construction of a hospital for company employees held ordinary and necessary expense) ; Rev. Rul. 131, 1953–2 CUM. BULL. 112 (assistance to employees who were tornado victims). A company payment for the benefit of employees may sometimes be justified as a charitable contribution. T. J. Moss Tie Co., 18 T.C. 188 (1952), petition to review dismissed, 201 F.2d 512 (8th Cir. 1953).

[152] Welch v. Helvering, 290 U.S. 111, 115 (1933) (Cardozo, J., declaring that the terms "ordinary and necessary" depend on "the ways of conduct and the forms of speech prevailing in the business world").

CHAPTER 8

CORPORATE APPROVAL

Close observance of the technical requirements of the law relating to approval by the corporation of executive compensation is of the utmost importance in safeguarding the interests of the corporation, its stockholders, and management. These requirements fall into three main categories: (1) contracting for compensation before the services are rendered; (2) disinterested dealing; and (3) stockholders' approval of the arrangement. In this chapter we shall discuss these three topics, other corporate approval problems, and the effect of the numerous revised corporation statutes enacted in recent years, largely under the influence of the Model Business Corporation Act proposed by the American Bar Association.

CONTRACTING IN ADVANCE

Presumptions. Frequently in small, closely held corporations, directors and officers who seek to be paid are unable to point to any contract or resolution providing for compensation or to any provision for payment in the charter or bylaws. When confronted with cases presenting this situation, the courts usually begin with the time-honored presumption that "directors and officers" are supposed to perform the duties of their office without pay, unless they have a valid, prearranged agreement with the corporation.[1]

[1] Air Traffic & Service Corp. v. Fay, 90 U.S. App. D.C. 319, 196 F.2d 40 (1952); Bassett v. Fairchild, 132 Cal. 637, 64 Pac. 1082 (1901); Angelus Securities Corp. v. Ball, 20 Cal. App.2d 423, 67 P.2d 152 (1937); Joy v. Ditto, 356 Ill. 348, 190 N.E. 671 (1934), *affirming* 271 Ill. App. 375, 190 N.E. 671 (1934); Johnson v. Tri-Union Oil & Gas Co., 278 Ky. 633, 129 S.W.2d 111 (1939); Fox v. Arctic Placer Mining & Mill Co., 229 N.Y. 124, 128 N.E. 154 (1920); Beacon Wool Corp. v. Johnson, 331 Mass. 274, 119 N.E.2d 195 (1954); First Nat'l Bank of Allen v. Daugherty, 122 Okla. 47, 250 Pac. 796 (1926); Althouse v. Cobaugh Colliery Co., 227 Pa. 580, 76 Atl. 316 (1910); Security Savings & Trust Co. v. Coos Bay Lumber & Coal Co., 219 Wis. 647, 263 N.W. 187 (1935). See 5 FLETCHER, CYC. CORPS. (perm. ed. 1952) §§ 2109–10; Tilden, *The Fiduciary Duty of Corporation Directors in Massachusetts,* 28 B.U.L. REV. 265, 279 *et seq.* (1948). *Cf.* Holmes v. Republic Steel Corp., 69 N.E.2d 396, 402 (Ct. Com. Pleas 1946), *mod. and aff'd,* 84 Ohio App. 442, 84 N.E.2d 508 (1948), discussed in text to note 183 *infra.*

Even though the agreement is prearranged, it must have valid consideration; when an officer-director was already obligated by an unexpired contract to give his services, cancellation of the contract and its replacement by a more favorable contract has been held without consideration and invalid. Dwyer v. Tracey, 118 F. Supp. 289 (N.D. Ill. 1954).

The cases show that this presumption, such as it is, in fact applies only to directors and director-officers. An officer who is not also a member of the board usually has no difficulty in recovering payment, subject to the usual principles of implied contract or *quantum meruit,* for valuable services rendered by him without previous formal agreement.[2]

In a few jurisdictions this "presumption" as to directors and director-officers is in fact a rigid rule of law.[3] But in most jurisdictions it serves merely as an initial position from which a court can attack the question of whether recovery is deserved in a particular case. After stating the presumption, the courts sometimes add a statement to the effect that if the director or director-officer has performed any services outside the orbit of his usual and ordinary duties, and if his conduct has not been such as to deprive him of any claim to equitable consideration, he should be paid.[4]

[2] Pease, Kolberg & Co. v. Bates, 85 Cal. App. 786, 260 Pac. 399 (1927); Kryger v. Railway Track Cleaner Mfg. Co., 46 Minn. 500, 49 N.W. 255 (1891); Smith v. Long Island R.R. Co., 102 N.Y. 190, 6 N.E. 397 (1886); Carr v. Kimball, 153 App. Div. 825, 139 N.Y. Supp. 253 (1st Dep't 1912), aff'd w.o. op., 215 N.Y. 634, 109 N.E. 1068 (1915); cf. Mather v. E. M. Co., 118 N.Y. 629 (1890). See 5 FLETCHER, *op. cit. supra* note 1, § 2111. However, recovery upon these principles will often not result in as liberal compensation as might have been received through a contract made in advance.

[3] In Pennsylvania, an officer or director cannot recover on an implied contract or in *quantum meruit.* He must have a contract, or his compensation must be fixed in the charter or bylaws. This is true whether he seeks a bonus or regular salary, and even though he has rendered services which are admittedly worth the amount sought. McKean v. Riter-Conley Mfg. Co., 230 Pa. 319, 79 Atl. 561 (1911); Althouse v. Cobaugh Colliery Co., *supra* note 1; Brophy v. American Brewing Co., 211 Pa. 596, 61 Atl. 123 (1905); Kilpatrick v. The Penrose Ferry Bridge Co., 49 Pa. 118 (1865). Compare the *Althouse* case with Fox v. Arctic Placer Mining & Mill Co., *supra* note 1, where the New York court on similar facts allowed recovery.

The Oklahoma courts take a position similar to that adopted in Pennsylvania. Gaines v. Gaines Bros. Co., 176 Okla. 583, 56 P.2d 863 (1936); Kirk Oil Co. v. Bristow, 154 Okla. 188, 7 P.2d 682 (1932); McCullock v. Perry, 150 Okla. 203, 1 P.2d 170 (1931); First Nat'l Bank of Allen v. Daugherty, *supra* note 1.

Under Delaware law an officer-director has been denied compensation on a *quantum meruit* basis. Air Traffic & Service Corp. v. Fay, *supra* note 1. See also Beacon Wool Corp. v. Johnson, *supra* note 1, where the court held bonuses paid directors to be gratuities, unless provided for by express contract made with a disinterested corporate representative, citing Lofland v. Cahall, 13 Del. Ch. 384, 118 Atl. 1 (1922), text to note 13 *infra.*

[4] King v. Grass Valley Gold Mines Co., 205 Cal. 698, 272 Pac. 290 (1928); Miller & Pardee, Inc. v. Pardee, 242 Ill. App. 233 (1926), aff'd w.o. op., 243 Ill. App. 602 (1927); Shaw v. Harding, 306 Mass. 441, 28 N.E.2d 469 (1940); and cases *supra* note 1; Mayer v. Oxidation Products Co., 110 N.J. Eq. 141, 159 Atl. 377 (1932). See generally 5 FLETCHER, *op. cit. supra* note 1, § 2114; BALLANTINE, CORPORATIONS 188 (rev. ed. 1946). For later cases, see Wiseman v. Musgrave, 309 Mich. 523, 16 N.W.2d 60 (1944); Morris v. North Evanston Bldg. Corp., 319 Ill. App. 298, 49 N.E.2d 647 (1943); Gauger v. Hintz, 262 Wis. 333, 55 N.W.2d 426

The courts have not been very definite as to what they mean by the "ordinary" or "usual" duties that a director or director-officer is supposed to perform for nothing. They may first look to the bylaws, but these may be ambiguous. Bylaw provisions as to particular duties of directors, such as attending board meetings, electing officers, and the like, are usually coupled with broad statements that the directors are to advance the corporate interests and control corporate policy. In the case of officers, the bylaws commonly provide that they shall perform all duties which are "incident to their office," or which are "usually vested" in that office,[5] or which are assigned to them from time to time by the directors.[6] Since in the usual case very little can be gleaned from the bylaws, the courts have adopted various rules of thumb to aid them in drawing the line between "ordinary" or "usual" duties, and duties which entitle a director or director-officer to compensation in the absence of an advance contract. One case seems to go so far as to hold that the only services which the officer-director should be expected to perform for nothing are those "such as any layman can perform without special knowledge or skill."[7] Then there is what might be called the "group" theory—only those services are gratuitous which the directors perform when acting as a body; if any director does work for the corporation as an individual, he should be paid for it.[8] However, in the typical case involving a director-officer, the court may say, "This man is a director; he is also the president"—or the secretary or treasurer or general manager, as the case may be—"and he has done something of value for this corporation." Then it looks at the services he has performed and says, without more, that ordinarily such an officer would or would not do that type of work.[9] If the director, acting as an officer, devotes

---

(1952); Hudson v. Belzoni Equipment Co., 211 Miss. 178, 51 So.2d 223 (1951). *Cf.* Production Machine Co. v. Howe, 327 Mass. 372, 99 N.E.2d 32 (1951) (salary held forfeited because of officer's serious breach of fiduciary duty).

[5] Corinne Mill, Canal & Stock Co. v. Topence, 152 U.S. 405 (1894); Jones v. Foster, 70 F.2d 200 (4th Cir. 1934); Vaught v. Charleston Nat'l Bank, 62 F.2d 817 (10th Cir. 1933); Langlois v. Merchant Inv. Co., 101 Colo. 438, 73 P.2d 1385 (1937); Joy v. Ditto, *supra* note 1.

[6] Johnson v. Tri-Union Oil & Gas Co., *supra* note 1.

[7] Fox v. Arctic Placer Mining & Mill Co., *supra* note 1; *cf.* Indurated Concrete Corp. v. Abbott, 195 Md. 496, 74 A.2d 17 (1950).

[8] Corinne Mill, Canal & Stock Co. v. Topence, *supra* note 5; Marcy v. Shelburne Falls & Colrain St. Ry., 210 Mass. 197, 96 N.E. 130 (1911); Fox v. Arctic Placer Mining & Mill Co., *supra* note 1.

[9] Bassett v. Fairchild, *supra* note 1 (vice-president and general manager); Pence v. West Side Hospital, 265 Ill. App. 500 (1932) (director and vice-president); Shaw v. Harding, *supra* note 4 (president, treasurer, and general manager); Ruttle v. What Cheer Coal Mining Co., 153 Mich. 300, 117 N.W. 168 (1908) (president, treasurer, and general manager); Ferrenbach v. Edward Fehlig & Co., 80 S.W.2d

all his time to the business, and manages all or the major part of the corporate activities, his services are certainly beyond the scope of "ordinary" duties.[10] The same is true of tasks of a professional or technical character.[11]

The cases would be more satisfactory if they drew a clearer distinction between the director who has no other position with the company and the director who is also an officer. The ordinary duties of a director are different from those of a director-officer. A director may do nothing more than attend the meetings of the board; if he is also an officer, his work is probably a good deal more extensive. But in deciding a case where a director-officer seeks compensation, the courts are influenced by the traditional concept that directors are to receive their rewards in forms other than direct monetary compensation from the corporation.[12]

Perhaps the reason for this form of treatment is that in small corporations the directors often fill all the chief executive positions, with a consequent paucity of cases in which directors who are not officers have sought compensation. The only case found in which directors claimed compensation for serving as directors is *Lofland v. Cahall*,[13] decided in Delaware in 1922. Even there four of the

---

705 (Mo. App. 1935) (vice-president and superintendent of construction); Fox v. Arctic Placer Mining & Mill Co., *supra* note 1 (mining engineer); Spalding v. Enid Cemetery Ass'n, 76 Okla. 180, 184 Pac. 579 (1919) (superintendent). For detailed examples of extraordinary services found compensable by the courts, see 5 FLETCHER, *op. cit. supra* note 1, § 2115.

[10] Navco Hardware Co. v. Bass, 214 Ala. 553, 108 So. 452 (1925); Bassett v. Fairchild, *supra* note 1; Johnson v. Tri-Union Oil & Gas Co., *supra* note 1; Kinsella v. Marquette Finance Corp., 16 S.W.2d 619 (Mo. 1929); Hunter v. Conrad, 132 Misc. 579, 230 N.Y. Supp. 202 (Sup. Ct. 1928).

[11] Ferrenbach v. Edward Fehlig & Co., *supra* note 9; Fox v. Arctic Placer Mining & Mill Co., *supra* note 1.

[12] See Chapter 9, text to notes 18 ff.; Robertson v. Schoonmaker, 158 Misc. 627, 285 N.Y. Supp. 204 (Sup. Ct. 1935); Caminetti v. Prudence Mutual Life Ins. Ass'n, 62 Cal. App. 2d 945, 146 P.2d 15 (1944), *reversing* 142 P.2d 41 (Cal. App. 1943). But *cf.* Rowland v. Demming Exploration Co., 45 Idaho 99, 260 Pac. 1032 (1927), where the court makes the distinction but allows the officer, even though a director, to recover.

[13] *Supra* note 3. Godley v. Crandall & Godley Co., 212 N.Y. 121, 105 N.E. 818 (1914), is frequently cited for the point that directors cannot recover in the absence of an express agreement. But there all but one of the directors were also managing officers. See Note, 32 MICH. L. REV. 672, 676 (1934). The nearest case involving directors as such seems to be Maclary v. Pleasant Hills, 109 A.2d 830 (Del. Ch. 1954), rejecting an attempt by corporate directors to justify issuance of shares to themselves *ex post facto* by references to their services. The Court's opinion indicates that at least one of the directors rendered only services normally expected of a director.

Only the following abstract was published in Pindell v. Conlon Corp., at 303 Ill. App. 232 (1940): "Director of manufacturing company could not recover on alleged contract to procure a merger with some other company, since a later contract with another company to manufacture ironing machines was not consummated by

seven directors were also officers. The court, however, applied the presumption with equal force to all seven.[14]

In some of the cases involving director-officers, a court's decision may depend on its interpretation of a statute or a bylaw. A statute under which a corporation is organized may prohibit payment to officers or directors for past services unless the payment is specifically authorized by the stockholders or directors; [15] or a bylaw may require that either the stockholders or the directors, or both, must authorize or vote upon the payment before the services are rendered. If the requirements of the statute or the bylaws are not complied with, compensation may be refused even by courts which might otherwise allow it.[16] An officer who is also a director of the corporation for which he is working cannot plead that he was ignorant of the bylaw provisions; he is presumed to have known what they are, and he is therefore controlled by them.[17] This presumption, however, may not extend to officers who are not stockholders and who are not members of the board of directors, and they may be able to secure compensation even in the face of an express prohibition in the bylaws.[18] They may be in the same position as other third parties

him, and even if it were, it would be within the scope of his duties as director, and no contract for compensation could be implied." The syllabus for the same case at 24 N.E.2d 882 is substantially the same. For a similar case involving an officer (not a director) see Portman v. American Home Products Corp., 201 F.2d 847 (2d Cir. 1953), *affirming* 98 F. Supp. 494 (S.D.N.Y. 1951).

[14] In Keenan v. Eshleman, 21 Del. Ch. 259, 2 A.2d 904 (1938), the same court that decided the *Lofland* case took a similar view in dealing with directors who were also managing executives.

[15] Henry v. Michigan Sanitarium & Benev. Ass'n, 147 Mich. 142, 110 N.W. 523 (1907) (charitable corporation; special statute); Triplett v. Fauver, 103 Va. 123, 48 S.E. 875 (1904); Georgetown Mercantile Co. v. First Nat'l Bank of Georgetown, 165 S.W. 73 (Tex. Civ. App. 1914). Bylaws adopted by the stockholders are generally valid notwithstanding the customary provision of state corporation laws that the board of directors shall manage the corporation. Ripley v. Storer, 1 Misc. 2d 281, 139 N.Y.S.2d 786 (Sup. Ct. 1955), *aff'd*, 286 App. Div. 844, 142 N.Y.S.2d 269 (1st Dep't 1955), *modified on other grounds*, 309 N.Y. 506, 132 N.E.2d 87 (1956).

[16] *In re* A. F. Brown Packing Co., 22 F.2d 419 (D. Md. 1927); Enders v. Northwestern Trust Co., 125 Ore. 673, 268 Pac. 49 (1928); Hudson v. Alaska Airlines, 43 Wash.2d 71, 260 P.2d 321 (1953); *In re* Queen City Plate Glass Co., 1 Ont. W.N. 863 (1910); cf. Francis v. Brigham-Hopkins Co., 108 Md. 233, 70 Atl. 95 (1908). But cf. Georgetown Mercantile Co. v. First Nat'l Bank of Georgetown, *supra* note 15, in which a non-director-officer was granted compensation even though a bylaw requirement had not been complied with.

[17] *In re* A. F. Brown Packing Co., *supra* note 16; Beers v. New York Life Ins. Co., 66 Hun 75, 20 N.Y. Supp. 788 (1st Dep't 1892); Enders v. Northwestern Trust Co., *supra* note 16.

[18] Pease, Kolberg & Co. v. Bates, *supra* note 2, noted 16 CALIF. L. REV. 435 (1928); see also Godley v. Crandall & Godley Co., *supra* note 13; Note, 19 MICH. L. REV. 96 (1920). Cf. BALLANTINE, *op. cit. supra* note 4, 191–92.

who deal with the corporation without actual notice of the bylaws.[19] But even though the directors comply with the restrictions of the by-laws, this does not prevent the court from exercising its equitable powers to inquire into the reasonableness of the compensation voted.[20]

The cases fall into five general groups: (1) when there is no agreement for payment of compensation; (2) when there is an informal agreement; (3) self-payment of compensation without any authorization; (4) a self-voted agreement to pay compensation; and (5) compensation retroactively voted or authorized. In the discussion which follows we are dealing (unless otherwise noted) with directors who are also officers. For brevity, we shall speak of them as "executives."

1. NO AGREEMENT. The executive may have rendered services for the corporation with no agreement whatsoever as to compensation.[21] When he seeks to be paid, or counterclaims for payment in a suit by the corporation or a minority stockholder, the court may allow recovery simply on the ground that in its judgment he has performed services clearly outside the scope of his duties, deciding this point in the manner indicated above or leaving it for the jury to determine.[22] The court may also insist that the executive show that he expected to be paid and that the other directors and officers understood that he would demand payment.[23] Merely doing the work is not enough to prove this expectation.[24] But if the executive has

---

[19] Pease, Kolberg & Co. v. Bates, *supra* note 2; see also Bank of Holly Springs v. Pinson, 58 Miss. 421, 38 Am. Rep. 330 (1880); *contra,* Putnam v. Ensign Oil Co., 272 Pa. 301, 308, 116 Atl. 285 (1922).

[20] Church v. Harnit, 35 F.2d 499 (6th Cir. 1929) *cert. denied,* 281 U.S. 732 (1930); Seitz v. Union Brass & Metal Mfg. Co., 152 Minn. 460, 189 N.W. 586 (1922). See also *infra* note 100.

[21] Corinne Mill, Canal & Stock Co. v. Topence, *supra* note 5; Jones v. Foster, 70 F.2d 200 (4th Cir. 1934) (counterclaim by officer in suit by corporation); Rosehill Cemetery Co. v. Dempster, 223 Ill. 567, 79 N.E. 276 (1906); Pindell v. Conlon Corp., *supra* note 13 (abstract of opinion); Taylor v. Citizens Oil Co., 182 Ky. 350, 206 S.W. 644 (1918); Notley v. First State Bank of Vicksburg, 154 Mich. 676, 118 N.W. 486 (1908); Ferrenbach v. Edward Fehlig & Co., *supra* note 9; Fox v. Arctic Placer Mining & Mill Co., *supra* note 1. *Cf.* Grean v. Grean, 274 App. Div. 279, 82 N.Y.S.2d 787 (1st Dep't 1948) (contract providing for fixed salary to officer with agreement to "devote only such time to the business of the Corporation as he in his sole judgment shall deem necessary" held not illusory).

[22] Corinne Mill, Canal & Stock Co. v. Topence, *supra* note 5; Jones v. Foster, *supra* note 21; Fox v. Arctic Placer Mining & Mill Co., *supra* note 1.

[23] Jones v. Foster, *supra* note 21; Shattuck v. Guardian Trust Co., 204 N.Y. 200, 97 N.E. 517 (1912); Graves v. Graves Co., 7 Tenn. App. 369 (1928). *Cf.* Holmes v. Republic Steel Corp., *supra* note 1.

[24] Portman v. American Home Products Corp., *supra* note 13 (officer of subsidiary not entitled to extra compensation for services beyond scope of position and inference of agreement held not warranted); Fox v. Arctic Placer Mining &

worked under a valid contract and been paid, and then has continued to work without a contract or other agreement, this may be sufficient to show that he and the other members of the board understood that he was not doing the work without the expectation of payment.[25] If the corporation is a very small one, where all the directors and stockholders knew what work the executive was doing, he may be able to recover.[26] There are, however, courts which take an extremely strict view in any case in which the executive does not have an express agreement.[27]

2. INFORMAL AGREEMENT. The executive may have rendered services under an informal agreement. Here the usual situation is that some or all of the officers and directors of a small corporation get together, talk things over, and agree on compensation to be paid, but neglect to embody their agreement in a formal contract or resolution. The informal agreement, however, may be sufficient to overcome any presumption that the executive should not be paid.[28] Similarly, entries on the minute books authorizing compensation,[29]

Mill Co., *supra* note 1; see also Gill v. New York Cab Co., 48 Hun 524, 1 N.Y. Supp. 202 (1st Dep't 1888); Kelsey v. Sargent, 40 Hun 150 (5th Dep't 1886).

[25] Ferrenbach v. Edward Fehlig & Co., *supra* note 9; Fox v. Arctic Placer Mining & Mill Co., *supra* note 1. Gillespie Land and Irrigation Co. v. Jones, 63 Ore. 535, 164 P.2d 456 (1945) (payment for services during 1940, 1941, and 1942 held to constitute implied promise to pay for services during 1943).

[26] Rosehill Cemetery Co. v. Dempster, *supra* note 21; Shattuck v. Guardian Trust Co., *supra* note 23.

[27] Air Traffic & Service Corp. v. Fay, *supra* note 1; Pindell v. Conlon Corp., *supra* note 13; Beacon Wool Corp. v. Johnson, *supra* note 1, and cases *supra* note 3. Particularly is this true where there is an element of fraud. See Taylor v. Citizens Oil Co., *supra* note 21; Notley v. First State Bank of Vicksburg, *supra* note 21.

[28] Vaught v. Charleston Nat'l Bank, *supra* note 5; National Loan & Inv. Co. v. Rockland Co., 94 Fed. 335 (8th Cir. 1899); Gettinger v. Heaney, 220 Ala. 613, 127 So. 195 (1930); Joy v. Ditto, *supra* note 1; Johnson v. Tri-Union Oil & Gas Co., *supra* note 1; Graves v. Graves Co., *supra* note 23. To the effect that a salary arrangement (including a percentage bonus) can be oral, see Young v. United States Mortgage & Trust Co., 214 N.Y. 279, 108 N.E. 418 (1915). See also *infra* note 141. As to the degree of definiteness required, see Holmes v. Republic Steel Corp., *supra* note 1 (simple promise of bonus, without yardstick, upheld); Ransome Concrete Machinery Co. v. Moody, 282 Fed. 29 (2d Cir. 1922) (prior informal agreement followed by later formal authorization held sufficient). On the other hand, the following promises have been held too indefinite: that the employee would receive "a satisfactory amount" [Mackintosh v. Kimball, 101 App. Div. 494 (1st Dep't 1905)]; that he would be paid "a fair share of my profits" [Varney v. Ditmars, 217 N.Y. 223 (1916)]; that the employer would "do well" by the employee [Jerome v. Wood, 39 Colo. 197, 88 Pac. 1067 (1907)]; that salary, fixed at a minimum, would be commensurate with earnings [Donovan v. Bull Mountain Trading Co., 60 Mont. 87, 198 Pac. 436 (1921)].

[29] Johnson v. Tri-Union Oil & Gas Co., *supra* note 1; see also Wineburgh v. Seeman Bros., 21 N.Y.S.2d 180 (Sup. Ct. 1940); Spalding v. Enid Cemetery Ass'n, *supra* note 9.

or the issuance by the board of directors of a note in payment for the services,[30] will be sufficient to entitle the executive to compensation either on an implied contract or in *quantum meruit*. The executive must, of course, prove that he has actually rendered valuable services.[31] A minority stockholder may not be able to set aside compensation paid under an informal agreement if the board of directors had been awarding such compensation for a number of years and during all this time the stockholders were aware of the facts.[32] Many cases hold that even though the agreement was informal all the directors and stockholders were familiar with it, accepted the benefits of the services, and should now pay for them. In very small corporations, indeed, the courts often do not pay much attention to the corporate form;[33] they treat the claim for services very much in the manner that they would treat a claim by one individual against another, especially where there are no minority stockholders or creditors who would be injured.[34]

3. SELF-PAYMENT. The executive who has helped himself to the corporate funds may be sued by the corporation or a minority stockholder who wants the money returned.[35] Where there is a total dis-

[30] Vaught v. Charleston Nat'l Bank, *supra* note 5; National Loan & Inv. Co. v. Rockland Co., *supra* note 28; Williams v. Williams Yellow Pine Co., 166 Miss. 803, 146 So. 143 (1933); *see also opin. on app. after jury's verdict,* 187 Miss. 425, 193 So. 1 (1940).

[31] Joy v. Ditto, *supra* note 1; see also Schulte v. Ideal Food Products Co., 208 Iowa 767, 226 N.W. 174 (1929); *cf.* Whitfield v. Kern, 122 N.J. Eq. 332, 192 Atl. 48 (1937), *aff'd in part and rev'd in part,* 125 N.J. Eq. 511, 6 A.2d 471 (1939).

[32] See, for example, Joy v. Ditto, *supra* note 1; Wineburgh v. Seeman Bros., *supra* note 29.

[33] See Sharon Herald Co. v. Granger, 97 F. Supp. 295 (W.D.Pa. 1951), *aff'd,* 195 F.2d 890 (3d Cir. 1952) where the District Court refers to the informal ways in which a small corporation may do business almost as a separate species of corporate practice; however, the case does not involve executive compensation.

[34] Vaught v. Charleston Nat'l Bank, *supra* note 5; Gettinger v. Heaney, *supra* note 28, 220 Ala. at 617, 127 So. at 198; Ruttle v. What Cheer Coal Mining Co., *supra* note 9; Hirsch v. Jones, 115 App. Div. 156, 100 N.Y. Supp. 687 (1st Dep't 1906), *app. dismissed,* 190 N.Y. 195, 83 N.E. 786 (1908); Graves v. Graves Co., *supra* note 23. But *cf.* Farris v. Farris Engineering Corp., 7 N.J. 487, 81 A.2d 731 (1951) (holding *ultra vires* payment of improperly authorized compensation to president of a family corporation).

For additional cases involving *quantum meruit* see Gauger v. Hintz, *supra* note 4; Gascue v. Saralegui Land & Livestock Co., *infra* note 47.

[35] Monterey Water Co. v. Voorhees, 45 Ariz. 338, 43 P.2d 196 (1935); O'Leary v. Seemann, 76 Colo. 335, 232 Pac. 667 (1925); Hall v. Woods, 325 Ill. 114, 156 N.E. 258 (1927); Stevenson v. Sicklesteel Lumber Co., 219 Mich. 18, 188 N.W. 449 (1922); Eskestrand v. Durant Hotel Co., 220 Miss. 867, 72 So.2d 207 (1954); Fields v. Victor Building & Loan Co., 73 Okla. 207, 175 Pac. 529 (1918); Collins v. Hite, 109 W. Va. 79, 153 S.E. 240 (1930); Security Savings & Trust Co. v. Coos Bay Lumber & Coal Co., *supra* note 1.

regard of corporate formalities, the courts usually accede to the plaintiff's demands.[36] This is true even though the board of directors may have later sought to ratify the self-payment.[37] Bad faith and fraud upon the corporation and stockholders are elements in many of these cases, but most courts seem to base their decisions merely on the fact that an executive has no authority to pay himself. Thus, in *Collins v. Hite,*[38] a minority stockholder sued the secretary-treasurer to force him to refund to the corporation money which he had paid out to himself as additional salary. The payments were unauthorized by the board of directors, of which the plaintiff and the defendant were members. After the payments had been made, the number of directors was increased, Hite was given a "white-washing," and the withdrawals were ratified. The court ordered the money returned, stating that Hite was taking money out of the pockets of the stockholders and giving it to himself.

In *Johnson v. Tri-Union Oil & Gas Co.,* however, where there were only three stockholders, all of whom were directors and officers, and where all the corporate transactions were conducted with complete informality, an officer who had paid himself was allowed to retain reasonable compensation for his services, being required to return only the excess.[39] The court emphasized that the defendant officer was largely responsible for the success of the business. In *O'Leary v. Seemann,*[40] the president of a corporation kept as payment for his services part of the money which he had received from selling corporate stock. At the suit of a minority stockholder he was compelled to return this fund to the corporation, on the ground that the taking was unauthorized. The court added, however, that he might

---

[36] Richardson v. Blue Grass Mining Co., 29 F. Supp. 658 (E.D.Ky. 1939); Flannery Bolt Co. v. Flannery, 16 F. Supp. 803 (W.D.Pa. 1935), *modified* 86 F.2d 43 (3rd Cir. 1936); Hall v. Woods, *supra* note 35; Brown v. De Young, 167 Ill. 549, 47 N.E. 863 (1897); Stevenson v. Sicklesteel Lumber Co., *supra* note 35; Bayer v. Yuckman, 281 App. Div. 860, 119 N.Y.S.2d 633 (1st Dep't 1953) (alleged increase in contractual salary not proved); Security Savings & Trust Co. v. Coos Bay Lumber & Coal Co., *supra* note 1; *cf.* Robertson v. Schoonmaker, *supra* note 12; Santarelli v. Katz, 270 F.2d 762 (7th Cir. 1959).

[37] Monterey Water Co. v. Voorhees, *supra* note 35; Lewis v. Matthews, 161 App. Div. 107, 146 N.Y.Supp. 424 (1st Dep't 1914); Fields v. Victor Building & Loan Co., *supra* note 35; Collins v. Hite, *supra* note 35.

[38] *Supra* note 35.

[39] *Supra* note 1. *Cf.* Adams v. Mid-West Chevrolet Corp., 198 Okla. 461, 179 P.2d 147 (1946), refusing to surcharge an officer-director with interest upon advances against salary subsequently earned, upon the ground that too "extensive" an audit would be required.

[40] *Supra* note 35; *cf.* Santarelli v. Katz, *supra* note 36 (executives required to repay amounts received on sale of scrap, a by-product of company's production).

have been allowed to retain a reasonable amount if he had proved that the board of directors had requested him to perform the services and that such services were valuable. These two cases took a fairly lenient attitude toward the defendant officers, but the authority of the *Johnson* case will probably not be extended beyond its own facts; and the statements in the *O'Leary* case are, of course, only dicta.

4. SELF-VOTED AGREEMENT. The executive may have performed services under a resolution or authorization passed by the board of directors which was "void" or "voidable" because the recipients of the compensation themselves voted for it.[41] Similarly, he may have completed the services and the board of directors may thereafter have enacted an "invalid" resolution authorizing payment.[42] The corporation itself or a minority stockholder may seek to enjoin payment,[43] or, if the executive has already been paid, to set aside the payment.[44]

[41] Heise v. Earnshaw Publications, 130 F. Supp. 38 (D. Mass. 1955); Todd v. Southland Broadcasting Co., 231 F.2d 225 (5th Cir. 1956), *cert. denied,* 352 U.S. 845 (1956); Skye v. Francis J. Skye Distributing Co., 305 Ill. App. 159, 26 N.E.2d 519 (1940); Francis v. Brigham-Hopkins Co., *supra* note 16; Shaw v. Harding, *supra* note 4; Briggs v. Gilbert Grocery Co., 116 Ohio St. 343, 156 N.E. 494 (1927). Compare OHIO REV. CODE, § 1701.60 (1955); Gauger v. Hintz, *supra* note 4. See also Gottlieb v. Heyden Chemical Corp., 90 A.2d 660 (1952), *on rehearing,* 91 A.2d 57 (1952), *on reargument,* 92 A.2d 594 (1952), *on retrial,* 99 A.2d 507 (Del. Ch. 1953), *aff'd,* 105 A.2d 461 (Del. Sup. Ct. 1954); Kerbs v. California Eastern Airways, 32 Del. Ch. 219, 83 A.2d 473 (1951), *rev'd,* 33 Del. Cir. 69, 90 A.2d 652 (1952), *pet. for reargument denied,* 91 A.2d 62 (1952), *on retrial,* 94 A.2d 217 (Del. Ch. 1953). For corporation laws relating to self-voted agreements, see text to notes 214 ff. *infra* and consult note 54, *infra.*

[42] Bassett v. Fairchild, *supra* note 1; Gottlieb v. Heyden Chemical Corp., *supra* note 41; Calkins v. Wire Hardware Co., 267 Mass. 52, 165 N.E. 889 (1929); State *ex rel.* Squire v. Miller, 62 Ohio App. 43, 23 N.E.2d 321 (1939).

[43] Holcomb v. Forsyth, 216 Ala. 486, 113 So. 516 (1927); Cook v. Malvern Brick & Tile Co., 194 Ark. 759, 109 S.W.2d 451 (1937); Sterling Loan & Inv. Co. v. Litel, 75 Colo. 34, 223 Pac. 753 (1924); Beha v. Martin, 161 Ky. 838, 171 S.W. 393 (1914); Jacobson v. Brooklyn Lumber Co., 184 N.Y. 152, 76 N.E. 1075 (1906); Sotter v. Coatesville Boiler Works, 257 Pa. 411, 101 Atl. 744 (1917); Russell v. H. C. Patterson Co., 232 Pa. 113, 81 Atl. 136 (1911); Schaffhauser v. Arnholt & Schaefer Brewing Co., 218 Pa. 298, 67 Atl. 417 (1907).

[44] Backus v. Finkelstein, 23 F.2d 531 (D. Minn. 1924), *app. dismissed,* 31 F.2d 1011 (8th Cir. 1929); Pece v. Tama Trading Co., 22 Cal. App. 2d 219, 70 P.2d 652 (1937); Angelus Securities Corp. v. Ball, *supra* note 1; Voorhees v. Mason, 245 Ill. 256, 91 N.E. 1056 (1910); Bates St. Shirt Co. v. Waite, 130 Me. 352, 156 Atl. 293 (1931); Francis v. Brigham-Hopkins Co., *supra* note 16; Shaw v. Harding, *supra* note 4; Calkins v. Wire Hardware Co., *supra* note 42; Miner v. Belle Isle Ice Co., 93 Mich. 97, 53 N.W. 218 (1892); Garwin v. Anderson, 334 Mich. 287, 54 N.W.2d 667 (1952); Barrett v. Smith, 185 Minn. 596, 242 N.W. 392 (1932); Putnam v. Juvenile Shoe Corp., 307 Mo. 74, 269 S.W. 593 (1925); Blancard v. Blancard & Co., 96 N.J. Eq. 264, 125 Atl. 337 (1924); Booth v. Beattie, 95 N.J. Eq. 776, 118 Atl. 257 (1922), *aff'd w.o. op.,* 123 Atl. 925 (1924); Raynolds v. Diamond Mills Paper Co., 69 N.J. Eq. 299, 60 Atl. 941 (1905); Davis v. Thomas &

In some cases the executive himself may sue on the "invalid" resolution.[45] But, regardless of the manner in which the question comes up, the courts have to decide what effect to give to the fact that the compensation was "self-voted." This is a problem which will be taken up later in this chapter, and the cases presently under discussion will be analyzed in some detail.[46]

5. RETROACTIVE COMPENSATION. The executive may have performed services for the corporation at a fixed salary under a validly prearranged agreement, but may have obtained or may seek to obtain additional compensation in the form of subsequently voted "bonuses" or "extra salary." Here, as in several of the other situations just discussed, we encounter the problem of whether a corporation can reward past services. That problem will be dealt with later in this chapter. The cases here under consideration are complicated by self-voting, overreaching, and other similar factors. In most of them the officer's conduct was flagrant, and the retroactive compensation was disallowed; in a few, the executive was found to have earned his pay and was allowed to keep it, even though it was retroactively voted.[47]

Davis Co., 63 N.J. Eq. 572, 52 Atl. 717 (1902); Atwater v. Elkhorn Valley Coal-Land Co., 184 App. Div. 253, 171 N.Y. Supp. 552 (1st Dep't 1918); Tilton v. Gans, 90 Misc. 84, 152 N.Y. Supp. 981 (Sup. Ct. 1915), *motion denied*, 168 App. Div. 908, 152 N.Y. Supp. 1146 (1st Dep't 1915); Von Herberg v. Von Herberg, 6 Wash. 2d 100, 106 P.2d 737 (1940).

[45] Pece v. Tama Trading Co., *supra* note 44; Mallory v. Mallory Wheeler Co., 61 Conn. 131, 23 Atl. 708 (1891); Skye v. Francis J. Skye Distributing Co., *supra* note 41; Kreitner v. Burgweger, 174 App. Div. 48, 160 N.Y. Supp. 256 (4th Dep't 1916); Chamberlain v. Chamberlain, Care & Boyce, Inc., 124 Misc. 480, 209 N.Y. Supp. 258 (Sup. Ct. 1925); Briggs v. Gilbert Grocery Co., *supra* note 41; State *ex rel.* Squire v. Miller, *supra* note 42. *Cf.* also Leon Farms Corp. v. Beeman, 240 S.W.2d 433 (Tex. Civ. App. 1951) and Hudson v. Alaska Airlines, *supra* note 16, in which promises of compensation made by officers contrary to resolutions of board of directors were held unenforceable.

[46] See especially text to notes 59 ff.

[47] In the following cases retroactive compensation was disallowed: Savage v. Lorraine Corp., 217 F.2d 378 (9th Cir. 1954); Dow v. River Farms of California, 110 Cal. App. 2d 403, 243 P.2d 95 (1952); Keenan v. Eshleman, *supra* note 14; Lofland v. Cahall, *supra* notes 3 and 13; Fidanque v. American Maracaibo Co., 33 Del. Ch. 262, 92 A.2d 311 (1952). In Todd v. Southland Broadcasting Co., *supra* note 41, the directors had retroactively voted themselves salaries and bonuses for prior periods; the court took the view that there is no consideration for bonuses and retroactive increases of salary except when there has been an express or implied understanding that they may be granted if conditions warrant; their grant by the directors alone will not sustain them against attack by the shareholders. See further, Bingham v. Ditzler, 309 Ill. App. 581, 33 N.E.2d 939 (1941); Sagalyn v. Meekins, Packard & Wheat, Inc., 290 Mass. 434, 195 N.E. 769 (1935); Godley v. Crandall & Godley Co., *supra* note 13; Carr v. Kimball, *supra* note 2; A. J. Ander-

We have noticed throughout the discussion in this section the emphasis placed by the courts on "self-dealing." It is now time to examine this problem more closely.

Self-Dealing

The Authorities. Any arrangement between a director and his corporation is, of course, subject to well-established rules against self-dealing—rules which have been laid down in hundreds of decisions.[48] The present analysis deals with only one phase of the kind of conduct usually characterized as self-dealing. It is limited to the self-voting of compensation.

First of all, what particular irregularities in the fixing of compensation constitute self-dealing? The irregularity may be due to the way in which the directors have voted at the meeting where compensation matters are passed upon.[49] Any resolution authorizing or confirming compensation is generally held to be self-voted if the vote of the executive who is to be paid is necessary to secure its adoption, in the sense that without his vote the resolution would not

---

son Co. v. Kinsolving, 262 S.W. 150 (Tex. Civ. App. 1924); Boyum v. Johnson, 127 F.2d 491 (8th Cir. 1942); Balch v. Investors Royalty Co., 7 F. Supp. 420 (N.D. Okla. 1934). See also Tarlow v. Archbell, 47 N.Y.S.2d 3 (Sup. Ct. 1943), aff'd w.o. op., 269 App. Div. 837 (1st Dep't 1945), aff'd w.o. op., 296 N.Y. 757 (1946) (complaint alleging, *inter alia*, payments for past services held to state good cause of action). As to retroactive compensation based on a previous promise of additional compensation not fixed in amount, see Holmes v. Republic Steel Corp., *supra* note 1, discussed in text to note 183 *infra*. As to widow's pension paid on account of deceased husband's services as president of employer corporation, see Moore v. Keystone Macaroni Mfg. Co., 370 Pa. 172, 87 A.2d 295 (1952), noted, 101 Pa. L. Rev. 153 (1952).

In the following, the grant to the officer was sustained as having been earned: Ransome Concrete Machinery Co. v. Moody, *supra* note 28; Buell v. Lanski, 232 Ill. App. 500 (1924); Gascue v. Saralegui Land & Livestock Co., 70 Nev. 83, 255 P.2d 335 (1953); Wood v. Myers Paper Co., 3 Tenn. App. 128 (1926). In Cook v. Malvern Brick & Tile Co., *supra* note 43, the cause was remanded to determine whether the increases were fair. As to "casual" bonuses and bonuses paid pursuant to "implied contract," see text to notes 28 ff. Retroactive compensation may be upheld as reasonable if it applies to a relatively short past period. Blish v. Thompson Automatic Arms Corp., 30 Del. Ch. 538, 64 A.2d 581 (1948); Francis v. Brigham-Hopkins Co., *supra* note 16; Russell v. H. C. Patterson Co., *supra* note 43. A contract for severance pay based on length of past service is enforceable, Montefalcone v. Banco di Napoli Trust Co., 268 App. Div. 636, 52 N.Y.S.2d 655 (1st Dep't 1945).

[48] See Stevens, Corporations 677–84, 755 (2d ed. 1949); Adams v. Mid-West Chevrolet Corp., *supra* note 39; Note, 175 A.L.R. 577 (1948).

[49] Except for statutory, charter, or bylaw provisions, a majority of the directors of a corporation is necessary to constitute a quorum to transact corporate business, including, of course, the authorization or ratification of executive compensation. 2 Fletcher, *op. cit. supra* note 1, § 419. For an example see Farris v. Farris Engineering Corp., *supra* note 34.

have passed.[50] Conversely, if the director does vote, but his vote is not necessary, this is not generally classed as self-voting.[51]

A conflict of authority exists as to the effect of the mere presence of an interested director necessary to constitute a quorum. In a number of jurisdictions, it is held that an interested director cannot form part of a quorum, even though he does not vote.[52] In other jurisdictions, it is considered immaterial if the director is present merely to make the necessary quorum and does not vote.[53] The latter view is favored by state legislation which permits the interested director to be counted as part of the quorum of the board and to vote, either generally or in regard to his compensation as an officer or employee of the corporation, provided that his self-interest is disclosed to the board.[54] In any event, a charter or bylaw provision per-

[50] Backus v. Finkelstein, *supra* note 44; Ransome Concrete Machinery Corp. v. Moody, *supra* note 28; Wight v. Heublein, 238 Fed. 321 (4th Cir. 1916), *affirming* 227 Fed. 667 (D.Md. 1915); Pece v. Tama Trading Co., *supra* note 44; Kerbs v. California Eastern Airways, *supra* note 41; Lofland v. Cahall, *supra* note 3; Buell v. Lanski, *supra* note 47; Francis v. Brigham-Hopkins Co., *supra* note 16; Shaw v. Harding, *supra* note 4; Putnam v. Juvenile Shoe Corp., *supra* note 44; Welchman v. Koschwitz, 21 N.J. Super. 304, 91 A.2d 169 (1952) (mutual stock purchase agreement among executives); Booth v. Beattie, *supra* note 44; Schaffhauser v. Arnholt & Schaefer Brewing Co., *supra* note 43; Von Herberg v. Von Herberg, *supra* note 44. See note, 32 MICH. L. REV. 672 (1934). Consult Landstreet v. Meyer, 201 Miss. 826, 29 So.2d 653 (1947); Elward v. Peabody Coal Co., 9 Ill. App.2d 234, 132 N.E.2d 549 (1956).

[51] Oil Fields Corp. v. Hess, 186 Ark. 241, 53 S.W.2d 444 (1932); Montreeville v. Victor Land & Mineral Co., 13 Cal. App. 2d 753, 57 P.2d 565 (1936); Miller & Pardee, Inc. v. Pardee, *supra* note 4; Clark v. American Coal Co., 86 Iowa 436, 53 N.W. 291 (1892); Carter v. Louisville R. Co., 238 Ky. 42, 36 S.W.2d 836 (1931); Wellington Bull & Co. v. Morris, 132 Misc. 509, 230 N.Y. Supp. 122 (Sup. Ct. 1928), *aff'd w.o. op.*, 226 App. Div. 868, 235 N.Y. Supp. 906 (1st Dep't 1929); *In re* Fergus Falls Woolen Mills Co., 41 F. Supp. 355 (D. Minn. 1941), *aff'd sub nom.* Boyum v. Johnson, *supra* note 47. However, in Vermont the presence of an interested director renders a contract between himself and the corporation voidable. VT. STAT. ANN., tit. 11, § 105 (1958).

[52] Holcomb v. Forsyth, *supra* note 43; Angelus Securities Corp. v. Ball, *supra* note 1; Laybourn v. Wrape, 72 Colo. 339, 211 Pac. 367 (1922); Kerbs v. California Eastern Airways, *supra* note 41, 90 A.2d at 659; Bates St. Shirt Co. v. Waite, *supra* note 44; Gascue v. Saralegui Land & Livestock Co., *supra* note 47; Butts v. Wood, 37 N.Y. 317 (1867); Rugger v. Mt. Hood Electric Co., 143 Ore. 193, 20 P.2d 412 (1933), *rehearing denied,* 143 Ore. 225, 21 P.2d 1100 (1933); Newcomber v. Mountain Springs Ice & Cold Storage Co., 63 So. Dak. 81, 256 N.W. 359 (1934); Mortenson v. Ballard, 218 Ark. 459, 236 S.W.2d 1006 (1951). See the Vermont statute referred to *supra* note 51.

[53] Buell v. Buckingham, 16 Iowa 284 (1864); Fountain v. Oreck's, Inc., 245 Minn. 202, 71 N.W.2d 646 (1955), *limiting* Jones v. Morrison, 31 Minn. 140, 16 N.W. 854 (1883); Hax v. R. T. Davis Mill Co., 39 Mo. App. 453 (1889). See Gumaer v. Cripple Creek Tunnel, Transp. & Mining Co., 40 Colo. 1, 90 Pac. 81 (1907), with which, however, compare the later case of Laybourn v. Wrape, *supra* note 52.

[54] CAL. CORPS. CODE (Deering 1948), § 820, considered in Levin v. Levin Inv.

mitting an interested director to be counted in making a quorum or requiring his presence has been held to remove the self-voting taint.[55]

The directors may see to it that no director votes for his own compensation as an officer. This is often done by "cross-voting," that is, several compensation items are brought up separately and each director refrains from voting on his own but does vote on all the others. Here the courts have taken the view that each director will be influenced by his knowledge that if he does not vote for the compensation of the other directors, they will not vote for his. Cross-voting, therefore, is generally regarded as self-dealing.[56]

A board of directors may sometimes be dominated by one of their own number, by a majority stockholder, by an important officer, or by someone else. In such a case, if the board votes compensation to this controlling personality, or to him and his group, the courts disregard the apparent regularity of the corporate procedure and decide the case in much the same manner as a "self-voting" case.[57]

Co., 123 Cal. App. 2d 158, 266 P.2d 552 (1954); 1951 NEV. STAT. 328 (identical with the California Code provision); under both statutes the director's self-interest must not only be disclosed but also recorded in the minutes of the board meeting. However, a statute will not automatically validate a contract if the contract is not fair and reasonable. Remillard Brick Co. v. Remillard-Dandini Co., 109 Cal. App. 2d 405, 241 P.2d 66 (1952); Kennerson v. Burbank Amusement Co., 120 Cal. App. 2d 157, 260 P.2d 823 (1953) (neither case involving executive compensation). As to the statutory treatment of transactions involving self-interest on the part of directors, see further notes 214 ff. *infra* and accompanying text.

[55] Piccard v. Sperry Corp., 48 F. Supp. 465 (S.D.N.Y. 1943), *aff'd*, 152 F.2d 462 (2d Cir. 1946), *cert denied*, 328 U.S. 845 (1946); Kaufman v. Shoenberg, 33 Del. Ch. 211, 91 A.2d 786 (1952); Sterling v. Mayflower Hotel Corp., 33 Del. Ch. 20, 89 A.2d 862 (1952), *aff'd and remanded*, 93 A.2d 107 (1952). *Cf.* Everett v. Phillips, 288 N.Y. 227, 43 N.E.2d 18 (1942); Francis v. Brigham-Hopkins Co., *supra* note 16; Adams v. Mid-West Chevrolet Corp., *supra* note 39; Mortenson v. Ballard, *supra* note 52.

[56] Angelus Securities Corp. v. Ball, *supra* note 1; Mallory v. Mallory Wheeler Co., *supra* note 45; Beha v. Martin, *supra* note 43; Sagalyn v. Meekins, Packard & Wheat, Inc., *supra* note 47; Barrett v. Smith, *supra* note 44; Wonderful Group Mining Co. v. Rand, 111 Wash. 557, 191 Pac. 631 (1920); Moore v. Herrink, 77 F.2d 96 (4th Cir. 1935). "No action could be taken without the affirmative vote of at least one of the three executive officers here involved. It is plain that as rational human beings each of these three knew that his own increase in salary probably depended upon his vote for a similar increase for one or both of the others." Rugg, Ch. J., in Sagalyn v. Meekins, Packard & Wheat, Inc., *supra* at 438, 439. *Contra,* Funsten v. Funsten Commission Co., 67 Mo. App. 559 (1896), involving, moreover, a single resolution. The majority rule applies to separate resolutions as well as to a single resolution. Angelus Securities Corp. v. Ball, *supra*; Steele v. Gold Fissure Mining Co., 42 Colo. 529, 95 Pac. 349 (1908) (single resolution); Beha v. Martin, *supra;* Davids v. Davids, 135 App. Div. 206, 120 N.Y. Supp. 350 (1909).

[57] Savage v. Lorraine Corp., *supra* note 47; Backus v. Finkelstein, *supra* note 44; Monterey Water Co. v. Voorhees, *supra* note 35; Bingham v. Ditzler, *supra*

The following discussion, then, will deal with those cases where the courts have looked upon the action of the board in fixing or awarding compensation as self-dealing. Some jurisdictions speak of self-voted resolutions or contracts for payment as "void"; others as "voidable." [58] The following compilation indicates what this means in terms of practical results:

1. Will an injunction restraining payment be granted at the suit of a minority stockholder or the corporation,[59] where suit is brought in advance of services and in advance of payment?

---

note 47; Matthews v. Headley Chocolate Co., 130 Md. 523, 100 Atl. 645 (1917); Lillard v. Oil, Paint & Drug Co., 70 N.J. Eq. 197, 56 Atl. 254 (1903); Boothe v. Summit Coal Mining Co., 55 Wash. 167, 104 Pac. 207 (1909); Monmouth Inv. Co. v. Means, 151 Fed. 159 (8th Cir. 1906); Beers v. New York Life Ins. Co., *supra* note 17. *Cf.* Steigerwald v. A. N. Steigerwald Co., 9 Ill. App. 2d 31, 132 N.E.2d 373 (1955), in which the Court disallowed increased compensation awarded the president by an executive committee on the ground that the committee, which was established by the president rather than the board of directors, was invalidly constituted under Illinois law. See also Shera v. Carbon Steel Co., 245 Fed. 589 (S.D.W.Va. 1917). For a discussion of the related question of self-payment, see *supra* text to notes 35 ff. Consult Kalisher v. Sussman, 314 Ill. App. 383, 41 N.E.2d 239 (1942); Elward v. Peabody, *supra* note 50.

[58] The terms "void" and "voidable" as used with reference to these corporate transactions are essentially useful abbreviations to distinguish judicial treatment which will not permit ratification except by all the stockholders and judicial treatment which will permit ratification by less than all the stockholders. *Cf.* opinion of Rifkind, J., in Piccard v. Sperry Corp., *supra* note 55, at 468. One California case goes so far as to hold such a resolution "void" in the sense that it cannot even be ratified by all the stockholders. Bassett v. Fairchild, *supra* note 1. See also McKey v. Swenson, 232 Mich. 505, 205 N.W. 583 (1925). As to the effect of ratification in "voidable" jurisdictions, see Kerbs v. California Eastern Airways, *supra* note 41, and Diamond v. Davis, 62 N.Y. S.2d 181 (Sup. Ct. 1945) and cases cited *infra* note 61. See also Shera v. Carbon Steel Co., *supra* note 57.
In at least one case, the Massachusetts Supreme Court adopted the view that a self-voted resolution is neither void nor voidable in the absence of fraud or an attempt to syphon off corporate profits in the guise of salary. Cook v. Cook, 270 Mass. 534, 541, 170 N.E. 455, 457 (1930). This has been said to be the Massachusetts rule. Tilden, *supra* note 1, at 280-81. See Landstreet v. Meyer, *supra* note 50, at 655, discussing this rule as an alternative to the "void" and "voidable" rules. But *cf.* Sagalyn v. Meekins, Packard & Wheat, Inc., *supra* note 47; Shaw v. Harding, *supra* note 4, and text infra to notes 71 and 73.

[59] In some cases involving wholly-owned subsidiaries, the attack may come from a stockholder of the parent company alleging that the latter, as controlling stockholder of the subsidiary, has allowed the subsidiary to pay excessive compensation to an executive [Gottfried v. Gottfried, 112 N.Y.S.2d 431 (Sup. Ct. 1952)] or has allowed the subsidiary to take other action favoring the parent's executives [Claman v. Robertson, 164 Ohio St. 61, 128 N.E.2d 429 (1955), in which the subsidiary sold shares of its stock to the executives of the parent and of itself]. See also Edmonson v. First Nat'l Bank of Birmingham, 256 Ala. 449, 55 So. 2d 338 (1951) (holding that beneficiary of trust does not have a cause of action against his trustee as the controlling stockholder of a corporation to recover damages for the payment of excessive compensation to the corporate executives, when the beneficiary was not himself a stockholder of the corporation).

A. *"Void" jurisdictions.* Cases in Alabama, Arkansas, Colorado, and Kentucky say "yes." [60]

B. *"Voidable" jurisdictions.* Delaware, New Jersey, New York, and West Virginia say "yes," as did an early Pennsylvania case,[61] although later Pennsylvania cases have taken a more generous attitude toward the officers and have refused to enjoin future payments if the stockholders have ratified the payments.[62] The injunction request is generally combined with a demand for refund of past payments, the courts' treatment of which is pointed out below.

2. Will an injunction be granted after services are rendered, but before payment?

No cases have been found. The answer should depend on the view taken as to the next question. If the compensation is held unreasonable on its face or the court holds that none can be allowed, an injunction will be issued.[63]

3. Can the corporation or a minority stockholder successfully sue to recover for the corporate treasury payments already made?

A. *"Void" jurisdictions.* An early California case set aside all compensation in excess of the reasonable value of the services, and a later California case reversed the trial court's granting of a non-suit and remanded the case, on the ground that self-voting required the action of the board to be looked into.[64] An Illinois case in 1910 held that the corporation could recover the excess over the amount the services were reasonably worth, but in no event more than the amount fixed in the resolution; the case was remanded for further proceedings.[65] In a Washington case, all the salaries which had been

[60] Holcomb v. Forsyth, Cook v. Malvern Brick & Tile Co., Sterling Loan & Inv. Co. v. Litel, Beha v. Martin, all *supra* note 43.

[61] Gottlieb v. Heyden Chemical Corp., *supra* note 41; Fidanque v. American Maracaibo Co., *supra* note 47; Prindiville v. Johnson & Higgins, 92 N.J. Eq. 515, 113 Atl. 915 (1921), *aff'd*, 93 N.J. Eq. 425, 116 Atl. 785 (1922) (dictum); Carr v. Kimball, *supra* note 2; Schaffhauser v. Arnholt & Schaefer Brewing Co., *supra* note 43; Browne v. Maxwell, 288 Pa. 398, 136 Atl. 232 (1927) (dictum); Collins v. Hite, *supra* note 35. But see Mayer v. Oxidation Products Co. (N.J.), *supra* note 4, where an injunction *pendente lite* was denied, on the ground that the wrongfulness of the payments had not been sufficiently established.

[62] Sotter v. Coatesville Boiler Works, *supra* note 43; Russell v. H. C. Patterson Co., *supra* note 43. See also Neff v. Twentieth Century Silk Corp., 312 Pa. 386, 167 Atl. 578 (1933); Wight v. Heublein, *supra* note 50, granting a "permanent" injunction for as long as the circumstances remained unchanged.

[63] See Dow v. River Farms Co. of California, *supra* note 47 (suit by executive's widow); Bassett v. Fairchild, *supra* note 1, and cases cited *infra* notes 66, 71, and 72.

[64] *Compare* Bassett v. Fairchild (Cal. 1901) with Angelus Securities Corp. v. Ball (Cal. App. 1937), both *supra* note 1; but in some instances the Court may uphold the compensation paid as proper. Levin v. Levin Inv. Co., *supra* note 54.

[65] Voorhees v. Mason, *supra* note 44.

paid under the resolution were set aside.[66] The authority of these California, Illinois, and Washington cases is weakened by later decisions in the same courts on related subjects.[67] A Maine case found no objection to self-voting where the directors owned all the common stock, and all the directors had acquiesced.[68] A Kentucky case allowed a reasonable amount for past services.[69] A Michigan case allowed a compromise settlement to stand with respect to allegedly excessive bonuses claimed by two executives.[70]

B. *"Voidable" jurisdictions.* Cases in Massachusetts and New Jersey ordered the executives to refund all compensation in excess of what the court found to be reasonable.[71] Cases in Illinois, Michigan, and Minnesota ordered an accounting to determine what excess over a reasonable amount the executives must return, the Michigan court saying that if any "wrong" had been done to the corporation the executives must refund *all* that they had received.[72] A federal case in the Second Circuit and cases in Maryland, Massachusetts, Missouri, New Jersey, New York, and Pennsylvania found that the executives had sustained the burden of showing that the amounts paid were reasonable or "not excessive," and therefore the compensation was not set aside.[73] In one New Jersey case, the court spoke of

[66] Wonderful Group Mining Co. v. Rand, *supra* note 56.

[67] See cases cited *infra* notes 72, 76, and 79, and connected text.

[68] Bates St. Shirt Co. v. Waite, *supra* note 44 (suit apparently brought by preferred stockholders who had taken over the corporation).

[69] Beha v. Martin, *supra* note 43.

[70] Garwin v. Anderson, *supra* note 44.

[71] Beacon Wool Corp. v. Johnson, *supra* note 1; Sagalyn v. Meekins, Packard & Wheat, Inc., *supra* note 47; Calkins v. Wire Hardware Co., *supra* note 42; Lillard v. Oil, Paint & Drug Co., *supra* note 57; Raynolds v. Diamond Mills Paper Co., *supra* note 44; Davis v. Thomas & Davis Co., *supra* note 44. But *cf.* Cook v. Cook, *supra* note 58.

[72] Dwyer v. Tracey, *supra* note 1; Buell v. Lanski, *supra* note 47 (suit by trustee in bankruptcy); Miner v. Belle Isle Ice Co., *supra* note 44; Backus v. Finkelstein, *supra* note 44.

[73] Ransome Concrete Machinery Co. v. Moody, *supra* note 28; Francis v. Brigham-Hopkins Co., *supra* note 16; Black v. Parker Mfg. Co., 329 Mass. 105, 106 N.E.2d 544 (1952); Shaw v. Harding, *supra* note 4; Putnam v. Juvenile Shoe Corp., *supra* note 44; Blancard v. Blancard & Co., *supra* note 44; Kranich v. Bach, 209 App. Div. 52, 204 N.Y. Supp. 320 (1st Dep't 1924); Gottfried v. Gottfried, *supra* note 59; Eisenberg v. Rodless Decorations, Inc., 106 N.Y.2d 822 (Sup. Ct. 1951); Murray v. Smith, 166 App. Div. 528, 152 N.Y. Supp. 102 (2d Dep't 1915), *modified on other grounds,* 224 N.Y. 40, 120 N.E. 60 (1918); Tilton v. Gans, *supra* note 44; Neff v. Twentieth Century Silk Corp., *supra* note 62; Hornsby v. Lohmeyer, 364 Pa. 271, 72 A.2d 294 (1950) (salaries held reasonable). See Landstreet v. Meyer, *supra* note 50 (salary of president reduced for the future but president allowed to retain compensation received in view of valuable services rendered); Indurated Concrete Corp. v. Abbott, *supra* note 7 (self-voted compensation without prior agreement held unjustified by nature of services). *Cf.* Skye v. Francis J. Skye Distributing Co. *supra* note 41. Massachusetts generally distinguishes between good faith and bad faith of directors; in the former situation they may retain compensation for services actually performed [*cf.* Daniel v. Briggs,

self-voting as an "unobjectionable incident" in a small family corporation, where it appeared that the executives were not being overpaid.[74] Similarly, a Tennessee case concluded that self-voting was the only way that salaries could have been fixed in a very small corporation, and therefore they need not be returned.[75] A Washington case held that a stockholder who was also a director was estopped from attacking payments because of participation and acquiescence in the action of the board.[76]

4. Can an officer who has rendered services, and who bases his claim on a self-voted resolution or contract, successfully sue the corporation?

A. *"Void" jurisdictions.* Two Ohio cases and a Texas case say "no." [77] However, in Ohio the officer may be able to recover if he pleads in *quantum meruit.*[78]

B. *"Voidable" jurisdictions.* A California case says "no," because the requirements of a California statute were not complied with.[79] A Connecticut case denied recovery on the ground that the corporation, by refusing to pay, had elected to avoid the compensation resolution.[80] A New York case and a federal case applying Delaware law declined to allow any recovery either on the resolution or in *quantum meruit.*[81] Later New York cases and an Illinois case allowed recovery because the services rendered were worth the amount voted.[82]

---

279 Mass. 87, 180 N.E. 717 (1932)] but in the latter situation all compensation is forfeited [*cf.* Lydia E. Pinkham Medicine Co. v. Gove, 298 Mass. 53, 9 N.E.2d 573 (1937), 303 Mass. 1, 20 N.E.2d 482 (1939) ; Cook v. Cook, *supra* note 58; Heise v. Earnshaw Publications, *supra* note 41]. *Cf.* RESTATEMENT, TRUSTS § 243, comment (a) ; RESTATEMENT, AGENCY §§ 456, 469. For similar cases in other jurisdictions see Edmonson v. First Nat'l Bank of Birmingham, *supra* note 59; Des Moines Bank and Trust Co. v. George M. Bechtel & Co., 243 Iowa 1007, 51 N.W.2d 174 (1952) ; Fountain v. Oreck's, Inc. (Minn.), *supra* note 53. *Cf.* Schick v. Riemer, 263 S.W.2d 51 (Mo. App. 1953) (dismissing complaint seeking to recover for benefit of minority stockholder).

[74] Booth v. Beattie, *supra* note 44. See Cook v. Cook, *supra* note 58.

[75] Wood v. Myers Paper Co., *supra* note 47.

[76] Von Herberg v. Von Herberg, *supra* note 44. See also 5 FLETCHER, *op. cit. supra* note 1, § 2129.

[77] Briggs v. Gilbert Grocery Co., *supra* note 41; State *ex rel.* Squire v. Miller, *supra* note 42; A. J. Anderson Co. v. Kinsolving, *supra* note 47 (counterclaim).

[78] Gilbert Grocery Co. v. Briggs, 121 Ohio St. 25, 166 N.E. 818 (1929) ; see also State *ex rel.* Squire v. Miller, *supra* note 42; as to these cases, compare the subsequent Ohio Corporation law, *supra* note 41.

[79] Pece v. Tama Trading Co., *supra* note 44.

[80] Mallory v. Mallory Wheeler Co., *supra* note 45. But *cf.* Massoth v. Central Bus Corp., 104 Conn. 683, 134 Atl. 236 (1926).

[81] Kreitner v. Burgweger, *supra* note 45; Air Traffic & Service Corp. v. Fay, *supra* note 1 (equities of situation held to preclude recovery as to particular services sued upon).

[82] Skye v. Francis J. Skye Distributing Co., *supra* note 41; Chamberlain v. Chamberlain, Care & Boyce, Inc., *supra* note 45; Garbarino v. Utica Uniform Co.,

The Effect of Self-voting: Some Conclusions. 1. In jurisdictions where the courts take the view that self-voted resolutions or contracts are "void," the court may sometimes rest its decision on the self-voting issue, and make no inquiry or at least only a cursory inquiry into the other elements in the case. As our analysis of the practical results of the cases shows, however, it is only in a few jurisdictions that the courts so emphasize the self-voting issue.[83] In a number of cases where the courts have called self-voted resolutions or contracts "void," reasonable compensation has been allowed; [84] this, as we have seen, is the same result reached in many cases where the resolutions or contracts are termed "voidable." It is apparent, then, that except in a few jurisdictions the difference in terminology is not a safe indication of the effect of self-voting.

2. Whether self-voted resolutions or contracts are said to be "void" or "voidable," self-dealing will cause a court to exercise its equity powers and inquire into the facts to see whether the rights of stockholders or creditors are being disregarded.[85]

3. Procedurally, self-dealing will place upon the recipients of the compensation the burden of showing that the amounts awarded are reasonable, or at least they must give the court information from which it may determine what is reasonable.[86] If there is evidence of fraud, overreaching, or mismanagement, the executives will not be able to enforce their compensation contracts or retain what they have already received.[87]

The New York Cases. The points just made are well illustrated in the results reached by the New York courts in a long series of

---

269 App. Div. 622, 58 N.Y.S.2d. 136 (4th Dept. 1945), aff'd w.o. op., 295 N.Y. 794, 66 N.E.2d 579 (1945). Recovery on *quantum meruit* was also allowed in Kenton v. Wood, 56 Ariz. 325, 107 P.2d 380 (1940); Francis v. Brigham-Hopkins Co., *supra* note 16; Blancard v. Blancard & Co., *supra* note 44. But *cf.* Will v. Will & Baumer Candle Co., 55 N.Y.S.2d 377 (Sup. Ct. 1945) (president; contract with his company for insurance policies on termination of employment held invalid, without considering value of services).

[83] Cases *supra* notes 60, 66, and 77.

[84] Bassett v. Fairchild, *supra* note 1 and cases *supra* notes 68, 69, and 78.

[85] Bassett v. Fairchild, *supra* note 1 and cases *supra* notes 64, 69, and 72; Comment, 41 YALE L.J. 109 (1931); Note, 46 HARV. L. REV. 828 (1933).

[86] Cases *supra* note 73; Comment, 42 YALE L.J. 419, 423 (1933).

[87] Dwyer v. Tracey, *supra* note 1; Backus v. Finkelstein, *supra* note 44; Lofland v. Cahall, *supra* note 3; Beacon Wool Corp. v. Johnson, *supra* note 1; Godley v. Crandall & Godley Co., *supra* note 13; Comment, 32 MICH L. REV. 672 (1934). See also, for justification of the reasonableness of restricted stock option plans and restricted stock options in terms of an adequate *quid pro quo,* Gottlieb v. Heyden Chemical Corp. and Kerbs v. California Eastern Airways, both *supra* note 41; Kaufman v. Shoenberg, *supra* note 55, and Eliasberg v. Standard Oil Co., 23 N.J. Super. 431, 92 A.2d 862 (1952), aff'd on op. below, 12 N.J. 467, 97 A.2d 437 (1953).

cases, beginning with *Godley v. Crandall & Godley Co.*,[88] decided by
the Court of Appeals in 1914. There the directors, who were already
receiving fixed salaries, voted to themselves as officers "additional
salaries" for the past year, and in two subsequent years they continued to draw their fixed salaries plus the increases. At the suit
of a minority stockholder, the court struck down the increases for all
three years. Said the court: [89]

• One fact is found which indubitably stamps the resolution of
November 14, 1906, as fraudulent. Whatever the power of directors
to vote salaries may be, they certainly had no power to vote increases
of salary to themselves for services already performed under a
stipulated salary. Under that resolution the directors paid to themselves an increase of $14,310 for services already performed. That
constituted nothing less than a gift to themselves of corporate funds
and of course was a fraud, and it was perforce of that resolution that
the increases were paid in subsequent years. . . . The resolution
was tainted with fraud and wholly void.

Self-dealing, then, with other elements, was deemed to constitute
"fraud." The other elements which tainted the directors' actions
were: (a) prior to the voting of the increases, the directors and
other employees were receiving bonuses based on their common
stock holdings; during the years when the directors received the
salary increases, these bonuses were discontinued as to the directors
but not as to the other employees; (b) there was no increase in the
work done by the directors commensurate with the increases in
salary; (c) the directors who had received the increases later dis-
solved the corporation and formed a new one, taking with them all
the business of the old corporation but excluding the plaintiff and
other minority stockholders from participation in the profits.

In another case, decided at about the same time as the *Godley*
case, the New York Supreme Court refused at the suit of a minority
stockholder to set aside self-voted compensation. Referring to the
factors which, coupled with self-voting, had caused the court in the
Godley case to strike down compensation, the Supreme Court in
Robbins v. Hill [90] emphasized that in the latter case there were no
"unlawful or fraudulent acts or practices, nor does it anywhere
appear by the evidence but what the salaries fixed were fair, reason-

---

[88] *Supra* note 13.
[89] *Id.* at 133.
[90] 81 Misc. 441, 142 N.Y. Supp. 637 (Sup. Ct. 1913), *aff'd w.o. op.*, 166 App.
Div. 899, 150 N.Y. Supp. 1074 (2d Dep't 1914), *aff'd w.o. op.*, 220 N.Y. 631, 115
N.E. 1033 (1917).

able, and just, and were in proportion to the services rendered by
those who performed the work for which the salaries were paid." [91]

The *Godley* case and the *Robbins* case show, then, that the New
York courts will scrutinize with great care the acts of executives
who have voted themselves compensation, but that the compensation
will not be set aside merely because it was self-voted. This is borne
out by many other cases.[92] The recipients of the compensation, however, must prove that they actually rendered services and that the
amounts voted were reasonable. If they fail to prove this, their
actions may be termed "fraudulent," and at the suit of the corporation or a minority stockholder they will be ordered to return to the
corporate treasury all that they have received or all in excess of a
reasonable amount.[93] And similar results will be reached if the self-
voting is coupled with other elements of fraud, overreaching, or
mismanagement.[94]

Several later New York cases deserve mention. In *Wineburgh
v. Seeman Bros.,*[95] a minority stockholder attacked as excessive the
salaries which the executives had voted to themselves and other
"key" employees, and also sought to recover additional compensation
which the directors had voted to themselves and other employees for
past services. The court, referring apparently to the self-voting,
called it a fraud "of the technical variety," and then without making
any further comment on the effect of self-voting went on to point
out that the executives had proved that the salaries were only minimum compensation which was brought up to a reasonable amount by
the granting of bonuses. No recovery, therefore, was allowed. On
similar facts, the same result was reached in *Anglo-American Equities Corp. v. Rollins & Sons;*[96] in *Eisenberg v. Rodless Decora-*

---

[91] 81 Misc. at 449.

[92] Cases *infra* note 93.

[93] Kranich v. Bach, *supra* note 73; Schall v. Althaus, 208 App. Div. 103, 203
N.Y. Supp. 36 (1st Dep't 1925); Atwater v. Elkhorn Valley Coal-Land Co., *supra*
note 44; Murray v. Smith, *supra* note 73; Carr v. Kimball, *supra* note 2; Chamberlain v. Chamberlain, Care & Boyce, Inc., *supra* note 45; Tilton v. Gans, *supra* note
44.

[94] Jacobson v. Brooklyn Lumber Co., *supra* note 43; Kreitner v. Burgweger,
supra note 45; Miller v. Crown Perfumery Co., 125 App. Div. 881, 110 N.Y. Supp.
806 (1st Dep't 1908), *affirming* 57 Misc. 383, 109 N.Y. Supp. 760 (Sup. Ct. 1908).

[95] *Supra* note 29.

[96] 258 App. Div. 878, 16 N.Y.S.2d 105 (1st Dep't 1939), *aff'd w.o. op.,* 282 N.Y.
782, 27 N.E.2d 200 (1940). Both appellate courts affirmed without opinion an
unreported master's decision. For the master's findings, to the effect that there was
no fraud or waste, consult his opinion beginning at p. 151 of the Record on Appeal,
282 N.Y. 782. *In accord,* Garbarino v. Utica Uniform Co., *supra* note 82. But *cf.*
Will v. Will & Baumer Candle Co. *supra* note 82.

tions; [97] and in *Gottfried v. Gottfried.*[98] In the first mentioned case, the only discussion of self-voting is in a dissenting opinion; in the other two, the court emphasizes approval by the stockholders. The *Gottfried* case has this additional feature of interest: the attack was made by a minority stockholder of the parent company against the compensation paid an executive of a wholly owned subsidiary who was also rendering gratuitous services to the parent company.

What, then, is the significance of these cases with regard to the effect of self-voting? It cannot be said that they overrule or are necessarily inconsistent with, the *Godley* and *Robbins* cases and the cases stemming from those decisions, since in both the *Wineburgh* case and the *Anglo-American* case there were specific findings that there was no fraud or wasting of corporate funds and, as indicated, in the *Eisenberg* and *Gottfried* cases the stockholders had given their approval. These cases do indicate, however, that the New York courts will investigate the actions of the board, and on all the evidence, without placing complete reliance on the self-voting issue, will decide on equitable principles whether or not compensation should be returned.[99]

Self-dealing and "Unreasonableness." In many of the self-dealing cases we have been discussing, there were charges that the compensation was excessive in amount. In numerous other cases, however, claims of unreasonableness were not accompanied by any charges of self-dealing. The cases involving unreasonableness, as a group, are discussed elsewhere, with certain additional conclusions drawn as to the effect of self-dealing on the determination of the issue of excessiveness.[100]

Practical Aspects. As a practical matter, what corporate procedure should be adopted in situations where the self-dealing prob-

[97] *Supra* note 73.

[98] *Supra* note 59, relying on Garbarino v. Utica Uniform Co., *supra* note 82, for the broad proposition that compensation of officers is in the first place fixed by the directors.

[99] See Volume II, Chapter 19. When repayment of compensation is ordered, reliance is usually not placed on self-dealing alone. See e.g., Stearns v. Dudley, 76 N.Y. S.2d 106 (Sup. Ct. 1947), *aff'd w.o. op.,* 274 App. Div. 1028, 86 N.Y.S.2d 478 (4th Dep't 1948). For other cases involving repayment, see Landstreet v. Meyer, *supra* note 50 and the Massachusetts cases cited *supra* note 73.

[100] Standards of reasonableness beyond which compensation paid executives becomes excessive are discussed in Volume II, Chapter 19. See also the discussions in Black v. Parker Mfg. Co., *supra* note 73; Gottfried, *supra* note 59; with regard to the reasonableness of consideration for stock options, see cases cited *supra* note 87.

lem is present? The discussion in the preceding pages would seem to indicate at least this much: Where compensation is to be voted to a single director who cannot be said to control or dominate the board, it will usually be sufficient if he withdraws from the meeting while his contract is being considered and voted upon. If compensation is being voted to more than one director and if the disinterested directors will constitute a quorum, all the interested directors should withdraw together in order to avoid the "cross-voting" situation. If a quorum of disinterested directors cannot be obtained, there are three alternatives: (a) voting by the entire board, including those interested, (b) cross-voting, (c) submission of the contracts to the stockholders. Of these alternatives, the last is clearly the most desirable, even when the charter or bylaws specifically authorize the presence or participation of an interested director. If a stockholders' meeting cannot be conveniently arranged, cross-voting is probably preferable to interested voting. In any doubtful case, submission of compensation contracts to the stockholders for their ratification and approval, at the earliest possible date, is a highly desirable precaution. More will be said on this subject in the following section.

Stockholders' Approval

Participation by stockholders in fixing and awarding compensation to executives may be considered in two aspects: first, the necessity for stockholder authorization prior to action by the board of directors, and, second, the effect of stockholder ratification of action which the board has taken.

Must Stockholders Give Prior Authorization for Salaries, Bonuses, and Special Rewards? Many cases contain statements to the effect that the sole power and authority to fix the compensation of directors belongs to the stockholders, and cannot be exercised by the board of directors without express authority in the charter or from the stockholders.[101] We have seen, however, that it is only in a rare case that a director seeks compensation for his services as a director; he usually wants to be paid for his services as an officer.[102] There seems to be no objection to the employment by the directors of one of their own number to act as an officer or employee of the corporation, and, in the absence of an express statutory, charter, or bylaw provision to the contrary, the board of directors has the power

[101] Cases *supra* note 1. See also *supra* text to notes 15 ff.
[102] See *supra* notes 13 and 14, and connected text. For a discussion of payment to directors for their services as such, see *supra* text to notes 12 ff.

and authority to fix the compensation he is to receive. In other words, in fixing the compensation of officers and employees of the corporation, whether or not they are members of the board, the directors need not first seek express authorization from the stockholders.[103]

Not only is this true when the directors seek to arrange for the payment of a regular salary to an officer or employee (whether or not also a director) in advance of his rendering services, but also when they seek to pay him through a profit-sharing arrangement.[104] It might be more accurate to say "a profit-sharing arrangement which does not go beyond customary limitations"; unrestricted profit-sharing will be referred to presently. As to other benefits, such as stock bonuses, stock options, pensions, annuities, and the like, the problem is more difficult. We start with the presumption that insofar as the arrangement is merely one for the compensating of employees, the directors have full authority; insofar as it is something else—a gift or a sale of stock—the local law may place the matter exclusively within the stockholders' power.[105] Where benefits in stock are in-

---

[103] Schulte v. Ideal Food Products Co., *supra* note 31; Wellington Bull & Co. v. Morris, *supra* note 51; Russell v. H. C. Patterson Co., *supra* note 43; and cases *infra* note 104; 5 FLETCHER, *op. cit. supra* note 1, §§ 2126 *et seq.*

[104] Wright v. McLaury, 81 F.2d 96 (7th Cir. 1936); Church v. Harnit, *supra* note 20; Ransome Concrete Machinery Co. v. Moody, *supra* note 28; Joy v. Ditto, *supra* note 1; Seitz v. Union Brass & Metal Mfg. Co., *supra* note 20; Putnam v. Juvenile Shoe Corp., *supra* note 44; Godley v. Crandall & Godley Co., *supra* note 13; Anglo-American Equities Corp. v. Rollins & Sons, *supra* note 96; Gallin v. Nat'l City Bank of New York, 152 Misc. 679, 704, 273 N.Y. Supp. 87, 115 (Sup. Ct. 1934); Wellington Bull & Co., Inc. v. Morris, *supra* note 51; Wineburgh v. Seeman Bros., *supra* note 29; Sotter v. Coatesville Boiler Works, *supra* note 43; *cf.* Richardson v. Blue Grass Mining Co., *supra* note 36. See also CONN. GEN. STAT., § 3387 (1930); N.J. STAT. ANN., tit. 14, §§ 14:9–1 *et seq.* (1939).

[105] Church v. Harnit, *supra* note 20; Putnam v. Juvenile Shoe Corp., *supra* note 44; Lillard v. Oil, Paint & Drug Co., *supra* note 57; Witt v. James McNeil & Bros., 296 Pa. 386, 146 Atl. 27 (1929); A. J. Anderson Co. v. Kinsolving, *supra* note 47; Security Savings & Trust Co. v. Coos Bay Lumber & Coal Co., *supra* note 1; Stout v. Oates, 217 Ark. 938, 234 S.W.2d 506 (1950) (stock bonuses concealed from minority stockholders considered to be preferential dividends requiring approval of all stockholders). As to requirements under state legislation of stockholder approval for stock option plans, see text to notes 221–28 *infra*.

In the case of companies whose shares are listed on the New York Stock Exchange, the policy of the Exchange requires stockholder approval before permitting the listing of shares subject to option in favor of directors, officers, or key employees, "regardless of whether or not such authorization is required by law, or by the company's charter." NEW YORK STOCK EXCHANGE COMPANY MANUAL A–118–120. Exceptions to this requirement may be made when options are issued under a plan in which all, or substantially all, of the employees participate or when options are issued to an individual, not previously employed by the company, as an inducement essential to his entering into a contract of employment with the company. *Id.* at A–120–21. Stockholder approval for this purpose means approval by a majority of all outstanding stock entitled to vote on the issuance of the options. *Id.* at B–18.

volved, counsel must trace back the authorization of the issue to its sources—the charter and the stockholders. The question of preemptive rights also enters.[106] After his search, counsel may decide that the issue needs no further authorization by stockholders, under the local law relating to stock issues; in such case, the remaining question, as to the use of stock in compensating employees, is a matter within the authority of the directors. Similarly, with pensions and related grants, the local law may condemn rewards based on past services, describing them as "gifts," while sustaining similar types of rewards designed as an inducement for the rendering of future services.[107] Here, again, the grant is—to the extent that it is bargained compensation for future services—within the power of the directors; to the extent that it is something else, it should be submitted to the stockholders.[108] The same may perhaps be said of an

[106] See text to notes 229--37 *infra*.

[107] See Volume II, Chapter 13. Thus, the grant of a stock option has been held an invalid gift of corporate funds when the option is based solely on past services with a mere "hope" of future services. Holthusen v. Edward G. Budd Mfg. Co., 52 F. Supp. 125 (D. Del. 1943); Rosenthal v. Burry Biscuit Co., 30 Del. Ch. 299, 60 A.2d 106 (1948). On the other hand, an option grant has been sustained if the optionee in consideration thereof agrees to enter or to continue in the company's employ. Holthusen v. Edward G. Budd Mfg. Co., 53 F. Supp. 488 (D. Del. 1943); Wise v. Universal Corp., 93 F. Supp. 393 (D. Del. 1950); see also stock option cases cited *supra* note 87; *cf.* Diamond v. Davis, 38 N.Y.S.2d 103 (Sup. Ct. 1942) *aff'd w.o. op.*, 265 App. Div. 919, 39 N.Y.S.2d. 412 (1st Dep't 1942), *aff'd w.o. op.*, 292 N.Y. 554, 54 N.E.2d 683 (1944). Of course the grant of a stock option, if invalid, would not be validated by a vote of anything less than all the stockholders of the corporation. Rosenthal v. Burry Biscuit Co., *supra*, at 110; Holthusen v. Edward G. Budd Mfg. Co., *supra*, 52 F. Supp., at 125. *Cf.* Fogelson v. American Woolen Co., 170 F.2d 660 (2d Cir. 1948) (pensions); Moore v. Keystone Macaroni Mfg. Co., *supra* note 47 (pension for executive's widow); Hoblitzell v. Howard, 30 N.J. Super. 159, 103 A.2d 625 (1954) *aff'd per curiam*, 18 N.J. 104, 112 A.2d 715 (1955) (corporation paying pension to employee of predecessor partnership). The Wisconsin statute specifically empowers the board of directors to authorize compensation to employees and their dependents for prior services. See note 220 *infra* and accompanying text.

A study of current proxy statements of major companies discloses a widespread practice of submitting compensation plans for approval by stockholders with a statement that in the opinion of counsel such approval is not necessary. E.g., Monsanto Chemical Co., Proxy Statement, Feb. 28, 1950, at 1; *cf.* Ekco Products Co., Proxy Statement, Mar. 17, 1950, at 4; Chrysler Corp., Mar. 15, 1951, at 8 (supplemental pension plan submitted to stockholders for their approval "because of the interest in it of employees who are directors"). Employment contracts sometimes provide that they shall not become effective unless approved by stockholders. Texas, App. II ¶ (9); Loew's Inc., Proxy Statement, Feb. 15, 1950, at 5. The du Pont Profit-Sharing Plan provides by its terms that it is to be resubmitted to stockholders every five years. See Proxy Statement, Mar. 10, 1950, at 7. This is likewise true of the General Motors Bonus Plan, pursuant to stockholder's resolution adopted in 1947. Consult also *supra* note 128 and related text.

[108] See Comment, 42 Yale L.J. 419 (1933).

"open-end" profit-sharing plan, under which the benefits may exceed any amount which the directors might reasonably have voted as straight salary; here we are coming perilously close to "gifts of corporate funds." [109]

In other words, submission of compensation plans to stockholders may be desirable as a precaution, to clear up doubts as to the borderline of the directors' power. Particularly is this true where the corporation is for the first time granting special benefits such as profit-sharing, pensions, or stock options. In certain companies these benefits have been granted for so many years, and their operation is so well understood and so well controlled, that submission adds but little. Yet it is noticeable that companies which have well-run bonus plans are usually among those which are most meticulous in reporting results to stockholders and in asking approval of any change.

Not only may submission to stockholders help clear up questions of the directors' power: it may also be helpful in resolving doubts as to the manner of exercise of that power. For example, where the board is largely composed of officers, it may be desirable to submit officers' compensation contracts to the stockholders, to help remedy possible objections based on self-dealing. This brings us to the question of the effect of stockholders' ratifying action.

Effect of Stockholders' Ratification. The whole question of ratification of management activities by stockholders is a difficult and involved one. We are limiting ourselves here to the cases involving ratification of payments to executives. In this field, most of the cases in which the courts have considered the effect of subsequent ratification by stockholders are those involving self-voting. In the majority of jurisdictions, as we have seen,[110] the courts regard self-voted compensation resolutions or contracts as "voidable," so that if the stockholders later ratify the action of the board, the defect may be cured.[111] Certainly this is true if all the stockholders are present at the stockholders' meeting and with full knowledge of the actions of the board ratify a voidable resolution or

---

[109] See Rogers v. Hill, 289 U.S. 582 (1933); Gallin v. Nat'l City Bank of New York, *supra* note 104; 46 HARV. L. REV. 828, 832 (1933). The North Carolina statute requires that a bylaw authorizing compensation for officers measured by corporate income or volume of business be renewed each five years by stockholder vote. See note 224 *infra*.

[110] See text *supra* to notes 60 ff.

[111] Ransome Concrete Machinery Co. v. Moody, *supra* note 28; Putnam v. Juvenile Shoe Corp., *supra* note 44; Yaeger v. Phillips, 128 N.Y.S.2d 376 (Sup. Ct. 1953); Kranich v. Bach, *supra* note 73; Chamberlain v. Chamberlain, Care & Boyce, Inc., *supra* note 45; Claman v. Robertson, *supra* note 59 (*semble*), where director's presence created necessary quorum; Bates St. Shirt Co. v. Waite, *supra* note 44.

contract.[112] Likewise, a stockholder who has voted by proxy in favor of ratification may not later be able to object.[113]

All stockholders, however, may not vote for ratification. In fact, steps toward ratification are usually taken by the majority of the stockholders, with the minority stockholder or stockholders either not present or objecting. Here the typical approach of the courts seems to be that ratification by the majority may validate the voidable acts of the board,[114] though the majority will not be permitted to "act in hostility to the interests of the corporation with the intention of defrauding the non-assenting stockholders." [115] Thus, even though there has been ratification by the majority, the court will investigate and strike down compensation if the evidence shows that it is unreasonable,[116] or that the stockholders were not fully acquainted with

[112] Hoblitzell v. Howard, *supra* note 107; Anglo-American Equities Corp. v. Rollins & Sons, *supra* note 96; Wellington Bull & Co. v. Morris, *supra* note 51; Wineburgh v. Seeman Bros., *supra* note 29; Boyum v. Johnson, *supra* note 47. Ratification by all common stockholders will not bind preferred stockholders. Hurt v. Cotton States Fertilizer Co., 159 F.2d 52 (5th Cir. 1947). In order to have an effective ratification of a compensation plan, stockholders must be advised as to all material elements of the plan and must also be requested to ratify the plan itself and not merely actions involved in its implementation. Berkwitz v. Humphrey, 163 F. Supp. 78, 93–94 (N.D. Ohio 1958) (holding invalid features of the "phantom stock" plan of Pittsburgh Consolidation Coal Company). But *cf.* Lieberman v. Becker, 155 A.2d 596 (Sup. Ct. Del. 1959) (upholding a similar plan of Koppers Company, Inc., App. LL, which was ratified by stockholders).

[113] Gottlieb v. Heyden Chemical Corp., *supra* note 41; Wellington Bull & Co. v. Morris, *supra* note 51. See also Holmes v. Republic Steel Corp., *supra* note 1.

[114] Ransome Concrete Machinery Co. v. Moody, *supra* note 28; Kaufman v. Schoenberg, *supra* note 55; Eliasberg v. Standard Oil Co., *supra* note 87; Booth v. Beattie, *supra* note 44; Yaeger v. Phillips, *supra* note 111; Claman v. Robertson, *supra* note 59; Sotter v. Coatesville Boiler Works, *supra* note 43; Russell v. H. C. Patterson Co., *supra* note 43; 5 FLETCHER, *op. cit. supra* note 1, §§ 2139 *et seq.* The *Yaeger* and *Claman* cases speak in terms of a "presumption of regularity" created by stockholder ratification.

[115] Fidanque v. American Maracaibo Co., *supra* note 47; Barrett v. Smith, *supra* note 44; Eliasberg v. Standard Oil Co., *supra* note 87; Yaeger v. Phillips, supra note 111; Godley v. Crandall & Godley Co., *supra* note 13; Atwater v. Elkhorn Valley Coal-Land Co., *supra* note 44. *Cf.* Collins v. Hite, *supra* note 35 (salary payments deemed "donation" or misappropriation though ratified by a majority of the stockholders). It has been said that non-voting stockholders are presumed to assent. Bookman v. R. J. Reynolds Tobacco Co., 138 N.J. Eq. 312, 48 A.2d 646 (1946).

[116] Fidanque v. American Maracaibo Co., *supra* note 47; Lillard v. Oil, Paint & Drug Co., *supra* note 57; Atwater v. Elkhorn Valley Coal-Land Co., *supra* note 44; Collins v. Hite, *supra* note 35; Landstreet v. Meyer, *supra* note 50. When a majority of the stockholders approve a stock option plan adopted by an interested board of directors, the Supreme Court of Delaware has in effect defined the scope of review as being whether the terms of the plan were so unequal as to amount to waste or whether the question was so close as to fall within the scope of business judgment. See Gottlieb v. Heyden Chemical Corp., *supra* note 41; Lieberman v. Becker, *supra* note 112, at 601; Beard v. Elster, 160 A.2d 731 (Sup. Ct. 1960). The scope of review for the action of a disinterested board of directors is consid-

the facts,[117] or that there was an attempt to deprive the minority of a share in the profits.[118] In some instances, the court is able to support its decision on two grounds, holding that ratification has cured the defect, and that the amounts were reasonable in any event.[119]

A few cases, arising in jurisdictions which describe self-voted arrangements as "void," indicate that ratification by a majority vote of stockholders cannot validate the directors' acts as against continued objection by a minority; but the actual decisions reached do not fully enforce this attitude.[120] Ratification is generally said, both in "voidable" and "void" jurisdictions, to be ineffective to validate fraudulent acts and misappropriations as against an objection seasonably taken and maintained by a minority.[121] Here, it is said, the majority could not originally have authorized the challenged acts, and cannot now achieve their ends through the mechanics of ratification. Yet even in such cases, laches may sometimes bar the minority's objection.[122]

---

erably more limited. See Beard v. Elster, *supra;* Forman v. Chester, 167 A.2d 442 (Sup. Ct. Del. 1961). See also Elster v. American Airlines, 167 A.2d 231 (Del. Ch. 1961) (approval by disinterested board of directors of action of interested option committee held effective).

[117] Camden Land Co. v. Lewis, 101 Me. 78, 63 Atl. 523 (1905); *cf.* Carr v. Kimball, *supra* note 2; Kaufman v. Shoenberg, *supra* note 55 (earlier communication to stockholders of terms of incentive compensation renders it unnecessary to do so again in proxy statement preceding meeting at which plan is voted on).

[118] Barrett v. Smith, *supra* note 44; Lowman v. Harvey Pierce Co., 276 Pa. 382, 120 Atl. 404 (1923); Holdridge v. Lloyd Garretson Co., 163 Wash, 1, 299 Pac. 657 (1931); Todd v. Southland Broadcasting Co., *supra* note 41. While shareholders may grant or ratify bonuses and retroactive compensation, they may not do so with the purpose of overreaching, or working a fraud on, a minority stockholder of the corporation.

[119] Putnam v. Juvenile Shoe Corp., *supra* note 44; Booth v. Beattie, *supra* note 44; Wineburgh v. Seeman Bros., *supra* note 29; Bookman v. R. J. Reynolds Tobacco Co., *supra* note 115.

[120] In McKey v. Swenson, *supra* note 58, the self-voted compensation was said, in spite of ratification by the officers in their capacity as majority stockholders, to be "wholly void . . . or at least [the facts] cast upon the officers the burden of showing the salaries were reasonable"; this they made no effort to do, and liability was imposed. In State *ex rel.* Squire v. Miller, *supra* note 42, a similar result was reached; the court, too, had other grounds for its decision. In both of these cases, there was no ratification by a disinterested majority. *Cf.* Holcomb v. Forsyth, *supra* note 43, and cases cited *supra* note 116.

[121] Fidanque v. American Maracaibo Co., *supra* note 47; Eliasberg v. Standard Oil Co., *supra* note 87; Yaeger v. Phillips, *supra* note 111; Pollitz v. Wabash R.R. Co., 207 N.Y. 113, 100 N.E. 721 (1921); Continental Securities Co. v. Belmont, 206 N.Y. 7, 18, 99 N.E. 138, 142 (1912). See Note, 4 U. CHI. L. REV. 495 (1937).

[122] See Markson v. Markson's Furniture Stores, Inc., 267 N.Y. 137, 195 N.E. 824 (1935); Riddle v. Mary A. Riddle Co., 142 N.J. Eq. 147, 59 A.2d 599 (1948); Lillard v. Oil, Paint & Drug Co, *supra* note 57.

While it is usually said that a director or officer may freely vote his shares in his own interest,[123] the courts will give more weight to ratification by a majority of disinterested stockholders than to ratification by an interested group. Those who have control of a majority of the stock, as well as of the board, are under a fiduciary obligation to the minority in all their relations with the corporation.[124]

The SEC and Stockholder Action. The solicitation of proxies with respect to securities listed on a national securities exchange is governed by proxy rules promulgated by the Securities and Exchange Commission,[125] and extension of such rules to many other securities has been sought.[126] These rules emphasize the necessity of disclosing the full terms of a compensation plan intended for the benefit of executives, if stockholder action with respect to such a plan is asked. The proxy rules also require disclosure of amounts paid—a type of disclosure which is required not only upon the submission of any executive compensation plan, but also upon the election of directors.[127] This subject is treated at length in the second volume of this work. The proxy rules do not require the submission of compensation plans to stockholders; they merely compel disclosure of compensation terms in case submission is made. The proxy rules may, in fact, have operated to discourage some companies from submitting their compensation plans to stockholder vote, thus taking the risk of relying solely on directors' action.

Submission to stockholders of compensation plans involving the issuance to executives of stock to be listed on a securities exchange may sometimes be required by the rules of the exchange.[128]

Investment companies registered under the Investment Company Act of 1940 face separate regulation; under Section 15(c) of that

[123] See United States Lines, Inc. v. United States Lines Co., 96 F.2d 148 (2d Cir. 1938); Kerbs v. California Eastern Airways, Inc., *supra* note 41 (ratification of profit-sharing plan approved though carried only by counting vote of interested shareholders-officers); Yaeger v. Phillips, *supra* note 111; Russell v. H. C. Patterson Co., *supra* note 43.

[124] See Lattin, *The Minority Stockholder and Intra-Corporate Conflict,* 17 Iowa L. Rev. 313, 332 (1932); Note, 28 Mich. L. Rev. 181 (1929). See Claman v. Robertson, *supra* note 59 (majority of disinterested shareholders must ratify) and cases cited *supra* note 121.

[125] SEC Reg. X-14 issued under § 14(a) of the Securities Exchange Act of 1934, 15 U.S.C. § 78n(a) (1952). See Feldman and Rothschild, *Executive Compensation and Federal Securities Legislation,* 55 Mich. L. Rev. 1115, 1145 (1957). Consult, generally, Dean, *Non-Compliance with Proxy Regulations: Effect on Ability of Corporation to Hold Valid Meeting,* 24 Cornell L.Q. 483 (1939).

[126] See Feldman and Rothschild, *supra* note 125, at 1140, n. 115.

[127] See Schedule 14A to SEC Reg. X-14, Item 7.

[128] See *supra* note 105.

Act, such companies must submit certain types of compensation contract to their stockholders for approval unless the contract has been adopted by a disinterested board of directors.[129]

OTHER PROBLEMS

Compensation as a Function of Employment. Rewards to executives and employees should be based on services performed for the company rather than on other considerations. Elementary as this proposition may seem, it is sometimes overlooked. Plans for paying bonuses to employee-stockholders, based on the size of their stockholdings rather than on the value of their services to the company, have been condemned by the courts. Thus, in *Scott v. P. Lorillard Co.,*[130] stockholders of the Lorillard Company sued to restrain the taking of a vote upon the adoption of a proposed bylaw which would have authorized an annual distribution of 5% of the company's profits "to and among those officers and employees of the company who have both been in the employ and owned common stock of the company as hereinafter stated as an extra dividend upon and in the proportion among such officers and employees of such shares of common stock thus owned by them respectively." The court, in granting the injunction, held that compensation to employees and officers could not be determined by a "factor entirely foreign to their employment." [131]

[129] Investment Company Act of 1940, § 15(c), 15 U.S.C. 80a–15(c).

[130] 108 N.J. Eq. 153, 154 Atl. 515 (1931), *aff'd,* 109 N.J. Eq. 417, 157 Atl. 388 (1931).

[131] 108 N.J. Eq. at 156. To the same effect, see Godley v. Crandall & Godley Co., *supra* note 13. Such plans have been held legal in New Jersey. Bookman v. R. J. Reynolds Tobacco Co., *supra* note 115 (holding that percentage compensation based on shares held by employees is proper under the New Jersey statute [N.J. STAT. ANN., tit. 14, § 14:9–1 (1939)]; the court also emphasized that the Lorillard case involved an injunction against the adoption of such a bylaw, as against the Reynolds Tobacco bylaw which had been in operation for 28 years). *Compare* Parsil v. Onyx Hosiery, Inc., 220 App. Div. 148, 221 N.Y. Supp. 174 (1st Dep't 1927), *aff'd w.o. op.,* 246 N.Y. 559, 156 N.E. 651 (1927); Lydia E. Pinkham Medicine Co. v. Gove, *supra* note 73. As to the propriety of an injunction against the holding of a meeting to approve a proposed bylaw or plan, see Holthusen v. Edward G. Budd Mfg. Co., 50 F. Supp. 621 (E.D. Pa. 1943). But *cf.* Berendt v. Bethlehem Steel Corp., 108 N.J. Eq. 148, 154 Atl. 321 (1931). For income tax purposes, payments under the R. J. Reynolds Tobacco Company incentive compensation bylaw were held entirely non-deductible by one court; a partial deduction was allowed by another court as to other taxable years. *Compare* R. J. Reynolds Tobacco Co. v. United States, 138 Ct. Cl. 1, 149 F. Supp. 889 (1957), *cert. denied,* 355 U.S. 893 (1957) *with* Com'r v. R. J. Reynolds Tobacco Co., 260 F.2d 9 (4th Cir. 1958), *affirming* T.C. Mem. Dec. 1956–161, 15 CCH TAX CT. MEM. 810 (1956).

Upon similar reasoning, compensation given in proportion to stockholdings will frequently not be deductible as a business expense (payment for personal services) under Section 162 of the Internal Revenue Code of 1954.[132]

Certain payments may be justified on grounds not directly related to services performed. Relatively small Christmas presents or bonuses given to all employees on an equal basis may be sustained as a proper means of creating and retaining general good will and high morale.[133] Certain types of payment by employers to or for the benefit of employees or their estates, such as payments under health and accident plans, wage continuation plans covering sickness or disability, and death benefit plans are given favorable treatment under the tax law.[134] Pension grants depend on other considerations.[135] Percentage payments, again, are sometimes, by reason of unexpectedly large corporate profits, found to be much in excess of what the parties originally had in mind; they may still be valid.[136] Apart from these exceptions or qualifications, the general principle still seems unquestionably sound: compensation should be based on the value of the services rendered.

Bylaw v. Contract v. Resolution. Compensation arrangements can be adopted in various ways. Baker, writing in 1938, studied thirty large industrial companies with definite profit-sharing compensation plans. He found that these plans were established through the following methods: sixteen by directors' resolution, six by con-

---

[132] See Volume II, Chapter 16.

[133] The value of turkeys, hams, and other items of nominal value at Christmas or on other holidays is not includible in income. See Rev. Rul. 59–58, 1959–1 Cum. Bull. 17. Generally, bonuses do constitute taxable compensation and are deductible by the employer. N. H. Van Sicklen, 33 B.T.A. 544 (1935); I.T. 1600, II-1 Cum. Bull. 184 (1923). Such bonuses have sometimes been quite substantial. E.g., N. Y. Times, Dec. 9, 1944, p. 13, col. 4, and Dec. 13, 1944, p. 16, col. 5 (describing the bonuses granted by Jack & Heintz Co., Inc. and Eastman Kodak Co. during World War II). See also Patton v. Com'r, 168 F.2d 28 (6th Cir. 1948). Consult, generally, Chapter 7, text to notes 105 ff.

[134] Health and accident plans and similar tax-favored employee benefit plans are discussed in Chapter 7. Voluntary payments made after death to an executive's widow may be vulnerable to attack by non-assenting shareholders. See Moore v. Keystone Macaroni Mfg. Co., supra note 47; Hoblitzell v. Howard, supra note 107.

[135] See Volume II, Chapter 19. For reimbursement payments and indemnity agreements, see WASHINGTON, CORPORATE EXECUTIVES' COMPENSATION 334 et seq., 369 et seq. (1942).

[136] Subject to qualifications discussed Ch. 4, text to notes 64 ff. The nature of such compensation as "contingent" may justify the higher amount paid. Gottfried v. Gottfried, supra note 59.

tract with executives, four by resolution and contract, three by bylaw, one not reporting.[137]

The directors' resolution is probably the traditional method: the directors, after electing the officers for a definite term (usually for one year), would resolve to pay them a stated sum for their services.[138] Later, when profit-sharing compensation plans came into vogue, the directors would hold out a promise of reward by voting to allocate a percentage of the profits to a bonus fund. The use of the resolution seems to have been associated originally with a "gift-offer" atmosphere; the directors might feel empowered to rescind or modify the resolution, without any sense of breaking a contract or subjecting the corporation to liability. This is to a certain extent reflected in the case law,[139] though today there seems little doubt that a resolution (not containing any clause permitting modification or revision) may bind the corporation as tightly as a formal agreement if the other party is invited to treat it as a basis of action in reliance and does in fact do so.[140] The directors' resolution, usually adopted subject to approval by stockholders, is still regarded as being particularly appropriate where a profit-sharing fund is created for the benefit of a large group, or for individuals to be selected at the close of the profit-sharing period.

Where a single executive is being employed, the resolution method is feasible, but offers no particular advantage to the executive. His bargaining position is usually strong enough to enable him to insist on the preparation of a formal contract with carefully worked-out provisions. It will ordinarily be advisable to have the directors adopt a resolution approving the final contract and authorizing its execution by the proper officers of the company.[141] Where the president

[137] Baker, Executive Salaries and Bonus Plans 200, 201 (1938).

[138] Consequently a promise made by a top executive to an executive of lower rank contrary to the terms of a governing board resolution is unenforceable against the corporation. Leon Farms Corp. v. Beeman, *supra* note 45; Hudson v. Alaska Airlines, Inc., *supra* note 16.

[139] See Burgess v. First Nat'l Bank, 219 App. Div. 361, 220 N.Y. Supp. 134 (2d Dep't 1927), and other cases discussed at Chapter 4, note 14. See also the following tenure and removal cases: Stevenson v. Higgins, 15 Ill. 110 (1853); O'Neal v. F. A. Neider Co., 118 Ky. 62, 80 S.W. 451 (1904); *Re* A. A. Griffing Iron Co., 63 N.J.L. 357, 46 Atl. 1097 (1899); Spahn v. Bielefeld & S. Co., 256 Pa. 543, 100 Atl. 987 (1917); Brindley v. Walker, 221 Pa. 287, 70 Atl. 794 (1908).

[140] 2 Fletcher, *op. cit. supra* note 1, § 431. A combination of formal documents is usually required of tax-exempt profit-sharing plans under § 401 of the Internal Revenue Code.

[141] Several factors enter here, full treatment of which lies beyond the scope of this book.

1. If the contract cannot be performed within a year, the Statute of Frauds requires that it be evidenced by a writing. See 2 Williston, Contracts §§ 495,

is receiving a contract, it may be well to name a particular vice-president as the officer empowered to execute the contract on the company's behalf.

Still a third method of arranging compensation is through bylaw provisions. In some corporations of small size, the entire executive payroll is thus provided for: the president is to receive $4,000, the secretary $2,500, and so on. Such a plan offers no attractions to the company of medium or large size, and seems useful in small companies only as a *modus vivendi* in situations where the stockholders do not have confidence in each other, or where they are simply dealing at arm's length.

Bylaws providing for special compensation, as distinguished from fixed salaries, are in fairly frequent use, even among companies of large size. The American Tobacco Company has perhaps the best-known of these bonus bylaws.[142] From the standpoint of the stockholders, such bylaws are subject to a serious disadvantage. They are rigid and hard to amend, even if they are found to operate unfairly toward stockholders. Further, they are relatively obscure and shadowy: a bylaw adopted ten or twenty years ago is not likely to come to the attention of a person buying stock today. The bylaw may quietly produce its results without being recalled to the stockholders' attention. From the standpoint of the executives, a bonus bylaw may be quite attractive—perhaps for the reasons just mentioned. There is also an additional point. In *Rogers v. Hill*,[143] the first *American Tobacco* case, the Supreme Court held that the bonus bylaw was "supported by the presumption of regularity and

500 (rev. ed. 1936). *Cf.* Young v. U.S. Mortgage & Trust Co., *supra* note 28. Formal corporate records may suffice. See 2 WILLISTON, *supra*, at § 568; 5 FLETCHER, *op. cit. supra* note 1, § 2206. See, however, Jacob v. Gratiot Central Market Co., 267 Mich. 262, 255 N.W. 331 (1934) (plaintiff has burden of showing that directors' resolution employing him was properly recorded in writing). Full formality thus seems desirable from the standpoint of both parties.

2. The hiring of a principal executive, particularly if the term is long or compensation substantial, should as a matter of precaution be made by the directors rather than by the company's president or other officers. See Lawton v. Contract Purchase Corp., 298 Mich. 712, 299 N.W. 777 (1941) (compensation in company stock must be authorized by directors); Heaman v. E. N. Rowell Co., 261 N.Y. 229, 185 N.E. 83 (1933) (contract for life employment is beyond power of president to authorize). And see Ginter v. Heco Envelope Co., 316 Ill. 183, 147 N.E. 42 (1925). See also the discussion of long-term contracts, Chapter 2, text to notes 11 ff.

3. Incidental advantages to the executive from a formal contract are illustrated in such cases as Realty Acceptance Corp. v. Montgomery, 51 F.2d 636 (3d Cir. 1930); Cuppy v. Stollwerck Bros., Inc., 216 N.Y. 591, 111 N.E. 249 (1916).

[142] See discussion, Chapter 3, text to note 66, *passim*. The bylaw is reprinted in App. U.

[143] *Supra* note 109.

continuity." [144] And in *Heller v. Boylan*,[145] the second *American Tobacco* case, the directors who had not received bonuses were sought to be held liable, on the ground that they had failed to supervise the computation of the bonuses. The court refused to impose liability, holding that the plan was the creature of the stockholders, not of the directors, and that the bylaw imposed the duty of computation on the treasurer rather than on the directors. This decision seems doubtful,[146] but it has placed an additional premium on the use of the bylaw method.

As to compensation plans adopted by stockholders' resolution, where a group plan is being adopted, this method has many advantages. It is somewhat less rigid than the bylaw device; the plan adopted is more likely to be reviewed at intervals, and the whole atmosphere is better. Much the same can be said of a stockholders' resolution confirming the directors' decision to enter into a contract with a single executive.

Compensation plans embodied in corporate charters, originally or through amendment, are seldom found. Though such a method would be of undoubted validity, it is too rigid for use in the average case. Further, a charter amendment of such a type might not be viewed with favor by the stockholders.[147]

Amendatory Contracts. The employment contracts of executives are frequently revised and amended. The executive becomes dissatisfied and seeks higher rewards, or the company seeks a downward revision. The typical situation is one where the officer or employee has contracted, let us say, to work for five years at the rate of $15,000 a year; after he has served for two years, he demands an increase to $20,000 a year and threatens to quit unless this is granted. Can the original contract be revised or amended so that the new agreement will bind the corporation? [148]

Here the contracting parties must cope with the elementary principle that an employee who is bound to perform under a preexisting contract cannot secure from his employer a legally enforce-

---

[144] *Id.* at 591.

[145] 29 N.Y.S.2d 653 (Sup. Ct. 1941).

[146] See Volume II, Chapter 19.

[147] See Jervis, *Corporate Agreements to Pay Directors' Expenses in Stockholders' Suits,* 40 COLUM. L. REV. 1192, 1202 (1940).

For a plan contained in a corporate charter, see BETHLEHEM STEEL, App. FF.

[148] At common law there are generally no specific requirements for amendatory contracts. 2 WILLISTON, *op. cit. supra* note 141, § 591. But see provisions such as N.Y. PERS. PROP. LAW, § 33-c, prohibiting oral change of written promises. See generally Note, 50 COLUM. L. REV. 700 (1950).

able promise to pay him something more for the same amount of work.[149] If the officer or employee, therefore, sues on the amended contract, he may be met with the defense that the promise of additional compensation is not supported by any consideration.[150] What new consideration can the employee furnish? Ordinarily it would seem that no new consideration is furnished by the employee's relinquishing his "right" to refuse to perform under the old contract and pay damages.[151] But if the employee agrees that in return for the increased compensation he will perform additional or different tasks, or that he will serve for a longer term than originally fixed, it would appear that the amendment should be upheld.[152]

It may perhaps be advisable to state specifically in the amended contract that the original contract has been rescinded by the mutual agreement of the parties on the theory that such a provision might operate to free both parties from any legal obligation, enabling them to enter into a new contract on any terms they desire.[153] However,

[149] 1 WILLISTON, CONTRACTS, *op. cit. supra* note 141, §§ 130, 130A. See also Dwyer v. Tracey, *supra* note 1 (president of company given amendatory contract increasing salary and granting stock option while decreasing services to be furnished to the corporation).

[150] 1 WILLISTON, *op. cit. supra* note 141, § 130A, note 16, and cases there cited. *Cf.* N.Y. PERS. PROP. LAW, § 33(2). The reasoning behind the "past services" cases might also be invoked.

[151] Western U. Teleg. Co. v. Brown, 253 U.S. 101, 40 Sup. Ct. 460 (1920); Dwyer v. Tracey, *supra* note 1; Blakeslee v. Board of Water Com'rs, 106 Conn. 642, 139 Atl. 106, 55 A.L.R. 1319 (1927); Duncan v. Cone, 16 Ga. App. 253, 85 S.E. 203 (1915); Prue v. Press Pub. Co., 117 App. Div. 854, 103 N.Y. Supp. 296 (2d Dep't 1907); *contra,* Rollins v. Marsh, 128 Mass. 116 (1880); Holmes v. Doane, 9 Cush. (63 Mass.) 135 (1851); Lattimore v. Harsen, 14 Johns. (N.Y.) 330 (1816); Evans v. Oregon & W. R. Co., 58 Wash. 429, 108 Pac. 1095 (1910); *cf.* Parrot v. Mexican Central Ry. Co., 207 Mass. 184, 93 N.E. 590 (1911). For criticism of these latter cases, see 1 WILLISTON, *op. cit. supra* note 141, § 130A; Barbour, *The "Right" to Break a Contract,* 16 MICH. L. REV. 106 (1917); Corbin, *Does a Pre-existing Duty Defeat Consideration?,* 27 YALE L.J. 362 (1918). *Cf.* Fraker v. A. G. Hyde & Sons, 127 App. Div. 620, 111 N.Y. Supp. 757 (1st Dep't 1908), where the plaintiff was hired at $10,000, but later was promised a bonus of 7% of earnings; the promise of a bonus was held enforceable, since the plaintiff had refrained from leaving the defendant's employ.

[152] Triangle Waist Co. v. Todd, 223 N.Y. 27, 119 N.E. 85 (1918); see also the stock option cases, *supra* note 87, and Kerbaugh v. Gray, 212 Fed. 716 (2d Cir. 1914); Haag v. Rogers, 9 Ga. App. 650, 72 S.E. 46 (1911); Duffy Bros. v. Bing & Bing, Inc., 217 App. Div. 10, 215 N.Y. Supp. 755 (1st Dep't 1926); Whitehouse v. Green, 81 Pa. Super. 386 (1923).

However, when the corporation's desire to secure the service of its executives for additional periods of time beyond the term of their existing contracts is the motive behind the grant of additional compensation, such as stock options, there need not presently exist personnel difficulties to justify such a plan. Kaufman v. Shoenberg, *supra* note 55, 91 A.2d at 793.

[153] Dover Copper Mining Co. v. Doenges, 40 Ariz. 349, 12 P.2d 288 (1932); Sasso v. K. G. & G. Realty & Const. Co., 98 Conn. 571, 120 Atl. 158 (1923), noted

in the situation we are discussing here, the officer or employee may be a member of the board which arranges for the amended contract; accordingly, if there is any evidence of fraud or overreaching, he might be denied recovery, not on any contractual basis but because he has violated his fiduciary obligation to the corporation.[154]

Employment contracts occasionally contain specific provisions to the effect that their terms contemplate merely a minimum compensation, to be raised at a later time to an amount representing a fair return for the employee's efforts and ability.[155] Such provisions may serve a purpose. They may indicate, first, that in return for faithful and efficient services on the part of the employee additional compensation was to be arranged from time to time,[156] and, second, that the parties have in mind an arrangement closely similar to a bonus plan. In other words, the compensation originally fixed may be re-

---

43 YALE L.J. 78 (1923); Schwartzreich v. Bauman-Basch, Inc., 105 Misc. 214, 172 N.Y. Supp. 683 (Sup. Ct. 1918), aff'd, 231 N.Y. 196, 131 N.E. 887 (1920), noted 7 CORNELL L.Q. 53 (1921). As to the problems involved where an employee seeks to enforce a promise of additional compensation for work already performed at a fixed rate of pay, see 1 WILLISTON, op. cit. supra note 141, § 130B. Compare discussion in text to notes 47 ff. supra.

[154] See discussion in text to notes 48 ff. supra.

[155] Thus, in a contract between Warner Bros. Pictures, Inc. and Sam E. Morris, dated Jan. 27, 1931, it was provided that Mr. Morris should be employed for a fixed term at a stated salary. The contract then stated:

Notwithstanding the foregoing, it is hereby agreed between the parties that at the expiration of each calendar year during the period of this contract, in the event that the earnings of First Party shall have increased during said respective years, Second Party shall have the privilege of addressing himself to the First Party, its officers and directors, for an increase in compensation to be paid to him for his services agreed to be rendered hereunder and thereupon and thereafter, the compensation payable to Second Party hereunder shall be such increased weekly amount above Two thousand dollars ($2,000.) and for such period of time, as shall be fixed by the officers and directors of First Party, but in no event less than Two thousand dollars ($2,000.) a week, during the balance of the term hereof.

Similarly, a contract between Esquire-Coronet, Inc. and D. A. Smart, dated Apr. 1, 1937, provided in ¶ 6:

It is understood that nothing herein contained shall prevent the Board of Directors of the Company from at any time increasing the compensation herein provided to be paid to Smart, either permanently or for a limited period, or of providing additional compensation to Smart based upon the earnings or business of the Company in the event the Board of Directors in its sole discretion, evidenced by a resolution adopted by all of the members of the Board of Directors of the Company, shall deem it advisable so to do in order to recognize and fairly compensate Smart for the value of his services to the Company; but nothing herein contained shall in any manner obligate the Board of Directors or any of the members thereof to make any such increase or provide any such additional compensation.

[156] See, for example, Fuller Co. v. Brown, 15 F.2d 672 (4th Cir. 1926); Roberts v. Mays Mills, 184 N.C. 406, 114 S.E. 530 (1922).

garded as a minimum, with higher rewards understood to be in the offing, dependent on the success of the company and the special merits of the employee.[157]

Tax problems are frequently created by changes in managerial compensation arrangements. Such problems are similar to those discussed in connection with changes in profit-sharing compensation.[158]

Employment of Executives by Controlling Stockholders. In many instances, an executive is not content to rely on the normal process of contracting with the corporation through its officers and directors. He may wish to deal directly with the controlling stockholders, seeking to obtain their personal guaranties as to his compensation, tenure, and powers as an executive.[159] He is particularly likely to seek to make such a contract obligating the controlling stockholders in cases where he is selling his own business in exchange for a share interest and for a remunerative office in a larger enterprise. Contracts of this nature have often been subject to judicial disapproval on the ground that the directors are being unduly restricted in their control of the corporate affairs or (which may or may not be the same thing) that minority stockholders may be injured.[160] Later cases, however, show more leniency and recognize that contracts between executives and controlling stockholders may often be advantageous to all parties interested in the corporation, including minority stockholders.[161]

[157] See, for example, Church v. Harnit, *supra* note 20; *In re* Knox Automobile Co., 229 Fed. 241 (D. Mass. 1915); Parsil v. Onyx Hosiery, Inc., *supra* note 131; Wineburgh v. Seeman Bros., Inc., *supra* note 29; Holmes v. Republic Steel Corp., *supra* note 1.

[158] For example, when an officer cancels the corporation's obligation to pay him accrued salary, has the officer received taxable income, and then made a gift? Or has there been an addition to corporate capital? See discussion in Chapter 4, text to note 59.

[159] Sometimes, too, an important stockholder may wish to supply additional compensation to the executives. For instances, see Deputy v. du Pont, 308 U.S. 488, 60 Sup. Ct. 363 (1940) (stockholder attempts to take tax deduction for such payments as his own business expense; deduction disallowed); Van Dusen v. Com'r, 166 F.2d 647 (9th Cir. 1948). However, when the controlling stockholder makes the promise on behalf of the corporation, the latter may be bound if the executive chooses to treat the controlling stockholder's promise as that of the corporation. Allen v. France Packing Co., 170 Pa. Super. 632, 90 A.2d 289 (1952).

[160] Meck, *Employment of Corporate Executives by Majority Stockholders,* 47 YALE L.J. 1079, 1080 (1938). See *In re* Petrol Terminal Corp., 120 F. Supp. 867 (D.C. Md. 1954) (company, on demand of majority shareholder, assured seller of stock to majority shareholder of an employment contract; even though the contract was ratified by the stockholders, it was declared void and against the best interests of the company).

[161] Meck, *supra* note 160, at 1090–92. See also Miller v. Vanderlip, 285 N.Y. 116, 33 N.E.2d 51 (1941), noted 54 HARV. L. REV. 1398 (1941).

There is still need for considerable care in drafting and adopting contracts of this nature. John F. Meck, Jr., offers the following suggestions : [162]

1. Make all the stockholders parties to the contract. If this is not possible, try to obtain their specific approval of it, or at least give them full notice of its terms.
2. Make the corporation itself, acting through its directorate, a party to the contract.
3. If the controlling stockholders are directors, avoid language which will bind them in their fiduciary capacity.
4. See that the contract provisions as to tenure, compensation, and powers are reasonable and fair.

Management by Other Corporations. The difficulties discussed in the preceding section may also arise in cases where a corporation contracts with a partnership or another corporation for the furnishing to it of executive management.

The traditional view is that such contracts are against public policy, in that they deprive the directors of their proper authority.[163] Such agreements have been frequently made, however, particularly among public utilities. In that field, certain restrictive legislation has been passed.[164] Yet in general it would seem fairly clear that the force of the traditional arguments has weakened.[165]

Distinguishable, even under the older view, are contracts in which the board of directors of Company A retains its authority, the agreement with Company B merely providing that the latter shall supply Company A with the services of certain executives, for a price to be paid by A to B.[166] This may in some instances and under certain circumstances be simply a device for reducing the taxes paid by the

[162] Meck, *supra* note 160, at 1098–99.

[163] Long Park, Inc. v. Trenton-New Brunswick Theatres Co., 297 N.Y. 174, 177 N.E.2d 633 (1948); Sherman & Ellis, Inc. v. Indiana Mutual Casualty Co., 41 F.2d 588 (7th Cir. 1930), *cert. denied*, 282 U.S. 293, 51 Sup. Ct. 107 (1930); Robinson v. Benbow, 298 Fed. 561 (4th Cir. 1924); see also Field v. Carlisle Corp., 68 A.2d 817 (Del. Ch. 1950), noted 34 MARQUETTE L. REV. 48 (1950); STEVENS, *op. cit. supra* note 48, at 654–55; Note, 61 HARV. L. REV. 1251 (1948). But *cf.* Schneider v. Greater M. & S. Circuit, Inc., 144 Misc. 534, 259 N.Y. Supp. 319 (Sup. Ct. 1932); Cullen v. Governor Clinton Co., 110 N.Y.S.2d 614 (1952) (unreasonable for directors to vote salaries to two officers of corporation who held similar offices in the management company).

[164] Public Utility Holding Company Act of 1935, 15 U.S.C., § 79m.

[165] See Schneider v. Greater M. & S. Circuit, Inc., *supra* note 163.

[166] Thus, in 1928, Warner Bros. Pictures, Inc., and Renraw, Inc., entered into a contract whereby the former would pay to Renraw, Inc. certain sums for the services of Harry M. Warner, Albert Warner, and Jack L. Warner. For the text of this contract, see Koplar v. Warner Bros. Pictures, Inc., 19 F. Supp. 173, 179–182 (D. Del. 1937).

executives,[167] or for regulating their individual interests in property used by A and B.[168]

Tax Reasons for Compliance with Formalities of Adoption.

One of the facts tending to support a claim that compensation is reasonable, so that the employing company may obtain a deduction under Section 162 of the Internal Revenue Code, is that the compensation has been paid pursuant to an express contract entered into prior to the rendition of the services and pursuant to formal authorization by the board of directors or stockholders.

Formal corporate action is not without evidentiary weight: In several instances, the absence of any formal corporate authorization or provision for the payment of amounts which the corporation had deducted as salaries has been emphasized to support disallowance of a claimed deduction.[169] But obviously such authorization or provision cannot of itself be of too great weight on the point of whether a deduction should be allowed.[170] While the courts may express reluctance to upset the judgment of the board of directors in fixing corporate salaries,[171] they do so if there are other facts which show that compensation has been paid in an attempt to evade taxes rather than in an effort to pay for services.[172] Except perhaps in some

[167] Compare the contract between General Motors Corp. and General Motors Management Corp., summarized in Volume II, Chapter 10; and see Comer v. Davis, 107 F.2d 355 (5th Cir. 1939); 1 MONTGOMERY, FEDERAL TAX HANDBOOK 789 (1940–41).

[168] Compare the contract between Loew's Inc., and the Mayer group, summarized in Volume II, Chapter 19.

[169] 105 W. 55th Street, Inc., 20 B.T.A. 711 (1930); Helmer, Dutton & Kehlenbrinck Realty Co., 21 B.T.A. 91 (1930); R. E. Cotter Co., 22 B.T.A. 436 (1931).

[170] Botany Worsted Mills v. United States, 278 U.S. 282, 49 Sup. Ct. 129 (1929); National Cottonseed Products Corp. v. Com'r, 76 F.2d 839 (6th Cir. 1935); Samuel Heath Co. v. United States, 2 F. Supp. 637 (Ct. Cl. 1933); East St. Louis Finance Co., 34 B.T.A. 1085 (1936).

[171] Toledo Grain & Milling Co. v. Com'r, 62 F.2d 171 (6th Cir. 1932); United States v. Philadelphia Knitting Mills, 273 Fed. 657 (3d Cir. 1921); L. Schepp Co., 25 B.T.A. 419 (1932).

[172] See Treas. Reg. §§ 1.162-7-8 (1958); Long Island Drug Co. v. Com'r, 35 B.T.A. 328 (1937), aff'd, 111 F.2d 593 (2d Cir. 1940); Brampton Woolen Co. v. Com'r, 45 F.2d 327 (1st Cir. 1930), where the court said (at 328):

Obviously, directors cannot technically contract with themselves; but it is well settled that when, as in this case, the directors, or a majority thereof, are also the executives and managing forces of the corporation, they may informally agree for reasonable compensation for their services rendered to their corporation. Of course such agreement, formal or informal, must be only for *reasonable* compensation.

See discussion, summarized in Volume II, Chapter 16.

instances in which compensation is paid on a percentage basis and the executives receive unexpectedly high remuneration because of increased business or a fortunate business deal,[173] the contract or a bylaw will not control if there is other evidence that the salaries are unreasonable.[174] About the most that can be said is that formal corporate action may create an inference that the salary allowances are reasonable.[175] Some courts, indeed, give it no weight at all, and decide the case just as though there had been no formal contract or agreement.[176] Similarly, in small, closely held corporations, the officers often withdraw compensation without formal authorization, and the courts do not appear to attach much significance to the failure to comply with technical corporate procedure.[177] The converse also holds true: if the officers who receive the compensation constitute or control the entire membership of the board of directors and dominate the stockholders' meetings, the courts will be justified in disregarding the corporation's reliance upon the strict observance of corporate formalities.[178] It is worth noting, however, that formal action in advance takes on added importance in cases involving profit participation.[179]

[173] Austin v. United States, 28 F.2d 677 (5th Cir. 1928); Thomas N. Perkins, 33 B.T.A. 606 (1935); California Vegetable Concentrates, Inc., 10 T.C. 1058 (1948); J. T. Flagg Knitting Co., 12 T.C. 394 (1949). But a mere increase in sales or profit stemming from outside circumstances, such as a war economy, without increased effort or services, does not of itself justify salary increases. Commercial Iron Works v. Com'r, 166 F.2d 221 (5th Cir. 1948); Ecco High Frequency Corp. v. Com'r, 167 F.2d 583 (2d Cir. 1948), cert. denied, 335 U.S. 825 (1948). Cf. Roth Equipment Co. v. Gallagher, 172 F.2d 452 (6th Cir. 1949).

[174] Long Island Drug Co. v. Com'r, supra note 172; Brampton Woolen Co. v. Com'r, supra note 172; E. Wagner & Son v. Com'r, 93 F.2d 816 (9th Cir. 1937); Frederick L. Watson, 25 B.T.A. 971 (1932).

[175] Indialantic, Inc. v. Com'r, 216 F.2d 203 (6th Cir. 1954); Mayson Mfg. Co. v. Com'r, 178 F.2d 115 (6th Cir. 1949) (reversing a tax court decision which disallowed in part the salary of a corporate president and stating that the case for deductibility was greatly strengthened by unanimous stockholder approval). Toledo Grain & Milling Co. v. Com'r, supra note 171; Benz Bros., 20 B.T.A. 1214 (1930); cf. Ox Fibre Brush Co. v. Blair, 32 F.2d 42 (4th Cir. 1929), aff'd sub nom. Lucas v. Ox Fibre Brush Co., 281 U.S. 115, 50 Sup. Ct. 273 (1930). But little weight may be given to such inferences. E. Wagner & Son v. Com'r, supra note 174.

[176] Long Island Drug Co. v. Com'r, supra note 172; Doernbecher Mfg. Co. v. Com'r, 30 B.T.A. 973 (1934), 80 F.2d 573 (9th Cir. 1935), 95 F.2d 296 (9th Cir. 1938); Samuel Heath v. United States, supra note 170.

[177] In re Concord Silversmiths Corp., 32 F. Supp. 128 (D.N.H. 1940); Helvering v. J. L. Brandeis & Sons, 75 F.2d 487 (8th Cir. 1935); Moore & Evans, 24 B.T.A. 45 (1931); Mobile Drug Co. v. United States, 39 F.2d 940 (D.S.D. Ala. 1930); Cataract Ice Co., 23 B.T.A. 654 (1931); Indiana Rubber & Insulated Wire Co., 20 B.T.A. 1201 (1930). For additional cases, see 2 MERTENS, LAW OF FEDERAL INCOME TAXATION (1961 Rvn.) §§ 12.88, 12.89.

[178] Lydia E. Pinkham Medicine Co. v. Com'r, 128 F.2d 986 (1st Cir. 1942); see Treas. Reg. § 1.162–7(b)(1) (1958).

[179] See Chapter 4, text to notes 73 ff.

The Problem of Rewarding Past Services. In several instances in this chapter and in other contexts we encounter the problem of whether a corporation may reward "past services." Succinctly stated, the question presented is whether payment for such services is without consideration and a "gift" of corporate funds which cannot be made without the unanimous consent of the stockholders. The problem presents itself in several forms which may, perhaps, be distinguished upon their facts. If an executive performs services without a prior agreement or with only an informal agreement, should his recovery from the corporation be barred by the past services doctrine? If he has contracted to work for $10,000 a year for five years, does a question present itself under the past services doctrine if he should receive an amendatory contract at the end of the second year raising his compensation for the remainder of the term to $15,000 a year? As we have seen, the courts will generally endeavor to compensate the executive in these two situations; in the one, at least if the services have been rendered in a justifiable expectation of payment;[180] in the other, if the agreed payment at the higher rate is confined to the unexpired period of the contract.[181]

A different problem is presented when additional compensation is granted for services which have already been rendered and which have been paid for at the agreed rate. In this situation, the grant of additional compensation has as a rule been declared invalid.[182]

Three important inroads have been made upon this general rule. The first is found in *Holmes v. Republic Steel Corp.*[183] In that case, the salary of Tom M. Girdler, chairman of the company's board of directors, had been fixed in February, 1940 at $175,000 a year "plus such additional amount, if any, as the Board of Directors may determine prior to Dec. 31, 1940." On December 23, 1940, the board voted to pay $50,000 for an annuity for Mr. Girdler and to pay him an additional $1,000 in cash. The Ohio Court of Common Pleas held that the payment of $51,000 to Mr. Girdler over and above his fixed salary of $175,000 was invalid.[184] But on appeal, with new oral evidence that Mr. Girdler had relied on the promise of additional

---

[180] See text to notes 23 ff. *supra.*

[181] See text to notes 153 ff. *supra.*

[182] See text to note 47 *supra.* Profit participation, under which the executive has initially been promised a share of the profits, constitutes part of his agreed compensation and is not retroactive compensation within the rule mentioned in the text. See Chapter 4, text to notes 79 ff. That past services do not constitute consideration for the grant of an option, see Holthusen v. Edward G. Budd Mfg. Co., *supra* note 107, 52 F. Supp. at 129, and see *supra* notes 104 and 107.

[183] 69 N.E.2d 396 (1946), *mod. and aff'd,* 84 Ohio App. 442, 84 N.E.2d 508 (1948).

[184] 69 N.E.2d 396 (1946).

compensation at the time of the February, 1940 resolution, the Ohio Court of Appeals upheld the additional payment.[185] The court thus decided that an executive may properly be granted compensation for services already rendered in addition to his fixed salary even though the additional compensation is not fixed in amount or by yardstick, provided the executive has been promised and has relied upon payment of such additional compensation before the services were rendered; in effect the court assimilated the rule here to the rule when no fixed salary has been agreed upon in advance.[186]

The second important inroad upon the rule prohibiting payment of additional compensation for past services was made in the case of *Blish v. Thompson Automatic Arms Corp.*[187] The defendant corporation, manufacturer of the well-known submachine gun, had been in poor financial condition for many years and in 1939 employed Russell Maguire to reorganize its finances. Mr. Maguire became a large stockholder, a director, and the president of the company. Aided by the government's rearmament program following the outbreak of World War II, he made the company a great financial success and lifted it to previously unknown prosperity. Much of this success was due to his ability as an organizer not only of finances, but also of production. Both in 1940 and in 1941 he received substantial pay increases which in each case were made retroactive for several months. The plaintiff brought a minority stockholder's action against the corporation and its directors complaining of various practices, including the payment of the retroactive increases in Mr. Maguire's compensation. On appeal, the Delaware Supreme Court decided in favor of the corporation and held that retroactive compensation, though generally prohibited, may be allowed when reasonable in the light of the services rendered.[188] In so holding, the

[185] 84 Ohio App. 442, 84 N.E.2d 508 (1948).

[186] *Cf.* Todd v. Southland Broadcasting Co., *supra* note 41. As to bonuses and similar retroactive increases of salary except where there has been an expressed or implied understanding that they may be granted if conditions warrant, there is no consideration for them. In the *Todd* case, contrary to a resolution not to take compensation until the corporation was liquid, the board of directors, acting as a management committee, voted themselves compensation for the previous year.

[187] *Supra* note 47, criticized in Note, 25 IND. L.J. 212 (1950).

[188] See Spaeth v. Journal Printing Co., 139 F. Supp. 188 (D.C. Alaska 1956) (burden of proof on defendant to show amount voted as retroactive salary increase was reasonable). As to application of the requirement of reasonableness to agreements fixing compensation prospectively, see Rogers v. Hill, *supra* note 109; Note, 17 MINN. L. REV. 433 (1933); Note, 25 N. CAR. L. REV. 479 (1947). The yardstick of reasonableness was explicitly rejected as inapplicable to a corporate resolution attempting to grant retroactive pay increases in Crichton v. Webb, 133 La. 167, 177, 36 So. 926, 932 (1904). But *cf.* Gascue v. Saralegui Land & Livestock Co., *supra* note 47. See also Hurt v. Cotton States Fertilizer Co., *supra* note 112 (contract fixing maximum limitation on salaries given restrictive interpretation so as to prevent retroactive pay increases).

Delaware court treated the problem almost as one involving prospective compensation.[189]

The consequences of the decision of the Delaware Supreme Court in *Blish v. Thompson Automatic Arms Corp.* are not easy to evaluate. They do not, however, appear to have been very great. Corporate proxy statements and other published information on compensation paid to corporate executives show no tendency to repeat the compensation pattern of Mr. Maguire. As far as reported cases indicate, the decision in the *Blish* case has also left little impress on later court decisions. The courts generally have continued to hold that services already rendered will not supply consideration for a subsequent increase in compensation for the same services.[190] Moreover, the Delaware Chancery Court itself has at least partially limited the scope of the *Blish* decision by its holding in *Fidanque v. American Maracaibo Co.*[191] that past services will not support an agreement with the president of the corporation to pay him a salary for future consulting services, when his physical ability to render such services is doubtful.

The third, and by far the most important inroad upon the rule precluding additional compensation for past services, is found in the pension cases. While there has as yet been no controlling decision upon the point, there has been an increasing trend towards the recognition of the validity of pension grants based in large part upon past services.[192] This trend is in keeping with present social policy which may, legally speaking, render the grant of a pension, if and when decided upon in the future by the employing company, an implied term of the employment contract.

In dealing with problems of rewarding past services the courts have tended to depend upon the factual situation involved, but in all instances the questions raised are basically similar: (1) Has there been a benefit to the corporation? (2) Has there been a fraud on the stockholders? (3) Were the payments within the corporation's

[189] Consult also cases sustaining grant of retroactive compensation *supra* note 47. In addition to cases to the contrary, also cited in that note, consult Diamond v. Davis, *supra* note 107, 38 N.Y.S.2d at 113; March v. Arch Rib Truss Co., 56 Cal. App. 2d 811, 33 P.2d 412 (1943); *In re* Wood's Estate, 299 Mich 635, 1 N.W.2d 19 (1941).

[190] Savage v. Lorraine Corp., Dow v. River Farms of California, Inc., and Moore v. Keystone Macaroni Mfg. Co., all *supra* note 47. The only exception found was Gascue v. Saralegui Land & Livestock Co., *supra* note 47. This case somewhat resembles Holmes v. Republic Steel Corp., *supra* notes 1 and 183, on its facts, in that in the *Gascue* case there also existed a corporate resolution indicating an understanding that the services of the executive whose compensation was challenged would be remunerated by the corporation.

[191] *Supra* note 47. See Chapter 6, text to notes 91 ff.

[192] See Chapter 6, text to note 92; also, Volume II. Chapter 13.

powers? (4) Was there sufficient consideration for the payment? All these questions seem to come down to one point. A business corporation is chiefly formed for the purpose of making a profit for the stockholders, and they are entitled to insist that dealings between the executive and the corporate treasury be regulated with that aim in view.[193] If a past service pension plan is honestly viewed by a disinterested board of directors and a majority of the stockholders as being a likely means of increasing the corporation's profits—by encouraging employees to stay in the service of the corporation—the essential test has been satisfied. If an amendatory contract or even a retroactive increase in compensation is honestly thought by a disinterested directorate to be desirable as a matter of business judgment, as tending ultimately to increase the profits of the corporation, then the action of the board is justified.[194] And if the executive has rendered valuable services without having any contract at all, it is even more clear that the best interests of the corporation may demand a payment to him corresponding to the reasonable worth of the services rendered.

State Legislation Relating to Corporate Approval

In the decade 1950–60 there were no less than sixteen major statutory revisions in state corporation laws,[195] and at the end of that decade several more were in progress.[196] In this great development of statutory law the largest single influence was the Model Business

[193] For a discussion of the problem of profit participation, see Chapter 3, text to notes 1 ff.; Chapter 4, text to notes 79 ff.

[194] The case of stock given for past services seems a different matter. The courts' traditional reluctance to allow stock to be issued for past services seems fully justified. A stock option may likewise present different problems.

As to stock, cf. Gascue v. Saralegui Land & Livestock Co. supra note 47.

[195] De Capriles, Survey of Corporate Developments, 1944–1959, 13 Vand. L. Rev., Dec. 1959, pp. 1, 4, lists thirteen major statutory revisions in this decade: Maryland and Wisconsin (1951), Florida and Oregon (1953), District of Columbia (1954), North Carolina, Ohio, and Texas (1955), Pennsylvania and Virginia (1956), Alaska and North Dakota (1957), and Colorado (1958). In addition, three states in 1959 enacted general revisions of their statutes relating to business corporations: Iowa [Iowa Code Ann., §§ 496A1–49A.146 (Supp. 1960) incorporating L. 1959, ch. 321 eff. July 1, 1959]; Alabama [Ala. Code Ann., §§ 1–101 (Supp. 1959) incorporating Ala. Laws 1959, Act 414, approved Nov. 13, 1959]; Connecticut [Conn. Gen. Stat. Ann., §§ 33–282–418 (1960) incorporating 1959 P.A. 618 eff. Jan. 1, 1961].

[196] See Lesher, Revision of the New York Corporation Statutes, 14 Bus. Law 807 (1959) (listing those in progress in early 1959). In 1961, New York enacted a new Business Corporation Law effective April 1, 1963, constituting Chapter 4 of the Consolidated Laws of New York. N.Y. Sess. Laws 1961, ch. 855.

Corporation Act of the Committee on Corporate Laws of the American Bar Association.[197]

The Model Business Corporation Act has served as a guide [198] to draftsmen of business corporation laws.[199] On the requirements of corporate approval for executive compensation, however, there have been notable statutory innovations which were not engendered by the Model Act.[200] On the whole, it is apparent that this is a field in which a good deal of useful borrowing takes place in the process of putting together a new act; the various enactments have an effect

---

[197] See Model Business Corporation Act (hereinafter cited as the MODEL ACT). For a history of the development of the MODEL ACT, see MODEL BUS. CORP. ACT ANN., § 1, ¶ 4, and Jennings, *The Role of States in Corporate Regulation and Investor Protection,* 23 LAW & CONTEMP. PROB. 191, 197–98 (1958). It should not be confused with the corporation statute recommended in 1928 by the Commissioners on Uniform State Laws as the "Uniform Business Corporation Act," and later redesignated as the Model Business Corporation Act, which formed the basis of the corporation statutes of four states: Louisiana (1928), Idaho (1929), Washington (1933), and Kentucky (1946). See 9 UNIFORM LAWS ANNOTATED 115 (1957). The Commissioners' model was used as source material for other corporate revisions (see Jennings, *supra*) but did not have the wide influence of the American Bar Association model and did not have an important bearing on the subject matter of this chapter, as is indicated by its draftsmen's policy of attempting "to avoid unalterable statutory regulation of matters of intra-corporate management and to give the incorporated group as much freedom in this regard as seems consistent with sound policy." 9 UNIFORM LAWS ANNOTATED, *supra* at 116. By 1939 the Commissioners' model had been withdrawn as a "Uniform Act" and redesignated as a "Model Act" on the basis that the subject was not one "upon which uniformity between the states is necessary or desirable." See 9 UNIFORM LAWS ANNOTATED *supra*; Jennings, *supra*.

[198] For a scholarly criticism of the Model Act, see Emerson, *Vital Weaknesses in the New Virginia Stock Corporation Act and the Model Act,* 42 VA. L. REV. 489 (1956); and also Harris, *The Model Business Corporation Act—Invitation to Irresponsibility?,* 50 NW. U.L. REV. 1 (1955); Jennings, *supra* note 197, at 198–205. Consult, also, Emerson, *The Roles of Management and Shareholders in Corporate Government,* 23 LAW & CONTEMP. PROB. 231 (1958). For alternative attitudes in the drafting of corporate statutes consult Katz, *The Philosophy of Midcentury Corporation Statutes,* 23 LAW & CONTEMP. PROB. 177 (1958).

[199] Between 1951 and the end of 1959, the substance of the MODEL ACT had been adopted by nine states: Wisconsin (1951), Oregon (1953), District of Columbia (1954), Texas (1955), Virginia (1956), Alaska and North Dakota (1957), Colorado (1958), and Iowa (1959). In addition, the MODEL ACT influenced the other seven states which revised their corporate statutes during that period: Maryland (1951), Florida (1953), North Carolina and Ohio (1955), Pennsylvania (1956), Alabama (1959), and Connecticut (1959). See authorities cited note 195 *supra.* The Business Corporation Law of New York adopted in 1961, *supra* note 196, is essentially based upon the MODEL ACT. See Lesher, note 196 *supra,* at 816.

[200] The California statute, which dates back to 1931, deals with the problem of self-interest of directors in a way which, although not followed by the MODEL ACT, has influenced North Carolina and perhaps other states that have dealt with the self-interest problem by provisions which do not have their counterpart in the MODEL ACT. See text to notes 214 ff. *infra.*

on each other and some states follow the lead of the Model Act in some areas but adopt quite a different approach in others.[201] We shall use the Model Act as a frame of reference, indicating the portions of it which relate to the subject matter of this chapter.

In the section of the Model Act setting forth the general powers of a corporation,[202] one clause [203] that has been widely adopted [204] empowers the corporation "to pay pensions and establish pension plans, pension trusts, profit-sharing plans, stock bonus plans, stock option plans and other incentive plans for any and all of its directors, officers and employees." [205] The purpose of this clause is evidently to avoid any possibility that such types of compensation would not be held to be within the scope of the implied powers of a business corporation. This clause makes directors as such eligible as a matter of corporate law to participate in the benefits listed; the participation of directors who are not also employees is unusual and, as a tax matter, not permitted under qualified pension and profit-sharing plans or restricted stock options.[206] Apart from this aspect, the clause is probably unnecessary in view of the entrenched position of these benefits in every stratum of industrial life.[207] Earlier corporate

---

[201] See discussion in Lesher, note 196 *supra*.

[202] MODEL ACT, § 4.

[203] MODEL ACT, § 4(p).

[204] See ALASKA COMP. STAT. ANN., § 36–2A–12(p) (Supp. 1957); COLO. CORP. ACT OF 1958, § 3(p), COLO. SESS. LAWS 1958, S.B. 14; ILL. STAT. ANN., ch. 32, § 5(o) (Supp. 1959); IOWA CODE ANN., tit. 19, § 496A.4(16) (Supp. 1959); N.C. GEN. STAT. § 55–17(10) (1960); N.D. 1943 REV. CODE, § 10–1904 (Supp. 1957); ORE. REV. STAT., § 57.030(16) (1955); TEXAS CIVIL STAT., art. 2.02(17) (1956); VA. CODE ANN., tit. 13.1, § 13.1–3(O) (1956). See also N.Y. BUS. CORP. LAW, § 202(a)(13).

[205] The Colorado statute, *supra* note 204, in adopting § 4(p), elaborated considerably on the list of employee benefits so as to include, in addition to those set forth in that section, "medical service, life, sickness, accident, disability or unemployment insurance, education, housing, social and recreational services and other similar aids and services." The Illinois statute, *supra* note 204, adds the power "to make the payments and issue the shares provided for therein."

[206] INT. REV. CODE OF 1954, § 401, relating to qualified pension and profit-sharing plans, limits the permissible class of beneficiaries to "employees." So does § 421, relating to restricted stock options. Directors have, however, been included in group life insurance plans. See, generally, Chapter 9, text to notes 57 ff.

[207] See MODEL BUS. CORP. ACT ANN., § 4(p), ¶ (1960); Latty, *Some Miscellaneous Novelties in the New Corporation Statutes*, 23 LAW & CONTEMP. PROB. 363, 369–70 (1958). The provision is somewhat analogous in its purpose to that of § 4(m) of the MODEL ACT, which authorizes corporations to make donations for the public welfare or for charitable purposes, and in time of war to make donations in aid of war activities. This provision has been adopted by a number of states which have followed the MODEL ACT and also exists in a variety of forms elsewhere. See, e.g., ALASKA COMP. STAT. ANN., § 36–2A–12(m) (Supp. 1957); N.C. GEN. STAT., § 55–17(6) (1960); ILL. STAT. ANN., ch. 32, § 5(m) (Supp. 1959); DEL. CODE ANN., tit. 8, § 122(9) (1953); MICH. STAT. ANN., tit. 21, § 21.10; N.Y. BUS CORP. LAW, § 202(a)(12).

statutes [208] had similar provisions at a time when supplementary forms of compensation were not as usual.

The clause does not deal with the power to grant supplementary forms of compensation as between the board of directors and the stockholders. In effect, it leaves these matters to the board of directors,[209] except as provided in other portions of the Model Act relating to employee stock sales and options [210] and the pre-emptive rights of stockholders.[211]

With reference to the compensation of a member of the board of directors, the Model Act provides only that "the board of directors shall have authority to fix the compensation of directors unless otherwise provided in the articles of incorporation." [212] This provision seems to be limited in its effect to doing away with any prima facie invalidity resulting from the participation of directors in the fixing of their own compensation; it does not deal with the question of invalidity when the vote of an interested director is needed to pass a compensation resolution. The Model Act does not specifically deal with the self-interest problem.[213]

[208] See N.J. Rev. Stat., § 14:9–1 (1937) (added by L. 1920, ch. 174); Pa. Stat., tit. 15, § 2852–316 (1936) (derived from Act of May 11, 1893, P.L. 42, § 1).

[209] Section 4(k) of the Model Act authorizes the corporation to elect or appoint officers and agents, define their duties and fix their compensation. Section 4(p) has been criticized for not requiring stockholder approval of incentive plans. See Harris, *supra* note 198, at 4. The view has been expressed that "under Section 4(p) a question remains open as to whether in a particular state adopting the section the power granted the corporation is to be exercised by the directors alone, the shareholders alone, or by both." Letter from Prof. Frank D. Emerson dated October 15, 1960 to one of the authors.

[210] Model Act, optional § 18A (1957 Addendum).

[211] Model Act, § 24.

[212] Model Act, § 33. This provision has been adopted in a number of states which have enacted the Model Act as a whole. See Alaska Comp. Stat. Ann., § 36–2A–41 (Supp. 1957); Colo. Corp. Stat. of 1958, § 34, Colo Sess. Laws 1958, S.B. 14; Iowa Rev. Code 1958, tit. 19, § 491.34; N.D. 1943 Rev. Code, § 10–1936 (Supp. 1957); Ore. Rev. Stat., § 47.180; Va. Code Ann., § 13–1–35 (Supp. 1956). Alabama and Connecticut also have adopted this provision of § 33 of the Model Act, except that Connecticut provides for negation of the directors' power in the bylaws rather than the Articles [See Ala. Rev. Code of 1958, § 21(24) (Supp. 1959); Conn. Gen. Stat. Ann., § 33–313 (1960)]. Indiana has a similar provision [Ind. Stat. Ann., § 25–208 (1960)]. See also N.Y. Bus. Corp. Law, § 713(c) which adopts this provision and adds to § 33 of the Model Act "for services in any capacity." The report of the New York Joint Legislative Committee to Study Revision of Corporation Laws states that the statute changes the law of New York by authorizing directors to fix their own compensation, since under present law no such authority exists unless first given by certificate of incorporation or bylaw provision. See *Supplement to Fourth Interim Report to 1960 Session of New York Legislature,* Legislative Doc. No. 15, p. 47 (1960).

[213] Jennings, *supra* note 197, at 201–02, criticizes this failure, with its result of leaving the self-interest problem to common law rules and to broad exculpatory clauses commonly inserted in charters and bylaws.

Some states have attempted specifically to legislate on the subject of self-interest. The broadest attack on the problem is that of the California statute which does not deal with compensation in terms but rather with the effect of self-interest of a director. The California law [214] provides that no corporate transaction in which a director is interested is void or voidable because such director is present at the meeting which authorizes the transaction, or because his vote is counted for this purpose, if the fact of the director's interest is disclosed or known and the transaction is approved in good faith by sufficient votes of disinterested directors or by sufficient votes of disinterested stockholders, or if the "contract or transaction is just or reasonable as to the corporation at the time it is approved"; it is provided that the interested director may be counted for the purpose of determining the presence of a quorum at the meeting which authorizes the transaction.[215]

North Carolina, which in this respect has modeled its statute [216] upon that of California, has the additional provision that in the case of services as a director or as an officer or employee "the standard of what is 'just and reasonable' is what would be paid for such services at arm's length under competitive conditions." [217]

A somewhat more limited approach to the problem of contracts with an interested director does away with the "void" or "voidable" body of case law by providing that the fact of interest will not of itself invalidate a transaction; the burden of establishing the validity of the questioned transaction is cast upon the party asserting validity.[218]

[214] ANN. CAL. CORP. CODE, § 820. See Caminetti v. Prudence Mutual Life Ins. Ass'n, *supra* note 12, which, in construing this section in a proceeding involving the compensation of a director and stockholder, held that when the interested party participated in the fixing of his own compensation, he was entitled to just and reasonable compensation, despite failure to comply with the requirement of approval by disinterested directors or stockholders. In this context, the question of what is just and reasonable becomes in effect one of *quantum meruit* with the burden of proof on the claimant.

[215] CAL. CORP. CODE, § 820.

[216] N.C. GEN. STAT., § 55–30 (1960). The first portion of the North Carolina statute [§ 55–30(a)] was taken from the MODEL ACT but is more explicit in that it spells out that a board of directors may compensate directors "for their services as directors, salaried officers or otherwise." The second subsection [§ 55–30(b)] corresponds to § 820 of the California Corporation Code with changes largely designed to protect minority stockholders; also, it explicitly imposes on the claimant the burden of proving that the transaction was just and reasonable at the time it was entered into or approved. The New York Business Corporation statute, in dealing with self-interest, was based upon the California law; it also incorporates § 33 of the MODEL ACT. See N.Y. BUS. CORP. LAW, § 7B. See also Everett v. Phillips, 288 N.Y. 277 (1942).

[217] N.C. GEN. STAT., § 55–30(b)(3) (1960).

[218] See MICH. STAT. ANN., § 21.13, subd. 5 (1937); VT. STAT. ANN., tit. 11, § 105 (1958) (but requiring that the contracting director not be present).

Several states have dealt with the particular question of self-interest in fixing compensation by spelling out in a specific statutory provision that the board of directors, with the affirmative vote of a majority of the directors then in office and irrespective of the personal interest of its members, may fix reasonable compensation for all directors for services as directors, officers, or otherwise.[219] One statute which has adopted this approach also provides that the board of directors may provide reasonable pensions and other benefits to directors, officers, and employees, and to their estates, families, dependents, or beneficiaries on account of prior services to the corporation.[220]

On the question of stockholder approval of executive compensation, the main area of legislative activity has been that of stock options for directors and officers. A variety of statutory patterns has emerged. The Model Act has an optional provision,[221] adopted in some states,[222] which requires that options issued to directors, officers, or employees be approved by a majority of the outstanding voting stock. A requirement of stockholder approval, sometimes accompanied by a right of appraisal for dissenting stockholders, had existed in some statutes antedating the Model Act.[223]

---

[219] ILL. STAT. ANN., ch. 32, § 157.33 (Supp. 1959); OHIO CODE ANN., tit. 17, § 1701.60 (Supp. 1959); WIS. STAT. ANN., § 180.31 (1957).

[220] WIS. STAT. ANN., § 180.31 (1957).

[221] MODEL ACT, § 18A (1957 ADDENDUM).

[222] See COLO. CORP. ACT OF 1958, § 19, COLO. LAWS 1958, S.B. 14; IOWA CODE ANN., tit. 19, § 496A.19 (Supp. 1959); N.D. 1943 Rev. CODE, § 10–1917 (Supp. 1957). The failure of most states which have followed the MODEL ACT to adopt this optional section may be explained by the fact that the section was promulgated in 1955 (see MODEL BUS. CORP. ACT ANN., § 18A, ¶ 4) after these states had adopted the MODEL ACT. Virginia, although following the MODEL ACT in many respects, has adopted a requirement that sales of stock and options to directors, officers, and employees be approved "in accordance with the authorization of the articles of incorporation or by a resolution of the stockholders." See VA. CODE ANN., § 13.1–17 (1956). This variation from § 18A thus permits the requirement of stockholder approval to be negated in the corporate charter. For adverse criticism, see Emerson, *supra* note 198, at 505–07. For a contrary view, see Gibson, *The Virginia Corporation Act of 1956,* 42 VA. L. REV. 445, 448 (1956).

[223] N.Y. STOCK CORP. LAW, § 14 (1951) (requiring approval of a majority of shares in connection with a plan for the issuance of stock to employees and giving dissenting stockholders a right of appraisal); N.J. REV. STAT., §§ 14:9–1, 14:9–2, 14:9–3 (1939) (requiring approval by a two-thirds vote of the stockholders, but providing that the procedure for adoption of plans for the issue or purchase and sale of stock to employees may be varied by provisions in the original articles of incorporation or in the original bylaws and giving a right of appraisal only to dissenting stockholders having stock issued prior to April 15, 1920). The requirement of these states as to stockholder approval is to be distinguished from requirements in states where such approval is necessary only in connection with extinguishing pre-emptive rights. See notes 229 ff. *infra* and accompanying text. The New York Business Corporation Law, effective April 1, 1963, *supra* note 196, abolishes all

North Carolina, whose corporate statute has been commended for innovations in the interest of minority stockholders,[224] requires that a majority of all outstanding voting shares of stock approve a stock option plan for a group of employees. The statute has a special provision applicable to a case in which "it is planned that 10% or more of shares being issued or optioned are to go, directly or indirectly to directors, or dominant stockholders"; in such a case the statute requires either that the issuance of the options be approved by two-thirds of the outstanding stock or be issued only after making a pre-emptive offer to the holders of the common stock.

On the other hand, some statutes, though providing for the issuance of employee stock options, have no requirement for stockholder approval unless the articles of incorporation provide for pre-emptive rights.[225] Under these statutes, the effect of the action of the board of directors is particularly important. The provision included in statutes patterned upon the Model Act,[226] as well as those of other states,[227] makes the judgment of the board of directors conclusive as to the adequacy of the consideration received for stock options.[228]

---

rights of appraisal on the part of dissenting stockholders but requires stockholder approval of a plan for the sale of stock to officers, directors or employees, such approval to be in the form of a vote or written consent of all shares entitled to pre-emptive rights; a similar approval of such a plan is required of stockholders entitled to vote even though they may not be entitled to pre-emptive rights. N.Y. BUS. CORP. LAW, §§ 505(d), 622(e). See Supplement to Fourth Interim Report to 1960 Session of the New York State Legislature, *supra* note 212, at 24–25. Such stockholder approval was required by the prior New York statute. N.Y. STOCK CORP. LAW, § 14.

[224] N.C. GEN. STAT., § 55–45(c) (1960). See Jennings, *supra* note 197. The North Carolina statute also contains a provision [§55–45(b)], apparently unique, that requires, in the case of a grant of an option for the purpose of securing or retaining the services of an employee, that either the option price be not less than 150% of the market price or that the action of the board of directors be authorized by a special resolution adopted by a majority stockholder vote, with any shares held by the employee not counted.

The North Carolina statute also provides [§55–16(a)(3)] that "no by-law authorizing compensation to officers measured by the amount of a corporation's income or volume of business shall be valid after five years unless renewed by the vote of the holders of a majority of the outstanding shares regardless of limitation on voting rights." See discussion in text to note 222, *supra*.

[225] CAL. CORP. CODE, §§ 397, 1107; PA. STAT. ANN., §§ 2852–611, 2852–612 (1952); OKLA. STAT. ANN., tit. 18, §§ 1.45, 1.47 (1953). See also IND. ANN. STAT., § 25.205(i) (1960) (no specific provision concerning the sale of shares to employees, but provision denying pre-emptive rights unless specifically granted). In Massachusetts, there are no pre-emptive rights as to shares of business corporations. MASS. ANN. LAWS, ch. 156, § 41 (1959).

[226] See MODEL ACT, § 18A and statutory provisions cited in note 222 *supra*.

[227] See DEL. CODE, tit. 8, § 157 (1953); MONT. REV. CODE ANN., § 15–801(10) (B) (1955); N.Y. STOCK CORP. LAW, § 69, N.Y. BUS. CORP. LAW, § 505(g), *supra* note 196.

[228] Provisions making director judgment conclusive on the value of stock options are similar to those making the judgment of the board of directors conclusive

Stockholder approval of an employee stock option plan may be required as the result of state law governing stockholders' pre-emptive rights.[229] The Model Act provides [230] for the existence of pre-emptive rights not only as to unissued shares but as to treasury shares, unless the articles of incorporation are to the contrary; in the case of a sale of shares to officers or employees of a corporation or of a subsidiary, it is provided that the corporation may make the sale without first offering the shares to its shareholders if the terms are approved by the holders of two-thirds of its voting stock. Except for the reference to treasury stock, this section of the Model Act is sub-stantially the same as an earlier Illinois statutory provision.[231] Pro-visions of this type which release pre-emptive rights upon approval of two-thirds of the shareholders have been adopted in a number of jurisdictions; [232] in some, the requirement is reduced to the vote of a simple majority.[233] Delaware has no statutory provision for the re-

---

as to the value of consideration received on the issuance of stock. See § 18 of the Model Act which contains such a provision, as do numerous state statutes. E.g., DEL. CODE ANN., tit. 8, § 152 (1952). The Delaware statute which makes the judgment of the board of directors conclusive as to consideration for the issuance of stock (without reference to stock options) was held inapplicable to consideration for executive stock options in Gottlieb v. Heyden Chemical Corp., cited *supra* note 41. Following this decision, the Delaware stock option section (§ 157) was amended to make the board's judgment conclusive as to the consideration received for stock options. 49 DEL. L. CH. 315, § 6, eff. July 8, 1953. The provision seems inapplicable to options granted before its enactment. See Beard v. Elster, *supra* note 116 (deal-ing with pre-1953 options and not citing statute); Bennett v. Breuil Petroleum Corp., 99 A.2d 236, 240 (Del. Ch. 1953). For the background of this provision, see *Making Stock Options Stand Up,* BUSINESS WEEK, Aug. 8, 1953, p. 99. For the view that this type of statute is of limited application, see Steadman, *Executive In-centive Arrangements,* 13 VAND. L. REV. 311, 336 (1959). In a case applicable to options granted after the enactment of the statute, the action of a board of directors was upheld on the ground that the board was disinterested, but without citing the statute. See Forman v. Chester, *supra* note 116.

[229] For a detailed discussion of the rules as to pre-emptive rights, see Volume II, Chapter 10. CONSULT MODEL BUS. CORP. ACT ANN., § 24 (1960), and Ford, *Share Characteristics Under the New Corporation Statutes,* 23 LAW & CONTEMP.. PROB. 264, 270–72 (1958).

[230] MODEL ACT, § 24.

[231] ILL. STAT. ANN., ch. 32, § 157.24 (1954).

[232] In addition to the Illinois statute, *ibid.,* see ALASKA COMP. STAT. ANN., § 36–2A–24 (Supp. 1957); TEX. CIV. STAT., art. 2.22, subd. D (1956); MD. ANN. CODE, art. 23, § 30(b)(7) (1957); N.D. REV. CODE, § 10–1924 (Supp. 1957); ORE. REV. STAT., § 57.136 (1955); D.C. CODE, § 29–907j (Supp. 1959).

[233] See COLO. CORP. ACT OF 1958, § 25; COLO. SESS. LAWS 1958, S.B. 14, as amended, SESS. LAWS 1959, ch. 83, § 5 (with provision permitting sale to directors, officers, and employees without stockholder approval as part of a concurrent sale of shares to the public or the shareholders when not more than 10% of the stock is being sold to the public or the shareholders and the price is not less than that of the concurrent offering); IOWA CODE ANN., § 496A.19 (1960 Supp.); LA. REV. STAT. ANN., § 12.28B (1950); MICH. STAT. ANN., § 21.24 (1937); OHIO CODE ANN., tit. 17, §§ 1701.15H, 1701.16, 1701.17 (Supp. 1959); PA. STAT. ANN., tit. 15, § 2852–612

lease of pre-emptive rights in connection with a sale of stock to employees but the result can be accomplished, according to a decision of the Chancery Court, by an amendment to the certificate of incorporation releasing the pre-emptive rights for the shares to be sold; such an amendment requires only a majority vote.[234]

In some states, pre-emptive rights are of less importance because of statutory provisions that such rights do not exist except as provided in the articles of incorporation.[235] A revision in 1955 [236] added to the Model Act an alternative version of the pre-emptive rights section which adopts this view.[237]

The Model Act and state legislation patterned upon it mark an important step in clarifying the need for and effect of stockholder approval of executive compensation. Although criticized in some quarters as not going far enough in requiring stockholder approval,[238] the legislation, representing the considered thought of an important segment of the corporate bar, does require or at least suggest the need for such approval in many contexts.

(1952); VA. CODE ANN., § 13.1–23 (1956). Prior to the adoption of the Business Corporation Law (effective April 1, 1963), *supra* note 196, the New York statute required that a plan for the sale of stock to employees receive approval by a majority vote of stockholders, whether or not pre-emptive rights existed, and gave dissenting stockholders a right of appraisal. N.Y. STOCK CORP. L., § 14. See also *infra* note 237 and accompanying text. The Business Corporation Law, which is applicable to existing as well as newly organized corporations [§ 103 (c)], continues the requirement of stockholder approval but abolishes the right of appraisal (see note 223, *supra*); pre-emptive rights generally continue to exist, unless otherwise provided in the certificate of incorporation, but such rights do not apply to shares issued or optioned under a plan providing for rights or options to purchase shares by officers, directors, or employees. N.Y. BUS CORP. L., § 622(3)(2). When pre-emptive rights exist, the adoption of the plan requires a majority vote of all shares having pre-emptive rights even though they do not otherwise have a right to vote. *Id.,* § 505(d).

[234] Gottlieb v. Heyden Chemical Corp., *supra* note 41.

[235] See statutes cited note 225 *supra.*

[236] MODEL ACT, § 24. See Ford, note 229 *supra.*

[237] See MODEL ACT, alternative § 24.

[238] See articles cited *supra* note 198.

CHAPTER 9

THE OUTSIDE DIRECTOR AND HIS REWARDS

In recent years there has been a noticeable trend toward paying outside directors fixed salaries and the practice, although by no means general, is now followed by a substantial number of business corporations.[1] While monetary rewards to directors have in the past been small, there has been a tendency to increase these rewards to more substantial figures, with a few leading companies paying from $10,000 to $15,000 a year.[2]

[1] A survey of the practices of 262 manufacturing companies made by the National Industrial Conference Board in 1960 showed that 39% of the companies in the survey paid fixed salaries (termed "retainers"). This is an increase over the 36% figure which was reported in 1958. See Mathes and Thompson, *Director's Compensation and Retirement,* 17 NICB Bus. Rec. 15 (Apr. 1960). A 1946 study showed that 20% of reporting companies followed the practice; only 3.6% did so in 1938. See Dickson, Compensation and Duties of Corporate Directors, NICB Studies in Business Policies No. 16, at 6 (1946). See also Fortune, Dec. 1933, p. 10, for the results of a still earlier survey.

Practices vary among different industries. A survey made by the NICB in 1958, which distinguished between practices in different kinds of business, showed that about 30% of the manufacturing industries surveyed paid regular salaries, 70% of the public utilities paid salaries, but no commercial banks reported their use. For transportation companies, the percentage was 30%; for merchandising companies, 20%; for insurance companies, 16%. See Ethe and Pegram, Corporate Directorship Practices, NICB Studies in Business Policies No. 90, at 29, 48 (1959).

Inside directors do not generally receive additional compensation for service on the board of directors. Mathes and Thompson, *supra,* at 16 (3 out of 4 companies paid no extra compensation to inside directors; of 76 companies that did, 5 out of 6 paid inside and outside directors alike).

[2] The Conference Board reported that in 1958 more than half of the manufacturing companies which followed the practice of paying salaries to directors paid $2,400 or more; the survey showed that manufacturing companies paid the largest amounts and that the amounts varied widely in other industries. See Ethe and Pegram, *supra* note 1, at 29 and Tables 19–23. In a 1960 survey confined to manufacturing companies, the Conference Board reported that two directors of a chemical company received retainers of $15,000 each. Ten companies reported an increase in the amount of retainers since 1958, while only one reported a reduction. See Mathes and Thompson, *supra* note 1, at 15. *Cf.* Smith, *Put the Board of Directors to Work!* 37 Harv. Bus. Rev. 41, 48 (May-June, 1958) (referring to flat compensation paid by some companies "in the range of $10,000 to $20,000," with compensation unrelated to number of meetings attended). The 1946 survey showed that of 2,089 directors in that survey more than one-half received less than $500. See Dickson, *supra* note 1, Table 19.

Outside directors may be called on for intensive work. Thus, from August 31 to October 27, 1960, TWA's fourteen outside directors, paid at the rate of $100 a meeting plus expenses, met a dozen times with one meeting lasting two days and a later meeting lasting six days. See N. Y. Times, Oct. 27, 1960, p. 52, col. 2.

Nevertheless, the prevalent custom is still to give directors a fee for each meeting attended.[3] The average amount of the director's regular meeting fee increased from $20 in 1933 [4] and $50 in 1946 [5] to $100 in 1960.[6] A substantial percentage of companies which pay salaries to directors also pay a regular meeting fee.[7] Directors who serve on committees sometimes receive additional fees or other compensation for attending committee meetings.[8] Other methods of compensating outside directors do not have wide currency.[9] Most companies reimburse directors for expenses incurred in attending meetings; [10] some grant flat expense allowances.[11] It is unusual for outside directors to be included in supplemental employee benefit plans.[12]

The pecuniary reward offered the outside director is usually not sufficient in itself to induce him to accept the responsibilities of a

[3] This was the case in three-fourths of the companies surveyed in 1960, a fraction that did not vary substantially from the 1958 survey. See Mathes and Thompson, *supra* note 1, at 16.

[4] See FORTUNE, Dec. 1933, p. 10.

[5] See DICKSON, *supra* note 1, at 6.

[6] The Conference Board survey in 1960 showed that only 6% of the reporting companies paid less than $50; of the balance, 45% paid $100 while 17% paid $50. Mathes and Thompson, *supra* note 1, at 15.

[7] This percentage was estimated at 45% in the 1958 survey and at about 33⅓% in the 1960 survey. See ETHE AND PEGRAM, *supra* note 1, at 29, 48; Mathes and Thompson, *supra* note 1, at 15.

[8] This practice was followed by one-third of the reporting companies in the 1960 survey and the most common fee was $100 per committee meeting. Mathes and Thompson, *supra* note 1, at 16. Incentive compensation and stock option plans sometimes provide for the payment of compensation to members of the committee which administers the plan.

[9] The tontine form of paying directors, with a fixed sum for each meeting which is divided among directors actually present, has now fallen almost completely into disuse. The survey in 1946 showed that 7 out of 535 companies followed this practice (DICKSON, *supra* note 1, at 7) ; the 1958 survey indicated that it was used by only 4 out of 470 manufacturing companies. ETHE AND PEGRAM, *supra* note 1, at 29. One of the companies reporting in the 1958 survey made the compensation of directors contingent upon profits. *Id.* at 50. For participation by directors in group insurance and pension plans, see text to notes 53 ff. *infra.*

[10] This was true of 75% of the companies covered by the 1960 survey. See Mathes and Thompson, *supra* note 1, at 16.

[11] *Ibid.*

[12] See text to notes 53 ff. *infra.* Including group life insurance, in which directors sometimes participate, the 1958 survey reported that such participation took place in less than 10% of all covered companies; group life insurance, reported in about 6% of the cases, was the prevalent type of benefit. See ETHE AND PEGRAM, *supra* note 1, at 50. In a 1956 survey, one company reported participation by outside directors in the company's retirement plan but "only to the extent that they are also active in other work for the company, such as the performance of consultant services." Baker and Thompson, *Corporate Directors' Pay Up Moderately*, 13 NICB BUS. REC. 1, 17 (July 1956).

director.[13] The director seems originally to have been thought of as simply a representative stockholder, perhaps one whose stock interest in the corporation was so large that he might be expected to give special attention to the corporate affairs. While this incentive is still important in small, closely held corporations operated by those who have not supplied the capital, it is not usually present in other corporations. Directors generally hold relatively few shares in the corporation which they are managing.[14] This tendency, a result of the current divorce of management from ownership, may be deplored,[15] but it can hardly be checked unless the law makes substantial shareholdings a necessary prerequisite to directorships.[16] A counteracting

[13] ". . . with the present tax structure that we have, the average man that you'd want is a highly successful individual and his present tax bracket would make those few thousand dollars that you're talking about, or even ten or twenty, completely inconsequential, or relatively so." BROWN AND SMITH, THE DIRECTOR LOOKS AT HIS JOB 134 (1957).

[14] See Gordon, *Stockholdings of Officers and Directors in American Industrial Corporations*, 50 Q.J. ECON. 622, 651 (1935–36) ; Atwood, *No Formula for Choosing Good Corporation Directors*, 24 PUB. UTIL. FORT. 595, 601 (1939). The 1958 survey by the National Industrial Conference Board showed that of 420 manufacturing companies, about one-fourth reported that none of their outside directors was the owner or representative of a sizable block of stock ; approximately one out of three of the outside directors was found to be or to represent a substantial stockholder. ETHE AND PEGRAM, *supra* note 1, at 16 and Table 8. The same relationship was found to exist in the case of 153 non-manufacturing companies. *Id.* at 19–20 and Table 12. See GILBERT AND GILBERT, *op. cit. infra* note 15.

[15] See GILBERT AND GILBERT, TWENTY-FIRST ANNUAL REPORT OF STOCKHOLDER ACTIVITIES AT CORPORATION MEETINGS DURING 1960, 153 *passim* (1959) (listing companies whose directors owned less than 25 shares or no common stock). For statements to the effect that stock ownership by directors is unimportant and conceivably disadvantageous to the company, see ETHE AND PEGRAM, *supra* note 1, at 17.

[16] At common law, directors were not required to be stockholders. 2 FLETCHER, CYC. CORP. § 299 (perm. ed. 1954). The ownership of stock for qualification as a director is required in a few states, chiefly in the West. E.g., MONT. REV. CODE, § 15–401 (1947) ; WYO. STAT., § 17–12 (1959). An Eastern state with this requirement is New Jersey, N.J. ANN. STAT., § 14:7–2 (1939). However, the minimum requirement is nominal and generally is set by the corporate charter or bylaws. A large minority of states, including such important incorporation states as California, Delaware, New York, and Texas, have no such requirement or allow it to be negated by the corporate charter or bylaws. E.g., N.Y. STOCK CORP. LAW, § 55; N.Y. BUS. CORP. LAW, §§ 701, 1401 (eff. Apr. 1, 1963). The Model Business Corporation Act, which has been adopted in whole or in part in a number of states (see Chapter 8, text to notes 197 ff.), provides that the directors of a corporation need not be stockholders unless its articles of incorporation or the bylaws so require. MODEL BUS. CORP. ACT ANN., § 33 (1960). Some states have stricter qualifications for directors of banking corporations than for other business corporations. Compare NEB. REV. STAT., § 21–112 (1954) with §§ 8–118 (requiring bank director to hold from $500 to $1,000 worth of stock, depending on the size of bank's capital) ; and N.Y. STOCK CORP. LAW, § 55 with N.Y. BANKING LAW, § 116 (requiring bank director to hold minimum of 10 shares with $1,000 par value). Only 4 out of 479

trend may be found in stock option, bonus, and purchase plans, which encourage the acquisition of stock by executives, but the average outside director, who is generally not a participant in such plans,[17] does not now look to dividends as an adequate return for his services. Supplementing, and perhaps surpassing, any monetary rewards offered by an outside directorship, are the intangible benefits attached to the position.

INTANGIBLE BENEFITS

Intangible incentives to serve on a board of directors usually result from the social and business prestige that may be derived from membership on the board. If the corporation is large and flourishing with a board of directors of high social and business standing, membership on the board may be sought after in much the same way as membership in an exclusive club and may bring with it appreciable advantages to the individual. Business advantage may take many forms, ranging from trivial perquisites to business opportunities.[18] Through membership on its board, a director may be in a position to furnish to the company underwriting, legal, or other services, or to supply materials or products used in the company's business. Which of these advantages a director is entitled to take, and which he must reject, is something which business morality has decided with varying degrees of definiteness during different eras in our economic history, subject to the ultimate control of the courts and the legislatures. It would seem that the standards observed by the business community have, in general and in the vast majority of cases, been reason-

---

manufacturing companies covered by the 1958 survey of the National Industrial Conference Board required their directors to own more than 100 shares; as to non-manufacturing companies, in almost all states an applicable state or federal statute required ownership of certain minimum par value of stock. No other required stock-holdings were found to exist except for the occasional nominal statutory requirement of one share. See ETHE AND PEGRAM, *supra* note 1, at 16–17, 20.

[17] See note 12 *supra.*

[18] For a discussion of the reasons why individuals act as directors, see RUML, TOMORROW'S BUSINESS 76, 80 *et seq.* (1945). Consult Fuller, *Restrictions Imposed by the Directorship Status on the Personal Business Activities of Directors,* 26 WASH. U.L.Q. 189 (1941); Maurer, *Boards of Directors,* FORTUNE, May 1950, p. 107, 108. Consult also BROWN AND SMITH, *supra* note 13, at 146–47: "Five chief inducements to individuals to take on the duties of directors were considered to be compensation, prestige of membership on certain boards, the high value attaching to personal associations with men and women of outstanding ability, personal interest in the work of the company, and the broadening of individual experience gained by insight into the workings of another company. None of these can be said to be more effective than any other. All must be relied on."

ably on a par with the standards set at any particular time by the law.[19]

Commencing in the 1930's legal standards have been appreciably raised and restrictions imposed upon the conduct of directors.[20] Standards of fiduciary obligation have reached a higher level.[21] Criticism of this trend seems in general to have been directed not so much at the moral standards set as at the real or supposed threat that liability will be inflicted on technical grounds quite apart from actual negligence or intentional breach of duty. As to our present problem, it seems sufficient to say that the outside director cannot expect to find his reward in the abuse of his position as director, nor does the average director seek to get his reward in that way.

Another form of reward, similar in many ways to those just discussed, is that which derives from control.[22] There is the power of

[19] For a discussion of corporate ethics involved in transactions by directors with their companies, see Wall Street Journal, Sept. 30, 1960, p. 1, col. 6 (discussing, *inter alia*, a tax transaction involving the sale to Georgia Pacific Corporation, by one of its directors, of timberland purchased by him for the purpose of such sale, the transaction having been motivated by tax considerations).

As the result of the discovery in 1960 that the president of Chrysler Corporation had a substantial interest in a supplier of that corporation, public attention was focused on the matter of conflicts of interest, but primarily on the part of employees rather than directors. See Wall Street J., Apr. 20, 1961, p. 20, col. 3 (Colonial Sand & Stone Co., Inc.) ; *id.,* p. 28, col. 1 (routine question at AT&T stockholders meeting) ; *id.,* Apr. 28, 1961, p. 1, col. 6 (discussion of corporate ethics). Consult FUCHS and THOMPSON, OUTSIDE BUSINESS INTERESTS OF KEY EMPLOYEES, 17 NICB BUS. REC., No. 11, p. 28 (Nov. 1960). For the Chrysler Corporation story, see N. Y. Times, July 22, 1960, p. 1, col. 2; Wall Street J., p. 5, col. 1; *id.* April 18, 1961, p. 1, col. 1. Consult Opinion of October 3, 1961, rendered to a Special Committee of the Board of Directors of Chrysler Corporation by Dewey, Ballantine, Bushby, Palmer & Wood (expressing opinions, *inter alia,* on the effect of gifts to, and entertainment of, executives by suppliers).

[20] An important factor in this development was the requirement under the Securities Exchange Act of 1934 that proxy statements used in soliciting proxies for stock registered on a national securities exchange disclose the amount of any material interest of any director in any material transactions since the beginning of the company's fiscal year or in any material proposed transactions. See 15 U.S.C. § 78n (1958) ; 17 C.F.R. § 240.14a-3 (Supp. 1960) and Schedule 14A, Item 7 (f).

[21] "The principles and practice of big business in 1959 seem to me considerably more responsible, more perceptive, and (in plain English) more honest than they were in 1929. The methods, morals, and social education of the leaders of big business actually seem to have improved substantially in a generation." Berle, *Foreword* to MASON, THE CORPORATION IN MODERN SOCIETY at xiii (1960).

[22] For discussions of the problem of "control," see BERLE AND MEANS, THE MODERN CORPORATION AND PRIVATE PROPERTY 69-70 (1932) ; BUREAUCRACY AND TRUSTEESHIP IN LARGE CORPORATIONS 19-20, 21 (TNEC Monograph 11, 1940); Taylor v. Standard Gas Co., 306 U.S. 307 (1939) ; Matter of H. M. Byllesby & Co. and the Byllesby Corp., 6 S.E.C. 639 (1940) ; Daimler Co. v. Continental Tyre & Rubber Co., [1916] 2 A.C. 307. For more recent discussions of the problem of control, see BERLE, THE TWENTIETH CENTURY CAPITALIST REVOLUTION (1954);

patronage—the semi-political power which is enjoyed through the opportunity to add people to the company's payroll, or at least to use one's influence in getting them added. There is the power which comes from the possibility of granting a contract to Mr. A rather than to Mr. B, so that the corporation will obtain its supplies from the former rather than from the latter.[23] We are not speaking now of transactions which would be in any sense describable as fraudulent or corrupt. We are speaking of situations in which the corporation will be positively benefited by dealing with Mr. A rather than with Mr. B. The director's exercise of power in such situations is directly beneficial to the company, but it may also be beneficial to the director himself—perhaps by directly or indirectly obtaining business for his own enterprise from Mr. A, perhaps by increased importance in the community, perhaps in other ways.

In dealing with this type of reward the law has not yet made its attitude entirely clear.[24] Many banking houses and brokerage firms have sought to have their representatives placed on the directorates of large corporations even when there was no immediate prospect that the corporation would issue new securities or would even hire a particular firm as underwriters. These banking houses have sought

---

LIVINGSTON, THE AMERICAN STOCKHOLDER (1958) ; MASON, *supra* note 21, and, in particular, Rostow, *To Whom and for What Ends Is Corporate Management Responsible?*, THE CORPORATION IN MODERN SOCIETY, 46 ff. (1960).

[23] See note 19 *supra* and related text.

[24] When the only benefit that the director may derive is not of a nature which can be measured in terms of money, the test which will be applied is doubtful. It may be that in such a situation the corporation or its stockholders will have no remedy. But in transactions involving a measurable financial benefit to the director, a majority of the courts, as in self-dealing in connection with compensation contracts (see Chapter 8, text to notes 48 ff.), attach significance not only to the fiduciary relation between the director and his corporation and its stockholders, but also to other factors: whether in approving the transaction, the board of directors acted in good faith with full knowledge of the facts; whether the transaction is fair from the corporation's standpoint; and whether the corporation was in fact represented in the transaction by directors other than the interested director in the sense that a majority of the board had no personal interest in the transaction; whether the presence of the interested director was necessary to make a quorum; or whether the interested director dominated other directors or presided at the meeting at which the vote was taken. E.g., Pepper v. Litton, 308 U.S. 295 (1939) ; Seagrave Corp. v. Mount, 212 F.2d 389 (6th Cir. 1954) ; Spirt v. Bechtel, 232 F.2d 241 (2d Cir. 1956) ; Bayou Drilling Co. of Texas v. Baillio, 312 S.W.2d 705 (Tex. Civ. App. 1958) ; Gauger v. Hintz, 262 Wis. 333, 55 N.W.2d 426 (1952), (dealing with usurpation of corporate opportunity) ; Liebman v. Auto Strop Co., 241 N.Y. 427, 150 N.E. 505 (1926). *Cf.* Johnston v. Greene, 121 A.2d 919 (Del. 1956), *reversing* Greene v. Allen, 114 A.2d 916 (Del. Ch. 1955). See generally 3 FLETCHER, *op. cit. supra* note 16, §§ 930-39 and cases cited; Note, 66 YALE L.J. 611 (1957) ; Note, 53 MICH. L. REV. 472 (1955) ; Note, 61 HARV. L. REV. 335 (1948) ; Berle, *Corporate Powers as Powers in Trust,* 44 HARV. L. REV. 1049 (1931).

directorships for reasons more remote and indirect. In many instances where they have been connected with issuance of the company's securities, they request representation on the board to protect the interests of the security holders to whom they consider themselves responsible and thereby to protect their own reputation and position in the financial community. Others have sought, and have been rewarded with, power.[25] The situation is very similar to that of a politician seeking office: the power involved may be his primary motivation. Such power-seeking need in no sense be corrupt. The traditional system of directors who receive only modest fees at best [26] has encouraged—or at least not discouraged—the man who seeks a directorship solely for the power it confers.

THE MOVEMENT FOR PAID FULL-TIME DIRECTORS

From time to time, arguments have been advanced in support of a system of "professional" directors: full-time within one organization or "well paid directors serving on boards of several non-competing organizations holding no executive position and representing no particular group." [27] Justice William O. Douglas, when he was chairman of the Securities and Exchange Commission, was an active proponent of such a system. "If directors are to perform their duties, honestly, efficiently and constructively," he said, "they should get paid for their work in proportion to the actual contributions made by them." [28] Similar recommendations have been made by some business leaders.[29]

[25] Out of 2,466 outside directors sitting on the boards of 431 manufacturing companies in 1958, occupations were represented in the following order: bankers, attorneys, corporate presidents, retired businessmen. Other occupations included consultants, insurance executives, and educators. ETHE AND PEGRAM, *supra* note 1, at 18–19, Table 9. Out of 2,037 outside directors sitting on the boards of 180 non-manufacturing companies, the largest single group represented was corporate presidents, followed by bankers, industrialists, and attorneys. *Id.,* at 21, Table 13. Women were found on only a small minority of the boards studied, chiefly when representing a substantial block of stock. *Id.* at 18. The failure to select women is a source of frequent complaint by the Federation of Women Shareholders in American Business, Inc.

[26] See text to notes 1, 2, and 13 *supra.*

[27] Dickson, *supra* note 1, at 18. See also *id.* at 4, 17–20.

[28] DOUGLAS, DEMOCRACY AND FINANCE 46, 47 (1940).

[29] See Paterson, *Wanted: Directors Who Direct,* N. Y. Times, Jan. 21, 1940 (Magazine) p. 6. *Cf.* Ruml, *Corporate Management as a Locus of Power,* address to American Bar Ass'n on Sept. 19, 1950 (suggesting four paid director-trustees, one each to represent the interests of customers, vendors, and employees, and the fourth to be selected by the remaining directors). A "public director" may be sought when there is conflict between management and an organized group of stockholders as in the case of the Segal Lock & Hardware Company. See N. Y. Times, Aug. 28, 1950, p. 25, col. 6 and 7.

Precedent for paid professional directors is found in the English system of compensating directors.[30] Opinions have varied as to the merits of the English system. On the one hand, it is claimed that it has created a class of "guinea pig" directors who are willing to lend their names for an annual stipend.[31] On the other, it is said by proponents of the system in the United States that a higher standard of service is produced.[32] The system of professional directors has not, however, taken root in the United States to any appreciable extent.[33]

State legislation sometimes authorizes the election of employee representatives to the corporate board of directors.[34] Although this practice is found in Western European countries, no corresponding pattern is discernable in this country and the idea has been adversely criticized.[35]

The enormous increase in the size of American corporations, which has given corporate management greater power and responsibility, often amounting practically to autonomy, has led to other suggestions for changing the character of corporate boards of directors. It has been suggested that the voting power should be taken from stockholders and that members of management should be treated as trustees subject to supervision by a new agency, governmental or non-governmental.[36] Suggestions of this nature have implications for management and control so far-reaching as to change the very

---

[30] In Swabey v. Port Darwin Gold Mining Co., 1 Megone 385 (C.A. 1889), each director received £200 per annum; in Salton v. New Beeston Cycle Co., [1899] 1 Ch. 775, aggregate of £5,000 per annum for all directors; in Inman v. Ackroyd & Best, Ltd., [1901] 1 K.B. 613, £125 per annum; in Diamond v. English Sewing Cotton Co., [1922] W.N. 327, £500 per annum. See also SAMUEL, SHAREHOLDERS' MONEY 121 (1933).

[31] See SAMUEL, *supra* note 30. Also see SPECTATOR, Aug. 24, 1951, p. 244.

[32] DOUGLAS, *supra* note 28, at 51.

[33] ETHE AND PEGRAM, *supra* note 1, at 18–19, state with reference to the prevalence of the "professional director" in a wide range of manufacturing and non-manufacturing corporations as of 1958:

The professional director is not represented to any real extent on the boards of corporations participating in the study. . . .

There is considerable resistance to the introduction of the career-type director in this country. Most company officials feel that the alleged advantages of professional directorships can be secured without the drawbacks which, they claim, would accompany such an innovation.

[34] See N.J. REV. STAT., § 14–9–1(d) (1937); MASS. ANN. STAT., ch. 156, § 23 (1959).

[35] See Blair, *Appraising the Board of Directors*, 28 HARV. BUS. REV. 101, 106 (Jan. 1950); Chayes, *The Modern Corporation and the Rule of Law*, THE CORPORATION IN MODERN SOCIETY 25, 41 (1960). Consult GILBERT AND GILBERT, *op. cit. supra* note 15, at 265.

[36] See Manning, *Review of The American Stockholder by J. A. Livingston*, 67 YALE L.J. 1477, 1490–91 (1958). Consult Rostow, *supra* note 22, at 56 ff.

basis of the corporate enterprise and at least at this juncture in our development seem highly theoretical. That such suggestions are put forward at all by thoughtful students of corporate practices, however, constitutes evidence that an unsolved problem does exist.

Outside v. Inside Directors

While the desirability of such proposals is largely in the realm of theory, the extent to which the board of directors should comprise individuals other than the company's own executives is a matter of debate and controversy. As a matter of practice, the trend appears to be towards greater use of outside directors.[37]

Officer boards are criticized on the grounds that the stockholders are not sufficiently represented, that outside views and the experience gained in other lines of business will not be made available, and that the officers may be tempted to reward each other too generously in the matter of salaries and bonuses.[38] In the case of an all-officer board, it is also said the president of the company is in effect given complete authority because of his control over his fellow directors.[39] Perhaps more fundamentally, it is argued that since it is the function of the board of directors to supervise management, it is too much to expect management to supervise itself.[40] Proponents of the inside board contend that it functions more expeditiously and efficiently because all its members have a more intimate knowledge of the prob-

[37] In the 1958 study of the National Industrial Conference Board, outside directors comprised a majority of the boards in 57% of the manufacturing companies surveyed and the percentage of outside directors increased from about 51% to more than 54% in the five-year period between 1953 and 1958. The preponderance of outside directors in non-manufacturing industries appears to be even more marked: Outside directors constituted a majority of the boards in 85% of non-manufacturing companies and this figure was well over 90% for banks, insurance companies, public utilities, and transportation companies. In companies of this type, employee directors constituted, according to this survey, 25% of the total number of directors as against 46% in the case of manufacturing companies. ETHE AND PEGRAM, *supra* note 1, at 16, 19. See *Managers Fade as Directors*, BUSINESS WEEK, June 27, 1959, p. 72.

[38] For an expression of stockholder viewpoints, see GILBERT AND GILBERT, *supra* note 15, at 152–55.

[39] See Rostow, *supra* note 22, at 46, 51; Smith, *supra* note 2, at 42.

[40] JACKSON, CORPORATE MANAGEMENT § 57 (1955). Consult, generally, COPELAND AND TOWL, THE BOARD OF DIRECTORS AND BUSINESS MANAGEMENT (1947); BAKER, DIRECTORS AND THEIR FUNCTIONS (1945); PALMER, *The Outside or Non-Management Director; What Shall He Look For in His Company?*, TRENDS IN MANAGEMENT-STOCKHOLDER RELATIONS (1960). Consult also MACE, THE BOARD OF DIRECTORS IN SMALL CORPORATIONS (1948). Presumably in connection with its conflict of interest problems, Chrysler Corporation in 1961 reduced the number of its employee-directors up for election so that outside directors would be in the majority. See Wall Street Journal, Apr. 19, 1961, p. 30, col. 1–2.

lems that come before it,[41] that outside directors do not have time to read even the material sent them in advance of meetings,[42] and that, in practice, the outside directors are dominated by the inside directors and, in particular, by the chief executive.[43]

The majority views the desideratum as the achievement of a balanced board, with representation by both inside and outside directors.[44] Views as to what this balance should be vary with different types of business activity. Proponents of cumulative voting argue that it results in a more balanced board.[45]

Between the two categories of inside and outside directors is the retired executive who is retained as a member of the board of directors and sometimes as a consultant. Such a director may have a deferred compensation contract which requires him to render these services; he is not subject to management control, although he will, of course, have closer ties to management than an unrelated outside director. The value of such a director to the board stems from his accumulated experience in management. It is notable, however, that an increasing percentage of companies has adopted policies of compulsory retirement for both management and outside directors,[46] with

[41] "Full-time directors, devoting their entire efforts to the Company's interests, can, in the Board's opinion, deal more effectively with the constant flow of intricate and far-reaching problems and serve the stockholders as they are entitled to be served. First-hand knowledge of the Company's business interests and its organization and personnel, derived from daily association with them, is essential for a director in this Company, with its complex and world-wide interests."
Standard Oil Co. of New Jersey, Proxy Statement for Annual Meeting on May 27, 1959, p. 15.
[42] Cf. BROWN AND SMITH, supra note 13, at 40.
[43] Id. at 45.
[44] See JACKSON, op. cit. supra note 40, § 59.
[45] The principal argument for cumulative voting, however, is that, in permitting minority representation, it promotes democracy in corporations. See GILBERT AND GILBERT, supra note 15, at 163 ff. Management is united in opposition to cumulative voting on the grounds, among others, that it would foster group loyalties and promote disharmony. Consult Whetten, Cumulative Voting for Directors, ATL. ECON. REV., Apr. 1959, p. 13; WILLIAMS, CUMULATIVE VOTING FOR DIRECTORS (1951).
[46] Mathes and Thompson report in their survey of manufacturing companies made in 1960 that 21% of the reporting companies have such policies and that a number of companies reported that they had adopted this policy since 1958. Mathes and Thompson, supra note 1, at 16. The 1958 survey had reported that among manufacturing companies, 14% provide for compulsory retirement of employee directors and 10% provide for compulsory retirement of outside directors. Slightly higher percentages had such policies among non-manufacturing companies. ETHE AND PEGRAM, supra note 1, at 23. In the 1960 survey, the retirement age was 70 in over 50% of the companies and 72 in another 28%. Mathes and Thompson, supra, at 17. Consult ABRAMS, AGE RESTRICTIONS ON DIRECTORS OF AMERICAN CORPORATIONS, GOOD NEWS FOR LATER LIFE 75 (1958) (of 80 national companies, 80% had no age barriers).

the retirement age of the latter group usually fixed somewhat higher than the former.[47]

A further question which goes beyond that of the proper balance between inside and outside directors on a particular board of directors is the relationship between outside directors and management.[48] The outside director is someone chosen for his knowledge and experience—often in a specialized field such as finance or corporate law—which will enable him to appraise the solutions by management of the internal and external problems of the company. He need not have operating experience in the company's particular field but he should understand the broad aspects of the problems of the company. It is not the outside director's function to solve operating problems but to be able to judge objectively how these problems are being handled by management. For the discharge of this function, management must be responsible for the preparation of significant information in a form that will enable the outside director to understand the problems of the company and to judge the progress of the company in its particular field.

LEGAL ASPECTS OF COMPENSATION TO DIRECTORS

What special legal problems are presented by payment of compensation to directors? From the strictly legal point of view, the difficulty with respect to such compensation is to find a source of authority to fix it. Who is to adopt the plan, and who is to fix the amount of pay? If the directors do so themselves, they will face criticism on the ground of self-dealing. Some jurisdictions, as we have seen in an earlier chapter, go so far as to say that a contract between a director and his company, not passed by a disinterested vote, is "void"; others speak of it as "voidable." [49] In line with this reasoning, we find a number of statements to the effect that directors have no power to grant each other compensation for their services as directors, unless there is some provision in the charter, statutes, or bylaws, or a resolution of a disinterested board, permitting them to do so.[50] In other words, the directors can compensate a member of

---

[47] See Mathes and Thompson, *supra* note 1, at 17.

[48] Consult JACKSON, *op. cit. supra* note 40, § 31–34a6.1; PALMER, *op. cit. supra* note 40; SMITH, *supra* note 2.

[49] See Chapter 8, text to notes 58 ff.

[50] 5 FLETCHER, *op. cit. supra* note 16, §§ 2109, 2110 and cases cited; STEVENS, CORPORATIONS § 162 (2d ed. 1949); Savage v. Lorraine Corp., 217 F.2d 378 (9th Cir. 1954); Beacon Wool Corp. v. Johnson, 331 Mass. 274, 119 N.E.2d 195 (1954); Flight Equipment & Engineering Corp. v. Shelton, 103 So.2d 615 (1958); Cahall v. Lofland, 12 Del. Ch. 299, 114 Atl. 224 (1921), aff'd, 13 Del. Ch. 384, 118 Atl. 1 (1922); Godley v. Crandall & Godley Co., 212 N.Y. 121, 131, 105 N.E. 818 (1914);

the board for his services as an officer or employee; they should leave to the stockholders the question of compensating directors for their services as such.

Case law has resulted in state legislation in a number of jurisdictions specifically authorizing the board of directors to fix the compensation of directors for their services as such.[51] In the absence of legislation, the safe course would be to have the compensation of directors approved, at least in general terms, by the stockholders. The disclosure required by federal securities legislation, although usually applicable only to compensation of officers and directors in the aggregate,[52] should give some protection against criticism. If the compensation voted to directors is more than nominal, the amount should be properly disclosed to stockholders, even when legislation authorizes the board to fix the compensation of its own members. Such, however, has not been general practice.

PARTICIPATION IN EMPLOYEE BENEFIT PLANS

As we have noted, it is not usual for outside directors to participate in employee benefit plans. Under the Internal Revenue Code, outside directors, since they are not "employees," [53] cannot participate in plans entitled to favorable tax treatment, such as qualified pension, profit-sharing and stock bonus plans,[54] restricted stock options,[55] and health and accident plans.[56] The favorable tax treatment accorded such plans is limited to employees. The same may be true for group life insurance,[57] although in practice outside directors have been included under group insurance policies.

To enable outside directors to participate in employee benefit plans, companies have occasionally conferred on them employee

---

Kalmanash v. Smith, 291 N.Y. 142, 51 N.E.2d 681 (1943); Polychronis v. Palace Meat & Grocery Co., 102 Utah 201, 129 P.2d 879 (1942). As to tax aspects, see Brampton Woolen Co. v. Com'r, 45 F.2d 327 (1st Cir. 1930).

[51] See Chapter 8, text to footnotes 212 ff.

[52] See Schedule 14A to SEC Reg. X-14, Item 7.

[53] See Treas. Reg. § 31.340(c)–1(f) (1957). Cf. note 12 supra, and connected text.

[54] INT. REV. CODE OF 1954, § 401. Cf. text to note 12, supra.

[55] Id. § 421. Outside directors might, however, be given unrestricted stock options.

[56] INT. REV. CODE OF 1954, §§ 105, 106.

[57] See Treas. Reg. § 1.61–2(d)(2) (1960), providing that "premiums paid by an employer on policies of group term life insurance covering the lives of his employees are not gross income to the employees, even if they designate the beneficiaries." It is questionable whether this provision would apply to non-employee directors.

status by making them members of management committees or part-time officers of the corporation or a subsidiary.[58] In a corporation in which, as a result of state legislation or otherwise, directors are not permitted to participate in a group insurance plan for employees, a supplemental insurance plan confined to directors may sometimes be installed. It is also possible to instal a separate retirement plan or formulate a separate retirement policy for directors and, in connection with compulsory retirement, there is a movement towards retirement pay for outside directors with long service.[59]

[58] *Cf.* Webb & Knapp, Inc., Proxy Statement for Special Meeting on July 26, 1955, p. 5 (Billy Rose granted option for 825,000 shares of common stock and elected vice-president, with permission "to carry on his usual activities in connection with the management and operations of the Ziegfeld Theatre and various realty and other personal interests"). See Webb & Knapp, Inc., Annual Report for 1958, p. 27 ("On February 25, 1959, Mr. Rose's employment was terminated for cause and such stock option has expired by its terms. Mr. Rose is contesting such termination and the status of his stock option in pending litigation with Webb & Knapp, Inc.")

[59] Consult KINSLEY AND THOMPSON, TENURE AND RETIREMENT OF DIRECTORS, 18 NICB BUS. REC., No. 5, at 30, 34 (May, 1961) (none of 205 firms surveyed provided directors with retirement income in the form of a pension as such, but retired directors received income when elected to honorary status or when retained as consultants). Occasionally, retired employees continue to share in profit-participation or profit-sharing plans. See KNOWLTON, PROFIT SHARING PATTERNS, Nos. 261, 286 (1954).

The Model Business Corporation Act authorizes as a corporate matter participation by directors in pension, profit-sharing and similar plans. See Chapter 8, text to notes 205–06.

APPENDIX

CORPORATE DOCUMENTS *

APPENDIX CONTENTS

Authors' Note. The contracts and plans set forth in the Appendix are deemed useful examples of draftsmanship and of corporate practice. They include a few that are no longer in effect selected to illustrate passages in the text.

GENERAL EMPLOYMENT CONTRACTS

APPENDIX A

FAIRBANKS, MORSE & CO.

CONTRACT WITH ROBERT H. MORSE

MEMORANDUM OF AGREEMENT made this 23 day of January, 1946, between FAIRBANKS, MORSE & CO., a corporation with its principal office at Chicago, Illinois (hereinafter called the Company), party of the first part, and ROBERT H. MORSE, party of the second part, WITNESSETH:

That the Company hereby agrees to employ the said party of the second part for a term of five (5) years, commencing on January 1, 1946, and terminating on December 31, 1950, as its General Manager with authority to manage and control all of its operations and to hire and discharge and fix the compensation of all of its employees, excepting the officers thereof elected from time to time by its Board of Directors.

During such term, said party of the second part agrees as General Manager to use his best endeavor, judgment, and energy to promote, improve, and advance the business and interests of the Company.

The Company agrees to pay said party of the second part for such services an annual salary of seventy-five thousand dollars ($75,000.00), such salary to be paid in equal monthly installments on the first day of each month during the term of employment.

In witness whereof the said party of the first part has caused this agreement to be executed in its corporate name by its proper officers, appointed by the Board, thereunto duly authorized, and its corporate seal to be attached, and said party of the second part has attached his hand and seal, all in duplicate, as of the day and date first above written.

FAIRBANKS, MORSE & CO.
By R. H. MORSE
President
S. T. KIDDOO
Vice Pres. & Treasurer
L. A. KEELER
Vice Pres. & Comptroller
C. H. POPPENHUSEN
Director

COMMITTEE
OF
THE
BOARD

(CORPORATE SEAL)
Attest:
E. T. SANDEEN
Assistant Secretary

Accepted:

ROBERT H. MORSE   (SEAL)

APPENDIX B

United States Rubber Company

CONTRACT WITH FRANCIS B. DAVIS

AGREEMENT dated as of January 1, 1938, by and between United States Rubber Company, a corporation organized and existing under the laws of New Jersey (hereinafter called the "Company"), party of the first part, and Francis B. Davis, Jr., of the City and State of New York (hereinafter called "Davis"), party of the second part;

Witnesseth :

Whereas, on or about January 15, 1929, Davis was elected Chairman of the Board of Directors and President of the Company and has since been in the employ of the Company in such capacities; and

Whereas, Davis, as Chairman of the Board of Directors and President of the Company, has operated, developed and expanded the business of the Company with conspicuous success and has assumed the responsibilities and is performing the duties of Chairman of the Board of Directors and President of the Company, to the great satisfaction of the Board of Directors of the Company; and

Whereas, the Board of Directors of the Company believe that the services of Davis in the future would be of great value to the Company and are desirous of retaining his services for a period of years and Davis has indicated his willingness to enter into an agreement upon the terms herein set forth, and

Whereas, Davis is eligible for rights or benefits under or participation in any bonus, profit-sharing, stock purchase or other plans or plan which at any time may have been or may hereafter be adopted by the Company for the payment of additional compensation or benefits to employees of the Company; and

Whereas, the execution by the Company of this contract has been authorized and approved by resolution adopted by the required number of the stockholders of the Company at the annual meeting held pursuant to due notice on April 19, 1938,

273

Now, Therefore, in consideration of the premises and of the mutual promises and agreements herein contained, the parties hereto agree as follows:

1. The Company hereby employs Davis and Davis hereby agrees to serve the Company in continental United States for the period of six years beginning January 1, 1938 and ending December 31, 1943, in an important managerial or executive capacity with such duties as may be assigned to him from time to time by the Board of Directors of the Company as constituted during such period, it being the expectation that Davis will continue to act as Chief Executive Officer of the Company. Said term of employment shall be subject to extension at the option of the Company from time to time for one or more periods but not beyond December 31, 1948, without the consent of Davis, and the Company shall, three months prior to the beginning of any extended term, give written notice to Davis of any election by it to extend the term of employment.

2. Davis shall devote all of his time and services exclusively to the business of the Company during the term of this Agreement. Davis shall enter into or conduct no other business and shall perform the duties of his office and those assigned to him by the Board of Directors of the Company with fidelity and to the best of his ability.

3. As entire compensation for his services: (a) The Company hereby agrees to pay Davis and Davis hereby agrees to accept from the Company, a yearly salary of $150,000. beginning January 1, 1938 and continuing during the period of actual service under this Agreement, such yearly salary being payable in equal monthly installments; (b) if the services of Davis under this agreement shall continue to December 31, 1943, the Company shall thereafter pay to Davis a retirement allowance of $75,000.00 a year, in equal monthly installments, from the beginning of his retirement upon the termination of his employment (as extended or not, as the case may be, and whether or not such termination shall be due to his becoming permanently incapacitated), to the end of his life, subject however, to termination by the Company in the event that Davis should engage, before or after retirement, in any commercial activity incompatible with the interests of the Company; or, (c) if the services of Davis under this Agreement shall not continue to December 31, 1943, due to his becoming permanently incapacitated, the Company shall pay to Davis a retirement allowance in an amount per year equal to that proportion of $75,000.00 which the period beginning January 1, 1938 and ending with his ceasing active service to the Company due to such incapacity, shall bear to the period from January 1, 1938, to Decem-

ber 31, 1943, such amount to be paid in equal monthly installments, from the beginning of such incapacity and retirement to the end of his life, subject, however, to termination by the Company in the event that Davis should engage, before or after retirement, in any commercial activity incompatible with the interests of the Company.

4. In consideration of the foregoing, Davis hereby agrees that during the term of this Agreement, except as herein otherwise in this Agreement mentioned, he shall be ineligible for rights or benefits under or participation in any bonus, profit-sharing, stock-purchase, or other plan or plans for the payment of additional compensation or benefits (other than Group Insurance) to employees of the Company which at any time may have been or may hereafter be adopted by the Company; and further, Davis shall, and hereby does, waive all unexercised rights which he may have under the Managers' Shares Plan of the Company to purchase shares of common stock of the Company in respect of any amounts which have been credited to the trustees under said Managers' Shares Plan.

5. Davis hereby retains any and all rights to purchase common stock of the Company under the option which was granted to him by the Agreement between the Company and him dated February 5, 1936, the Company hereby agreeing that by the execution of this Agreement, said Davis does not thereby surrender up to the Company his said rights under said option but said presently existing option shall and does hereby remain in full force and effect according to the terms and conditions set forth in said Agreement of February 5, 1936, and Davis shall also remain eligible and does not waive eligibility to participate from time to time in the Stock Option Plan of the Company as the same may from time to time be amended or revised.

6. At all times after his retirement from active service hereunder, Davis will hold himself available to the Company for general advice and consultation.

7. The parties hereto agree for themselves and for their respective heirs, administrators, executors, successors and assigns, that all disputes and differences arising out of the interpretation, construction or performance of this contract shall be settled and finally determined in the City of New York by arbitration pursuant to the Arbitration Law of the State of New York, as follows: Each party shall appoint an arbitrator. If the two arbitrators so appointed are unable to agree within thirty days after their appointment, they shall select a third arbitrator. The decision in writing of the three arbitrators, or of any two of them, shall be final and binding upon the parties to the arbitra-

tion, and the parties hereto agree that judgment may be entered in the Supreme Court of the State of New York upon any decision or award so rendered. If either party fails to appoint his arbitrator within thirty days after notice in writing requiring him to do so, the arbitrator appointed by the other party shall act for both, and his decision in writing shall be final and binding upon all parties to the arbitration, as if he had been appointed by consent. Each party shall pay the expenses of the arbitrator chosen by him and shall pay one half of the expenses of any third arbitrator who may be chosen hereunder.

8. This Agreement cancels as of January 1, 1938, the terms of employment of Davis by the Company set forth in any previous agreement entered into by Davis and the Company.

IN WITNESS WHEREOF the parties hereto have executed this Agreement as of the day and year first above written.

UNITED STATES RUBBER COMPANY
By ERIC BURKMAN
Secretary
F. B. DAVIS, JR. (L.S.)

Attest:
O. W. GREINER
Assistant Secretary

[N.B. *The deferred compensation provisions of this contract should be compared with those of a later contract reproduced as App. HH.*]

APPENDIX C

COLUMBIA BROADCASTING SYSTEM, INC.

CONTRACT WITH FRANK STANTON

AGREEMENT between COLUMBIA BROADCASTING SYSTEM, INC. (hereinafter called "Columbia"), a corporation organized and existing pursuant to the laws of the State of New York and having its principal office at 485 Madison Avenue, New York 22, New York, and FRANK STANTON (hereinafter called "Stanton"), of 25 East 83rd Street, New York 28, New York.

WITNESSETH :

1. Stanton has been in the employ of Columbia since October 14, 1935, and has been since January 9, 1946, and is now, the President of Columbia.

2. Columbia and Stanton desire that Stanton shall (a) continue in the employ of Columbia on a full-time basis for an additional period and (b) after the termination of such period shall perform advisory and consultative services on a part-time basis for Columbia and its wholly owned subsidiary corporations.

3. The Board of Directors of Columbia has authorized the execution and delivery to Stanton of an agreement providing for such employment and such advisory and consultative services on the terms hereinafter set forth.

Now, THEREFORE, in consideration of the foregoing premises and the mutual covenants hereinafter contained, Columbia and Stanton hereby agree as follows :

FIRST: A. Columbia hereby employs Stanton as a senior executive of Columbia for the period (hereinafter called "the employment period") commencing as of January 2, 1949 and, except as otherwise provided in part B of this Article FIRST, ending on December 31, 1958, and Stanton hereby accepts such employment and agrees to perform such services as a senior executive of Columbia as shall from time to time be reasonably assigned to him by Columbia's Board of Directors, and, except during usual vacation periods and reasonable periods of illness or other incapacitation and except to the extent reasonably required for the supervision of his own investments, to

277

devote his entire time and attention to the business of Columbia during the employment period.

B. Columbia may terminate the employment period as of any date subsequent to December 31, 1953 by giving Stanton not less than 30 days' prior notice of such termination and by paying the sum of $100,000 to Stanton on or prior to the date of termination specified in such notice, and, in such event, the employment period shall terminate on the date specified in such notice.

C. Columbia shall pay to Stanton, and Stanton shall accept from Columbia, for Stanton's services provided for in part A of this Article FIRST (i) compensation at the rate of $100,000 per annum, which shall be payable on the last day of each calendar week during the employment period, and (ii) if Columbia's Board of Directors in its sole and absolute discretion shall so determine, such additional compensation (either under any plan or plans adopted pursuant to the authority heretofore granted by Columbia's Stockholders, or under any other bonus or additional compensation plan or plans, or otherwise) as Columbia's Board of Directors shall so determine, which shall be payable at such time or times and in such manner or manners as Columbia's Board of Directors shall so determine. Stanton acknowledges receipt from Columbia of payments at the rate above provided for the period from January 2, 1949 to the date of the execution and delivery of this Agreement.

SECOND: A. Columbia hereby retains Stanton to perform, and Stanton hereby agrees to perform, during the period (hereinafter called "the consultative period") commencing on the first business day after the termination of the employment period (whether the same shall terminate on December 31, 1958 or on any earlier date pursuant to a notice given by Columbia as provided in part B of Article FIRST hereof) and ending on December 31, 1968, such advisory and consultative services on a part-time basis for Columbia and its wholly owned subsidiary corporations as Columbia's Board of Directors or senior executives shall from time to time request, subject to the conditions that (1) such services shall be performed in such place or places within the United States of America as Stanton shall from time to time specify, (2) Stanton shall not be required to devote a major portion of his time to the performance of such services and (3) Stanton shall not be required to perform such services during usual vacation periods and reasonable periods of illness or other incapacitation.

B. Columbia shall pay to Stanton, and Stanton shall accept from Columbia, for Stanton's services provided for in part A of this Article SECOND, compensation at the rate of $25,000 per annum, which shall be payable on the last day of each calendar week during the consultative period.

THIRD: Stanton agrees that, unless Columbia shall consent thereto, he will not at any time during either the employment period or the consultative period engage in any activity which, at the time of his entering upon such engagement, shall be competitive with any business then carried on by Columbia or by any other corporation directly or indirectly controlled by Columbia. Stanton shall be free, however, without such consent, to purchase, as investment or otherwise, stocks or other securities of any corporation which shall have any security listed upon any recognized securities exchange.

FOURTH: All notices and consents given under this Agreement shall be in writing, and, if given by Stanton, shall be addressed to Columbia at its address hereinbefore set forth, or at any other address of which it shall have given notice to Stanton in the manner provided in this Article FOURTH, for the attention of any of its officers other than Stanton, and shall be delivered to such officer by hand or mailed to Columbia by registered mail, and, if given by Columbia, shall be addressed to Stanton at his address hereinbefore set forth, or at any other address of which he shall have given notice to Columbia in the manner provided in this Article FOURTH, and shall be delivered to Stanton by hand or mailed to him by registered mail.

FIFTH: In the event that Columbia, or any corporation resulting from any merger or consolidation referred to in this Article FIFTH, shall at any time be merged or consolidated into or with any other corporation or corporations or in the event that substantially all of the assets of Columbia shall be sold or otherwise transferred to another corporation, the provisions of this Agreement shall be binding upon and inure to the benefit of the corporation resulting from such merger or consolidation or to which such assets shall be so sold or transferred; this Agreement shall not be assignable by Columbia or by any corporation resulting from any such merger or consolidation or to which such assets shall be so sold or transferred, except to the continuing corporation in or the corporation resulting from, and as an incident of, any such merger or consolidation or to the corporation to which such assets shall be so sold or transferred and as an incident of such sale or transfer. This Agreement shall not be assignable by Stanton.

SIXTH: Stanton's rights under the pension plan of Columbia as now in effect shall not be diminished by the payments to be made to Stanton by Columbia under this Agreement.

SEVENTH: This Agreement shall be construed in accordance with the laws of the State of New York.

IN WITNESS WHEREOF Columbia has caused this Agreement to be executed by one of its officers thereunto duly authorized and its corporate seal to be hereto affixed and attested, and Stanton has hereto subscribed his name and affixed his seal, this 18th day of April, 1949.

COLUMBIA BROADCASTING SYSTEM, INC.
By WILLIAM S. PALEY
Chairman of the Board

Attest:
JULIUS F. BRAUNER

FRANK STANTON   (L.S.)

APPENDIX D

Wm. Filene's Sons Company

CONTRACT WITH HAROLD D. HODGKINSON

1. THIS AGREEMENT executed in Boston, Massachusetts, on this first day of June, 1944, by Wm. Filene's Sons Company, a Massachusetts corporation, hereinafter referred to as "the Employer" and Harold D. Hodgkinson, of Boston, Massachusetts, hereinafter referred to as "the Employee."

2. The expression "employment period" as hereinafter used means the period beginning with June 1, 1944 and ending at the close of December 1949, or at the time of the death of the Employee, whichever first occurs.

3. The Employer hereby employs the Employee to act as a Manager of the Employer's business for the employment period and agrees to pay to the Employee compensation for said employment and services rendered thereunder as follows:

A. During the employment period and subject only to the provisions of the succeeding subparagraph B hereof the sum of five thousand (5,000) dollars monthly.

B. If at any time during the employment period the Employee shall concede, or a reputable physician (who may be chosen by the Employee) shall certify to the Employer that the Employee is incapacitated from actively participating in the management of the Employer's business, and that such incapacity is likely to continue for not less than six (6) months, the Employee shall thereafter until the end of the employment period, or until the Employer shall concede, or a reputable physician (who may be chosen by the Employee) shall certify to the Employer that such incapacity has terminated, whichever event first occurs, receive payment at the rate of $2,083.33 per month instead of at the rate provided in the preceding subparagraph A.

C. If the parties hereto do not, prior to the expiration of the employment period, enter into a contract in writing for the Employer's employment of the Employee for a further period, and if the Employee shall during the calendar year 1949 have offered to the Employer to enter into a contract (in the form hereto attached marked "A," which offer the Employer shall have declined) then the Employee shall after the expiration of the employment period receive payment at the rate of $2,083.33 per month as long as it shall be the fact (but not after any time when it shall not be fact) that the Employee:

(a) is still living, and

(b) is not engaged in the conduct or management of any business of substantial size, nor in any employment which yields the Employee substantial compensation, and

(c) does not have in any competing business an aggregate investment resulting from his having advanced on loan or contributed to capital or expended for the purchase of shares of stock or of an interest in such shares or in a business or having expended in one or more of the ways aforesaid a sum or sums amounting in the aggregate to not less than five hundred thousand (500,000) dollars, and

(d) is neither an officer nor a director of a corporation, nor a member of a partnership, which conducts a competing business, nor the proprietor of a competing business.

D. "Competing business" as above used means a business which is conducted in whole or in part in one or more of the following States, to wit: Ohio, New York, New Jersey and the New England States, and is not conducted by any of the following corporations, to wit: Federated Department Stores, Inc., Wm. Filene's Sons Company, Abraham & Straus, Inc., The F. and R. Lazarus and Company, Bloomingdale Bros., Inc., the R. H. White Company, The John Shillito Company, or a subsidiary of any of the foregoing, but is in whole or in part substantially similar to such business, or to some substantial part of such business, as now is, or at the end of the employment period shall be, conducted by one or more of said corporations.

E. Except as above provided, the Employee shall not be deemed to be engaged in the conduct or management of a business merely by reason of his having an investment in the business or of his being a director of the corporation which conducts it.

F. If the Employer shall during the calendar year 1949 have requested the Employee to enter into a contract for the Employer's employment of the Employee in the form hereto attached marked "A" and the Employee shall have declined to enter into such contract, then, in lieu of the provision for the payment at the rate of $2,083.33 per month in the preceding subparagraph numbered C, the amount to be paid to the Employee shall be at the rate of $1,041.66, but in other respects the provisions of the preceding paragraphs numbered C, D and E shall apply.

G. From and after the time when the employment period shall have terminated both under this contract and under any renewal or extension thereof so that the Employee shall cease to be actively employed in the business of the Employer and the Employee shall also cease to be entitled to receive any payments under paragraph C or paragraph F hereof, the Employer shall thereafter pay to the Employee and his executors and administrators in the installments hereinafter set out an aggregate sum determined by multiplying fifteen thousand (15,000) dollars by the number of years that the Employee shall, after June 1, 1944, have continued in the active employment of the Employer and at that rate for a fractional part of a year; provided that said aggregate sum shall not exceed seventy-five thousand (75,000) dollars. Said aggregate sum determined as aforesaid shall be paid to the Employee and his executors or administrators in one hundred and twenty (120) equal monthly installments.

4. The Employee agrees that during the employment period

(1) he will faithfully and in conformity with the directions of the Employer's Board of Directors perform the duties of his employment hereunder, which duties (as the Employer agrees) shall be of substantially the same character as those which he has performed for the Employer during the year immediately preceding the employment period; and that he will devote to the performance of his said duties all such time and attention as they shall reasonably require, taking, however, from time to time (as the Employer agrees that he may) reasonable vacations;

(2) he will not become actively associated with or engaged in any businesses other than those of the corporations hereinabove named, and he will no nothing inconsistent with his duties to the Employer.

5. The Employer agrees that during the employment period the Employee shall be allowed reasonable traveling expenses and shall be furnished office space and accommodations suitable to the character of his position with the Employer and adequate for the performance of his duties hereunder.

6. This agreement supersedes, cancels and annuls any and all previous contracts, arrangements or understanding between the parties hereto with respect to the employment of the Employee.

In Witness Whereof the parties hereto have hereunto and to a duplicate hereof set their signatures, on the day and year first above written, the Employer by Lincoln Filene its President thereunto duly authorized by its Board of Directors.

> Wm. Filene's Sons Company
> By Lincoln Filene
> Its President
> Harold D. Hodgkinson

―――

[N. B. The Agreement marked "A" attached to the preceding contract is the same as the foregoing contract except for the omission of subdivision "F" of paragraph 3.]

APPENDIX E

FAIRCHILD ENGINE AND AIRPLANE CORPORATION

CONTRACT WITH J. CARLTON WARD, JR.

AGREEMENT dated May 9, 1940, as amended April 30, September 17, 1942, February 22, 1944, and April 1, 1948, between FAIRCHILD ENGINE AND AIRPLANE CORPORATION, a Maryland corporation (hereinafter called the Corporation), and J. CARLTON WARD, JR., of Hartford, Connecticut (hereinafter called Ward).

In consideration of the mutual agreements hereinafter set forth the parties hereto have agreed, and do hereby agree, as follows:

1. The Corporation hereby employs Ward to perform the services and to discharge the duties of President of the Corporation, or, if at any time during the term hereof he shall cease to be President of the Corporation, to perform such services and duties of an executive character, in an office or position of comparable dignity, as shall be assigned to him by the Board of Directors of the Corporation. Such employment shall extend for a period beginning not later than October 1, 1940, and continuing until terminated in the manner provided in paragraph 8 hereof.

2. Ward accepts the employment specified in paragraph 1 hereof for the term therein specified and for the compensation hereinafter provided for and, during such employment, will devote his entire time, energy and skill to the service of the Corporation and the promotion of its interests and will not engage in any business competing with or of a character similar to the business of the Corporation nor take part in any activities detrimental to the best interests of the Corporation.

3. As compensation for the services to be rendered to the Corporation by Ward under this Agreement, the Corporation will make the following payments to Ward during the term of his employment hereunder:

(a) a minimum salary of Fifty Thousand Dollars ($50,000) per year, payable in equal semi-monthly installments, and, in addition,

(b) an amount equal to 4% of the annual net income of the Corporation (as hereinafter defined) during each year or portion thereof

285

of such employment, payable not later than March 1 of each year beginning March 1, 1941, or as soon thereafter as the annual net income of the Corporation may be determined.

4. The term "annual net income of the Corporation" as used herein shall mean the consolidated net earnings of the Corporation and its subsidiaries during the fiscal year available for dividends on its capital stock, as determined by the annual audit of the independent public accountants regularly employed by the Corporation, after deducting:

(a) all taxes applicable to the year in question;

(b) all compensation payable to officers of the Corporation and its subsidiaries including the amounts payable to Ward under this Agreement, for such year or any part thereof;

(c) provision for amortization of development costs, it being understood that all development costs which heretofore have been, or hereafter prior to the termination of Ward's employment hereunder shall be, capitalized, and all other development costs not previously charged off, shall be charged against the earnings of the Corporation during the years 1941 through 1943, inclusive; and

(d) the amount of all dividends paid during the year in question on all stock representing additional capital invested in the Corporation after April 1, 1948.

In determining the annual net income of the Corporation for the purposes of this Agreement, there shall be excluded any capital gains and capital losses, and there shall not be deducted the amount of any reserves for contingencies, post-war adjustments and the like, set up by the Corporation while the United States is at war, whether out of earnings or surplus, until such reserves shall be applied in whole or in part to costs or expenses which would normally be treated as proper charges against income. The decision of the independent public accountants regularly employed by the Corporation with respect to any accounting question relating to the determination of such net income shall be conclusive upon the Corporation and Ward. The amounts of such net income payable to Ward hereunder in respect of part of any fiscal year of the Corporation shall be in the same proportion to the entire net income for such year as such part of a year bears to the full year.

5. Ward will use his best efforts to commence his employment hereunder by not later than October 1, 1940, but if his employment shall not have commenced by such date, the Corporation may elect, upon fifteen (15) days' notice to Ward (given in writing or by tele-

graph or cable), to terminate this Agreement, and upon such termination Ward shall be under no further obligation to the Corporation.

6. All inventions, improvements, processes and devices made, discovered or developed by Ward during the term of his employment hereunder which may be directly or indirectly useful in, or which relate to, the design and manufacture of aircraft or aircraft engines or parts thereof, shall be the property of the Corporation, and upon request Ward shall surrender to the Corporation all drawings, sketches, models and other data and records relating to such inventions, improvements, processes and devices. Upon the request and at the expense of the Corporation, Ward will make application in due form for United States letters patent and foreign letters patent on, and will assign to the Corporation all his right, title and interest to, said inventions, improvements, processes and devices, and will also execute any instruments necessary or which the Corporation may deem desirable in connection with any continuations, renewals or reissues of such letters patent or in the conduct of any proceedings or litigation in regard thereto.

7. Nothing in this Agreement contained shall prevent the consolidation of the Corporation with, or its merger into, any other corporation, or the sale by the Corporation of all or substantially all its properties or assets, or the assignment by the Corporation of this Agreement and the performance of its obligations hereunder to any subsidiary or affiliated corporation; and this Agreement shall, subject to the provisions of this paragraph, inure to the benefit of, and be enforceable by, any corporate successor to or assignee of, the Corporation.

8. (a) Ward's employment hereunder shall terminate on December 31, 1957, subject, however, to earlier termination if any of the following events shall first occur:

(i) Ward's death or disability, for physical or mental causes, to continue his employment under this Agreement; or

(ii) a determination by the Board of Directors of the Corporation that Ward shall have failed duly and faithfully to perform his obligations under this Agreement; or

(iii) a determination by Ward that, by reason of his physical or mental condition, it is advisable for him to retire; or

(iv) a determination by Ward that, by reason of a major change in the management of the Corporation, he will be unable to work harmoniously and effectively with the new management of the Corporation;

provided, however, that not less than ninety days' written notice shall be required for termination of Ward's employment pursuant to (ii), (iii) or (iv) above; and provided further that, notwithstanding any other provision of this Agreement, the Corporation shall have the right, with or without cause, to terminate Ward's employment hereunder at any time upon one year's written notice to Ward.

(b) In consideration of the services to be rendered by Ward before and after the termination of his employment hereunder, the Corporation shall, beginning with the date of such termination, pay to Ward, as deferred compensation, in substantially equal semi-monthly installments, the sum of Thirty-two thousand five hundred dollars ($32,500) per year, either

(i) for the remainder of his life, if such termination shall occur either on December 31, 1957, or earlier by reason of his complete disability or pursuant to (a) (iii) above or to the Corporation's right to terminate upon one year's notice; or

(ii) for the next ensuing 10 years, if such termination shall occur pursuant to (a) (ii) or (iv) above.

(c) If Ward's employment hereunder shall have been terminated by reason of his death, or for any other reason and Ward shall have died before receiving deferred compensation payments for a period of 10 years, such payments shall be made or continued to his wife, if and so long as she shall survive him, until the total amount of such payments to Ward and his wife shall aggregate Three hundred and twenty-five thousand dollars ($325,000).

(d) Ward agrees, and the Corporation's obligation to pay deferred compensation to Ward under the provisions of this paragraph 8 is subject to the condition, that after the termination of his employment hereunder and during all periods in which he shall be entitled to receive such deferred compensation, Ward

(i) shall not engage in any business competing with or of a character similar to the business of the Corporation nor take any part in any activities detrimental to the best interests of the Corporation;

(ii) shall continue to comply with the provisions of paragraph 6 of this Agreement relating to inventions, patents and the like; and

(iii) shall render such consultant services to the Corporation as may be reasonably requested by the Corporation from time to time.

(e) Notwithstanding any of the provisions of this paragraph 8, no deferred compensation shall be payable to Ward if and so long as he is in the regular fulltime employ of the Corporation and receiving compensation for such employment.

(f) The deferred compensation payable to Ward or to his wife under the provisions of this paragraph 8 shall be reduced by the amount, if any, which may be distributable to either of them at any time under any pension or similar retirement plan of the Corporation which may hereafter be adopted.

(g) The deferred compensation payable under the provisions of this paragraph 8 shall not be subject in any manner to anticipation, alienation, sale, transfer, assignment, pledge, encumbrance or charge, and any attempt so to anticipate, alienate, sell, transfer, assign, pledge, encumber or charge the same shall be void; nor shall such compensation be in any manner liable for, or subject to, the debts, contracts, liabilities, engagements or torts of Ward or of his wife.

(h) In view of its obligations under this paragraph 8, the Corporation shall have the right, at its own expense, to take out life or disability insurance on Ward for its own benefit in such amount as it shall see fit, and Ward agrees to cooperate with the Corporation, at its request, in obtaining such insurance.

IN WITNESS WHEREOF the Corporation has caused this Agreement to be executed in its corporate name by its President and its corporate seal to be hereunto affixed and attested by its Secretary and Ward has hereunto set his hand and seal on the day and year first above written.

(CORPORATE SEAL)
Attest:
W. H. SCHWEBEL
    Secretary

                  FAIRCHILD ENGINE AND AIRPLANE CORPORATION
                  By

                          S. M. FAIRCHILD
                              President
                    J. CARLTON WARD, JR.   (L.S.)

                                March 18, 1949

J. Carlton Ward, Jr., Esq.,
30 Rockefeller Plaza,
New York 20, N. Y.

Dear Mr. Ward:

This is to confirm that the Agreement between us dated May 9, 1940, as heretofore amended, has been further amended, as of April

1, 1948, by changing subparagraphs 8(a), (b), (c) and (e) to read as follows:

"8. (a) Ward's employment hereunder shall terminate on December 31, 1957, subject, however, to earlier termination if any of the following events shall first occur:

"(i) Ward's death or disability, for physical or mental causes, to continue his employment under this Agreement; or

"(ii) a determination by Ward with the concurrence of the Board that, by reason of his physical or mental condition, it is advisable for him to retire; or

"(iii) a determination by Ward that, by reason of a major change in the management of the Corporation, he will be unable to work harmoniously and effectively with the new management of the Corporation;

provided, however, that not less than ninety days' written notice shall be required for termination of Ward's employment pursuant to (ii) or (iii) above;

"(b) Notwithstanding any other provision of this Agreement, the Corporation shall have the unqualified right to terminate Ward's employment hereunder at any time upon ninety days' written notice to Ward.

"(c) In consideration of the services to be rendered by Ward before and after the termination of his employment hereunder, the Corporation shall, beginning with the date of such termination but only in the event that such termination if it shall occur pursuant to (a) (ii) or (iii) above, takes place on or after July 1, 1950, pay to Ward, as deferred compensation, in substantially equal semi-monthly instalments, the sum of Twenty-five thousand dollars ($25,000) per year, either

"(i) for the remainder of his life, if such termination shall occur either on December 31, 1957, or earlier pursuant to (a) (i) above or by exercise of the Corporation's right to terminate pursuant to (b) above; or

"(ii) for the next ensuing 10 years, if such termination shall occur pursuant to (a) (ii) or (iii) above.

If Ward's employment hereunder shall have been terminated pursuant to (a) (i) or (b) above, or for any other reason after July 1, 1950, and Ward shall have died before receiving deferred compensation payments for a period of 10 years, such payments shall be made or continued to his wife, if and so long as she shall survive him, until the total amount of such payments to Ward and his wife shall aggregate Two hundred and fifty thousand dollars ($250,000).

"(e) Notwithstanding any of the provisions of this paragraph 8, no deferred compensation shall be payable to Ward (i) if and so long as he is in the regular full-time employ of the Corporation and receiving compensation for such employment, or (ii) if at any time Ward shall have failed duly and faithfully to perform his obligations under this Agreement."

Very truly yours,

FAIRCHILD ENGINE AND AIRPLANE CORPORATION

By _____
President

Confirmed:

J. Carlton Ward, Jr.

APPENDIX F

LERNER STORES CORPORATION

CONTRACT WITH BENJAMIN J. TIMONER

THIS AGREEMENT dated this 20th day of April, 1951, made and entered into by and between LERNER STORES CORPORATION, a Maryland corporation, having its principal office at 7 East Redwood Street, Baltimore 2, Maryland, sometimes hereinafter referred to as the "Corporation," and BENJAMIN J. TIMONER, of Woodmere, Long Island, New York, hereinafter referred to as "Timoner,"

WITNESSETH:

WHEREAS, the Corporation is the owner of all the shares of issued and outstanding capital stock of Lanes Fourteenth Street Corporation, a New York corporation (a subsidiary of the Corporation), which will operate a store, now in process of construction, on leasehold premises at the southeast corner of 14th Street and Fifth Avenue, Borough of Manhattan, City of New York, which new store it is presently proposed to operate under the name of "Lanes" (which store is hereinafter referred to as "Lanes") and which it is expected will be opened in approximately the Fall of 1951; and

WHEREAS, the Corporation desires to employ or cause to be employed the said Timoner as General Manager of Lanes for a period of approximately three (3) years, commencing on or about July 1, 1951, or prior thereto with the mutual consent of the Corporation and Timoner, and terminating on August 31, 1954, on the terms and conditions set forth herein, plus such further period or periods (hereinafter referred to as the "renewal period" or "renewal periods"), and upon such terms and conditions therefor as may be subsequently mutually agreed upon between the parties hereto:

NOW, THEREFORE, IT IS AGREED by and between the parties hereto as follows:

SECTION I.

The Corporation agrees to employ or cause to be employed the said Timoner in the capacity of General Manager of the store herein referred to as Lanes, for a period of approximately three (3) years commencing on or about July 1, 1951, or commencing on such earlier date as may be mutually agreed upon between the parties hereto, and ending August 31, 1954, and for each renewal period of this agreement subsequent to August 31, 1954, and Timoner hereby accepts such employment upon the terms and conditions hereinafter set forth.

During the period of employment under the provisions of this agreement, Timoner agrees to act as General Manager of Lanes, to devote his knowledge, ability and his working time and energy, subject to the right to receive reasonable vacations and subject to absences on account of temporary illnesses, to the business and interests of Lanes in an efficient, trustworthy and businesslike manner, and to perform such other duties from time to time as may be appropriate to the office of General Manager of Lanes, subject, however, to the supervision and control of the Board of Directors, the President, and the General Manager of the Corporation.

Section II.

For his services as such General Manager of Lanes, Lerner Stores Corporation agrees to pay or to cause to be paid to Timoner during his period of such employment:

(a) a salary at the annual rate of Forty-five thousand Dollars ($45,000), payable monthly, subject to adjustment as provided in Section IV hereof;

(b) provided this agreement shall not have been terminated by the Corporation pursuant to the provisions of Section VIII hereof, then in addition to the payments provided in paragraph (a) and (c) of this Section II, the Corporation shall also pay or cause to be paid to said Timoner, as deferred compensation, during the ten (10) successive years following the termination of his employment under this agreement, an amount equal in the aggregate to thirty-three and one-third per cent. (33-1/3%) of the aggregate salary theretofore paid or payable to him, prior to such termination of employment, pursuant to the provisions of paragraph (a) of this Section II, said payments of such deferred compensation to be made to him in equal monthly installments following the termination of his employment; and

(c) an amount equal to three per cent. (3%) of the amount if any, by which the net profits (as hereinafter defined) of Lanes during the preceding operational year in which the said Timoner shall be employed under this agreement exceeds the sum of Three hundred thousand Dollars ($300,000), payable as provided in this Section II.

The said Timoner shall have no right, except with the approval of the Board of Directors of the Corporation, to anticipate any of the payments provided to be made to him by the foregoing paragraph (b).

The additional compensation referred to in the foregoing paragraph (c) shall be payable as soon after the end of the operational year (as hereinafter defined) of Lanes as the amount thereof shall be ascertained, as provided in Section III hereof.

The term "operational year" of Lanes shall for the purpose of the first operational year under this agreement commence on the first day of the month in which the store herein described as Lanes shall be formally opened for business and shall terminate on the day preceding one (1) year from the anniversary of such commencement. Each successive operational year thereafter shall commence on the day following the termination of the preceding operational year.

Section III.

"Net profits," under the abovementioned Section II, shall mean the net profits of the store described as Lanes after deduction of all proper charges, including without limitation interest, rentals, depreciation and amortization on plant and equipment, computed in accordance with good accounting practice, but before income and excess profits taxes. The certificates of the Treasurer of the Corporation shall be conclusive and binding upon the Corporation, Lanes and Timoner with respect to the amount of such net profits and the additional compensation, if any, payable to Timoner under the provisions of paragraph (c) of Section II hereof.

Section IV.

In the event of Timoner's death during the period of his employment under this agreement, this agreement shall terminate as of the last day of the month in which such event occurs, and Timoner's salary hereunder shall cease at that date and the additional compensation under Section II, paragraph (c), hereof for the full fiscal year during which such event occurs shall be computed as therein and in Section III provided, and Timoner's administrators or executives shall be paid an amount of such additional compensation, if any, proportionate to the elapsed number of months of such operational year, including the month in which such event occurs; but shall be entitled to no further payments under Section II, paragraph (c).

In the event of Timoner's death during the period of his employment under this agreement, or thereafter and prior to the time when

Timoner shall have received full payment of the amounts payable to him under the provisions of paragraph (b) of Section II hereof, the full balance of the amount of deferred compensation payable to him and unpaid at the time of his death shall immediately become due and payable to his administrators or executors, but without any interest thereon.

In the event of Timoner's permanent disability or incapacity during the period of his employment hereunder, Timoner's salary shall cease as of the last day of the month in which such event occurs, and the additional compensation under Section II, paragraph (c), hereof for the full operational year during which such event occurs shall be computed as therein provided, and Timoner shall be paid an amount of such additional compensation proportionate to the elapsed number of months of such operational year, including the month in which such event occurs, and shall be entitled to no further payment under Section II, except the amounts payable thereafter to him pursuant to the provisions of paragraph (b) of Section II. Permanent disability shall be deemed to have occurred if Timoner shall have been disabled from performing his duties hereunder for an aggregate of four (4) months during any operational year of Lanes. Sickness not constituting permanent disability shall not reduce any payment under Section II.

SECTION V.

The term "renewal period" as used herein means a period of renewal occurring at the end of the original term of this agreement on August 31, 1954, or any renewal thereof, either

(a) by written agreement of the parties extending the time for employment of Timoner; or

(b) by failure to give notice as herein provided in this Section V.

Unless either party to this agreement gives to the other party notice in writing of his intention not to renew this agreement at least sixty (60) days before the terminal date of this agreement, or of any renewal period thereof, then this agreement shall be automatically renewed for a period of one (1) year beginning with the day following said terminal date, or the terminal date of the renewal thereof, on the terms and conditions herein set forth.

SECTION VI.

Timoner agrees that during the period of this agreement he will not engage in any business, directly or indirectly, in competition with the business of Lanes, the Corporation, or any subsidiary thereof.

Section VII.

This agreement shall not be assignable by Timoner without the written consent of Lanes or the Corporation, except that if Lanes shall merge or consolidate with or into, or transfer substantially all of its assets, including good will, to another corporation or other form of business organization, this agreement shall bind and run to the benefit of the successor of Lanes and/or the Corporation resulting from such merger, consolidation or transfer; provided, however, that no such merger, consolidation or transfer shall enlarge the right of Timoner to compensation pursuant to the provisions of paragraph (c) of Section II hereof; it being intended that in any event the amount of compensation payable to Timoner under the provisions of paragraph (c) of Section II hereof shall be determined by the net profits of the store at the southeast corner of 14th St. and Fifth Avenue, New York, N.Y., referred to in the first recital hereof as "Lanes."

No assignment by Timoner by pledge or otherwise of any right to receive any payments hereunder from Lanes or from the Corporation or any successor thereto shall be valid unless approved by the Board of Directors of Lanes and consented to in writing by Lanes and the Corporation, or their respective successors.

Section VIII.

This agreement may be terminated by either of the parties hereto on thirty (30) days' written notice as follows:

(a) by Lerner Stores Corporation in the event of a violation of any of the covenants, terms and provisions hereof to be performed by Timoner under this agreement for a period of sixty (60) days; and

(b) by Timoner in the event of the non-payment to him of any amounts payable to him hereunder within sixty (60) days after the same shall be due and payable in accordance with the terms and provisions of this agreement.

Section IX.

This agreement shall inure to the benefit of Lerner Stores Corporation, its successors (by merger, consolidation or otherwise) and assigns.

Section X.

Any notice addressed to Lerner Stores Corporation shall be deemed sufficiently given if mailed, postage prepaid, by registered mail, addressed to Lerner Stores Corporation, c/o Harold M. Lane, 354 Fourth Avenue, New York 10, N.Y., or to such other address as may be specified by written notice to Timoner.

Any notice addressed to Timoner shall be deemed sufficiently given if mailed, postage prepaid, by registered mail addressed to him at 323 Eastwood Road, Woodmere, Long Island, New York, or such other address as may be specified by written notice to Lerner Stores Corporation.

Section XI.

This agreement comprises the entire agreement between the parties. This agreement may not be modified orally.

In witness whereof, the parties hereto have hereunto and to a duplicate counterpart hereof set their signatures on the day and year above written, Lerner Stores Corporation by Harold M. Lane, its Executive Vice-President, with its corporate seal affixed hereto, attested by one of its Assistant Secretaries, thereunto duly authorized by its Board of Directors.

APPENDIX G

Stylon Corporation

ALFRED KOEHLER

June 11, 1954

Mr. Alfred Koehler
491 Huntington Avenue
Boston, Mass.

Dear Mr. Koehler:

This will confirm arrangements made this day wherein it was mutually agreed that effective January 1, 1954 your employment as Sales Manager of Stylon Corporation and its subsidiaries shall be as set forth herein below.

As Sales Manager you will be in full charge of sales of Stylon Corporation and its subsidiaries and directly responsible to the President of the Corporation for the performance of your duties as such. We shall expect your total effort in maintaining and promoting sales of the Company's products with particular emphasis on the following.

1. Setting up distributorships.
2. Direct sales and supervision of same.
3. Supervision of Sales Manager—Central and Western Division.
4. Supervision of salesmen.
5. Sales promotion and customer relations.

Your compensation will be as follows:

1. Effective January 1, 1954, annual salary of $12,500.00 payable in equal monthly or weekly installments as you may elect.
2. Effective January 1, 1954, additional compensation of $5,000.00 for the 12 month period commencing January 1st in each year when sales in the Eastern Division, representing the territories not specifically assigned to the Central and Western Division, exceed $2,000,000.00 during the said period.
3. Additional compensation, effective January 1, 1954, for the 12 month period commencing January 1st in each year of

½% of all sales in excess of $2,000,000.00 during the said period in the territories not specifically assigned to the Central and Western Division.

You will be reimbursed for travel and incidental expense expended by you in carrying on your duties upon submission of detailed weekly expense statement.

You will be required to give thirty days written notice to the Company's office at Milford, Mass. in the event you wish to terminate your employment and correspondingly will be given 30 days written notice in the event Stylon wishes to terminate your employment. In the event of termination, your regular and additional compensation shall be adjusted pro rata as of the termination date.

I trust the foregoing clearly expresses the arrangements mutually agreed on today at the Stylon Corporation offices at Milford, Mass. and shall appreciate receiving acknowledgment of your assent thereto by your signature on the duplicate copy of this letter.

Very truly yours
STYLON CORPORATION

Approved: /s/ Alfred Koehler   /s/ Joseph Mass
————————————   ————————————————
ALFRED KOEHLER   JOSEPH MASS, PRESIDENT

APPENDIX H

GENERAL BAKING CO.

GEORGE L. MORRISON

October 19, 1950

Mr. George L. Morrison,
420 Lexington Avenue
New York 17, N.Y.

Dear Sir:

This will confirm the understanding between the undersigned (herein called the "Company") and you (herein called "Morrison") as follows:

1. The Company hereby employs Morrison in an executive capacity, subject to the powers by law vested in the Board of Directors and officers of the Company, for a period of 5 years, commencing November 1, 1950 and terminating October 31, 1955, at the following salary:

(a) During such period as Morrison shall hold the office of President of the Company, such salary shall be at the rate of $85,000 per annum, payable in appropriate installments to conform with the Company's regular payroll payment dates.

(b) During such period as Morrison shall not hold the office of President of the Company, such salary shall be at the rate of $42,500 per annum, payable in appropriate installments to conform with the Company's regular payroll payment dates.

Morrison hereby accepts such employment and agrees during the period thereof to devote as much of his time as shall be necessary to the faithful performance of such duties as may be reasonably assigned to him from time to time by the Board of Directors of the Company. In the event that Morrison shall become incapacitated for any reason from performing such duties, he or the Company may terminate his employment under this paragraph 1. Morrison and the Company may by mutual agreement extend or lessen the period of employment provided for in this paragraph 1.

2. The Company hereby employs Morrison in an advisory and consulting capacity for a further period commencing on the date of

termination for any reason of Morrison's employment under paragraph 1 hereof and terminating on October 31, 1960, at a compensation at the rate of $21,250 per annum, payable in appropriate installments to conform with the Company's regular payroll payment dates. Morrison hereby accepts such employment and agrees during such further period to give to the Company his advice and judgment upon all matters as to which the Company shall reasonably desire to consult with him. In the event that Morrison shall become incapacitated for any reason from performing such advisory and consulting services, he shall nevertheless be compensated as in this paragraph 2 provided until October 31, 1960, or his death, whichever shall first occur, provided that if such incapacity shall arise prior to October 31, 1955 such compensation shall be reduced to an annual rate which is such percentage of $21,250 as shall equal the percentage which the number of full months of Morrison's service to the Company in any capacity from May 1, 1940 (the date of the first employment of Morrison by the Company) to the date of such incapacity shall be of 186 (the number of full months from May 1, 1940 to October 31, 1955). Morrison and the Company may by mutual agreement extend from year to year the further period of employment provided for in this paragraph 2, provided that Morrison shall not be incapacitated from performing his duties hereunder.

3. Morrison agrees during the full period of his employment pursuant to this agreement not to engage or have any financial interest in any business competing with or of a character similar to the business conducted by the Company.

4. If at the next meeting of stockholders of the Company this agreement shall not be ratified and approved by a majority of the stockholders of the Company present and entitled to vote, then this agreement shall terminate as of the last day of the month in which such meeting shall be held.

If the foregoing is in accordance with your understanding, please constitute this a binding agreement between us by executing the enclosed copy hereof in the space provided at the bottom thereof and returning the same to us.

Very truly yours,
GENERAL BAKING COMPANY

By (Signed) T. S. OLSEN
Executive Vice President

The foregoing is hereby accepted as of the day first above written.

(Signed) GEORGE L. MORRISON
George L. Morrison

APPENDIX I

Ford Motor Company

CONTRACT WITH ERNEST R. BREECH

A g r e e m e n t

THIS AGREEMENT, made this 16th day of May, 1946, to be effective as of July 1, 1946, between Ford Motor Company, a Delaware corporation, hereinafter called "the Employer," and Ernest R. Breech of Birmingham, Michigan, hereinafter called "the Employee,"

W i t n e s s e t h :

In consideration of the covenants and agreements hereinafter set forth, the parties hereto do hereby agree as follows:

1. For the purposes of this Agreement:

(a) The term "the Employer" shall include Ford Motor Company and any corporate or other successor to the business of manufacturing motor vehicles under the trademark or trade name "Ford," presently conducted by Ford Motor Company.

(b) The "employment hereunder shall have terminated" when, whether as a result of resignation, dismissal, death, incapacity, notice of termination of employment given by either party to the other, or for any other reason other than retirement as provided in Section 8 hereof, the Employee shall have ceased to serve the Employer on a full-time basis, except for reasonable vacation periods and other reasonable leaves of absence, under this or some subsequent employment arrangement.

(c) The Employee shall be "engaged in a competing business" if, as proprietor, partner, trustee, employee or director, he is engaged or participates in the operation or management of an enterprise which (1) is engaged in the business of manufacturing in the United States motor vehicles of a type which are sold in competition with motor vehicles manufactured by the Employer, and (2) is one of the three largest manufacturers (on the basis of units manufactured or sold) of passenger motor vehicles in the United States.

2. The Employer shall employ the Employee, and the Employee shall serve the Employer in an executive capacity, hereinafter more particularly described, for the twelve (12) months' period commencing July 1, 1946 and expiring June 30, 1947. From and after July 1, 1947, and from and after July 1 of each year thereafter, and until June 30 of the following year, employment hereunder shall continue upon the terms and conditions stated in this Agreement, unless on or prior to September 1 of any such year, the Employer or the Employee shall notify the other in writing (a) of a desire to renegotiate the provisions of Sections 4 and/or 5 hereof, or (b) of the termination of employment hereunder. If prior to September 1 of any such year notice of a desire to renegotiate such provisions shall have been received, and if prior to such date renegotiation of such provisions shall not have been completed, and no notice of termination shall have been given, employment hereunder shall continue upon the terms and conditions stated in this Agreement, until June 30 of the following year. If notice of termination shall have been given prior to September 1 of any year, employment hereunder shall cease on August 31 of such year. Anything herein to the contrary notwithstanding, the Employer shall have the right to dismiss the Employee and the Employee shall have the right to resign, with or without cause, at any time. No termination of employment, however effected, shall relieve the Employer of its obligations under Sections 6 and 7 of this Agreement.

3. Throughout the period of employment hereunder, except for reasonable vacation periods and other reasonable leaves of absence, the Employee shall devote his best efforts and all of his business time and attention to the affairs of the Employer, including, but without limitation, the affairs of subsidiary and affiliated companies, except that the Employee may be a member of the Board of Directors of other non-competitive companies as may be agreed upon in writing with the President of the Employer.

4. Throughout the period of employment hereunder, the Employee shall have the title of Executive Vice-President. He shall report and be responsible only to the President and to the Board of Directors, and, subject only to this limitation shall exercise all the powers and functions of the chief executive officer. All other officers and employees of the Employer shall be under his general supervision and direction and shall report to the Employee, and through him to the President and to the Board of Directors. Subject to the control of the President and the Board of Directors, he shall have immediate supervision and direction of the Employer's business and affairs.

Throughout the period of employment, he shall be a member of the Board of Directors, and of any other governing or executive committees. In the absence of the President, he shall preside at all meetings of any such governing or executive committees, if any.

5. As compensation hereunder, the Employer shall pay, and the Employee shall accept:

(a) Basic compensation of $150,000 per year, payable in equal monthly installments on the last day of each month during his employment hereunder.

(b) Such bonus, supplemental or incentive compensation or other payments, if any, as may be awarded from time to time by the Employer in its sole discretion.

6. In consideration of the making of this Agreement, the Employer, from and after employment hereunder shall have terminated, shall make payments as follows:

(a) If such termination of employment occurs prior to the attainment by the Employee of age 65, the Employer shall make payments to the Employee of $50,000 per year for ten (10) successive years; provided, however, that from and after the attainment by the Employee of age 65, or if deceased, from and after the 65th anniversary of his birth, such payments shall be reduced to $25,000 per year;

such payments to be made on or before each July 1, commencing with the July 1 next succeeding the date on which employment hereunder shall have terminated; the making of such payments, and each of them, to be subject only to the condition that the Employee (without having first procured the written consent of the Employer) shall not have engaged in a competing business in the United States during such period of ten (10) successive years, beginning with the date when employment hereunder shall have terminated. It is agreed that the Employee, by so engaging in such competing business during said ten (10) year period, without having first procured the written consent of the Employer, shall automatically forfeit all rights to any subsequent contingent payments coming due thereafter. The Employer, in such written consent, may specify the terms on which the consent is given and the amounts of subsequent contingent payments, which amounts may be less than those specified herein.

7. The right of the Employee to receive the contingent payments hereinbefore provided for, but not the retirement income hereinafter provided for, pursuant to this Agreement, shall inure to the benefit

of his executors, administrators, personal representatives and assigns. Any of the annual contingent payments which fall due upon or after the death of the Employee shall be paid to any person designated by the Employee, in a writing duly acknowledged and filed with the Employer prior to the date of the Employee's death, as the one to receive such payments, and in the absence of such designation, to such person as may furnish the Employer with evidence of appointment as representative of the estate of the Employee. The receipt of any such person for such payments shall release the Employer of any further obligation in respect thereof. "Person," as used in this Section 7, may include one or more individuals, trusts, firms or corporations.

8. In the event that the Employee shall remain in the employ of the Employer under this or any other agreement until he shall have reached the age of 60, at any time thereafter, either at his or the Employer's option, he may be retired, in which event the Employer agrees to pay to him throughout the remainder of his life a retirement income of $25,000 a year, payable in equal monthly installments, on the first day of each month, commencing with the month immediately following the month in which his retirement shall occur, and ending upon his death.

9. Neither the Employee, nor his estate or his assigns, shall under any circumstances have any option or right to require payments under Sections 6 and 7 hereof otherwise than in accordance with the terms hereof or after the terms and contingencies herein specified have been met.

WITNESS the hands and seals of the parties hereto this 16th day of May, 1946.

FORD MOTOR COMPANY

By /s/ HENRY FORD II
President

Attest:

/s/ H. E. SCHLUCHTER
Secretary

/s/ ERNEST R. BREECH   (L.S.)

Witnessed by:

/s/ JAMES B. GORDON

SPECIAL CLAUSES FOR EMPLOYMENT
CONTRACTS

APPENDIX J

BURLINGTON MILLS CORPORATION

CONTRACT WITH J. SPENCER LOVE

THIS AGREEMENT, made this 30th day of April, 1954 between BURLINGTON MILLS CORPORATION (hereinafter sometimes referred to as the "Corporation"), party of the first part, and J. SPENCER LOVE, residing at 1610 Granville Road, Greensboro, N. C. (hereinafter sometimes referred to as "Love"), party of the second part.

WITNESSETH:

WHEREAS, the Corporation as of December 6, 1950 entered into an Agreement with Love pursuant to which, among other things, his full time employment with the Corporation and its subsidiaries was extended for the period to and including November 30, 1957; and

WHEREAS, Love is an important and very valuable executive of the Corporation, being Chairman of the Board of Directors and Chief Executive Officer of the Corporation and a recognized leader in the textile industry, and the Corporation deems it to be in its interest and in the interest of its stockholders to secure the services of Love for an additional term of years to end July 5, 1961; and

WHEREAS, the Corporation, as an incentive to Love to continue his employment with the Corporation and its subsidiaries for such additional term and to increase his proprietary interest in the Corporation, desires to enter into this Agreement with him containing the terms and conditions hereinafter set forth and to grant him an option to purchase, on different terms, 75,000 shares of the Common Stock of the Corporation in lieu of the option he now has to purchase 30,000 shares of such Common Stock; and

WHEREAS, Love has indicated his willingness to execute this Agreement with respect to such employment and option upon the terms and conditions hereinafter set forth;

Now, THEREFORE, in consideration of the premises and the mutual agreements hereinafter contained, and in consideration of Ten Dollars ($10.00) paid by the Corporation and Love each to the other, the receipt of which is hereby acknowledged, and for other good and valuable considerations, the parties hereby agree as follows:

FIRST: This Agreement effective April 30, 1954 shall supersede the Agreement, dated December 6, 1950, between the Corporation and Love with reference to his employment after said April 30, 1954 and the option heretofore granted him to purchase 30,000 shares of Common Stock of the Corporation, and said Agreement, dated December 6, 1950, shall be deemed terminated and cancelled and of no further force and effect as at the close of business on said April 30, 1954.

SECOND: The Corporation agrees to employ, or to cause one or more of its subsidiary companies to employ Love, and Love agrees to serve the Corporation and such of the Corporation's subsidiary companies as may be designated by the Corporation, upon the terms and conditions hereinafter set forth.

THIRD: The employment of Love hereunder shall commence April 30, 1954 and shall continue for a period ending July 5, 1961.

FOURTH: Love agrees to serve the Corporation and such of the Corporation's subsidiary companies as may be designated by the Corporation, faithfully and to the best of his ability, under the direction of the Board of Directors of the Corporation and of such subsidiary companies, devoting his entire time, energy and skill during the regular business hours of such employment, and perform from time to time such services as said Board of Directors shall request, and to act as Director, Chairman of the Board of Directors, Chairman of the Executive Committee and Finance Committee, and any other officer of the Corporation and of any of its subsidiary companies as said Board of Directors shall request, without further compensation. It is understood and agreed that Love in connection with such duties and responsibilities will be required to travel to and from the various offices and places of business of the Corporation and its subsidiary companies wherever located, and the Corporation agrees to maintain, at its own expense, at such offices and places of business such secretarial, personnel, telephone, transportation facilities, equipment and other services as Love shall deem necessary for the adequate performance of his duties and responsibilities and in the interest of the business of the Corporation and its subsidiary companies.

FIFTH: The Corporation agrees to pay or cause one or more of its subsidiary companies to pay to Love, commencing as of April 30,

1954 and continuing during the period of the term hereof as salary for his services the sum of One Hundred Thousand Dollars ($100,000.00) per annum, payable in equal monthly installments.

SIXTH: It is expressly understood and agreed that Love shall not be entitled to, and that the Corporation, its subsidiary companies and management shall be released from any and all obligations to pay to Love, any additional compensation, contractual profit sharing interest, bonus or other similar payments for any and all period or periods of time whatsoever by reason of his employment or otherwise, except as expressly provided for in this Agreement and in the Retirement System and Profit Sharing Plan of the Corporation and its Affiliated Companies with respect to Love's participation therein and except amounts deferred for fiscal years prior to October 4, 1953 as now on the books of account of the Corporation.

SEVENTH: It is understood and agreed that the services required of Love by this Agreement include the duty of entertainment which Love shall deem to be in the interest of the Corporation's business, and the Corporation hereby appropriates and makes available to him for this purpose, beginning April 30, 1954, a sum of Thirty-five Thousand Dollars ($35,000) per annum, payable in such amounts and at such times as Love shall request.

In arriving at the indicated fixed aggregate annual expense allowance for necessary entertainment, the Corporation has carefully appraised the amount of such entertainment that Love may be required to dispense, if his services are to be productive of the maximum benefits which the Corporation expects to derive therefrom.

The Corporation reposing confidence in Love recognizes that such entertainment may be so diversified and casual as to make the maintenance of complete and accurate records thereof inconvenient, impracticable, and virtually impossible for Love, and therefore the Corporation will not require that expense vouchers for such entertainment be furnished to it.

The Corporation acknowledges that Love has recently established a residence in Greensboro, N. C., and may hereafter maintain residences at other locations, and that the Corporation has received and will receive the benefit of the use of such residences, their personnel, facilities and appurtenances as they are devoted to the entertainment of persons in the Corporation's interest, the holding of conferences and meetings concerning the Corporation's problems and the conduct of other business on behalf of the Corporation, all without direct compensation from the Corporation.

Therefore, in consideration of the continuation of the above described benefits, the Corporation agrees to reimburse Love for expenses incurred in travel of like frequency as heretofore, or as increased by necessity of the Corporation's interests, to and from each of such locations and to maintain, at its own expense, secretarial and other personnel, telephone and other services, equipment and transportation facilities at these points as may be necessary or appropriate in the conduct of the Corporation's business; and Love agrees to release the Corporation from any claim arising from the aforesaid use of any residence, its facilities and appurtenances owned or used by him.

It is understood that this annual lump sum allowance of Thirty-five Thousand Dollars ($35,000.00) per annum is provided for entertainment expenses only and shall be in addition to any reimbursement required to be made to Love to cover expenses he may have incurred while traveling to and from such residences and places of business, and while traveling on any and all other engagements devoted immediately and directly to the business of the Corporation, for all of which such additional expenses he will be expected to render expense accounts, which shall be paid by the Corporation.

EIGHTH: It is understood and agreed for the purposes of this Employment and Option Agreement that if Love is drafted for military service, or with the consent of the Board of Directors of the Corporation volunteers for governmental service, military or otherwise, and is thereby prevented from devoting his entire time, energy and skill to his employment under Article FOURTH of this Agreement, his failure so to do shall not be termed a breach of this Agreement or in any way constitute a cause for or of itself constitute a cessation of his employment during the period of such military or governmental service, but in any such event the Corporation shall have the right to reduce, during the period of such military or governmental service, the compensation payable to Love under this Agreement to such amount as the Board of Directors of the Corporation, in its sole and absolute discretion, shall fix and determine, and Love agrees to accept during the period of his military or governmental service such amount as shall be fixed and determined by said Board of Directors, in payment of, and in full discharge and release of this Corporation and its subsidiaries of and from their obligations to pay to him, during such period the sum provided for in Articles FIFTH and SEVENTH hereof. In no event, however, shall the compensation fixed and determined in accordance with this Article be paid to Love after July 5, 1961, and such compensation shall cease upon commencement prior thereto of any of the payments provided for in Article NINTH hereof.

NINTH: In further consideration of the foregoing, the Corporation and Love hereby agree as follows:

(a) The Corporation shall pay to Love if living or to others in the event of his death the following additional sums upon the terms and conditions and for the periods hereinafter set forth:

(1) the sum of $4,166.66 per month for a fixed and definite period to begin on July 6, 1961 or on such earlier date as Love shall die or his full time active employment hereunder be terminated in the manner hereinafter provided because of his disability and to end July 31, 1971; and

(2) If the death or disability of Love occurs on or before July 5, 1961, while he is in the full time active employment of the Corporation and while this Agreement is in full force and effect, the Corporation shall pay to him if living or to others (as hereinafter provided) in the event of his death the following sums in addition to those provided in sub-paragraph (1) above: (i) an amount equal to the balance of the monthly salary then payable to Love up to the end of the month in which death occurs or in which his full time active employment is duly terminated because of disability, (ii) an amount each month thereafter for the next three successive months, but not beyond July 5, 1961, equal to his monthly salary at the time of death or such termination because of disability, and (iii) an amount after said three months' period payable monthly to and including July 5, 1961 equal to $2,083.33 per month.

Payments of the aggregate monthly sums hereinabove provided for in sub-paragraphs (1) and (2) shall begin at the time set forth therein and be an obligation of the Corporation for the respective periods specified, which said periods are hereinafter sometimes referred to as the "Certain Periods"; *provided,* however, that if after July 5, 1961 Love is in the full time active employment of the Corporation, the aggregate monthly sums then payable to him shall be deferred during the period or periods of such employment but the total amount so deferred shall be paid to him upon his subsequent retirement or disability in equal monthly installments for the remainder of said Certain Periods, along with the monthly sums above specified then currently payable during his retirement or disability for the remainder of said Certain Periods.

Subject to the foregoing provisions, the aggregate monthly sums hereinabove provided for, including any such sums deferred for payment upon the retirement or disability of Love, shall be paid to Love as stated if living, otherwise to Love's wife, Martha Eskridge Love, if living, for said Certain Periods.

If Love's said wife predeceases Love, then upon Love's death all payments deferred and/or remaining to be paid for said "Certain Periods" shall be paid in a lump sum, and without diminution because of prepayment, to Love's children born of said wife, Martha Eskridge Love, in equal shares; but if any of Love's said children shall predecease him, leaving issue surviving, such child's share shall be paid to the issue of such child *per stirpes,* or if any of Love's said children shall predecease him leaving no issue surviving at Love's death, then the share of such deceased child shall be paid to the surviving child or children of Love born of said wife, Martha Eskridge Love, and the surviving issue of any such deceased child *per stirpes* and not *per capita.*

If Love's said wife survives him but dies before all such payments have been made, then and in such event, the deferred and/or monthly payments remaining to be paid for said Certain Periods shall be paid in a lump sum, and without diminution because of prepayment, as follows: (i) the same shall be paid to such persons, firms or corporations, and in such proportions, as Love's said wife shall, in her absolute discretion, designate and appoint in a will or codicil executed by her after Love's death; *provided that,* no such designation or appointment shall be effective unless in any such will or codicil Love's said wife shall expressly, specifically and directly refer to and dispose of such payments; it being the intention hereof that no such payments shall pass by reason of any general residuary clause or other similar general provision in any will or codicil executed by Love's said wife; (ii) if any such payments shall not be disposed of by Love's said wife as above provided, the same shall be paid in a lump sum to Love's children born of said wife, Martha Eskridge Love, in equal shares, but if any of Love's said children shall predecease Love's said wife and leave issue surviving, then the share of such deceased child shall be paid to its issue *per stirpes* and not *per capita,* or if any of Love's said children shall predecease Love's said wife and leave no issue surviving, then the share of such child shall be paid to the surviving child or children of said Love born of said wife, Martha Eskridge Love, and the surviving issue of any such deceased child *per stirpes* and not *per capita.*

For the purposes of sub-paragraphs (1) and (2) above, the obligations of the Corporation and its subsidiary companies to make the monthly and other payments aforesaid upon the disability of Love shall not become effective unless and until all of the following conditions are met: (i) Love shall become physically or mentally incapable (excluding infrequent and temporary absences due to ordinary illnesses) of properly performing the services required of him in accordance with his obligations under Article FOURTH hereof, (ii) such incapacity shall exist or be reasonably expected to exist for more than 90 days in the aggregate during any period of twelve consecutive months, and (iii) either Love or the Corporation shall have given the other thirty days' written notice of his or its intention to terminate the active employment of Love because of such disability.

(b) In addition to the sums to be paid to Love or others in accordance with sub-paragraph (a) above, if Love be living at the expiration of said Certain Periods on July 31, 1971, the Corporation shall pay to him thereafter the sum of $4,166.66 per month during the remainder of his lifetime, but only during the remainder of his lifetime, which monthly payments shall commence August 1, 1971 and shall continue up to and including the end of the month in which his death shall occur. The last monthly payment due to Love for the month in which his death shall occur shall be paid to his legal representatives unless previously paid to Love during such month prior to his death.

(c) Love agrees that, upon cessation of his full time active employment by reason of his retirement or mental or physical disability and during the Certain Periods above mentioned, he will, while not prevented from so doing because of such disability, serve the Corporation and its subsidiary companies in an advisory and consultative capacity and in the performance of important special assignments relating to the business, management, financial, personnel and public relations of the Corporation and its subsidiary companies, be available for such purposes at such times and places as shall be reasonable, and act as a director and/or member of any Committee of the Board of Directors of the Corporation or any of its subsidiary companies, as the Corporation may from time to time request, all without further compensation except that Love, while serving as a member of said Board of Directors or Committee shall be entitled to receive and shall be paid fees and shall be reimbursed for his expenses as in the case of other directors and members thereof who are not full time active employees or officers of the Corporation.

TENTH: Love expressly agrees, as a condition to the performance by the Corporation and its subsidiary companies of their obligations hereunder, that during the term of this Agreement and the Certain Periods specified in Article NINTH hereof, he will not, directly or indirectly, render any services of an advisory nature or otherwise to or become employed by or participate or engage in any business materially competitive with any of the businesses of the Corporation and its subsidiary companies, without the written consent of the Corporation first had and obtained.

ELEVENTH : In further consideration of the foregoing, the Corporation hereby grants to Love the right and option to purchase Seventy-five thousand (75,000) shares of Common Stock, par value $1.00 per share, of the Corporation subject to the provisions hereinafter set forth. Said Option may be exercised by Love, subject to the limitations and conditions hereinafter set forth in Article THIRTEENTH hereof, in whole at any time or in part from time to time during the period, and only during the period, from the date hereof to and including the close of business on July 5, 1961, by giving to the Corporation notice in writing to that effect; provided, however, that notwithstanding the foregoing, if Love should become totally disabled or should die during the interval from April 5, 1961 to and including July 5, 1961, while he is in the full time active employment of the Corporation or of any parent or subsidiary of the Corporation as provided for in Article FOURTH hereof, then said Option may be exercised within three months after the effective date of the termination of such employment because of such total disability or the date of the legal qualification of the executors or administrators of his estate in the event of his death (provided diligent efforts are made and such qualification is obtained within a reasonable time after his death) by giving the Corporation notice in writing to that effect. This option may be exercised only for lots of Fifteen thousand (15,000) shares or more, and the purchase price to be paid with respect to said shares of Common Stock in the event of exercise of this Option shall be $10.45 per share.

TWELFTH : The Corporation shall within thirty days after the receipt by it of notice of exercise of said Option cause certificates for the number of shares with respect to which such Option is exercised to be issued in the name of Love or his executors, administrators or other legal representatives, heirs, legatees, next of kin or distributees, or to be properly endorsed or accompanied by separate stock powers duly executed, and to be delivered to Love or his executors, administrators or other legal representatives, heirs, legatees, next of kin or distributees, together with revenue stamps or checks in an amount sufficient to pay any and all Federal and State stock transfer taxes required on such delivery. Payment of the purchase price for the shares with respect to which this Option is exercised shall be made to the Corporation upon the delivery of such stock. The Corporation shall give the person or persons entitled to same at least five days' notice of the time and place for delivery and for the payment of said purchase price. It is expressly understood and agreed that the Corporation shall not be required at any time to authorize the issue and sale of any Common Stock of original issue upon exercise of this Option, but shall be obligated upon such exercise to transfer and deliver the number of shares so purchased out of shares then issued and outstanding and held or acquired from time to time by the Corporation for its own account. It is further expressly understood and agreed that in the event the Corporation does not have sufficient shares of Common Stock in its treasury to deliver to Love or other persons entitled to the same upon receipt of notice of exercise of this Option, then the Corporation shall purchase or acquire sufficient shares to enable it to deliver within thirty days after receipt by it of such notice the number of shares required to be so delivered pursuant to such notice.

THIRTEENTH : It is further understood and agreed as follows :

(a) The Option herein granted to Love shall not be transferable by Love other than by will or the laws of descent and distribution, and shall be exercisable, during his lifetime, only by him ; and

(b) Said Option may be exercised by Love only while he is in the full time active employment of the Corporation or of a parent or subsidiary of the Corporation as provided for in Article FOURTH hereof, or within three months after the date he ceases to be so employed, except that in the event of his total disability or death while so employed or within three months after the date he ceases to be so employed, then said Option may be exercised within three months, but not later than three months, after the effective date of the termination of such employment because of such total disability, or, in the event of his death as aforesaid, may be exercised by his executors, administrators, or other legal representatives, heirs, legatees, next of kin or distributees within three months, but not later than three months, after the date of the legal qualification of the executors or administrators of his estate provided diligent efforts are made and such qualification is obtained within a reasonable time after his death.

(c) Notwithstanding the provisions of sub-paragraph (b) next above, if the employment of Love shall be terminated by the Corporation without cause (other than on account of his death or physical or mental disability) prior to the close of business on July 5, 1961, then such Option may be exercised during the period, but only during the period, to and including July 5, 1961 by Love or, in the event of his death after such termination, by his executors, administrators or other legal representatives, heirs, legatees, next of kin or distributees during said period within three months, but not later than three months, after the date of the legal qualification of the executors or administrators of his estate provided diligent efforts are made and such qualification is obtained within a reasonable time after his death.

In no event, however, shall the Corporation be obligated in any respect under the option provisions of this Agreement unless notice in writing of exercise of this Option is duly given to the Corporation within the time and in accordance with the provisions hereinabove set forth in Article ELEVENTH and this Article for the exercise of such Option. Further, the provisions of this Agreement with respect to said Option shall become null and void and inoperative immediately at the expiration of the period hereinabove provided in sub-paragraphs (b) and (c), respectively, for the exercise of such Option in the event of cessation of employment, death or physical or mental disability of Love unless exercised within said period and in accordance with the provisions set forth therein. The provisions of this Agreement with respect to said Option shall also become null and void and inoperative immediately upon any attempted sale, assignment, transfer or other disposition by Love of said Option or any of his right, title and interest therein; provided, however, that nothing herein shall be construed as prohibiting Love upon his death (at any time while he has the right to exercise such Option) from providing for the disposition of said Option or his right, title and interest therein by will or as prohibiting the transfer of said Option by the laws of descent and distribution.

FOURTEENTH : It is understood and agreed that if the Corporation shall issue any additional shares of stock by way of a stock dividend on, or split-up, subdivision or reclassification of outstanding Common Stock, then this Option shall be deemed to cover such additional shares to the extent that the same would have been issued to Love had this Option been exercised in its entirety and the shares of Common Stock then remaining subject to this Option been delivered to Love at the time of such dividend, split-up, subdivision or reclassification, and there shall be a corresponding proportionate adjustment of the Option price per share hereinabove set forth so that in the aggregate the Option price for all shares then covered shall be the same as the aggregate Option price for the shares of stock remaining subject to said Option immediately prior to the issuance of such additional shares.

If there shall be any capital reorganization, or consolidation or merger of the Corporation with any other corporation or corporations, or any sale of all or substantially all of the Corporation's property and assets to any other corporation or corporations, the Corporation shall take such action as may be necessary to enable Love to receive upon any subsequent exercise of this Option, in whole or in part, in lieu of any shares of Common Stock of the Corporation, the share or shares of stock, securities, or other assets as were issuable or payable upon such reorganization, consolidation, merger or sale in respect of or in exchange for such shares of Common Stock.

FIFTEENTH: It is understood and agreed that the exercise of the Option herein provided for and the delivery of the shares subject thereto will be contingent upon the Corporation's being furnished by Love, his legal representatives, or other persons entitled to exercise such Option with a representation in writing that at the time of such exercise it is his or their intention to acquire the shares being purchased for investment and not with a view to distribution.

SIXTEENTH: The Option provided for in this Agreement is intended to qualify as a restricted stock option within the meaning of Section 130–A of the Internal Revenue Code, as enacted by Section 218 of the Revenue Act of 1950, as amended, and shall be so construed; provided, however, that nothing herein shall be deemed to be or interpreted as a representation, guarantee or other undertaking on the part of the Corporation that such Option is or will be determined to be a restricted stock option within said Section of the Internal Revenue Code, as enacted by Section 218 of the Revenue Act of 1950, as amended.

SEVENTEENTH: This Agreement cancels and terminates, as of the date of delivery hereof, the existing Option and provisions with respect thereto contained in the Agreement, dated December 6, 1950, between the Corporation and Love.

EIGHTEENTH: Any notice to be given by Love hereunder shall be sent by registered mail to the Corporation at its offices, 301 North Eugene Street, Greensboro, N. C., and any notice from the Corporation to Love shall be sent by registered mail to Love at 1610 Granville Road, Greensboro, N. C. Either party may change the address to which notice in writing is given to the other in accordance with the terms hereof.

NINETEENTH: Except as hereinabove otherwise expressly provided, Love agrees on behalf of himself and of his survivors named in Article NINTH hereof and of his executors and administrators, heirs, legatees, distributees and any other person or persons claiming any benefits under him by virtue of this Agreement, that this Agreement and the rights, interests, and benefits hereunder shall not be assigned, transferred, pledged or hypothecated in any way by Love or any such survivor, executor, administrator, heir, legatee, distributee, or other person claiming under Love by virtue of this Agreement and shall not be subject to execution, attachment or similar process. Any attempted assignment, transfer, pledge, or hypothecation or other disposition of this Agreement or of such rights, interests and benefits contrary to the foregoing provisions, or the levy of any attachment or similar process thereupon, shall be null and void and without effect.

IN WITNESS WHEREOF, Burlington Mills Corporation has caused this Agreement to be executed in its corporate name by its corporate officer thereunto duly authorized, and Love has hereunto set his hand and seal, as of the 30th day of April, 1954.

BURLINGTON MILLS CORPORATION

By /s/ J. C. COWAN
Vice Chairman of the Board

(CORPORATE SEAL)

/s/ J. SPENCER LOVE   (L.S.)
J. Spencer Love

APPENDIX K

AMERICAN CYANAMID COMPANY

FORM OF EMPLOYMENT AGREEMENT
(Non-Disclosure and Invention Clauses in Effect on April 19, 1961)

THIS AGREEMENT, made as of the   day of   , 19 , between   a corporation organized and existing under the laws of the State of   , with general offices at (hereinafter referred to as the "COMPANY") and residing at (hereinafter called the "EMPLOYEE"), Social Security No. ——

WITNESSETH:

In consideration of the EMPLOYEE's employment by the COMPANY, and of the covenants hereinafter set forth, it is mutually agreed as follows:

(1) EMPLOYMENT. The EMPLOYEE shall be and hereby is employed by the COMPANY, and the EMPLOYEE shall faithfully and to the best of his ability perform services for the COMPANY as directed by it, devoting all of his working time to such services. Such employment shall continue until the EMPLOYEE's retirement date under any applicable retirement plan, subject to the right of either the EMPLOYEE or the COMPANY to terminate the employment on one day's notice if given during the first six months of continuous employment, or on notice if given thereafter; and subject to the right of the COMPANY to terminate the employment at any time in the event of default or non-performance by the EMPLOYEE of any of the provisions of this Agreement. In the event of notice, the EMPLOYEE shall remain for the full notice period if so requested by the COMPANY, but the COMPANY reserves the right at any time to pay the EMPLOYEE his full salary for any required notice period and to terminate the employment immediately or at any time during such period.

(2) COMPENSATION. The COMPANY shall pay and the EMPLOYEE shall accept, in full payment for the latter's services, the salary

of

Dollars ($) per   . The COMPANY reserves the right to raise the salary of the EMPLOYEE or to pay bonuses under any plan which the COMPANY may from time to time inaugurate, without changing the provisions and rights under this Agreement.

(3) HEADQUARTERS. The EMPLOYEE shall make his headquarters at such place or places as the COMPANY from time to time believes to be to the interest of the COMPANY and may accordingly direct. Whenever, the EMPLOYEE is so directed to change his headquarters under circumstances reasonably requiring a change of residence, he shall be reimbursed for reasonable expenses of moving in connection therewith; and during the time he may be away, in the service of the COMPANY, from the headquarters assigned to him, he shall receive personal expenses for traveling, communicating, lodging and subsistence.

(4) CONFIDENTIAL INFORMATION. The EMPLOYEE shall not, during the term or after the conclusion of his employment under this Agreement, disclose to a third party any confidential information relative to the business of the COMPANY or of any of its subsidiary or affiliated companies obtained by him while in its or their employ, without the written consent of an executive officer of the COMPANY; and further, upon leaving the employ of the COMPANY, the EMPLOYEE shall not take with him, without like consent, any drawing, blueprint, or other reproduction, or any special data, tables, calculations, letters or other documents or copies thereof, or any confidential information pertaining to the COMPANY or to any of its subsidiary or affiliated companies.

(5) IMPROVEMENTS AND INVENTIONS. With regard to any and all improvements and inventions which the EMPLOYEE may conceive or make either solely or jointly with others (whether during the term of his employment, or during such period thereafter, not exceeding one year, for which the COMPANY shall have notified the EMPLOYEE in writing, prior to the expiration of his employment, that it will continue to pay the EMPLOYEE amounts equivalent to his then salary, provided said payments are made or tendered), which in any way affect the goods or materials produced, sold or used by the COMPANY or any of its affiliated or subsidiary companies, or which may affect any methods, processes or apparatus used in connection with the production or treatment of such goods or materials, or which are or may be or may become capable of being used in the business of the COMPANY or of its affiliated or subsidiary companies, such improvements and inventions shall at all time(s) and for all purposes be re-

garded as acquired and held by the EMPLOYEE in a fiduciary capacity for, and solely for the benefit of, the COMPANY. The EMPLOYEE shall promptly disclose to the COMPANY, and upon its request assign to the COMPANY, all such improvements and inventions; and thereupon said improvements and inventions shall become and remain the property of the COMPANY, whether or not patent applications are or have been filed thereon. The EMPLOYEE shall from time to time, upon request and at the expense of the COMPANY, make application, through the patent solicitors of the COMPANY, for letters patent of the United States, and of any and all other countries designated in such request, on said improvements and inventions, and shall promptly assign all such applications to the COMPANY or according to its order; and without charge for his services beyond the payments herein provided for, the EMPLOYEE shall give to the COMPANY, its attorneys and solicitors, all reasonable and requested assistance in preparing said applications, and from time to time on request of the COMPANY shall execute all papers and do all things that may reasonably be required in order to protect the rights of the COMPANY and vest in it or its assigns the improvements, inventions, applications, and letters patent herein provided for. Time actually spent by the EMPLOYEE at such work at the request of the COMPANY after the termination of his employment or, in case the COMPANY pays the EMPLOYEE during an extended period as above provided, then after the termination of such extended period, shall be paid for by the COMPANY at a reasonable rate, but no termination of this Agreement shall release the EMPLOYEE from his obligations under this Agreement as to any and all improvements and inventions.

(6) Nothing in this Agreement shall be construed to limit the EMPLOYEE's participation in any insurance plan, medical plan, retirement plan, or other employee benefit arrangement to which he would otherwise be entitled in the absence of this Agreement.

(7) ASSIGNABILITY. This Agreement shall enure to the benefit of any assigns, successors in business, or nominee of the COMPANY; and the EMPLOYEE specifically agrees on demand to execute any and all necessary documents in connection therewith, including any necessary documents to effect transfers of title of patents or patent applications, in the United States and in foreign countries, on inventions referred to in paragraph (5) of this Agreement.

(8) This Agreement supersedes all previous contracts for personal services between the COMPANY and the EMPLOYEE. This Agreement constitutes the entire understanding between the parties hereto with reference to the subject matter hereof and shall not be

changed or modified except by a written instrument signed by both parties.

In witness whereof the COMPANY has caused this Agreement to be executed in duplicate by a proper and duly authorized officer thereof, and the EMPLOYEE has signed this Agreement in duplicate, as of the day and year first above written.

················ (COMPANY)

By ····················

Vice-President

Secretary

············· (EMPLOYEE)

APPENDIX L

DEVOE & RAYNOLDS COMPANY, INC.

CONTRACT WITH WILLIAM C. DABNEY
(*Inflation Clause*)

AGREEMENT entered into as of December 1, 1952, between DEVOE & RAYNOLDS COMPANY, INC., a New York corporation (hereinafter called the "Corporation"), and WILLIAM C. DABNEY (hereinafter called the "Employee").

WITNESSETH:

The parties hereto covenant and agree as follows:

1. For the purposes of this Agreement:

(a) The term "Corporation" shall include Devoe & Raynolds Company, Inc., party hereto, and any corporation successor to the business presently conducted by Devoe & Raynolds Company, Inc.

(b) The term "Employee" shall mean William C. Dabney and, except as used in Paragraph 4 hereof, shall also include his legal representatives.

(c) The term "Additional Compensation Plan" shall mean the Corporation's Officers' and Key Employees' Additional Compensation Plan, as amended, which reads as set forth in Schedule 1 hereto.

(d) The term "Period of Employment" shall mean the period commencing December 1, 1952 and ending at the close of the fiscal quarter in which the Employee attains age 65, or when, whether as a result of resignation, death, incapacity or any other reason, the Employee ceases to serve the Corporation or a subsidiary or affiliated corporation on a full-time basis, whichever date shall first occur.

(e) The term "Retirement Date" shall mean the date when, whether as a result of resignation, death, incapacity or any other reason, the Employee ceases to serve the Corporation or a subsidiary or affiliated corporation on a full-time basis.

(f) The term "Employee's Aggregate Contingent Compensation" shall mean the lower of

(i) the sum of $1,282.33 multiplied by the number of months in the Period of Employment, or

(ii) an amount equal to the aggregate amount the Employee would be entitled to receive under the Additional Compensation Plan for the Period of Employment assuming the continuance of the Additional Compensation Plan without change and participation therein by the Employee at the rate of twelve and one-seventh per cent. (12 1/7%) per annum.

(g) The Employee shall be "engaged in a competing business" if, as proprietor, partner, trustee, employee or director, he is engaged or participates in the operation or management of a business which has gross receipts in excess of One million Dollars ($1,000,-000) per annum from the manufacture or distribution of paints, varnishes or lacquers.

(h) The term "Cost of Living Index Number" shall mean the index number under the heading "All Items" in the Consumer Price Index (as revised January, 1953) published for each month by the Bureau of Labor Statistics of the United States Department of Labor or, in the event of the discontinuance thereof, a similar number in any appropriate index selected by the Board of Directors of the Corporation.

(i) The term "Base Index Number" shall mean the Cost of Living Index Number for the month most recently available at the end of the month in which the Retirement Date occurs.

2. The Corporation shall pay to the Employee, subject to the contingencies set forth in Paragraph 4 hereof, an amount computed as provided in Paragraph 3 hereof (hereinafter called "contingent adjusted compensation") each month during the seven-year period next following the Retirement Date.

3. The contingent adjusted compensation to be paid each month to the Employee, as provided in Paragraph 2 hereof, shall be an amount (hereinafter called the "Base Amount") equal to one eighty-fourth (1/84) of the Employee's Aggregate Contingent Compensation, increased or decreased from time to time, as hereinafter provided, so as approximately to reflect increases or decreases in the cost of living during the seven-year period next following the Retirement Date. To reflect said increases or decreases, the Base Amount for any month shall be increased or decreased by that percentage which shall equal the percentage by which the Cost of Living Index Number most recently available on the first day of such month shall exceed or be less than the Base Index Number.

4. In addition to the contingent adjustments hereinabove provided for, the contingencies upon which payments of contingent adjusted compensation, and each of them, shall be made or continued are the following:

(a) that the Employee, if then living, shall, during the seven-year period next following the Period of Employment, make himself available for advice and consultation in such manner as the Corporation may reasonably request and, if so requested, shall serve on any committee or board that may be established to consider and make recommendations respecting the business of the Corporation and shall participate in the meetings thereof when reasonably requested by the Corporation (it being agreed that the Corporation shall reimburse the Employee for his reasonable travelling expenses incurred in performing the duties required by this subparagraph (a)); and

(b) that, during the seven-year period next following the Retirement Date, the Employee shall not be engaged in a competing business without having first procured the written consent of the Corporation.

Either or both of the foregoing contingencies specified in this Paragraph 4 may be eliminated by action of the Board of Directors of the Corporation if said Board shall determine that such elimination shall not be prejudicial to the interests of the Corporation.

5. The contingent adjusted compensation provided for in this Agreement is not in lieu of, or substitution for, any right of the Employee to receive a salary or to participate in the Additional Compensation Plan, or any right of the Employee in, under, or to participate in, any pension, retirement, group life, health, or accident insurance, or other employees' benefit plan, now in existence or which may hereafter become effective for employees of the Corporation; and any payments to or for the benefit of the Employee on account of or under any one or more of the foregoing shall be in addition to any and all payments of contingent adjusted compensation pursuant to this Agreement.

6. The Employee shall not have any power of anticipation, alienation, or assignment of payments hereunder and no person shall acquire any right whatsoever in respect thereof by reason of any sale, assignment, transfer, claim or judgment.

7. This Agreement may be assigned by the Corporation to any corporation which shall succeed to the business of the Corporation by a merger, consolidation, or transfer of all or substantially all the assets

of the Corporation and which shall expressly assume the obligations and liabilities to be performed by the Corporation under this Agreement by an instrument in writing delivered to the Employee.

8. Any notice to be given under this Agreement to the Corporation shall be deemed to have been effectively given to the Corporation when mailed, postage prepaid, addressed to it at the principal office of the Corporation, 787 First Avenue, New York 17, N. Y., or such other address as the Corporation may hereafter designate.

Any notice to be given under this Agreement to the Employee shall be deemed to have been effectively given to the Employee when mailed, postage prepaid, addressed to the Employee at Upper River Road, Louisville, Kentucky, or such other address as the Employee may hereafter designate.

IN WITNESS WHEREOF the Corporation has caused this Agreement to be signed in its corporate name by its President or one of its Vice Presidents thereunto duly authorized and its corporate seal to be hereunto affixed and to be attested by its Secretary or one of its Assistant Secretaries, and the Employee has hereunto set his hand and seal, all as of the day and year first above written.

DEVOE & RAYNOLDS COMPANY, INC.

By ....
Vice President

Attest:

....
Secretary

....
Employee

PROFIT-PARTICIPATION CONTRACTS

APPENDIX M

Fairbanks, Morse & Co.

SUPPLEMENTAL CONTRACT WITH ROBERT H. MORSE

MEMORANDUM OF AGREEMENT made this 23 day of January, 1946, between Fairbanks, Morse & Co., a corporation with its principal office at Chicago, Illinois, (hereinafter called the Company), party of the first part, and Robert H. Morse, party of the second part, this agreement to be a rider to contract executed on the 23 day of January, 1946, between said parties,
Witnesseth:

The Company also agrees to pay him additional compensation for each year of the term hereof, which additional compensation shall be ascertained in the following manner:

(a) From the net profits of the Company for each calendar year there shall be deducted a sum equalling four percent (4%) of the sum of its average outstanding Common Capital Stock during such year and its surplus and undivided profits at the beginning of such year as shown by its books of account, which deductions are hereinafter referred to as "Capital Earnings." The remainder after the deduction of such "Capital Earnings" from the said net profits is hereinafter referred to as the "Balance of Profits."

(b) "Net Profits of the Company" as used herein shall mean the net profits for the calendar year for which such additional compensation is being determined, as audited and certified by the Certified Public Accountant regularly auditing the Company's accounts.

(c) Such annual additional compensation shall be that proportion of the annual salary paid to said party of the second part during such year as said "Balance of Profits" shall bear to said "Capital Earnings" above described, provided, however, that such additional compensation in any year shall not be less than the sum of fifteen thousand dollars ($15,000.00) for each calendar year during the term hereof.

(d) The valuation of the fixed assets of the Company as shown upon its books on the first day of the term hereof, less proper annual depreciation shall be the basis used in determining the surplus and undivided profits of the Company, any additions thereto being on the basis of the cost of such additions to the Company.

(e) Nothing contained in this agreement shall be construed to give the party of the second part any interest in or to the surplus or net profits of the Company, it being agreed that the annual profits thereof are being adopted herein as a standard by which to measure the amount of the additional compensation payable under this agreement.

(f) Such additional compensation shall be payable to said party of the second part for each calendar year during the term hereof upon the net profits of the Company for such year being determined as herein provided by the Board of Directors of the Company.

In witness whereof the said party of the first part has caused this agreement to be executed in its corporate name by its proper officers, appointed by the Board, thereunto duly authorized, and its corporate seal to be attached, and said party of the second part has attached his hand and seal, all in duplicate, as of the day and date first above written.

FAIRBANKS, MORSE & CO.
By R. H. MORSE
  President

  S. T. KIDDOO
  Vice Pres. & Treasurer

  L. A. KEELER
  Vice Pres. & Comptroller

  C. H. POPPENHUSEN
  Director

COMMITTEE OF THE BOARD

(CORPORATE SEAL)
Attest:
E. T. SANDEEN
  Assistant Secretary

Accepted:
ROBERT H. MORSE (SEAL)

ALLIED STORES CORPORATION

CONTRACT WITH CHARLES E. McCARTHY

AGREEMENT made as of the 1st day of February 1950 between ALLIED STORES CORPORATION (hereinafter referred to as "Allied"), a Delaware corporation, party of the first part, and CHARLES E. MCCARTHY (hereinafter referred to as "McCarthy"), party of the second part.

WITNESSETH:

1. Allied hereby agrees to employ McCarthy as President with such duties as shall be assigned to him by the Chairman of the Board and McCarthy hereby accepts such employment, upon the terms and conditions hereinafter set forth. The period of employment shall commence as of February 1, 1950 and continue until terminated as hereinafter provided. McCarthy agrees during the period of employment to devote substantially all of his time and attention to the business of Allied and to the performance of his duties hereunder, but he shall, with the prior approval of the Board of Directors of Allied, be permitted to serve on The Boards of Directors or Committees of other corporations.

2. As compensation for his services hereunder, Allied agrees to pay McCarthy (a) a salary at the rate of $50,000 per annum, payable monthly; plus (b) an amount equal to $3/4$ of 1% of the amount, if any, by which the net profits of Allied for each fiscal year of employment hereunder shall exceed the annual dividend requirement on all preferred stock of Allied during such year; but the amount of such additional compensation for any year shall not exceed $75,000. Such additional compensation shall be payable as soon after the end of each fiscal year as the amount thereof can be ascertained.

"Net profits" under the above paragraph shall mean the consolidated net profits of Allied and its subsidiary companies before dividends on its preferred stock, after deduction of all salary and additional compensation accruing to McCarthy hereunder, all taxes (including federal taxes on income and excess profits) and all proper charges, all computed in accordance with good accounting practice. "The annual dividend requirements on the preferred stock of Allied" for each year shall mean the aggregate amount of dividends which became payable on the preferred stock of Allied outstanding in the hands of the public on the four quarter-yearly dividend dates during such year. The certificate of the firm of public accountants selected as the regular auditors of Allied by its Board of Directors, Executive Committee or by its stockholders shall be conclusive and binding upon McCarthy and Allied with respect to the amount of such net profits, dividend requirements, and the additional compensation, if any, payable to McCarthy under the above paragraph.

3. The employment of McCarthy shall terminate (a) in the event of the selection of a successor as President, (b) McCarthy's permanent disability, (c) McCarthy's death; or (d) McCarthy notifies Allied of its termination, whichever shall first occur.

In the event of such termination of employment other than on a January 31, McCarthy's salary under Section 2 (a) shall cease as of the last day of the month in which such event occurs and the additional compensation under Section 2 (b) hereof for the year during which such event occurs shall be computed as therein provided, and McCarthy or his administrators or executors shall be paid an amount of such additional compensation, if any, proportionate to the elapsed number of months of such year, including the month in which such event occurs but shall be entitled to no further payment under Section 2 (b).

Permanent disability shall be deemed to have occurred if McCarthy shall have been disabled from performing his duties hereunder for six calendar months. Sickness not constituting permanent disability shall not reduce any payments under Section 2.

4. In the event of the termination of McCarthy's employment with Allied pursuant to Section 3 and provided no new employment contract is at the time agreed upon by Allied and McCarthy, Allied agrees to pay to McCarthy as a retirement allowance for the remainder of his life $20,000 per annum payable monthly.

5. All payments under Section 4 shall (a) cease if McCarthy becomes an officer, director or employee of a corporation or a member or an employee of a partnership which conducts a business, or personally conducts a business, competing with that of Allied or any of its subsidiaries, or (b) be suspended while McCarthy is an officer, director or employee of a publicly-owned corporation, even though not competing, from which he receives compensation in excess of $20,000 per annum.

A decision of the Board of Directors of Allied as to what is a competing business or a publicly-owned corporation shall be final and binding thereafter upon Allied and McCarthy.

6. Allied has heretofore adopted a Retirement Annuity Plan for its executives and employees to which payments are being made for McCarthy's benefit. The payments to McCarthy under Section 4 of this agreement shall be reduced in an amount equal to the Retirement Annuity payments made to McCarthy by the Equitable Life Assurance Society under said Plan, provided that if McCarthy has elected to receive a reduced Retirement Annuity under the contingent annuitant option provided for in the Plan, the reduction will be in an amount equal to the Retirement Annuity payment which he would have been entitled to if he had not adopted the contingent annuitant option.

7. The employment agreement between the parties hereto, dated February 1, 1948, is hereby terminated as of January 31, 1950 including Section 4 of such agreement providing for a retirement allowance, and the provisions of Section 4 of this agreement shall be applicable in lieu thereof.

8. No assignment by McCarthy by pledge or otherwise of any right to receive payment hereunder from Allied, will be recognized by Allied.

IN WITNESS WHEREOF the parties hereto have executed this agreement as of the day and year first above written.

ALLIED STORES CORPORATION
By   B. EARL PUCKETT
        Chairman of the Board

C. E. McCARTHY

APPENDIX O

UNIVERSAL PICTURES COMPANY, INC.
AND
UNIVERSAL CORPORATION

CONTRACTS WITH WILLIAM A. SCULLY

AGREEMENT made and entered into this 4th day of March, 1941, by and between UNIVERSAL PICTURES COMPANY, INC., a corporation duly organized and existing under and by virtue of the laws of the State of Delaware, hereinafter referred to as "Universal," party of the first part, and WILLIAM A. SCULLY, of Forest Hills, Long Island, New York, hereinafter referred to as "Scully", party of the second part,

WITNESSETH :

Scully is presently employed by Universal under an agreement dated the   day of December, 1937.

The parties hereto desire to modify the provisions of the aforesaid agreement and to extend the term thereof, all upon the terms and conditions hereinafter set forth.

Now, THEREFORE, in consideration of the premises and of the mutual covenants, promises and agreements hereinafter set forth, the parties hereto have agreed and do hereby agree as follows:

FIRST: Universal hereby employs Scully as General Sales Manager of Universal, for a period of seven (7) years, commencing as of January 1, 1941 and ending on December 31, 1947.

It is agreed that the duties of Scully shall be such as are fixed by the Board of Directors of Universal but they shall be of a dignity consistent with the standing and experience of Scully in the industry, and that the duties of Scully shall at all times include the general supervision of sales in the territory of the United States of America, the general management of the sales organization and personnel, including district managers, branch managers and salesmen, and the engagement and discharge of the personnel of the sales organization; the determination of the number and location of such personnel and the salaries to be paid; with respect to all of the foregoing, Scully shall

331

have full exclusive power and authority subject only to the approval of the President or, in the absence of the President, from such person as the President may designate, all as authorized by the Board of Directors of Universal.

Scully hereby accepts such employment and agrees to devote his exclusive business and working time to Universal and its subsidiaries during the term hereof and to perform the said services for Universal conscientiously and to the full limit of his ability.

Scully agrees that during the term hereof he will not have any financial interest, directly or indirectly, in any other person, firm or corporation engaged in any business competitive to Universal's except that Scully may acquire and own an interest in securities of any company listed on any recognized public exchange.

Scully may continue to hold any directorships, trusteeships or executorships, if any, which he now has but shall not assume any new ones without the authorization of the Board of Directors of Universal first had and obtained.

SECOND: Subject to the provisions of Paragraph FIRST hereof, Scully shall make his headquarters in New York City, New York.

When Scully is absent from his headquarters on business of Universal, he shall be paid, in addition to the compensation herein provided, reasonable traveling and living expenses. If his absence, as aforesaid, is required for a period of two (2) weeks or longer, then Scully shall also be paid the reasonable traveling and living expenses of Mrs. Scully.

Scully shall also be entitled to reimbursement for entertainment and other expenses incurred by him in the performance of his duties hereunder for Universal. Such expenses shall be paid promptly as vouchers therefor are presented by Scully.

THIRD: Provided that Scully shall fully and completely keep and perform the duties and obligations on his part to be kept and performed under the terms of this agreement, Universal shall pay to Scully and Scully shall accept the following:

(a) During the first two (2) years of the term of this agreement, *i.e.*, from January 1, 1941 through December 31, 1942, the sum of One thousand five hundred dollars ($1,500) per week, payable weekly.

(b) During the last five (5) years of the term of this agreement, *i.e.*, from January 1, 1943 through December 31, 1947, the sum of One thousand seven hundred fifty dollars ($1,750) per week, payable weekly.

In addition to the fixed compensation hereinabove provided for, Universal agrees, during each year, to pay to Scully a percentage of the consolidated net profits of Universal and subsidiaries before providing for Federal and State taxes based on income but after providing for the amounts payable as additional compensation based upon consolidated net profits to all other officers or employees of Universal, as follows:

A. During the first two years of the term of this agreement, as follows:
    (a) One-half ($\frac{1}{2}$) of one percent (1%) on the first $1,000,-000 of such net profits;
    (b) Three-fourths ($\frac{3}{4}$) of one percent (1%) on the second $1,000,000 of such net profits;
    (c) One-half ($\frac{1}{2}$) of one percent (1%) on the next $500,-000 of such net profits;
    (d) One percent (1%) of such net profits in excess of $2,-500,000.

B. During the last five years of the term of this agreement, as follows:
    (a) One-half ($\frac{1}{2}$) of one percent (1%) of the first $2,500,-000 of such net profits; and
    (b) One percent (1%) of such net profits in excess of $2,500,000.

If, for any Universal fiscal year during the term of this agreement, rates of Federal or State taxes based on income are increased so that the ratio of such taxes, payable by Universal, to its taxable income is increased over the ratio for the fiscal year ended November 2, 1940, then the percentages of net profits payable to Scully under the terms hereof shall be decreased by the percentage of such increase in taxes, *e.g.,* taking the net profit of Universal and subsidiaries for the fiscal year ended November 2, 1940 as $3,000,000 and the income taxes payable thereon as $900,000, the ratio of the taxes to net profits is thirty percent (30%). If in any subsequent fiscal year the ratio should be forty percent (40%), then there is a ten percent (10%) increase in taxes for the purposes of this agreement and, consequently, the percentage of net profits of Universal payable to Scully under the terms of this agreement would be decreased by ten percent (10%). It is understood and agreed, however, that if for any one or more fiscal years the net profit of Universal, after provision for Federal and State taxes on income of Universal, is equal to or greater than the sum of $2,400,000, then for any such fiscal year or years, the reduction in the percentages of net profits of Universal payable to Scully under the terms hereof shall apply only to the excess of net profits over $2,400,000 and as to the first $2,400,000 of net profits, Scully shall be entitled to and shall receive the percentage above provided for without reduction of any kind.

Such additional compensation based upon Universal's net profits, as above provided, shall be paid to Scully for each Universal fiscal year ending during the term of this employment, commencing with the fiscal year that started November 2, 1940.

For the last two (2) months of the term of this agreement, Scully shall receive the additional compensation based upon one-twelfth (1/12th) of one percent (1%) of the first $2,500,000 of net profits, determined as above provided, and one-sixth (1/6th) of one percent (1%) of the net profits, determined as above provided, in excess of $2,500,000 during the fiscal year 1947/48.

For the purposes of determining the additional compensation based upon the net profits of Universal, payable to Scully hereunder for each year, the net profits shall be computed without including therein any funds (hereinafter referred to as "pounds sterling"), the remittance of which is restricted, from Great Britain, as presently constituted. Price, Waterhouse & Co. or such other firm of public accountants employed by Universal to make an annual audit of its books of account shall, at the end of each fiscal year, prepare a statement showing the net profits of Universal for the fiscal year in question which shall set forth fully the net profits of Universal without including pounds sterling, the remittance of which is restricted. The statement prepared by Price, Waterhouse & Co., or such other firm of public accountants employed by Universal to make an annual audit of its books, shall also show the amount of pounds sterling, the remittance of which is restricted.

The additional compensation shall be paid to Scully promptly upon the completion of the statement above provided to be prepared by Price, Waterhouse & Co. or such other auditors as Universal uses, based upon the net profits without including therein the pounds sterling, the remittance of which is restricted.

At such time as the restrictions on the remittance of the pounds sterling, specified as net profits in any statement furnished as aforesaid, are lifted, then the net amount in dollars received by Universal on the sale of such restricted pounds sterling shall be added to the net profits in dollars of the fiscal year during which the pounds sterling, originally restricted, accrued. Universal shall recompute the net profits for such fiscal year and the additional compensation payable to Scully thereon, under the provisions of this agreement, and pay to Scully the difference between the amount actually due and the amount theretofore paid to Scully; provided, however, that where dollars, by reason of the sale of restricted pounds sterling, are available for adjustment of payments on account of net profits for previous fiscal years, no more than one fiscal year shall be adjusted or paid in any twelve (12) months' period but adjustments and payments shall continue annually until completed.

It is understood and agreed by and between the parties hereto:

(1) That where remittance quotas are granted out of current earnings in any fiscal year by any of the fiscal authorities having jurisdiction, the amount in dollars of such remittances shall be included in the net profits of the current fiscal year.

(2) As and when the restrictions against remittances are lifted as to funds blocked in preceding years, the pounds sterling earliest restricted shall be deemed the first available for remittance.

(3) In the event that any funds previously blocked are used by Universal for its own purposes as permitted by the fiscal authorities of Great Britain having jurisdiction, the amount thereof in dollars at the current rate of exchange shall be deemed to have been remitted for the purposes of this agreement and shall be credited to the net profits for the fiscal year during which the pounds sterling so used and restricted accrued and paid.

Universal represents and warrants that at the year ended November 2, 1940, it had blocked in Great Britain approximately Three hundred ninety thousand pounds (£390,000). As and when restrictions on the remittances are lifted in regard to these pounds sterling, Scully shall have no interest therein. However, if after November 2, 1940 any pounds sterling blocked to that date are used by Universal and charged against its income in any year subsequent to November 2, 1940, then the amounts so charged to income by Universal shall be added back to the net profit upon which Scully's percentage is to be computed.

Universal shall, with the remittance of the amount due Scully under the terms hereof, deliver to Scully a copy of the audited statement of Price, Waterhouse & Co., or such other auditors as Universal may then be using. Such statements shall be deemed to be conclusive unless, within ninety (90) days thereafter, Scully shall submit to Universal written objections to any of the items set forth in the said statement. In the event that the parties hereto cannot agree upon an adjustment of such protested items, it is agreed that any difference of opinion shall be submitted to arbitration as herein provided.

For the foregoing purposes, Universal agrees that Scully shall have the right at all reasonable hours to inspect and audit such books and records of Universal as are relevant to the provisions of this agreement.

Any and all disputes arising under this Paragraph THIRD between Universal and Scully shall be decided by arbitration in the City of New York under the laws of the State of New York. Each party, by written notice, may appoint an arbitrator and demand that the other party appoint its arbitrator within five (5) days after the receipt of such notice. The two arbitrators so selected shall appoint an umpire. If, within ten (10) days after their appointment, the two arbitrators shall be unable to agree upon an umpire, the umpire shall be selected by the American Arbitration Society. Within twenty (20) days after the foregoing notice demanding arbitration has been sent by either party to the other, the two arbitrators and the umpire shall commence the arbitration proceedings and proceed to an award with reasonable dispatch. Any award so rendered shall be final and binding upon the parties hereto and may be enforced in accordance with the laws of the State of New York.

FOURTH : Scully shall be entitled to take a vacation or vacations aggregating thirty-one (31) days during each year with full pay, and such vacation periods shall be cumulative so that if during any one or more years Scully does not take the entire vacation permitted hereunder, he may add the unused periods to such other vacations as he may take during the term of this agreement.

FIFTH : In the event that Scully shall become physically or mentally disabled or incapacitated so that he cannot carry on his duties hereunder for a period of six (6) consecutive months, Universal, at its election, may at any time thereafter terminate this agreement. Until such termination, however, the compensation shall be paid to Scully in accordance with the provisions hereof. In the event of such termination or in the event of the death of Scully, Scully or his estate shall nevertheless be entitled to and be paid the additional compensation payable to him under the terms hereof, for the year during which such termination or death took place.

SIXTH : It is understood and agreed that the services to be rendered under the terms of this agreement by Scully are of a special, unique, unusual, extraordinary and intellectual character, which give them a peculiar value, the loss of which cannot be reasonably or adequately compensated in damages in an action at law, and that a breach by Scully of any of the provisions contained in this agreement will cause Universal irreparable injury and damage. Scully hereby expressly agrees that Universal shall be entitled to injunctive and other equitable relief to prevent a breach of this agreement by Scully. This provision, however, shall not be construed as a waiver of any other rights that Universal may have in the premises for damages or otherwise.

SEVENTH: Each and all of the several rights, remedies and options of both parties hereunder shall be construed as cumulative, and no one of them as exclusive of the other or of any right or priority under this contract or pursuant to law.

EIGHTH: No waiver by either party of any breach of any duty, obligation or agreement to be kept or performed hereunder shall be deemed to be a waiver of any preceding or succeeding breach of the same or any other duty, obligation or agreement.

NINTH: This agreement shall enure to the benefit of and be binding upon the successors and assigns of Universal in the event that any corporation succeeds to or acquires all of the assets of Universal and in the event of a merger or consolidation of Universal with any other corporation.

In the event of a merger or consolidation of Universal with any corporation other than one with which it is now affiliated, Scully may at any time, but no later than thirty (30) days after the consummation of such merger or consolidation, elect to cancel and terminate this agreement. Such election shall be addressed to Universal at No. 1250 Sixth Avenue, New York City, New York, mailed registered mail, and specify the date upon which Scully elects that this agreement shall terminate and come to an end, which date shall be no later than thirty (30) days after the date of such notice. Thereafter, this agreement shall terminate and come to an end on the date specified in the notice of cancellation aforesaid, with like force and effect as though the date therein specified had been the expiration date of this agreement under its terms and, further, Scully shall be entitled to receive pro rata additional compensation, computed to the nearest month of the termination, based upon the percentage of the net profits of Universal for the fiscal year in which such termination took place.

TENTH : The agreement heretofore executed by and between the parties hereto, dated the   day of December, 1937, is hereby cancelled and terminated as of January 1, 1941.

ELEVENTH : This agreement shall be governed and construed by and according to the laws of the State of New York.

TWELFTH : This agreement shall be subject to the approval of the stockholders of Universal, entitled to vote thereon, and of the approval by the stockholders of Universal Corporation, entitled to vote thereon, of the agreement entered into by it with Scully concurrently with the execution hereof, and unless and until so approved by the stockholders of both corporations, shall not be binding upon the parties hereto.

IN WITNESS WHEREOF, Universal has caused these presents to be executed by its officers thereunto duly authorized and its corporate seal to be hereunto affixed, and Scully has hereunto set his hand and seal, the day and year first above written.

UNIVERSAL PICTURES COMPANY, INC.

By   J. CHEEVER COWDIN
Chairman of the Board

Attest :

PEYTON GIBSON   WILLIAM A. SCULLY   (L.S.)
Secretary

AGREEMENT made and entered into this 4th day of March, 1941, by and between UNIVERSAL CORPORATION, a Delaware corporation, hereinafter referred to as "the Corporation", party of the first part, and WILLIAM A. SCULLY, of Forest Hills, Long Island, New York, hereinafter referred to as "Scully", party of the second part,

WITNESSETH:

The Corporation is the owner of all of the outstanding shares of Second Preferred Stock and approximately ninety-two percent (92%) of all of the Common Stock of Universal Pictures Company, Inc.

The parties hereto entered into a certain agreement under date of the   day of December, 1937.

Universal Pictures Company, Inc., concurrently with the execution hereof, has entered into an employment agreement with Scully, modifying the previous agreement between the said parties.

The best interests of the Corporation and its affiliates would be served if Scully's holdings of the Corporation's stock were materially increased because his personal ownership of a larger investment in the Corporation, or his right to purchase the same, would act as an incentive to him to make the Corporation's stock more valuable and would insure his loyalty to the welfare of the Corporation and its security holders.

In consideration of the premises and of the execution of the aforesaid employment agreement by the said Scully with Universal Pictures Company, Inc., and as an inducement for him so to do, and of other good and valuable consideration, the receipt whereof is hereby acknowledged, the parties hereto have agreed and do hereby agree as follows:

FIRST: The Corporation agrees to, and does hereby guaranty the full and faithful performance by Universal Pictures Company, Inc. of all of the terms, conditions and agreements on its part to be kept and performed under and pursuant to the employment agreement dated the 4th day of March, 1941, executed concurrently herewith by the said Universal Pictures Company, Inc. and Scully.

SECOND: In order to enable Scully to have a greater participation in the management of the Corporation and its subsidiary and affiliated corporations:

The Corporation hereby agrees to issue to Scully, in place and in exchange for all of the five-year Warrants issued to the said Scully under and pursuant to the aforesaid agreement, dated December , 1937, a like number of valid Warrants to Purchase Common Stock (Voting Trust Certificates) of the Corporation, representing the right to purchase on or before April 1, 1956, Common Stock (Voting Trust Certificates) of the Corporation at Ten dollars ($10.) per share, which said Warrants shall contain all of the terms, conditions and provisions of the Warrants presently outstanding and as to which the Chase National Bank of the City of New York is the Transfer Agent, and which were originally authorized by resolutions duly adopted at a meeting of the Board of Directors of the Corporation held on March 25, 1936.

The Corporation further agrees to issue to Scully at the end of each year of his employment, under the agreement between the said Scully and Universal Pictures Company, Inc., executed concurrently herewith, valid Warrants for the purchase of Three thousand (3,000) shares of Common Stock (Voting Trust Certificates) of the Corporation, on or before April 1, 1956, at Ten dollars ($10.) per share, which said Warrants shall contain all of the terms, conditions and provisions of the Warrants presently outstanding and as to which the Chase National Bank of the City of New York is the Transfer Agent, and which were originally authorized by resolutions duly adopted at a meeting of the Board of Directors of the Corporation held on March 25, 1936.

In the event that at any time during the term of this agreement the Corporation issues an additional number of shares of Common Stock or other stock of a class equal to the Common Stock as a stock dividend, or in the event that at any time during the term of this agreement the Corporation, by amendment of its certificate, shall split up the outstanding number of shares of Common Stock into a greater number of shares, then in either of these events a proportionate adjustment shall be made in the number of Warrants thereafter to be issued to Scully under the terms hereof or in the price to be paid by Scully on the exercise of the rights granted under the Warrants thereafter issued for the rights therein granted.

THIRD: In the event that the agreement between Scully and Universal Pictures Company, Inc., executed concurrently herewith, is terminated by reason of the provisions of Paragraph FIFTH thereof, or in the event of the death of Scully, Scully or his estate shall nevertheless be entitled to the number of Warrants issuable to him hereunder for the year during which such termination or death took place.

In the event that the said agreement between Scully and Universal Pictures Company, Inc. is terminated by Scully by reason of the provisions of Paragraph NINTH thereof, Scully shall be entitled to receive a pro rata number of Warrants, computed to the month nearest the date of termination, for the year in which such termination takes place.

FOURTH: The agreement between Scully and the Corporation, dated December , 1937, is hereby cancelled and terminated as of January 1, 1941.

FIFTH: This agreement shall be subject to the approval of the stockholders of the Corporation, entitled to vote thereon, and the approval by the stockholders of Universal Pictures Company, Inc., entitled to vote thereon, of the agreement executed concurrently herewith by the said Universal Pictures Company, Inc. and Scully, and unless and until so approved by the stockholders of both corporations, shall not be binding upon the parties hereto.

IN WITNESS WHEREOF, the Corporation has caused these presents to be executed by its officers thereunto duly authorized and its corporate seal to be hereunto affixed, and Scully has hereunto set his hand and seal, the day and year first above written.

UNIVERSAL CORPORATION

By J. CHEEVER COWDIN
Chairman of the Board

Attest:

  PEYTON GIBSON
   Secretary

WILLIAM A. SCULLY (L.S.)

UNIVERSAL PICTURES COMPANY, INC.
ROCKEFELLER CENTER
NEW YORK

March 4, 1941.

Mr. William A. Scully
Forest Hills, N. Y.

Dear Mr. Scully:

This is to confirm our understanding and agreement with regard to the employment agreement executed between yourself and the undersigned concurrently with the execution hereof.

In the event that the stockholders of the undersigned do not approve said agreement within sixty (60) days from the date hereof, or within such further period as may be mutually agreed upon, then and in that event either party may cancel and terminate the said agreement executed concurrently herewith by giving written notice, mailed registered mail, to the other, of its or your election so to do. Upon such cancellation the agreement between yourself and the undersigned, executed on the   day of December 1937, shall continue to be and remain in full force and effect.

It is also understood and agreed between us that in the event the aforesaid employment agreement, executed concurrently herewith, is invalidated for any reason, then and in such event the agreement between us, dated the   day of December 1937, shall be and remain in full force and effect.

> Very truly yours,
> UNIVERSAL PICTURES COMPANY, INC.
> By   J. CHEEVER COWDIN
> Chairman of the Board

APPENDIX P

SAFEWAY STORES, INCORPORATED

CONTRACT WITH HERBERT WILCOX

May 15, 1950

Mr. Herbert Wilcox
Safeway Stores, Incorporated
300 Mercer Street
Jersey City, New Jersey

Dear Mr. Wilcox:

Our understanding of the arrangement under which you are to be compensated as Division Manager of the Company's New York Division is as follows:

Your salary as Division Manager of said Division, unless changed as herein provided, shall be $40,000.00 per year. In addition to this salary you will receive a bonus computed as follows:

If the combined net profits of all operations under your control, after first deducting the amount of salary and bonus payable, exceed the sum of $800,000.00 in any one Company fiscal year, you shall be paid a bonus equal to 5% of all such profits in excess of $800,000.00. For bonus purposes, the profits of the operations under your control shall be computed as herein outlined.

Said net profits shall be computed after first deducting federal income and excess profits taxes, state income taxes, franchise taxes and all other taxes which have not been directly charged to expense and after deducting the pro-rata share of administrative office expense and service company upcharges applicable to these operations. The administrative office expense shall be prorated over all divisions in direct proportion to the total sales in each division. Service company upcharges shall be allocated against company operations benefiting from the services rendered by such companies as determined from time to time by the administrative office. The amount of income and excess profits taxes (as well as all other taxes computed in a similar manner) to be deducted shall, at the option of the President of this Company (herein referred to as "President") be determined by either (1) applying to your operations the average tax rates applicable to the Company as a whole, or (2) by looking upon the operations under your control as a separate business entirely distinct from other Company operations, and using the earnings of and the capital invested in your operations, computing the amount of tax upon such operations at the rates prescribed by law. In the event the second method is used, no consideration whatsoever shall be given to the profits and losses of other operations of the Company. The Controller of this Company, or in his absence an Acting Controller designated by the President, shall determine all questions which may arise as to the amount of taxes or net profits to be used in the bonus computation. Such determination shall be conclusive and binding upon both the Company and you. Your continued service to the end of the fiscal year as Division Manager of the New York Division shall be a condition precedent to your right to receive the bonus provided for herein for such year.

Your salary and bonus for 1950 shall be computed on a pro-rata basis, commencing with the date when you report for duty at New York. Thereafter your bonus shall be computed annually, with payment thereof to be made as soon as conveniently possible after the close of the fiscal year. If the approval of the President is first obtained, you may ask for and receive an advance on the bonus payable to you for any year.

If you are transferred or sever your connections with the Company, your salary and bonus shall be computed upon a pro-rata basis to the date upon which you are transferred, or to the date upon which you sever your connections with the Company.

The President may at his discretion, at any time and from time to time, change any provisions in this arrangement, including but not being limited to, the percentage of net profits upon which your bonus is computed, or he may rescind or terminate this arrangement in its entirety. Any such change, recision or termination may, at his option, be made retroactive to the beginning of the fiscal year.

The provisions hereof which relate to the payment of remuneration are subject to all laws and governmental regulations now or hereafter in effect and in no event is remuneration in excess of the amount permitted by such governmental laws and regulations to become payable hereunder.

The sole purpose of this memorandum is to record our mutual understanding as to the amount and method of computing the remuneration which you are to receive and it is not our thought or intention to have it constitute an employment contract. This letter will confirm the fact that no employment contract exists between you and the Company.

If the above is in conformity with your understanding, please signify your acceptance by signing and returning the duplicate copy of this letter.

Very truly yours,
SAFEWAY STORES, INCORPORATED
By L. A. WARREN

President

Accepted:

HERBERT WILCOX
Date: June 5, 1950

SPECIAL PROFIT-PARTICIPATION CLAUSES

APPENDIX Q

New England Theatres, Inc.

(Excerpts from contract with Martin J. Mullin and Samuel Pinanski, September 7, 1948.)

By separate written agreement, New England has, for the term and upon the terms and conditions therein set forth and provided, employed M & P Theatres Corporation (a Massachusetts corporation, hereinafter referred to as "M & P") to have supervision of the operation and management of certain theatres, real estate properties and other businesses in which New England has an interest. Under the terms of said agreement, New England has agreed to pay to M & P a proportionate part, determined as provided in said agreement, of the total costs incurred by M & P in managing the theatres, real estate properties and other businesses managed by M & P for any corporation for which it furnishes management service (which total costs are called in said agreement ("Home Office Costs"). Certain other corporation [sic] in which New England owns capital stock have similar management agreements with M & P. The expression "New England's Share of Home Office Compensation" as used anywhere in this agreement shall mean for any period the total amount payable by New England to M & P for that period on account of such "Home Office Costs," increased by such proportionate part of the amount payable to M & P for that period on account of such "Home Office Costs" by each corporation in which New England owns capital stock as shall correspond to the percentage which the capital stock owned by New England in such corporation bears to the total capital stock thereof. The expression "capital stock" as used anywhere in this agreement means capital stock entitled to participate in the earnings of the corporation after preferred-stock requirements, if any, have been met or provided for.

*   *   *

2. (a) New England agrees, subject to the provisions of paragraph 8 hereof, to pay to Mullin and Pinanski (one-half to be paid

to each) a combined Percentage Compensation (hereinafter referred to as "Percentage Compensation") of fifteen per cent. (15%) of its consolidated net earnings as defined in paragraph 2 (c) of this agreement for the accounting period beginning January 4, 1948 and ending January 1, 1949, computed and payable as provided in this agreement, after deducting from such fifteen per cent. (15%) of such consolidated net earnings for such accounting period a sum equal to eighty-five per cent. (85%) of New England's Share of Fixed Compensation for such accounting period; provided, however, that such Percentage Compensation payable by New England shall in any event be not less than an amount which, when added to New England's Share of Fixed Compensation, shall result in a total of not less than Fifty-five Thousand Dollars ($55,000). New England's Share of Fixed Compensation shall be construed to mean such proportionate part of the total Fixed Compensation as shall correspond to the percentage which New England's Share of Home Office Compensation bears to the total "Home Office Costs" incurred by M & P as hereinbefore referred to.

(b) The consolidated net earnings of New England and the Percentage Compensation payable to Mullin and Pinanski by New England shall be computed as of January 1, 1949, for the accounting period from January 4, 1948 through January 1, 1949, the date as of which said computation is to be made being hereinafter referred to as the "Computation Date." Within one hundred twenty (120) days after the Computation Date an audit of the books of New England and its Subsidiaries for such accounting period (such period being hereinafter referred to as the "Computation Period"), a computation of the consolidated net earnings of New England for the Computation Period, and a computation of the Percentage Compensation payable to Mullin and Pinanski by New England for the Computation Period shall be made. Such audit and such computation of consolidated net earnings and Percentage Compensation shall be made by Price, Waterhouse & Co. or by any other accountant or accountants (who may be the regular accountants for New England and who shall be hereinafter referred to as the "Accountants") selected by New England and approved by Mullin and Pinanski, whose approval shall not be unreasonably withheld. The Accountants' computations of consolidated net earnings and Percentage Compensation, made in the manner hereinafter provided, shall be final and binding upon New England and upon Mullin and Pinanski for the purpose of this contract. The amount of Percentage Compensation determined by the Accountants to be payable to Mullin and Pinanski by New England for said Computation Period shall be paid to Mullin and Pinanski by New England not later than one hundred thirty (130) days after the expiration of such Computation Period.

New England hereby further agrees that if and when any dividend or distribution shall be paid after January 3, 1948 and prior to January 1, 1952, out of earnings which shall have accrued after June 27, 1936 and prior to January 4, 1948, by any corporation in which New England shall have a capital stock interest at the time of such payment (excepting, however, any corporation which is a Subsidiary) then New England shall promptly thereafter pay to Mullin and Pinanski an amount equal to fifteen per cent. (15%) of that portion of such dividend or distribution which the capital stock owned by New England in such corporation bears to the total outstanding capital stock thereof, less fifteen per cent. (15%) of any taxes attributable to the receipt of such dividend or distribution.

(c) For the purpose of computing the Percentage Compensation of Mullin and Pinanski, the consolidated net earnings of New England for the Computation Period shall be the amount by which

(A) the gross earnings and income of New England from all sources during the Computation Period, applicable to the Computation Period (it being understood, however, that such gross earnings and income shall not include capital gains and capital receipts (including in capital gains from the purchase or redemption of any of New England's securities or obligations at a discount and from the sale or other disposition of real estate or tangible personal property, leases, securities or other investments) but shall include (without limiting the generality of the foregoing) (i) all dividends or distributions paid to New England out of earnings accrued after January 3, 1948 except dividends or distributions paid or payable by Subsidiaries of New England, and (ii) an amount equal to such proportionate part of the consolidated net earnings (ascertained and determined in the same manner as herein set forth for determining the consolidated net earnings of New England) for the Computation Period of each Subsidiary of New England, as the amount of the capital stock of such Subsidiary held by New England bears to the total outstanding capital stock of such Subsidiary)
exceed

(B) the sum of the following items:

(i) All expenses paid or accrued during the Computation Period, applicable to the Computation Period, in the operation of the business of New England, including the amounts paid or payable to M & P by New England for the Computation Period and interest charged on money borrowed for corporate purposes but excluding salaries of directors or other corporate officers as such, and also excluding interest upon debts created for the purpose of paying dividends.

(ii) All taxes (including, but without limiting the generality of the foregoing, all corporation and franchise taxes and federal and state income and excess profits taxes), assessments and insurance paid or accrued by New England during the Computation Period and applicable to the Computation Period, said income taxes to be computed after giving effect to the deduction, as an expense, of the Percentage Compensation and New England's Share of Home Office Compensation applicable to the Computation Period; it being understood that the income and excess profits taxes deductible under this subdivision (ii) are the income and excess profits taxes actually paid or payable in respect of the Computation Period by New England.

(iii) All other charges of New England, paid or accrued, applicable to the Computation Period, which are of a character which would generally be regarded as operating expenses for the Computation Period by corporations conducting a business similar to that of New England, including ordinary current repairs to and minor replacements of and additions to and maintenance expenditures upon, the properties or equipment of New England (provided, however, that if in the Computation Period any capital gain or receipt shall result from recovery for loss of or damage to property of which there shall not be full repair or replacement during such Computation Period, any expenditure for such repair or replacement during any subsequent Computation Period, if any, shall not be deducted), and including depreciation, applicable to the Computation Period, at fair rates not in excess of those taken by New England of all properties and equipment owned by New England from time to time, but excluding capital payments and capital losses (including in capital losses, without limiting the generality of the foregoing, losses from the purchase, or redemption of any of New England's securities at a premium, and losses from or in respect of sales or other disposition or real estate or tangible personal property, leases, securities or any other investments or losses from or in respect of obligations of others to New England not created during the period of any employment of Mullin and Pinanski by M & P); it being understood and agreed that, although losses actually taken from or in respect of obligations of others to New England created after June 27, 1936 shall be included in the charges of New England under this subdivision (iii), there shall not in any event be included in such charges of New England any losses which are, or have in any Computation Period been, reflected in the net losses referred to in subdivision (iv) of paragraph 5 of an agreement between the parties and others dated October 14, 1938, or in the net losses referred to in subdivision (vi) of paragraph 5 of an agreement between the parties and others dated January 31, 1936, or in the net losses referred to in subdivision (iv) of paragraph 2 of this agreement.

(iv) Such proportionate part of the net losses (as hereinafter defined) for the Computation Period sustained by each Subsidiary of New England as the amount of capital stock of such Subsidiary held by New England bears to the total outstanding capital stock of such Subsidiary. For the purpose of this subdivision (iv), the net loss of each Subsidiary for the Computation Period shall be deemed to be the amount by which the aggregate of all the items corresponding, with respect to such Subsidiary, to the items specified in subdivision (i), (ii) and (iii) above, deductible by such Subsidiary during the Computation Period, and the net loss (ascertained and determined as in this subdivision (iv) provided) sustained by the Subsidiaries of such Subsidiary during the Computation Period exceeds the gross income of such Subsidiary (ascertained and determined in the manner herein provided for determining the gross income of New England) for the Computation Period,

(d) The term "Subsidiary" as used in subdivisions (a), (b) and (c) of this paragraph 2 shall include only corporations in which New England (or any Subsidiary as herein defined) holds at least fifty per cent. (50%) of the capital stock, or in which New England and Publix Netoco Theatres Corporation, a Delaware corporation, (hereinafter referred to as "Publix Netoco"), or any Subsidiaries of either as herein defined, together hold at least fifty-one per cent. (51%) of the capital stock, and if there is more than one class of stock, the term "capital stock" shall be deemed to mean stock entitled to participate in the earnings of such corporations after preferred-stock requirements, if any, have been met or provided for.

(e) In making a computation of consolidated net earnings and Percentage Compensation with respect to New England in the manner provided above, there shall not be included in the gross earnings and income of New England income derived by New England, either directly or indirectly, through subsidiaries or otherwise, from properties not served by M & P; and there shall not be included in the expenses or charges of New England to be deducted from gross earnings and income any expenses or charges (including all taxes) incurred by New England, either directly or indirectly, through subsidiaries or otherwise, in connection with or attributable to properties not served by M & P or attributable to income from such properties.

(f) In making a computation of consolidated net earnings of and Percentage Compensation with respect to New England in the manner provided above, (1) there shall be excluded any earnings, income, losses, or charges of New England or any Subsidiary attributable (i) to the construction or operation of a television broadcasting station or the obtaining of the necessary licenses or permits therefor or the supplying of services in connection therewith or the ownership or leasing of any television equipment or other property in connection therewith, or (ii) to the business of selling television receivers or other television equipment, including, without thereby limiting the foregoing generality, any interest on monies borrowed for any of the foregoing purposes, and (2) all income and excess profits taxes of New England and of any such Subsidiary shall be computed after such exclusion and as though the foregoing items of earnings, income, losses, or charges did not exist.

(g) In the event that the holders of the "non-Paramount interest" (as hereinafter defined) in any corporation, in which either New England or Publix Netoco shall have an interest, either directly or indirectly, through subsidiaries or otherwise, shall be willing to enter into an agreement with Mullin and Pinanski whereby such holders will agree to pay to Mullin and Pinanski fifteen per cent. (15%) of such holders' pro rata share of the earnings of said corporation or of dividends or other distributions paid to such holders by such corporation, New England hereby consents to the making of such agreement by Mullin and Pinanski with such holders of such "non-Paramount interest"; it being understood, however, that any such agreement, and all payments of percentage compensation thereunder, shall be made by such holders of the "non-Paramount interest" and not by the corporation itself. "Non-Paramount interest," as used herein, shall mean capital stock of any corporation not held or owned, directly or indirectly, by New England or Publix Netoco. New England also consents to the making of an agreement between Mullin and Pinanski and Publix Netoco whereunder Publix Netoco shall agree to pay compensation to Mullin and Pinanski as an inducement to Mullin and Pinanski to continue to act, for any period, through their said employment by M & P, as General Managers of theatres, real estate properties and other businesses in which Publix Netoco shall have an interest.

(h) If at any time subsequent to the expiration of said Computation Period and prior to January 1, 1952 an adjustment shall be made with respect to any income, charges or expenses (applicable to such Computation Period) of New England, a proper accounting thereof shall thereupon be made by and between New England and Mullin and Pinanski.

3. New England (in so far as it legally may) agrees with Mullin and Pinanski, and each of them,

(a) to cause the election of said Samuel Pinanski as President, and of said Martin J. Mullin as Vice-President, and of both as directors, of said New England and to cause the continuance of each of them in such offices until January 1, 1949 or such earlier date as his employment by M & P shall have terminated, such earlier date being hereinafter in this paragraph 3 referred to as the "Date of Termination";

(b) to cause the election of said Samuel Pinanski as President, and of said Martin J. Mullin as Vice-President, and of both as directors, of said M & P and to cause the continuance of each of them in such offices until January 1, 1949 or the Date of Termination; and New England further agrees that the present provisions of the By-Laws of M & P limiting the Board of Directors to four and requiring the affirmative vote of not less than three of the directors to effect action by such Board of Directors, shall remain until January 1, 1949 or the Date of Termination.

APPENDIX R

BLOOMINGDALE BROS., INC.

(Excerpt from contract with M. Schaap, February 2, 1935.)

As used in this agreement the expression "net earnings" means the amount of the net earnings of the employer available for addition to surplus or distribution to the stockholders of the employer as dividends, and shall be determined according to the usual practice of the employer and approved accounting methods. In determining the basic net earnings upon which the amount payable to the employee under clause 3B above is calculated the amount of the dividends on the preferred stock of the employer accrued during the fiscal year in question shall be deducted; but there shall not be deducted in determining "net earnings" or "basic net earnings" for the purpose of this agreement the amount payable under said clause 3B to the employee hereunder or the amount payable to Harry A. Hatry under a similar clause designated as 3B in an agreement of even date between this corporation and said Harry A. Hatry. (par. 3D)

APPENDIX S

JONES & LAUGHLIN STEEL CORPORATION

(Excerpt from contract with L. M. Parsons, March 1, 1938.)

(b) And as an incentive to second party to promote and increase the business and profits of the party of the first part, the party of the first part agrees and binds itself to pay to the party of the second part, for the fiscal years 1938, 1939, 1940, 1941 and 1942, one-half of one per cent. (½ of 1%) of all net profits earned by first party in each of said years in excess of Four million two hundred thousand ($4,200,000.00) Dollars (equivalent to the amount of the annual dividend on 600,000 shares of cumulative seven per cent. preferred stock of the party of the first part).

"Net Profits" as used in this Agreement, it is agreed by the parties, means profits after deduction of provision for depreciation and depletion, interest charges and all taxes.

This additional compensation, if any, shall be payable to the party of the second part after the close of each fiscal year upon completion of the audit of the books and accounts of the party of the first part by certified public accountants, and said net profits so determined by the books and accounts of the party of the first part, shall be conclusive and binding upon both parties to this Agreement.

PROFIT-PARTICIPATION PLANS

APPENDIX T

American Optical Company

INCENTIVE COMPENSATION PLAN

The Board of Trustees of American Optical Company has established an incentive compensation plan for officers, executives, and supervisory employees, which Plan is to be known as the American Optical Incentive Compensation Plan.

The administration of the Plan shall be delegated by the Board of Trustees of the Company to the Executive Committee of the Board, none of which may participate in any distribution of the amounts appropriated for incentive compensation under this Plan. The Executive Committee shall formulate, within the general scope of the Plan, rules, regulations, and restrictions for the distribution of the amounts appropriated by the Board of Trustees.

The following terms as used in the American Optical Incentive Compensation Plan, herein called the Plan, shall have the following meanings:

"Net Income" shall mean net income, as determined by the Board of Trustees of the Company, ascertained from its books maintained in accordance with generally accepted accounting principles before (a) Federal income and excess profits taxes and other taxes of the type which are for the year for which net income is calculated, allowable as a credit against Federal income and excess profits taxes, and (b) incentive compensation in accordance with this Plan, but after all other taxes, and all charges and reserves deemed necessary or advisable by said Board. There shall be excluded from such net income non-recurring or extraordinary items, income on any funds excluded from net worth as provided below, and any income not realized or readily convertible into dollars at an exchange rate deemed favorable by the Board at the time of the appropriation. Income earned in any year in foreign currency and so excluded from net income for that year may be included in net income for the first subsequent year in which conversion into dollars of a sum equal to the amount of such foreign income has occurred or becomes possible at an exchange rate which the Board deems favorable. Net income as so determined for any year shall not, for incentive compensation purposes, be subject to subsequent adjustment.

"Net worth" shall mean the excess of assets of the Company over its liabilities (exclusive of capital and surplus) as determined by the Board of Trustees of the Company ascertained from its books maintained in accordance with generally accepted accounting principles, excluding, however, such amount of cash or investments as the Board of Trustees may deem to be in excess of current working capital needs or as the Board may have reserved or appropriated for a general or specific purpose.

"Salary" shall mean the compensation of an employee computed at regular rates of pay excluding any overtime and incentive compensation payments, but including in the case of salesmen, commissions paid during the fiscal period.

The Board of Trustees shall deduct from net income an amount which, when reduced by the estimated income and excess profits taxes thereon (which for the purpose of this calculation shall not exceed 50%), would be equal to 5% of the net worth of the Company at the beginning of the taxable year. They shall then appropriate an amount which shall not exceed 20% of the balance of such net income for distribution to officers, executives, supervisory and other employees in accordance with the Plan as outlined herein. The sum so appropriated shall not, however, be in excess of an amount equal to 60% of the total salaries of all officers, executives, supervisory and other employees who are recommended, as described subsequently herein, to participate in the Plan for the fiscal year, and the sums distributed, together with the salaries of the participants, shall not exceed reasonable compensation for the participants' services.

The amount of incentive compensation so determined shall be appropriated by the Board of Trustees as soon after the end of each calendar year as audited statements are available and adequate consideration can be given thereto, shall first be divided into two parts, of which not more than 60% shall be allocated for distribution among officers and senior executive employees, and not less than 40% shall be allocated for distribution among other executive and supervisory employees, and said sums shall be distributed among employees selected from the executive and supervisory group on the following basis:

(a) 50% of the sum so appropriated, pro rata to each participant in the ratio of the amount of his salary to the aggregate salaries of all participants for the calendar year;

(b) 50% of the sum so appropriated, in accordance with the best judgment of the Executive Committee as to the individual contribution of each participant to the Company during the calendar year.

The distribution of the 50% (b) appropriated by the Board of Trustees for the specific distribution shall be made upon the recommendation of the chief executive officer of the Company to the Executive Committee of the Board of Trustees, and shall be based upon unusual and outstanding effort or accomplishment in the advancement of the Company's interests during the year. The Executive Committee of the Board of Trustees, within the limits of the appropriation by the Board of Trustees, shall have sole discretion as to the amount of each specific distribution. An employee shall have no fixed or vested right under the Plan until a sum has been appropriated and allocated to him by the Executive Committee for distribution pursuant to the Plan.

The Board of Trustees reserves the unrestricted right at any time to terminate or amend this Plan, and appropriation may be deferred by the Board of Trustees if deemed advisable to conserve working capital or for other purposes. It is the present intention of the Board of Trustees not to terminate or amend the Plan except at the beginning of a new calendar year with respect to its prospective operation.

APPENDIX U

AMERICAN TOBACCO COMPANY

(Article XII of the By-laws, as adopted by stockholders on March 13, 1912, and as amended on April 6, 1960.)

ARTICLE XII

Section 1. (A) As soon as practicable after the end of the year 1957 and of each year thereafter, if the net profits earned by the Company during such year, as hereinafter defined, exceed the sum of $15,500,000, there shall be made available for allotment, subject to Section 8 hereof and as hereinafter provided, an amount equal in the aggregate to 5% of the first $6,000,000 of such excess, 4% of the next $2,700,000 thereof, 3% of the next $2,700,000 thereof, 2% of the next $2,700,000 thereof, and 1% of the balance thereof.

(B) Of such aggregate amount 20% shall be allotted to the person or persons who during such year held the office of the President and 16% shall be allotted to each of the persons who during such year held the office of one of the two Senior Vice-Presidents, as incentive compensation, in addition to the fixed salary of each of such persons for such year, subject, however, to Section 8 hereof. If any such office shall have been vacant at any time during the year, the amount to be allotted to the incumbent or incumbents of such office for such year shall be reduced proportionately. If any such office shall have had more than one incumbent during the year, the amount to be allotted in respect of such office shall be divided among the different incumbents in the proportion of their respective periods of incumbency during the year. Nothing herein contained shall give any incumbent of any office any right to claim to continue therein, or any other right except as herein specifically expressed.

(C) The balance of 48% of such aggregate amount shall be available for allotment to other key employees, as provided in Section 2 hereof, in addition to the fixed salary of each of such employees for such year, subject, however, to Section 8 hereof.

Section 2. (A) As soon as practicable after the end of the year 1957 and of each year thereafter, a committee, to be known as the Incentive Compensation Committee, consisting of the President and

358

the Senior Vice-Presidents or Senior Vice-President then in office, shall designate a Management Group to participate in such allotment, which group shall consist of all salaried employees of the Company whose salaries during all or any part of such year were at or above a salary rate determined by such Committee, but which rate shall in no event be less than $30,000 per annum. A person who during part of such year has held the office of President or Senior Vice-President may be included in the Management Group for the portion of the year during which he was in the employ of the Company but did not hold either of such offices, and the allotment to such person as a member of the Management Group shall be in addition to the allotment to which he is entitled under Section 1(B).

(B) Within 60 days after receipt from the independent public accountants of the certificate to be furnished pursuant to Section 7 hereof showing the aggregate amount available for allotment, said balance of 48% of such aggregate amount shall then be allotted (subject, however, to Section 8 hereof) among the members of such Management Group as follows:

(1) One-half of such balance, or 24% of such aggregate amount, shall be allotted to all members of such Group pro rata according to the proportion which the highest fixed salary rate during each such year of each member of said Group bears to the total of the highest fixed salary rates for such year of all the members of said Group. In the case of any members of such Management Group who were employed by the Company during less than all of any such year, the pro rata computation hereunder shall be adjusted proportionately to include such members only for their full calendar months of employment during such year. In the case of any members of such Management Group who have held the office of President or Senior Vice-President during part of any such year, the pro rata computation hereunder shall be adjusted proportionately to include such members as if they had been employed during such year only during the full calendar months of their employment in capacities other than as President or Senior Vice-President.

(2) So much of the remaining balance of 24% of such aggregate amount as the Incentive Compensation Committee determines, in its sole discretion, shall be allotted among the members of such Management Group to such individuals in said Group, and in such amounts as to individuals as the Incentive Compensation Committee, in its sole discretion, shall determine.

(C) In addition to the foregoing, there shall also be available for allotment to such Management Group within the 60-day period specified in paragraph (B) of this Section any amount, not in excess of 16% of such aggregate amount, which is not allotted in such year to the Senior Vice-Presidents or Senior Vice-President pursuant to Section 1(B) hereof by reason of vacancy at any time during such year in either or both of such offices. So much of such additional amount as the Incentive Compensation Committee determines, in its sole discretion, shall be allotted (subject, however, to Section 8 hereof) among the members of such Management Group to such individuals in said Group, and in such amounts as to individuals as the Incentive Compensation Committee, in its sole discretion, shall determine.

Section 3. (A) No part of such aggregate amount available for allotment as shall not have been allotted, under Sections 1 and 2 hereof, within such 60-day period, for any year may be carried forward for subsequent allotment.

(B) As used in Sections 2 to 5, inclusive, of this Article the word "Company" means The American Tobacco Company and its subsidiaries (except J. Wix & Sons Limited) included in the consolidated financial statements set forth in the annual reports for each year to the stockholders of The American Tobacco Company, together with such other subsidiaries or affiliates (which may include J. Wix & Sons Limited) as the Incentive Compensation Committee shall expressly designate for any such year.

(C) All decisions of the Committee pursuant to the provisions of this Article shall be binding and conclusive on all interested parties.

Section 4. (A) Payment to each President and Senior Vice-President, of the amounts payable to them under Section 1(B) hereof, and to each of the allottees of the Management Group of the amount of his total allotment, under Sections 2(B) and 2(C) hereof, with respect to any year shall be made as follows:

(1) One-half thereof shall be payable in cash as soon as practicable.

(2) Subject to Section 8 hereof, the balance, being one-half thereof, shall be contingently payable as hereinafter provided.

(B) All amounts contingently payable to all persons hereunder, such persons being hereafter referred to as "participants," shall be payable in cash in ten equal annual contingent installments, one such installment to be paid on the last business day in January, or as soon as practicable thereafter, in each of the ten years following the close of the year in which the participant's employment by the Company terminates: but all such payments shall be subject to the following conditions:

(i) If any participant ceases to be employed by the Company within a period of five years from the close of any year for which an allotment is made to him hereunder, the part of his allotment with respect to such year which is contingently payable in installments as aforesaid shall be reduced to the proportion thereof which the number of completed calendar quarter-years from the beginning of such five year period to the termination of employment bears to twenty; provided, however, that the provisions of this subdivision (i) shall have no application to any termination of employment (a) by death or (b) under such circumstances that the participant is eligible for retirement benefits (including early retirement), severance benefits or disability benefits under the Company's Retirement Plan, or (c) for other reasons deemed by the Board of Directors not detrimental to the Company's interests.

(ii) Payment of all unpaid installments shall be contingent upon the participant's not having, since the termination of his employment with the Company, accepted employment with, or rendered personal service to, any competitor of the Company or engaged in any activity in competition with the Company, except as expressly approved by the Company.

(iii) Payment of each such installment shall be conditioned upon the participant's having during the year preceding such payment been available to the Board of Directors, or any representative designated by the Board of Directors, for consultation, at such times and places, upon prior written notice, as the Board or such representative may reasonably request, having due regard to the age, health and convenience of the participant; provided, however, that the participant is to be reimbursed for all expenses in connection therewith, and if said participant is more than 100 miles from the Company's principal offices, such consultation may at his option be at the place where he then is located and may be, at the Company's option, either by personal visit to him by the representative of the Company for such purpose, or by written communication.

(iv) Subject to Section 5 hereof, no such installment may be transferred by any participant in any manner whatsoever, including transfer by operation of law. If any participant is, in the opinion of the Board of Directors, incapable of handling his affairs, or makes or suffers any attempted transfer, whether voluntary or involuntary, of any contingent installment, then in the discretion of the Board of Directors payment thereof to such participant shall cease and payments may be made or applied to or for the benefit of such participant or his spouse, children, or other dependents, or any of them, in such manner and in such proportion as the Board of Directors shall from time to time deem proper, subject, however, to the other provisions hereof.

(C) Any portion of any allotment which terminates by reason of noncompliance with its conditions shall revert to the Company.

Section 5. Any of the said annual contingent payments that may fall due after death of a participant shall be paid in such installments as herein provided, either to such person as shall furnish evidence satisfactory to the Company that under the last will and testament of the participant or for other reason such person is authorized in law to receive such payment, or, in the discretion of the Company, to such person as shall furnish the Company with evidence of appointment as representative of the estate of the participant; provided, however, that the Incentive Compensation Committee may, in its sole discretion, accelerate one or more of such payments. The Company may rely upon any opinion of counsel in determining the person entitled to receive such payments and the receipt of any such person for such payments shall release the Company from any further obligation in respect thereof. The word "person" as used in this Section may include one or more individuals, firms, trusts or corporations.

Section 6. For the purpose of this Article, the term "net profits earned by the Company" in any year is defined to mean the net income stated by the independent public accountants who have audited the Company's books as fairly reflecting the consolidated results of the operations for such year of the Company and its subsidiaries included in the consolidated financial statements set forth in the annual report for such year of the Company to the stockholders, but adjusted to exclude (1) the financial statements of J. Wix & Sons Limited from such consolidated financial statements as if it were an unconsolidated subsidiary and (2) all gain in excess of loss (net of federal tax applicable thereto) resulting from sales or other dispositions of land, buildings, good will, brands, trade-marks and investments in subsidiaries or other companies.

Section 7. At the time of rendering their report with respect to the financial statements of the Company and its consolidated subsidiaries, such public accountants shall also furnish to the Company their written certificate stating the aggregate amount available for allotment for such year, and the amounts thereof to be allotted to the President and to each Senior Vice-President, and the amount available for allotment to the Management Group, pursuant to this Article without reference to Section 8 hereof, which certificate as to the amounts available and payable hereunder shall be binding and conclusive on all interested parties, and no one claiming hereunder shall have a right to question the same, or to any examination of the books or accounts of the Company or subsidiaries.

Section 8. After the amounts to be allotted under Sections 1(B), 2(B) and 2(C) hereof with respect to any year have been determined for all participants without reference to this Section, the amount that, but for this Section, would be contingently payable pursuant to subparagraph (2) of Section 4(A) hereof to each participant for such year shall be reduced by a sum equal to the amount apportioned to such participant for such year under the Profit-Sharing Plan of The American Tobacco Company.

Section 9. This Article may be repealed only by the action of the stockholders of the Company, and not by the Directors. Upon the unanimous recommendation of the Incentive Compensation Committee, this Article may be amended or modified by the Directors in accordance with Article XI, except that, without the approval of the stockholders of the Company, no such amendment or modification shall be made which increases the aggregate amount payable hereunder or alters the amount thereof payable hereunder to the President and Senior Vice-Presidents.

APPENDIX V

GENERAL MOTORS CORPORATION

BONUS PLAN

(First adopted by stockholders on August 27, 1918 and as amended on May 27, 1957.)

1. The purpose of this plan is to provide incentive and reward to employes who contribute to the success of the enterprise by their invention, ability, industry, loyalty or exceptional service, through making them participants in that success. The term "employes" shall mean persons employed by General Motors Corporation or any subsidiary in which the Corporation owns directly or indirectly substantially all of the common stock and shall include employes who are also directors of the Corporation or of any such subsidiary.

2(a). The Corporation shall maintain a reserve for the purposes of this plan and the General Motors Stock Option Plan, to which shall be credited for each year an amount which the independent public accountants of the Corporation determine and report to be 12% of the net earnings after deducting 5% on net capital, but not in excess of the amount paid out as dividends on the common stock of the Corporation during that year, all as hereinafter provided, except that for any year the Bonus and Salary Committee may in its discretion direct that a lesser amount be credited.

(b). Before the determination of bonus awards each year by the Committee, the independent public accountants of the Corporation shall determine and report the total amount available in the reserve. The Committee may award bonuses which, when added to the Contingent Credits then to be conditionally credited under the General Motors Stock Option Plan and the amount of the charge to the reserve pursuant to paragraph 11(b), total the amount available in the reserve as determined and reported by the independent public accountants, but the Committee shall not be obliged to award as bonus the full amount so authorized to be awarded. Bonus awards under this plan, Contingent Credits under the General Motors Stock Option Plan, amounts chargeable to the reserve pursuant to paragraph 11(b) and such other amounts arising out of the operation of this plan and the General Motors Stock Option Plan as the Committee may determine shall be charged to the reserve. The reserve shall be deemed for all purposes a single, continuous reserve. Balances retained in the reserve each year shall, except to the extent otherwise directed by the Committee, be carried forward and be available in a future year or years.

(c). In the event that the amount determined and reported by the independent public accountants in any year as available for credit to the reserve should for any reason later prove to have been more than 12% of net earnings after deducting 5% on net capital, the reserve shall be debited and the appropriate account of the Corporation shall be credited by the amount of such excess, except that if the amount credited to the reserve was less than the amount determined and reported by the accountants, the amount required for adjustment shall be reduced by such difference; and if the amount in the reserve is less than the amount of such adjustment, the reserve shall be reduced immediately upon any subsequent credit to the reserve until the amount of the adjustment has been completely offset. In the event that the amount determined and reported by the independent public accountants as available in the reserve should for any reason later prove to have been overstated, the amount then or subsequently available in the reserve shall be reduced accordingly.

Any excess credits or charges to the reserve and any overstatement of the amount available in the reserve, however occasioned, shall thus be corrected exclusively by adjustment of the reserve then or subsequently available and not by recourse to any person.

3(a). The term "net earnings" as used in this plan shall mean, for each year, the amount reported in the annual statement of income which is transferred to earned surplus as shown by the annual statement of surplus, plus the amounts of the credit for such year to the reserve for the purposes of this plan and the General Motors Stock Option Plan and interest on debt included in net capital as defined in paragraph 3(b) and less all amounts credited to income for such year pursuant to paragraph 8(b) of this plan and paragraphs 5(b) and 5(c) of the General Motors Stock Option Plan or as a result of any direction of the Bonus and Salary Committee under paragraph 2(b) of this plan that any amount of the reserve is not to be carried forward. Interest on debt shall include charges or credits arising out of premium or discount paid or received with respect to such debt.

(b). The term "net capital" as used in this plan shall mean the total of capital stock and surplus, plus debt of General Motors Corporation, as shown on the balance sheet as of the end of the year preceding the year for which the net earnings are taken, less any treasury stock (other than stock held in the special account provided for in paragraph 10(a)), plus or minus a proportionate allowance for any change during the year, based on the period of such change. in the amount of capital stock, surplus, or debt, from newly issued or finally retired capital stock (except treasury stock previously deducted) or from increase or decrease in the outstanding principal of debt.

The term "debt" as used in this plan shall mean the unpaid principal amount of all indebtedness of General Motors Corporation as principal and not as surety or guarantor, having a maturity at the time of its creation of more than one year, independent of acceleration, and evidenced by a bond, debenture, or promissory note.

(c). The terms "balance sheet," "statement of income," and "statement of surplus" as used in this plan shall mean, for each year, those statements of General Motors Corporation and consolidated subsidiaries certified by the independent public accountants of the Corporation and contained in the Corporation's annual report to stockholders.

4. Full power and authority to construe, interpret and administer this plan shall be vested in the Bonus and Salary Committee as from time to time constituted pursuant to the By-Laws of the Corporation. Decisions of the Committee shall be final, conclusive and binding upon all parties, including the Corporation, the stockholders and the employes, provided, however, that the Committee shall rely upon and be bound by the amount of net earnings, the amount of net capital, the maximum amount which may be credited to the reserve, the total amount available in the reserve, the total amount to be charged to the reserve pursuant to paragraph 11(b) and the value of stock for award purposes, all as reported by the independent public accountants.

5(a). An employe shall be eligible for consideration for bonus if at the end of the year he is receiving a salary at or above such monthly rate (which may differ with respect to employes outside the United States from the rate with respect to employes in the United States) as the Bonus and Salary Committee shall from year to year determine, but the Committee may, in its discretion, award bonuses to employes receiving salaries below the eligible monthly rate in special cases. A person whose employment terminates during the year or who is granted a leave of absence during the year, and who at the time of such termination of employment or granting of leave is receiving a salary at or above the eligible monthly rate established for that year by the Committee, may, at the discretion of the Committee and under such rules as the Committee may from time to time prescribe, be awarded a bonus with respect to the period of his services during the year. An employee whose compensation under a contract of employment is determined in whole or in part on a commission basis or by the earnings of a dealership or of a sales or service branch (whether or not separately incorporated) shall not be eligible for bonus for the period during which his compensation is so determined, nor shall such compensation be charged against the reserve, but the Bonus and Salary Committee shall have exclusive jurisdiction to approve, disapprove, modify or amend all plans to compensate employes, otherwise eligible for bonus, in whole or in part on a commission basis or by the earnings of a dealership or of a sales or service branch. A person who is compensated on the basis of fee or retainer, as distinguished from salary, shall not be eligible for bonus for the period during which he is so compensated.

(b). Membership on a committee of directors shall not itself render a person eligible for bonus. Membership on the Bonus and Salary Committee or on the Audit Committee shall render a person ineligible for an award of bonus.

6. The Bonus and Salary Committee shall have discretion with respect to the determination of each bonus award. Recommendations for bonus awards shall be made to the Committee by the Chairman of the Board of Directors, the President and the Chairman of the Financial Policy Committee, jointly, under such procedure as may from time to time be prescribed by the Committee except that no such recommendations shall be made with respect to employes of the Corporation or of any subsidiary who were in the year for which a bonus is awarded members of the Board of Directors or the Operations Policy Committee or the Financial Policy Committee, but such bonus shall be dealt with exclusively by the Bonus and Salary Committee under such procedure as it may determine. The aggregate amount of bonus awarded in any year to executives who are also granted stock options in such year pursuant to the General Motors Stock Option Plan shall be 75% of the aggregate amount of bonus which would have been awarded to such executives under this plan, in the opinion of the Committee, if they were not being granted such stock options under the General Motors Stock Option Plan.

Upon final determination of bonus awards by the Committee, each award of $1,000 or less (cash or stock of equivalent award value) shall be paid at the time of award. Each award of more than $1,000 shall be paid in annual instalments of 20% or $1,000, whichever is greater, the first such instalment at the time of award, and the remaining instalments in January of each succeeding year (until the full amount of the award is paid) if earned out by the beneficiary by continuing service to the Corporation, at the rate of 1/12th of the amount of the first instalment for each complete month of service beginning with January of the year of the determination, except that if it shall be determined that a beneficiary has acted or conducted himself in a manner inimical or in any way contrary to the best interests of the Corporation, such beneficiary shall lose any right to receive any portion of any instalment or amount that would otherwise have been earned out subsequent to the first of the month in which such act or conduct first occurred, provided that no instalment or amount delivered or paid prior to the date of such determination shall be required to be returned. The determination as to whether any act or conduct of a beneficiary is inimical or in any way contrary to the best interests of the Corporation shall be made by the Bonus and Salary Committee under such procedure as may from time to time be prescribed by the Committee and shall be made in the absolute discretion of the Committee. Any determination so made, including any determination of the time at which such act or conduct first occurred, shall be conclusive.

7(a). Bonus awards for any year shall be in cash or in General Motors stock or partly in cash and partly in General Motors stock, as the Bonus and Salary Committee in its discretion shall determine.

(b). With respect to bonus awards which become payable partly or wholly in cash, the amount of cash payable at the time of award shall be paid forthwith to the beneficiaries. The remaining cash shall be retained by the Corporation (without liability for interest) pending its being earned out by and paid to the beneficiaries at the times specified.

(c). With respect to bonus awards which become payable partly or wholly in General Motors stock, the shares payable at the time of award shall be delivered forthwith to the beneficiaries. The remaining stock shall be retained by the Corporation as treasury stock pending its being earned out by and delivered to the beneficiaries at the times specified. On each dividend payment date after March 31 of the year of an award of stock, the record date for which occurs after the date of the award but prior to the date of the registration of all such awarded stock in the name of the beneficiary, the Corporation shall (except as otherwise provided in paragraph 8(b)) pay to the beneficiary, with respect to any such awarded stock not registered in his name on or prior to such record date, an amount equal to the value of the dividends which the beneficiary would have received if such stock had been registered in his name on such record date.

8(a). A beneficiary whose employment terminates by dismissal for cause or who voluntarily terminates his employment shall, unless otherwise determined in connection with the termination of his employment, lose any right to earn out his unearned bonus awards. A beneficiary whose employment terminates for any reason other than by death or as set forth in the preceding sentence shall, unless otherwise determined in connection with the termination of his employment, retain all rights to earn out unearned bonus awards.

If it shall be determined that a beneficiary who was permitted to retain his rights to earn out his unearned bonus awards upon termination of employment has, after such termination of employment, engaged, directly or indirectly, in any activity which is in competition with any activity of the Corporation or any subsidiary or has, either prior to or after such termination of employment, otherwise acted or conducted himself in a manner inimical or in any way contrary to the best interests of the Corporation, such beneficiary shall, unless otherwise determined, lose any right to earn out his unearned bonus awards as of the first of the month in which such competitive activity or such act or conduct first occurred; provided that no instalment or amount delivered or paid prior to the date of any such determination shall be required to be returned.

Each determination provided for in this paragraph 8(a) shall be made by the Bonus and Salary Committee under such procedure as may from time to time be prescribed by the Committee and shall be made in the absolute discretion of the Committee. Any determination so made, including any determination of the time at which such competitive activity or such act or conduct first occurred, shall be conclusive.

(b). A beneficiary who loses his rights to earn out unearned bonus awards shall receive forthwith all earned-out portions of bonus awards and all amounts, if any, payable in accordance with the provisions of paragraph 7(c) with respect to such earned-out stock, but not with respect to unearned stock. As to any instalment payable in stock, a fractional share shall not be delivered but shall instead be purchased by the Corporation at the closing market price of the stock on the date of termination of earning-out rights. The unearned portions of bonus awards, including unearned stock at its award value, shall be credited to income of the Corporation and any such unearned stock shall be transferred at such award value from the special treasury stock account designated for purposes of this plan and the

General Motors Stock Option Plan to the account for treasury stock which is held for other corporate purposes.

9. If a beneficiary dies, his unpaid and undelivered bonus awards and dividend equivalents shall be paid and delivered to his legal representatives or to the persons entitled thereto as determined by a court of competent jurisdiction, at such times and in such manner as if the beneficiary were living.

10(a). The Bonus and Salary Committee shall from time to time recommend to the Corporation the purchase of stock, in such amounts as the Committee may determine, for purposes of this plan and the General Motors Stock Option Plan. Stock purchased pursuant to any such recommendation shall be valued at cost and placed in a special account designated for purposes of this plan and the General Motors Stock Option Plan. The Bonus and Salary Committee may before the close of any year and before bonus awards for such year are determined recommend to the Corporation the transfer to the special account of other treasury stock held by the Corporation. Stock placed in the special account pursuant to such recommendation shall be placed therein at the average value at which all treasury common stock (other than stock held for purposes of this plan and the General Motors Stock Option Plan) is carried on the Corporation's books or at a value per share equal to the average of the daily closing market prices of General Motors common stock on the New York Stock Exchange during such year or the portion preceding such transfer, whichever value is higher.

(b). Stock shall be valued for purposes of bonus awards under this plan at the average value, determined and reported by the independent public accountants, at which all stock (other than stock held in respect of bonuses awarded under this plan or in respect of Contingent Credits conditionally credited under the General Motors Stock Option Plan) is carried in the special account provided for in paragraph 10(a) on such date as may be fixed by the Bonus and Salary Committee.

11(a). Any corporation in which General Motors Corporation owns an interest but the employees of which are not eligible for bonus under this plan because General Motors Corporation does not own directly or indirectly substantially all of the common stock may without regard to the limitations of this plan have a separate bonus plan. A bonus provision under such separate bonus plan shall not be included in or considered a part of the provision under the Corporation's plan nor shall awards made under such separate bonus plan be charged against the reserve maintained for the purpose of this plan and the General Motors Stock Option Plan. The income from and investment in such other corporation shall not be excluded from net earnings or net capital as herein defined.

(b). Any corporation in which General Motors Corporation owns directly or indirectly substantially all of the common stock and which is incorporated, or does substantially all of its business outside of the United States, may have a separate bonus plan. The Bonus and Salary Committee shall have exclusive jurisdiction on behalf of the Corporation, to approve, disapprove, or suggest amendments to all such plans. In each year in which there shall be a bonus provision under such a separate bonus plan, such provision shall, prior to the determination of bonus awards for such year under this plan, be charged against the reserve maintained pursuant to paragraph 2(a) to the extent of the amount available therein, provided that, if for any reason less than all of the net income of any such corporation for the year is included in the consolidated net income of the Corporation, there shall be charged to the reserve to the extent of the amount available therein only that part of such provision which bears the same relationship to the total thereof as the amount of the net income for the year of such corporation which is included in the consolidated net income of the Corporation bears to the total net income of such corporation for the year, all as determined and reported by the independent public accountants.

12. While it is contemplated that bonuses will be awarded annually, the Bonus and Salary Committee shall have the right from time to time to modify or suspend this plan; provided, however, that no modification of the plan by the Committee without approval of the stockholders shall increase the maximum amount which may be credited to the reserve pursuant to paragraph 2(a) or charged against the reserve as hereinabove provided, or change the provisions of paragraph 6 with respect to the aggregate amount of bonus which may be awarded in any year to executives who are also granted stock options in such year, or render any member of the Bonus and Salary Committee or of the Audit Committee eligible for an award of bonus.

13. The expenses of administering this plan and the dividend equivalents which become payable hereunder shall be borne by the Corporation and not charged against the reserve.

14. In the event of a change in the Corporation's fiscal year, this plan shall apply, with pro rata adjustment in the deduction for net capital, to any intermediate period not consisting of twelve months and shall then apply to each fiscal year following.

15. Every right of action by or on behalf of the Corporation or by any stockholder against any past, present or future member of the Board of Directors, officer or employe of the Corporation arising out of or in connection with this plan shall, irrespective of the place where action may be brought and irrespective of the place of residence of any such director, officer or employe, cease and be barred by the expiration of three years from whichever is the later of (a) the date of the act or omission in respect of which such right of action arises or (b) the first date upon which there has been made generally available to stockholders an annual report of the Corporation and a proxy statement for the annual meeting of stockholders following the issuance of such annual report, which annual report and proxy statement alone or together set forth, for the related period, the amount of the credits to the reserve for the purposes of this plan and the General Motors Stock Option Plan and the aggregate bonus awards; and any and all right of action by any employe (past, present or future) against the Corporation arising out of or in connection with this plan shall, irrespective of the place where action may be brought, cease and be barred by the expiration of three years from the date of the act or omission in respect of which such right of action arises.

16. This plan as hereby modified shall become effective as of January 1, 1957.

APPENDIX W

General Motors Corporation

STATEMENT BY SPECIAL COMMITTEE TO REVIEW BONUS PLAN

The By-Laws of the Corporation provide that the Bonus Plan be presented by the Directors for action at a stockholders' meeting at least once in every five years. The Plan was last submitted at the annual meeting in 1952. In anticipation of presenting it to stockholders this year, the Board of Directors in July, 1956 appointed a special committee, consisting of the undersigned members of the Board, to review the Bonus Plan in the light of its objectives and make recommendations with respect to the Plan. Based on the conclusions and recommendations of the Special Committee, the Board of Directors has adopted, subject to the approval of stockholders, an incentive program consisting of the Bonus Plan, which is being continued with certain modifications, and a related General Motors Stock Option Plan. None of the members of the Special Committee will be eligible under the proposed program.

In its study which led to the recommendation that a stock option plan be adopted, the Committee carefully considered the relationship of any such plan to the Bonus Plan. The Committee decided that it would not be desirable to add a stock option plan to the Corporation's present incentive compensation structure without an adjustment in the case of executives exercising options. As a result, the General Motors Stock Option Plan provides that such executives will not receive certain payments of supplemental compensation which they might otherwise receive.

The Special Committee made a thorough study of the Bonus Plan and its operation and is unanimous in its conclusion that the basic theory and objectives of the Bonus Plan are sound; that the incentive which has been provided by the Plan over the years has been a very significant factor in the success of General Motors; and that as a result of the operation of the Plan the earnings of the Corporation have been substantially greater than they otherwise would have been. Accordingly, the Committee has recommended that the basic concept of the Bonus Plan and its fundamental provisions be continued.

373

Since 1947, the formula for determining the amount that may be credited annually to the bonus reserve has been 12% of net earnings after deduction of 5% of net capital. The Special Committee gave extensive consideration to the question as to whether or not some modification should be recommended in this formula. It noted that over the ten year period since the formula became effective, the aggregate amount credited to the bonus reserve by the Bonus and Salary Committee has been less than the maximum amount available under the formula and the awards over the period as a whole have been less than the amount credited. It is also recognized, however, that the Bonus Plan must be designed to operate over a period of time and must contemplate years of varying levels of business activity and resulting profits.

The Committee concluded that the discretionary power of the Bonus and Salary Committee to credit and award less than the maximum available under the formula had proved highly effective in the past, and could be relied upon in the future, as a means of limiting total bonus awards if desirable to do so. Accordingly, the Committee has recommended that the 12% after 5% formula be continued unchanged. The Committee did, however, recommend, and the Bonus and Salary Committee has directed, that the unawarded balance in the Corporation's bonus reserve at the end of 1956, which amounted to approximately $19,800,000, be restored to income of the Corporation in 1957.

The Special Committee concurs in the belief, long held in General Motors, that substantial stock ownership by its management is an important factor in the success of any enterprise. The relatively large stockholdings in General Motors Corporation by its executives have played an important role in bringing the Corporation to its position of industrial leadership. However, high personal income tax rates have, for some time, reduced the portion of bonus awards that the executives have been able to retain as an investment in General Motors stock. The Committee further noted the steadily increasing use in recent years of stock option plans by other industrial companies.

The General Motors Stock Option Plan recommended by the Special Committee is described in detail in the Proxy Statement. The Plan contemplates that options may be granted each year, for the five years 1958 through 1962, to principal executives selected by the Bonus and Salary Committee. Under the options the executives will be permitted to purchase General Motors Corporation common stock at a price equal to 100% of the fair market value of the stock at the time the option is granted. An option will not become exercisable until the executive has completed 18 months of employment after it is granted and will expire not later than ten years after it is granted. The Committee has contemplated that the number of executives who might be selected in 1958 to receive options would be in the area of 250. Over the five year period, the number of shares for which options may be granted may not exceed 4,000,000 shares for all executives, equivalent to 1.4% of the shares now outstanding, or 75,000 shares for any one executive, which is 1.9% of the total number of shares for which options may be granted, such limits being subject to appropriate adjustment in the event of a stock split, etc. If an option terminates for any reason without having been exercised in full, options may be granted to other executives with respect to the unpurchased shares.

As set forth in the Proxy Statement, the Bonus Plan has been modified in certain respects to permit the concurrent operation of that Plan and the Stock Option Plan. The modified Bonus Plan also incorporates several other modifications recommended by the Special Committee. These modifications include certain changes which will have the effect of reducing the amount of bonus which would otherwise be available for award under the Bonus Plan: namely, changes in the definitions of "net earnings" and "net capital" for the purposes of the 12% after 5% formula and changes in the provisions of the Bonus Plan relating to the separate bonus plans of the Corporation's overseas manufacturing subsidiaries. The more important modifications of the Bonus Plan, including those referred to in this Statement, are discussed in detail in the Proxy Statement.

Since most of the members of the Special Committee either hold, or represent, large stock interests in the Corporation, their interest is identical with that of the stockholders. As previously stated, they will not be eligible to receive an award of bonus or a stock option under the proposed incentive program. The Special Committee believes that the incentive program now being submitted to stockholders is consistent with the definite policy which has been followed by the Corporation since the Bonus Plan was first adopted in 1918 and which, in the opinion of the Committee, has been one of the firmest foundations of the Corporation's success. In brief, this policy recognizes the wisdom of an incentive program whereby men of outstanding ability are attracted to and retained in the service of the Corporation and are provided the opportunity to achieve substantial stock ownership. It is the Committee's belief that aggressive and imaginative leadership was never more essential to business success than it is today and that, accordingly, the adoption of the proposed incentive program is of first importance for the maximum well-being of the Corporation in the future.

The Committee therefore recommends, as in the best interests of the Corporation and the stockholders, that the stockholders approve the incentive program as submitted.

SPECIAL COMMITTEE TO REVIEW BONUS PLAN
ALBERT BRADLEY, *Chairman*
HENRY C. ALEXANDER
LAMMOT DU P. COPELAND
HENRY B. DU PONT
EARLE F. JOHNSON
ALFRED P. SLOAN, JR.

April 16, 1957

APPENDIX X

E. I. du Pont de Nemours and Company
BONUS PLANS "A", "B", AND "C"
(As approved by stockholders on April 11, 1960)

I. Purposes

The purposes of the Company's Bonus Plans are: (a) to provide greater incentive for employees continually to exert their best efforts on behalf of the Company by rewarding them for services rendered with compensation that is in addition to their regular salaries; (b) to attract to and retain in the employ of the Company persons of outstanding competence; and (c) to further the identity of interests of such employees with those of the Company's stockholders generally.

II. Plans

Under the Company's Bonus Plans employees who have contributed in an unusual degree to the success of the Company by their inventions, ability, industry and loyalty may be granted additional compensation in the form of bonuses awarded under one or more of the following Plans:

Plan "A"

Bonus awards under Plan "A" may be granted for conspicuous service of any nature, such as—

(a) an invention or improvement which results in a profit, saving or important benefit, or in a reduction of risk of personal injury or damage to the Company's property,

(b) unusually ingenious solution of a business or technical problem,

(c) perseverance and persistency of a character that results in demonstrating a proposition (in some instances against either internal or external opposition) that results in a saving or important benefit to the Company, or

(d) an accomplishment by an employee of a character far beyond that which might be expected of one occupying his position.

377

Plan "B"

Bonus awards under Plan "B" may be granted to those who have contributed most in a general way to the Company's success by their ability, efficiency and loyalty, consideration being given to ability to succeed to more important managerial responsibility in the Company.

Plan "C"

Bonus awards under Plan "C" may be granted to employees in important managerial or other responsible positions who concurrently are, or otherwise would be, recommended for bonus awards under Plan "B".

III. FORM OF AWARDS

Plans "A" and "B"

1. Bonuses under Plans "A" and "B" may be awarded in acquired common stock of this Company, or in cash to be invested in new common stock issued directly to the beneficiaries, or in cash, or in two or more of said forms.

2. The Bonus and Salary Committee shall determine the portion of each bonus award under Plans "A" and "B" to be paid in cash and the portion to be delivered to the beneficiary in the form of common stock.

Plan "C"

3. Bonuses under Plan "C" may be awarded in the form of either—

(a) "dividend units", or
(b) "dividend units" accompanied by a stock option to purchase common stock of this Company.

Each "dividend unit" shall entitle the holder thereof to receive for a term of years, under terms and conditions consistent with Article XV hereof, cash payments from the Company equivalent in amount or value to the interim and year-end dividends (other than stock dividends) declared as such by the Board of Directors and paid during such term on one share of common stock of this Company. Changes in capitalization, or special distributions to common stockholders, shall not give rise to equivalent payments to a "dividend unit" holder, but the number of his "dividend units" shall be equitably adjusted pursuant to paragraph 3(a) of Article XV.

4. The Bonus and Salary Committee shall determine the form of each "C" bonus award and prescribe the terms and conditions applicable thereto consistent with Article XV hereof.

IV. LIMITATIONS ON BONUS AWARDS

Plan "A"

1. Bonus awards under Plan "A" may be granted irrespective of the Company's earnings.

Plan "B"

2. Bonus awards under Plan "B" shall be made from the "B" Bonus Fund which the Company shall establish and to which shall be credited annually an amount to be determined by the Bonus and Salary Committee. This amount shall not exceed 20% of the "bonus net income," and shall not be credited until the independent public accountants employed by the Committee on Audit have certified the maximum amount which in their opinion may be so credited to the "B" Bonus Fund.

3. The term "bonus net income" for any year, as used in this Plan, shall mean the amount of net income as shown in the Statement of Consolidated Income of this Company and its subsidiaries set forth in the Annual Report to the Stockholders for such year; adjusted, however, by—

    (a) deducting the amount of any income, net after Federal taxes applicable thereto, derived from the Company's investment in General Motors Corporation common stock which has been included in computing said net income, and

    (b) adding any amount which has been deducted in computing said net income with respect to any provision for the "B" Bonus Fund, and

    (c) deducting an amount equal to 6% of the "bonus net capital employed," as defined in paragraph 4 of this Article.

4. The term "bonus net capital employed" for any year, as used in this Plan, shall mean the average of the amounts of issued and outstanding Capital Stock and Surplus as of December 31st of such year and December 31st of the preceding year, as shown in the Consolidated Balance Sheets of this Company and its subsidiaries set forth in the Annual Reports to the Stockholders, after adjusting said amounts, however, by—

(a) deducting the amount at which the Company's investment in General Motors Corporation common stock is included in said Consolidated Balance Sheets, and

(b) adding to the Surplus as stated in the later of such Balance Sheets any amount which has been deducted in computing net income with respect to any provision for the "B" Bonus Fund, as described in paragraph 3(b) of this Article.

5. It shall not be incumbent upon the Bonus and Salary Committee to make "B" bonus awards for each year having an aggregate value equal to the entire amount available in the "B" Bonus Fund. Any unawarded portion of said Fund shall be carried forward and be available for "B" bonus awards in a succeeding year or years, and while "B" bonus awards in the aggregate for any year may exceed the amount credited for that year to the "B" Bonus Fund, they shall not exceed the total amount in said Fund.

Plan "C"

6. The number of "dividend units" which may be awarded under Plan "C" to any employee for any year shall not exceed 5,000.

7. The aggregate number of "dividend units" which may be awarded under Plan "C" for any year shall not exceed one and one-half times the number obtained by dividing the excess, if any, of the amount certified by the independent public accountants as the maximum amount which may be credited for such year to the "B" Bonus Fund, as hereinabove provided, over the actual amount credited to such Fund by—

(a) the average value per share of all stock to be used (awarded or sold) for "B" bonus purposes for that year, or

(b) the average of the daily closing prices for the Company's common stock on the New York Stock Exchange during the calendar year for which such "C" bonuses are awarded, if "B" bonus awards for that year are to be entirely in cash;

provided, however, that no "dividend unit" shall be awarded which would cause the cumulative number of "dividend units" awarded during any five consecutive years to exceed 500,000. No "dividend units" shall be awarded for any year until the independent public accountants have certified the maximum number of "dividend units" which in their opinion may be awarded for that year.

8. When a "C" bonus award is in the form of "dividend units" accompanied by a stock option, the number of shares subject to the

option shall not exceed one and one-third times the number of the accompanying "dividend units."

V. ELIGIBILITY FOR BONUS AWARDS

Plan "A"

1. Bonus awards under Plan "A" may be granted to any employee, without limitation as to length of service, each case being considered on its merits.

Plans "B" and "C"

2. Bonus awards under Plans "B" and "C" may be granted to any employee who, on January 1st of the year in which the awards are made, has been in the continuous employ of the Company at least two years. In special cases awards may be made by the Bonus and Salary Committee to employees with less than two years' service.

Plans "A", "B" and "C"

3. For the purpose of determining eligibility under these Plans, the term "employee" may include—

(a) a person performing services on a consultant basis.
(b) a former employee who, before severance of employment, rendered services for which bonus awards would have been recommended if he had continued in the employ of the Company (in the case of a former employee who would have been recommended for a bonus but for death, an award or awards may be granted to the surviving spouse or to the estate of such employee), and
(c) an employee of a subsidiary in which this Company shall directly or indirectly own fifty per cent or more of the outstanding voting stock (the term "bonus plan company" as used hereinafter shall mean a company whose employees are eligible for bonus awards under these Plans).

VI. BONUS CUSTODIAN

Plans "A" and "B"

The Finance Committee shall appoint a Bonus Custodian who shall perform the duties assigned to him under the "A" and "B" Bonus Plans.

VII. Bonus Awards

Plan "A"

1. Where a bonus under Plan "A" is to be awarded for services which it is believed will result in continuing financial benefit to the Company, the amount of which is determinable over a period of years, the bonus shall take the form of a three-part bonus based upon profits or savings over a five-year period. The first award may be made after the close of the year in which the improvement or benefit has been in regular operation for six months or more and the practicability of the scheme demonstrated on a reasonably representative commercial basis. If justified by the continued financial benefit resulting from such conspicuous service, second and third awards may, in the discretion of the Executive Committee (or the Bonus and Salary Committee if the beneficiary is a Director of the Company), be made after the close of the third and fifth years of the period, based upon reconsideration of the case and recalculation of the profits or savings which have resulted to the Company.

2. Where a bonus under Plan "A" has been recommended for services which it is believed will not result in continued financial benefit to the Company, or which cannot be evaluated in money, the bonus shall take the form of a first and final award, the amount being determined on such basis as may be fixed by the Executive Committee (or the Bonus and Salary Committee if the beneficiary is a Director of the Company).

Plan "B"

3. The Bonus and Salary Committee shall determine each year the total amount of the "B" Bonus Fund to be distributed. Bonuses under Plan "B" for any calendar year shall be awarded as soon as practicable after the close of such calendar year.

Plans "A" and "B"

4. An award under Plan "A" or "B" in the form of cash to be invested in new common stock of the Company shall be conditioned upon such investment and the Bonus Custodian shall procure from each beneficiary of such an award a signed subscription for the number of shares available to him at the price fixed therefor. Such subscription agreement shall provide that the stock is to be issued in the name of the beneficiary and is to be subject to the applicable provisions of these Plans.

Plan "C"

5. Subject to the limitations prescribed in Article IV, the Bonus and Salary Committee shall determine each year the total number of "dividend units" to be awarded and the total number of shares to be optioned. Bonuses under Plan "C" for any calendar year shall be awarded simultaneously with the award of "B" bonuses.

Plans "A", "B" and "C"

6. Annually upon the granting of awards under these Plans, each beneficiary shall be informed of his bonus award by the head of his department or company and that such award is subject to the applicable provisions of these Plans.

VIII. Stock for Awards Under Plans "A" and "B"

1. With respect to the portion of bonus awards under Plans "A" and "B" to be delivered in common stock, the Finance Committee shall determine whether, and to what extent, such portion of the awards shall be in cash to be invested in new common stock issued directly to beneficiaries, or in common stock acquired by the Company. When the Finance Committee has determined that the stock portions of bonuses are to be awarded in the form of common stock acquired by the Company, it may authorize the Treasurer to purchase the stock and place it in appropriate bonus accounts, "A" and "B", established for that purpose, or may direct the Treasurer to transfer into said bonus accounts any previously acquired treasury stock, not held for bonus purposes.

2. Stock so purchased shall be placed in the bonus accounts at cost thereof to the Company, and any previously acquired treasury stock transferred into said bonus accounts shall be placed therein at the following valuations:

(a) In the "A" bonus account, at a value per share substantially equal to the market value of such stock on the New York Stock Exchange at the time the transfer is authorized.

(b) In the "B" bonus account, at a value per share substantially equal to the average of the daily closing prices for such stock on the New York Stock Exchange during the calendar year for which the bonuses are to be awarded; or if transferred prior to the close of said year, at the average of the daily closing prices from January 1st to the date such transfer is authorized.

If the stock in either of the bonus accounts, "A" or "B", is not currently required for bonus purposes, the Treasurer shall transfer such stock to the treasury stock account at the average value at which all shares in such bonus account are carried on the books of the Company.

3. The value per share at which acquired stock will be awarded in any year under Plans "A" and "B" shall be an amount equal to the average value at which all shares in the bonus account are carried on the books of the Company on such date as may be fixed by the Bonus and Salary Committee. Before any bonuses in the form of acquired stock are awarded, the Bonus and Salary Committee shall obtain a certificate from the independent public accountants setting forth their opinion as to such award value per share. The value (price) per share at which new common stock is to be sold to beneficiaries under Plans "A" and "B" shall be fixed and determined by the Board of Directors. Payment for new common stock shall be made by the beneficiaries through the Bonus Custodian from bonuses awarded in cash to be invested in such stock.

IX. RECOMMENDATIONS AND GRANTING OF BONUS AWARDS

Plans, "A", "B" and "C"

1. Bonus awards to members of the Board of Directors shall be determined by the Bonus and Salary Committee. Recommendations for bonus awards to employees who are not members of the Board of Directors shall be made under Plans "B" and "C" to the Bonus and Salary Committee by the Executive Committee, and under Plan "A" to the Executive Committee by heads of departments.

2. Final action on all awards under Plans "B" and "C", and on any awards to members of the Board of Directors under Plan "A," shall be taken by the Bonus and Salary Committee. The Executive Committee shall take final action on all awards under Plan "A" to employees who are not members of the Board of Directors. At the discretion of the Bonus and Salary Committee bonus awards granted to employees of a subsidiary company may be made subject to approval by the board of directors of such company.

3. The Executive Committee may authorize the heads of departments to award bonuses under Plan "A" not exceeding in value such amount as that Committee shall fix from time to time for any first and final award or any award under a three-part bonus; such awards to be granted in accordance with rules, consistent with this Plan, adopted by said Committee.

4. The term "heads of departments" shall be deemed, for the purpose of this Article, to include the presidents of subsidiary companies.

X. Commitments of Beneficiary

Plans "A" and "B"

The Bonus Custodian shall procure from each beneficiary an irrevocable power of attorney with respect to any shares not immediately deliverable to the beneficiary hereunder, which power shall provide that—

(a) the beneficiary shall not sell, assign or pledge any of such stock remaining in the custody of the Bonus Custodian;

(b) the Bonus Custodian shall receive and hold any stock dividend declared on the stock in his custody, and any certificates of stock resulting from a split-up or other change in such stock, to be released to the beneficiary as provided by Article XII hereof; and

(c) in case the beneficiary leaves the service of the bonus plan companies, or is dismissed, stock in the custody of the Bonus Custodian may be sold and settlement made as hereinafter provided in Article XIII.

XI. Rights of Beneficiary

Plans "A" and "B"

An award in stock of the Company, or the investment of a cash award in stock of the Company, shall vest in the beneficiary all the rights of a stockholder in such stock, subject (1) to the right of the Bonus Custodian to possession of certificates evidencing a portion of the stock as herein provided, and (2) to the right of the Company to purchase such stock, as provided in Article XIII hereof.

XII. Delivery of Bonus Awards

Plans "A" and "B"

1. When any part of a three-part bonus is awarded under Plan "A", certificates of stock, or cash, as the case may be, shall be delivered as directed by the Executive Committee (or Bonus and Salary Committee if the beneficiary is a Director of the Company) within not more than 18 months. When any bonus of a value of less than such amount under $2,000 as may be determined from time to time by the Bonus and Salary Committee is awarded under Plan

"A" or Plan "B", certificates of stock, or cash, as the case may be, representing such awards, shall be delivered to the beneficiary promptly.

2. When any award is made to a surviving spouse or to the estate of a deceased employee, cash or certificates of stock, as the case may be, representing such award shall be delivered at such times and in such manner as if the employee were living; provided, however, that if it shall be demonstrated that earlier release or delivery of the stock or cash is necessary to avoid hardship, the Bonus and Salary Committee may authorize such acceleration of release or delivery as it deems suited to the circumstances.

3. Except as provided in paragraphs 1 and 2 of this Article, certificates of stock, or cash, as the case may be, representing one-fourth of any bonus award shall be delivered to the beneficiary promptly; and certificates for the balance of any such award involving stock shall be delivered to the Bonus Custodian who shall hold the same for release to the beneficiary. The Bonus Custodian shall release and deliver to the beneficiary the certificates in his custody, and the Company shall pay the balance of a cash award to the beneficiary, in three equal annual installments, the first installment to be delivered after the end of the year in which the award is made; provided, however, that should such beneficiary leave the service of the bonus plan companies, settlement shall be made in the manner hereinafter described.

4. No fractional share of stock shall be delivered under either Plan.

Plan "C"

5. When an award is made under Plan "C", each beneficiary shall be furnished promptly with an appropriate written statement of the terms and conditions applicable to his award as fixed by action of the Bonus and Salary Committee in accordance with Article XV.

XIII. FORFEITURE OF BONUS AWARDS

Plans "A" and "B"

1. The Bonus Custodian shall open an account with each beneficiary to whom a bonus is to be delivered in accordance with Article XII, paragraph 3, crediting him immediately with one-fourth of such bonus award, in shares or cash, as the case may be, and crediting him, with respect to the remaining three-fourths, at the rate of 1/48th of the total award, for each completed month of service beginning with January of the year in which the award was made.

2. A beneficiary shall forfeit the portion of the award not yet credited to his account—

(a) if the beneficiary is dismissed or leaves the service of the bonus plan companies for any reason other than his death, or retirement pursuant to the provisions of the pension or retirement plan of such a company, or

(b) if the beneficiary retires pursuant to the provisions of the pension or retirement plan of a bonus plan company, and if following such retirement the Bonus and Salary Committee, or the Executive Committee, with respect to awards made under their respective authorities, after a hearing at which the beneficiary shall be entitled to be present, shall find that he has wilfully engaged in any activity which is harmful to the interests of any such companies;

provided, however, that he may continue a beneficiary under either or both Bonus Plans "A" and "B" to such extent and under such conditions as the Bonus and Salary Committee, or the Executive Committee, may determine with respect to awards made under their respective authorities.

3. In the event of forfeiture as hereinabove provided, the beneficiary shall receive the cash and stock represented by the net accumulated credits in his account, except that any fractional interest in whole shares shall be paid in cash at the market value thereof. The portion of the forfeited award represented by stock (including shares in which the beneficiary has a fractional interest) shall be sold by the Bonus Custodian to the Treasurer of the Company at the market value, and the proceeds from the sale of such forfeited stock, together with the cash portion of the forfeited award, shall be credited to the appropriate Company account (in the case of an award under Plan "A"), or to the Company's "B" Bonus Fund (in the case of an award under Plan "B").

Plan "C"

4. Bonus awards under Plan "C" are subject to forfeiture as and to the extent provided in Article XV.

XIV. Death of Bonus Beneficiary

Plans "A" and "B"

1. Upon the death of a beneficiary of an "A" or "B" bonus award the Bonus Custodian shall release the undelivered shares held in his

custody for such beneficiary, and the Company shall release the undelivered installments of cash awards, and said shares and cash shall be delivered to, or in accordance with the directions of, the executor or administrator of his estate at such times and in such manner as if the beneficiary were living; provided, however, that if it shall be demonstrated that earlier release or delivery of the stock or cash is necessary to avoid hardship, the Bonus and Salary Committee may authorize such acceleration of release or delivery as it deems suited to the circumstances.

Plan "C"

2. Upon the death of a beneficiary of a "C" bonus award, the rights of the beneficiary's estate or of his executor, administrator, legatees or distributees with respect to the "C" bonus award shall be as provided in Article XV.

XV. TERMS AND CONDITIONS OF "C" BONUS AWARDS

1. The Bonus and Salary Committee shall fix the terms and conditions of "dividend units" and stock options awarded under Plan "C", subject to the following limitations and restrictions:

"Dividend Units"

(a) Subject to forfeiture as hereinafter provided, "dividend units" awarded for any year shall remain in effect as follows:

(i) If not awarded in conjunction with a stock option, "dividend units" shall remain in effect until the beneficiary's death or the 85th anniversary of his birth, whichever is later.

(ii) If awarded in conjunction with a stock option, "dividend units" shall remain in effect only until the exercise of such option. Upon partial exercise of such option only that proportion of the "dividend units" which corresponds to the proportion of the option then unexercised shall remain in effect. If at the expiration of the option any portion thereof has not been exercised, a corresponding portion of the "dividend units" shall continue in effect until the beneficiary's death or the 85th anniversary of his birth, whichever is later.

(b) During the beneficiary's lifetime "dividend units" shall not be transferable or assignable.

(c) Upon the death of a beneficiary prior to his 85th birthday, his "dividend units" then in effect and rights thereunder shall pass to, or in accordance with the directions of, the executor or administrator of his estate.

(d) A beneficiary shall forfeit all rights under "dividend units" included in an award—

(i) if within the 10-year period following the date of such award the beneficiary is dismissed or leaves the service of the bonus plan companies for any reason other than his death, or retirement pursuant to the provisions of the pension or retirement plan of such a company, or

(ii) if the beneficiary retires pursuant to the provisions of the pension or retirement plan of a bonus plan company within the 10-year period following the date of such award, and if within one year following such retirement but not later than the end of the 10-year period the Bonus and Salary Committee, after a hearing at which the beneficiary shall be entitled to be present, shall find that he has wilfully engaged in any activity which is harmful to the interests of any of such companies;

provided, however, that such "dividend units" may continue in effect to such extent and under such conditions as the Bonus and Salary Committee may determine.

(e) When circumstances are deemed justifiable by the Bonus and Salary Committee, it may, upon agreement with the beneficiary, or his representatives in the event of his death, authorize lump-sum payment in cancellation of his outstanding "dividend units."

(f) No payments shall be made in respect of fractional "dividend units".

Stock Options

(g) The price per share of the stock which is the subject of the option shall in no case be less than the average of the high and low prices of the stock on the New York Stock Exchange on the date of the granting of the option, or, if no sale of the stock shall have been made on such Exchange on that date, on the next preceding date on which there was such a sale.

(h) A stock option shall in no case be exercisable at a faster rate than—

(i) to the extent of 50% of the number of shares under the option, after January 1 of the year following the year of grant, or after the expiration of 10 months following the date of grant, whichever is later,

(ii) to the extent of an additional 25% of the number of shares under the option, upon or after the expiration of one year following the date established in (i) above, and

(iii) to the extent of the remaining 25% of the number of shares under the option, upon or after the expiration of two years following the date established in (i) above.

(i) A stock option shall in no case be exercisable after the earliest of—

(i) 10 years from the date of its grant, or

(ii) 1 year after death of the optionee, or

(iii) 3 months after retirement of the optionee pursuant to the provisions of the pension or retirement plan of a bonus plan company; provided, however, that if the optionee should die within the 3-month period following his retirement the option period may be extended to one year after his death, but not beyond 10 years from the date of its grant, or

(iv) termination of the optionee's employment with the bonus plan companies, for any reason other than his retirement as provided in subparagraph (iii) or his death;

provided, however, that the optionee may terminate any option, or any portion thereof, prior to its expiration, by written notice to the Company bearing the signature and seal of the optionee, which notice shall be final, conclusive and binding.

(j) During his lifetime only the employee to whom an option is granted may exercise it. It shall not be transferable, except that, in the event of the optionee's death, the option (to the extent provided in paragraph (k) below) shall be exercisable by, or in accordance with the directions of, the executor or administrator of his estate.

(k) Upon the death of the optionee or his retirement pursuant to the provisions of the pension or retirement plan of a bonus plan company, whichever shall first occur, the number of shares subject to option shall be limited to that number of shares which the optionee could have purchased under the terms of his option on the date of his death or retirement, and the option as to the remainder of the shares shall terminate.

2. The Finance Committee shall periodically determine whether, and to what extent delivery of stock upon exercise of options shall be in new common stock issued for that purpose, or in common stock acquired by the Company. When the Finance Committee has determined that delivery of stock upon exercise of options shall be in common stock acquired by the Company, it may authorize the Treasurer to purchase the stock required, in its discretion, for such purpose.

3. In the event of any stock dividend, split-up, reclassification or other analogous change in capitalization, or any distribution to common stockholders other than interim or year-end dividends declared as such by the Board of Directors, the Bonus and Salary Committee shall make such adjustments, in the light of the change or distribution, as it deems to be equitable, both to the beneficiaries and the Company, in—

(a) the number of "dividend units" outstanding,
(b) the number of shares and prices per share applicable to outstanding stock options, and
(c) the limitation set forth in paragraphs 6 and 7 of Article IV with respect to the maximum number of "dividend units" which may be awarded to any employee for any year and the aggregate number which may be awarded to all employees during any five consecutive years.

XVI. Bonus and Salary Committee

The Bonus and Salary Committee shall be elected pursuant to the By-Laws of the Company, and the members thereof shall be ineligible for bonus awards while serving on said Committee.

XVII. Expenses of Administering Plans

All expenses and costs in connection with the operation of these Plans shall be borne by the Company and no part thereof shall be charged against the "B" Bonus Fund.

XVIII. Amendments to Plans

While it is the present intention of the Company to award bonuses annually, the Board of Directors reserves the right to modify these Plans from time to time or to repeal the Plans entirely, or to direct the discontinuance of awarding bonuses either temporarily or permanently; provided, however, that no modification of these Plans shall operate to annul, without the consent of the beneficiary, a bonus award already granted hereunder; provided, also, that no modification without approval of the stockholders shall increase the maximum amount which may be credited to the "B" Bonus Fund as hereinabove provided or change the limitations in paragraphs 6, 7 and 8 of Article IV, except by way of adjustments hereinabove expressly provided for.

XIX. INTERPRETATION

Plans "A" and "B"

1. Wherever reference is made in Bonus Plans "A" and "B" to "stock" or "shares," it shall be deemed to include any stock dividends on, or any division of or substitution for, stock resulting from an award.

Plans "A", "B" and "C"

2. A beneficiary shall be considered to have retired pursuant to the provisions of the pension or retirement plan of a bonus plan company only in the event his retirement has been pursuant to Section III, or Section IV A (1), (2), (3), or (4), covering age and voluntary retirements, optional retirement with reduced pension, and disability retirement of the Company's Pension and Retirement Plan or similar provisions of such a plan of another bonus plan company.

3. The decision of the Bonus and Salary Committee with respect to any questions arising as to interpretation of these Plans, including the severability of any and all of the provisions thereof, shall be final, conclusive and binding.

APPENDIX Y

E. I. du Pont de Nemours and Company

COMMUNICATION FROM BONUS
AND SALARY COMMITTEE

May 3, 1957

To: Board of Directors

E. I. du Pont de Nemours and Company

From: Bonus and Salary Committee

For some time now this Committee of the Board of Directors has studied the Company's Bonus Plans to make sure they are doing the best possible job for the long-term interests of the stockholders. As the result, the Committee is convinced it would be in the best interests of the Company, its stockholders, and its employees to amend the bonus program by: (1) reducing the amount of "B" Bonus awards, and (2) substituting awards under a proposed new Bonus Plan "C."

In essence, Plan "C" would give key employees what might be called a terminating "limited partnership" in the business in the form of "dividend units." In most cases the employee would also be awarded a "restricted stock option," affording him the opportunity to buy a permanent ownership in lieu of the "limited partnership." This would be accomplished by awards in either of the following forms:

(a) "dividend units," or
(b) "dividend units" accompanied by the right to buy Common Stock from the Company.

A "dividend unit" would entitle the beneficiary to receive, for a term of years, cash payments from the Company equal to the interim and year-end dividends (other than stock dividends) paid on one share of Common Stock of the Company.* No equivalents would be paid for stock dividends, other changes in capitalization, or special distributions to stockholders, but an equitable adjustment would be made in the number of the employee's "dividend units." The maximum term of years would be until the death of the beneficiary, or until

* 1956 Common Stock dividends were $6.50 a share.

393

his 85th birthday, whichever came later. During the beneficiary's lifetime the payments would be made only to him, but if he died before he was 85, the payments would continue to his heirs until that anniversary was reached.

In alternative (b), where the "dividend units" were in conjunction with stock options, they would be canceled in proportion to the number of shares of Common Stock purchased under the option. In either (a) or (b) the "dividend units" would be forfeitable for 10 years after grant, but not later than one year after the beneficiary's retirement.

The price per share of the stock optioned would not be less than the market price on the date the option was granted. The option period would not be more than 10 years. Except in case of death, an option could be exercised only by the employee to whom it was granted. It could be exercised while he was working for the Company, or within three months after his retirement, but would be canceled if he left the Company.

"Dividend units" do not give the recipient any shares of the Company's stock, which he could receive under Bonus Plan "B." Therefore, it is planned that the employee would be awarded one and one-half "dividend units" for each share of stock, or its cash equivalent, that would have been awarded him under Bonus Plan "B." At the same time, the number of shares of Common Stock optioned to any individual would not be more than one and one-third times the number of "dividend units" awarded him.

Recognizing that conditions may change from year to year, this Committee believes that had Plan "C" been in effect for 1956, "B" Bonus awards to some 50 to 75 employees would have been reduced by amounts ranging from 25% to 70%. For example, "B" Bonus awards to the President and to a Vice-President Member of the Executive Committee would have been reduced about like this:

"B" Bonus Award for 1956	*President*	*Vice-President Member of the Executive Committee*
Actual Award (common stock and cash)	$410,000	$250,000
Award If Plan "C" Had Been in Effect (entirely in cash)	125,000	100,000
Reduction in "B" Bonus Award	$285,000	$150,000

The number of "dividend units" and shares optioned in each "C" Bonus award would have been calculated as follows: in the case of the

President the REDUCTION IN "B" BONUS AWARD ($285,000) would have been divided by the value per share ($210.96) at which Common Stock was awarded for "B" Bonuses for 1956. The resulting figure would have been multiplied by one and one-half, giving the President 2,025 "dividend units." The number of shares optioned to him would have been one and one-third times the number of "dividend units" awarded. Therefore, he would have been granted an option, good for no more than 10 years, to buy from the Company 2,700 shares of its Common Stock. The price of this stock would have been the market price on the award date last February. This would have worked out at something like $182 a share, making a total purchase price of $491,400.

Applying the same formula, a Vice-President Member of the Executive Committee would have been awarded as "C" Bonus 1,065 "dividend units" and an option to purchase 1,420 shares of stock, the total purchase price coming to $258,400.

By this method of awarding "C" Bonuses, the grants of "dividend units" would be uniformly related to reductions in "B" Bonus awards. It is true that some "dividend units" might remain in effect longer than others, because of the different ages of the employees receiving them. Despite this, the Committee believes it would be best for the Company to grant the "dividend units" without regard to the age of the employees.

The advantage to the Company and the stockholders of the "C" Bonus Plan is this: awards of "B" Bonus in cash or purchased Common Stock mean less money available for the Company's use. The substitution of "dividend units" would save money for use in the business. This money, put to work as profitably as the other assets, would give additional earnings more than enough to cover the cost of the "dividend unit" payments. And if the Company continues to prosper, as we expect it will, we believe that many of those getting "C" Bonus awards will use their options, and buy stock. For every four shares they buy, three "dividend units" would be canceled; use of the whole option would cancel all the "dividend units." No further payments would be made on them. Other "dividend units" would, of course, expire upon the death of the employee holding them, or on the 85th anniversary of his birth.

Whenever payments under a "dividend unit" ceased, all the earnings made possible by the increase in investment resulting from that reduction in "B" Bonus awards would be fully available for the benefit of the Company and its stockholders. In addition, the Company would have the use of the money received from those buying new stock on options.

Because the "dividend unit" payments would be viewed as a cost of the increased earnings made possible by the additional investment resulting from the reductions in "B" Bonus awards, they would be charged against income, and not against the "B" Bonus Fund. Tax counsel has advised us that the "dividend unit" payments should be tax deductible. Dividends paid on stock delivered under the "B" Bonus Plan are not tax deductible.

Taking all this together, it would seem that the operation of Plan "C" should improve the position of the Company and its stockholders.

The Bonus and Salary Committee believes that Plan "C" would also be good for the Company and its stockholders because it would strengthen the ties between the Company and its key employees. These employees carry primary responsibility for the Company's success, and this Plan would effectively reward them for their contribution to that success. Stock options would give them an opportunity for greater stock ownership than under the Company's present Bonus Plans. On the other hand, even if an employee does not use his stock options, the current and future importance to him of the "dividend units" should insure his constant striving to improve earnings and promote the Company's interests.

Your Committee also knows that the Company will not be able to attract and hold persons of outstanding ability unless it provides opportunities at least as attractive as those offered by other companies. The increasing popularity of "restricted stock options" throughout industry will, we fear, put this Company at a competitive disadvantage unless Plan "C" is adopted.

We have been advised by the Internal Revenue Service that the stock options that would be awarded under Plan "C" would qualify as "restricted stock options." Hence, the employee would have no taxable income from receiving or using the option. At the same time, the Company would not be entitled to any tax deduction in connection with the sale.

As has been said, if Bonus Plan "C" is adopted by the Board and approved by the stockholders, it is planned that at the start awards under the Plan would be made to about 50 to 75 key employees. Experience may prove the wisdom of widening the group. It is not possible now to say which employees would receive "C" Bonuses. Neither can it be said now to what extent such awards would replace "B" Bonus awards.

Bonus Plan "C," integrated with the present Bonus Plans "A" and "B," and accompanied by additional information helpful to an understanding of the proposal, is attached to this communication. The Bonus and Salary Committee recommends that the Plan be adopted by the Board and presented to a special meeting of stockholders in 1957 in order that it can be applied to this year's bonus awards to be made in 1958.

BONUS AND SALARY COMMITTEE

J. W. McCoy, Chairman

Donaldson Brown

H. F. du Pont

W. F. Harrington

Hugh R. Sharp, Jr.

APPENDIX Z

The American Sugar Refining Company

INCENTIVE COMPENSATION PLAN

Section 1. Purpose

The purpose of this Plan is to provide greater incentive to employees in managerial and other important positions, who contribute materially to the success of the Company, by making them participants in that success.

Section 2. Definitions

As used in this Plan, the following terms shall have the following meanings.

(a) "Company" means The American Sugar Refining Company and its successors and assigns.

(b) "Employee" means any person, including any officer, employed by the Company or any of its wholly-owned domestic subsidiaries at any time during the year on a salary basis. Any person who serves the Company only as a director shall not be considered an employee.

(c) "Committee" means all members of the Board of Directors of the Company, except those who are employees and therefore eligible to receive awards under the Plan and those who are employed by any subsidiary of the Company.

(d) "Subsidiary" means a corporation a majority of the outstanding shares of voting stock of which is owned by the Company directly or indirectly. "Wholly-owned domestic subsidiary" means a corporation organized under the laws of one of the states of the United States of America or the District of Columbia, all of the outstanding shares of voting stock of which, other than directors' qualifying shares, are owned by the Company directly or indirectly.

(e) "Adjusted net earnings" means, with respect to any year, an amount determined as follows: Net Income for the Year as set forth in the Statement of Consolidated Income and Surplus for the Company and its subsidiaries in the annual report to stockholders for such year shall be increased by any special credits, and decreased by any special charges, made for such year to surplus which represent adjustments to consolidated net income as previously reported to stockholders for periods subsequent to January 1, 1958. The resulting figure shall then be adjusted to exclude (i) gains and losses on the sale or other disposition or revaluation of real estate, buildings, machinery, equipment and capital stock of corporation, (ii) amounts of awards or portions thereof forfeited under the Plan during the year and (iii) reductions and increases in the provision for federal taxes attributable to items (i) and (ii). The resulting figure as so adjusted shall be the "adjusted net earnings."

(f) "Incentive plan net earnings" means, with respect to any year, adjusted net earnings for such year plus the amount of the credit for such year to the incentive compensation reserve (established pursuant to Section 3 below) and minus the amount of the reduction in the provision for federal taxes attributable to such credit.

(g) "Incentive base" means, with respect to the year 1958, $8,000,000. With respect to any year after 1958, "incentive base" means $8,000,000 plus 5% of an amount equal to (i) adjusted net earnings for the period from January 1, 1958, to the beginning of such year less (ii) the aggregate amount of dividends (other than dividends payable in capital stock of the Company) paid, and other distributions made, on the capital stock of the Company during such period. In no event shall "incentive base" mean, with respect to any year, an amount less than $8,000,000.

SECTION 3. DETERMINATION OF INCENTIVE COMPENSATION RESERVE

For each year in which the dividend requirements of the 7% preferred stock are met and dividends of $1.60 or more per share are paid on the common stock of the Company and the incentive plan net earnings for the year equal or exceed the incentive base for the year, there shall be credited for such year to a reserve to be maintained on the books of the Company and called the "incentive compensation reserve" an amount equal to, in the aggregate, 2% of such amount of the incentive plan net earnings for the year as is equal to the incentive base for the year and, on any incentive plan net earnings for the year in excess of such incentive base, 3½% of the first $500,000 of such excess, 5% of the next $500,000 of such excess, 7½% of the next $1,000,000 of such excess and 10% of the balance thereof.

In the event of any recapitalization affecting, or any combination or split-up of, or any stock dividend on, the common stock of the Company, the foregoing dividend requirement of $1.60 per common share shall be adjusted proportionately.

All awards of incentive compensation made by the Committee, as hereinafter provided, shall be charged to the incentive compensation reserve. This reserve shall be deemed a single continuous reserve and any unawarded balance remaining in the reserve in any year shall be carried forward and be available for awards in any future year or years.

The firm of independent public accountants employed by the Company to audit its books and accounts for the year shall, as promptly as practicable after the end of the year, determine, and certify such determination to the Committee, the total amount of the incentive compensation reserve available for incentive awards as of the end of such year, that is, the aggregate of (i) the amount of the credit for such year to the reserve and (ii) the amount of any balance in the reserve which was credited thereto for prior years and has not been awarded. All determinations so made and certified shall be final, conclusive and binding upon the Company and all persons having any interest therein.

Section 4. Determination and Payment of Incentive Awards

After the close of each year and after receipt of the determination by the independent public accountants of the amount in the incentive compensation reserve, the Committee may, in its sole discretion, make incentive awards for such year to such employees as it may select (or to the executor or administrator of the estate of any such employee), and in such amounts as it may determine, in order to carry out the purpose of this Plan. An award may be made to any person who shall have been an employee at any time during the year for which such award shall be made. An award may also be made, as the Committee in its sole discretion may determine, to the executor or administrator of the estate of any employee if the employee dies during such year or thereafter but prior to the making of such award.

Awards may be made for the year regardless of the amount credited for the particular year to the incentive compensation reserve but the aggregate amount of awards made shall not exceed the total amount certified by the independent public accountants, in accordance with Section 3 above, as available for incentive awards. No award to any employee for any one year (or to the executor or administrator of the estate of any employee) shall exceed 40% of the employee's basic annual salary rate at the end of the year for which the award is made (or at the termination of his employment if his employment is terminated during the year).

The Committee at the time of making an award shall determine, in its sole discretion, whether payment of such award is to be immediate in whole or in part or deferred in whole or in part. Payment of the amount of an award which is deferred shall be contingent upon the fulfillment of conditions as hereinafter provided.

In case the payment of any employee's award is wholly or partly deferred, there shall be set up on the books of the Company a "deferred contingent account" for such employee and there shall be credited to such account the amounts of all deferred contingent awards made to such employee. In no event shall interest be paid or accrued on any award.

The amount credited to the employee's deferred contingent account shall, subject to the conditions set forth below in Section 5, be paid to the employee after termination of his employment in ten equal annual instalments, one such instalment to be paid on the last day of January, or as soon as practicable thereafter, in each of the ten years following the year in which termination of his employment occurs, provided that, if the employee should retire prior to age 60 under the pension plan of the Company, or of a subsidiary, other than for disability, the payment of such instalments shall not commence until the year following that in which the retired employee attains the age of 60 years. Leave of absence authorized by the Company shall not be considered termination of employment.

If the employee dies, any amount remaining unpaid in his deferred contingent account shall be paid to, or in accordance with the directions of, the executor or administrator of his estate in the following manner.

(a) If employment of an employee is terminated by death, payment of such amount shall be made in ten equal annual instalments, one such instalment to be paid as soon as practicable after the employee's death and one of the remaining nine instalments to be paid on the last day of January, or as soon as practicable thereafter, in each of the nine succeeding years following the year in which payment of the first instalment occurs.

(b) If the employee dies after termination of his employment and there has been no forfeiture of his rights under this Plan as provided in Section 5, payment of such amount shall be made at such times and in such manner as if the employee were still living. If such employee had retired prior to age 60 under the pension plan of the Company, or of a subsidiary, other than for disability, and had not attained the age of 60 years before his death, it shall be assumed for the purposes of this sub-paragraph (b) that he attained the age of 60 years on the date of his death.

The Committee may in its sole discretion authorize the acceleration of payment of any unpaid instalments of any deferred contingent award upon written application of the employee or other persons entitled thereto.

Section 5. Conditions of Payment of Deferred Contingent Awards; Forfeiture

No payment of any instalment of a deferred contingent award shall be made and all rights under this Plan of the employee or other persons to the payment thereof shall be forfeited if any one or more of the following events shall occur prior to the time of such payment.

(a) The employee voluntarily terminates his employment with the Company or any subsidiary without the consent of the Company; provided, however, that termination of employment as the result of the employee's retirement under the Company's pension plan or that of a subsidiary, or his death or disability, shall not be considered voluntary termination of employment for the purpose of this subparagraph (a).

(b) The employee is discharged for willful, deliberate or gross misconduct.

(c) The employee after termination of his employment with the Company, or any subsidiary, shall fail to make himself available for advice and consultation at reasonable times and places if physically able to do so when requested by the Company.

(d) The employee after termination of his employment with the Company, including subsidiaries, shall be employed by any competitor of, or engage in any activity in competition with, the Company or a subsidiary without the written approval of the Company.

The amounts of any awards or portions thereof forfeited shall be credited to the net income or surplus of the Company in the year in which the forfeiture occurs and shall not be restored to the incentive compensation reserve.

Section 6. Source of Award Payments

All awards shall be paid in cash from the general funds of the Company or its wholly-owned domestic subsidiaries and no special or separate fund shall be established or other segregation of assets made to assure the payment of any award.

Each wholly-owned domestic subsidiary shall be charged each year with the amount, if any, awarded under the Plan to its employees for such year.

Section 7. General Conditions

No employee or other person shall have any claim or right to be granted an award under this Plan.

Neither this Plan nor any action taken thereunder shall be construed as giving to any employee the right to be retained in the employ of the Company.

An employee's right to the payment of a deferred contingent award may not be assigned or transferred except by will or by the laws of descent and distribution.

Any corporation in which the Company owns an interest, other than corporations that are wholly-owned domestic subsidiaries as of the effective date of this Plan, may, notwithstanding the existence of this Plan and without regard to the provisions thereof, have a separate incentive compensation plan, provided that no person receiving an award under such other plan may receive an award under this Plan with respect to the same period.

Section 8. Administration of Plan

This Plan shall be administered by the Committee which shall have full power and authority to interpret, construe and administer the Plan and any part thereof and the Committee's interpretations and constructions thereof and actions thereunder, shall be binding and conclusive on all persons for all purposes.

The Committee shall have the power to adopt rules and regulations for the administration of the Plan, and to amend or repeal any rule or regulation so adopted.

Any expense incurred in the administration of the Plan shall be borne by the Company and not charged against the incentive compensation reserve.

Section 9. Amendment

This Plan may be amended, suspended, terminated or reinstated in whole or part by the Board of Directors of the Company but no such action shall adversely affect any right or obligation with respect to any award theretofore made, nor shall any amendment affect the provisions of the Plan governing the computation of the amount to be credited to the incentive compensation reserve each year so as to increase such amount unless such amendment is approved by action of the stockholders. In the event that the Company or any subsidiary merges with or into another corporation or acquires substantially all of the stock or assets of another corporation, the Board of Directors shall at such time consider whether amendment of the Plan is advisable in the light of such merger or acquisition.

Section 10. Effective Date and Continuance of Plan

This Plan shall be effective as of January 1, 1958. No credit to the incentive compensation reserve shall be made on account of incentive plan net earnings for any year beginning after December 31, 1962, unless the Board of Directors of the Company recommends continuance of the Plan and such continuance is approved by stockholder action prior to December 31, 1963.

APPENDIX AA

General Electric Company

INCENTIVE COMPENSATION PLAN

Section I. Purpose of Plan and Determination of Incentive Compensation Reserve

(1) The purpose of this Plan is to provide a means of paying incentive compensation, in addition to salaries, to employees (including officers) of General Electric Company and of its consolidated affiliates (hereinafter sometimes referred to as the Consolidated Group) in managerial and other important positions who contribute materially to the success of the Company's business by their ability, ingenuity and industry, and to reward such contributions by making them participants in the results of that success. To this end the Plan provides for the establishment of an incentive compensation reserve the maximum amount of which is dependent upon the profits realized by the Consolidated Group, from which payment may be made to such employees of such compensation.

(2) There shall be maintained an Incentive Compensation Reserve (hereinafter called the "Reserve"). To this Reserve there shall be credited for each year such amount as may be appropriated by the Board of Directors of the General Electric Company for that purpose not exceeding an amount equivalent to 10% of the excess, if any, of the net earnings of the Consolidated Group for such year, as defined in paragraph (3), over an amount equivalent to 5% of the average capital investment of the Consolidated Group for such year as defined in paragraph (4).

(3) The term "net earnings of the Consolidated Group" as used in this Plan shall mean for each year (a) the consolidated net earnings (as defined hereinafter) of the General Electric Company and the consolidated affiliates, plus (b) the amount credited to the Reserve for such year which shall have been deducted as an expense of operations in determining such consolidated earnings, and (c) interest paid or accrued on any indebtedness which is included in capital investment. Consolidated net earnings for the purposes of this Plan shall be the consolidated net earnings which are reported in the Company's Annual Report to its share owners, as approved

405

by the Independent Public Accountants who have examined the accounts of the Company for the applicable year. Such consolidated net earnings may include capital and other gains and losses from transactions other than in the ordinary course of business, and dividends and other income received by members of the Consolidated Group from investments in corporations other than members of the Consolidated Group. In adding to consolidated net earnings, for the purpose of determining net earnings of the Consolidated Group, the deductions made for the amount credited to the Reserve under paragraph (2) of this Section I and for interest paid or accrued on indebtedness included in the average capital investment (as defined hereinafter), no adjustment shall be made for any reduction in income taxes payable by any corporation in the Consolidated Group which reduction may be attributable to such deductions.

(4) The term "average capital investment of the Consolidated Group" for any year, as used in this Plan, shall mean the average book value of the General Electric Company's capital stock plus the average amount of indebtedness of the Consolidated Group which is interest-bearing, and is evidenced by a bond, note or other written evidence of indebtedness, exclusive of any such bond, note or other indebtedness, which is payable to a non consolidated affiliate. Such average book value and average amount of indebtedness shall consist of the average of the applicable amounts as of the beginning and end of the applicable year. Book value of the Company's capital stock shall consist of the sum of (a) the par value of all issued capital stock of the General Electric Company, whether such stock is outstanding or is held in the treasury of the Company, and (b) the aggregate amount of the consolidated earned and capital surplus of the Consolidated Group, i.e., the aggregate amount of the consolidated reinvested earnings of the Consolidated Group, plus the investment in excess of the par value of capital stock.

(5) Prior to the determination by the Board of Directors of the amount to be credited to the Reserve for any year, the Independent Public Accountants of the General Electric Company shall determine and report to the Board of Directors of the Company (a) the maximum amount which may be appropriated and credited to the Reserve for that year under the Plan, and (b) the amount of any balance in the Reserve which has been carried forward from prior years.

(6) A consolidated affiliated corporation shall pay or accept charges for all allotments from the Reserve, and dividend equivalents contingently credited to employees of such corporation under the provisions of Section V.

SECTION II. ADMINISTRATION OF THE PLAN

(1) The Plan shall be administered by a committee appointed by the Board of Directors of the Company from among its own number (hereinafter called the "Committee"). The membership of the Committee may be reduced, changed, or increased from time to time in the absolute discretion of the Board of Directors. No member of the Committee shall be eligible for an allotment awarded while he is serving upon the Committee.

(2) The Committee shall have full power to construe and interpret this Plan, and to establish and amend rules and regulations for its administration. Similarly the determination of those who may participate in incentive compensation under the Plan, and the amount of individual allotments to such participants shall rest in the absolute discretion of the Committee. The determinations provided for in the next preceding sentence may be delegated to one or more officers and/or managers of the Company in accordance with such rules and regulations as may be prescribed or adopted by the Committee from time to time, except that the Committee itself shall determine the individual allotments to be made to officers of the Company and to other individuals reporting directly to the Chairman of the Board, the President, or a Group Executive.*

(3) As soon as practicable after determination by the Board of Directors of the amount to be credited to the Reserve for any year, the Committee shall determine the total amount which is to be allotted from the Reserve for that year but such total allotment may not exceed the sum of (a) the amount credited to the Reserve for that year, and (b) the amount of any balance carried forward from prior years as determined and reported by the Independent Public Accountants of the Company in accordance with paragraph (5) of Section I of the Plan.

SECTION III. PAYMENT OF ALLOTMENTS TO PARTICIPANTS

(1) Allotments under the Plan to officers of the General Electric Company, and to such other executives of members of the Consolidated Group as the Committee may, in its absolute discretion select, shall be divided into two approximately equal parts. The first of such parts shall be used to determine the nearest number of full shares of General Electric common stock which such part would purchase at the closing market price on the New York Stock Exchange on the nearest day of sale preceding the date of allotment and this first part

* As amended by the Board of Directors of General Electric Company October 26, 1956, and April 23, 1958.

(hereinafter referred to as a "contingent allotment"), shall be contingently payable in the number of shares of General Electric common stock so determined in the manner and subject to the conditions set forth in Section IV of the Plan. The second of said parts, constituting the remainder of the total allotment, shall be paid in cash as soon as is practicable.

(2) Allotments under the Plan to all other participants shall be paid in full as soon as is practicable. Such payments may, in the absolute discretion of the Committee, be made wholly or partly in cash, in General Electric common stock, or in other securities. For the purpose of such distribution, General Electric common stock shall be valued at the closing market price on the New York Stock Exchange on the nearest day of sale preceding the date of allotment, and other securities at their fair market value on the day of allotment as determined by the Committee, which determination shall be conclusive.

(3) No participant shall have any right with respect to any allotment, contingent or otherwise, until such allotment or written notice thereof shall have been delivered to him.

(4) There shall be deducted from all payments of allotments and dividend equivalents under the Plan, any taxes required to be withheld by the Federal or any State or local government and paid over to such government for the account of such participant. In the case of payments made in General Electric common stock or in other securities, the employer company shall have the right to retain and/or to sell without notice sufficient securities to pay the amount of tax required to be paid over by it in respect of such payment, remitting any balance to the participant. In lieu thereof, however, the Committee may permit a participant receiving a payment in securities to pay or reimburse the employer company for any taxes required to be paid over by it in respect of such payment upon such terms and conditions as the Committee may prescribe.

SECTION IV. CONTINGENT ALLOTMENTS

(1) Subject to the conditions set forth in paragraph (3) of this Section IV of the Plan, payment of contingent allotments shall be made in equal annual installments commencing April 1, or as soon thereafter as is practical, of the year following the year in which the participant's employment with General Electric Company, including its affiliates, terminates. The number of such installments shall be fifteen if employment terminates at age 65 or over, sixteen if employ-

ment terminates at age 64, seventeen if employment terminates at age 63, eighteen if employment terminates at age 62, nineteen if employment terminates at age 61, and twenty if employment terminates prior to age 61.* If the aggregate number of shares of General Electric common stock contingently payable to a participant at the time his employment terminates, is not divisible by the applicable number of installments into whole shares, each installment except the last shall be determined on the basis of the nearest number of whole shares which is divisible by the total number of installments contingently payable and the last installment shall consist of the total contingent allotment minus the sum of all previous payments.

(2) Any contingent allotments, or remaining unpaid portion thereof, which become payable after the death of a participant, shall be paid in installments to his legal representatives. If the death of a participant occurs after the termination of his employment, the number of such installments shall be the remaining number which otherwise would have been paid to the participant, and if termination of employment is attributable to death, the number of such installments shall be in accordance with paragraph (1) of this Section IV. However, the Committee shall possess absolute discretion in either event to accelerate the time of payment of any such allotments, or remaining unpaid installments thereof, to the extent that it deems equitable or desirable under the circumstances.

(3) Payment of contingent allotments shall be subject to the following conditions:

(a) If the participant's service with General Electric Company, including its affiliates, terminates (whether voluntarily or by dismissal but otherwise than as a result of death, disability, retirement under the Company's Pension Plan or under circumstances deemed by the Committee not to be contrary to the interests of General Electric Company or any of its affiliates) within a period of three years following the close of the fiscal year for which a contingent allotment has been made for his account, such allotment shall be reduced to the nearest number of whole shares calculated by multiplying such allotment by a fraction, the numerator of which is the number of full quarter-years during which he remained in the employ of General Electric Company or one

* As amended by the Board of Directors of General Electric Company May 21, 1954, applicable to incentive compensation payable from earnings in 1954 and thereafter.

of its affiliates following the close of the fiscal year for which such allotment was made, and the denominator of which is twelve. The amount by which any such allotment has been so reduced shall be forfeited.

(b) If, without the written consent of the Committee, the participant at any time during the period following the termination of his employment in which period he would otherwise be entitled to receive payment of contingent allotments credited to him, engages in the operation or management of a business, whether as owner, partner, officer, employee, or otherwise, having a net worth in excess of $5,000,000, which at such time is in competition with General Electric Company or one of its affiliates, any and all contingent installments thereafter due him shall be forfeited. The determination as to whether a participant is engaged in the operation or management of such a business and as to whether such business is in competition with General Electric Company or any of its affiliates shall be made by the Committee in its absolute discretion and the decision of the Committee with respect thereto, including its determination of the time at which the participation in such competitive business commenced, shall be conclusive.

(c) Any allotment or portion thereof forfeited under (a) or (b) of paragraph (3) of this Section IV, shall revert to the Reserve and shall be added to the amount of the balance in the Reserve. The value of any such forfeited allotment or portion thereof shall be determined on the basis of the stock price originally employed to determine the amount of the allotment.

SECTION V. DIVIDEND EQUIVALENTS CREDITABLE TO CONTINGENT ALLOTMENTS

(1) Each contingent allotment shall during the period and to the extent it remains unpaid or unforfeited, be contingently credited with amounts equivalent to the dividends which would have been declared within such period in respect to the General Electric stock represented by such allotment if such stock were issued and outstanding (such amounts being hereinafter called "dividend equivalents"). Such dividend equivalents shall be contingently credited on the date of record as of which a dividend is declared.

In the event that any such dividend would have been payable in property other than cash or General Electric common stock, then the Committee in its absolute discretion may contingently credit as the dividend equivalent the fair market value of such property at the time of payment of such dividend.

(2) The cumulative amount of such dividend equivalents credited to any installment payment made under Section IV of the Plan shall be payable or distributable at the time of payment of such installment. For the purpose of determining the cumulative amount of such credits which is applicable to any installment payment, such installment payment shall be deemed to have been made out of the earliest unpaid contingent allotment or portion thereof. Payment of such dividend equivalent accumulations shall be subject to the same conditions as those pertaining to the contingent allotment to which such dividend equivalent accumulations apply.

(3) The aggregate amount of dividend equivalents contingently credited under this Section V shall be charged to the operating expenses of the employing member of the Consolidated Group at the time such credits are made, and shall be in addition to any amounts that may be credited to the Reserve under this Plan. Any dividend equivalent contingently credited to any allotment which is forfeited under the provisions of Section IV shall revert to the company to which it was charged and shall be credited to the operating costs of such company as of the time of forfeiture.

Section VI. Scope of Plan *

(1) Employees of any company in the Consolidated Group who, at the end of any year or at the end of their employment by such company, receive salaries at a rate of $15,000 or more per annum (adjusted in proportion to increases or decreases made by the Committee in the General Electric Exempt Salary Structure) shall be eligible for selection by or under the authority of the Committee, for participation in the Plan for that year. The Plan, however, shall not apply to employees of any company in the Consolidated Group who are not eligible to participate in the Plan pursuant to the provisions of the preceding sentence.

(2) Nothing in this Plan shall be construed as preventing the Company or any of its consolidated affiliates from establishing sales commission plans for employees who, though eligible under paragraph (1) above, are not selected for participation under this Plan, nor shall the Plan be construed as affecting the power of the respective Boards of Directors of such companies (which may act through

* As approved by the Share Owners and amended by the Board of Directors of General Electric Company April 23, 1958.

duly authorized Committees of such Boards) to adopt or to authorize the adoption of other incentive compensation plans (including sales commission plans) applicable to employees receiving salaries at a rate of less than $15,000 per annum (adjusted in proportion to the increases or decreases above referred to in the General Electric Exempt Salary Structure).

(3) The Plan shall not apply to employees of any other company in which the Company has a stock interest, the balance sheet and operating results of which are not consolidated with those of the Company for purposes of its Annual Report to share owners, and any such company may, notwithstanding the existence of this Plan, have a separate plan or plans for the payment of incentive compensation to its employees including its employees in managerial or other important positions.

(4) The Board of Directors of the Company may in its discretion determine for each year which affiliated corporations of the Company shall be included in the Consolidated Group.

SECTION VII. GENERAL CONDITIONS

(1) The Board of Directors may from time to time amend, suspend or terminate in whole or in part, and if terminated, may reinstate any or all of the provisions of the Plan, except that (a) no amendment, suspension or termination may, without his consent, apply to the payment to any participant of any allotment (contingent or otherwise) made to him prior to the effective date of such amendment, suspension or termination and (b) no amendment may be made which will increase the amount which may be appropriated to the Reserve under the Plan without prior approval of the holders of the common stock of the Company given at a meeting of such stockholders. Without limiting the generality of the foregoing, the Board of Directors may, subject to the limitations contained in this paragraph (1) of Section VII of the Plan, amend or rescind any provision of the Plan so as to increase, reduce or eliminate the proportion of total allotments which is contingently payable, change the number of installments or the medium in which contingent allotments are payable, or modify the period of time during which any such installments shall be paid and the contingencies under which any such installments shall be paid.

(2) The place of administration of the Plan shall be conclusively deemed to be within the State of New York and the validity, construction, interpretation, administration and effect of the Plan, and

of its rules and regulations, and the rights of any and all persons having or claiming to have an interest therein or thereunder, shall be governed by, and determined exclusively and solely in accordance with, the law of the State of New York.

(3) The selection of any employee for participation in the Plan shall not give such participant any right to be retained in the employ of any member of the Consolidated Group and the right and power of the employer company to dismiss or discharge any participant is specifically reserved. Nor shall any such participant or any person claiming under or through him have any right or interest, whether vested or otherwise, in this Plan, or in the Reserve, or in any allotment hereunder, unless and until all the terms, conditions and provisions of the Plan that affect such participant have been complied with as specified herein.

(4) Any decision or action taken or to be made by the Company, or the Board of Directors, or the Committee, arising out of or in connection with the construction, administration, interpretation, and effect of the Plan and of its rules and regulations shall lie within their absolute discretion and shall be conclusive and binding upon all participants and any person claiming under or through any participant.

(5) The Board of Directors and the Committee may rely upon any information supplied to them by any officer of the Company or by the Company's Independent Public Accountants, in connection with the administration of the Plan.

(6) No member of the Board of Directors or of the Committee shall be liable for any act or action, whether of commission or omission, taken by any other member, or by any officer, agent, or employee; nor, except in circumstances involving his bad faith, for anything done or omitted to be done by himself.

(7) The Committee shall conduct its business and hold meetings as determined by it from time to time and any action taken by the Committee at meetings duly called shall require the affirmative vote of at least a majority of its members then in office.

SECTION VIII. GENERAL DEFINITIONS

For the purposes of the Plan, unless the context otherwise indicates, the following definitions shall be applicable:

(1) The term "Company" means General Electric Company.

(2) The term "Consolidated Group" means General Electric Company and all affiliated corporations of General Electric Com-

pany, the financial results of which for the year in question are consolidated with those of General Electric Company for purposes of the latter's Annual Report to its share owners.*

(3) The term "affiliate" or "affiliated corporation" means any corporation more than 50% of whose voting stock is owned directly or indirectly by General Electric Company.

(4) The term "officers" refers solely to officers of the parent General Electric Company.*

(5) The use of the masculine gender shall also include within its meaning the feminine.

(6) The use of the singular shall also include within its meaning the plural and vice versa.

SECTION IX. EFFECTIVE DATE

(1) This Plan as herein amended shall be applicable for the calendar year 1950 and subsequent years.

* As amended by the Board of Directors of General Electric Company April 23, 1958.

APPENDIX BB

GENERAL ELECTRIC COMPANY

RULES FOR THE ADMINISTRATION OF INCENTIVE COMPENSATION PLAN *

I. DEFINITIONS

As used in these rules the term

"Company" means all corporations in the "Consolidated Group" as defined in Section VIII of the Plan.

"Officer" means an Officer of the parent General Electric Company.

"Applicable Officer" means the Officer (or his successor) having managerial responsibility over a participant for the period for which incentive compensation is to be allotted.

"Applicable Manager" means the manager (or his successor) having managerial responsibility over a participant for the period for which incentive compensation is to be allotted.

"Applicable year" means the year for which incentive compensation is to be allotted.

"Annual paid salaries" means salaries paid for the applicable calendar year.

"Board of Directors" means the Board of Directors of the parent General Electric Company.

"Committee" means the Compensation Committee of the Board of Directors.

II. DETERMINATION OF TOTAL ALLOTMENT FOR APPLICABLE YEAR FROM INCENTIVE COMPENSATION RESERVE

As soon as practicable after the Board of Directors shall have determined the amount to be credited to the Incentive Compensation Reserve for the applicable year, the Committee will, pursuant to Section II(3) of the Plan, determine the maximum amount which may be allotted from the Reserve for that year. The amount so determined by the Committee will constitute the amount available for

* Adopted by the Compensation Committee of the Board of Directors of General Electric Company May 23, 1958.

allotment to eligible individual participants in accordance with these rules; all such allotments shall, however, be subject to the approval of the Committee as provided for in these rules.

III. ELIGIBILITY

Employees of the Company

    a. who, at the end of the applicable year or at the end of their employment in the Company within the applicable year, receive a salary at a rate of $15,000 or more per annum (adjusted in proportion to increases or decreases made by the Committee in the General Electric Exempt Salary Structure subsequent to April 23, 1958); and

    b. who shall have completed at least 12 months of continuous service with the Company (including its non-consolidated affiliates) by December 31 of the applicable year; or

    c. who having on that date completed less than 12 months of such service, are specifically approved by the Committee as provided in Article VII of these rules;

shall be eligible for selection as participants.

IV. GENERAL

1. Allotments to individual participants shall be determined on the basis of an appraisal of the participant's contribution to, and performance with, the Company during the applicable year.

2. The selection of an employee as a participant for any year is not to be construed as an assurance that he will be allotted any incentive compensation for any such year, or that he will be selected as a participant for any future year.

V. SELECTION OF PARTICIPANTS AND DETERMINATION OF ALLOTMENTS

1. The Committee shall select those in the following positions who are to participate in the Plan, and determine the allotments to each such participant:

    a. employees occupying the position of Chairman of the Board, President, or Group Executive,

    b. employees in positions reporting directly to the Chairman of the Board, the President, or a Group Executive,

    c. employees in positions evaluated in position levels above 24 of the Exempt Salary Structure, and

    d. all other employees who are Officers of the Company.

2. The Chairman of the Board is authorized (with power to delegate such authority) to select as participants employees other than those covered by Paragraph 1 of this Article V, and to determine the allotments to such participants. All allotments made under this Paragraph 2 shall be deemed to be tentative until approved by the Committee as provided in Article VII.

VI. PROCEDURE

There shall be submitted to the Committee:

1. A statement, certified by the Comptroller, showing in connection with the Committee's selection of participants and determination of allotments under Paragraph 1, Article V the names, positions, position levels, changes in salary rates during the preceding year ending March 1, annual paid salaries, incentive compensation allotments for the preceding two years, and prospective pension benefits of, and stock options granted to, such employees.

2. A summary, certified by the Comptroller, and signed by the Chairman of the Board, of the tentative allotments made by or under the authorization of the Chairman of the Board under Paragraph 2, Article V, which summary shall show for each major operating unit and consolidated affiliate and for the Services of the Company as a group:

    a. the total number of participants allotted incentive compensation,

    b. the aggregate of the annual paid salaries of the allottees,

    c. the aggregate amount of the allotments, and

    d. the ratio which the aggregate of such allotments bears to such aggregate annual paid salaries.

3. A statement, certified by the Comptroller, and signed by the Chairman of the Board, showing the tentative allotments made by or under the authorization of the Chairman of the Board under Paragraph 2, Article V to those participants:

    a. whose allotments exceed 100% of their respective annual paid salaries, or

    b. who shall have completed less than 12 months of continuous service with the Company by December 31 of the applicable year, or

    c. whose allotments include a contingent allotment.

Such statement shall show the names, positions, position levels, changes in salary rates during the preceding year ending March 1, annual paid salaries, incentive compensation allotted for the current year and allotments for the preceding two years and prospective pension benefits of, and stock options granted to, such participants.

VII. APPROVAL BY THE COMMITTEE

The approval by the Committee of the documents called for by Article VI shall, subject to such changes or revisions as it may direct, constitute an approval by the Committee of the allotments which are included or reflected in such documents, and the delivery of such allotments (or of notice of contingent allotments) shall thereby be authorized.

VIII. MANNER AND TIME OF PAYMENT OF APPROVED ALLOTMENTS

1. Except as to allotments made pursuant to Section III(1) of the Plan (relating to contingent allotments), unless the Committee otherwise directs

    a. allotments to participants whose service with the Company terminated prior to the delivery of the allotments shall be payable entirely in cash (less any withholding taxes required by law),

    b. all other allotments (less any withholding taxes required by law) shall be payable approximately 50% in cash and 50% in General Electric Common Stock, which stock shall, pursuant to Section III(2) of the Plan, be valued at the closing market price thereof on the New York Stock Exchange on the nearest day of sale preceding the date of approval of allotments by the Committee.

2. Delivery of all allotments approved pursuant to these rules shall be made as soon as possible after approval of such allotments by the Committee.

IX. REMOVALS AND TRANSFERS

1. Participants whose employment with the Company is terminated because of retirement, disability, or other reason except death:

    a. after the close of the applicable year but prior to the actual distribution of allotments for such year, may be awarded a full allotment for that year.

    b. after the beginning but prior to the end of the applicable year may be awarded an allotment for that year based upon the actual period of their employment with the Company within the year.

2. Participants whose employment with the Company is terminated because of death :

    a. after the close of the applicable year but prior to the actual distribution of allotments for such year shall be awarded a full allotment for that year,

    b. after the beginning but prior to the end of the applicable year shall be awarded an allotment for that year based upon the actual period of their employment with the Company within the year.

3. Participants transferred during the applicable year from one component of the Company to another may be awarded an allotment through the component in which he is employed at the end of the applicable year even though the amount thereof is based on the contribution made in each component in which he was employed during the year.

X. APPLICATIONS FOR CONSENT OF COMMITTEE UNDER SECTION IV (3) (b) OF THE PLAN

Applications of contingent allottees for the consent of the Committee, pursuant to Section IV (3) (b) of the Plan, to engage in business in competition with the Company, shall be made in writing, and filed with the Chairman of the Board, who shall as soon thereafter as practicable submit such application to the Committee, with his recommendation as to such application and a statement of the considerations upon which such recommendation is made.

XI. AMENDMENT OR RESCISSION OF THESE RULES

The Committee reserves the right to amend or rescind these rules in whole or in part at any time without notice.

APPENDIX CC

Ford Motor Company

SUPPLEMENTAL COMPENSATION PLAN

Purpose

1. The purpose of this Plan is to make provision for the payment of supplemental compensation to employees who contribute to the success of the Company, thus affording to them an incentive for and a means of participating in that success.

Supplemental Compensation Reserve

2. The Company shall establish and maintain a Supplemental Compensation Reserve (hereinafter referred to as the "Reserve") to which shall be credited for each year (commencing with the full calendar year (1955) an amount equal to 6% of the Income * for such year, after first deducting from the amount of such Income an amount equal to 10% of the Capital Employed in the Business; provided, however, that the amount of such credit shall be adjusted, if necessary, so that the credit made to the Reserve for any year will not have the effect of reducing Net Income for such year to an amount less than 6% of the Capital Employed in the Business.

3. The Reserve shall be a single, continuous reserve. The unawarded amount in the Reserve in any year shall be carried forward and be available for awards in a future year or years. The Audit and Compensation Committee shall have the full and exclusive power and right to determine the year or years in which the unawarded amount of the Reserve thus carried forward shall be used for awards, and the extent to which it shall be so used in any such year. Each such determination shall be in the sole discretion of such Committee and need not be with reference to either the results of the operations of the Company for such year or years or the credit or credits to the Reserve for such year or years. The Reserve shall not be debited except (a) to reflect awards duly made pursuant to the provisions of this Plan, (b) to reflect any adjustment made pursuant to Para-

* The following terms are defined in Paragraph 20 of this Plan: Committee, Subsidiary, Eligible Subsidiary, Affiliate, Employee, Income, Net Income, Capital Employed in the Business, and Debt.

graph 5, or (c) pursuant to action by the stockholders at a meeting duly called and held for such purpose.

CREDITS AND DEBITS TO THE RESERVE

4. After the close of each year, and as promptly as practicable after they shall have completed their review and audit for such year of the accounts of the Company for the purpose of certification, the Company's independent public accountants shall determine and report in writing to the Audit and Compensation Committee (a) the amount creditable to the Reserve for such year in accordance with the provisions of Paragraph 2, which amount forthwith, and without any further action, shall be credited to the Reserve; and (b) the total amount of the Reserve (after giving effect to such credit, to all debits on account of the full amount of all awards for prior years, whether or not such awards or any part thereof shall have been paid, and to all other credits, debits and adjustments that may have been made pursuant to the provisions of this Plan).

5. If it shall be determined by the Company's independent public accountants, or if it shall be determined in connection with any claim or proceeding with respect to this Plan, that the amount credited to the Reserve for any year pursuant to the provisions of Paragraph 4 is more or less for any reason than the amount properly creditable thereto pursuant to the provisions of this Plan, the only consequence shall be that an adjustment shall be made in the Reserve in the year in which such determination is made by crediting the amount of the deficiency or debiting the amount of the excess to the Reserve. If the adjustment involves a reduction in the Reserve and if the amount in the Reserve prior to adjustment is less than the amount of such adjustment, the amount in the Reserve shall be written off immediately and adjustment of the remainder of such excess shall be effected by the reduction of any amount or amounts subsequently creditable to the Reserve. No other adjustment on account of such determination shall be made in any year, including, but without limitation thereto, any adjustment of the Capital Employed in the Business for any year prior to the year in which such determination is made or any adjustment of awards (whether or not paid) made hereunder prior to such determination. Any excess credit to the Reserve, however occasioned, may be corrected solely in the manner and to the extent provided above, and neither any such credit nor the making of any award (whether or not paid) in excess of the unawarded balance of the Reserve in reliance upon such credit shall result, directly or indirectly, in the adjustment of any award or recourse to or charge

against any recipient of an award under the Plan, any employee, officer or director of the Company or of any Subsidiary thereof, any member of the Audit and Compensation Committee or any member of the Executive Committee, or any other person whomsoever.

AWARDS

6. a. After the close of each year, and as promptly as practicable after the Audit and Compensation Committee shall have received the report of the Company's independent public accountants pursuant to Paragraph 4, such Committee shall:

(1) determine the maximum total amount of all awards to be made for such year, which amount, in the sole discretion of the Committee, may be equal to or greater or lesser to any extent than the total amount credited to the Reserve for such year, but shall not exceed the total amount of the Reserve (after giving effect to the credit for such year), all as reported to such Committee pursuant to Paragraph 4, and

(2) make all awards for such year to such members of the Administration Committee and such members of the Executive Committee as may be deemed by the Audit and Compensation Committee to be entitled to awards (and to the spouse, children or legal representatives of any of such members in accordance with the provisions of Paragraph 7), in each case in such amount as it in its sole discretion may determine.

b. The Executive Committee then shall make all awards for such year to such Employees of the Company other than members of the Administration Committee or members of the Executive Committee, and shall recommend all awards for such year to be made by Eligible Subsidiaries to such of their Employees, as may be deemed by the Executive Committee to be entitled to awards (and to the spouse, children or legal representatives of any of such Employees in accordance with the provisions of Paragraph 7), in each case in such amount as it in its sole discretion may determine; provided, however, that the aggregate amount of awards so made and recommended, when added to the aggregate amount of awards made by the Audit and Compensation Committee for such year, shall not exceed the maximum total amount of all awards to be made for such year as determined by the Audit and Compensation Committee pursuant to Paragraph 6a(1).

Persons to Whom Awards May Be Paid

7. An award of supplemental compensation may be made under this Plan to: (a) any person who shall have been an Employee at any time during the year for which such award shall be made, and (b) to the spouse, children, or legal representatives, as the Committee in its sole discretion shall determine, of any such person whose employment shall have been terminated by reason of his death during such year or thereafter but prior to the making of such award.

8. No award of supplemental compensation shall be made to any person who at the time shall be, or at any time during the year for which such award is made shall have been, a member of the Audit and Compensation Committee.

Payment of Awards and Conditions Thereon

9. a. *Payment of Certain Awards.*

Each award of $2,000 or less shall be paid, subject to the provisions of Paragraph 11, on or before March 31 of the year next succeeding that for which the award is made.

b. *Payment of Other Awards.*

Each award other than an award referred to in Paragraph 9a shall be payable, subject to the provisions of Paragraphs 9c and 11, as follows:

(1) Each award for the year 1955 shall be paid as follows, until the full amount of the award is paid: one-fourth of the award, or $1,500, whichever shall be greater, on or before March 31, 1956; one-half of the award (but in no event more than the remainder of the award) on January 10, 1957; and the remainder, if any, of the award on January 10, 1958; provided, however, that if any unpaid installment of the award would be less than $500 in amount, it shall be paid at the same time that the next preceding installment is payable.

(2) Each award for the year 1956 and for each subsequent year shall be paid as follows, until the full amount of the award is paid: one-fourth of the award, or $1,500, whichever shall be greater, on or before March 31 in the year next succeeding that for which the award is made, and one-fourth of the award, or $1,500, whichever is greater (but in no event

more than the remainder, if any, of the award), on January
10 of each of the next three succeeding years; provided,
however, that if any unpaid installment of the award would
be less than $500 in amount, it shall be paid at the same time
that the next preceding installment is payable.

c. *Conditions.*

Anything hereinbefore to the contrary notwithstanding, the right
of any Employee to receive under Paragraph 9b(1) or 9b(2) payment of any installment of an award subsequent to the first installment shall accrue only if during the entire period from the making of
the award until Decembr 31 of the year preceding that in which such
installment is payable he shall have earned out such installment (a)
by continuing in the employ either of the Company or any Subsidiary
thereof, or (b) if terminated from such employment for a reason
other than death, by (i) refraining from (A) engaging in the business of manufacturing automobiles, trucks, tractors, farm implements,
aircraft engines or industrial engines in competition with the Company or any Subsidiary or Affiliate thereof, (B) entering the service
of any organization so engaged in such business (or any Subsidiary
or Affiliate of such an organization) and (C) personally engaging
in, or entering the service of any organization that is engaged in,
consulting work or styling or engineering activities for any organization so engaged in such business (or any Subsidiary or Affiliate of
such an organization), and (ii) making himself available, upon request, at reasonable times and upon a reasonable basis to consult
with, supply information to, and otherwise cooperate with the Company or any Subsidiary thereof with respect to any matter that was
handled by him or under his supervision while he was in the employ
of the Company or any Subsidiary thereof. In the event of nonfulfillment of these conditions, no further installment shall be paid to such
Employee; provided, however, that the nonfulfillment of the condition specified in subclause (b)(i) of this Paragraph 9c may at any
time (whether before, at the time of or subsequent to termination
of his employment) be waived by the Audit and Compensation Committee in the case of any Employee who at any time shall have been
a member of the Administration Committee or a member of the
Executive Committee, and by the Executive Committee in the case
of any other Employee, upon the Committee's determination that
in its sole judgment there has not been and will not be any substantial
adverse effect upon the Company or any Subsidiary or Affiliate

thereof by reason of the nonfulfillment of such condition. In the case of an Employee whose employment shall have been terminated by reason of his death, the right to receive payment of any installment of an award to him unpaid at the time of his death shall be governed by the provisions of Paragraph 11.

d. *Form of Payment.*

Each award of supplemental compensation shall be paid from the general funds of the Company or, in the case of an award by an Eligible Subsidiary, from the general funds of such Eligible Subsidiary. Neither the Reserve nor any part thereof shall be represented by any special or separate fund, and no special or separate fund shall be established or other segregation of assets made to assure payment of any such award. No Employee or other person shall have under any circumstances any interest whatever, vested or contingent, in any particular property or asset of the Company or of any Eligible Subsidiary by virtue of any award of supplemental compensation or any unpaid installment thereof.

e. *Interest not Payable.*

No interest shall be payable to any person upon any award or installment thereof, whether contingent or otherwise.

f. *Determination of Fulfillment of Conditions.*

Any question of controversy that may arise as to whether there has been fulfillment of any condition set forth in Paragraph 9c with respect to the payment of any installment of an award, or as to whether such nonfulfillment should be waived, shall be determined by the Audit and Compensation Committee in the case of an Employee who at any time shall have been a member of the Administration Committee or a member of the Executive Committee, and by the Executive Committee in the case of any other Employee.

g. *Disposition of Installments not Earned Out.*

In the event it shall be determined that the right to receive payment of any unpaid installment of an award shall not have accrued by reason of nonfulfillment of any condition set forth in Paragraph 9c and such nonfulfillment shall not have been waived as provided in Paragraph 9c, the amount of such unpaid installment shall again be credited to the Reserve but shall not be included in determining Income or Net Income.

Awards to Persons in Foreign Branches

10. Anything in this Plan to the contrary notwithstanding, the Executive Committee, during each year or after the close thereof, may make awards of supplemental compensation for such year to such persons (other than Employees, as defined in Paragraph 20) regularly employed at a salary by foreign branches of the Company at any time during such year as may be deemed by such Committee to be entitled to awards, in each case in such amount as it in its sole discretion may determine; and may provide for the payment of each such award at such time or times, in one payment or in installments, in such currency or currencies, and upon such conditions, as such Committee in its sole discretion may deem advisable, taking into consideration the laws, customs and other circumstances of the country or countries involved. Each such award shall be paid out of the funds of the branch employing the person to whom it is made. The Reserve shall not be debited to reflect any such award, and the amount of any such award shall not be taken into consideration for the purposes of Paragraph 6.

Effect of Death

11. In the event of the death of any person to whom an award shall have been made, each installment (if any) of such award unpaid at the time of death shall be paid to the legal representatives of such person at such time (or as soon thereafter as practicable) and otherwise as if such person were living and had fulfilled all applicable conditions as to earning out set forth in Paragraph 9, provided such conditions shall have been fulfilled by such person until the time of his death (unless the nonfulfillment thereof shall have been or shall be waived as provided in Paragraph 9). In the event of an award to a person after his death, the first installment and each subsequent installment (if any) of such award shall be paid to his legal representatives, and in the event of an award to the spouse, children or legal representatives of a person who shall have died before the award was made, the first installment and each subsequent installment (if any) of such award shall be paid to such spouse, children or legal representatives, as the case may be, in each such event at such time (or as soon thereafter as practicable) and otherwise as if such person were living and had fulfilled all applicable conditions as to earning out set forth in Paragraph 9. If the aggregate amount of unpaid installments of awards made to a person but payable to his legal representatives in accordance with the foregoing provisions of

this Paragraph 11 shall be less than $5,000, then the amount so payable, in the sole discretion of the Committee, may be paid to the spouse or children of such person instead of to such legal representatives, and such payment shall discharge all obligations to such spouse, children and legal representatives.

LIMITATIONS

12. No Employee or other person shall have any claim or right (legal, equitable or other) to be awarded supplemental compensation; and no director, officer or employee of the Company or any Subsidiary thereof or any other person shall have authority to enter into any agreement with any person for the award or payment of any supplemental compensation, or to make any representation or warranty with respect thereto.

AUTHORITY

13. Except as otherwise herein expressly provided, full power and authority to construe, interpret and administer this Plan shall be vested in the Audit and Compensation Committee; provided, however, that such Committee shall be bound by the determination of the Company's independent public accountants as to the amount creditable to the Reserve and the total amount of the Reserve. The Audit and Compensation Committee and the Executive Committee each may at any time adopt or terminate, and may from time to time amend, modify or suspend, such rules, regulations, policies and practices as they in their sole discretion may determine in connection with the performance of their respective responsibilities under this Plan.

INDEMNIFICATION AND EXCULPATION

14. Each person who is or shall have been a member of the Audit and Compensation Committee or a member of the Executive Committee shall be indemnified and held harmless by the Company against and from any and all loss, cost, liability or expense that may be imposed upon or reasonably incurred by him in connection with or resulting from any claim, action, suit or proceeding to which he may be a party or in which he may be involved by reason of any action taken or failure to act under this Plan and against and from any and all amounts paid by him in settlement thereof (with the Company's written approval) or paid by him in satisfaction of a judgment in any such action, suit or proceeding, except a judgment in favor of the Company based upon a finding of his bad faith; subject, however, to the condition that upon the institution of any claim,

action, suit or proceeding against him, he shall in writing give the Company an opportunity, at its own expense, to handle and defend the same before he undertakes to handle and defend it on his own behalf. The foregoing right of indemnification shall not be exclusive of any other right to which such person may be entitled as a matter of law or otherwise, or any power that the Company may have to indemnify him or hold him harmless.

Each member of the Audit and Compensation Committee, each member of the Executive Committee, and each director, officer and employee of the Company or of any Subsidiary thereof shall be fully justified in relying or acting upon any report made by the Company's independent public accountants and upon any other information furnished in connection with the administration of this Plan by any person or persons other than himself. In no event shall any person who is or shall have been a member of the Audit and Compensation Committee, a member of the Executive Committee, or a director, officer or employee of the Company or any Subsidiary thereof be liable for any determination made or other action taken or any omission to act in reliance upon any such report or information, or for any action (including the furnishing of information) taken or any failure to act, if in good faith.

Access of Independent Public Accountants and Committee to Information

15. The Company's independent public accountants shall have full access to the books and records of the Company and its Subsidiaries, and the Company shall furnish to such accountants such information as to the financial condition and operations of the Company and its Subsidiaries as such accountants may from time to time request, in order that such accountants may take any action required to be taken by them under this Plan. The Vice President-Finance or, in the event of his absence or disability to act, the principal accounting officer of the Company (now designated as the "Controller") or, in the event of the absence or disability to act of such Vice President and Controller, any Assistant Controller of the Company, shall furnish to the Committee such information as the Committee may request to assist it in carrying out this Plan. Neither such accountants, in reporting amounts creditable to the Reserve and the total amount of the Reserve, nor the Vice President-Finance, Controller, any Assistant Controller, or any other director, officer or employee of the Company, in furnishing information to such accountants or to the Committee, shall be liable for any error therein,

if such accountants or other person, as the case may be, shall have acted in good faith.

LIMITATIONS OF ACTIONS

16. Every asserted right of action by or on behalf of the Company or by or on behalf of any stockholder against any past, present or future member of the Audit and Compensation Committee, member of the Executive Committee, or director, officer or employee of the Company or any Subsidiary thereof, arising out of or in connection with this Plan, shall, irrespective of the place where such right of action may arise or be asserted and irrespective of the place of residence of any such member, director, officer or employee, cease and be barred upon the expiration of three years (a) from the date of the alleged act or omission in respect of which such right of action arises, or (b) from the date upon which the Company's Annual Report setting forth the amount of the credits to the Reserve and the aggregate amount of the awards of supplemental compensation to all or any part of which such action may relate is made generally available to stockholders, whichever date is later; and every asserted right of action by or on behalf of any employee, past, present or future, or any spouse, child, or legal representative thereof, against the Company or any Subsidiary thereof arising out of or in connection with this Plan shall, irrespective of the place where such right of action may arise or be asserted, cease and be barred by the expiration of three years from the date of the alleged act or omission in respect of which such right of action arises.

ADMINISTRATION EXPENSE

17. The entire expense of administering this Plan shall be borne by the Company and shall not be charged against the Reserve.

FINALITY OF DETERMINATIONS

18. Each determination made pursuant to the provisions of this Plan by the Audit and Compensation Committee, the Executive Committee, or the Company's independent public accountants shall be final and shall be binding and conclusive for all purposes and upon all persons, including, but without limitation thereto, the Company, the stockholders, the Audit and Compensation Committee and each of the members thereof, the Executive Committee and each of the members thereof, and the directors, officers, and employees of the Company and its Subsidiaries, and their respective successors in interest.

AMENDMENTS

19. The Audit and Compensation Committee shall have the right to amend or modify this Plan at any time and from time to time; provided, however, that no such amendment or modification shall affect any right or obligation with respect to any award theretofore made, nor shall any such amendment or modification, unless previously approved by the stockholders, in any manner affect the provisions of this Plan governing the computation of the amount to be credited to the Reserve each year or prohibiting the making of awards of supplemental compensation to members of the Audit and Compensation Committee. Full right is reserved by the stockholders of the Company to amend, modify, suspend or terminate this Plan at any time and in any manner they deem advisable; provided, however, that no such amendment, modification, suspension or termination shall affect any right or obligation with respect to any award theretofore made.

DEFINITIONS

20. As used herein:

a. The term "Committee" shall mean, unless the context otherwise requires, the following as they from time to time may be constituted:

(1) The Audit and Compensation Committee, with respect to all matters affecting members of the Administration Committee or members of the Executive Committee (including, but without limitation thereto, members who are also officers or directors of the Company).

(2) The Executive Committee, with respect to all matters affecting employees other than members of such Committee or members of the Administration Committee.

b. The term "Subsidiary" shall mean, as applied with respect to any person or legal entity specified, a person or legal entity a majority of the voting stock of which is owned or controlled, directly or indirectly, by the person or legal entity specified.

c. The term "Eligible Subsidiary" shall mean, for any particular year for which awards are made, any corporation (i) all of the voting stock of which, except for qualifying shares, is owned, directly or indirectly, by the Company at any time during such year, (ii) the accounts of which are consolidated with the accounts of the Company in the Company's consolidated financial statements for such year, and (iii) which the Audit and Compensation Committee of the Company in its sole discretion shall have determined should be regarded as eligible for the purposes of this Plan for such year.

d. The term "Affiliate" shall mean, as applied with respect to any person or legal entity specified, a person or legal entity that directly or indirectly, through one or more intermediaries, controls or is controlled by, or is under common control with, the person or legal entity specified.

e. The term "Employee" shall mean any person who is regularly employed by the Company or an Eligible Subsidiary at a salary (as distinguished from a pension, retirement allowance, severance pay, retainer, commission, fee under a contract or other arrangement, or hourly, piecework or other wage) and is enrolled on the active employment rolls of the Company or an Eligible Subsidiary maintained in the United States, including, but without limitation thereto, any Employee who also is an officer or director of the Company or an Eligible Subsidiary.

f. The term "Income" shall mean, for the purpose of computing the amount which may be credited to the Reserve for any year, the Net Income of the Company for such year, plus (i) provision for United States Federal income and excess profits taxes, (ii) provision for supplemental compensation (in an amount which shall be equal to the amount creditable to the Reserve), and (iii) interest on Debt, all as shown by or included in the Company's Consolidated Statement of Income as certified by the Company's independent public accountants. Such Consolidated Statement of Income shall be set forth in the Company's Annual Report for such year.

g. The term "Net Income" shall mean, for the purpose of computing the amount which may be credited to the Reserve for any year, the net income for such year after all charges (including (i) provision for United States Federal income and excess profits taxes, (ii) provision for supplemental compensation [in an amount which shall be equal to the amount creditable to the Reserve], and (iii) interest on Debt), all as shown by or included in the Company's Consolidated Statement of Income as certified by the Company's independent public accountants.

h. The term "Capital Employed in the Business" shall mean the total capital (including capital stock, capital account in excess of par value of stock, surplus, and earnings retained for use in the business, but excluding the amount of any treasury stock at that date), plus Debt, all as shown on or included in the Company's Consolidated Balance Sheet, as certified by the Company's independent public accountants, all as of the end of the year immediately preceding that for which the credit to the Reserve is computed, plus or minus an allowance, proportionate to the fraction of the year involved, for any changes in total capital or Debt during the year for which the credit to the Reserve is computed arising from (a) any issuance of capital stock, any sale of treasury stock, any purchase of capital stock, any retirement of capital stock other than treasury stock, (b) any increase or decrease in Debt, or (c) any addition to or elimination from the Consolidated Balance Sheet of a Subsidiary or foreign branch of the Company. Such Consolidated Balance Sheet and such allowance shall be set forth in the Company's Annual Report for the year for which the credit to the Reserve is computed.

i. The term "Debt" shall mean the unpaid principal of all indebtedness of the Company or of any of its Subsidiaries, whether an Eligible Subsidiary or otherwise, as principal and not as surety or guarantor, included in the Company's Consolidated Balance Sheet, as certified by the Company's independent public accountants, which indebtedness has a maturity at the time of its creation of more than one year, independent of accerelation, and is evidenced by a bond, debenture, or promissory note.

APPENDIX DD

Federated Department Stores, Inc.

GROUP PLAN PROVIDING DEFERRED PROFIT SHARING

Section 1. Definitions

1.1. "Plan" means the Executive Contingent Compensation Plan of Federated Department Stores, Inc. as described in this instrument.

1.2. "Company" means Federated Department Stores, Inc. or any successor company.

1.3. "Committee" means the Committee appointed to administer the Plan as provided in Section 8.

1.4. "Fiscal Year" means the fiscal year of the Company as established from time to time.

1.5. "Participant" means a person to whom an allotment has been made for any fiscal year pursuant to the Plan and whose cash or stock allotments have not been wholly forfeited or distributed.

1.6. "Allotment" means the amount allotted to a participant for any fiscal year pursuant to Section 3.1.

1.7. "Cash Allotments" of a participant at any time mean the sum of all amounts, including interest equivalents, theretofore contingently credited to him pursuant to Section 4.2, less the amounts thereof theretofore forfeited or distributed.

1.8. "Stock Allotments" of a partipant at any time mean the aggregate of all stock equivalents and dividend equivalents theretofore contingently credited to him pursuant to Section 4.3, less the amounts thereof theretofore forfeited, distributed, or changed to cash allotments.

1.9. "Termination of Service" or similar expression means the termination of the participant's employment as a regular employee of the Company. Disability, whether temporary or permanent, shall not be considered termination of service, as long as the participant is receiving at least one-half the salary paid prior to disability. A participant who is merely rendering advisory service at a substantially reduced salary will be considered to have terminated his service. A participant who is on temporary leave of absence, whether with or without pay, shall not be deemed to have terminated his service.

SECTION 2. ELIGIBILITY AND SELECTION OF PARTICIPANTS

2.1. Any executive of the Company or of any Division of the Company shall be eligible to be selected as a participant in the Plan for any fiscal year if at the end of such fiscal year:

(a) he qualifies under the eligibility requirements then in effect established by the Committee pursuant to Section 8.3; and

(b) he is not a member of the Committee.

None of the present Directors of the Company may participate in the Plan. Any future Director, not a present Director, may participate provided he is otherwise eligible to participate in the Plan.

2.2. At the end of each fiscal year the Committee shall select, subject to the approval of the Board of Directors of the Company, the participants to whom allotments are to be made for such fiscal year from eligible executives recommended to it by:

(a) the Chief Executive Officer of the Division by which the participant is employed, concurred in by the President of the Company; or

(b) the President of the Company if the participant is employed by the Central Office of the Company. The selection of a participant for any fiscal year shall not entitle such participant to an allotment for any subsequent fiscal year for which he is not selected for an allotment.

SECTION 3. DETERMINATION OF AMOUNT TO BE ALLOTTED TO EACH PARTICIPANT

3.1. At the end of each fiscal year the Committee shall allot, subject to the approval of the Board of Directors of the Company, to each participant selected for such year an amount determined by the Committee, but not less than 10% nor more than 20% of the participant's compensation from the Company for such fiscal year, including bonuses. The Committee shall notify each participant promptly in writing of any allotments made to him.

3.2. Each allotment shall be contingently credited as provided in Section 4 and shall be contingently distributable only in the manner and subject to the conditions set forth in Sections 5 and 6.

SECTION 4. CASH AND STOCK ALLOTMENTS AND CONTINGENT CREDITS

4.1. The entire amount of each allotment to each participant shall be contingently credited to him either as a cash allotment or as a stock allotment in accordance with the participant's election.

Such election shall be made in writing by the participant not later than 10 days after he has received written notice of the allotment from the Committee, but the Committee may extend the time for making an election in any case. If the participant shall fail to make an election within such period with respect to any allotment, he shall be deemed to have elected to have such allotment contingently credited as a stock allotment.

4.2. (a) If a cash allotment is elected, the participant shall be contingently credited with the dollar amount of the allotment.

(b) The cash allotments of each participant shall be contingently credited, at the end of each fiscal year, with an interest equivalent, which shall be an amount equal to $2\frac{1}{2}\%$ of the cash allotments of such participant at the end of the preceding fiscal year.

4.3. (a) If a stock allotment is elected, the participant shall be contingently credited with a stock equivalent which shall be the number of full shares of common stock of the Company that could be purchased with the amount of the allotment at the closing price of such stock on the New York Stock Exchange on the nearest day of sale preceding the date on which the Committee sends notification of the allotment to the participant, and with the dollar amount of any part of such allotment that is not convertible into a full share.

(b) The stock allotments of each participant shall be contingently credited, at the end of each fiscal year, with a dividend equivalent which shall be an amount determined by multiplying the dividends payable, either in cash or property (other than common stock of the Company), upon a share of common stock of the Company to a stockholder of record during such fiscal year, by the number of shares in the participant's stock allotments at the end of the preceding fiscal year. In case of dividends payable in property, the dividend equivalent shall be based on the fair market value of the property at the time of distribution of the dividend, as determined by the Committee. If at the end of any fiscal year the dollar amounts credited to the stock allotments of a participant equal or exceed the closing price of 10 shares of common stock of the Company on the New York Stock Exchange on the nearest preceding day of sale, such amount shall be treated as if it were a stock allotment made on such date and such dollar amount shall be reduced accordingly.

(c) If at any time the number of outstanding shares of common stock of the Company shall be increased as the result of any stock dividend or split-up, the number of shares contingently credited to each participant's stock allotments shall be increased in the same proportion as the outstanding number of shares of common stock is increased, or if the number of outstanding shares of common stock of the Company shall at any time be decreased as the result of any combination of outstanding shares, the number of shares contingently credited to each participant's stock allotments shall be decreased in the same proportion as the outstanding number of shares of common stock is decreased. In the event the Company shall at any time be consolidated with or merged into any other corporation, there shall be contingently credited to each participant's stock allotments, in lieu of the common stock of the Company then contingently credited thereto, the stock or securities given in exchange for a share of common stock of the Company upon such consolidation or merger, multiplied by the number of shares of common stock then contingently credited to the stock allotments of the participant.

4.4 (a) At the election of a participant any stock allotment contingently credited to him in any year may be changed to a cash allotment subject to the following conditions

(i) Such change of election may be made only as of the last day of the fifth fiscal year of the Company following the fiscal year in which the allotment was made.

(ii) An election to change a stock allotment to a cash allotment shall be made in writing to the Committee not more than 20 days prior or 10 days subsequent to the end of the Company's fiscal year as of which such change is made.

(b) If a participant elects to change a stock allotment to a cash allotment in accordance with this Section 4.4.

(i) Such participant shall be contingently credited with the same dollar amount as would have been contingently credited to him at the time such allotment was made had he then elected to have it contingently credited as a cash allotment, but no interest equivalents shall be contingently credited thereto for the fiscal year in which change of election is made or for any fiscal year prior thereto. Beginning with the fiscal year following the fiscal year in which the change of election is made, such allotment shall thereafter be contingently credited with an interest equivalent in accordance with Section 4.2 (b). For all other purposes such allotment shall thereafter be treated as if it had been contingently credited to the participant as a cash allotment in the year in which it was originally made.

(ii) The stock allotments of the participant shall be reduced by the stock equivalent contingently credited on account of such allotment and all dividend equivalents and dollar amounts attributable to such allotment contingently credited in accordance with Section 4.3.

SECTION 5. FORFEITURES

5.1 On the termination of a participant's service with the Company, he shall forfeit:

(a) 100% of any cash or stock allotment and any interest or dividend equivalent contingently credited to him in the fiscal year next preceding the year in which his termination of service occurred; and

(b) 25% of any cash or stock allotment and any interest or dividend equivalent contingently credited to him in the second fiscal year preceding the year in which his termination of service occurred; and his cash and stock allotments shall be reduced accordingly.

Such forfeiture and reduction shall not apply, however, in case of termination of service:

(a) attributable to death, disability or discharge; or

(b) for any reason after the participant has attained age 60 and has been a participant for at least a period of 5 years; or

(c) attributable to any other reason approved by the Committee.

5.2 If, without the written consent of the Company, the participant:

(a) at any time prior to or following his termination of service shall make an investment of $100,000 or more in a competing business, either in the form of a stock purchase, contribution to capital, loan or otherwise; or

(b) at any time prior to his termination of service shall be employed to give advice or assistance to a competing business; or

(c) at any time following his termination of services shall render personal services to a competing business, either as owner, partner, director, officer, employee or otherwise; the entire amount of the participant's cash and stock allotments shall be forfeited and cancelled.

5.3. A "competing business" shall be any business which:

(a) at the time of determination is substantially similar to the whole or a substantial part of the business conducted by the Company or any of its subsidiaries or affiliates; and

(b) at the time of determination is conducted in a city or within 25 miles from the boundaries of a city in which the Division of the

Company by which the participant is or was employed, as the case may be, is conducting a retail business, or in which any Division is conducting a retail business in case he is an employee of the Central Office of the Company; and

(c) had net sales at all its locations, including sales in leased departments, during its fiscal year preceding that in which the participant made such investment or first was employed to give such advice or assistance or rendered such personal service, in excess of: (i) $25,000,000 if the participant is an employee or former employee of the Abraham & Straus Division or the Bloomingdale Bros. Division or the Central Office of the Company; or (ii) $7,000,-000 if the participant is an employee or former employee of any other Division of the Company. The foregoing net sales figures are based on the January, 1950, price level and shall be adjusted in each subsequent year by the same percentage as any change in the U.S. Bureau of Labor Statistics Department Store Inventory Price Index.

5.4. If the Company shall be adjudicated or determined to be insolvent by a court of competent jurisdiction either in bankruptcy or otherwise, all cash and stock allotments of all participants shall thereupon be forfeited and cancelled.

Section 6. Distribution

6.1. Distribution of the cash and stock allotments of a participant contingently credited to the end of the fiscal year in which termination of his service occurs shall be made in approximately equal annual installments commencing March 1 following the end of the fiscal year in which termination of his service occurs. If termination occurs at or after the date on which the participant has attained age 65, such distribution shall be made in approximately ten equal annual installments. The number of installments shall be increased by one for each year of the participant's age under 65 at the time of termination of his service, but the number of installments shall not exceed fifteen in any case. Interest or dividend equivalents contingently credited in a fiscal year after that in which termination of service occurs shall be distributed on March 1 of the fiscal year following the fiscal year in which credited.

6.2. Any cash or stock allotments or remaining undistributed installments thereof, which become distributable after the death of a participant, shall be distributed in installments, as provided in this Section 6, to such person or persons, or the survivors thereof, including corporations, unincorporated associations or trusts, as the participant may have designated in writing delivered to the Committee. The participant may from time to time revoke or change any such designation by writing delivered to the Committee. If there is no unrevoked designation on file with the Committee at the time of the participant's death, or if the person or persons designated therein shall have all predeceased the participant or otherwise ceased to exist, such distributions shall be made to the participant's estate.

6.3. If the death of the participant occurs after the termination of his service, the number of installments remaining to be paid shall be the number which otherwise would be distributable to the participant, and if death occurs before the first installment has been distributed, the number of installments shall be ten.

6.4. Distribution of the cash allotments of a participant shall be made in cash. Distribution of the stock allotments of a participant may be made by delivery of the number of shares of common stock of the Company contingently credited hereto (using only treasury shares) and by payment of the balance, if any, in cash with the last installment. The Committee may, however, distribute wholly or partly in lieu of any installment of common stock of the Company, cash in an amount equal to the closing price of said stock on the New York Stock Exchange on the nearest day of sale preceding the date on which such common stock is distributable. The Committee may, with the consent of the person or persons entitled to receive distribution of the next installment of any cash or stock allotments, make other changes in the time or medium of distribution of the entire undistributed amount thereof.

6.5 The Company shall deduct from the amount of all distributions under the Plan any taxes required to be withheld by the federal or any state or local government. In case distributions are made in shares of common stock of the Company, the Company shall have the right to retain the number of shares having a then market price equivalent to the amount of the said tax required to be withheld in respect of such distributions. In lieu thereof, however, the Committee may permit a recipient receiving a distribution in common stock to reimburse the Company for any such taxes required to be withheld by the Company, upon such terms and conditions as the Committee may prescribe.

SECTION 7. RIGHTS OF PARTICIPANTS

7.1. No participant or any other person shall have any interest in any fund or in any specific asset or assets of the Company by reason of any cash or stock allotments or interest or dividend equivalent contingently credited to him hereunder, nor the right to exercise any of the rights or privileges of a stockholder with respect to any common stock contingently credited to his stock allotments, nor any right to receive any distribution under the Plan except as and to the extent expressly provided in the Plan. Nothing in the Plan shall be deemed to give any officer or any employee of the Company any right to participate in the Plan, except to such extent, if any, as the Committee may determine in accordance with the provisions of the Plan.

7.2 Neither the adoption of the Plan, the making of any allotments nor any action of the Board of Directors of the Company or the Committee shall be held or construed to confer on any person any legal right to be continued as an employee of the Company.

7.3. No participant shall have the right to assign, pledge or otherwise dispose of (except as provided in Section 6 hereof) any cash or stock allotments, nor shall the participant's contingent interest therein be subject to garnishment, attachment, transfer by operation of law, or any legal process.

SECTION 8. ADMINISTRATION OF THE PLAN—COMMITTEE

8.1. The Plan shall be administered by a Committee of not less than three nor more than six Directors of the Company appointed from time to time by the Board of Directors of the Company to serve at the pleasure of the Board of Directors. No participant may be a member of the Committee.

8.2 A majority of the members of the Committee shall constitute a quorum for the transaction of business. All action taken by the Committee at a meeting shall be by the vote of a majority of those present at such meeting, but any action may be taken by the Committee without a meeting upon written consent signed by all the members of the Committee.

8.3. The Committee shall from time to time establish eligibility requirements for participation in the Plan and rules for the administration of the Plan that are not inconsistent with the provisions of the Plan.

8.4. The determination of the Committee as to any disputed question arising under the Plan, including questions of construction and interpretation, shall be final, binding, and conclusive upon all persons. Without limiting the generality of the foregoing, the determination of the Committee as to whether a participant has terminated his service and the date thereof, or the cause to which termination of service is attributable, or whether an employee has made an investment in or was employed to give advice or assistance or rendered personal services to a competing business, shall be final, binding, and conclusive.

SECTION 9. AMENDMENTS, ETC.

9.1. The Board of Directors of the Company may, in its absolute discretion, without notice, at any time and from time to time, modify or amend, in whole or in part, any or all of the provisions of the Plan, or suspend or terminate it entirely; provided, that no such modification, amendment, suspension or termination may, without his consent, apply to or affect the payment or distribution to any participant of any cash or stock allotments, interest or dividend equivalent contingently credited to him for any fiscal year ended prior to the effective date of such modification, amendment, suspension or termination.

SECTION 10. EFFECTIVE DATE

10.1. This Plan shall be effective beginning with the fiscal year commencing January 29, 1950.

APPENDIX EE

Kennecott Copper Corporation and Subsidiaries

EXECUTIVE INCENTIVE COMPENSATION PLAN

1. Purpose.

The purpose of the Plan is to provide an incentive to certain employees of the Company and certain of its subsidiaries who occupy key executive positions and contribute in a notable degree to the success of the Company and such subsidiaries by invention, ability, industry or exceptional service.

2. Definitions.

(a) "Company" shall mean Kennecott Copper Corporation. "Participating Subsidiary" shall mean such of the wholly owned subsidiaries of the Company as the Board of Directors of the Company may from time to time designate as within the Plan. The term "Subsidiary" shall mean any corporation more than 50% of the voting stock of which is owned by the Company or any other Subsidiary of the Company.

(b) "Committee" shall mean the Directors, not less than 3 in number, appointed by the Board of Directors of the Company from among their number to administer the Plan in accordance with the provisions hereof. Such Directors, while serving on the Committee, shall not be eligible to participate in the Plan. Members of the Committee shall be entitled to receive the customary fee payable for attendance at meetings of committees of the Board of Directors.

(c) "Consolidated Net Income" as used in the Plan, shall mean, for each year, the consolidated net income of the Company and its consolidated Subsidiaries for such year, after provision for all taxes for such year but adjusted so as not to take into account the amounts, if any, allocated at any time to the Reserve for Compensation Awards pursuant to the provisions of the Plan, all as determined by the Company and certified by its independent accountants.

(d) "Consolidated Net Worth" as used in the Plan shall mean the aggregate amount of the consolidated capital stock and surplus (excluding surplus reserves and contingency reserves) of the Company and its consolidated Subsidiaries as at the beginning of the year for which Consolidated Net Income is being determined, all as determined by the Company and certified by its independent accountants.

(e) "Participant" shall mean any full-time salaried employee of the Company or of a Participating Subsidiary to whom an award is made hereunder.

(f) "Reserve" as used in the Plan, shall mean the account entitled "Reserve for Compensation Awards," referred to in Section 3 hereof.

3. RESERVE.

The Company shall maintain a reserve account entitled "Reserve for Compensation Awards," to which shall be credited each year during which the Plan remains in effect an amount which shall not exceed one per cent (1%) of the amount remaining after deducting from Consolidated Net Income an amount equivalent to six per cent (6%) of Consolidated Net Worth. The actual amount so to be credited in each year within the foregoing limitation shall be the aggregate of the awards in respect of such year made by the Committee and approved by the Board of Directors in accordance with Section 4 hereof.

4. AWARDS.

For each calendar year during which the Plan is in effect, the Committee shall determine, in its discretion, on or before March 1 of the following year, the employees who shall participate in awards in respect of such year, the respective amounts of such awards to be made to such Participants and the resulting aggregate amount of such awards to be credited to the Reserve with respect to such year in accordance with Section 3 hereof.

No awards shall be made in respect of any year after March 1 of the following year, and no credits to the Reserve shall be made with respect to any year in excess of the aggregate of the awards for such year so made by the Committee. No awards for any year shall become final until the aggregate amount of such awards has been submitted to and approved by the Board of Directors.

Awards made to each Participant shall be debited to the Reserve and credited to an individual account to be maintained by the Company or a Participating Subsidiary for each Participant, the amounts credited to the account of each Participant to be designated "A" award or "B" award as the case may be, in accordance with Section 5 hereof.

5. Payment of Awards to Participants.

Awards made to Participants shall be either "A" or "B" awards as the Committee, in its discretion, shall determine.

An "A" award for any year shall be paid to a Participant, or in the event of the death of a Participant, to his beneficiary or if no beneficiary has been designated or if a beneficiary who has been designated dies prior to the receipt of the final payment, to the personal representative of the Participant, in one hundred twenty (120) equal monthly installments, commencing with the first calendar month following the day upon which employment ceases by death or otherwise or the day upon which the award is made, whichever is the later.

A "B" award for any year shall be paid to a Participant, or in the event of the death of a Participant, to his beneficiary or if no beneficiary has been designated or if a beneficiary who has been designated dies prior to the receipt of the final payment, to the personal representative of the Participant, in equal installments over a five-year period, commencing with the calendar year following the year in respect of which such award is made. With respect to any "B" award, the Committee may, in its sole discretion, in special circumstances, upon submission of evidence satisfactory to the Committee, accelerate payments to a Participant, his beneficiary or personal representative.

A participant shall be entitled to designate, from time to time, one or more beneficiaries to whom payments shall be made which become due after the death of the Participant.

6. Termination of Payment of Awards.

No Participant shall have a vested right to any award, or part thereof, made to him until a payment is due him as provided in Section 5 above, and in the event a Participant voluntarily terminates his employment (other than by normal, early or disability retirement, as those terms are described in the Retirement Plan of the Company for Salaried Employees) or is discharged for cause, no payments shall thereafter be made to him pursuant to the Plan, and the Participant, his beneficiary or personal representative shall have no further claim against the Company or any Participating Subsidiary hereunder. Further, no payments shall be made to a Participant, and neither such Participant, his beneficiary nor personal representative shall have any further claim hereunder if, without the consent of the Company, the

Participant, either directly or indirectly, is paid or employed by, or has a controlling interest in, a competitor of the Company or of any Subsidiary of the Company. Employment with a competitor, for the purpose of the Plan, shall be deemed to include, among other things, membership on the Board of Directors or any committee of the Board of Directors of, or partnership in, such a competitor. For the purposes of the Plan, a competitor shall be deemed to include any person, firm, partnership, corporation or other organization which customarily produces or manufactures one or more of the products customarily produced or manufactured by the Company or any Subsidiary of the Company, or any products competitive therewith.

Notwithstanding the foregoing, the Committee may determine, in its discretion, that awards made to a Participant shall not be forfeited by reason of such termination or discharge, but shall be paid in accordance with the provisions of the Plan, where, in the judgment of the Committee, the particular circumstances warrant such a determination.

In the event that the amount of any award made to a Participant pursuant to the Plan is forfeited, the amount of such forfeited award standing in the account of such Participant shall be debited to such account and credited to the appropriate account of the Company or Participating Subsidiary and shall no longer be subject to the provisions of the Plan.

7. PARTICIPATION.

An employee eligible to be a Participant hereunder shall participate in awards only to the extent that the Committee may from time to time determine, and any Participant who participates in one year may be excluded from participation in any other year.

8. TERM.

The Plan shall become effective upon approval thereof by vote of the holders of a majority of the capital stock of the Company present or represented and voting thereon at the annual meeting of stockholders during the year 1956, or at any adjournment thereof. The first year for which awards may be made shall be the calendar year 1956. The Plan shall continue until such time as it shall be terminated by action of the Board of Directors of the Company, provided, however, that the Plan, if not theretofore terminated, shall be submitted to the stockholders for action with respect thereto at a stockholders' meeting at least once in every five years.

9. ADMINISTRATION.

Full power and authority to construe, interpret and administer the Plan shall be vested in the Committee as from time to time constituted by the Board of Directors; provided, however, that upon any termination of the Plan, amounts already awarded to Participants shall, subject to the provisions of Section 6 regarding forfeitures, continue to be paid in accordance with the provisions of the Plan. Except as expressly provided in the Plan, decisions of the Committee shall be final, conclusive and binding upon all parties, including the Company, Participating Subsidiaries, employees and Participants and their beneficiaries and personal representatives.

No interest shall be paid at any time on any awards made to Participants.

The expenses of administering the Plan shall be borne by the Company.

APPENDIX FF

Bethlehem Steel Corporation

(Article Tenth of Certification of Incorporation, as adopted by stockholders in 1936, and amended by stockholders on November 10, 1959)

Tenth. In order to provide an incentive to increased efficient and profitable management there is hereby established a Special Incentive Compensation Plan.

The persons who shall be eligible to receive special compensation under said Plan shall be the persons who shall be in the employ of the Corporation or in the employ of one or more of its subsidiary companies and shall be directors of the Corporation. Said persons are hereinafter in this Article Tenth collectively referred to as executives of the Corporation. Effective July 1, 1959 the special compensation under said Plan shall consist of "dividend units," as follows:

For each fiscal year commencing with the year ending December 31, 1960, there shall be credited to the executives of the Corporation, upon the publication by the Corporation of its Annual Report to Stockholders for such year, "dividend units" hereinafter described representing 2% of the consolidated net income for such year. The "dividend units" to be credited for any fiscal year shall be credited to the persons who shall have been the executives of the Corporation in that year (or to the estates of any of them who shall have died in the meantime) and shall be divided among such executives (or their estates) in the ratio of the cash compensation (including fixed salary and cash payments on "dividend units") which such executives, respectively, shall have received as such executives for that year to the aggregate amounts of such compensation so received by all such executives for that year.

For the purpose of determining the number of "dividend units" to be credited to executives for any fiscal year each unit shall be taken at a value equal to the average of the high and low prices of a share of Common Stock of the Corporation on the New York Stock Exchange on the first business day of such fiscal year. Fractional units shall not be credited.

Each "dividend unit" will entitle the holder to receive from the Corporation a cash payment equal to each cash dividend that shall be paid on one share of Common Stock of the Corporation after the crediting of the unit and during the lifetime of the executive (but in any event until the fifteenth anniversary of the termination, by death or otherwise, of his service with the Corporation and its subsidiary companies). The payments to be so made on the "dividend units" will be subject to the earlier termination of such units as hereinafter described. In the event of any stock dividend, split-up, reclassification, or analogous change in capitalization, a corresponding change shall be made in the number of "dividend units" then outstanding.

During the lifetime of the executive of the Corporation to whom "dividend units" shall be credited, such "dividend units" shall not be transferable or assignable, and said payments thereon shall be made only to him, but if he dies before the expiration of the aforesaid 15-year period, the rights under his "dividend units" shall pass to his estate.

All rights under "dividend units" credited to an executive of the Corporation shall be terminated if, within a period of five years following the date when such units were credited to him, the service of such executive shall be terminated for any reason other than death or retirement pursuant to the Pension Plan of the Corporation or voluntary termination of service with the consent of his employer, or if at any time the Board of Directors shall find that he has wilfully engaged in any activity which is harmful to the interests of the Corporation.

For the purposes of this Article Tenth, "consolidated net income" for any fiscal year shall be the consolidated net income of the Corporation and its subsidiary companies consolidated as shown in the Annual Report to Stockholders of the Corporation for such year. For the purposes of the provisions of this Article Tenth relating to the crediting of "dividend units," the term executives of the Corporation shall not be deemed to include (a) any person who shall have reached age 70 (except that persons who reached age 66 on or before March 31, 1959, shall so long as otherwise qualified be deemed to continue as executives until March 31, 1964), or (b) any person who is designated an honorary officer of the Corporation.

The amounts of the respective fixed salaries of the executives of the Corporation shall be determined by the Board of Directors or by any one or more committees (none of which shall consist of less than three members) appointed by the Board of Directors from among its members; provided, however, that none of the executives of the Corporation shall as a member of the Board of Directors or of any such committee thereof have any vote in the determination of the amount that shall be paid to him as a fixed salary.

Anything herein contained to the contrary notwithstanding, the aggregate amounts paid on all "dividend units" subsequent to July 1, 1959, plus the aggregate fixed salaries paid to the executives of the Corporation in excess of an amount equal to $90,000 per month for the period elapsed subsequent to such date, shall not at any time exceed 4% of the aggregate cash dividends paid on the Common Stock of the Corporation subsequent to such date.

The Board of Directors, acting for the Corporation as the owner, direct or indirect, of capital stock in any other corporation, shall have power in its discretion to approve any plan for the payment of incentive compensation to the officers and employees of said other corporation which shall be based on the net earnings of said other corporation or in any manner which will make the amount of said incentive compensation dependent upon the results accomplished by them or any of them, and the Board of Directors shall also have power to adopt similar plans for the payment of incentive compensation to officers and employees of the Corporation engaged in the conduct and operation of businesses relating to physical properties directly owned or operated by it; provided, however, that no such other incentive compensation shall be paid to any person in respect of any calendar quarter-year by the Corporation or any corporation any of the stock of which shall, at the time, be owned directly or indirectly by the Corporation, if any cash compensation of such person for any part of the same calendar quarter-year shall be the basis for the crediting of "dividend units" to him.

DEFERRED COMPENSATION ARRANGEMENTS

APPENDIX GG

Union Carbide Corporation

INCENTIVE PLAN

ARTICLE I. The Board of Directors of the Corporation may from time to time, within five years from the date of approval of this Plan by the stockholders, grant Incentive Awards to officers and other employees of the Corporation and its Subsidiaries, such Incentive Awards to be in the form of either (a) Options to purchase capital stock of the Corporation, or (b) Dividend Equivalents with an accompanying Option to purchase an equal number of shares of capital stock of the Corporation, or (c) Dividend Equivalents only. A "Dividend Equivalent" means the right to receive for a specified period of time cash payments from the Corporation or a Subsidiary equivalent in value to dividends (other than stock dividends) paid during such period on one share of stock of the Corporation. The number of shares optioned under (a), the number of Dividend Equivalents with accompanying Options awarded under (b) and the number of Dividend Equivalents awarded under (c) shall not in total exceed 5% of the shares of capital stock of the Corporation outstanding on December 31, 1958. No single Participant shall be granted in the aggregate more than 2% of such total authorized hereunder.

ARTICLE II. Incentive Awards shall be granted to such officers and employees of the Corporation and of its Subsidiaries, including members of the Board of Directors who are also salaried officers, and in such amounts and forms as a Committee of the Board of Directors shall determine. No member of this Committee shall be eligible for Incentive Awards.

The Committee shall have authority to interpret and administer this Plan and to determine the provisions of Incentive Awards subject to the conditions of this Plan.

ARTICLE III. Options to purchase capital stock are subject to the following conditions:

450

1. The option price shall not be less than 95% of the fair market value per share of the Corporation's capital stock on the date of granting the Option, such fair market value to be the mean between the highest and lowest quoted selling prices on the New York Stock Exchange on such date, or if there are no sales on such date, on the next preceding date on which there were sales, provided, however, that the Committee with the approval of the Board of Directors, may make such adjustments to the option price as may be permitted for restricted stock options under the Internal Revenue Code as now in effect or as it may hereafter be amended.

2. An Option shall expire on the earliest of (a) ten years after date of grant; (b) three months after termination of employment of the Participant for any reason other than death.

3. An Option prior to its expiration as specified in paragraph 2 above shall become exercisable at any time after the first anniversary of the granting of the Option with respect to not more than $33\frac{1}{3}\%$ of the total number of shares covered, at any time after the second anniversary with respect to not more than an additional $33\frac{1}{3}\%$, and at any time after the third anniversary with respect to the balance of the shares.

4. An Option may be exercised with respect to a part or all of the shares covered by the Option and the purchase of such shares effected either (a) by payment in cash of the option price for such shares, or (b) when exercised during employment by the Corporation or its Subsidiaries, by execution and delivery to the Corporation of an unconditional contract to pay the purchase price within five years. If shares are purchased under (b), the purchaser shall pay interest on the unpaid balance of the purchase price at such rate as may be determined by the Board of Directors, provided that such rate of interest shall not be less than 2% per annum. The shares with respect to which an Option has been exercised under (b) shall be issued and delivered to the purchaser and pledged by the purchaser as collateral security for payment of the unpaid balance of the purchase price, and shall be released from such pledge proportionately as such unpaid balance is paid to the Corporation. If the employment of a Participant is terminated for any reason other than death or Retirement, any unpaid balance under any contract entered into prior thereto by such Participant for the purchase of shares of stock shall become due and payable three months after such termination. "Retirement" as used in this Plan means a retirement under the Corporation's retirement program.

5. Only the Participant may exercise his Option during his lifetime. The Option shall not be transferable, except that, in the event of the Participant's death during his employment or within three months after termination of his employment, the Option shall be exercisable by the executor or administrator of his estate or the distributee within one year of the Participant's death but not after ten years from the date of its grant. Such exercise of an Option after a Participant's death shall be limited to not more than the number of shares with respect to which the Option could have been exercised on the date of the death of the Participant. If the Option is exercised after the death of a Participant, the Corporation shall have the right, in lieu of issuing and delivering shares of stock, of returning the option payment and paying the amount by which the fair market value on the New York Stock Exchange on the date of the exercise of the Option exceeds the option price with respect to the number of shares for which the Option was exercised.

ARTICLE IV. Dividend Equivalents are subject to the following conditions:

1. Unless forfeited as hereinafter provided, Dividend Equivalents shall remain in effect for such period of time as the Committee shall specify but in no event beyond the Participant's death. The exercise of an Option accompanying Dividend Equivalents shall terminate a corresponding part of such Dividend Equivalents.

2. Dividend Equivalents will be forfeited if the Participant's employment is terminated during his lifetime for any reason other than Retirement, except that if in the opinion of the Committee it will be in the best interests of the Corporation to continue said Dividend Equivalents they shall be continued to the extent specified by the Committee and approved by the Board of Directors. Dividend Equivalents will also be forfeited if the Committee finds, after a hearing at which the Participant shall be entitled to appear, that the Participant has at any time engaged in any activity harmful to the interests of or in competition with the Corporation or its Subsidiaries.

3. Dividend Equivalents may not be pledged, assigned or transferred for any reason.

4. The granting of Dividend Equivalents shall be upon the condition that if a Participant should retire before the expiration of his Dividend Equivalents he shall thereafter be available until such expiration to render such consultant or advisory services for the Corporation as the Corporation may request and as may be reasonable considering his personal circumstances and the number of Dividend Equivalents granted.

ARTICLE V. In the event of any change in capital, shares of capital stock or any special distribution to the Stockholders, the Board of Directors shall make equitable adjustments in the number of Dividend Equivalents then outstanding and which may thereafter be granted and in the number of shares and prices per share applicable to Options then outstanding and in the number of shares which are available for grant of Options thereafter.

APPENDIX HH

CHRYSLER CORPORATION

CONTRACT WITH K. T. KELLER

AGREEMENT, made as of the first day of January, 1951, between K. T. KELLER, residing at No. 19366 Cumberland Way, Palmer Woods 3, Michigan (hereinafter called "Keller"), and CHRYSLER CORPORATION, a Delaware corporation having its principal office at 341 Massachusetts Avenue, Detroit 31, Michigan (hereinafter called "Chrysler").

Keller served Chrysler as a major Executive beginning April 1, 1926, and as President of Chrysler from July 22, 1935, until November 3, 1950. Of that period from August 29, 1940, until November 3, 1950, the By-Laws of Chrysler provided that the President subject to the control of the Board of Directors should have general charge and control of all the business and affairs of Chrysler and Keller exercised such charge and control. On November 3, 1950, contemplating reaching his normal retirement date under Chrysler Corporation Salaried Employees' Retirement Income Indenture, dated as of April 30, 1941, as amended, Keller advised the election of a new President to strengthen the management. The Directors requested Keller to remain in active charge of the Corporation. Keller resigned as President and the Board of Directors elected him Chairman of the Board and amended the By-Laws so as to provide that the Chairman of the Board should have general charge and control of all the business and affairs of Chrysler. Chrysler thereafter fixed Keller's salary as Chairman of the Board at $300,000 a year beginning as of January 1, 1951.

Chrysler contemplates submitting for the approval of its stockholders at the annual meeting of the stockholders of Chrysler on April 17, 1951, a proposal for a Supplemental Pension Plan for Salaried Employees, which Chrysler and Keller propose shall not include Keller.

Chrysler in view of Keller's experience in general charge and control of all of its business and affairs is desirous of having Keller continue to have general charge and control of all the business and affairs of Chrysler during a period of five (5) years from the first meeting of the Board of Directors of Chrysler following the annual meeting of stockholders on April 17, 1951, and therefore to act as Chairman of the Board for that period and thereafter render such advisory and consulting services to Chrysler as Chrysler may reasonably request and not take other employment or render services to others than Chrysler without the consent of Chrysler. Keller is willing to exercise general charge and control of all the business and affairs of Chrysler and accordingly to serve as Chairman of the Board for the period specified and thereafter to render services to Chrysler and not take other employment or render services to others without Chrysler's consent.

Now, THEREFORE, in consideration of the mutual undertakings hereinafter set forth, the parties agree as follows :

1. Chrysler employs Keller as Chairman of the Board of Chrysler with general charge and control of all the business and affairs of Chrysler subject to the Board of Directors for a period of five (5) years from the first meeting of the Board of Directors of Chrysler following the annual meeting of stockholders on April 17, 1951, and Keller accepts employment as Chairman of the Board of Directors of Chrysler and agrees for that period to accept election as a Director of Chrysler and as Chairman of the Board and as a member of the Finance Committee, and to devote his time, or as much of his time as the Board of Directors of Chrysler shall request, to the general charge and control of all the business and affairs of Chrysler and its subsidiary corporations, in the capacity of Chairman of the Board and as a Director and a member of the Finance Committee of Chrysler.

2. Chrysler will pay Keller for performing his services as Chairman of the Board at the rate of $300,000 per year.

3. Chrysler agrees that the Board of Directors of Chrysler will nominate Keller one of the persons for whom the proxies that Chrysler solicits for the annual meetings of stockholders of Chrysler in each of the years 1951, 1952, 1953, 1954 and 1955, will be voted for Director if Keller is able and willing to serve, and that if the stockholders elect Keller as a Director at any of those meetings the Board of Directors will elect Keller Chairman of the Board if Keller is able and willing to serve.

4. If the stockholders at any one or more of the annual meetings mentioned in Paragraph 3 fail to elect Keller a Director, or if the Board of Directors after the stockholders at any one or more of those annual meetings have elected Keller a Director, fail to elect him Chairman of the Board, and he is able and willing to serve, then for each of those years in which Keller shall fail of election as Chairman of the Board through failure of election either as a Director or as

Chairman of its Board, Chrysler shall pay to Keller as liquidated damages and Keller shall receive as liquidated damages the sum of $300,000 payable half monthly during that year in equal instalments as long as he is willing and able to serve, and Keller will not take other employment or render services to others than Chrysler without the consent of Chrysler during that year.

5. When Keller's employment as Chairman of the Board of Directors of Chrysler terminates, as provided in Paragraph 1 above, or by mutual agreement or by Keller being no longer willing or able to serve, or by reason of Keller having failed of election as a Director or as Chairman of the Board and Chrysler shall have paid him liquidated damages in the amount and over the period as specified in Paragraph 4, then Keller will render such advisory and consulting services to Chrysler as Chrysler may reasonably request, and will not take other employment or render services to others than Chrysler without the consent of Chrysler, and Chrysler will pay Keller for life at the rate of Seventy-five Thousand Dollars ($75,000) a year, payable half-monthly.

6. Chrysler and Keller expressly agree that Keller shall not be subject to removal under Section 1 of Article V of the By-Laws of Chrysler or any similar provision as Chairman of the Board by the Board of Directors during any term for which he shall have been elected Chairman of the Board pursuant to the terms of this agreement.

7. Chrysler and Keller agree that the validity of this agreement or of any of the provisions thereof shall be determined under and according to the laws of the State of Delaware, under which Chrysler is incorporated, and the contract and its provisions shall be construed according to the laws of the State of Delaware.

IN WITNESS WHEREOF Keller has hereunto set his hand and seal and Chrysler has caused its corporate name to be hereunto subscribed by the hand of its Vice-President thereunto duly authorized and its corporate seal to be hereunto affixed by its Assistant Secretary as of the day and year first above written.

K. T. KELLER   (L.S.)

CHRYSLER CORPORATION
By NICHOLAS KELLEY
Vice-President

Attest:
KENNETH M. EYESTONE
Assistant Secretary
[SEAL]

APPENDIX II

The Texas Company

CONTRACT WITH W. S. S. RODGERS

THIS AGREEMENT, entered into as of the first day of June, 1949, and amended December 17th, 1949, by and between THE TEXAS COMPANY (hereinafter referred to as the "Company") and W. S. S. Rodgers, of New York City, Chairman of the Board of Directors of the Company (hereinafter referred to as "Rodgers"),

WHEREAS, Rodgers entered the employ of the Company in 1915 and (except during the period of his military service in World War I) has been in the continuous employ of the Company since that time, having become Assistant to the President in 1926, Vice President and a Director of the Company in 1928, President in 1933, and having served as Chairman of the Board of Directors of the Company since 1944; and

WHEREAS, in recognition of the increased burden assumed by Rodgers during World War II (for which, because of certain wartime Federal salary stabilization statutes, he received no corresponding increase in compensation) and in recognition of his essential role in the development of the Company's interests and operations in the Eastern Hemisphere, the members of the Board of Directors of the Company, commencing in 1942, engaged in discussions among themselves and with Rodgers regarding an employment agreement to provide for appropriate compensation for services rendered by him, and to this end the Board of Directors of the Company, by resolution duly adopted in 1945, created a Special Committee of the Board for the purpose, among others, of negotiating such an agreement with Rodgers; and

WHEREAS, in recognition of the fact that on March 1, 1951, Rodgers will be eligible for complete retirement under the Company's Pension Plan, the Board of Directors desires to secure the continuation of his active services for the Company on a full-time basis for two years after that date; and

WHEREAS, the Board of Directors of the Company is desirous of obtaining the benefit of Rodgers' long experience in the industry and his unique knowledge of the Company and its affairs, particularly with reference to its interests and operations in the Eastern Hemisphere, in a consulting and advisory capacity or for assistance in connection with litigation or legislation which may arise affecting the interests of the Company for a period of five years after March 1, 1953, and to have the option during such period of recalling him for active service to the Company or to any of its associated or affiliated companies during any emergencies.

Now, THEREFORE, THIS AGREEMENT WITNESSETH THAT:

In consideration of the premises herein stated, and the mutual covenants and promises herein contained, the said parties hereto, intending to be legally bound, have agreed as follows:

(1) Except in the event of his earlier death or disability which incapacitates him therefor, Rodgers will devote his full time to the services of the Company until March 1, 1953, in such key executive, administrative, advisory or directorial capacity as may be designated by, and which shall make him responsible only to, the Board of Directors of the Company. The Company hereby engages Rodgers for, and he agrees to perform, such services. The Company will compensate Rodgers for such services at the rate of $150,000 per annum until March 1, 1953, payable in equal monthly installments; provided, however, that in the event of his earlier death or disability which incapacitates him for the services provided in this paragraph (1), such compensation shall cease and he shall receive no further payments hereunder except as and to the extent provided by paragraph (2) or paragraph (3), as the case may be.

(2) For a period of five years from and after the date on which he ceases to render the services provided in paragraph (1), Rodgers will, except in the event of his earlier death or disability which totally incapacitates him for the services required under this paragraph, continue faithfully to serve the Company in an advisory and consulting capacity and will render advice and assistance to the Company in connection with its business affairs and with respect to any proposed legislation or litigation affecting the Company's interests, when reasonably called upon at any time to do so by either the Company's Board of Directors or its Executive Committee. The Company hereby engages Rodgers for, and he agrees to perform, such services.

The Company will compensate Rodgers for such services by delivering to him annually, in equal quarterly installments, during each year of the said five-year period, 1200 fully paid and non-assessable shares of Capital Stock of the Company, of the par value of $25 per share; provided, however, that in the event that prior to any such delivery the stock of the Company shall be reclassified, or proportionately increased or decreased, including the payment of any stock dividend, or in case of merger or consolidation, then the securities to be thereafter deliverable to Rodgers shall be automatically increased or decreased or changed as to class or otherwise appropriately adjusted, as the case may be; and provided further that it shall be a condition to the delivery of any securities under this Agreement that Rodgers or any other recipient thereof shall represent in writing to the Company that it is the then intention of the recipient to acquire and hold such stock for investment and not with a view to subsequent sale or other disposition; and provided further that in the event of his death or disability which totally incapacitates him for the services required under this paragraph (2) before the end of such five-year period, such compensation shall cease and he shall receive no further payments or deliveries hereunder except as and to the extent provided by paragraph (3).

(3) In the event of Rodgers' death or disability which totally incapacitates him for the services required hereunder at any time from and after the date of this Agreement and before the end of the five-year period provided in paragraph (2), no further payments or deliveries shall be made under paragraphs (1) or (2) hereof, but the Company will then pay or deliver to him or to the recipient or recipients designated by him in writing (or in default of any such designation, to his estate) an amount of cash and stock or of stock alone, as the case may be, equal to such proportion of the total compensation which would have been payable to Rodgers hereunder had he continued to serve to the end of the five-year period provided by paragraph (2) and not theretofore paid to him, as the number of days during which he has actually performed services under this Agreement from and after June 1, 1949 bears to the total number of days in the period from June 1, 1949 to the end of the said five-year period.

The amount payable or stock deliverable pursuant to this paragraph (3) shall be payable or deliverable in ten equal annual installments except that in the event of Rodgers' death any balance may, in the discretion of the Board, be paid immediately in one lump sum.

(4) At any time after Rodgers ceases to perform the full-time services required by paragraph (1) hereof and prior to March 1, 1958 or his earlier death or total disability, the Board of Directors

shall have the right and option to recall him on a temporary, month-to-month basis for full-time duties and services to the Company or to any of its associated or affiliated companies, in any key executive, administrative, advisory or directorial capacity designated by, and which shall make him solely responsible to, its Board of Directors, whenever the Board of Directors of the Company shall, in its sole discretion, determine that there exists an emergency affecting either the country or the Company; provided, however, that without his consent no continuous period of such full-time service shall be extended beyond eight calendar months nor shall the aggregate of all periods of such full-time service exceed eight calendar months in any one twelve calendar month period. In the event that any one such continuous period of full-time services exceeds ninety days or that the aggregate of all periods of full-time service rendered in any one year exceeds one hundred and eighty days, the Company will compensate Rodgers therefor, on a monthly basis, by the payment to him of such amounts as, when added to the value of any other compensation received by him for such period or periods under paragraph (2) of this Agreement, will make his total remuneration for such period or periods at least equal to the rate of compensation then normally payable for such duties and services.

(5) Rodgers will continue to serve as both a director and member of the Executive Committee of the Company after he ceases to render the services provided in paragraph (1) for so long a period of time as may be requested by the Board of Directors of the Company (subject to any necessary election or approval by the stockholders of the Company). For such services he shall receive, in addition to any and all other payments under this Agreement, the customary fees for attendance and expenses received at that time by the other non-management directors.

(6) In the event that, for any reason other than his death or disability which incapacitates him for the services required hereunder, Rodgers shall voluntarily leave the employment of the Company before March 1, 1953 or shall at any time while he is still receiving compensation payments hereunder fail to render the services required of him hereunder, or in the event that at any time while any payments of any kind are being made hereunder to or for the benefit of Rodgers, he shall, without the written consent of the Board of Directors or of the Executive Committee of the Company, accept employment with or render services of any kind to any other oil company or organization engaged in any phase of the oil industry for profit

other than any of the Company's associated or affiliated companies, then in any of such events this Agreement and all of his rights and all of the Company's obligations hereunder shall forthwith terminate.

(7) Nothing herein contained shall affect the right of Rodgers to participate in and receive benefits under and in accordance with the then current provisions of the Company's present Group Life Insurance and Pension Plan, but he shall not be eligible to participate in any other pension, profit sharing or incentive compensation plan of the Company.

(8) This Agreement shall be binding upon and inure to the benefit of the parties hereto and any successors to the business of the Company, but neither this Agreement nor any rights hereunder shall be assignable by Rodgers.

(9) This Agreement is subject to approval at a meeting of the stockholders of the Company. To this end it shall be submitted to the stockholders at a meeting thereof, not later than the annual meeting to be held in 1950. Pending such meeting, the Company shall continue to compensate Rodgers for his services at the present rate. Upon such approval, such compensation shall be deemed to have been paid, and such services shall be deemed to have been rendered, pursuant to paragraph (1) hereof. Failing such approval, this Agreement shall be of no force and effect.

IN WITNESS WHEREOF, the Company has caused its corporate name to be subscribed hereunto by a Special Committee of non-management Directors duly authorized thereto by resolutions of the Board of Directors adopted May 27, 1949 and December 16, 1949, and its corporate seal to be affixed and attested by its Secretary, and Rodgers has hereunto set his hand and seal, all as of this first day of June, 1949.

THE TEXAS COMPANY
By ROBERT C. SHIELDS
L. J. NORRIS
J. H. LAPHAM
Special Committee

Attest:
    W. G. ELICKER
       Secretary
    [SEAL]
WITNESS:
    OSCAR JOHN DORWIN   W. S. S. RODGERS   (L.S.)

APPENDIX JJ

The Goodyear Tire & Rubber Company

CONTRACT WITH P. W. LITCHFIELD

THIS AGREEMENT, made this 31st day of March, 1947, effective as of January 1, 1947, between THE GOODYEAR TIRE & RUBBER COMPANY, an Ohio corporation with its principal office at Akron, Ohio (hereinafter called the Employer), and P. W. LITCHFIELD, of Akron, Ohio (hereinafter called the Employee),

WITNESSETH :

WHEREAS, the Employee has heretofore been serving as chief executive of the Employer, holding the office of Chairman of the Board of Directors, and has been reelected to such office at the meeting of the Board of Directors held on March 31, 1947; and

WHEREAS, the Employee has previously been employed under an arrangement for compensation under which, unless terminated by the Board of Directors during the first six months of the calendar year (amended to three months for the year 1947 and thereafter), he is entitled to receive as compensation for such calendar year, in addition to a fixed salary of $100,000 per annum, an amount (not in excess of $75,000) equal to 1% of the balance of consolidated net earnings of the Employer and its subsidiaries remaining after deducting from such earnings 5% of consolidated average book value of the outstanding capital stocks of the Employer; and

WHEREAS, the Employer and Employee desire to change the basis of compensation of employment from and after January 1, 1947, to the basis hereinafter provided for,

Now, THEREFORE, in consideration of the premises and of the mutual covenants herein contained, THE PARTIES HERETO AGREE AS FOLLOWS :

1. For the purposes of this agreement :

(a) The term "Employer" shall include The Goodyear Tire & Rubber Company, a party hereto, and any corporation succeeding to the business presently conducted by The Goodyear Tire & Rubber Company.

462

(b) The Employee shall cease to be employed by the Employer when, whether as a result of resignation, dismissal, death or any other reason, he ceases to serve the Employer or a subsidiary or affiliated company on a full-time basis under this or a subsequent employment arrangement.

(c) The Employee shall be "engaged in a competing business" at any time if, as proprietor, partner, trustee, employee or director, he is engaged or participates in the operation or management of a business selling any product or products of the kind or character which the Employer or a subsidiary is selling at the time the Employee ceases to be employed by the Employer and the sales of which by the Employer and its subsidiaries during the fiscal year preceding the year in which the Employee ceases to be employed by the Employer represent in dollar volume 5% of the total sales of the Employer and its subsidiaries for such year.

2. The Employer agrees to employ the Employee, and the Employee agrees to serve the Employer, during the term of this agreement as chief executive of the Employer. The Employee shall hold the office of Chairman of the Board of Directors or such other office as the parties may mutually approve. During the term of this agreement the Employee shall, under the direction of the Board of Directors, devote his best efforts and attention to the affairs of the Employer and its affiliated companies.

3. The term of this agreement shall commence January 1, 1947, and shall end as follows:

(a) The Employer or the Employee may end the term of this agreement on any December 31st by at least sixty days' prior written notice to the other.

(b) If the Employee shall not be reelected as Chairman of the Board of Directors or such other office as may be agreed upon between the parties at any time at which his term of office shall expire, the term of this agreement shall end at such time.

(c) If the Employee shall die or become incapacitated from performing his duties hereunder, the term of this agreement shall end with the last day of the month in which such death or incapacity occurs.

(d) The term of this agreement may be ended at any time by mutual agreement of the parties.

4. For his services performed during the term of this agreement the Employer shall pay to the Employee:

(a) Fixed compensation at the rate of $100,000 per annum to March 31, 1947, and thereafter at the rate of $125,000 per annum, payable in equal monthly instalments on the last day of the month during such term; and

(b) Contingent compensation at the rate of $75,000 per annum during the term of this agreement, payable as herein provided. Payment of the total amount to which the Employee shall become entitled during the term of this agreement under this paragraph (b) shall be made (subject to the contingencies hereinafter mentioned) in ten equal annual instalments on January 15 of each year, commencing with the January 15 next succeeding the year in which the Employee ceases to be employed by the Employer within the meaning of Section 1(b) of this agreement.

The contingencies upon which such contingent payments and each of them shall be made or continued are the following:

(i) That the Employee shall have duly performed his services hereunder pursuant to Article 2 hereof during the term of this agreement.

(ii) That the Employee shall not have engaged in a competing business as above defined during the period of three years, beginning with the date when the Employee ceased to be employed by the Employer (within the meaning of Section 1(b) hereof), without having first procured the written consent of the Employer. It is agreed that the Employee by engaging in such competing business during said three-year period without first having procured the consent of the Employer in writing, will automatically forfeit all rights to any subsequent contingent payments becoming due thereafter (but not to any contingent payments becoming due theretofore). The Employer in such written consent may specify the terms on which the consent is given and the amounts of subsequent contingent payments, which amounts may be less than those specified herein.

(iii) If in any calendar year after the Employee shall have ceased to be employed by the Employer (within the meaning of Section 1(b) hereof) the business compensation of the Employee (that is, the total compensation received by the Employee directly or indirectly as an employee or officer of a business organization other than the Employer), together with the amount of contingent compensation payable hereunder on the next succeeding January 15th, before adjustment for any deduction required by the provisions of this paragraph (iii), shall have exceeded an amount equal to 75% of the annual average compensation received by the Employee from the Employer during the three years next preceding the date on which the Employee shall have ceased to be employed by the Employer (other than bonuses, profit sharing or other special compensation), the amount of such excess shall be deducted from the contingent compensation otherwise payable to the Employee on (but only on) such next succeeding January 15th. The Employee shall furnish to the President of the Employer at his request a certified copy of the Employee's federal income tax return and such additional information as the President of the Employer may request to assist in the determination of the amount payable to the Employee under the provisions of this paragraph (iii) in any year.

5. All annual contingent payments which fall due hereunder after the death of the Employee shall be paid to his executors, administrators or such other person or persons as shall, under the last will and testament of the Employee or otherwise, be entitled thereto.

6. Neither the Employee nor the estate of the Employee nor any other person shall under any circumstances have any option or right to require payment for services of the Employee performed hereunder during the term of this agreement, other than in accordance with the terms hereof and after the contingencies herein specified have been met, but this agreement shall not affect the Employee's right to compensation for services other than those performed hereunder during the term of this agreement.

7. This agreement and all rights and benefits hereunder are personal to the Employee, and neither this agreement nor any right or interest of the Employee herein or arising hereunder shall be subject to voluntary or involuntary alienation, assignment or transfer.

IN WITNESS WHEREOF, the Employee has executed this agreement and The Goodyear Tire & Rubber Company has caused this agreement to be executed by its officers thereunto authorized, all at Akron, Ohio, this 31st day of March, 1947.

THE GOODYEAR TIRE & RUBBER COMPANY

By ....

President

Attest:

....

Secretary

....

P. W. LITCHFIELD

APPENDIX KK

The Texas Company

INCENTIVE COMPENSATION AGREEMENT

AGREEMENT, dated   , between The Texas Company, a corporation organized under the laws of the State of Delaware (hereinafter called the "Company"), and of   (hereinafter called the "Employee")

Whereas, for some time past, the Employee has rendered faithful and efficient services to the Company and is now one of its valued employees; and

Whereas, the Company desires to continue to receive the benefit of the Employee's services, more surely to identify the Employee's interest with the Company's future and success, and to provide an Incentive Compensation Plan as an incentive, in addition to ordinary compensation and benefits under the Company's Group Life Insurance and Pension Plan for the Employee to devote his best efforts to the service of the Company, and, to this end, the Company deems it appropriate to enter into a written agreement with the Employee that will provide a basis for compensation which will reflect, to the extent hereinafter provided, the growth and prosperity of the Company as evidenced by the market value of its stock;

Now, therefore, in consideration of the premises and of the mutual covenants and agreements hereinafter set forth, the parties hereto hereby covenant and agree as follows:

Incentive Compensation Account

1. The Company shall establish records containing an account to be designated as the Employee's "Incentive Compensation Account," which shall be used as a basis for determining the amount of payments to be made to the Employee, his estate or his personal representatives, as and subject to all of the terms and conditions hereinafter provided.

2. The Company shall promptly credit to the Incentive Compensation Account   units (hereinafter referred to as

466

the "Units"), each of which shall, for the purposes of this Agreement, be deemed to be the equivalent of one share of the Company's Capital Stock, of the par value of $25 per share, outstanding at the date hereof. The Capital Stock, or other securities of the Company, of the class or classes, which, from time to time, may be represented by the Units credited to the Incentive Compensation Account pursuant to the provisions of this Agreement, are hereinafter sometimes collectively referred to as the "Stock" or "Stock of the Company."

3. If, and whenever, the Company shall declare and pay a dividend (other than a stock dividend), whether in cash or property, upon its issued and outstanding Stock, or shall make any distribution with respect thereto, including the distribution of rights to subscribe for or warrants to purchase any of the Company's Stock or any securities of any other company at a price less than their then fair market value, there shall be credited to the Incentive Compensation Account the dollar amount of such cash dividend or the cash equivalent of such property dividend, as would have been paid upon, or the fair market value of such other distribution as would have been made with respect to, the number and class of Stock represented by the Units credited to the Incentive Compensation Account had such Stock been issued and outstanding, full paid and non-assessable, on the day on which such dividend or other distribution was declared. For the purposes of this paragraph, the Board of Directors shall make all determinations of fair market values, cash equivalents and dollar amounts in its absolute and uncontrolled discretion, and all such determinations shall be final and conclusive for all purposes hereunder.

4. No interest shall be allowable or payable in respect of any Units or dollar amounts which may at any time be credited to the Incentive Compensation Account.

MATURITY

5. This Agreement shall mature upon the date of the occurrence of the first of the following events:

(a) The Employee retiring at age 65 or in case his employment by the Company continues for all or any part of the two years from age 65 to 67, then at the date of retirement but not later than age 67;

(b) The Employee being retired by action of the Board of Directors after he has attained age 55;

(c) The Employee being retired at any age by action of the Board of Directors for reason of disability;

(d) The death of the Employee;

(e) The dissolution, liquidation, or winding up of the Company, whether voluntary or involuntary, or the voluntary sale, conveyance or transfer of all or substantially all of its property and assets; or

(f) The merger of the Company into another corporation, or the consolidation of the Company with one or more corporations, if one of such other corporations or a new corporation shall be the resulting or surviving corporation, unless prior to the effective date of such merger or consolidation it shall be determined by the Board of Directors of the Company that the active term of this Agreement shall survive such merger or consolidation.

PAYMENTS AFTER MATURITY

6. (a) After this Agreement shall have matured, the Company, subject to the other provisions hereof, shall pay to the Employee an amount of Stock computed to be the then equivalent of the Units then credited to his Incentive Compensation Account, together with all cash amounts theretofore credited to such Account, in ten approximately equal annual instalments (except that fractional shares of Stock shall not be delivered but payment made in the largest number of full shares deliverable), the first such payment to be made at any time within one year after the maturity of this Agreement, as may be determined by the Board of Directors in its absolute and uncontrolled discretion; provided, however, that if the maturity of this Agreement shall have resulted from the death of the Employee or his retirement by action of the Board of Directors for reason of disability, or if the Employee shall die or become disabled after the maturity of this Agreement but before all of such annual instalment payments have been made hereunder, the Board of Directors, in its absolute and uncontrolled discretion, may cause such payment, or the balance of such payments, to be made to him, his estate or his personal representative, as the case may be, in a single payment or in such monthly or annual instalments, extending over a period not in excess of eleven years from the date of maturity, as it may in its sole discretion determine.

(b) The delivery of any Stock pursuant to subparagraph (a) above shall automatically effect a ratable reduction in the number of Units remaining credited to the Incentive Compensation Account.

(c) Any dollar amounts credited to the Incentive Compensation Account pursuant to the provisions of paragraph 3 hereof after this

Agreement shall have matured, shall be added to the next succeeding payment made pursuant to subparagraph (a) above.

TERMINATION OF EMPLOYMENT

7. If, prior to the happening of any of the events enumerated in paragraph 5 of this Agreement, the employment of the Employee by the Company shall terminate for any cause whatsoever, all rights and obligations of the Company and the Employee hereunder forthwith shall cease and determine, unless the Board of Directors of the Company, in its absolute and uncontrolled discretion, shall elect to mature this Agreement as of the date of termination of employment of the Employee as to all or some portion of the Units and cash (if any) then credited to the Incentive Compensation Account in which event the Company, subject to the other provisions of this Agreement, shall pay the aggregate of the Stock computed hereunder to be the then equivalent of such matured Units, together with the amount of cash applicable thereto, as so determined by the Board, in the manner provided in paragraph 6 of this Agreement or, if the Board of Directors in its sole discretion shall so determine, in a single payment to be made within ninety days after the date of termination of employment of the Employee.

RECLASSIFICATION, MERGER, ETC.

8. If, and whenever, the Company shall take any action which results in its issued and outstanding Stock being reclassified, or proportionately increased or decreased, including the payment of any stock dividend, the number of shares and the class of Stock represented by each Unit which has theretofore been credited to the Incentive Compensation Account shall be simultaneously increased or decreased or changed as to class, as the case may be, in like manner as if such Stock had been issued and outstanding, full paid and nonassessable, on the day on which such Units were credited, and each of such Units shall thereafter be deemed to be the equivalent of such increased or decreased number and such changed class of Stock.

9. Upon the merger of one or more corporations into the Company, or upon a consolidation of the Company and one or more corporations in which the Company shall be the surviving corporation, each Unit credited to the Incentive Compensation Account shall thereafter be deemed to be the equivalent of (and the term "Stock" as used herein shall thereafter include) the shares of stock or other securities of the Company which, pursuant to the terms of such merger or consolidation as effectuated and without taking into

account any changes therein which might have taken place had such Stock then been issued and outstanding, would have been issued with respect to the Stock theretofore represented by such Unit had such Stock been issued and outstanding, full paid and non-assessable, on the day on which such merger or consolidation became effective.

10. Except as hereinbefore expressly provided, the issue by the Company of shares of Capital Stock or other securities for cash, property, or labor or services, either upon direct sale or upon the exercise of rights or warrants to subscribe therefor, or upon conversion of shares or obligations of the Company convertible into such stock or securities, or otherwise, shall not affect, and no adjustment by reason thereof shall be made with respect to, the number or class of Stock represented by the Units credited to the Incentive Compensation Account; nor, except as otherwise expressly provided in paragraph 3 of this Agreement, shall such Account be entitled to any credit with respect to or on account of any rights or warrants to subscribe for or to purchase shares of stock or securities of the Company which may at any time be issued.

DELIVERY OF STOCK

11. In any case where any Stock may be deliverable hereunder it shall be a condition to the delivery thereof that the Employee or other recipient shall represent in writing to the Company that it is his then intention to acquire and hold such Stock for investment and not with a view to subsequent sale or other disposition. Unless and until such Stock shall have been so delivered, all in accordance with the provisions of the preceding sentence, the Employee shall not, under any circumstances, have any interest whatsoever in any of the Stock represented by the Units which may from time to time be credited to his Incentive Compensation Account.

COVENANTS OF THE EMPLOYEE

12. The Company's obligation to make any payment pursuant to any of the provisions of this Agreement shall be contingent upon the fulfillment at the time of the following conditions:

(a) That the Employee has not engaged in or performed, and is not then engaging in or performing any services, whether full time or part time or on a consulting or advisory basis, for any other business organization in connection with any matter in respect of which the interest of such other business organization is or might reasonably be expected to be adverse to or inconsistent with that of the Company. If, at any time, the Board of Directors shall determine, in its absolute and uncontrolled discretion, that the Employee has violated this condition (a), this Agreement shall thereupon terminate, the Company shall have no further obligations hereunder and all of the rights of the Employee hereunder shall thereupon cease and determine; provided, however, that if the Employee shall furnish to the Board of Directors proof adequate and satisfactory to it that (i) the violation was unintentional and not in grossly negligent disregard of this condition (a), and (ii) the activities deemed by the Board of Directors to constitute such violation have been discontinued, the Board of Directors may, in its absolute and uncontrolled discretion, waive such violation in which event this Agreement shall remain in full force and effect as though such violation had not occurred.

(b) That, after his regular full-time employment with the Company has terminated and so long as this Agreement remains in effect, the Employee shall, unless physically incapacitated therefor, have rendered advisory and consultative services to the Company at reasonable compensation whenever reasonably requested so to do. If, at any time, the Board of Directors shall, in its absolute and uncontrolled discretion, determine that this condition (b) has not been fulfilled, this Agreement shall thereupon terminate, the Company shall have no further liability hereunder and all of the rights of the Employee hereunder shall forthwith cease and determine.

(c) Upon receipt of each and every payment under this Agreement, the Employee shall certify to the Company in writing that he has complied with all of the terms and conditions of this Agreement, and, in the absence of notice to the contrary, the Board of Directors may rely upon such certification for all purposes under this Agreement.

COMMITTEE OF DIRECTORS

13. The Board of Directors of the Company may delegate to a committee consisting of three or more of its members full power and authority to have and to exercise in its behalf all of the rights, powers and privileges herein reserved to the Company or its Board of Directors, and any action taken or omitted pursuant to this Agreement, and any determination made hereunder, by any such committee shall be final, conclusive, and binding on the Company and on the Employee as though made by the Board of Directors.

MISCELLANEOUS

14. Nothing herein contained shall require the Company to segregate physically, or otherwise earmark, any cash or any of the Stock which may at any time be represented by Units credited to the Incentive Compensation Account.

15. Anything in this Agreement to the contrary notwithstanding, if at any time specified herein for the making of any payment to any person, any law or regulation of any governmental authority having jurisdiction in the premises shall require the Company to withhold, or to make any deduction for, any taxes or take any other action in connection with the payment then to be made, such payment shall be deferred until such withholding or deduction shall have been provided for by the Employee or other appropriate action shall have been taken.

16. In case of any uncertainty, or any dispute as to the person or persons to whom the Company shall be obligated to make any payment provided hereunder, the Board of Directors of the Company shall have full power to determine the matter and any payment made pursuant to such determination shall fully discharge all obligation of the Company with respect thereto.

NOTICES

17. The Company shall give the Employee written notice of any event maturing this Agreement under subparagraphs (b), (c), (e) or (f) of paragraph 5 hereof.

18. Any notice which either party hereto may be required or permitted to give to the other shall be in writing, and may be delivered personally or by mail, postage prepaid, addressed as follows: To the Company, at 135 East 42nd Street, New York 17, N. Y., or at such other address as the Company, by notice to the Employee, may designate in writing from time to time; to the Employee, at the address hereinabove specified, or at such other address as the Employee, by notice to the Company, may designate in writing from time to time.

ASSIGNMENT

19. This Agreement shall bind and inure to the benefit of the respective heirs, personal representatives, legatees, distributees and successors of the respective parties hereto; *provided,* that the Employee shall not assign this Agreement, or any of his rights or inter-

ests herein or any cash or Units at any time credited to the Incentive Compensation Account.

IN WITNESS WHEREOF, the Company has caused this Agreement to be executed by its duly authorized officers, under its corporate seal, and the Employee has hereunto set his hand and seal, all as of the day and year first above written.

THE TEXAS COMPANY

By ....

President

.... [L.S.]

Attest:

....
       Secretary

APPENDIX LL

KOPPERS COMPANY, INC.

DEFERRED COMPENSATION UNIT PLAN

I. PURPOSE.

The purpose of this Plan is to enable the Company to attract to and retain in its employment over the years persons of outstanding competence, and to promote the stockholder point of view among key employees of the Company.

II. DEFINITIONS.

(a) "Company" means Koppers Company, Inc., or any company successor thereto by merger, consolidation, liquidation or other reorganization which has made provision for adoption of this Plan and the assumption of the Company's obligations thereunder, as well as any subsidiary 51% or more of the outstanding common stock of which is owned by the Company.

(b) "Common Stock" means shares of the Common Stock of Koppers Company, Inc.

(c) "Administrative Committee" means the committee established by the Board of Directors of the Company pursuant to Article III hereof.

(d) "Employee" means any person, including an officer of the Company (whether or not he is also a director thereof), who is employed by the Company on a full-time basis, who is compensated for such employment by a regular salary, and who, in the opinion of the Administrative Committee, is one of the key personnel of the Company in a position to contribute materially to its continued growth and development and to its future financial success. The term does not include persons who are retained by the Company as consultants only.

(e) "Participant" means an Employee who is awarded Deferred Compensation Units hereunder.

(f) "Retirement" means a severance from the Company's employment upon or after attainment of age 65 pursuant to retirement rights under the Company's Employees Cooperative Retirement

Plan for salaried employees as now in effect or as hereafter amended, or earlier retirement on a Disability Pension pursuant to rights under said Plan.

(g) "Termination Date" shall mean the date of a Participant's severance from employment with the Company by death, Retirement, resignation, discharge or otherwise.

(h) "Fair Market Value" of the Common Stock shall be the price at which the last sale of Common Stock was made on the New York Stock Exchange on the date in question. If there is no transaction in the Common Stock on the New York Stock Exchange on that day, then the Fair Market Value shall be the last bid price for the Common Stock on said Exchange on that day.

III. ADMINISTRATION.

(a) The Board of Directors of the Company shall establish an Administrative Committee consisting of three or more members of the Board who are ineligible to become Participants, and who shall serve at the pleasure of the Board of Directors, to administer, construe and interpret this Plan. No member of the Administrative Committee shall be liable for any act done or determination made in good faith.

(b) The construction and interpretation by the Administrative Committee of any provision of this Plan shall be final and conclusive. It shall determine, subject to the provisions of this Plan:

(i) The Employees who shall participate in the Plan from time to time; and

(ii) The number of Deferred Compensation Units (sometimes hereinafter called "Units") to be set aside for each Participant.

(c) The Administrative Committee may, in its discretion, delegate its duties to an officer or employee, or a committee composed of officers or employees of the Company, but may not delegate its authority to construe and interpret this Plan, or to make the determinations specified in Items (i) and (ii) of Paragraph (b) of this Article III.

IV. ESTABLISHMENT OF DEFERRED COMPENSATION UNITS.

The Company shall set up an appropriate record (hereinafter called "the Special Ledger") and thereafter from time to time enter therein the name of each Participant, the number of Units awarded to him by the Administrative Committee, and an amount equivalent to the Fair Market Value of an equal number of shares of Common Stock on the day such Units were awarded him.

V. Aggregate Number of Units.

The aggregate number of Units standing in the Special Ledger to the credit of Participants at one time shall not exceed 100,000, and the aggregate number of Units awarded to any one Participant shall not exceed 5,000, provided however, that upon severance of any Participant from employment with the Company, any Units therefore awarded him shall no longer be considered outstanding for the purposes of this Article V.

VI. Credits to the Account of Participants.

(a) So long as this Plan remains in effect the Company shall credit to each Participant's account in the Special Ledger throughout the term of his employment with the Company, amounts equal to dividends payable in cash or property paid from time to time on issued and outstanding shares of Common Stock equal to the number of Units in his account, so that the amount of each such credit will be equivalent to dividends which the Participant would have received had he been the owner of the number of shares of Common Stock equal to the number of Units in his account. No such credit shall be made with respect to any dividend paid after a Participant's Termination Date or after any date of termination of this Plan, even though the record date is prior thereto.

(b) There shall be credited to each Participant's account in the Special Ledger an amount which shall be equal to the excess, if any, of the aggregate Fair Market Value on his Termination Date of that number of shares of Common Stock which is equal to the number of Units then standing to his credit over the aggregate Fair Market Value of such shares on the date or dates the Units were awarded him, all subject, however, to the provisions of Paragraphs (c) to (g), inclusive, of this Article VI.

(c) When a Participant's employment with the Company is severed other than by death or Retirement, then all or any part of the credit under the provisions of Paragraph (b) of this Article VI may be credited to the Participant's account only if the Administrative Committee shall authorize the same after consultation with the President of the Company. If such severance occurs within five years from the date he became a Participant, then all or any part of the credits theretofore made to his account under the provisions of

Paragraph (a) of this Article VI will be paid him only in exceptional circumstances in the discretion of the Administrative Committee after consultation with the President.

(d) When a Participant's employment with the Company is severed by death or Retirement, he or his Beneficiary or Beneficiaries designated pursuant to Paragraph (b) of Article VII hereof shall have the option, exercisable in writing filed with the Secretary of the Company on or before his Termination Date (or in the event of his death, within thirty days thereafter), to have his credit under the provisions of Paragraph (b) of this Article VI determined by using the Fair Market Value of the Common Stock as of a Selected Value Date in lieu of his Termination Date; provided however, that such Fair Market Value may not exceed the highest price at which a sale of the Common Stock was made on the New York Stock Exchange between the date such employee became a Participant and his Termination Date. The Selected Value Date shall be any date within a three-year period immediately following his Termination Date which he or his Beneficiary or Beneficiaries may designate by notice in writing to the Secretary of the Company not less than three days prior to the date so designated. If no such designation is made, then his Selected Value Date shall be the third anniversary of his Termination Date. If such option shall be exercised, no credit shall be made to such Participant's account in the Special Ledger under the provisions of said Paragraph (b) until the Selected Value Date, except as provided in Paragraphs (f) and (g) of this Article VI.

(e) Any Participant whose employment with the Company is severed other than by death or Retirement shall have an option to choose a Selected Value Date, as provided in Paragraph (d) of this Article VI, only upon consent thereto being granted by the Administrative Committee.

(f) If the Board of Directors of the Company shall terminate this Plan within five years from its effective date, no credit under the provisions of Paragraph (b) of this Article VI shall be made thereafter to the account of any Participant; provided however, that if the date of such termination occurs after a Participant's Termination Date and prior to his Selected Value Date, then such Participant shall be entitled to any credit resulting under the provisions of said Paragraph (b) from the use of the Fair Market Value of the Common Stock as of the date of termination of this Plan in lieu of such Participant's Selected Value Date.

(g) If the Board of Directors of the Company shall terminate this Plan more than five years after its effective date, then each Participant who has not received a credit under the provisions of Paragraph (b) of this Article VI shall be entitled to any credit resulting thereunder from the use of the Fair Market Value of the Common Stock on the date of termination of this Plan in lieu of each such Participant's Termination Date or Selected Value Date, as the case may be, and any credit so resulting shall be entered in the Special Ledger to the account of each such Participant as of the date of termination of this Plan, but no other credits under the provisions of said Paragraph (b) shall be made thereafter to the account of any Participant.

VII. PAYMENT OF BENEFITS.

(a) Upon severance of any Participant from the employment of the Company there shall be paid to him, or in the event of his death to the person or persons designated under the provisions of Paragraph (b) of this Article VII, the aggregate amounts then standing to his credit in the Special Ledger, plus any amount thereafter credited to him under the provisions of Paragraph (b) of Article VI hereof. Such amounts shall be payable in quarter-annual installments over a ten-year period immediately following his Termination Date, the first such payment to be made within three months immediately following his Termination Date.

(b) Each person upon becoming a Participant shall file with the Secretary of the Company a notice in writing designating one or more Beneficiaries to whom payments otherwise due the Participant shall be made in the event of his death while in the employment of the Company or after severance therefrom, subject however to the provisions of Paragraph (c) of this Article VII.

VIII. AGREEMENT TO CONTINUE EMPLOYMENT AND TO CONSULT.

(a) Each Participant, as a condition to the awarding to him of Units hereunder, shall agree that he will remain in the employment of the Company or one of its subsidiaries (subject to the right of the Company or such subsidiary to terminate his employment at any time) for a period of five years from the date of such award or until Retirement prior to the expiration of such five-year period.

(b) As a condition to the receipt of benefits hereunder, each Participant, upon severance of his employment with the Company, shall execute an Agreement with the Company whereby, in consideration of the receipt of such benefits, he agrees to hold himself available to the Company for reasonable consultation in so far as his health permits, throughout a period of ten years following his Termination

Date, and whereby he further agrees not to engage in any business or practice or become employed in any position in competition with the Company, or which is otherwise prejudicial to the interests of the Company. In the event of any breach of such Agreement by the Participant, the Board of Directors of the Company, by written notice to such Participant, may cause his benefits to be suspended. Thereafter, if the Board of Directors shall find that the Participant has continued to violate such Agreement for a period of one month following such suspension, the Board may permanently cancel his benefits hereunder and thereupon all rights of such Participant under this Plan shall terminate.

IX. LIMITATION OF RIGHTS.

(a) The Administrative Committee may at any time prior to a Participant's Termination Date reduce the number of or cancel all Units standing to his credit in the Special Ledger; provided however that any such action shall not affect the rights of any such Participant with respect to amounts therefore credited to him under Paragraph (a) of Article VI hereof.

(b) Nothing in this Plan contained shall be construed to:

    (i) Give any employee of the Company any right to be awarded any Units other than in the sole discretion of the Administrative Committee.

    (ii) Give Participant any rights whatsoever with respect to shares of Common Stock of the Company.

    (iii) Limit in any way the right of the Company to terminate a Participant's employment with the Company at any time; or

    (iv) Be evidence of any agreement or understanding, express or implied, that the Company will employ a Participant in any particular position or at any particular rate of remuneration.

X. ADJUSTMENT IN NUMBER OF UNITS.

In the event of any stock dividend on the Common Stock or any split-up or combination of shares of the Common Stock appropriate adjustment shall be made by the Administrative Committee in the aggregate number of Units which may be awarded under this Plan, in the maximum number of shares which may be awarded to any one Participant, and in the number of Units standing to the credit of each Participant in the Special Ledger; provided however, that the Administrative Committee shall not be required to establish any fractional Units.

XI. Non-Alienation of Benefits.

No right or benefit under this Plan shall be subject to anticipation, alienation, sale, assignment, pledge, encumbrance or charge, and any attempt to anticipate, alienate, sell, assign, pledge, encumber or charge the same shall be void. No right or benefit hereunder shall in any manner be liable for or subject to the debts, contracts, liabilities or torts of the person entitled to such benefit. If any Participant or Beneficiary hereunder should become bankrupt or attempt to anticipate, alienate, sell, assign, pledge, encumber or charge any right or benefit hereunder, then such right or benefit shall, in the discretion of the Administrative Committee, cease and determine, and in such event, the Company may hold or apply the same or any part thereof for the benefit of the Participant or Beneficiary, his or her spouse, children or other dependents, or any of them, in such manner and in such proportion as the Administrative Committee may deem proper.

XII. Amendment or Termination of Plan.

(a) The Board of Directors may terminate this Plan at any time.

(b) The Board of Directors may amend this Plan at any time, except that without approval by a vote of the holders of a majority of the outstanding Common Stock:

> (i) The aggregate number of Units which may be awarded to all Participants and the aggregate number of Units which may be awarded to any one Participant may not be increased except as provided in Article X hereof; and
> (ii) This Article XII may not be amended.

(c) Any amendment or termination of this Plan shall not affect the rights of Participants or Beneficiaries to payments in accordance with Article VII of amounts standing to the credit of Participants in the Special Ledger at the time of such amendment or termination.

XIII. Effective Date of Plan.

This Plan shall become operative and in effect on such date as shall be fixed by the Board of Directors of the Company, in its discretion, after approval and authorization thereof by a vote of the holders of a majority of the outstanding Common Stock.

APPENDIX MM

SYLVANIA ELECTRIC PRODUCTS, INC.

CONTRACT WITH DON G. MITCHELL

January 1, 1956

Mr. Don G. Mitchell
Chairman of the Board and President
Sylvania Electric Products Inc.
1740 Broadway
New York 19, New York

Dear Mr. Mitchell:

Sylvania Electric Products Inc. (hereinafter referred to as "Sylvania") is desirous of retaining your services for at least another five years commencing January 1, 1956. To this end, I am authorized by the Board of Directors of Sylvania to offer you a contract under the following terms to induce you to remain with Sylvania for at least this five year period.

1. Sylvania hereby agrees to employ you in such capacity and to perform such duties on a full time basis as its Board of Directors from time to time shall determine for the five year period commencing January 1, 1956, so long as you are able, physically and in all other respects, to perform the duties required of you by the Board. You agree to perform faithfully and devote your full time and energies in the capacity and to the duties determined by the Board during this five year period so long as you are physically able. You also agree faithfully to serve as Chairman of the Board and/or President of Sylvania if duly elected by the Board at any time or times during this five year period.

2. Your annual compensation during such five year period, while you are so employed, will be at the rate of $150,000 per annum. In addition, Sylvania agrees to pay you, as deferred compensation, $50,000 (or a *pro rata* portion thereof if a portion of a year is involved) for each year of your service as set forth in paragraph one herein, subject to the conditions referred to in paragraph three herein, such deferred compensation to be paid to you in ten equal

481

annual installments over a ten year period commencing with the date
you cease to be an employee of Sylvania (whether or not you continue as a Director) or cease to be able to carry out your duties as set
forth herein. Also, while you are an employee during such five year
period, you will participate in the Company's Savings and Retirement
Plan and Group Insurance Program, and may also receive benefits
from time to time under the Stock Option Plan. During such five
year period, however, you will not participate in the Executive Compensation Plan.

3. The payment to you of each of the ten annual installments of
the deferred compensation referred to in paragraph two herein is
expressly conditioned on the following:

   (a) That during such ten year period you do not enter into the
       employ of any company in the electrical or electronics in-
       dustry which, in the opinion of Sylvania's Board of Di-
       rectors, is a substantial competitor of Sylvania; and
   (b) That during such ten year period you hold yourself avail-
       able for such consultative or advisory services, or the like,
       as the Board of Directors of Sylvania deems reasonable.

4. In the event that you should die during the five year period
referred to in paragraph one herein, Sylvania agrees that the amount
of deferred compensation determined pursuant to paragraphs two
and three herein shall be paid to your estate in a lump sum. In the
event that you should die during the ten year installment period
referred to above, the balance (not already paid to you) of such deferred compensation shall be paid to your estate in a lump sum, provided you have fulfilled all the conditions of paragraph three. Notwithstanding the foregoing, at any time during your lifetime, but
not after the end of the ten year installment period, you may elect by
written designation filed with Sylvania's Board of Directors (which
election may be changed by you during your lifetime from time to
time prior to the end of such period) to have the appropriate lump
sum payment referred to in this paragraph paid to your estate over a
specified period of years or to a designated beneficiary or beneficiaries
in various proportions either in a lump sum or over a specified
period of years.

5. This agreement shall be binding on Sylvania and any successor company into or with which Sylvania may be merged, consolidated, or to which Sylvania may sell, or distribute by way of
liquidation or otherwise, substantially all its assets.

If you agree to the foregoing arrangement, please sign the duplicate original of this letter where indicated below and return it to me.

Sincerely,
Chester F. Hockley
Chairman of the Directors'
Salary Committee

Agreed to this 5 day
of March, 1956.
/s/ Don G. Mitchell
Chairman and President

APPENDIX NN

FEDERATED DEPARTMENT STORES, INC.

CONTRACT WITH FRED LAZARUS

THIS AGREEMENT made in the City of Cincinnati, State of Ohio, this 13th day of April, 1950, between FEDERATED DEPARTMENT STORES, INC., a Delaware Corporation (hereinafter called the "Employer"); and FRED LAZARUS, JR., of the City of Cincinnati and State of Ohio (hereinafter called the "Employee"), WITNESSETH:

WHEREAS, the Employee has been in the service of the Employer or its constituent companies for a period of more than forty-five (45) years, and during the past 5 years has been President and General Manager of the business of the Employer, and it is the desire of the parties hereto to enter into an agreement to provide for:

(a) The employment of Employee for a three (3) year period on the terms and conditions set forth herein, plus such further period or periods, and upon such terms and conditions therefor, as may be subsequently mutually agreed upon between the parties hereto; and

(b) To provide for a retirement allowance for Employee from and after the period of active employment covered by this agreement or after the period of active employment covered by any subsequent agreement and for the benefits the Employer may receive from Employee's knowledge and experience during the period of retirement and from the other terms of this agreement; and under certain conditions hereinafter set forth to provide for a pension for a limited period for members of his family after his death;

Now, THEREFORE, IT IS AGREED by and between the parties hereto as follows:

1. The Employer agrees to and does employ the said Employee as President and General Manager of the business of said company for a period beginning with the date hereof and ending August 31, 1953, and further agrees to pay him during said period of active employment a salary of One Hundred and Forty-five Thousand Dollars ($145,000.00) per year, payable monthly, and at the same rate for any fraction of a month unexpired at the termination of said period of active employment.

The term "period of active employment," as used herein, means the period beginning with the date hereof and ending August 31, 1953, or on the last day of any renewal period, as hereinafter provided, or at the time of the previous death or retirement of said Employee.

The term "retirement," as that term is used herein, begins when either:

(1) The failure of the parties before the close of business on August 31, 1953, or on the last day of any renewal period, to enter into a contract for the Employer's employment of the Employee for a further period of at least one (1) year and the cessation of Employee's employment by Employer as a result thereof; or

(2) The failure so to agree before the end of any renewal period of this agreement, in case it should be renewed on the same or similar terms, whether for one year or more, by mutual agreement of the parties hereto or otherwise, and the cessation of Employee's employment by Employer as a result thereof; or

(3) The failure of Employee, during the period of active employment of this agreement, or any renewal thereof, to render services to the Employer for a continuous period of twelve (12) months, because of Employee's physical or mental disability during said period, and action by the Board of Directors of Employer to end Employee's active employment by reason thereof. If there should be any dispute between the parties as to Employee's physical or mental disability at any time, such question shall be settled by the opinion of an impartial reputable physician agreed upon for the purpose by the parties or their representatives, or failing agreement within ten (10) days of a written request therefor by either party to the other, then one designated by the then president of the Cincinnati Academy of Medicine. The certificate of such physician as to the matter in dispute shall be final and binding on the parties.

2. If the Employee performs his duties in accordance with this agreement during the period of active employment, then, if the Employee is living at the end of said period, he shall thereafter receive a retirement allowance, payable monthly, at the rate of Fifty-five

Thousand Dollars ($55,000.00) per year, as long as it shall be the fact (but not after any time when it shall not be the fact) that the Employee

(a) is still living, and

(b) is not engaged in any employment or proprietary business which yields the Employee compensation from said employment or net income from said proprietary business equal to or in excess of Fifty-five Thousand Dollars ($55,000.00) per year; provided, however, that if the Employee's retirement from active employment is due to Employer's unwillingness to renew his employment contract at the end of any period of employment or renewal period for at least one year on the same terms as during the last period of employment or renewal period then ending, but the Employee is willing to renew for at least one year on such terms, then the provisions of this paragraph (b) shall not apply; and

(c) does not have, in any competing business, as hereinafter defined, an aggregate investment resulting from his having advanced on loan or contributed to capital or expended for the purchase of shares of stock or of an interest in such shares, or in a business, or having expended in one or more of the ways of aforesaid, a sum or sums amounting in the aggregate to not less than Five Hundred Thousand Dollars ($500,000.00); and

(d) is not an officer, director or employee of the corporation nor a member of a partnership nor trustee of a business trust, which conducts a competing business, nor the proprietor of a competing business.

"Competing business," as used herein, shall mean a business (a) which is substantially similar to the whole or a substantial part of the business now or at the end of the period of active employment, conducted by Employer, or any of its subsidiaries, or subsidiaries of subsidiaries, or affiliates, or substantially similar to some substantial part of said business, and (b) which is being conducted in a city or within a radius of twenty-five (25) miles from the outer limits of a city where Employer, or any of its subsidiaries, or subsidiaries of subsidiaries, or affiliates is at the time of the commencement of the engagement by Employee in such competing business conducting a retail store.

Before Employer may refuse to pay to Employee the retirement allowance to which he would otherwise be entitled during retirement because of his failure to comply with the provisions of the foregoing paragraphs (b), (c) or (d) of this Section 2, or the following Section 9, Employer shall give to Employee at least thirty (30) days' notice in writing of its intention to cease making the payments and the reason therefor. Such notice shall be served by a delivery thereof in hand to the Employee or by sending the same by registered mail return receipt requested addressed to the Employee at 707 Race Street, Cincinnati, Ohio unless some other address shall previously have been designated in writing to the Employer by the Employee. Employee shall have thirty (30) days after the delivery of mailing of said notice in which to cure any alleged default and to put himself in compliance with the terms of this agreement for the receipt of such pay, and if he shall do so within said thirty (30) day period, then he shall be entitled to receive said monthly payments unless and until he subsequently disqualifies himself from receiving them. Any waiver by the Employer of the right to discontinue making said monthly payments to Employee shall not be construed as a waiver of any subsequent matter that would give rise to the right of Employer to discontinue said monthly payments.

3. On the death of the Employee, provided he is then in the active employment of Employer and has performed his obligations under this agreement up to that time, in accordance with the terms thereof, Employer will pay to the surviving widow or issue, or both, of Employee for a period of ten (10) years, in equal monthly installments, the sum of Fifty-five Thousand Dollars ($55,000.00) per year, subject to the conditions hereinafter stated. If the Employee should die during retirement, but before the end of ten (10) years from the end of his period of active employment, then the Employer will pay to the surviving widow or issue, or both, of Employee, for the remaining period of ten (10) years from the end of his period of active employment, in equal monthly installments, the sum of Fifty-five Thousand Dollars ($55,000.00) per year, subject to the conditions hereinafter stated.

4. Said annual payments to the widow or issue of Employee, as set forth in the preceding Section 3 hereof, shall be made only in case the consolidated net earnings of Employer, before income taxes, and before minority interests in subsidiary companies, but excluding items charged or credited directly to surplus (hereinafter termed "consolidated earnings"), in the fiscal year preceding the year in which such payments are to be made, are at least Five Million Five Hundred Thousand Dollars ($5,500,000.00). If Employer had no consolidated earnings during said preceding fiscal year, then the widow and issue of Employee shall receive nothing during the year following that in which Employer had no consolidated earnings. If Employer had consolidated earnings during the preceding fiscal year, but less than Five

Million Five Hundred Thousand Dollars ($5,500,000.00), then the widow and issue will receive the proportion of Fifty-five Thousand Dollars ($55,000.00) that the consolidated earnings during said preceding fiscal year bear to Five Million Five Hundred Thousand Dollars ($5,500,000.00). If payment at the rate of Fifty-five Thousand Dollars ($55,000.00) per year is not made either in whole or in part in any year or years (a year for this purpose shall be deemed to be the year beginning with Employee's death, or any anniversary thereof, and ending one year thereafter), any deficiency therein, or the aggregate of any deficiencies, shall be paid in any succeeding year or years in which said widow and issue are entitled to payments in accordance with the terms of this contract, when the consolidated earnings for the preceding fiscal year are in excess of Five Million Five Hundred Thousand Dollars ($5,500,000.00), such deficiency or deficiencies to be made up only by the payment of not more than one per cent (1%) of the amount by which the consolidated earnings of the Employer for the preceding fiscal year exceeded Five Million Five Hundred Thousand Dollars ($5,500,000.00).

"The preceding fiscal year" as used herein, shall be construed to mean the Employer's fiscal year, the last day of which most nearly precedes the first day of the one in which the payments are to be made, unless the date of ending of the fiscal year and the date for the determination of the commencement of the payments coincide, in which event, "the preceding fiscal year" shall mean the one ending on that coinciding date.

Consolidated earnings, as herein defined, shall be determined from the items in the annual report submitted to the stockholders of Employer, certified by independent certified public accountants employed by Employer, whose certificate as to such consolidated earnings shall in case of dispute be final, binding and conclusive on the parties hereto for the purpose of this agreement.

5. Employee may by writing delivered to Employer during Employee's lifetime designate the person or persons among his widow and issue who are to receive the payments after his death, and the proportions in which they are to receive the amounts payable under the provisions of Sections 3 and 4 hereof, if he designates more than one. He may also designate which person or persons shall succeed to the rights of the person or persons designated in case the designated person or persons shall die and in what proportions he or they shall receive them. The Employee may change his designation from time to time and the last designation in writing filed with the Employer before his death will control. Failing any designation the payments

will be made to his widow, if she is living, and if not, to the living children in equal proportions. If neither his widow nor any child is living, the payments will be made to the Employee's issue in equal proportions, *per stirpes*. If the Employee should make a designation to more than one person and one of the persons to whom the designation is made shall die before the payments are completed, then failing any other designation by the Employee, the payments that were being made to the deceased beneficiary shall be made to the surviving designated widow or issue in the same proportions as they were respectively receiving payments previously. In case there should be a complete failure of widow and issue of Employee before the payments provided in Section 3 and 4 hereof are completed, then the payments shall cease. In no event shall any payment of any nature be made to any person under the terms of Sections 3, 4 or 5 of this agreement more than ten (10) years after (a) the death of Employee, or (b) the end of the period of his active employment, whichever is earlier.

Words in the masculine herein may be interpreted as feminine, and words in the singular as plural, and vice versa, where the sense requires.

6. The Employee agrees that during the period of active employment (a) he will faithfully and in conformity with the directions of Employer's Board of Directors, perform the duties of his employment hereunder, which duties (as the Employer agrees) shall be of substantially the same character as those ordinarily performed by persons in similar positions, and that he will devote to the performance of said duties all such time and attention as they shall reasonably require, taking, however, from time to time (as the Employer agrees that he may), reasonable vacations; and (b) he will not, without the express consent of the Board of Directors of Employer, become actively associated with or engaged in any business during the period of active employment other than that of Employer, or its subsidiaries or affiliates, and he will do nothing inconsistent with his duties to the Employer.

7. The Employer agrees that during the period of active employment, the Employee shall be allowed reasonable traveling expenses and shall be furnished office space, assistance and accommodations suitable to the character of his position with the Employer and adequate for the performance of his duties hereunder.

8. Unless one party to this agreement gives to the other party notice in writing of the intention not to renew this agreement, at least one hundred and twenty (120) days before the terminal date of this agreement or of any renewal thereof, then this agreement

shall be renewed for a period of one (1) year beginning with the day following said terminal date, on the terms and conditions herein set forth other than the period of employment.

9. Employee agrees during the period of retirement, while he is receiving payments from Employer, as a condition of receiving such payments, to render such services of an advisory or consultative nature as the Employer may reasonably request, in order that the Employer may continue to have the benefit, in this manner, of his experience and knowledge of the affairs of Employer, and his reputation and contacts in the trade. Employee shall be available for advice and counsel to the officers and directors of the Employer at all reasonable times by telephone, letter or in person, wherever he may be. Employee's illness or other incapacity during the period of retirement shall not in any event affect his right to payments at the rate herein provided after retirement. Any expense incurred by Employee in connection with such consultation and advice shall be paid by the Employer.

10. So far as Employee reasonably can, he will not at any time permit the use of the name "Lazarus" as the whole or any part of the business or trade name of any other person, firm or corporation, competing in whole or in part with the business of Employer, or any of its subsidiaries, or subsidiaries of subsidiaries, or affiliates.

11. This agreement shall bind and run to the benefit of the successors and assigns of Employer, including any corporation or other form of business organization with which the Employer may merge or consolidate or to which it may transfer substantially all of its assets, including good will. The Employee may not, however, assign his interest in this agreement or any part thereof without the written consent of Employer.

12. This agreement and all questions arising in connection therewith shall be governed by the laws of the State of Ohio.

13. Subject as hereinafter provided, this agreement supersedes and cancels and annuls, any and all previous contracts, arrangements or understandings between the Employee and Employer or any of its subsidiaries, with respect to the employment of the Employee; provided, however, that this agreement shall not be effective unless and until it shall have been approved at a meeting of the stockholders of the Employer, and provided, further, that if this agreement shall not have been approved at a meeting of the stockholders of the Employer prior to August 1, 1950, or any later date which may be agreed to in writing by the Employer and the Employee, this agreement shall be deemed to have been abandoned, and the agreement

dated December 17, 1947 between the Employer and the Employee shall remain in full force and effect, except that the time within which either party to such agreement may give to the other party notice of intention not to renew such agreement shall be extended until 15 days after August 1, 1950, or such later agreed date, and if notice of intention not to renew such agreement is given within such extended period, the Employee shall be deemed to have retired under such agreement dated December 17, 1947 as of September 1, 1950, or as of the date of such notice if such date is subsequent to September 1, 1950.

IN WITNESS WHEREOF, the parties hereto have hereunto and to a duplicate hereof, set their signatures on the day and year above written, the Employer by Walter Rothschild, its First Vice-President and Jacob J. Kaplan its Secretary, thereunto duly authorized by its Board of Directors.

APPENDIX OO

American Home Products Corporation

EMPLOYMENT AGREEMENT WITH
WALTER SILBERSACK

AGREEMENT made this 3rd day of January, 1958, but effective as of January 1, 1958, by and between AMERICAN HOME PRODUCTS CORPORATION (herein referred to as "American Home") and WALTER SILBERSACK (herein referred to as "Silbersack").

Witnesseth :

Whereas, American Home and Silbersack entered into an Employment Agreement dated March 10, 1950, effective as of January 1, 1950, which agreement was amended on November 5, 1953, December 27, 1956, and September 19, 1957; and

Whereas, American Home and Silbersack desire to consolidate said agreement, and the amendments thereto, and to add thereto, in this as a new single instrument.

Now, therefore, in consideration of the premises and in order to induce Silbersack to continue in his employment with American Home, it is agreed between the parties hereto as follows:

1. In the manner and subject to the conditions hereinafter stated, American Home agrees to pay Silbersack for each year, or portion thereof, in which Silbersack has been or shall be employed by American Home, additional compensation for the indicated periods in the amounts stated for such periods:

    A. From January 1, 1941, through December 31, 1953— $12,500.00

    B. From January 1, 1954, through December 31, 1956— $22,500.00

    C. From January 1, 1957, through December 31, 1957— $25,000.00

    D. From and after January 1, 1958—$30,000.00;

such amounts to be in addition to such regular or other compensation as may be mutually agreed upon between American Home and Silbersack from time to time.

2. The additional compensation referred to in Paragraph 1 above shall be subject to the conditions hereinafter set forth in Paragraphs A and B below:

A. During the period of additional compensation payments, Silbersack shall not become or serve as an officer, director or employee of any individual, partnership or corporation, nor the owner of any business, nor a member of a partnership which conducts a business in competition with American Home or any of its subsidiaries.

B. During the period of additional compensation payments, Silbersack shall consult with American Home in an advisory capacity on policy matters and with respect to important decisions relating to sales, advertising, production, financial and other matters when requested to do so and at such reasonable and convenient times and places as may be mutually agreed upon.

3. In the event that Silbersack breaches either or both of the conditions set forth in Paragraphs A and B of Paragraph 2 hereof, he shall forfeit all rights to additional compensation to which he may then or thereafter be entitled.

4. Subject to the foregoing conditions, the total additional compensation to which Silbersack may be entitled under this agreement shall be paid to Silbersack in 180 equal monthly installments commencing with the first day of the month following termination of employment of Silbersack with American Home for any reason whatsoever.

5. In the event Silbersack shall die prior to the receipt of any or all of such additional compensation and is survived by his wife, Eleanor, then such additional compensation as remains unpaid shall be paid to his said wife in the manner and amounts payable to Silbersack as if he were alive and performed the conditions required of him in this agreement. In the event that Silbersack shall die prior to the receipt of any or all of such additional compensation and his said wife not survive him, or, if surviving him, die before receiving any or all of such additional compensation unpaid at his death, then such additional compensation as remains unpaid shall be paid to Silbersack's estate in the amount payable to Silbersack as if he were alive and had performed the conditions required of him in this agreement.

6. It is further agreed that Silbersack during his lifetime shall not be entitled to commute, encumber, sell or otherwise dispose of

his right to receive the additional compensation payments provided for hereinabove, which payments and the right thereof are expressly declared to be non-assignable and non-transferable during his lifetime, and in the event of any attempted assignment or transfer thereof, American Home shall have no further liability under this agreement.

7. American Home agrees that it will make adequate provision for such obligation and for its discharge.

8. In consideration of the above, Silbersack agrees to continue his employment as President and General Manager of American Home and to devote his time and best efforts to the interest of American Home and its business and that of its subsidiary companies.

9. This agreement supersedes all employment agreements entered into between Silbersack and American Home prior to the date hereof.

IN WITNESS WHEREOF, the parties hereto have hereunto set their hands this 3rd day of January, 1958, effective as of January 1, 1958.

AMERICAN HOME PRODUCTS CORPORATION

Attest:

By   ALVIN G. BRUSH
_____
Chairman of the Board

Gilbert S. McInerny
_____
Secretary

WALTER SILBERSACK
_____
Walter Silbersack

Witness:

Herbert E. Carnes
_____

MANUFACTURERS TRUST COMPANY

AGREEMENT WITH HORACE C. FLANIGAN

This agreement made at New York, N.Y., this 18th day of November 1957, by and between Manufacturers Trust Co., a New York banking corporation, hereinafter referred to as the 'trust company,' and Horace C. Flanigan, hereinafter referred to as as 'Flanigan,' witnesseth:

Whereas Flanigan has been employed by the trust company for more than 25 years and during that period has had an important part in its management and has contributed substantially to its growth and success; and

Whereas since 1951 Flanigan has been and is now employed by the trust company on a full-time basis as chief executive officer and now has the title of 'chairman of the board of directors'; and

Whereas the trust company desires to make provision for the continuance of Flanigan's employment as chief executive officer and to obtain the continued benefit of Flanigan's advisory and consulting services as a part-time employee when he ceases to be chief executive officer; and

Whereas Flanigan is willing to render the services provided for herein on the terms and conditions herein set forth: Now, therefore, in consideration of the premises and the mutual covenants and agreements herein contained the parties hereto agree as follows:

1. So long as the board of directors of the trust company shall determine, Flanigan agrees to serve the trust company as the chief executive officer on a full-time basis at a salary at the rate of $125,000 per annum payable in approximately equal instalments on the customary salary payment dates of the trust company. At any time after November 18, 1959, Flanigan may elect on 30 days' written notice to the trust company to terminate his services as chief executive officer at the expiration of such 30-day period with the same effect hereunder as if such termination were determined by the board of directors of the trust company.

2. On the termination of Flanigan's services as chief executive officer of the trust company under paragraph 1 hereof and for a period

of 5 years from that date, Flanigan agrees to continue as a part-time employee during such 5-year period and render such advisory and consulting services to the trust company as may be reasonably required by the board of directors of the trust company, and subject to their supervision and control. Flanigan shall be required to devote in the aggregate up to but not exceeding one-half of his time during regular business hours to such services. Flanigan, however, shall be required to render such services only at such times and to such extent as his health permits and does not unduly interfere with his other activities which he may be engaged in during the other half of his time not committed to the trust company. Flanigan's annual salary under this paragraph 2 shall be at a rate equal to the sum of $50,000 per annum plus the annual pension Flanigan would have been entitled to receive under the trust company's pension plan, as then in force, if he retired at the conclusion of his services under paragraph 1 hereof, and shall be payable in approximately equal instalments on the customary salary payment dates of the trust company. In the event that Flanigan becomes physically or mentally incapable of performing the services provided for in this paragraph 2, the board of directors of the trust company shall have the right to terminate the period provided for as of a date to be determined by the board of directors.

3. During the period of part-time employment provided for in paragraph 2 hereof the trust company shall provide for Flanigan a suitable office in the building occupied by its branch at Fifth Avenue and 43d Street in the city of New York, and shall also provide him with such secretarial and other services as he may reasonably require in carrying out his obligations under said paragraph 2.

4. During the period provided for in paragraph 1 hereof as well as during the period provided for in paragraph 2 hereof, the trust company shall pay, or reimburse Flanigan for, expenses paid or incurred by Flanigan in performing his obligations under paragraphs 1 and 2 hereof of the same general nature and to the same general extent now being paid or reimbursed to Flanigan.

5. During the periods provided for in paragraphs 1 and 2 hereof, Flanigan, in addition to the salary payments provided for in said paragraphs, shall participate in and be covered by such pension, profit sharing, insurance, and other benefit plans as are provided by the trust company for its active employees, and he shall not be treated as a retired employee until the completion of his employment under paragraph 2 hereof.

6. As a further inducement to Flanigan to enter into this agreement, the trust company, upon the termination of his employment

under paragraph 2 hereof, agrees to pay to Flanigan an aggregate amount equal to $25,000 for each full year, and proportionately for each fraction of a year, of his service under paragraphs 1 and 2 hereof, which aggregate amount shall be payable at the rate of $25,000 per annum, and such annual amount to be payable in approximately equal installments on the customary salary payment dates of the trust company. In the event of Flanigan's death prior to the payment in full of the sums provided for in this paragraph 6 hereof, and whether such death occurs before or after the completion of his period of employment under paragraphs 1 and 2 hereof, the balance shall be paid to Flanigan's legal representative promptly after the qualification of such legal representative.

7. During the period provided for in paragraphs 2 and 6 hereof, Flanigan agrees that he will not directly or indirectly engage in any business which is competitive with the business of the trust company.

8. The obligation of the trust company to make the payments provided for in paragraph 6 hereof shall be conditioned upon Flanigan's due performance of his obligations under paragraphs 1, 2, and 7 hereof.

9. This agreement shall inure to the benefit of and be binding upon the trust company, its successors and assigns (including without limitation any corporation which might acquire all or substantially all of the trust company's assets and business or with which the trust company may be consolidated or merged).

10. This agreement shall be governed by the laws of the State of New York.

In witness whereof the parties hereto have executed this agreement the day and year first above written.

Attest:

J. F. ADAMS
MANUFACTURERS TRUST CO.
By E. S. HOOPER,
H. C. FLANIGAN

RETIREMENT CONTRACT

APPENDIX QQ

Avco Manufacturing Corporation

CONTRACT WITH IRVING B. BABCOCK

THIS AGREEMENT, entered into as of April 22, 1948, between Avco Manufacturing Corporation, a corporation organized and existing under the laws of the State of Delaware and having its principal place of business in the City of New York, New York, hereinafter referred to as "Avco," and Irving B. Babcock, of Detroit, Michigan, hereinafter referred to as "Babcock";

Witnesseth:

That whereas, Babcock has heretofore been employed by Avco pursuant to an employment contract bearing date of December 28, 1944 for a term of three (3) years, commencing February 1, 1945 and expiring January 31, 1948, and pursuant to said contract has served Avco as its President and Manager and has also acted as an executive officer and/or director of several of the subsidiary and affiliated corporations of Avco; and

Whereas, it has now been mutually agreed that Babcock shall retire from the Presidency of Avco as of the date hereof and thereafter from time to time and whenever so requested to do by the Chairman of the Board of Directors of Avco shall retire and resign from any other executive positions which he now holds or may hereafter hold in any of Avco's subsidiary or affiliated corporations, but Avco desires to continue to utilize and avail itself of the services of Babcock as a Consultant to Avco and in such other official or non-official relationships to Avco or any of its subsidiary or affiliated companies as Avco may hereafter request, and upon the terms and conditions hereinafter set forth; and

Whereas, Babcock, to the extent permitted by his health, desires to furnish such personal services to Avco and its subsidiary and

498

affiliated companies and to perform such duties and assume such responsibilities as from time to time may be entrusted to him during the period of this agreement;

Now, THEREFORE, the premises considered, the parties hereto mutually covenant and agree each with the other as follows:

FIRST: Avco hereby employs Babcock and Babcock hereby agrees to accept employment with Avco as Consultant and Advisor to its management and to the executives of its subsidiary and affiliated corporations for a term commencing April 22, 1948 and to end June 30, 1951 unless such employment is sooner terminated as hereinafter provided.

SECOND: Babcock, during the term of such employment, agrees to devote to the business and affairs of Avco and its subsidiary and affiliated corporations such time and attention as his health may permit and as may be reasonably required and usefully utilized, it being agreed by the parties that Avco shall have first call upon and the prior right to utilize Babcock's services to the extent of fifty per cent (50%) of his normal working time in each year during the term of this agreement. In the event that Avco during any twelve (12) month period commencing on this date, or any anniversary thereof, shall request the utilization of Babcock's services in excess of the fifty per cent (50%) of his normal working time contemplated by this agreement and Babcock shall accede to such request and furnish such services, an appropriate adjustment reflecting the increased call on his time shall be mutually agreed upon and paid by Avco. The services to be rendered by Babcock shall be rendered by him under the general direction of the Chairman of the Board and Chief Executive Officer of Avco, which, as the employer, shall retain full direction and control of the means and methods by which Babcock performs the services for which he is employed hereunder. Specifically, Babcock agrees to act as Consultant and Advisor to the management of Avco and its subsidiary and affiliated companies, to assist the officers of the corporation in the solution of manufacturing problems, in contract negotiations and in the sale of Brill buses and other products, and to advise to make recommendations with respect to the operations of Avco's various manufacturing plants and subsidiaries, including ACF-Brill Motors Company and The Nashville Corporation. Babcock also agrees that during the term of such employment he will engage in no other business activities competitive with Avco or any of its subsidiary or affiliated corporations without the written consent and approval of the Chairman of the Board of Directors of Avco first had and obtained.

THIRD: The services which are to be rendered by Babcock pursuant to the foregoing undertaking are to be rendered in the City of New York or at the various offices and plants of Avco in the United States of America as may be determined from time to time by the Chairman of the Board of Avco. Babcock, however, shall be at liberty to maintain his own principal office and residence in the City of Detroit, Michigan, and whenever absent from Detroit on account of the performance of services under this agreement, shall be reimbursed for all expenses reasonably incurred by him in the performance of his duties hereunder. Avco also agrees to continue the employment of Babcock's Detroit secretary at a rate no greater than the salary in effect during the twelve (12) months preceding the execution of this agreement and also to pay one-half (½) of Babcock's Detroit office rent and expense not exceeding Two Thousand Dollars ($2,000) annually. Babcock, however, shall reimburse Avco quarterly or semi-annually at Avco's election for one-half (½) of the total cost to Avco incurred in the employment of his secretary, including social security taxes and payments made for her benefit to any insurance or retirement plan in which she is eligible to participate. Such payments shall be made by Avco and Babcock while this contract remains in full force and effect but, if this contract and Babcock's employment hereunder is terminated by Babcock, Avco's responsibility to continue the employment of his secretary and to pay any portion of his Detroit office expense shall likewise immediately terminate. If termination of this contract, is, however, otherwise effected by reason of Babcock's death or incapacity, Avco agrees to pay his Detroit secretary two (2) months' severance pay and, in addition, to pay one-half (½) of the cost of terminating his Detroit office lease, not exceeding, however, an additional Two Thousand Dollars ($2,000).

FOURTH: Subject to adjustment only in the event that Avco calls upon Babcock for more than fifty per cent (50%) of his normal working time and services in any twelve (12) month period, Avco agrees to pay or cause to be paid to Babcock as compensation for the services to be rendered hereunder a salary at the rate of Fifty Thousand Dollars ($50,000) annually, payable in monthly or semi-monthly installments, which salary may be allocated by Avco between itself and its various subsidiary and affiliated corporations in such manner and amounts as Avco may from time to time determine. In consideration of the payment of such salary and without any additional compensation therefor, Babcock agrees to serve any of Avco's subsidiary or affiliated corporations in any official position which he may now hold or to which he may be hereafter elected, provided, however, that in addition to such salary at the rate of Fifty Thousand Dollars ($50,000) annually and his reasonable expenses incurred in behalf of the corporation to be paid as hereinbefore provided, Babcock shall also be entitled to receive from time to time any directors' fees which are paid by New York Shipbuilding Corporation, ACF-Brill Motors Company and The Nashville Corporation to directors who are not salaried employees of said corporations as long as said corporations continue to pay such directors' fees and Babcock remains a member of their Boards of Directors eligible to receive such compensation. Babcock further agrees, however, at any time hereafter, upon the request of the Chairman of the Board of Directors of Avco, to tender for immediate acceptance his resignation from any position or office which he now holds or may hereafter hold as an officer of Avco or any of its subsidiary or affiliated corporations, and also, upon similar request, to tender his resignation as a Director of any of Avco's subsidiary or affiliated corporations which do not solicit proxies for stockholders' meetings and to the Boards of which he was elected to represent Avco as controlling stockholder.

FIFTH : During the period of his employment hereunder, Babcock shall be eligible to participate in Avco's Extra Compensation Annuity Plan, and shall be entitled to participate in such group life and other insurance plans as are offered by Avco to its officers and employees, and in the Pension and Retirement Plan if same is maintained in full force and effect, and upon retirement at the attained age of sixty (60) at the expiration of this contract of employment, June 30, 1951, it is further understood and agreed that Babcock may retire under the provisions of the Avco Pension and Retirement Plan, subject, however, to all applicable provisions thereof.

SIXTH: In the event Babcock shall for any reason become incapacitated to perform the duties contemplated by this agreement, and if such incapacity shall continue for a period of three months or more, the Board of Directors of Avco, acting in good faith and without fraud, passion, prejudice or caprice, may terminate this agreement. Babcock shall also have the right to cancel and terminate this agreement at any time on three months' notice to Avco.

IN WITNESS WHEREOF, Avco has caused this agreement to be signed by its officers thereunto duly authorized and its corporate seal to be hereunto affixed, and Babcock has hereunto set his hand and seal as of the day and year first above written.

AVCO MANUFACTURING CORPORATION
By   VICTOR EMANUEL
        Chairman of the Board

Attest:
    R. S. PRUITT
    Secretary

                    IRVING B. BABCOCK

MODEL CONTRACT

APPENDIX RR

A Model Form of Compensation Contract

(Authors' Note: This model form of contract combines in one document various clauses set forth and discussed in this volume, with a few changes, principally those made necessary as the result of combining in a single document the major clauses discussed in the volume and to complete the document. The form is intended solely to illustrate points discussed in the text and must of course be adapted by counsel to the circumstances of each individual situation and to any applicable special legal requirements of the state of execution or of incorporation.)

AGREEMENT made as of the first day of _____,

19 , between _____, a _____
　　　　　　　　(name of corporation)　　　　　　(state of incorporation)

corporation (the Company), and _____,
　　　　　　　　　　　　　　　　(name of executive)

residing at _____, in the City of _____,

State of _____ (the Executive).

RECITALS

The Executive has been a valued employee and key executive of the Company for many years and the parties wish to provide for his continued employment and future services upon the terms and conditions set forth in this agreement.

NOW, THEREFORE, IT IS HEREBY MUTUALLY AGREED AS FOLLOWS:

1. The Company agrees to and hereby does continue the Executive in its employ, and the Executive agrees to and hereby does continue in the employ of the Company, as general manager of the Company in charge of the operation of its business and affairs, subject to the supervision and direction of its Board of Directors, for a period commencing with the date of this Agreement and ending on .... 19.., unless such period is extended by written agreement of the parties or is sooner terminated pursuant to the provisions of paragraph 5(a) below. [Discussed in Chapter 2, text to footnotes 9 ff.]

2. The Executive agrees to continue to devote all of his time, attention, skill, and efforts to the performance of his duties as general manager of the Company, and to the performance of all the duties of office of President of the Company and of any subsidiary or subsidiaries of the Company, if elected, all under the supervision and direction of their respective boards of directors. [Discussed in Chapter 2, text to footnotes 20 ff.]

3. (a) For all services to be rendered by him in any capacity hereunder (including services as an officer, director, member of any committee or otherwise), the Company agrees to pay the Executive, so long as he shall be employed hereunder,

    (i) a fixed salary at the rate of $...... per annum, payable in equal monthly installments at the end of each month; [Discussed in Chapter 2, text to footnotes 24 ff.]

    (ii) an additional sum (hereinafter sometimes referred to as "the Executive's percentage compensation") equal to ..% of the adjusted consolidated net earnings of the Company and its subsidiaries for each calendar year, or portion thereof, during his employment hereunder beginning January 1, 19.., such sum to be computed and payable as provided in paragraph 3(b) below, and [Discussed in Chapter 3, text to footnotes 18 ff.]

    (iii) upon the termination of his employment, except as otherwise provided and subject to the conditions set forth in paragraph 7 below, contingent compensation equal to the sum of $........ for each period of twelve months that the Executive shall have been employed hereunder, each such sum, if and to the extent payable, to be paid in 120 equal monthly installments at the end of each month commencing in January of the calendar year next following termination of the Executive's employment. [Discussed in Chapter 5, text to footnotes 5 ff.]

(b) The adjusted consolidated net earnings of the Company and its subsidiaries, for the purpose of computing the Executive's percentage compensation under the provisions of paragraph 3(a) above, shall be determined in accordance with accepted accounting practice within 90 days after the end of each calendar year by the independent accounting firm employed by the Company as its auditors. The computation by such accounting firm of the net earnings and of the Executive's percentage compensation, made in the manner herein provided, shall be in all respects final and binding upon the Company and upon the Executive, and the Company shall pay such compensation to the Executive within 120 days after the end of the calendar year in question. For the purpose of computing the Executive's percentage compensation, the adjusted consolidated net earnings of the Company and its subsidiaries for the above-mentioned period shall be the consolidated net earnings of the Company and its subsidiaries for such period, as certified by the Company's independent auditors for the purposes of the Company's annual report to stockholders for such period, plus all amounts charged against such consolidated net earnings in respect of the following:

(i) Taxes of the United States and foreign governments (including, but without limitation, excess profits taxes) based upon or measured, in whole or in part, by income of the Company or its subsidiaries but exclusive of state and territorial taxes and taxes imposed by political subdivisions thereof; [Discussed in Chapter 3, text to footnotes 54 ff.]

(ii) Profit participations, if any, which may be payable by the Company under any plan or agreement, including this agreement, other than a profit-sharing plan qualified under Section 401 of the Internal Revenue Code or any statutory provision that may hereafter be enacted to replace such section;

(iii) All items of non-recurring loss or other extraordinary charge which, by reason of size, character, or other factors, did not, in the sole and uncontrolled judgment of the Board of Directors, arise in the ordinary and usual course of the business of the Company and its subsidiaries, including expenses properly attributable to such loss or charge; less, however, all amounts included in such consolidated net earnings in respect of items of capital gain, non-recurring profit, or other extraordinary credit which, by reason of size, character, or other factors did not, in the sole and uncontrolled judgment of the Board of Directors, arise in the ordinary and usual course of the business of the Company and its subsidiaries, after deducting expenses properly attributable to such gain, profit, or credit, except and to the extent that the Board of Directors, in its sole and uncontrolled judgment, shall find that the Executive was responsible for such gain, profit, or credit and shall direct the inclusion, in whole or in part, of such gain, profit, or credit in the computation of consolidated net earnings.

4.   The Executive agrees that during the period of his employment he will not have any other corporate affiliations without the approval of the Board of Directors of the Company. The Executive further agrees that during the period of his employment, and during a further period of two years after leaving the employ of the Company, whether upon the expiration of this contract or otherwise, he will not directly or indirectly, for his own benefit, or for or with any person, firm or corporation whatsoever other than the Company, engage in the production or the manufacture or the distribution of any products similar to those manufactured or sold by the Company during such period of employment. [Discussed in Chapter 2, text to footnote 30.]

5.   Notwithstanding anything herein contained,
    (a) In the event that the Executive shall, during the term of his employment hereunder, fail to perform his duties hereunder owing to illness or other incapacity and such illness or other incapacity shall continue for a period of more than ...... months, the Company shall have the right, by notice sent by registered mail addressed to him at ...., to terminate the Executive's employment hereunder as of a date (not less than 30 days after the date of the sending of such notice) to be specified in such notice, and the Executive shall be entitled to receive (i) his fixed compensation as provided in paragraph 3(a)(i) hereof to the last day of the calendar month in which such notice shall be sent, (ii) percentage compensation for the year in which such notice shall be sent, computed as provided in 5(c) hereof, and (iii) contingent compensation for each period of twelve months prior to the last day of the calendar month in which such

notice shall have been sent (without proration for any period of less than twelve months) ; provided, however, that if, prior to the date specified in such notice, the Executive's illness or incapacity shall have terminated and he shall have taken up and performed his duties hereunder, the Executive shall be entitled to resume his employment hereunder as though such notice had not been given. [Discussed in Chapter 2, text to footnotes 32 ff.]

(b) In the event of the Executive's death during the term of his employment hereunder, the Executive's legal representatives shall be entitled to receive (i) his fixed compensation as provided in paragraph 3(a)(i) hereof to the last day of the calendar month in which the Executive's death shall have occurred, (ii) percentage compensation for the year in which his death took place, computed as provided in 5(c) hereof, and (iii) contingent compensation for each period of twelve months prior to the month in which his death took place (without proration for any period of less than twelve months).

(c) In computing the Executive's percentage compensation for the year in which his employment terminated as the result of death or disability under this paragraph 5, the Executive's contingent compensation shall be computed as if the Executive had been employed throughout such year and the amount so computed shall be multiplied by a fraction the denominator of which shall be twelve and the numerator of which shall be the number of months during such year that the Executive was employed by the Company, including as a full month for the purpose the month in which notice of termination became effective or death took place as the case may be.

6. (a) The Company will not consolidate or merge into or with another corporation, or transfer all or substantially all of its assets to another corporation, unless such other corporation (hereinafter referred to as the "Successor Corporation") shall assume this agreement, and upon such assumption the Executive and the Successor Corporation shall become obligated to perform the terms and conditions hereof and the term "Company" as used in this agreement shall be deemed to refer to such Successor

Corporation; provided, however, that although the Executive shall be an executive of the Successor Corporation, he need not be designated as chief executive of the Successor Corporation, and his duties shall be such as shall be prescribed by the Board of Directors of the Successor Corporation. [Discussed in Chapter 2, text to footnotes 38 ff.]

(b) In the event of such a consolidation, merger or sale, the Executive's percentage compensation shall, as to subsequent operations, be based as nearly as may be upon the earnings attributable to the assets owned by the Company at the time of any such consolidation, merger or sale, and shall be determined by the independent accounting firm employed by the Successor Corporation as its auditors, the determination of such accounting firm to be final and binding upon the Successor Corporation and upon the Executive. [Discussed in Chapter 3, text to footnotes 101 ff.]

7. The contingent compensation provided for in paragraph 3(a)(iii) above shall be payable if and when but not unless:
   (a) The employment of the Executive shall have been terminated
      (i) by retirement of the Executive in accordance with any provision of the Employees' Retirement Plan of the Company, as in effect at the time of such retirement; or
      (ii) by the death or disability of the Executive; or
      (iii) by the Company for any reason other than dishonesty or wrongful conduct on the part of the Executive; or
      (iv) as the result of circumstances not deemed by the Board of Directors of the Company in its sole judgment to be prejudicial to the interests of the Company; and

   (b) The Executive shall, if and as long as such contingent compensation shall be paid and without additional compensation, fee, or other payment by the Company (other than payment or reimbursement of reasonable actual out-of-pocket travel and other disbursements)

(i) render such consulting and advisory services as the Company may from time to time reasonably request, having in mind the Executive's health, residence, and personal circumstances, in connection with any matter on which the Executive was working at the time of the termination of his employment or with respect to which the Executive might be expected to have special competence by reason of his former employment by the Company or otherwise;

(ii) continue to serve on the Board of Directors of the Company if elected, provided that the Executive shall not be under obligation to serve on any committee of the Board;

(iii) refrain (independently of and without reference to the second sentence of paragraph 4 hereof), after the expiration of a period of thirty (30) days from the mailing to him of written notice by the Secretary of the Company of a direction to do so, from engaging in the operation or management of a business, whether as owner, stockholder, partner, officer, employee or otherwise, which at the time of the termination of the Executive's employment shall be in competition with the Company or any of its subsidiaries, provided that ownership as an investor of not more than five per cent (5%) of the outstanding shares of stock of any company listed on a national securities exchange or having at least one hundred (100) shareholders shall not in itself constitute a violation of these provisions;

(iv) refrain from disclosing to unauthorized persons information relative to the business of the Company or any of its subsidiaries which he shall have reason to believe is confidential; and

(v) refrain from otherwise acting or conducting himself in a manner which he shall have reason to believe is inimical or contrary to the best interests of the Company.

In the event that the Executive shall fail to comply with any provision of paragraph 7(b) hereof, the Company's obligation to make any further payment of the contingent compensation provided for in paragraph 3(a) (iii) above shall forthwith terminate, but the Executive shall not have any obligation to repay to the Company any payments theretofore made to him. [Discussed in Chapter 5, text to footnotes 31 ff.]

8. It is contemplated that in performing services hereunder the Executive will be required to incur entertainment expense in the interests and on behalf of the Company and in furtherance of its business. To defray such expense the Company agrees to make available to the Executive sums not to exceed a total of $........ per annum. Subject to such limitation in amount, the Company at the end of each month during the period of this agreement will, upon submission of appropriate bills or vouchers, pay all such expense incurred by the Executive during such month, such payment to be made either directly to the payee named in such bills or vouchers, or to the extent paid by the Executive, by reimbursement of the Executive. The Executive agrees to maintain adequate records, in such detail as the Company may reasonably request, of all expenses to be reimbursed by the Company hereunder and to make such records available for inspection as and when reasonably requested by the Company. The provisions of this paragraph are not intended to apply to travelling expense or to business expense (other than entertainment) incurred by the Executive with the specific approval of the Company and such expense, as and when incurred, shall be separately paid, or reimbursed to the Executive by the Company, upon submission of appropriate bills or vouchers and upon his maintenance of adequate records, but otherwise without reference to the provisions of this paragraph. [Discussed in Chapter 7, text to footnotes 9 ff.]

9. The Executive, by written notice to the Company during his lifetime signed by him and witnessed by at least two persons, may designate one or more persons or entities (including a trust or trusts or his estate) to receive his contingent compensation, or any balance thereof, and, notwithstanding the provisions of paragraph 6 hereof, any other compensation payable to him under this agreement, in the event of his death prior to full payment thereof, and if he shall designate more than one, the proportion in which each is to receive such payments. He may also designate the person or persons who shall succeed to the rights of the person or persons originally designated in case the latter should die. He may from time to time change any designation so made and the last written notice given by him before his death shall be controlling. In the absence of a designation made by the Executive pursuant to this paragraph 9 or, in the event of the

death of a person to whom payments were being made pursuant to this paragraph 9 before such payments are completed and, failing any other designation by the Executive, such payments, or any balance thereof, shall be paid to the legal representatives of the Executive. The person or persons entitled to payments pursuant to the provisions of this paragraph 9 are referred to in this agreement as the Executive's Beneficiary.

10. Nothing in this agreement shall be construed as limiting or restricting any benefit to the Executive, his legal representatives or Beneficiary, under any pension, profit-sharing or similar retirement plan, or under any group life or group health or accident or other plan of the Company, for the benefit of its employees generally or a group of them, now or hereafter in existence, nor shall any payment under this agreement be deemed to constitute payment to the Executive, his legal representatives, or Beneficiary in lieu of or in reduction of any benefit or payment under any such plan.

11. (a) This agreement shall enure to the benefit of the Executive's legal representatives and Beneficiary but, except as authorized by paragraph 9 hereof, neither this agreement nor any right or interest under this agreement, shall be assignable by the Executive or by his Beneficiary without the Company's prior written consent.

(b) Except as authorized by paragraph 6 above, this agreement shall not be assignable by the Company.

12. (a) Any notice to the Company under this agreement shall be deemed to have been given if and when delivered in person to an officer of the Company (other than the Executive) or if and when mailed by registered mail to the Company at its principal office in the City of ...., State of ...., or such other address as the Company may from time to time designate in writing by notice to the Executive given pursuant to paragraph 12(b) hereof.

(b) Any notice to the Executive under this agreement shall be deemed to have been given if and when delivered to him in person or if and when mailed by registered mail to the Executive at his address hereinabove given or such other address as the Executive may from time designate in writing by notice to the Company given pursuant to paragraph 12(a) above.

(c) Any notice to the Executive's Beneficiary under this agreement shall be deemed to have been given if and when mailed by registered mail to such Beneficiary in care of the Estate of the Executive given in or pursuant to paragraph 12(b) hereof, or at such other address or respective addresses as such Beneficiary may from time to time respectively designate in writing to the Company by notice or notices given pursuant to paragraph 12(a) hereof.

13. (a) No amendment or modification of this agreement shall be deemed effective unless and until executed in writing by the parties hereto with the same formality attending execution of this agreement.

(b) No term or condition of this agreement shall be deemed to have been waived, nor shall there be any estoppel to enforce any provision of this agreement, except by written instrument of the party charged with such waiver or estoppel executed with the same formality attending execution of this agreement.

14. This agreement having been executed and delivered in the State of ...., its validity, interpretation, performance and enforcement shall be governed by the laws of that State.

IN WITNESS WHEREOF, the Company has caused this agreement to be executed and its seal to be affixed thereto by its officers thereunto duly authorized, and the Executive has signed and sealed this agreement, as of the day and year first above written.

[Seal]   _____
                                [Company]

                           By _____
                                         President

Attest:

_____
            Secretary

[*Acknowledgments in the form prescribed in the state of execution*]

TABLE OF CASES

(Cases from Volume I and Volume II have been listed cumulatively. Volume II begins on page 537.)

TABLE OF CASES

TABLE OF CASES

TABLE OF CASES

TABLE OF CASES

TABLE OF CASES

TABLE OF CASES

TABLE OF CASES

TABLE OF CASES

TABLE OF CASES

TABLE OF CASES

TABLE OF CASES

TABLE OF CASES

TABLE OF CASES

INDEX

INDEX

INDEX

INDEX

INDEX

tax-favored status, 657–60
requirement for, 659–60
types of, recognized by Internal Revenue Code of 1954, 658

Radio Corporation of America, incentive plan, 933–41
Ralston Purina Company, 813
litigation on stock offering, 813
Rand, James H., Jr., 904
Raskob, John J., 897–98
Reasonable compensation, 23–29, 562–67;
see also "Reasonableness" of compensation under tax laws
bargaining power of executives, 24
ceiling on executive compensation, 26–27
closely held company, 852–67
"business judgment" rule, 852
cases, 853, 870–74
profit participation, 854–55
court inquiries into, 208
difficulty in finding formula, 23
Heinz Company plan, 566
informal agreement, 209–10
judicial attitude, summary of, 867
Koppers Company plan, litigation on, 564–65
"no agreement" cases, 208–9
Pittsburgh Consolidated Coal Company plan, litigation on, 562–63
market appreciation and value of services, court's holding on, 563, 565
profit-participation plans, 97–102
qualified retirement plans, 668–69
retroactive compensation, 213–14
self-payment of compensation, 210–12
self-voted agreements, 212–13
standards, 855–63
increased compensation, 857
industry comparison, 856
intra-company comparison, 856–57
loss of purchasing power, 859–60
previous earnings, 856
size of amount, 861–62
success of company, 857–59
tax cases, 863
tax rates, 860–61
trend of decisions, 862–63
stock option, 573–75
burden of proof on plaintiff, 575
stockholders' litigations following 1950 tax statute, 573–74
tax aspects, 97–102, 241–42

"Reasonableness" of compensation, under tax laws, 758–73
burden of proof, 769–73
cases, 763–67
compensating employees of subsidiaries, 768–69
unacceptable compensation arrangements, 760–63, 771
Reconstruction Finance Corporation, 774–75
Regent Corporation, 897–98
Registration of securities with SEC;
see Securities and Exchange Commission
Remington Rand Corporation, stockholder litigation, 904–5
Renegotiation Acts, 786–88
profit limitation under, 787–88
Republic Steel Corporation, 243
stockholder litigation, 904
Reserves, for profit-participation plan, 101
Resignation, termination of contract because of, 46
Resolution method of establishing compensation agreements, 233–35
profit-participation plans, 56
self-dealing, 214–25
stockholders, 236
"Restricted" stock, in unrestricted stock option, 589–90
excessive restrictions, 590
lapse or removal of restrictions, 590
Restricted stock option, 590–98; *see* Stock option
Restricted Stock Option Plan, 601–12
Restrictions imposed on executives, in salary contracts, 44
Restrictions on bonus stock, tax effect of, 547–50
corporate deduction, 549–50
limitation of value, 548–49
the *Salvage* rule, 547–48
Retirement benefits, 104
Retirement contracts, examples of, 498–502
Retirement income credit, in qualified plans, 706
Retirement plans, 30
for directors, 267
non-qualified; *see* Non-qualified retirement plans
qualified; *see* Qualified retirement plans
Retroactive compensation, 213–14

INDEX

INDEX

INDEX

INDEX

INDEX